Everything Is Now

The 1960s New York Avant-Garde—Primal Happenings, Underground Movies, Radical Pop

J. Hoberman

VERSO
London • New York

This paperback edition first published by Verso 2026
First published by Verso 2025

The manufacturer's authorized representative in the EU for product safety (GPSR) is LOGOS EUROPE, 9 rue Nicolas Poussin, 17000, La Rochelle, France Contact@logoseurope.eu

1 3 5 7 9 10 8 6 4 2

Verso
UK: 6 Meard Street, London W1F 0EG
US: 207 East 32nd Street, New York, NY 10016
versobooks.com

Verso is the imprint of New Left Books

ISBN-13: 978-1-80429-089-7
ISBN-13: 978-1-80429-088-0 (US EBK)
ISBN-13: 978-1-80429-087-3 (UK EBK)

British Library Cataloguing in Publication Data
A catalogue record for this book is available from the British Library

Library of Congress Cataloging-in-Publication Data
A catalog record for the hardback edition of this book is available from the Library of Congress

Typeset in Minion by Hewer Text UK Ltd, Edinburgh
Printed and bound by CPI Group (UK) Ltd, Croydon CR0 4YY

In memory of intended readers Callie Angell (1948–2010),
Mel Gordon (1947–2018), and Suze Rotolo (1943–2011)

Contents

Acknowledgments

As a collective saga, *Everything Is Now* draws largely on first-hand reporting, published memoirs, online oral histories and interviews. Participants and witnesses with whom I spoke on multiple occasions are David Gurin, Ken and Flo Jacobs, Joan MacIntosh, P. Adams Sitney, Amy Taubin and Richard Goldstein. Other interviewees included Vince Aletti, Penny Arcade, Gordon Ball, Mari-Claire Charba, Paula Cooper, Dan Drasin, Ben (Morea) Eagle, Dean Fleming, Richard Foreman, Ernie Gehr, Mimi Gross, Jerome Hiler, Hettie Jones, Larry Kardish, Lucy Lippard, Barbara Moore, Richard Schechner, Michael Snow, and Terri Thal. In addition, I used interviews with Tony Conrad, Diane di Prima, Judith Malina, Richard Preston, and Ron Tavel conducted in 1997 in the course of writing *On Jack Smith's Flaming Creatures*.

Autobiographical or otherwise, the writings of Jane Alpert, Gordon Ball, Amiri Baraka, Stefan Brecht, John Cale, Diane di Prima, Joe Flaherty, Grace Glueck, Hettie Jones, Jill Johnston, Richard Kostelanetz, Jonas Mekas, Ed Sanders, Susan Sherman, and Andy Warhol (with Pat Hackett) were extraordinary helpful, as were historical works by Peter Doggett, Brandon W. Joseph, Nadja Millner-Larsen, Benjamin Piekut, Melissa Rachleff Burtt, David C. Viola, and Midori Yamamura. I have on occasion paraphrased material from my books *The Dream Life: Movies, Media and the Mythology of the Sixties* and *On Jack Smith's Flaming Creatures*, as well as my chapter on underground movies in *Midnight Movies*, written with Jonathan Rosenbaum, whom I thank.

Most of my research was done at Columbia University's Butler Library; some at the New York Library for the Performing Arts, as well as the New York City Municipal Archives. I am indebted to John Klacsmann, Anthology Film Archives; Gregg Pierce, The Andy Warhol Museum; Jonathan Pouthier, the Centre Pompidou; Allison Chomet, Fales Library and Special Collections and Elizabeth Miseo, Boris Lurie Foundation for their assistance. M. M. Serra, Film-Makers' Cooperative and Johann Kugelberg, proprietor of the gallery Boo Hooray, were extraordinarily helpful. Scholars and researchers who generously shared their research include Henry K. Miller, John Powers, Matt Rosen, Steve Watson, and especially Chuck Smith.

I owe a special debt of gratitude to Ed Leffingwell, with whom I worked on the 1997 Jack Smith exhibit at P.S.1 and who, before he died, left me material he had planned to use in a never-written biography of Smith. I also benefited from moral support from Tim Barry, Danny Czitrom, David Fresko, Edith Kramer, Andrew Lampert, Tom Robbins, Jay Sanders, Adam Shatz, Art Spiegelman, and Elisabeth Sussman. I thank them all along with my editor Kelly Burdick, my production editor Nick Walther, my sometime savior Andy Hsiao and my lifelong helpmate Shelley Hoberman.

Introduction

Cultural innovation comes from the margins and is essentially collective. "Art is not produced by one artist, but by several," the Surrealist painter Max Ernst maintained. "It is to a great degree the product of their exchange of ideas with one another."[1]

New York City in the 1960s was one such cradle of artistic innovation. Boundaries were transgressed, new forms created. A collective drama was played out in coffeehouses and bars, at openings and readings, in lofts and storefront theaters and ultimately the streets. The dramatis personae were an assemblage of penniless filmmakers, marginal musicians, former painters and performing poets, as well as less classifiable and hyphenate artists, including political organizers. A significant few were émigrés from Europe or Asia, profoundly affected by their experience of World War II.

Some of these actors were associated with specific art movements: Avant Rock, Black Arts, Conceptual Art, Destruction Art, Fluxus, Free Jazz, Guerrilla Theater, Happenings, Mimeographed Zines, Pop Art, Protest-Folk, Ridiculous Theater, Stand-Up Poetry, Structural Film, Underground Comix, and Underground Movies. These tendencies were fluid and cross-pollinating (interstitial artists were not uncommon), and although art is not produced by a single individual—there were also movements of one.

1 Quoted in "Eleven Europeans in America," *Museum of Modern Art Bulletin* 13, 4–5 (September 1946): 17.

Largely free of established institutional support, drawing sustenance from urban detritus, artists produced work that was taboo-breaking and confrontational—not least regarding the established art world. A good deal of the new art could be (and was) considered anti-art. Consequently, artists often clashed with the police, the courts, the law, and authority in general. By the mid-'60s various artistic subcultures had coalesced into an entire counterculture that overlapped the struggle for civil rights, the peace and anti-war movements, Black nationalism, women's and gay liberation, the campaign for sexual freedom and the legal assault on censorship, as well as forms of direct-action anarchy.

At the same time, New York itself went through convulsive changes. The transformations of the 1959–71 period were physical as well as political, demographic, and economic. Jobs disappeared, welfare rolls lengthened, crime rose, heroin flooded poor neighborhoods. The city was the site of demonstrations, insurrections, strikes, trials, sit-ins, be-ins, bombings, and, as a muse, all manner of public theater—one giant happening on an epic urban stage. *Everything Is Now* chronicles that happening.[2]

Born in 1949 and brought up in New York, I lived through this period. Written in my seventies, *Everything Is Now* is an act of remembrance, underscored by a sense of belatedness. Although too young to have participated in most of these events I evoke, I am old enough to have experienced what might be termed the normalization of cultural craziness that characterized the 1960s. As a young adult, I also benefited from the era of cheap rents—perhaps the greatest facilitator of artistic innovation.

Everything Is Now is divided into two sections ("Subcultures" and "Counterculture") and organized in eleven more-or-less chronological chapters. Each chapter is broken down into a dozen or so delineated narratives. A former journalist (forty years with the *Village Voice*), I appreciate a good story and in researching this book discovered more than a few. Newspapers pride themselves in providing the "first rough

2 It is also a map. Paris is filled with plaques marking the former dwelling places of distinguished artists and writers. New York is not, hence my emphasis on specific addresses and locations, often marking buildings that (New York being New York) no longer exist.

draft of history" and, to my mind, there would be no history of the '60s avant-garde without them.

Much performative work exists only as reported or advertised in the underground press. To write this book, I not only interviewed witnesses and participants but read through virtually every copy of the *Voice* between late 1958 and early 1972, along with much of the *East Village Other*, *Rat*, and the *New York Free Press*. At heart, *Everything Is Now* is a tribute to those who wrote for the alternative weeklies as well as other cultural reporters. It is through their eyes that we might know how new work, alarming or exhilarating or both, was received.

At the Factory: Bob Dylan, Andy Warhol, Barbara Rubin, Gerard Malanga (September 1965). © Nat Finkelstein Estate / courtesy of Elizabeth Murray Finkelstein.

Subcultures, 1959–66

Original poster, *The Connection* (1959).

1

The Connections, 1958–60

In which the Beat Generation is absorbed by TV and the movies as an as-yet-underground counterculture coalesces around Village coffeehouses, Jonas Mekas sees new things developing. The Living Theatre has a hit "jazz play," *The Connection*, Allan Kaprow stages New York's first Happening, Ornette Coleman introduces *The Shape of the Jazz to Come*, and a *Village Voice* writer envisions a Hipster General Strike.

> *Early morning in the universe . . .*
>
> —Jack Kerouac, first line of *Pull My Daisy* (1959)

Thursday, November 6, 1958: President Eisenhower threatens resumed nuclear testing as the Air Force delays its third attempt to catapult a rocket around the moon and Cuban rebels capture a third commercial air flight.

A three-judge federal panel in Mississippi has dismissed a suit charging that qualified voters have been barred from the polls because of their race. In New York, incalculably wealthy Nelson A. Rockefeller celebrates his election as governor, having handily defeated another rich man, W. Averell Harriman, while brother David Rockefeller proposes transformation of lower Manhattan's old city into a new "superblock" business district.

That evening the Brandeis University Club of New York holds a forum at the Hunter College Playhouse, posing the question, "Is There a Beat Generation?" This subject, the Brandeis dean of students explains in introductory remarks, "is of literary interest, as a social phenomenon, and some would consider as a symptom of the alienation which many young people experience in adapting to the standards and the problems of our society."

To answer the question, the Brandeis Club invited young British novelist Kingsley Amis, the editor of the then liberal *New York Post*, self-identified "unreconstructed radical" James Wechsler, and Princeton anthropology professor Ashley Montagu to meet the "laureate of the Beat Generation," Jack Kerouac. Another, implicit, question: Why did Kerouac, who enjoyed and suffered no small amount of publicity in the months following the publication of his epochal novel *On the Road*, accept the invitation?

In a hostile review of Kerouac's latest novel *The Dharma Bums*, the *New York Times* gave the writer his soubriquet and derisively referred to his fans as "Beejees" (for Beat Generation). Kerouac's own term, coined by his comrade Allen Ginsberg, was "subterraneans," which he took for the title of a hastily written novella inspired by his brief, intense love affair with Alene Lee, an African American woman who passed through the Beat circle. Published by Grove Press in early 1958, *The Subterraneans* was dismissed by the *New York Times* book columnist David Dempsey, who considered the novel notable only for its "schizophrenic disintegration of syntax" and intended exclusively for the "coterie world" from whence it came.[1]

The *New York Times* ignored the Brandeis Club event; as befitted the Beejee paper of record, the *Village Voice* covered it on page one. The previous week's edition had included Allen Ginsberg's lengthy defense of *The Dharma Bums* as well as the first installment of "Movie Journal," a regular column by Jonas Mekas, a thirty-seven-year-old Lithuanian immigrant who had arrived in New York ten years earlier from a German displaced persons camp, edited a magazine called *Film Culture* and lived in poverty with his brother Adolfas on Avenue B.

Two weeks before, the *Voice* ran an article in which Professor Roger

1 The observation was truer than Dempsey knew. Lee, a figure so subterranean that she is referred to in some Kerouac biographies by her fictional name Mardou Fox, actually reviewed *The Subterraneans* in the *Village Voice*, as A. Lee. Her scathing put-down blows off Kerouoc's fictional subterranean pals as "a superior order of poseurs" and the novel itself, concluding with the question, "Are our senses now to be assaulted by long-winded tortuous accounts of erotic experiences which verge on secondary self-masturbation?"

Shattuck compared the early twentieth-century French avant-garde and the Beat Generation, graciously noting that "the only organ which had begun to articulate the feelings and the context of the so-called beat generation and to oblige its members to see themselves without indulgence is a little newspaper in New York," that is, the *Village Voice*. "In its informal interviews, heated letters from readers of all shapes and addictions, and unstereotyped literary and social criticism," Shattuck continued, "one can begin to perceive what has happened. The total engagement in life which Existentialism taught immediately after the last war has evolved mysteriously into the total disengagement of the cool cat who doesn't lift a finger for anyone and lives skin deep."

True or not, Marc Schleifer's *Voice* piece was appropriately cool. Reporting on the event as theater, Schleifer noted the overflow crowd straining to get in, the moderator's bilious demeanor ("when the evening's festivities of hoots, cheers, insults, and poetry were over, I feared for his supper") and characterized the cast: Amis was perplexed but friendly; Montagu appeared "slightly amused and slightly sleepy"; Wechsler looked angry, glaring at the Beat Laureate with incredulous incomprehension.

Kerouac—dressed in a checkered flannel shirt and black jeans—had prepared an essay. He began his manic spiel by asking "Does the world exist?," connected the word "beat" to "beatitude" and went on to cite James Dean, Humphrey Bogart, Laurel and Hardy, Popeye the Sailor, Lester Young, and the Shadow (voiced on the radio by Orson Welles) as Beat precursors, embodying America's "wild self-believing individuality." America, he pointed out, was changing. College kids were now referring to people as "hung up," a hip phrase synonymous with "bugged," which he first heard used on Times Square back in the 1940s.

Schleifer described the writer dashing off and on stage a dozen times, clowning with a hat, stumbling into the audience and dragging poet Allen Ginsberg up from his seat to take a bow. The Beats were happening. Kerouac was performing Kerouac.

2

On the Road had appeared fourteen months before, unexpectedly hailed by the *New York Times*. The critic, forty-ish freelance writer Gilbert Millstein, anointed the book "the testament of the Beat Generation" in a notice that not only made Kerouac a bestselling author and generational spokesman but transformed him into a star.

Continuing to push the bandwagon, Millstein suggested Kerouac's box-office potential to Max Gordon, owner of the venerable Village Vanguard, a cellar nightclub just across Seventh Avenue from the *Village Voice* office. Gordon booked Kerouac as the Christmas week attraction on a bill that included bop trombonist J. J. Johnson and the young singer Beverly Kenney, whose act included an original composition, "I Hate Rock and Roll." Kerouac was packaged as a jazz poet. Gordon insisted on having the house pianist noodle behind him.

The twenty-two-year-old *Voice* reporter Howard Smith interviewed the chain-smoking, coffee-swilling, already boozed-up Kerouac backstage. "The drink, the sweat, the smoke, the nerves are taking effect," Smith wrote in his page-one piece. Clinging to the Beat credo of spontaneous authenticity, Kerouac was uncertain what to read. Smith compared him to "a frightened MC on his first job." Still, the room—deemed by Smith to be filled with agents, gladhanders, and Madison Avenue types—seemed appreciative. Dan Wakefield, a Vanguard regular, reviewing for *The Nation*, attended a subsequent set. He found Kerouac distastefully soused as well as unrehearsed and the audience "cold."

The Vanguard performance was judged a disaster (although Steve Allen caught Kerouac's act and would book him on his TV show). On the other hand, Kerouac's first movie appearance, in which he is heard but unseen, would be a triumph. In the radioactive glow of the Millstein review, twenty-one-year-old would-be producer Leo Garen approached Kerouac to write a play. Supposedly knocked off in a single night, *The Beat Generation* reprised key characters from *On the Road*, including stand-ins for Kerouac's hero Neal Cassady, Ginsberg, and Kerouac himself, now somewhat older and even, after a fashion, settled down. Garen could not get the play produced but some months later it came to the attention of the painter Alfred Leslie and photographer Robert Frank, a Kerouac buddy, who had collaborated with him on a New York-to-Florida road trip commissioned but never published by *Life* magazine.

Frank, thirty-four, and Leslie, thirty-one, planned a movie composed of three half-hour segments and thought that *The Beat Generation*'s third act might work as one. In late 1958, around the time Kerouac clowned at Hunter, they were able to raise funds from a pair of Wall Street investors looking for a tax write-off. By the time that the Cuban insurrectionist Fidel Castro entered Havana (January 8, 1959), Frank and Leslie were shooting *The Beat Generation* in Leslie's loft in an old office building on the used-book stretch of Fourth Avenue, around the corner from the Tenth Street galleries. Victorious Revolution in the air![2]

The two weeks of filming coincided with John Cassavetes's shooting retakes for his independent 16mm feature, *Shadows*. Not yet thirty, Cassavetes had fashioned an impressionistic drama from thirty hours of footage shot during the summer of 1957. The movie was largely unscripted; it was cast with Cassavetes's acting students and based on dramatic improvisations. The conflict experienced by an interracial family was daring; the seedy Times Square locations felt real; the posturing of actor Benito Carruthers (was he imitating James Dean or playing a character imitating James Dean?), as well as the Charles Mingus jazz score, signified a hipster milieu. Most impressive, however, was the film's authenticity.

Prizing spontaneity, Cassavetes did not edit out blown lines and awkward miscues. *Shadows* was a movie about getting into show business acted by people in the same position. Jonas Mekas first saw *Shadows* in November 1958 at one of the three free midnight screenings Cassavetes organized for prospective exhibitors at the Paris Theater. Knocked out, Mekas championed the film to which his journal *Film Culture* gave its first annual Independent Film award.[3]

Shadows featured acting students. *Pull My Daisy* had real stars, the poets Ginsberg, Gregory Corso, and Peter Orlovsky (all playing themselves). The supporting cast included painters Larry Rivers and Alice Neel, gallery director Richard Bellamy, the dancer Sally Gross (later employed as a model in *Life* magazine's seven-page spread "Squaresville U.S.A. vs. Beatsville"), and Delphine Seyrig, a young French actress (then married to painter Jack Youngerman) who had come to New York to study the Method.

---

2 Kerouac was being courted by Hollywood producer Jerry Wald, interested in filming *On the Road*, maybe even with Marlon Brando. The deal never materialized, although *The Subterraneans* was acquired by MGM.

3 Editing on *Shadows* was delayed when Cassavetes took a gig as a piano-playing hipster private eye in a half-hour TV show. *Johnny Staccato* usually opened with Cassavetes jamming at a "MacDougal Street" jazz cellar called Waldo's. Produced in Los Angeles but set in a nocturnal Manhattan populated by creeps, junkies, and show-biz bottom-feeders, the show regularly complicated its back-lot geography with an assortment of Manhattan locations—sometimes annotated by Cassavetes. Times Square's neon wilderness was a frequent backdrop, and several *Shadows* cast members put in fleeting appearances.

Sweetly self-aggrandizing, *Pull My Daisy* celebrates a certain lifestyle—embodied by the poets, who play themselves, and Rivers in the Neal Cassady role, a railway brakeman named Milo. Kerouac is invisible but ubiquitous, describing the action in a humorous and grandiloquent monologue recorded as he watched the edited film, interspersed with sound effects and music by twenty-nine-year-old composer David Amram, a regular at the Five Spot, a onetime Bowery dive bar that for the past two years had been the hippest jazz joint in New York.[4]

Hardly a road film, *Pull My Daisy* was a home movie. Frank's studiedly casual compositions emphasize the minutiae and mild squalor of loft living, punctuating the interiors with occasional poetic cutaways to the street. The action encompasses a single day and is largely restricted to a single setting. A character known only as the Wife (Seyrig) makes breakfast for her young son (Pablo Frank) and hustles him off to school. As the boy goes through the door, her husband's pals, Ginsberg and Corso, come tumbling in, and, ignoring the Wife, amuse themselves by declaiming poetry, drinking wine, smoking pot, and clowning around. Eventually, the man of the house, Milo (Rivers), returns from work, Orlovsky in tow.

The Wife's genteel aspirations and latent squareness become apparent when she informs Milo that she's invited the Bishop (Bellamy) for afternoon tea. Accompanied by his sister (Gross) and mother (Neel), the youthful Bishop is confounded by the unruly poets, most memorably when, after a discussion of Buddhism, "Peter the Saint" wonders if baseball and alligators are holy. A freeform jam session begins. The child Pablo reemerges in his bathrobe as the Bishop and his entourage retreat from the loft in confusion. The Wife loses her temper ("all the time we give them wine and beer . . . all these beatniks in the house") and starts to cry. Milo, in turn, gets angry and storms into the night with his feckless friends, treating them to an exhibition of tap dancing on the stairs.

Frank and Leslie would later compete for credit, but the author of *Pull My Daisy* is also its *auteur*. Kerouac's commentary effectively directs the film. (So fluid and immediate that it was taken for spontaneous, his reading was in fact constructed out of three separate takes.) Not just

4 Amram had also played the French horn behind Kerouac in New York's first poetry-jazz reading held at the Tenth Street Brata Gallery a month after the Millstein review in October 1957.

introducing a new cinema, *Pull My Daisy* heralded the coming Golden Age of Bardic Verse.[5]

3

That winter, coffeehouse poetry readings took root in New York.[6] Carved from the dank basement of a Greenwich Village tenement at 116 MacDougal Street, the main venue was the Gaslight Poetry Café. The joint opened in February 1959. The first readings were by Corso and Ginsberg, followed by Ted Joans, thirty-four-year-old former stockbroker Taylor Mead, and twenty-five-year-old Brooklyn-born Diane di Prima.

Conveniently downstairs from another Beat hangout, the Kettle of Fish bar, the Gaslight was born in illegality. According to the legend, John Mitchell—a Brooklyn-bred Beat Generation fellow traveler in his mid-thirties who had once roomed with the ancient Village character Maxwell Bodenheim, fathered a child with Jack Kerouac's lost love Alene Lee, started the Café Figaro at the intersection of Bleecker and MacDougal and having started it, profitably flipped it—had dug deeper into the cellar floor to create more head room below the exposed pipes and, like a convict tunneling toward freedom, needed to find a way to surreptitiously dispose of the dirt. Still, the ceilings felt oppressively low.

Only 110 patrons were allowed but Mitchell regularly crammed in more. Because sound traveled up the airshaft into the building's residential floors, he instituted a practice by which, rather than applaud, appreciative patrons snapped their fingers—a new and further signifier of hipness! According to the poet Ed Sanders, the finger-snap applause was an arrangement worked out with police. In his comic, semi-fictional memoir *Tales of Beatnik Glory*, Sanders writes that the finger-snaps were "inadequate to satisfy the approval-hungry needs of some poets."

> For a very few, when they had completed their poems, and the audience was enthused, there was a flurry of snaps like someone crashing

5 Kerouac and Ginsberg both performed significant readings as *The Beat Generation* went into post-production. On February 5, 1959, Ginsberg premiered "Kaddish" in the McMillin Theatre at his alma mater, Columbia University. Ten days later he joined Ted Joans, LeRoi Jones, Gregory Corso, and Kerouac for a reading at the Artist's Studio on East Third Street. Thanks to *Voice* photographer Fred McDarrah's iconic image, Kerouac—checkered shirt, arms extended—was the star.

6 Coffeehouse poetry readings, often with jazz accompaniment, had been popular in San Francisco's North Beach for the past five years. By 1959, the scene had become a tourist attraction, suffering from the commercialization that had not yet arrived in New York.

through twiggy underbrush. But after a poet who was not well received or not understood (not humorous) there were a pitiful four or five snaps then a dissolving silence.

By May, Joans was reading around the corner at Café Bizarre, another coffeehouse cave located in a former stable at 106 West Third Street, and twenty-four-year-old poet Hugh Romney, an eventual Gaslight mainstay, was next door at the Caravan Café, 102 West Third Street. A few blocks away, at 165 Bleecker Street, twenty-two-year-old Larry Poons and two painter friends opened the Epitome, a venue that not only hosted junior Beats like the twenty-five-year-old ex-con Ray Bremser but was a favored hangout for a group of young artists, among them Dick Higgins and Al Hansen, who had taken John Cage's composition course at the New School for Social Research.

There was even a merchant's organization, the Washington Square South Association, distributing store-window posters urging patrons not to contribute to the panhandlers who, attracted by the tourists, had wandered down. The association was opposed by Israel "Izzy" Young, the thirty-one-year-old proprietor of the Folklore Center, a tiny store down MacDougal from the Gaslight that served as a folksingers' hangout, selling finger picks, songbooks, and records, often at absurdly low prices. Devoted to the music, he organized concerts and readings and dispensed advice. The scene's benign Dutch uncle, Young told *Voice* reporter John Wilcock that these panhandlers (many of whom resided at the Greenwich Hotel, a $1.25-a-night flophouse off MacDougal on Bleecker) were human beings and a storekeeper had no right to tell patrons not to hand a down-and-outer some change.

As coffeehouses proliferated, those unwilling to deal with the local Mob or navigate the bureaucratic labyrinth necessary to obtain a liquor license became de facto cabarets and, before long, the New York police began issuing summons. Such harassment would continue for the next several years on what the *Voice* called "the main drag of the poetry set."[7]

7 A 1926 New York City ordinance defined a cabaret as an establishment that featured dancing and other forms musical entertainment along with the sale of food or drinks. Cabarets were licensed by the Department of Consumer Affairs and from 1940 through 1967 entertainers were required to have a cabaret card, which could be revoked at the discretion of the police. (Although several times amended, the cabaret law was not repealed until 2017.)

There were more formal readings at Julian Beck and Judith Malina's Living Theatre, newly moved to a shabby four-story building, once a prominent department store, on the corner of Fourteenth Street and Sixth Avenue. Merce Cunningham had his dance studio on the top floor while the theater occupied floors two and three. The Becks, then in their mid-thirties, were part of an older avant-garde, but soon merged with the Beats. Lawrence Ferlinghetti, the dean of the North Beach scene, read several times at the Living Theatre in 1959 (an event consecrated with page-one coverage in the *Voice*).

Ginsberg and LeRoi Jones were regulars. There were films as well. Maya Deren premiered her last competed work, *The Very Eye of Night*, at the Living Theatre in February 1959 but it was *The Connection*, a drama by twenty-seven-year-old Chicago-born, one-time shipfitter Jack Gelber, that, opening in July, put the theater on the map.

Gelber's "jazz play" was scarcely as antic as *Pull My Daisy* but there was a family resemblance. *The Connection* concerned a filmmaker's foredoomed attempt to document a gaggle of heroin addicts hanging around a cold-water loft waiting for their daily dose of the drug they call "junk," "smack," or most often "shit." It also fit with the Becks' interest in Luigi Pirandello: The play, directed by Malina, purported to be an actual conclave of drug addicts, a quartet of jazz musicians among them, being paid (with heroin) to play themselves in a movie. The proscenium was porous. The supposed screenwriter, seated in the audience, periodically objected to the actors' alterations of his dialogue.

Act I had the junkies impatiently awaiting their connection, known as Cowboy. Intermittently, the musicians jammed, including alto saxophonist Jackie McLean (who two years previously had his cabaret card revoked for alleged drug use). After intermission, Cowboy—Carl Lee, son of the blacklisted actor Canada Lee, dressed in angelic white and wearing shades—materialized at the pad to minister to each of his customers in turn. This was "offstage." Or rather, it occurred behind the closed door of an actual onstage toilet. In the dramatic climax, the loft's proprietor, a whiny hipster unsubtly named Leach (Warren Finnerty), demanded more dope and, divine retribution, died of an overdose.

Ranting soliloquies alternated with prolonged musical improvisations. When not nodding out or ragging on each other, the members of the racially integrated cast questioned their roles and mocked the straight world for its unacknowledged addictions; they not only scrutinized the audience but followed them into the lobby during intermission. While not unaware of *The Connection*'s clever gloss on Samuel Beckett's *Waiting for Godot*, which had arrived on Broadway in 1956, or Eugene O'Neill's *The Iceman Cometh*, successfully revived off-Broadway the same year, the daily press was dismissive. According to the *New York Times*'s second-string critic, *The Connection* was "nothing more than a farrago of dirt, smalltime philosophy, empty talk and extended runs of 'cool' music." But the *Village Voice* made the play a cause: Jerry Tallmer's long, analytical review was seconded in the letters column with endorsements from Allen Ginsberg as well as the *Voice*'s co-founder Norman Mailer.[8]

Robert Brustein, who to his good fortune had *The Connection* as the subject of his first *New Republic* review, was another supporter; British critic Kenneth Tynan praised the play in *Harper's*. Eventually, the *New York Times*'s senior critic Brooks Atkinson came to see for himself and left impressed, not least by the spectacle of the "mangled theatregoers" who came "tottering down the stairs to the street in various frames of mind—horror, revulsion, terror or ironic amusement." Among them were Leonard Bernstein, Lillian Hellman, Tennessee Williams, and Laurence Olivier.

Atkinson had the pithiest formulation: *The Connection* was "more like an experience than a play." Indeed, Living Theatre associate Larry Rivers, himself a formidable drug user, would outrageously maintain that the musicians were being given real heroin; others recall them occasionally passing out mid-performance. One historian writes that, over the course of the play's three-year run, some fifty spectators fainted at the sight of Leach sticking a needle in his arm.

The first few months of *The Connection*'s 722-performance run coincided with a drug panic in the Village. That fall, having planted five

8 Dominating the *Voice*'s 1960 Obie awards, *The Connection* was named Best All-Around Production and Best New Play—in a season that included local premieres of Jean Genet's *The Balcony*, Edward Albee's *The Zoo Story*, and Beckett's *Krapp's Last Tape*—while Finnerty was singled out as Best Actor. The play was also an event in the commodification of cool. Grove Press published it in paperback, as it would Kerouac's monologue for *Pull My Daisy*; Blue Note brought out an LP. If not a sensation, *The Connection* was at least a Thing. I know that because even my parents—Museum of Modern Art members and musical comedy–loving *New Yorker* readers—drove into the city from Queens to get a taste. And I remember that because my mother's annoyed account of the actors panhandling the audience during intermission impressed itself on my eleven-year-old brain.

undercover detectives disguised as beatniks in the MacDougal–Bleecker Street area, the NYPD's narcotic squad staged a well-publicized "dope raid." One member of the squad, twenty-six-year-old George Bermudez, learned to play the bongos, memorized Oscar Wilde's "Ballad of Reading Gaol," and read original poems including "Junkie's Woe."

4

The Connection fused certain European ideas with more indigenous aesthetic notions. On one hand the Becks were interested in not only Pirandello but also Bertolt Brecht and the Theater of the Absurd. (A fascination with the French surrealist Antonin Artaud would soon follow.) On the other, the Living Theatre was attuned to the spontaneity of jazz and Beat poetry and the authenticity of Method acting, and it had an affinity to the underground theater pieces, eventually called "happenings," staged for the past few summers at the Sun Gallery in Provincetown by the young painter Red Grooms.

The form arrived in New York in early October when painter Allan Kaprow, a thirty-two-year-old Rutgers art instructor and co-founder of Hansa Gallery, staged *18 Happenings in 6 Parts* at the new Reuben Gallery, a loft on Fourth Avenue, between Ninth and Tenth Streets, a few blocks down from the studio where *Pull My Daisy* was shot. Two months later, Grooms presented his play *The Burning Building* in an abandoned boxing gym on the third floor of a building one block from the approach to the Williamsburg Bridge. "It was a crummy place," Grooms recalled. He dubbed it the Delancey Street Museum.

A continuation of *The Walking Man*, shown in September at the Sun Gallery, Grooms's new piece had a correspondingly casual feel. Part slapstick, part shadow play, named for its single jerrybuilt set, *The Burning Building* involved lit candles, verbal non sequiturs, a pair of comic firefighters, a human clock, various offstage crashes, and escalating pandemonium as the young Pasty Man (Grooms), aflame with passion, follows the Girl in the White Box (Joan Herbst) into the Firemen's Den. After ten minutes, the Firemen chase him into the audience, after which he surprisingly doubles back to somersault down from the top of the rickety Burning Building.

The Burning Building presented Kerouac's "wild self-believing individuality" for its own sake. The piece lasted ten minutes; the opening night audience of neighborhood friends demanded four encores.

Audiences varied over the nine performances. One gala night, the sculptor Claes Oldenburg led thirty people down from his opening at the Judson Gallery. But only Oldenburg's buddy, painter Jim Dine, showed up a few days later on a snowy weeknight for a performance that had to be canceled after irate neighbors complained.

Grooms explained his methodology: "I pretty much improvised it before we went on stage. If we had a rehearsal, it was one day before. And then it was likely playing backyard football. You make the play up right on the spot, saying this is what we are going to do." Kaprow's piece was more formal. For two years, he had sat in on John Cage's New School classes on musical composition, applying Cage's ideas regarding randomness and the ordinary with brief pieces that, in addition to sound, involved activities and images. Highly specific, the poster for *18 Happenings* announced in block letters that

> SLIDES WILL BE SHOWN. TAPE-RECORDED SOUNDS, PRODUCED ELECTRONICALLY, WILL COME FROM FOUR LOUDSPEAKERS. THERE WILL BE LIVE SOUNDS PRODUCED. WORDS WILL BE SPOKEN. HUMAN ACTIONS WILL OCCUR OF DIFFERENT BUT SIMPLE KINDS. IN ADDITION THERE WILL BE NON-HUMAN ACTORS. THERE WILL BE A DANCING TOY AND TWO CONSTRUCTIONS ON WHEELS. THE SAME ACTION WILL NEVER HAPPEN TWICE. THE ACTIONS WILL MEAN NOTHING CLEARLY FORMULABLE SO FAR AS THE ARTIST IS CONCERNED. IT IS INTENDED, HOWEVER, THAT THE WHOLE WORK IS TO BE INTIMATE, AUSTERE, AND OF SOMEWHAT BRIEF DURATION.

Evidently structured, with a more developed script than Kaprow would use again, *18 Happenings* had been well rehearsed, although several members of the Living Theatre were puzzled in that the "acting" seemed to be the performance of simple tasks and the performers were mainly painters: Red Grooms, Lucas Samaras, Bob Thompson, Robert Whitman, Sam Francis, Jay Milder, and, in at least one performance, Robert Rauschenberg and Jasper Johns, who were actually painting.

Upon entering, members of the audience—limited to one hundred—received a set of instructions directing them through each of three rooms. The spaces varied in size and lighting. One had a string of Christmas bulbs, another an illuminated blue globe, and the last a row of spotlights. Prompted by a bell, spectators followed their scripts, moving through the gallery from room to room to watch a series of performed events. In taking their cues, they also became performers.

Each of the three rooms featured six actions for a total of eighteen. The rooms were separated by plastic sheets. Thus, spectators were aware of happenings in other rooms but, Kaprow stressed, none would "fully" experience the entire *18 Happenings*. The gallery walls held several large collages and five full-length mirrors. The audio cacophony included a sound collage of French poetry (plus Allen Ginsberg's "Howl"), interspersed with ads, motivational speeches, and the ambient sounds of a delicatessen.

Voice theater critic J. H. Livingston described the event as "a hurly-burly of noise and time and action, where human activity was double distilled in one room while vague happenings were unfolding in the other two." Among the activities, Livingston observed were two men bending over a board and playing a game of blocks, a woman squeezing oranges into a glass and drinking the juice and two painters separated by a rectangular canvas that they painted simultaneously. A man wandered around wearing a sandwich board, another lit matches. Not all the performers were human. A phonograph was encased in a robot figure and, more disturbingly, a windup Black Sambo children's toy executed a tap dance.

The breaks during which spectators changed rooms might be as long or longer than the actions themselves. The future science fiction writer and essayist Samuel Delany, who attended the piece as a teenager, remembered being confused by the lengthy pauses: "After a while, a leotarded young woman with a big smile came in and said, 'That's it.' For a moment, we were unsure if that was part of the work or the signal that it was over. But then Kaprow walked by the door and said, 'Okay, it's over now.'" Judging from the poster, Delany "assumed that the work, regardless of its content, would be rich, Dionysian, and colorful." Instead, it was "spare, difficult, minimal, constituted largely by absence, isolation, even distraction."

Livingston was also impressed. He wondered if the piece was Dada then decided it was not. *18 Happenings* had an object-like opacity and indifference. "There is a shattering awareness of unawareness. Things are looking at us, but we cannot see them." The piece was "not theater but display, a demonstration, and the over-all effect is wonderment . . . an event of high originality and at times beauty and revelation."

5

18 Happenings seemed to signal something new. So too *Pull My Daisy*, which had its long-awaited premiere on Wednesday night, November 11, at Cinema 16—the subscription film society run by Amos and Marcia Vogel that was the preeminent venue for experimental films—billed with the revised version of *Shadows*.[9]

Jonas Mekas promoted both films in the *Voice*. Reviewing the Cinema 16 show, he embraced *Pull My Daisy* and disowned Cassavetes's "virtual remake" of *Shadows*, explaining in a subsequent *Voice* column that unnamed "distributors" had corrupted Cassavetes, persuading him to reshoot and re-edit to the film to be more suitable for commercial theaters.

> The result was a bastardized, hybrid movie which had neither the spontaneity of the first version, nor the innocence, nor the freshness. It is this second version that the producers are now sending to festivals and trying to sell . . . All the virtues which I am bestowing on *Shadows* concern the first version of the film and only this version.[10]

Privately, Mekas realized that he had seen his own imagined film, writing in his personal journal after the show that "this fateful night I realized that what I have to say, if I have anything to say, I'll be able to say it only as an artist."

> My realization that I was betrayed by the second version of *Shadows* was the last stone [*sic*]. It helped me realize that what I was talking about, what I really saw in the first version of *Shadows*, nobody else really saw: I was pursuing my own ideal, my own dream. They didn't know what they had: a blind man's improvisation which depended on chance accidents.

---

9 TV watchers could have seen Cassavetes's most recent episode of *Johnny Staccato*, "Murder in Hi Fi," wherein a mobster's daughter is foisted off as a singer at Johnny's club. Warning her about "the pitfalls of beatnik living," Staccato winds up defending her against one of her father's apish minions.

10 Between Mekas's two columns, the argument consumed the *Voice*'s letter page. Cassavetes and Amos Vogel wrote in to defend the new *Shadows*; Ben Carruthers wrote in support of Mekas. Long thought to be lost, the original *Shadows* (or at least an earlier version) turned up at the 2004 Rotterdam Film Festival. Although full of surprises, it included many familiar scenes. Nor was it devoid of narrative. On the contrary: There was a radical concentration of activity, a frantic round of parties, performances, and pickups that begged to be diluted.

The underground had yet to surface. *Pull My Daisy* and *18 Happenings* were anticipated by the wild street performances that twenty-four-year-old photographer Jack Smith improvised, and which his friend, the twenty-three-year-old painter Ken Jacobs, had begun filming in late 1956. The two men met in a City College night-school film class taught by the onetime Dadaist Hans Richter and, as Jacobs put it, "found common cause." Smith was intrepid as well as inspired, dressing up in not quite drag, not exactly garbage, striking poses or cavorting—as documented by Jacobs often in film-saving fast motion—in the empty streets around Washington Market. "I filmed him as my Don Quixote at odds with New York, challenging its sleepwalking citizens," Jacobs later wrote. He would recall Smith pushing a paperback copy of *On the Road* into his hands, saying, "It's about us."

Star Spangled to Death, the epic Smith vehicle that Jacobs began shooting in 1957, shortly before John Cassavetes started *Shadows* and several months before Viking published *On the Road*, would be the quintessential example of the movie that Mekas now extolled. After disowning *Shadows*, he used his *Voice* column to herald a new epoch in American cinema. Like *The Connection*, *Pull My Daisy*, which Mekas previewed when it was still called "The Beat Generation," pointed "toward new directions, new ways out of the frozen officialdom and midcentury senility of our arts." More than the first flowering of some new aesthetic, *Pull My Daisy* renewed the promise of the medium. It was a return to origins, "to where the true cinema first began, to where Lumière left off."

While affording Mekas license to wipe clean the slate and reinvent the movies virtually from scratch, *Pull My Daisy* suited his other needs. Not for the last time would Mekas hitch his wagon to an avant-garde star. Five days after *Pull My Daisy*'s premiere, Kerouac—who by then had two LPs in release—appeared on network TV in anticipation of a third LP, reading selections from *On the Road* and *Visions of Cody* on the *Steve Allen Plymouth Show*. Leslie and Frank would be stars soon enough. Introduced by Kerouac, *The Americans*, published by Grove Press, was Frank's extraordinarily influential (and no less controversial) collection of photography in January 1960. By the end of the year, Leslie—a rising second-generation Abstract Expressionist soon to be included in a show at the Museum of Modern Art—brought out an ambitious one-shot review, *The Hasty Papers*, which, among much else, included writing by *Pull My Daisy* collaborators Corso, Ginsberg, Kerouac, Orlovsky, and Alice Neel.

The movement with which *Pull My Daisy* was associated had occasioned considerable media attention. As heralded by the *Life* magazine spread "Squaresville U.S.A. vs. Beatsville," autumn 1959 was the Season of the Beatnik. *Pull My Daisy* was even reviewed in *Time*—the magazine's fourth piece on the Beats that year. A few months after it opened, the *New York Times Book Review* devoted its front page to Lawrence Lipton's quasi-sociological account of beat life in Venice, California, *The Holy Barbarians*. Inspired by Ted Joans's beatnik loft parties, Fred McDarrah created Rent-a-Beatnik, a service that provided extroverts like Joans to enliven suburban cocktail parties. A few months later, a *Voice* reader spotted a "Beatnik Kit"—beret, sunglasses, and paste-on beard—in the window of a downtown novelty store.

There was also a serious side. Around the time Kerouac appeared at Hunter, a group of University of Chicago students had published a nine-page excerpt from William Burroughs's *Naked Lunch* in the university literary magazine, *The Chicago Review*. Attacked by a *Chicago Daily News* columnist for facilitating "one of the foulest collections of printed filth" he'd seen publicly circulated, the panicked administration suppressed the upcoming issue, which was to have a second helping of *Naked Lunch* plus poems by Kerouac and Gregory Corso.

The student editors, Irving Rosenthal and Paul Carroll, resigned and started a new magazine, *Big Table* (title suggested by Kerouac), which, in March 1959, published the complete contents of the banned issue. Although the Chicago post office refused to send the "obscene" material through the mail and impounded the magazine, copies circulated in San Francisco and New York.[11]

6

Autumn 1959 brought a third epochal event. "In the jazz circles of New York in the fall of 1959, there was an unusual feeling of apprehension and anticipation in the air," the poet A. B. Spellman, then living on the Lower

11 In June 1960, the American Civil Liberties Union took the case to court and won. (The judge, Julius Hoffman later presided over the trial of the Chicago Seven.) Charges were dismissed in July 1961; by then, Rosenthal had moved to New York City, where he became close to the poets Allen Ginsberg, Ira Cohen, and John Wieners, with whom he lived for a time.

East Side, would recall. On November 17, alto saxophonist Ornette Coleman's Quartet—Don Cherry on cornet, Charlie Haden on bass, and Billy Higgins on drums—made its New York debut at the Five Spot.

The Five Spot was discovered in the mid-'50s as an alternative to the Cedar Bar, on University Place near Eighth Street, which had become a magnet for tourists and art groupies. There was no scene but there was a piano (and beer was 15 cents). The joint, which until 1955 had been beneath the Third Avenue El, was run by Joe and Iggy Termini, who inherited it from their father. It was small, with a capacity of one hundred. A neighborhood painter and amateur musician encouraged Joe Termini to apply for a cabaret license. Avant-garde jazzmen like David Amram and the pianist Cecil Taylor brought painters from the Cedar.

The Termini brothers were hip enough to let Billie Holiday (who had lost her cabaret card) perform unannounced and to book Thelonious Monk (whose cabaret card had been suspended) for several extended gigs beginning in July 1957. Larry Rivers, who claimed to have persuaded Joe Termini to engage Monk, produced evenings of poetry and jazz. The bar even took out an ad in LeRoi Jones's "little magazine" *Yūgen*, advertising it as the home of Monk, jazz poetry, and "America's Leading Painters, Sculptors, Composers, Actors, Poets, PEOPLE."

Some years later *New York Times* jazz critic John S. Wilson cited the Five Spot as an example of what would come to be seen as artist-driven gentrification: "When the El came down, the appearance of open skies, fresh air, and sunshine brought new residents into what had been a drab neighborhood where Cooper Square joins the Bowery. Many of the newcomers were artists and musicians." A "fever spot of coolness" per *Voice* arts editor Jerry Tallmer, the Five Spot tolerated artists and oddballs like Harry Smith who just came to listen.[12]

Monk paved the way for Coleman, after the jazz critic Martin Williams and jazz pianist John Lewis urged Joe Termini to hire him for a two-week gig. Coleman was "a walking myth," Spellman wrote, "a

12 Some even stood outside to hear the music and there were other appeals. The Five Spot had an old-fashioned phone booth wherein the musicians used to get high. Dave Van Ronk, living across the street at 15 Cooper Square with a group of traditional jazz buffs, used to sneak into the booth and pick the remnants of marijuana joints off the floor: "Those guys did not smoke homemade; they had really good dope, so we would collect all these roaches and make new joints out of them, and get bombed out of our birds, basically on the house."

small, bearded man striding out of the woods of Texas and into New York's usually closed jazz scene, with a band of acolytes who played only toy instruments." Coleman's ax was a white plastic saxophone but, for Spellman, "everything about this man was distinctive: his style of playing, his style of dress, his personal history."

A genius born in poverty who had spent his Depression-era childhood living by the railroad tracks in Fort Worth, Texas, Coleman was almost entirely self-educated. He taught himself to play the saxophone and—"a teenage honker," in Spellman's phrase—toured with several R&B bands and even a minstrel show, enduring isolation and indignity before arriving in Los Angeles in the early 1950s, a kook in the land of kookiness, so weird that the Communist Party attempted to recruit him. Nonetheless, Coleman found a sympathetic helpmeet, the poet Jayne Cortez, and managed to gather some disciples—the trumpeter Don Cherry, as eccentric as he, New Orleans drummer Ed Blackwell, and later, a white bassist, Charlie Haden.

Coleman had serious supporters among the writers of the highbrow *Jazz Review*, but the Termini brothers hedged their bets, inviting a host of jazz influentials—Columbia Records' John Hammond, Atlantic founder Ahmet Ertegun, jazz radio deejay Symphony Sid—as well as critics for a double debut. Coleman's Quartet was paired with the Art Farmer–Benny Golson Jazztet, featuring the young pianist McCoy Tyner. Other notables included painters Robert Rauschenberg, Larry Rivers, and Franz Kline; writers Jack Kerouac, James Baldwin, LeRoi Jones, and Norman Mailer (whose essay "The Mind of an Outlaw," declaring himself a pot-smoking anti-establishment rebel, had just appeared in *Esquire*), and conductor-composer Leonard Bernstein, who, by some accounts, attempted to jam with Coleman.

Voice jazz critic Bob Reisner was there as well. The Coleman Quartet "threw away the key, which they claim gives them a greater musical freedom," he wrote. "They sounded their barbaric yawps to the great delight of many who are eagerly awaiting a new sound." Reisner preferred the Jazztet but admitted to having been knocked "off kilter by the Coleman group." He returned a few nights later and found them sounding "better and surer." Others were more emphatic. Canadian pianist Paul Bley, who had jammed with Coleman in Los Angeles, deemed the Jazztet slick, smooth, and "very modern": "Ornette played one set and turned them into Guy Lombardo."

Not all musicians were so approving. "When I arrived in New York," Coleman recalled, "all I got was a wall of hostility"—much of it from established jazz musicians. "I think he's jiving, baby," veteran trumpeter Roy Eldridge asserted. "He's putting everybody on." More temperate, the revered saxophonist Coleman Hawkins suggested that Coleman only needed "seasoning—a lot of seasoning." The pianist Red Garland, a fellow Texan and sometime Miles Davis sideman, called Coleman a faker while Davis suggested that Coleman was "all screwed up inside." The drummer Max Roach was so incensed that after Coleman finished a set, he followed him into the Five Spot kitchen and socked him in the jaw.[13]

John Cage made music identical with noise (or the absence of noise). Ornette Coleman did something similar by subtracting melody and abstracting jazz into pure sound. He inspired similar outrage but also, unlike Cage, professional jealousy. From a musician's point of view, Coleman not only rendered even the most contemporary jazz old fashioned but skipped the well-trodden career path, having paid no dues as sideman to an acknowledged master.

Coleman was immediately snapped up by Atlantic records, the label of Ruth Brown and Ray Charles. Recognizing that they had something like a Jazz Kerouac, Atlantic promoted their new star with a brazenly titled first LP, *The Shape of Jazz to Come*.[14]

7

If Ornette Coleman was the future, something else was in the air. Like, to whom did the music belong? Chicago-based filmmaker Edward Bland's thirty-four-minute polemic *The Cry of Jazz* addressed the question to painful effect, dramatizing an argument between the racially mixed members of a Chicago "jazz appreciation club" in a manner as provocatively stilted and crudely didactic as anything by Brecht.

Debate is triggered when one of the whites carelessly equates jazz with rock 'n' roll. The Black musician Alex sets him straight, then goes

13 Johnny Staccato hated Coleman in advance. Hardly shy about dismissing fellow musicians (or indeed anyone) as "square," Johnny is himself a moldy fig. He disdains bebop and is driven crazy when in the gloriously demented "Wild Reed" episode (first telecast December 3, 1959), an obnoxious hophead sax player (Harry Guardino, one of Ben Carruther's buddies in *Shadows*) attempts to make like Ornette.

14 Originally scheduled for two weeks, Coleman's gig it was extended to ten, through January 1960.

on to maintain that "the Negro alone created jazz." Incredulous and hopelessly square, the whites are incapable of understanding this essentialist position; they can't comprehend what Alex means by "the hazard of being Negro" in America nor why he sees jazz as the triumph of the African American spirit. His characterization of improvisation as "the joyous celebration of the present" in the face of a "futureless future" likewise whizzes over their heads. Meanwhile, shots of impoverished ghetto streets and roach-infested slum apartments are accompanied by extended passages of Sun Ra's ensemble making joyfully raucous noise.

First shown in New York at Cinema 16 in February 1960, *The Cry of Jazz* set off a heated discussion on a panel that included the filmmakers—Bland and scenarist Mark Kennedy—and jazz critic Marshall Stearns. Filling in for James Baldwin, the novelist and jazz critic Ralph Ellison was particularly incensed, stating that the travails of African American life were a crucible "out of which strong people can come." (Here Kennedy interrupted to remark that he wasn't sure that Jews benefited much from their suffering under the Nazis.)

Whites in the audience also took issue. Kenneth Tynan, present at the Cinema 16 screening, reported that soon after one irate man stormed out, "a policeman came in and took the names of the people who were participating in the debate: It seemed that someone had put through an anonymous telephone call, alleging that the meeting was a deliberate attempt to stir up racial antipathy." The movie was praised in the *Voice* by Jonas Mekas, who, responding to complaints it was an anti-white film, wrote, "It's about time somebody made one."

As 1959 ended, David McReynolds, a socialist-pacifist sometime *Voice* contributor who had recently decried the Beat Generation's apolitical alienation, published a manifesto entitled "The Hipster General Strike." New York was plagued by destructive "slum clearance," pointless juvenile gang wars, and Madison Avenue mendacity, not to mention indifference to the suffering poor. New York was a city "from which justice has taken holiday and compassion is on an indefinite leave of absence." More locally, McReynolds cited the "morality drive" launched by the police to shut down the poetry cafés and run the folksingers out of Washington Square, as well as "the trumped-up and much-trumpeted narcotics raid in the Village" apparently designed to transform the Beats into "public scapegoat #1."

McReynolds cited Allen Ginsberg's paraphrasing of Plato's *Republic*: "When the mode of music changes, the walls of the city shake." He was not thinking of Ornette Coleman or Sun Ra but rather an unnamed young Trinidadian who celebrated his graduation from high school by leading a steel band through the streets of the Bronx—a crime for which he was hauled into court and admonished against any such further such expression of "public joy."

Public joy was precisely what New York needed. McReynolds proposed a general strike against city hall to be held in the spring. He called upon artists, poets, and Zen meditators to prepare for the day when motorcyclists from Brooklyn and "roving bands of boppers" from East Harlem would converge in Washington Square, joining

> a wonderful assemblage [of] folksingers and dancers, bongo drummers and poets—the whole mighty column marching joyous through the streets, past [NYU's] Tishman project, right down to City Hall and there, finally, sustained and inspired by magic horns of jazz, the hip population of our city would march seven times around the City Hall, while we stand by the hundreds of thousands to watch.

And then, "perhaps—just perhaps—the walls of indifference would crumble, injustice fall broken to the ground."

It was all happening! "Alas and unfortunately, this is nothing but fantasy," McReynolds concluded, and yet he had been granted a vision of that which, in the next decade, would, however imperfectly, come to pass.[15]

15 McReynolds failed to foresee that six weeks after his article ran, the revolt would begin in Greensboro, North Carolina, when four African American college freshmen sat down at the "white" end of a lunch counter inside a Woolworth five-and-dime and after they were refused service, continued to sit. Within days their numbers swelled to eighty-five and sit-ins spread to Durham and Raleigh—a Political Happening that gave folk-singers, jazz musicians and Beejees something new to consider.

Installation photo, *The Doom Show* (December 1961). Courtesy of Boris Lurie Art Foundation.

2

Primitives of the New Era, 1960–61

In which Manhattan neighborhoods are decimated and young artists take urban detritus for their material. Across the continent, another young New York artist completes the first underground film, *The Flower Thief*. Jonas Mekas makes his own movie and names a movement. Yoko Ono hosts performances in her loft. Boris Lurie's No!art dramatizes nuclear jitters and Claes Oldenburg opens *The Store*.

> *A walk down 14th Street is more amazing than any masterpiece of art.*
>
> —Allan Kaprow, "The Principles of Modern Art," *It Is: A Magazine for Abstract Art* (Autumn 1959)

For fifteen years New York City—and specifically Manhattan—was understood to be the Prime Target and hence Ground Zero in a nuclear war. "The intimation of mortality is part of New York now," E. B. White wrote in 1949; it was present "in the sound of jets overhead, in the black headlines of the latest edition." Children entering kindergarten were issued dog tags. (I was one.)

Ruins were already present. Since the end of World War II, huge chunks of Manhattan had been leveled in the name of urban renewal, the new term for "slum clearance." Buildings, entire blocks, even whole neighborhoods might disappear as if overnight, often rebuilt in the form of brutalist public housing projects. Many of these were on the Lower East Side.

In the 1950s, a red brick palisade of high-rise public housing went up along Avenue D. Many LES residents, arrived since the war, were Puerto Rican; the area's remaining Jews were mostly concentrated in older, less monumental public housing south of Delancey Street. "They were tearing down block after block," the artist Aldo Tambellini recalled. "It looked like a bombed-out area from World War II." Tambellini found inspiration in the rubble: "I vividly remember a dismembered wall remaining standing from an old synagogue with a big mural of the Lion of Judah."

Greenwich Village was more contested. There were plans to demolish the neighborhood south of Washington Square; the god-like master builder Robert Moses sought to extend Fifth Avenue through Washington Square. Although his "emergency road" was defeated, new apartment buildings sprouted, and renovated brownstones appeared among the dilapidated cold-water flats west of Sixth Avenue. The newly finished luxury development Washington Square Village was a fortress amid the tenements and loft buildings south of Bleecker Street—eventually to be cleared in favor of the three concrete slabs called Silver Towers.

During the summer of 1959, the *Village Voice* reported an outbreak of vandalism in the South Village, as well as violence: "Attacks by neighboring youths on beatniks, particularly Negroes, have occurred with disturbing frequency." Art D'Lugoff, proprietor of the neighborhood's largest music venue, the Village Gate—opened the previous year in a former flophouse on the corner of Thompson and Bleecker—saw local resentment in the epidemic of smashed windows. The South Village was increasingly "cosmopolitan" even as aggressive slum clearance facilitated the incursion of upper-middle-class housing.

Harlem and East Harlem had public housing projects. So did the area around Pennsylvania Station, not to mention Brooklyn and Queens or the Bronx, which Moses bifurcated with two colossal expressways. Few of these developments were as ambitious as the Lincoln Square Renewal Project, which despite four years of community resistance obliterated the largely Black and Puerto Rican neighborhood of San Juan Hill to create space for the Lincoln Center for the Performing Arts.

"You cannot rebuild a city without moving people," Moses explained at the May 1959 groundbreaking, an event attended by President Dwight D. Eisenhower and that was deemed sufficiently significant to broadcast live in New York City classrooms (or at least mine). “You cannot make an omelet without breaking eggs.”

2

Ken Jacobs, working as a building superintendent nearby, used the San Juan Hill rubble as a movie set. A movie without a script, shot with a windup, spring-driven Bell and Howell 16mm camera, Jacobs's *Star Spangled to Death* evolved out of Jack Smith's improvised performances. Fearless in making a public spectacle of himself, Smith animated the sooty neorealism of '50s New York with outlandish fantasy, appearing variously as in the guise of a sheik, playing matador, dressed as a bishop, a turbaned odalisque, and an indescribable walking trash heap. Moreover, he engaged his environment. Confounding visitors to the Central Park Zoo with his cardboard headdress, erupting gauze-festooned on the Bowery to consternate a conclave of winos or materializing on St. Mark's Place wearing a paper crown and brandishing a toilet plunger.

Smith's own project was the Hyperbole Photography Studio, a storefront off Cooper Square, which he used to recruit customers seeking to have their picture taken as models for his exotic tableaux. “People were made to look like they were in a scene from a movie,” Jacobs later explained. “The most important thing was to bring the actors in connection with each other.” Smith was playful, not least in his cheerful morbidity. Smiling subjects were swaddled in fabrics, the ambiguity of their poses suggestive of necrophilia or death.

Jacobs conceived *SSTD* in symbolic terms. But the allegory invariably dissolves in the desperate lyricism of the mise-en-scène—there are no establishing shots—and manic immediacy of Smith's performances, not to mention the quasi-documentary moments when the police appear, or a bystander attempts to grab the camera. According to Jacobs, Smith was an existential creature embodying “The Spirit Not of Life But of Living.” His foil was short, emaciated Jerry Sims, a quasi-derelict who wandered one day into the Hyperbole (and who would, for Jacobs, suggest a traumatized survivor of a Nazi concentration camp).

Smith's antics and Sims's misery are punctuated with shards of found footage (a World's Fair promotional short, Richard Nixon's “Checkers” speech) and scenes of the “Two Evils” (Bill Carpenter and Gib Taylor) hanging out in garbage dumps and playgrounds, rocking back and forth amid dismembered bicycles and abandoned toys, like Jewish men in synagogue. (Jacobs has said that he was inspired by a documentary on autistic children, most likely part of the program *The Brain: Restricted Medical and Psychiatric Films*, shown at Cinema 16 in April 1958.)

More bored than malicious, the Two Evils deprive Sims of the consolation he received from hugging his toy dolls, although at the end of the film, his suffering is redeemed. In the climactic cast party, Sims is permitted to set fire to a campaign poster for the movie's bête noire, gubernatorial candidate Nelson Rockefeller. Everyone warms their hands in the blaze.

Jacobs was not the only young artist to take urban detritus as material. Boris Lurie, a thirty-five-year-old painter yet to make a sale, had begun collaging tabloid newspapers and porn magazines, inaugurating a mode he would call "No!art." Mark di Suvero, twenty-seven, was scavenging industrial wooden beams from downtown construction sites, hauling the material to his studio in a former sail factory around the corner from the Fulton Fish Market. Aldo Tambellini, thirty, recently arrived from upstate New York and living in a storefront at 217 East Second Street, collected washbasins and pipes from demolished buildings south of Delancey, affixing them with nails and tin cans and sometimes coating them with plaster cement.

Tambellini considered his storefront studio a community space. Working with Puerto Rican neighbors, he expanded his backyard sculpture garden into a fenced-off, newly cleared empty lot along East Houston Street. "We are the primitives of a new era," he proclaimed in a 1961 drawing of two spherical orbs. As a child, Tambellini had lived through the bombing of his hometown of Lucca, Italy; Lurie was a Latvian Jew who has survived three Nazi concentration camps. Di Suvero was also displaced, albeit not so drastically, by the war; his father, a Jewish Italian naval attaché in China, brought the family to California. A less traumatized foreign-born junk collector was thirty-one-year-old sculptor and Yale-educated son of a Swedish diplomat, Claes Oldenburg.

Living on East Fourth Street, a few blocks north of the same three-acre construction site Tambellini harvested, Oldenburg was picking up rags, ripping apart cardboard boxes and stuffing his studio with worn burlap bags. He had had a piece in the Reuben Gallery's *Below Zero* group show and now with a younger Reuben artist, Jim Dine, had taken a three-month residence in the basement gallery at the Judson Church, a Romanesque edifice originally built just off Washington Square as a mission for the poor.

3

Under the rubric "Ray Gun," Oldenburg and Dine installed a pair of complementary environments. Dine's was *The House*, where bedsprings dangled from the ceiling and the walls were adorned with tapestries made from his wife's discarded clothes. The space was otherwise filled with egg crates and shiny objects that, retrieved from the street, Dine had painted pink and green. To reach his cozy-crazy nest one had to pass through Oldenburg's less ingratiating *The Street*, where, rather than repurposed dresses, the walls were covered with sooty cardboard and strips of newspaper.

On the evening of February 29, 1960, and the two that followed, Oldenburg and Dine presented a medley of dramatic *Ray Gun Spex*, so branded to avoid using Kaprow's term "happenings." Oldenburg's piece was *Snapshots from the City*; Dine's *The Smiling Workman*. In addition, they invited Al Hansen, Dick Higgins, Allan Kaprow, and Robert Whitman to contribute work. (No longer much interested in the form he pioneered, Red Grooms bowed out.)

Theorizing what some preferred to call "painters' theater," Oldenburg distinguished between the cerebral artists like Kaprow (influenced by John Cage) and those like Grooms, Dine, and himself, who were more expressive. Actually, Oldenburg did have ideas. Like many downtown artists, including Kaprow, he was interested in the French surrealist de jour Antonin Artaud, whose translated manifestos, including "The Theater of Cruelty," Grove Press published in late 1958.

Oldenburg was introduced to Artaud's writings by his Chicago Art Institute classmate, Richard O. Tyler, a World War II veteran who had been stationed in Tokyo in the aftermath of the city's 1945 firebombing and who proposed projects that took Artaud literally. A man of arcane interests and multiple talents, Tyler set up a print shop in the basement of a small, near-derelict Greek Revival building on the Avenue D end of East Fourth Street. Employed as the building janitor, he found Oldenburg a studio on the top floor.

A one-man counterculture, Tyler published manifestos and editions of his oversized woodcut prints, hawking them from the "bookbarrow" wheeled out each day and positioned in the tiny Judson Church courtyard. In addition to the Uranian Press, Tyler organized the Uranian

Alchemy Players, a group he characterized as "'Old Bohemians,' shell shocked Vets, beatnik dopers, hustlers & street people" who liked to smoke pot and improvise what Oldenburg recalled as anti-music using "various instruments in all the 'wrong' ways." Often timed to coincide with "planetary occurrences," these lengthy stoned jams were convivial, ceremonial, and sometimes performed at the Judson.

Tyler's subterranean reputation was furthered by a page-one story in the April 6, 1960, *Voice*: "He is a printer, artist, editor, writer, Jungian thinker of sorts, and a businessman," J. R. Goddard explained. The piece, pegged to Tyler's exhibition of woodcuts at the Judson Gallery, referred to the Uranian Alchemy Players' upcoming performance of *Frog's Shock Dream*. According to Oldenburg, Tyler proposed to gather the church audience to witness a friend of his with a metal plate in his head tied up on stage and clobbered with a baseball bat. (Tyler deemed Oldenburg suitable for the active role.) At the piece's climax bombs would be hurled into the space to panic an already alarmed audience. Unsurprisingly, the Judson nixed the idea although Oldenburg credited Tyler's notions of theatricalized "suffering and cruelty" with influencing his *Snapshots from the City*.

Originally, Oldenburg contemplated staging *Snapshots* outside in the wintry air, with Thompson Street blocked by a strategically stalled car. The result, suggesting some performances in *Star Spangled to Death*, would have been clamorous and potentially violent. Moved into the cramped Judson basement, the piece was still uncomfortable. The audience was kept waiting for fifteen minutes in the dark before Oldenburg and his partner Patty Muchinski—he a homeless "rag man," swaddled in tattered bandages and dirty underwear, she a "street chick" wearing a rat-like mask with engorged braids—appeared dramatically framed in the doorway of an adjoining room.

Oldenburg's unseen studio assistant Lucas Samaras flicked the lights at varying intervals thirty-two times to create a series of primitively stroboscopic frozen tableaux vivants. Longer dark intervals were accompanied by recorded car honks, sirens, and shouts over which one heard the artist's retching moans, Muchinski's yips, and miscellaneous "backstage" clatter. Spectators jostled to see these briefly illuminated tableaux. Rag Man and Street Chick scuffled and writhed, striking various agonized poses before executing a shambolic shimmy to the ground. Nothing in *18 Happenings* was nearly so exciting or funny.

Adapting the "Theater of Cruelty," Oldenburg linked his and Muchinski's staged suffering to the audience's actual discomfort. According to early notes, the illuminated activities ranged from "walking like a stripper" and drinking alcohol from a bottle to fighting off an attacker or dying in a car crash. Al Hansen saw them in a more apocalyptic light, characterizing the piece as "a Shinbone Alley aftermath of Hiroshima in Manhattan," with Oldenburg and Muchinski "charging about, dying."

> There were shreds of buildings—objects made of cardboard with blackened edges—and Claes moved about like a modern mummy waving a bottle and being a cross between a Bowery bum and an accident victim. It was very hard to see because the space was so cramped.

Stan VanDerBeek, who filmed the piece as *Snapshots of* [sic] *the City* had a similar sense, describing it as "a black statement about the City in which two people represent the populace after a bomb raid."[1]

Following *Snapshots*, the audience proceeded from Oldenburg's *Street* down a short hallway to Jim Dine's even smaller room for *The Smiling Workman*. The piece was a solo performance, even a psychodrama. Dressed entirely in red and humming to himself, the artist made signs ("I love what I'm doing"), purported to drink paint (actually, tomato juice), poured some over his head, and dove through a canvas. The performance lasted less than a minute.

4

There was another, more obvious art-historical event that month, uptown. With coverage by newsweeklies, television networks, and radio stations, the Museum of Modern Art hosted the Swiss artist Jean Tinguely's self-destroying "meta-matic" sculpture, *Homage to New York*.

Tinguely assembled his monstrous jerry-built gadget, twenty feet high and thirty feet long, in one of the Buckminster Fuller geodesic domes then exhibited in the MoMA sculpture garden, using discarded bicycles and baby carriages and junk found on Canal Street. Set in

1 The associations were topical: Six months after taking office, Governor Rockefeller came out with a statewide civil defense plan that among other things would make fallout shelters mandatory in all new buildings, including private homes, and require owners of existing buildings to provide fallout protection. Thus, a fallout shelter sign sprouted, most unconvincingly, in my apartment building's basement "carriage room."

shuddering motion, the machine created its own smoke screen. The audience, which included New York's governor (a MoMA trustee), booed when a fireman felt compelled to use a heavy CO_2 fire extinguisher to smother the flaming piano, and cheered as the machine shook, gyrated, and ultimately collapsed into rubble. Yet even as Tinguely was setting up his contraption, *Time* ran a story on *Ray Gun*. Happenings had gone national.

Time investigated "an obscure basement gallery in Manhattan's Greenwich Village" where visitors "trooped from room to room, artfully littered with nets and old bottles, the walls splashed with weird designs and slogans," pondering "a new kind of art show that was half picture and half theater." Albeit "ignored by the serious critics, [the happenings were] thoroughly enjoyed by uncritical crowds." The newsweekly's verdict: "It was beat, man . . . Real children might do better." As if to make the writer's point, the page was dominated by rat-muzzled (and unidentified) Muchinski and screaming Oldenburg, bending their knees as if in some moronic dance.

Stanley Fisher, a thirty-five-year-old Brooklyn schoolteacher, snagged an even more outrageous *Snapshot* photo, this one by Fred McDarrah, to plaster on the cover of his new "anthology of rebellion," *Beat Coast East*. The image of Rag Man sprawled on the floor, dirty feet all but brushing the camera lens, might be easily read as a beatnik pad of indescribable, squalid degradation. (Indeed, it was read as such by the teenaged me when, some three or four years later, I saw the magazine for sale in the Paperbook Gallery on Sixth Avenue.)

Beat Coast East featured the usual suspects (Corso, Ginsberg, Kerouac, Diane di Prima, LeRoi Jones). It also included a cheerful, Ginsbergian riff by stand-up poet Hugh Romney, "Three [ambivalent] Poems for Cuba" by Daisy Aldan, and a detail from *Les Lions*, the title and centerpiece of Boris Lurie's first one-man show—an eight-by-six-foot collage of clippings, ads, headlines, and art reproductions trapped in a web of painted color. Seen through squinted eyes, it appeared to be a layered allover abstraction, albeit populated by small pinups cut from girlie magazines. Smaller and not quite as busy, Lurie's *Liberty or Lice* was finished days ahead of the show, incorporating, among other things, a headline noting the May 2 gas-chamber execution of Caryl Chessman, placed in ominous proximity to a large Jewish star.

Les Lions opened in May 1960 at the March Gallery, a tenement cellar at 95 East Tenth Street, around the time that a more respectable, minimalist version of *The Street* was installed at the Reuben Gallery around the corner at 61 Fourth Avenue. Lurie's show was reviewed in the *Voice* but, befitting its basement location akin to the Gaslight and other MacDougal Street dives, not by an art critic.

The June 16 installment of Bill Manville's *Voice* column "Saloon Society" described a long night of drinking that began once the bars opened at 10:00 p.m., having been closed for Election Day (a primary that brought some victories for the Village's reform Democrats) and, thanks to a buddy's bottle of applejack, was able to continue, after the bars closed, in Washington Square. Around 6:00 a.m. a "party of beats" paraded through the square "dancing, jigging along the paths to their East Side jungle pads." An hour or so later, the drones appeared—early people on their way to work and disapproving mothers of small children.

At 8:00 a.m. the first bars reopened. Manville and his cronies were staggering west toward the Hudson when they were intercepted by an artist named Boris Lurie, who persuaded them to reverse course to his show at March Gallery and likely flourished a key to open the basement where his paintings and collages were displayed. Hopelessly hungover or miraculously re-intoxicated, Manville devoted the rest of his column to Lurie's "disturbing nightmares."

> Arab refugees side by side with atom-bomb texts and green Salem cigarette ads, headlines about junkies breaking through photos of babies burning. *Les Lions* sitting in the shade of trees growing by the side of a lush river of Friendly Aunt Mother's Home-Made Southern-Style Instant Frozen Less-Work-for-You Tomato Juice. Obsessively repeated throughout the paintings, girls. Naked girls, pinup girls, corset and brassiere-in-the-*Times Magazine* section girls. Marilyn, Brigitte, Liz and Jayne.

Lurie's "bizarre, strange, hallucinatory, and shocking paintings" inspired Manville to bardic poetry.

> Advertisements for Revlon Beautyglo driven into the heart of a story on a leper colony in Africa. *Life* magazine taken to its final ultimate, absurd, and frightening conclusion, pain and death given no more space and attention than pictures of Elsa Maxwell's latest party. And

> all of us spectators at our own death, hovering over it all in narcotized detachment, bored as gods with The Bomb, yawning over The Election, coming to a stop at last only to linger over the tender dream photos of Marilyn.

Manville, a former adman, may have been nobody's idea of a beatnik but—entranced by the March basement—he was in sync with a cultural moment. *Time*'s disapproval notwithstanding, the Beat continued that spring with several explanatory paperbacks, Fred McDarrah's photo collection *The Beat Scene* and Seymour Krim's mass-market anthology *The Beats*, as well as two LPs purportedly recorded "live" in beatnik coffeehouses: the Gaslight's *Beat Generation Jazz Poetry* and Café Bizarre's *Assorted Madness, Beat Generation Poetry, Beat Erotica by the Beat and the Unbeat*. By way of an uptown promotion, the Record Hunter sponsored a "beatnik invasion of the midtown bourgeoisie" in which an assortment of Beat poets and painters occupied the emporium's display window across Fifth Avenue from the Forty-Second Street Library.

MGM's adaptation of *The Subterraneans*, Jack Kerouac's quickly written follow-up to *On the Road*, would open in late June to universal derision. Jonas Mekas called it "the trashiest, phoniest, not to say stupidest masterpiece of Hollywood Anno 1960" and compared the acting to the insane asylum scene in the recent Tennessee Williams adaptation *Suddenly Last Summer*. (But hadn't *Pull My Daisy* also been crazy?) Meanwhile, two months earlier, the first truly underground Beat movie had its world premiere in a storefront coffeehouse 3,000 miles west of Café Bizarre.

A 16mm film of indeterminate length made by Ron Rice, *The Flower Thief* starred the poet Taylor Mead traipsing through San Francisco along with a cluster of North Beach habitues. *Pull My Daisy* consecrated a Beat aristocracy. Rice—a decade younger than Kerouac and Ginsberg—was more like the unknown beatnik, raking over the coals of the dying North Beach scene.

5

Not yet twenty-five when he shot *The Flower Thief*, Rice was a Bronx-born high school dropout. Discharged for an unspecified "physical disability" four months after enlisting in the Air Force, Rice briefly took art classes at Cooper Union. He was excited by Mekas's spring 1959 columns on *Pull My Daisy* and, inviting the writer for a beer at the Cedar Tavern, asked how he might learn filmmaking. (Mekas directed him to an Eighth Avenue camera store that sold outdated film stock.)

That summer, Rice made his way to Provincetown, where he shot an 8mm movie he would describe as "partly about a painter's exhibition and partly footage of a girl running nude through the sand dunes." (More significantly, the post–Labor Day season in Provincetown brought Red Grooms's *The Walking Man*, a series of enigmatic, clownish actions performed at the Sun Gallery by a cast of five using material from the town dump.) Back in New York, Rice decided to travel west and, armed with an old 16mm Eastman Kodak camera, set out for Squaw Valley, Utah, to film the Winter Olympics.

After touching down in Utah, Rice turned up in North Beach, where he frequented the Coffee Gallery. Located on the district's shabby main drag, upper Grant Avenue, the Coffee Gallery functioned as the community nerve center. The walls were covered with personal notices and posted announcements; the atmosphere as characterized by one San Francisco journalist was one of "more or less near-anarchy."

There the charismatic Rice met a group of older poets, including recently returned Taylor Mead and two local stars. One was the African American poet Bob Kaufman, editor of *Beatitude*, author of the "Abomunist Manifesto," a onetime organizer for the Communist-led Maritime Union and leader of a 1958 Beat protest march, given to holding forth with effusive monologues, his centrality to the scene buoyed by tourists as well as fellow Beats. The other was the green-haired, Berlin-born performance artist ruth weiss, credited as the first poet in San Francisco to read poetry to jazz.

Rice asked Kaufman to be in his movie (he is, briefly) and weiss to write a script. Imagining a 3:00 a.m. encounter between a local and a tourist, she gave him the film's title and wrote a part for Mead. Rice jettisoned the script but kept the title as well as Mead. (weiss subsequently made the film as *The Brink*, a forty-minute tour of San Francisco filtered through the musings of two lovers, "He" and "She," more evocatively free-associative than linear.)

Born to wealth in Grosse Pointe, Michigan, the peripatetic Mead, then thirty-five, had once been a broker at Merrill Lynch. He also studied acting in Los Angeles and New York, was present in San Francisco for the birth of the North Beach scene in 1955, bounced back to New York to join the Beat poets who began reading at the Gaslight in 1959, then went on the road back to the Beach, where he made a splash at the Coffee Gallery, sharing first prize with Kaufman in a "read off."

North Beach had been under fire for the better part of two years. In May 1958, *The San Francisco Examiner* ran a three-part exposé of the Beat Generation's "headquarters" and the sinister antics occurring "far out in the faceless jungle of nothingness." Two lurid incidents—a drunken suicide and a rape/murder—triggered police occupation that summer. Much of the harassment was racial, and Kaufman was arrested twice. The raids were ongoing when Rice arrived.

Mead imagined *The Flower Thief* as the scene's "death-knell," a pensive eulogy. In his memoir, he wrote that Rice thought of him "wandering through various locations, some in the process of being torn down and associating with the last twenty or so genuine intellectual wastrels in the area." In any case, the look was proudly primitive. Rice used outdated army-surplus 16mm film to document Mead's arbitrary tour of San Francisco's bohemian quarter. Mead was impressed with Rice's energy. He "didn't sit around theorizing on a 'project' or how to make a movie. He made the movie. He believed in 'pushing the button.'" (According to Mead, Rice also financed the movie by forging checks on his girlfriend's account.)

Affect alternating between the wistfully infantile and dementedly fey, frequently dragging an outsized teddy bear in a child's red wagon, Mead clowns around town. Sites range from jazz bars and downtown street corners to the beach-side Playland amusement park on San Francisco's western edge and a vast derelict loft belonging to the scene's frequently busted, 300-pound paterfamilias Eric "Big Daddy" Nord. Although nothing if not pre-sexual, Mead appears to find love, picked up by a good-looking kid in the film's final sequence (a fantasy surely more his than Rice's).

To call *The Flower Thief* self-indulgent is to state the obvious—and miss the point. Unscripted and (unlike *Pull My Daisy*) genuinely haphazard, filled with goofy non sequiturs, less talented than persistent, *The Flower Thief* was something like the scene's home movie, premiering at the Coffee Gallery on a borrowed 16mm projector. Rice's then friend, the future producer Barry Clark, stood at the door asking for donations: "I don't recall any contributions, any applause, or any comments," he would later write. "The whole thing felt like a dismal failure." According to Mead, a histrionic Rice had to be talked out of burning his film.

Still, he persevered. Rice screened *The Flower Thief* several times in North Beach that spring, making changes according to the audience suggestions, including bathing the film in blue dye to render it more "avant-garde." Mead was furious. "Who got your ear? What fuck headed asshole buzzed you into changing that film?" he wrote Rice after one June screening. "Are you going to listen to every asshole diddley bop in San Francisco and the Bagel Shop?" Mead was angry that some of his scenes were cut and his performance badmouthed. "I see that anyone can flatter you with a little attention and laugh at the 'movie director' behaving like a wild man and you will fall for it. Don't drink."

Mead calmed down after the next screening. In a more paternal mode, he cautioned impetuous Rice (now tinkering with the movie in hopes of attracting Hollywood attention) to leave well alone:

> You're trying too hard—the whole thing should take place in the same atmosphere of ease and collaboration in which we filmed it but now that you smell money you are getting nervous . . . Don't worry too much about the reaction of the San Francisco audiences—this is rather a square city—all the shows that arrive here are the second string out of New York.

Reassuringly, he ended his note, "Don't worry about the bathroom scene—it is great. We are great—the movie is great." Mead urged him to send *The Flower Thief* to New York.[2]

---

2 There are no records of any further North Beach screenings although *The Flower Thief* was re-edited at least once more by Dr. Francis J. Rigney, a San Francisco psychiatrist sympathetic to the Beats and the co-author of *The Real Bohemia* (a "sociological and psychological study of the 'Beats'"), written mainly in 1959 and published two years later. Rice stayed with Rigney for a time while Rigney recut the film, adding a signed introduction, dated 1961:

> The film you are about to see is a mixture of fact and fantasy. These have been fused in a way that gives the film its own internal logic. At times it faithfully documents life in San Francisco's Grant Avenue bohemian colony [sic] known to most as beatniks. At times there is a plot but only in the loosest sense of the word. There were no rehearsals. The acting was spontaneously generated by a peculiar mystique between

The scene had shifted east. Ginsberg returned to New York in late 1958, taking an apartment at 170 East Second Street. Corso was back in the Village. Kerouac was living with his mother on Long Island. Soon after *The Flower Thief* was shown in North Beach, Bob Kaufman left San Francisco, with his wife Eileen and infant son Parker, for an apartment at 42 St. Mark's Place shared with the jazz vibraphonist Dave Pike, a sometime sideman with Paul Bley. A few months later Kaufman moved into the same building as Ginsberg and, along with Ginsberg, Corso, and Kerouac, read at the Gaslight.

Mead remained in San Francisco to star in two more movies, Vernon Zimmerman's 16mm *Lemon Hearts* and Bob Chatterton's 8mm *Passion in a Seaside Slum*, each just short of half an hour and largely based on Mead's improvised routines. Chatterton described *Passion in a Seaside Slum* as "a fantasy on third sex relationships," recommending it to "those who wish to delve further into the psyche of Taylor Mead." *Lemon Hearts* was similar.

Zimmerman, who learned his craft assisting Rice on *The Flower Thief*, would boast that *Lemon Heart* was produced for $50, provided by Mead's cousin-by-marriage, the Broadway star Richard Kiley. On one hand the movie documents the construction sites and derelict Victorian houses produced by the "redevelopment" of San Francisco's Western Addition, particularly Japantown and the largely African American Fillmore neighborhood. On the other hand, the movie showcases Mead. Appearing as a score of different characters, he hula-hoops in drag, impersonates a Spanish dancer, slouches around with Ruth Etting's rendition of "Love Me or Leave Me," makes faces and spits. Sometimes accompanied by bongos, he is heard reciting his poems on the soundtrack: "I'm a genius and all that jazz, jazz, jazz."

Mead moved on to Los Angeles, settling briefly in the city's bohemian quarter, Venice. He was back in New York by 1961, reading at the Gaslight and elsewhere, but it would be another eighteen months before *The Flower*

---

the director and the actor. The film was made in 1960 at a time when most outsiders were condemning and berating these bohemians as ineffectual, humorless frauds.

Another version of the film was distributed by the Audio Film Center in San Francisco, which rented a print to the East Bay group that later became Canyon Cinema. It was shown in Los Angeles, under the auspices of the Society for Cinema Arts at the Coronet Theatre, the venue for the West Coast premiere of *Pull My Daisy*, as well as the Riviera-Capri (now New Beverly), which also screened avant-garde or underground movies in the early '60s.

Thief followed him. Meanwhile, several Beat movies were in production. Robert Frank was adapting an Isaac Babel story, *The Sin of Jesus*, as his solo follow-up to *Pull My Daisy*. Shirley Clarke had secured the rights to *The Connection* and Jonas Mekas was shooting *Guns of the Trees*.

6

Spring 1960 had been filled with portents. In April, Communist youth groups from fifteen countries, including the United States, gathered in Havana to express their support for Fidel Castro's fight against "Yankee imperialism." On May Day the Soviet ground defenses shot down an American U2 spy plane, waiting nearly a week to make the news public. In the interim, a protest held in City Hall Park against the annual nationwide civil defense drill resulted in twenty-six arrests. A group of Lower East Side teenagers took advantage of the deserted streets to rob a grocery store.

Guns of the Trees was Jonas Mekas's contribution to the zeitgeist. The movie took its subject (and itself) seriously, contemplating human existence in the glare of annihilation and the shadow of the atomic bomb, in New York City circa 1960 A.D. Mekas even imagined that *Guns* might change the world, writing in his diary, "What I want to achieve—ideally—with my film: is to overthrow the government. All governments."

For a year or more, Mekas had been extolling what he called the New American Cinema, heralded first by *Shadows* and then *Pull My Daisy*. Indeed, *Guns* can be seen as a would-be synthesis of *Shadows*'s "texture of dark, lonely streets, bars and neon lights" (as Mekas praised it in the British Film Institute's magazine *Sight and Sound*) and *Pull My Daisy*'s spontaneous hijinks and Beat pad. The stars were Argus Spear Julliard, Frances Stillman, Mekas's brother Adolfas, and Benito Carruthers, the intense twenty-four-year-old actor who stole *Shadows* with his precocious Method performance and who, just as importantly, agreed with Mekas that the film had been ruined by Cassavetes's second "commercial" cut.

Guns had Hegelian aspirations—the star of *Shadows* meets Allen Ginsberg, who, never seen on-screen, declaims a poetic soundtrack as Kerouac had in *Pull My Daisy*—but it was far more schematic than its models. The movie concerns two young couples. One pair (Stillman and Adolfas) is white and gloomy. The other (Spear Julliard and Carruthers) is Black and life-affirming. As in *Shadows*, the principal characters are generally named for their actors. Argus is happily pregnant. She and Ben frisk through various locations and make love in what looks like a cold-water loft as militantly sullen Frances rails against the ugliness of the world. Actually, Frances has already committed suicide. The movie is a flashback in which her bereaved lover, the black-clad Gregory (Adolfas), tries to figure out why.

Unlike *Pull My Daisy* and *The Flower Thief*, *Guns of the Trees* was seriously Beat and hence close to self-parody. Yet it was also engagé. There were intimations that the Beat Generation might be growing into a full-fledged oppositional counterculture. Not just bohemian poets but peace demonstrators and even the youthful supporters of presidential candidate Adlai Stevenson were being termed "beatniks." So were the folk-singers who played in Washington Square, the teenage kids who flocked on weekends to MacDougal Street coffeehouses, and Jonas Mekas's crew.

As various city agencies attempted to regulate or shut down MacDougal Street, *Guns of the Trees* experienced its own legal vicissitudes. *Sunday Junction*, Mekas's first attempt at feature filmmaking—directed by a hero of the Polish resistance, Edouard de Laurot, né Edward Lada Laudański—had been abandoned back in 1957, Mekas recalled, due to "insufficient funds and constant bickering with the police." Making *Guns* of *the Trees* entailed similar problems. Mekas's diary details all manner of official harassment, not only in the city but in its environs.

The filmmakers were chased out of Catskill woodlands and run off Long Island ponds. On July 14, Connecticut authorities arrested them for "trespassing" on a public lake. The cops were particularly tough on Adolfas because he had grown a beard for his part. On July 25, the filmmakers infiltrated the wetlands around Idlewild Airport. "During the shooting on the beach," Mekas wrote, "a group of truck drivers stopped their trucks and came to watch us work. One said: 'You are either communists or beatniks.'" (Which was worse? The previous week's *Voice* had published a plaintive account of anti-beatnik persecution at the Newport Jazz Festival.)

Their jeep repeatedly broke down. Their Arriflex camera needed repairs. Equipment was stolen. Money ran out in mid-August and Mekas required a $750 loan from the owner of the New Yorker Theater, Dan Talbot. When shooting resumed at the end of the month, the filmmakers were chased off the "demolished ruins on 9th Avenue near 28th Street," the site—"a field of nothing"—that was to be a mammoth housing development sponsored by the International Ladies' Garment Workers Union. Even an abandoned railyard in the Bronx was off-limits.

Unlicensed filming was itself subversive. At one point, Mekas was prevented from shooting at the Fulton Fish Market—the police considered them too close to the naval base in New York Harbor. (As if in retribution, the city's waterfront was soon after flooded by Hurricane Donna and, as Mekas noted, "all hell broke loose.") On September 25, Mekas reported that he and his crew were questioned and searched as part of the security surrounding Nikita Khrushchev's notorious shoe-pounding appearance at the United Nations. In early November, *Guns of the Trees* wrapped (albeit temporarily).

Mekas returned to his *Village Voice* column, reporting the Village abuzz with "Young Cinema" activity, not just Shirley Clarke's adaptation of *The Connection* and Robert Frank's *The Sin of Jesus* but also novelist Harold "Doc" Humes's *Don Peyote*. Humes, Mekas noted, was suing the New York Police Department for roughing up his crew: "How well I know it, from my own experiences this summer." There was another persecution that season. On the night of October 20, 1960, the hipster monologuist Lord Buckley, performing at the Jazz Gallery on St. Mark's Place, was busted on stage by undercover members of the vice squad—his cabaret card revoked for failure to report a 1943 marijuana arrest.[3]

When Buckley suffered a fatal stroke less than a month after his arrest, he became the first show-biz martyr of the '60s. The Jazz Gallery hosted a memorial event in early December that mixed Bebop royalty and raconteurs, among them kindred spirit Babs Gonzalez, who introduced his new song "Old MacDonald Did the Twist." The evening of "supercharged excitement" peaked, per *Voice* jazz critic Bob Reisner, when Dizzy Gillespie called Ornette Coleman up on stage. Coleman requested his own drummer, Ed Blackwell. Cautioning Coleman "with a smile" not to play too fast,

---

3 Although the engagement was Buckley's first New York gig in a decade, Judith Malina recalls him being around in 1959, attending rehearsals for *The Connection*, present in the lobby on opening night, and inspiring the intermission routine in which the actors panhandled the audience for money to score. "The way that each actor came out and did their little shtick was really inspired by the way that Lord Buckley did his shtick."

> Gillespie announced that they were going to play five tunes at once. After the first number, Diz gleefully suggested that they play blues. Ask anyone who was there who carved whom. The answer will depend on their hipness or, as Lord Buckley used to say, "his double hipness."[4]

On November 8, 1960, John F. Kennedy was elected president by the narrowest of margins. Bob Kaufman, as obstreperous a barroom personality in the Village as he had been in North Beach, was arrested after an altercation in a MacDougal Street coffeehouse and committed to Bellevue, and the Reuben Gallery reopened at a new location, a storefront on 44 East Third Street that had formerly housed a flooring business. The first Happening, staged just before the election, was Jim Dine's *Car Crash*.

Even more than *The Smiling Workman*, the twenty-minute performance was a psychodrama—inspired by two car accidents the artist had survived the previous year. Dine whitewashed the performance space, still cluttered with shelves holding rolls of linoleum and cork, and added fifty folding chairs so that, as Jill Johnston noted in her *Village Voice* review, the audience was "an active component." Lights and various sorts of red crosses hung from the ceiling.

Unlike *The Smiling Workman*, *Car Crash* had a cast. Seated atop a high stepladder, Patty Muchinski was combination chorus and observing angel as three anthropomorphized cars, small flashlights affixed to their headgear, careened around the space amid honks and traffic noise. Dine, largely sprayed silver, was the protagonist car. Accompanied by the sounds that might precede a crash (ignition keyed, gears shifting, acceleration, screeching tires), Dine moved to a blackboard on which he drew images of cars with such vehemence the chalk kept breaking. His face was contorted. The word "help" was repeated on an unfurling roll of paper towels. As the cast joined in with Dine's grunts and moans, he abruptly exited.

---

4 Doc Humes, Buckley's newly appointed agent, had planned to feature him (as well as Ornette Coleman) in an "improvisational" movie, an update on Cervantes titled *Don Peyote*. The thirty-four-year-old writer called for a grand jury investigation into the NYPD Cabaret Bureau. To that end, he organized a Citizens Emergency Committee. As the co-founder of *The Paris Review*, Humes was well connected, rallying Norman Mailer, Norman Podhoretz, George Plimpton, Grove Press publisher Barney Rosset, playwright Jack Gelber, and Assemblyman Mark Lane. The NYPD responded with a massive investigation of the city's cabarets, finding hundreds of violations, and fourteen outstanding parking tickets issued to Humes, who was briefly jailed as a scofflaw.

Dine's distress was such that Al Hansen was moved to tears. Outside in the lobby, he found Dick Higgins drying his eyes, which were wet from laughter. According to Dine, "Kaprow once said, 'You're the one who does the funny Happenings.' He likes classification . . . But they were not funny. *Car Crash* was not laughed at; the spectators tittered like they do at nudes in museums—kids get embarrassed and laugh."

That same weekend, the March Group—Boris Lurie, John Fischer, Stanley Fisher, and Sam Goodman—held its first exhibition. All four artists were Jews. Fischer (the youngest of the group, born in Belgium in 1930) was a refugee who managed to escape the Nazis as a teenager. Lurie called the *Vulgar Show* a "group manifestation" inspired by the "courage of the Beat poets, Castro's insurrection, our own desperation," and he considered it an exorcism. Stepping back from his pinup collages, he showed older canvases of inflated, dismembered women while Goodman and Fisher packed the basement with crude collages and ramshackle constructions.

Advertised by a collage scribble-scrabble flier of unsurpassed crudeness, the show (which changed over the course of the month) more than justified its name. The work was brutally childish, aggressively artless, and far more primitive than Dine's *House* or even Oldenburg's *Street*. Repeatedly evoking nuclear war, Fisher's brief mission statement might have been written for *Guns of the Trees*. It began by asserting that "Art has ended. The world and being [sic] collapsed" and asking, "Who are you?"

The final question was suitably apocalyptic: "Can we confront again the speed of death in H-bomb blasts and retain our corpse of clay or must we watch the kaleidoscope of paint immured in motion sickness of that final day?" Following Lurie, the March group would term their work "No!art."

7

"Some artists remind us of real or impending disasters," Jill Johnston wrote in the *Voice*. "Others couldn't care less about anything outside of a canvas and a pot of paint if that's what they happened to be involved in." Johnston was thinking specifically about the composer La Monte Young.

Inspired largely by John Cage, who followed several stints teaching at Black Mountain College with a class in experimental composition at the New School for Social Research from fall 1956 to summer 1960, a kindred art gang was coalescing. Young, a twenty-five-year-old sometime saxophonist who claimed to have jammed with Ornette Coleman and Don Cherry in Los Angeles, arrived from Berkeley in December 1960 on a prestigious traveling scholarship in music composition. The poet Susan Sherman, who lived for a time with Young and his girlfriend, the poet Diane Wakoski, while a student at Berkeley, was properly overawed: "La Monte knew more about music than anyone I had ever met, than I ever imagined it was possible to know," while Wakoski, still an undergraduate, was already acknowledged as "the opinionated matriarch of the San Francisco/Berkeley poetry scene."

A dandy in a black velvet suit and voluminous cape ("possibly taken more seriously as a character than a composer," per Johnston), Young teamed up with the nascent Japanese American conceptual artist Yoko Ono, twenty-seven, who sat in on Cage's New School class (her then husband, Toshi Ichiyanagi, was a student). Together, Young and Ono organized a six-month series of two-evening concerts at Ono's loft—a grimy, low-ceiling space with a $50 monthly rent on the top floor of 112 Chambers Street. The loft had no heat. Electricity was furnished from the space below via extension cord. Ono somehow managed to maneuver a piano into the space but Young cautioned the prospective attendees on his mailing list to "come prepared to sit on the floor." The notice also included the capitalized warning that THE PURPOSE OF THIS SERIES IS NOT ENTERTAINMENT (not a caveat one was likely to find at a performance of Oldenburg's *Ray Gun Spex*).

The first Chambers Street concert introduced Young's protégé Terry Jennings. The next two featured Ichiyanagi and another of Young's associates, Joseph Byrd. Among those involved as accompanists were pianist and Cage associate David Tudor, electronic composer Richard Maxfield (who took over Cage's New School class), Diane Wakoski, the dancer Simone Forti, and the musician-painter Larry Poons, as well as Cage students Dick Higgins, Alison Knowles, and Jackson Mac Low.[5]

A powerful personality, born to a Mormon family in an Idaho log cabin, Young largely monopolized the Chambers Street events. Years later, he maintained that he had had an affair with Ono, who, only

5 Subsequent events included a performance by Mac Low (which involved several other poets, Robert Kelly and John Perrault, as well as Wakoski), Maxfield, and Young, a dance recital choreographed by Simone Forti with Steve Paxton, Yvonne Rainer, and Forti's then husband, the artist Robert Morris, who followed up with an installed "environment." Three and a half years later Johnston would recall the concerts as "the equivalent of the underground cinema without the publicity."

wishing to be as famous as he, made her loft available for his projects. Be that as it may, Ono was an active participant in the concerts. She and Young were both involved in creating "instructional pieces" although hers took the form of performative paintings. *Kitchen Piece* involved hurling leftover food from the refrigerator onto a canvas and then setting the canvas on fire. (Cage cautioned her to apply a fire retardant first.)

A few weeks into the Chambers Street calendar, Ono gave her first solo concert, *A Grapefruit in the World of Park*, as part of an Evening of Contemporary Japanese Music and Poetry at the Village Gate. Ichiyanagi and Toshiro Mayuzumi supplied the music. Ono read a text about a grapefruit abandoned after a picnic that she had written six years earlier while a student at Sarah Lawrence and published in the college newspaper. In the background, Ichiyanagi, Young, and Cage performed according to her instructions: laughing, playing atonal music, and making noise, including that of a toilet flushing. "Far out was the phrase for last night's program at the Village Gate," the *New York Times* reported.[6]

Inspired by the Chambers Street concerts, George Maciunas, a twenty-nine-year-old Lithuanian émigré who had attended Maxfield's New School composition class (where he met Hansen, Kaprow, Mac Low, and Young, all future associates of Maciunas's art movement Fluxus), began hosting similar events uptown at the AG Gallery (Madison Avenue and Seventy-Fourth Street). The programs ran through July.

The gallery's closing show included three of Ono's instruction paintings, including a picture of a grapefruit, *Painting to Be Stepped On*. Due to unpaid electricity bills, the gallery was only open during the daytime. It was during Ono's show that Ray Johnson, another Cage colleague, having attended Black Mountain, staged his first "Nothing"

6 The *Times* employed the same phrase when Ono reprised *A Grapefruit in the World of Park* for a packed audience at Carnegie Recital Hall in November 1961. The "far-out music" was performed in near total darkness: "Against a taped background of mumbled words and wild laughter a girl spoke earnestly about peeling a grapefruit, squeezing lemons and counting the hairs on a dead child. Musicians in the corner made their instruments go squeep and squawk." Reviewing for the *Voice*, Jill Johnston was unimpressed with Ono's "theater of events," writing that she was "alternately stupefied and aroused, with longer stretches of stupor." Arousal was prompted by Yvonne Rainer performing an exercise in "excruciating slow motion"; stupefaction by Ono's finale, concluding the evening with "amplified sighs, breathing, gasping, retching, screaming—many tones of pain and pleasure mixed with a jibberish [sic] of foreign-sounding language that was no language at all."

performance. Once attendees had gathered in an empty room, Johnson made his appearance carrying a large, corrugated cardboard box of wooden spools that he emptied down the staircase, creating a hazardous means of egress.

In March, Young and Ono had organized a concert at Judson Church by Cage disciple Philip Corner. That same month, which also saw Allen Ginsberg give his first reading of "Kaddish" at Columbia University, Cage's most celebrated student, Allan Kaprow, staged *A Spring Happening*, a frightening, surprisingly brutal "rebirth" performed twelve times over six nights at the Reuben Gallery. The aesthetic was Artaud's Theater of Cruelty. A few spectators resisted but most were herded single file into a dark, narrow tunnel. "The unwitting audience has no choice in the matter," Jill Johnston explained in her *Village Voice* review. "Once situated in the long narrow dark cattle car, or tomb or womb, or subway, one is already affected."

Peering through narrow slits, members of the audience could see red walls covered with chicken wire, cardboard, and newspapers. Lights flickered, then went out. In the darkness, the audience heard rumbling, booming, and crashing as, unbeknownst to them, a man on the tunnel roof hurled metal drums down on a tile floor. "Claustrophobia contracts to panic," Johnston wrote. "Terrible things are about to happen." These included the repeated sound of a stifled bell, persistent hissing as matches were lit and extinguished, the buzz of a power saw.

In the gloom, two men could be glimpsed menacing each other with cudgels, first in slow motion and then accelerated. The tunnel began to shake. Suddenly, Johnston witnessed "the most terrifyingly beautiful scene of a naked girl." Crouched down, a spring of collard greens dangling from her mouth, she seemed to be looking for something but she herself was the object of a hunt, tracked by searchlight, until two men found and smothered her with a blanket. The noise level increased, the walls appeared to collapse and a man pushing a power lawn mower forced the audience out into the light.

Johnston was clearly disturbed. "Nobody need know any specific intention or specific imagery. One knows simply violence, fear, extreme relief, death and life crowding close together." Whatever foreboding *A Spring Happening* may have had was reinforced less than a month later, when, sponsoring a doomed invasion at the Bay of Pigs, the new

Kennedy administration blundered into an abortive attempt to overthrow Fidel Castro.

Nowhere in America were more nuanced positions taken on the Cuban Revolution than in New York. As the debate over Cuba intensified, several of the more politically minded Beat journals, including *Yūgen*, *Kulchur* (founded in early 1960, and subsequently abandoned, by Marc Schleifer), *The Provincetown Review* and *The Second Coming* (already preparing a special Cuba issue) organized a protest vigil at the UN. Norman Mailer commandeered the *Voice* front page for an open letter to JFK. The time was ripe for the truculent anti-Americanism of the *Involvement Show*, opening at March Gallery on Bay of Pigs weekend.

Writing in *Art News*, Jack Kroll cited the show's atmosphere of "tone deaf subversion." Standing out amid the chaos: Boris Lurie's hyper-cluttered six-by-six-and-a-half-foot canvas collage *Lumumba is Dead* (*Adieu Amérique*). The title alludes to Patrice Lumumba, the first democratically elected prime minister of the newly independent Congo, murdered in a US-backed putsch in early 1961. A field of newspaper clippings and bare-breasted pinups harvested from girlie magazines and underwear ads provide the dizzying ground for a large, red-and-black swastika flag through which peaked a news photo of the Nazi desk-murderer Adolf Eichmann.

The *Involvement Show* included work by poets Ted Joans and Jerome Rothenberg. Kroll was inspired to a bit of poetry himself, writing of *Lumumba is Dead* that "all our tramps on the trampoline of the mass and underground-mass mediums concoct [Lurie's] goodbye Valentine to our sugar-boat society."

8

Jonas Mekas finally had some good news. A few days into the *Involvement Show,* the *New York Times* announced that composer Gian Carlo Menotti's recently established Festival of the Two Worlds, held in Spoleto, Italy, was to feature a program of American independent films including such recent films as *The Connection*, *Guns of the Trees*, and *The Flower Thief* (which guest programmer David Stone had likely seen in Los Angeles).

Had the movement arrived? *Pull My Daisy* was playing downtown at Dan Talbot's newly acquired Charles Theater; *Shadows* was enjoying a Village run at the 8th Street Playhouse. Ron Rice wasn't attending the

Spoleto festival but, assuming Mekas would be there, wrote to tell him of *The Flower Thief*, name-dropping his star, Taylor Mead, as someone known to Mekas's *Village Voice* colleague Fred McDarrah. For his part, Mekas took out a series of ads in the *Voice* offering shares in *Guns*.

Stone must have been shown a rough cut as Mekas didn't get his first answer print until June 1961, sixteen days before the movie had its premiere. Completed, *Guns* was appropriately strident. Mekas punctuated the action with blasts of white light and high frequency noise. Allen Ginsberg recited "Sunflower Sutra" and there were intermittent folk songs provided by Sara Wiley, Caither Wiley, and Tom Sankey (who a few years later composed the pioneer off-off-Broadway, anti-sellout folk rock musical *The Golden Screw*). Adding to the existential drama, a pair of satiric mimes occasionally appeared, and a monk (the poet Frank Kuenstler) wandered through the proceedings searching for his lost faith. Not exactly *The Flower Thief*.

Even Ben has a crisis, ranting about strontium 90 in the rain, the execution of Caryl Chessman in California's gas chamber, and "Nixon (Nixon!) running for president." While these topical references might require footnotes, the interpolated footage of peace marches, Hurricane Donna, and a last-minute addition of the April 1961 "Beatnik Riot" (discussed next chapter) spoke for themselves, as did the mutely eloquent shots of despoiled industrial landscapes in and around New York. However tiresome the movie's over-articulated angst, one need only look through the two-dimensional drama to see a raw and heartfelt document, an homage to a sooty, ungentrified city and the hard rain falling on its earnest bohemian inhabitants.[7]

According to Gregory Markopoulos, who attended the festival with his stream-of-consciousness feature *Serenity*, festival director Menotti walked out of *Guns*, a countess fainted, and the clergy banned the film. "It literally drills into the spectator," he wrote. "I think it lacks aesthetic sense, but Jonas does get his message across in a rather Dada fashion." After his return Mekas wrote a statement: "*Guns of the Trees* deals with the thoughts, feelings and anguished strivings of my generation faced

7 Reviewing *Guns* in the *Voice*'s August 10, 1961, issue, the arts editor Jerry Tallmer began with a spirited defense of his film critic: "No feature of the *Village Voice* has stirred up more of a storm over the years than the Movie Journal customarily supplied in this space." As for the film, "*Guns of the Trees* has some of the virtues and all of the faults of its young, seeking, bewildered creator."

with the moral perplexity of the time." Such thoughts, feelings, and strivings were not unique.

At the end of a column mainly devoted to the Charles Theater, a moldering 700-seat movie house on Avenue B, a few blocks north of Tompkins Square Park, reopened by Dan Talbot, owner of the Upper West Side's preeminent revival house, the New Yorker, Mekas put in a plug for a rough cut of Ken Jacobs's *Star Spangled to Death*, screening that weekend and looking for backers. The history of American art would have been altered if Jacobs raised the money and summoned the strength to finish his mammoth underground film.[8]

Star Spangled had also stalled for personal reasons. Jacobs was no longer on good terms with his star (and muse), Jack Smith. That summer, Jacobs attempted a reconciliation, inviting Smith to meet him in Provincetown, where, having failed to find a dishwashing job at a hotel in the Poconos, he had hitchhiked. Ready to play, Smith hitched to Cape Cod from New York with a wicker basket full of props (boater hats, granny gowns, Atlantic City T-shirts, and teddy bears).

9

Provincetown, summer of 1961: The jazz pianist Mose Allison was in residence in Atlantic House, and *La Dolce Vita* was in heavy rotation at Provincetown's Art Cinema (*Breathless* played there too, as did *Pull My Daisy* on a bill with Josef von Sternberg's *The Blue Angel*).

Directed by young academic Richard Schechner, the East End Players staged productions of *No Exit*, *Krapp's Last Tape*, and several Ionesco plays, as well as a version of Sophocles' *Philoctetes* on the beach in North Truro. There was an art exhibit to benefit the Freedom Riders, work contributed by thirty-odd artists including Hans Hofmann (whose classes Jacobs was still "auditing") and George Segal.

The fourth issue of *The Provincetown Review* included poems by Allen Ginsberg, LeRoi Jones, and Diane di Prima, fiction by Susan Sontag, Rosalyn Drexler's first published piece (an autobiographical sketch), plus art by Elaine de Kooning and Franz Kline. *The Provincetown*

8 Had *Star Spangled to Death* appeared by 1962 or 1963 it would be understood as the quintessential film of the period—predating *Pull My Daisy* or even the Beat Generation. It was finally finished, in digital form, in 2004. The movie was meant to be endless. Jacobs later said that he "wanted there always to be a question as to whether the film would last, would it die, would it at any moment fall off the projector."

Review was also in court. The previous issue of Bill Ward's ambitious literary magazine, published during summer of 1960, included an excerpt from Hubert Selby's *Last Exit to Brooklyn* in which Tralala, a waterfront prostitute, suffers a brutal, graphically described gang rape. An eighteen-year-old kid from Warwick, Rhode Island, purchased a copy in the Lobster Pot on Commercial Street and got Ward to sign it. His parents discovered the periodical, filed a complaint with the Provincetown police, and on July 14, nearly a year after the magazine was purchased, Ward was arrested for selling obscenity to a minor. The trial was set for a month later in Boston.[9]

Nevertheless, tourists, artists, art students, and beatniks strolled the streets, some famous (like Gregory Corso), others still obscure—notably Jacobs and Smith (who, coincidentally, had had a photograph published in last summer's *Provincetown Review*). Washing dishes for 65 cents an hour, Jacobs was hired by the newly renovated Crown & Anchor on Commercial Street to spear trash on the beach. Smith also found a restaurant job, from which he was soon fired for stealing food.

As Jacobs and Smith had amused themselves with street theater in New York, they began performing their *Human Wreckage Revue* on the beach, teaming up with two Rhode Island School of Design (RISD) students, Alice Meyers and Florence Karpf, passing the hat while a third student, nicknamed Martha the Scorch, provided their antics with a bluesy accompaniment. After the police chased them off, the abstract expressionist painter who managed the Crown & Anchor allowed Jacobs and Smith to perform their revue there for a few days.

In addition to making drawings to sell, Jacobs worked up a few posters for Richard Schechner's East End Players. Smith may have auditioned for the director, who, not surprisingly, was shocked by his extravagant performances. Jacobs, however, documented one. After shooting some footage of Smith skidding down the dunes, Jacobs brought his star to the venerable Alden Street Cemetery at the edge of town. Dressed in a nightgown with wings, crowned with a soft petasos

9 I interviewed four then-young people who spent the summer of '61 in Provincetown. Not one remembered this incident. The entire transcript of the trial was published in the issue that appeared the following summer: "EDITOR JAILED." Judge Robert A. Welsh, the son and grandson of Massachusetts judges, quickly found Ward guilty. The case was dismissed as quickly on appeal, largely because the minor who purchased the obscene material was not in fact a minor.

and wielding a scepter that incorporated a crocheted doll, Smith's Fairy Vampire skipped amid the graves, balanced on the cemetery fence, and posed with a leer in front of a large crypt. Jacobs had two rolls of Kodachrome II and used them both.

The men had a jealous quarrel over Karpf. She went back to RISD. Smith returned to New York. Jacobs remained in Provincetown past the end of the season. There at the Sun Gallery, site of Red Grooms's 1959 happenings and Oldenburg's 1960 show of collaged newspapers and burnt-edged cardboard, he presented *The Death of P'town* and *Little Stabs at Happiness*, a half dozen camera rolls, most shot with Smith during the making of *Star Spangled to Death*. If the progression of Grooms to Oldenburg to Jacobs was natural, P'town was predictably unappreciative. Jacobs was booed. "The people who ran the gallery were terrific," he remembered, "but not the audience."

10

Back in New York the scene was heating up. In early October, Mekas's so-called New American Cinema was featured at several venues. The Provincetown Playhouse hosted Stan VanDerBeek's "American Underground Cinema." A Tenth Street gallery was advertising "experimental films." On Avenue B, the Charles was back and open for business—a pair of young film enthusiasts, Walter Langsford and Ed Stein, acquired the theater from Dan Talbot.

That same month, Maya Deren, the filmmaker who for nearly twenty years had personified American avant-garde cinema, died age forty-four of a cerebral hemorrhage. Her death was a shock. "No one had known she was even in hospital, was ill, was anything but what she always was," Jerry Tallmer wrote in the *Voice*. No less than her rival in exoticism, the diarist Anais Nin, or the poet e. e. cummings (then being evicted from his Patchen Place apartment), or Willem de Kooning (currently facing charges for a Cedar Tavern brawl), Deren was a heroic Villager and more.

Her role as an advocate for avant-garde film was assumed by Mekas, and her status as the paradigmatic avant-garde filmmaker by twenty-eight-year-old Stan Brakhage. Deren had had reason to criticize both men (Mekas for championing *Pull My Daisy*, Brakhage for making the childbirth film *Window Water Baby Moving*). Following Tallmer's obituary, Mekas was free to proclaim Brakhage "the most original film artist in America today"—a preeminence that for Mekas had been confirmed by a show at the Charles in August that included the first American screening of Brakhage's controversial *Anticipation of the Night*.

For the first time, Brakhage's protagonist was fully the entity behind the camera. The movie is silent; the only rhythm is visual, with the handheld 16-millimeter camera used to dynamic effect—smearing light or blurring the image to achieve special effects that more timid filmmakers might consider mistakes. Brakhage brought *Anticipation of the Night*, along with a half dozen other films, to the international film competition at the 1958 Brussels World's Fair.

Brakhage won an award, although *Anticipation of the Night* supposedly caused a riot. Consequently, Amos Vogel—whose Cinema 16 distributed Brakhage's previous films—declined to take it on. Brakhage angrily refused to give Vogel any of his future films. Their conflict contributed to the forming of the Film-Makers' Cooperative in early 1962. Still, Cinema 16 was advertising a "New American Cinema" series that featured both *The Flower Thief* and *Guns of the Trees*, the latter ambiguously promoted as "the best-loved or most-hated film on this year's program."

Not yet seen in New York, *The Flower Thief* was better suited than *Guns* to the current art-world juggernaut. In October 1961, less than a year after the *Ray Gun Spex*, not five months after Martha Jackson brought Grooms, Kaprow, Oldenburg, and Dine uptown in her wide-ranging *New Forms–New Media in Painting and Sculpture* show, the Museum of Modern Art opened a contextualizing exhibit, *The Art of Assemblage*.

Curated by William Seitz, who also wrote the catalog, the show focused mainly on European old masters. Kurt Schwitters was represented by some thirty pieces. (Although not yet recognized as a master, Joseph Cornell was also well represented.) *Homage to New York* was acknowledged, praised for having "magnificently but inefficiently sawed, shook, and burned itself to rubble and extinction." Robert Rauschenberg and the San Francisco–based assemblagist Bruce Conner were virtually the only young American artists included although Seitz had been trekking down to Tenth Street for months, observing happenings at the Judson and Reuben galleries; he photographed *Car Crash* and may have considered including one of Lurie's collages in the show.

Indeed, Seitz might well have been thinking of Lurie and Oldenburg (name-checked in the catalog) when he described certain artists who rather than approaching a "vernacular repertoire" (hot rods, mescaline, faded flowers, pinups, trash, juke boxes, hydrogen explosions were his examples) in a "mystical" or aesthetic manner were rather "fearfully dark, evoking horror or nausea, the anguish of the scrap heap; the images of charred bodies that keep Hiroshima and Nagasaki before our eyes." (In a word, "No!art.")

Seitz understood that anti-authoritarian protest art could acknowledge the struggle for racial equality and the immorality of capital punishment. However, the idea very much displeased the *New York Times* art critic John Canaday. A decade older than Seitz at fifty-four, Canaday trashed the show, declaring *Assemblage* "a secondary art form at best and a viciously prostituted one at worst." The critic could have been describing *Snapshots from the City* when he declared that over half the exhibit seemed devoted to "the aesthetic counterparts of the social deficiencies that land people in the clink on charges of vagrancy."

MoMA, the *Times* critic charged, was catering to an unspecified "coterie." Indeed, three days before Seitz's show was disassembled, the *New York Herald Tribune* profiled Aldo Tambellini under the headline SCULPTOR HUNTS JUNK FOR FIERCE FORMS. Visiting Tambellini's storefront studio, the reporter Don Ross found a small, emotional man living amid "big overwhelming plaster sculptures that bristle with the points of long nails, jagged pipes, tin cans, trowels, rusted automobile wheels and even parts of toilets and washing machines all he has found on the streets or in vacant lots or bought at junkyards." The artist "literally sleeps with his work," Ross joked, pointing out that Tambellini's bed frame was an ornamental iron fence salvaged from a demolished synagogue.

Out in Coney Island and even more radical, the twenty-seven-year-old abstract painter Ralph Ortiz had begun ripping apart and reordering mattresses and chairs—what he called "Archeological Finds"—and spraying their remains with a clear fixative. Back on the Lower East Side, Boris Lurie and Claes Oldenburg were preparing major exhibitions. The *Doom Show*, which Lurie organized at the March Gallery along with Sam Goodman and Stanley Fisher, filled the cramped cellar with dismembered dolls and defaced, paint-splashed dummies. Detritus hung from the tin ceiling.

Fisher's statement termed the current Cold War situation "a cul-de-sac which makes the Nazi crematoriums relatively innocuous" and cited the March Gallery's ambition to spearhead demonstrations on and discussions of the madness of "atomic war." Quite likely the March Group was aware of Julian Beck's concurrent effort to organize a general strike for peace. The *Voice* critic Suzanne Kiplinger reported going from reading twelve pages on fallout shelters in the current issue of *Consumer Guide* to the March Gallery, which, she imagined, was presenting "the results of a thermonuclear ground burst." She found the show sufficiently shocking although she faulted the blinding overhead light. More temperate, Jill Johnston wrote a capsule review in *Art News* describing it as "a show of protest [that] isn't pretty to look at," "a chamber of horrors [that] leaves little to be desired" except the ability to reach beyond people who already support the movement.

Acknowledging "The Bomb" as a ready-made subject, *Times* critic Brian O'Doherty reported a group of young people in "a grubby little gallery" were protesting with a vehemence recalling the belief of primitive doctors "that purgatives and emetics cure everything." The artists "have mutilated toys, singed dolls, attacked machines and ravaged the girlie magazines for material." The *Doom Show* was "neo-dada journalism" and "neo-Fascist social protest."

Such "dada" was the particular form of those artists who, traumatized by their experience of World War II, arrived in New York during the 1950s. Lurie, who had survived a two-day slaughter of Latvian Jews, as well as several Nazi concentration camps, may have been the most extreme case; however, younger artists including Aldo Tambellini, Yoko Ono, the puppeteer Peter Schumann, and the sculptor Hans Haacke endured severe bombing raids in Italy, Japan, and Germany, respectively. The Japanese painter Yayoi Kusama and Korean musician Nam June Paik also suffered as children during the war. Lithuanians Jonas Mekas and George Maciunas lived under German occupation at a time when their Jewish neighbors were being massacred. All made art that was stridently anti-authoritarian as well as anti-art. Some, like Schumann, were militant pacifists.

For O'Doherty, the March Gallery cellar had "the ugliness of a mutant's pornography collection," suggesting "the private gallery of one of the guards at Belsen." *The Store*, by contrast, was a smash that (unlike the *Doom Show*) made history. Located at 107 East Second Street in a space Oldenburg had rented as a studio, Ray Gun Mfg. Co., for the past six months, *The Store* was part Orchard Street notions shop, part luncheonette, and part Avenue D bodega complete with Puerto Rican votive candles, selling everything from hot dogs and gooey slices of pie to sneakers and frocks, souvenirs and watches, all made of chicken wire and painted plaster, at prices ranging from $34.99 (toy ray gun) to $899.95 (free-standing bride mannequin).

Unlike the *Doom Show* (or *The Street*), *The Store* was welcoming and abundant—less an installation than an environment. Visitors could be shoppers, admiring and even handling the items on display walls. Writing in *Kulchur*, Frank O'Hara was moved to poetry: "You find cakes your mother never baked, letters you never received, jackets you never stole when you broke into that apartment, and a bride that did not pose for Rembrandt's famous Jewish ceremony." The show was so popular that Oldenburg kept it open through January, although it supposedly lost money ($285) and much of its inventory remained unsold.

Noting *The Store*'s "appalling fidelity to the facts," *New York Times* critic Stuart Preston considered it more social comment than art—a satire of American consumer capitalism. Like his neighbor Aldo Tambellini, if more pleasingly, Oldenburg fused art and trash.[10]

11

The Store was also a theater. Beginning in late February 1962 and continuing through March, Oldenburg used his store's cramped back rooms (home to previous proprietors) to stage an ambitious series of "real events" that, not unlike *Star Spangled to Death*, dealt with what he called America's "consciousness." Oldenburg compared these happenings to newsreels and staged them as matched pairs with a repertoire cast. (Thanks to their presence in his and other artists' happenings, Oldenburg's now wife Patty Muchinski and studio assistant Lucas Samaras were the art-world equivalent of underground movie stars.)

Store Days I and II mixed naturalistic and fantastic events, reflecting on New York City and the Lower East Side, representing what Oldenburg called "the atmosphere of the slums." (The Statue of Liberty turned up in

10 Tambellini had his first and only one-person show, titled *Black and White*, at the Brata gallery in November 1962. The paintings were minimal but expressive circular forms—a mode continued by the young painter Ben Morea, who met Tambellini at the show and became part of his group, the Center. Other core members included sculptors Jackie Cassen and Ron Hahn, painter Peter Martinez, and photographer Don Snyder; the Center also had a friendly affiliation with the Umbra group of Black poets.

various ways.) *Nekropolis* I and II were more sinister and violent. If, as Oldenburg said of *Store Days*, the idea was to evoke "people dead to their experience," *Nekropolis*, as suggested by its title, evoked the dead.

Jill Johnston reviewed these in the *Voice*, writing mainly on *Nekropolis* I, in which Samaras and Muchinski (wearing men's clothing) performed a sluggish pas de deux that wound up with Muchinski in a bathtub, water up to her chin, behaviors that struck Johnston as reptilian brain activities. "I enjoyed the heavy slow clamor of these bulky creatures crawling and messing around in that bulky environment of burlap, paper, paint and other assembled junk." Oldenburg, she noted, "made wonderful nondescript jungle sounds and heaved his considerable weight from mound to mound like a natural denizen."

Store Days I had featured a meal of courses ripped from magazine ads. *Nekropolis* II has a similar scene in which "three customers, faces whitened, all jabbered at once in various languages and did incredible things to the fake food that never stopped arriving . . . A 'monster' stumbled in, went to sleep, was kicked out by the proprietor. A 'bride' was ushered in, undressed, laid out, carried off." Then everyone put on tinfoil masks. "This is immediate, elemental theater," Johnston concluded, "the more so perhaps because Oldenburg is an authentic slob." He was also, like Di Suvero, Jacobs, Lurie, Ortiz, Smith, and Tambellini, something of a rubble-rouser.

Ray Gun took a break after *Nekropolis*; performances resumed in April. *Injun* I and II evoked the violent settling of the Old West, *Voyages* I and II were more literary with references to *The Tempest* and Rip Van Winkle, and *World's Fair* I and II were satirically anti-patriotic. None of these were about any one thing, of course. Far more important than even the semblance of plot were the activities and the set. Oldenburg would tell art historian Barbara Rose that his cluttered mise-en-scène and use of people as props were influenced by Jack Smith. Oldenburg had visited Smith's East Fifth Street apartment and seen the fantastic tableaux of nude and costumed figures that Smith called "plastiques," which he and his friend, the poet Piero Heliczer, later assembled in a handmade portfolio. Known as *The Beautiful Book*, it foreshadowed the movie ultimately titled *Flaming Creatures*, which Smith would begin filming that summer.

The affinity went two ways. Oldenburg's expressive use of junk dragged off the street foreshadowed Smith's subsequent loft theater, as did his use of slow motion, which was characterized by the young critic Susan Sontag, in an early description of Oldenburg's theater, as a mixture of ceremoniousness and ineffectuality. Smith may or may not have visited *The Store* but Ken Jacobs did. So did Sontag, brought by her friend, the painter Martha Edelheit, herself a Reuben Gallery artist. Attending Ray Gun productions in the company of her eleven-year-old son, David Rieff, Sontag found a subject. Her subsequent essay on these "esoteric" spectacles, "Happenings: An Art of Radical Juxtaposition," was one of the first serious appreciations of the mode.

Sontag's unequalled description notes that Happenings tend to discomfit their audiences and end in confusion. The basic structure is "an asymmetrical network of surprises, without climax or consummation." Linking the "preoccupation with materials" in messy, crowded, disorderly "Environments" with Assemblage, of which Happenings are an extension, Sontag coins a wonderful term: "Radical Juxtaposition." She recognizes an affinity to Buster Keaton's deadpan slapstick and the terrifying "humor" that prompts spectators to laugh. But mainly in discussing the de-emphasis of the word to privilege spectacle, she introduces Artaud, on whom she will publish an essay four years hence in *Partisan Review*, as the Happenings' aesthetic forebear.

Showing off all she knew about the new subterranean sensibility (the essay also contains a long parenthesis on camp, cut from the version published in *Against Interpretation*), the twenty-seven-year-old critic also nailed it. Written for *The Second Coming* in 1962, her brilliant essay was not published until the journal's penultimate, January 1965 issue (and then it introduced the script for Allan Kaprow's *Eating*). By then, Happenings had peaked as a form if not a subject of academic interest.[11]

11 *The Drama Review* (*TDR*) devoted its winter 1965 issue to what guest editor Michael Kirby called "The New Theater" (scripts by Oldenburg, Whitman, and Higgins, an interview with John Cage, a lecture by La Monte Young, and material on Fluxus); the same year, Higgins's Something Else Press published Al Hansen's *Primer on Happenings and Time/Space Art*, and Dutton brought out Kirby's anthology *Happenings*, which established a pantheon, with scripts and statements by Kaprow, Grooms, Whitman, Dine, and Oldenburg. The word "happening" had conquered the world. "What's happening?" was the question of the age. The year 1965 also brought the TV special *What's Happening, Baby*, co-produced by the US Office of Economic Opportunity and hosted by radio disc jockey Murray the K. Two years later, the Supremes had a number one song titled "The Happening."

12

In early 1962, however, Happenings were still happening. The Ray Gun Theater continued through May. In March, the New York Poets Theater, founded by Diane di Prima, Alan Marlow, and LeRoi Jones (and recently fined by the city for performing without a license at the Off-Bowery Theater, 84 East Tenth Street), took up temporary residence in a Times Square theater, the Maidman Playhouse, for an ambitious series of performances that included dance works by Fred Herko and Yvonne Rainer; a "variety program" featuring Simone Forti and La Monte Young; Ray Johnson's *Second Nothing*; Happenings by George Brecht and Robert Whitman; and a revival of Allan Kaprow's *Spring Happening* that left Jill Johnston unimpressed: "Invite a lot of people, hire a boiler room, get a naked girl, make a lot of noise and turn off the lights and I suppose you have the makings of something terribly shocking."

The *Voice* now had "Off-Off-Broadway" listings that included everything from the Ray Gun Theater and plays staged at Café Bizarre and Caffe Cino to the coffeehouse monologist Theodore and Dick Higgins's "chance play" *Inroads Rebuff'd* at the Judson Church, where the Uranian Alchemy Players also performed in Peter Schumann's *Totentanz*.[12]

"Something weird took place" in the church sanctuary, Howard Smith reported in the *Voice*. The dancers who really weren't dancers doubled as musicians who didn't really play music.

> Voices, a drum, violin, trumpet, flute, saxophone, tambourine, harmonica, bells, and someone clapping his hands are used as instruments to produce sounds in alternating currents of funeral dirges, kindergarten bands, primitive rituals, and a diabolic symphony warming up.

Smith noted that throughout the performance, the participants (and even some of the audience) wore "ghostly gray-white masks that in

12 A twenty-seven-year-old sculptor and dancer, Schumann left Germany in late 1961, moving with his wife, Russian-born Elka Leigh Scott, to Richard Tyler's East Fourth Street block. Unable to recruit any of the Judson dancers for his projects, he successfully enlisted the Uranians, who first performed the *Totentanz* in November 1961 in Washington Square and then again as part of a peace march the following February. In 1963, the Schumanns founded the Bread and Puppet Theater, originally housed in the same Delancey Street loft that had been Red Grooms's museum.

themselves create an instant supernatural atmosphere of impending doom." Judson was not pleased although the death dance was repeated two weeks later at the church's Hall of Issues.

A few months later, July 12, 1962, Aldo Tambellini orchestrated New York's first political Happening in front of the Museum of Modern Art. After a brief association with the Brata Gallery (a brawny, leftish co-op that also supported the young Japanese émigré painter Yayoi Kusama), Tambellini formed his own group, having decided that even Tenth Street co-ops were corrupt. He had been distributing a broadside manifesto called *The Screw* for several months before leading a protest with a picket line in front of the Museum of Modern Art.

Everyone in *The Event of the Screw* was accessorized with screw paraphernalia. Wearing a black tie clipped with a mini gold screw, Tambellini declaimed the "Manifesto of the Screw." A Lower East Side doo-wop group billed as the Belltones sang the "Song of the Screw" as leotarded Elsa Tambellini did her best to dance while squeezed into a five-foot papier-mâché screw. The performance ended when public school teacher Mira Fine presented MoMA with a hardware screw painted gold and placed on a velvet cushion, thus symbolically reciprocating the royal screw the museum gave artists. Similar awards were bestowed upon the Whitney and Guggenheim Museums.[13]

Although more installation than Happening, *Doomshow* was filmed as the latter by the anti-nuclear activist Ray Wisniewski, who, back in August 1958, had borrowed Mekas's Bolex to film the demonstrations meant to mar the three-day celebration of the nuclear-powered USS *Nautilus* when it entered New York Harbor following the submarine's successful voyage beneath the North Pole. There was a fracas. The camera fell into the ocean. Wisniewski dove after it. "Being a good swimmer, he managed to retrieve it, but it never worked well again," Mekas would recall long after he bought a second Bolex to make *Guns of the Trees*. Wisniewski filmed the *Doomshow*'s deinstallation, perhaps with that very camera.

A frantic fifteen minutes, appropriately black-and-white, set entirely in the cramped murk of the March Gallery basement, the *Doomshow*

13 A photo of the event made the front page of New York's largest Spanish-language daily *El Diario*. A flowery caption evoked the Knight of La Mancha and his boon companion, friend Sancho, seeming to suggest that the spectacle of a girl dressed as a *tornillo* accompanied by a Puerto Rican group urging "artists in an anonymous generation to arise" was a hallucination worthy of the Illustrious Manchego.

movie has a score that mixes Ray Charles with gallery chatter and police sirens. It's possible to make out some of the exhibit's larger, more grotesque items—Sam Goodman's *Burnt Doll with Flowers* or the bomb-shaped, pendulous inflatable breasts of his *Female Fetich*. But basically, the show is just a stage for activity. People "walk" the dummies as a crutch seems to move by itself. Baby dolls are abused. A woman appears to get dressed. A child plays with a toy rifle. Indeed, children, mainly Stanley Fisher's small daughters, are ubiquitous (as in many scenes from *Star Spangled to Death*). They contribute to the spirit of play. One rides her tricycle into the assemblage. Toward the end, as people start tossing the artwork around, a twist party breaks out mid-detritus to coalesce around a burning baby doll.

"A ritual fire dance in a cellar on Tenth Street in the shadow of the shadow over [the nuclear test site] Christmas Island" is how Wisniewski described *Doomshow*'s fallout shelter antics in the *Film-Makers' Cooperative Catalog*. In addition to a paragraph of praise from Jonas Mekas, Wisniewski also included excerpts from a letter written to the Coop that began, "I lost *Doomshow* Tuesday evening on the D train," and concluded, "Maybe it's better that way: *Doomshow*, was there ever a *Doomshow*? Let it lie, wherever it is, jammed up someone's vein, say, dead and dead it might LIVE as myth." But the city that swallowed Wisniewski's film spit it back out.

3

The Freedom Jazz, 1961–63

In which the coffeehouse wars continue and beatniks riot in Washington Square. LeRoi Jones declares a Jazz Avant-Garde and is busted for publishing William Burroughs, Lenny Bruce gives his greatest performance, and a kid calling himself Bob Dylan arrives in the Village to reinvent himself as a protest singer. Mimeographed poetry magazines proliferate, the struggle for Black rights accelerates, and, with the Cuban Missile Crisis, nuclear jitters peak.

It was as if the music was leading us.

—Amiri Baraka on Ornette Coleman's *Free Jazz*
(*The Autobiography of LeRoi Jones*)

Around one o'clock on a Sunday morning in early January 1961, the fire department shut down the Gaslight Poetry Café . . . again. Not six months earlier, the *Village Voice* ran a page-one story ominously headlined GASLIGHT, BEATNIK SPA, EXTINGUISHED FOREVER. The place was eulogized: "Poetry, singing—and an occasional brawl—made it famous." Sick of the tumultuous neighborhood the South Village had become, owner John Mitchell threatened to move to the Caribbean.

South of Washington Square and east of Sixth Avenue, Greenwich Village was less a neighborhood than a territorial free-for-all. Urban planners and real estate developers joined forces to fight a tenuous coalition of neighborhood activists and night-life entrepreneurs like Mitchell and Art D'Lugoff.

On another front, the latter were themselves pitted against the police and other municipal authorities (including the Mob) who had allied with the community's indigenous, working-class, largely Italian families in opposition to the burgeoning Beat element (drawn to the South Village by relatively cheap rents and relaxed social mores). Paradoxically, the Beats were united with their hostile neighbors in disdain for the swarm of weekend tourists courted by the coffeehouse entrepreneurs.

Race was also a factor. "The general resentment the locals felt toward the white bohemians was quadrupled at the sight of the black species," Amiri Baraka recalled in *The Autobiography of LeRoi Jones*. Interracial couples drew hostile stares. Black and Italian teens repeatedly scuffled in Washington Square. During the summer of 1960, the *Voice* had articulated fears of a full-scale "rumble" in the park. Izzy Young told the press that "some people don't want Negroes down here."[1]

The socialist journal *Dissent* was preparing a special-issue portrait of New York. "The biggest change in the composition of the Village beat scene and in Village life generally, is the far greater absolute number and far greater percentage of Negroes," the sociologist Ned Polsky declared in his contribution. Although the Village was scarcely easier for African Americans to rent apartments in than other white neighborhoods, the area was home to some notable Black writers, including Lorraine Hansberry, Claude Brown, and James Baldwin, as well as James Farmer, who had coined the term "Freedom Ride" while serving as the national director of the Congress of Racial Equality (CORE), the most prominent of New York civil rights organizations.[2]

The Village was also populated by white supporters of civil rights. In the spring of 1961, NAACP organizer Medgar Evers addressed one of the several rallies held in Washington Square near the Judson Memorial Baptist Church, where the socially progressive new minister, Rev. Howard Moody, was pleased to officiate interracial weddings. In 1960, the Village Gate hosted several benefits for CORE as well as a regular

1 The irony, as J. R. Goddard pointed out in the *Voice*, was that before the late nineteenth-century influx of Italian immigrants, the area around Bleecker and MacDougal had been New York's preeminent African American neighborhood.

2 A more Bohemian cluster of Black poets, painters, and musicians, LeRoi Jones among them, lived on the Lower East Side, where rents were cheaper and landlords less discriminatory, particularly in the area known as Cooper Square, notable for the Five Spot and its spin-off the Jazz Gallery.

Sunday night "Cabaret for Freedom." Coincidentally or not, the Gate was repeatedly cited by the NYPD Cabaret Bureau for dimming its lights during performances.

Interviewed by the *Voice*, D'Lugoff wondered "why should a non-syndicate enterprise in a syndicate-ridden business be faced with perpetual harassment by the Police Department . . . They are trying legally to drain me and get me out of business. We are treated like criminals."[3]

2

The battle for the Village had been joined in the mid-1950s. The blocks around Seventh Avenue and Sheridan Square, where the *Village Voice* had its office, had been the neighborhood's prime entertainment zone. But as the Italian espresso *caffès* transformed into Americanized coffeehouses, the tenement blocks south of Washington Square proved a magnet for Beat poets, folksingers, and all manner of stand-up extroverts.

The blind composer-musician Moondog worked the street. The freakish ukulele-strumming, falsetto-voiced Tiny Tim was a favorite at lesbian bars. Brother Theodore (last name Gottlieb), a German-born concentration-camp survivor, introduced an element of Weimar Berlin to the scene with his sardonic audience-baiting rants. Tourists followed. Weekends were hell. Outer borough kids clogged the sidewalks, New Jersey cars cruised the narrow streets. In vain the police attempted to enforce a Sabbath Law: "If religion is demanded on MacDougal Street, I insist on it for Forty-second Street," Izzy Young told the *Voice*.

Beneath the festive banner hung from a second-floor fire escape, the Gaslight sold dishwater espresso and provided free entertainment. A bit more than a year after it opened, Mitchell's coffeehouse got national attention when newsman Mike Wallace used the 116 MacDougal stoop as a location for a TV report on the Beats. By the summer of 1960, the Gaslight was a home for poets turned hip raconteurs, including the joint's "entertainment manager" Hugh Romney (later the hippie-jester Wavy Gravy) and the jazz drummer turned stand-up comic Steve Ben Israel (soon to join the Living Theatre), as well as apostles of the folk revival.

3 According to Gaslight habitue Terri Thal, D'Lugoff was one of only two Village club owners who got away without paying the police. (The other was Joe Marra, who ran the Night Owl Café, which opened a few years later at 118 West 3rd Street and would become the neighborhood citadel of folk rock.)

Poets read for free. The musicians who initially served to clear the house expected to get something. One step up from busking, the Gaslight was a "basket house," a venue that paid the talent from the money audience would pitch in at the door. When a cover charge was established, some were paid by the week, although conditions did not necessarily improve. Even dressed up with some hanging imitation Tiffany lamps, the place, according to its frequent performer and eventual manager, Dave Van Ronk, a bearish, Brooklyn-born twenty-four-year-old high school dropout, was "hopelessly filthy"—a rat- and roach-infested tenement basement.

Summer 1960, the *Voice* ran J. R. Goddard's three-part series on MacDougal Street's "fruitcake inferno." Café Bizarre was furnished like a spook house with flying bats and black drapes. The poet Ray Bremser's wife Bonnie worked there as a waitress: "Everything about it was gross, intentionally grotesque and designed to hustle tourists." It was also a firetrap, she recalled, "always packed and very hot." The management sent its provocatively ghoulish waitresses walking in the neighborhood—bleached hair, dead-white make-up, heavy eyeshadow, garish sarapes draped over purple leotards.

South Village residents were not only agitated by tourists and visiting teenage hordes but publicity. Incredibly, the Coffee House Association hoped to institute an annual Mardi Gras—the theory being that given "the school-integration situation," New Orleans had lost its luster as a vacation destination—and thus drive the locals crazier.

The fire department closed the Gaslight for the first time less than a month after the Wallace interview. The police had determined that, liquor or no, coffeehouses were cabarets. Some blamed the striptease joints on West Third Street for the escalating anti-coffeehouse campaign. Others suspected that Carmine DeSapio, the recently defeated Democratic Party boss, long suspected of Mob connections, was attempting to shore up his neighborhood base.[4]

4 The last boss of Tammany Hall, the once-notorious Manhattan Democratic Party organization, DeSapio anointed Robert F. Wagner Jr. as New York City mayor in 1953 and W. Averell Harriman as New York governor in 1954. In 1961, however, he lost the district leadership of Greenwich Village (a post he held for two decades) to an insurgent reformer. The same year Wagner would win re-election running a reform campaign that denounced his former patron. DeSapio was then defeated twice more as district leader by another reform candidate, future mayor Edward I. Koch.

"The shops selected were of course non-Italian," Polsky noted in his essay, "although hardly any commercial establishment within blocks of the area doesn't have fire violations." The Gaslight and Café Bizarre were particular targets and café operators filed suit, charging "resentment by local residents against the influx into the neighborhood of certain minority and racially mixed groups." Mitchell was briefly arrested for riling up a crowd while jawing with the local fire chief, who later told reporters that he had planned to close Café Bizarre as well as the Commons (across MacDougal from the Gaslight) but backed down for fear of a riot.

After the Gaslight and Bizarre were shuttered for overcrowding, the *New York Times* reported a "beatnik protest." Organized by Mitchell and Bizarre owner Rick Allmen, leader of the self-serving Coffee House Association, some eighty demonstrators marched through the Village in pouring rain, pelted from the fire escapes with garbage and redundant water balloons. Crossing Sixth Avenue and marching up West Tenth Street, the protestors besieged the local firehouse. There, the Bizarre's current headliner, international songstress (and schoolteacher) Varda Karni, Israeli by way of Paris, led the group in an improvised version of the Depression-era union anthem "I Don't Want Your Millions, Mister" that, referring to the fact coffeehouses did not sell alcohol, went "We Don't Want Your Whiskey, Mister."

3

The coffeehouse boom coincided with that of bardic poetry as well as folk music. Readings migrated east from North Beach and east again from MacDougal Street to the art galleries of East Tenth Street. The key venue was Mickey Ruskin's Tenth Street Coffeehouse, which began hosting Monday night open readings in fall 1960, around the time Lord Buckley was busted at the Jazz Gallery. One poet recollected these as "brutal and exhausting" competitive jam sessions: "Everyone was pushing and demanding to be heard." Heckling was not uncommon. Young poets came to make themselves known while established ones read to burnish their reputations.

In those days, aspiring poet Steve Kowit recalled, Berkeley student Diane Wakoski was "Poetry Queen" of the Tenth Street. One Monday she brought "a large and rather peculiar-looking entourage." Kowit vaguely recognized Wakoski's boyfriend La Monte Young "dressed heroically in a maroon cape." The others included Jackson Mac Low, along with Julian Beck and Judith Malina, and other members of the Living Theatre, which had recently staged Mac Low's "chance" theater piece *The Marrying Maiden*. The play, which varied with each performance, was based on words taken from the *I Ching*. *New York Times* reviewer Brooks Atkinson deemed it unintelligible "gibberish." More recently, Mac Low had brought the piece to a West Village coffeehouse, Phase 2. *Voice* critic Michael Smith thought it "looked and sounded like recreation time in the booby hatch." Now he planned to read at the Tenth Street.

"When his turn came," remembered Kowit, "Mac Low read an interminable piece that seemed utterly disembodied and pointless—even more pointless than the earnest poetry of the ordinary avant-garde." Indeed, that pointlessness seemed the point. As Mac Low's reading far exceeded the customary five-minute set, "a wave of grumbling spread through the audience," escalating into whistles, catcalls, and Bronx cheers until "somebody jumped out of their seat to tell Mac Low to get the fuck off the stage before he kicked his lights out."

Mac Low quickly finished, gathered his papers, and made a dignified return to his table, after which the entourage left en masse. Commotion ensued, coalesced into an impromptu meeting and resulted in a formal apology to Mac Low and an invitation to read by himself two nights later. Unexpectedly, the solo performance was a hit, "boring as hell and utterly exhilarating," according to Kowit. "Immediately, everyone took to writing Jackson Mac Low poems: aleatoric concoctions based on chance operations."

The readings outgrew the Tenth Street's capacity. In June 1961, Ruskin and Bill Mackey opened Les Deux Mégots (meaning "the two butts," as in cigarette butts, a riff on the legendary French café Les Deux Magots) at 64 East Seventh Street, a larger storefront tucked amid the tenements on the far side of Second Avenue. Weekly open readings alternated with invited ones featuring LeRoi Jones and Bob Kaufman among many others. Les Deux Mégots was roomier and more performative than the Tenth Street.

One of the first events, reported in the *Voice* as an expression of the "espresso underground," was a four-hour debate on "The Art of Protesting" (and screwing The System) that featured thirty-seven-year-old poet Tuli Kupferberg (a "red-diaper" child of Communist parents and apostle of Wilhelm Reich), *Realist* editor and Lenny Bruce disciple Paul Krassner, thirty, and Doc Humes, basically pitting this trio of anarchists against the sober pacifists in the audience, estimated at two hundred.

Les Deux Mégots could be a show. Taylor Mead was a regular and Tiny Tim an occasional participant. But it also "exuded a warm and electric atmosphere of friendliness and camaraderie," Calvin Hernton wrote, citing the racially mixed ownership of Ruskin and Mackey. However, the place changed hands and in March 1963 the scene moved around the corner to Café le Metro at 149 Second Avenue.

Meanwhile, the folk scene traveled south from Cambridge. In the April–May 1960 issue of the leftist folk zine *Sing Out!*, Izzy Young reported Joan Baez "singing in every nightclub in the Boston area" and that the new Club 47 off Harvard Square opened on the understanding that Baez would appear there at least once a week. In New York, he added, "folk-singing seems to be moving from the living room concert hall and hootenanny to the Coffee House and Night Club."

In early 1960, the *Voice*'s forty-ish jazz critic Bob Reisner wrote a mock irate manifesto on the "menace" of folk music, complaining that "the humble, monotonous, skimmed-milk folk song is pushing classical and jazz records out of homes." A week later, a younger *New York Times* music critic, Robert Shelton, published a genuinely angry rejoinder to Reisner's "exercise in Philistinism, illogic, snobbishness, and misinformation." Still, one of Reisner's points seemed valid: Just as what he called "honestly primitive folk music" was being denatured and commercialized, so folk music was the latest "shortcut to becoming an 'entertainer.'"

Indeed, that spring, J. R. Goddard soon after reported on twenty-three-year-old Carolyn Hester, THE LITTLE GIRL WITH THE BIG NEW VOICE, a beautiful Texan who'd come to New York to study acting and was now making her debut at a new club, a former saloon with a high ceiling and a tiny stage, Gerde's Folk City, on West Fourth Street, a few blocks east of Washington Square toward the no man's land separating the Village from the Lower East Side. (The switch to folk was Izzy Young's idea. He briefly managed the joint but was forced out by the owner Mike Porco.)

The scene bred local stars as well. Not two months later, Goddard gave a page-one profile to Dave Van Ronk, whose "passionate wail" was currently wowing the Commons. Performing ragtime and blues with an asthmatic growl, Van Ronk—who made his debut at Café Bizarre and continued to perform at benefits for the Young People's Socialist League—was a genuine original, albeit a throwback to the moldy fig jazz of the pre–Five Spot Village.

Café Bizarre and three other coffeehouses were fined for lacking cabaret licenses even as Shelton gave the movement its *New York Times* imprimatur: "Folk music is leaving the imprint of its big country boots on the night life of New York in unparalleled fashion, from the grimiest Greenwich Village espresso joint to the crooked-finger elegance of the Waldorf Astoria."

Shelton namechecked Len Chandler, Karni, Hester, and especially Van Ronk, all of whom appeared at the Gaslight, the Commons or Café Wha?, another former stable around the corner at 115 MacDougal, "graceless grottos so subterranean one expects Jean Valjean to be their waiter."

4

It was a few months later that someone called a false alarm on the Gaslight. Fire trucks jammed MacDougal Street; firemen barged in on the crowd digging Chandler, a Gaslight regular recruited by Hugh Romney (by then was living upstairs).

Singing the Georgia Seas Island stevedore song "Pay Me My Money Down," Chandler smoothly improvised new lyrics for the occasion: "Don't you be alarmed/It's only a fire drill." A single cop showed up, mediating a heated discussion between John Mitchell and a fire department lieutenant.

Mitchell, recalled by Van Ronk as "the world's foremost maniac" and "a magnet for trouble," not to mention "one of the least diplomatic men on earth," received three summonses, including one for operating a cabaret without a license. Meanwhile, identical violations were issued to the Commons. Later known as the Fat Black Pussycat, the Commons had opened, like the Gaslight, in 1959 and served Mitchell as an alternative base of operations during the summer of 1960 when the fire department shut down the Gaslight, presumably to allow him to install the leaky sprinkler system that Van Ronk thought added to the steam bath ambience.

But this was a chilly winter night. Sometime after 2:00 a.m., a weary building inspector appeared to close the premises. Perhaps inspired by Chandler, a regular presence at civil rights protests, some thirty patrons employed a tactic introduced by SNCC less than a year before. More cops arrived at the Gaslight, followed by three police wagons but, unlike the sit-ins in North Carolina, there were no arrests. The sit-in morphed into a sleep-in and ultimately a snore-in.

Indeed, before dawn the order to vacate was itself vacated, although an additional summons noted the absence of a "no spitting" sign in the kitchen. The "Beatnik Sit-In" made the *New York Times* and the *Village Voice* front pages: GASLIGHT NIGHT OF TRAVAIL SPARKED BY FALSE ALARM. Mitchell beat the charges, then went to the state crime commission to complain of police shakedowns, blaming harassment on his decision to stop paying off the cops. (By late spring, he would also sell the Gaslight.)

The Gaslight specialized in hip comedy, and the absurdity of the January bust cum snore-in must have surely furnished material for Hugh Romney. A poet whose humorous declarative lists were credibly Ginsbergian (*I have interesting hair formations on my stomach / I brush my teeth every morning with Gleem toothpaste*), Romney could also free-associate scenarios in a half dozen voices. He was a disciple of Lord Buckley and sometime protégé of another Buckley acolyte, thirty-six-year-old stand-up comedian Lenny Bruce, who a year later would secure Romney his lone recorded gig in San Francisco.[5]

Although he was born in Mineola, Long Island, and riffed in a pronounced New York accent, Bruce was not a Village product. He picked up much of his jazz cadence and hipster vocabulary from Buckley, with whom he had worked LA strip joints. Like the Beat Generation and Ornette Coleman, Bruce brought an improvisational

5 The LP, *Third Stream Humor*, demonstrates Romney's facile mastery of voices (including Lord Buckley's) and flair for surreal pothead humor. During the summer of 1963, Romney assembled a cabaret act for the Fat Black Pussycat called the Phantom Theater, which consisted of himself, Moondog, and Tiny Tim. J. R. Goddard was so taken with it he published a page-one story, GHOULS AT THE PUSSY CAT. Tiny Tim, a "long-haired grotesque who sounds equally convincing as Rudy Vallee or an old-time vaudeville queen singing love duets with himself," was the main subject: "'T T' does more than evoke the '20s and '30s," Goddard wrote:

> Patriotic songs become particularly ridiculous when he sings them. And whether intentional or not, his crooner-queenly ballads get double-edged as they satirize those sentimental times too . . . Watch that marvelous clown's face, the ridiculous banjo, the constant swaying of his body, and the reaction is far different. Hysterically funny, yet funny on so many levels. Tim is a surrealist who can leave your senses jangled and your belief in popular Americana badly cracked.

The same trio appeared that summer at the Living Theatre. One wonders which gig was the move-over.

West Coast sensibility to town. Bruce developed an underground reputation in New York in the spring of 1959 with a series of gigs at The Den, a tiny club beneath the Duane Hotel, on Madison Avenue at Thirty-Seventh Street, where he introduced "Religions Inc." and "Father Flotski's Triumph," among other routines.

None other than Kerouac's herald Gilbert Millstein profiled Bruce for the *New York Times Magazine*: "Using the argot of hipsters and jazz musicians, Lenny Bruce blows sharp social comment." But the *Times* TV critic was less impressed when Bruce appeared on Channel 13's *One Night Stand*: "He is reputed to be a darling of the 'beatnik' set, which describes him reverently as being 'far out' . . . Most of his comments on jazz, modern art and other topics were in the tedious idiom of the chin-whisker crowd." Somewhat better press was supplied by *Time*'s July 1959 report on "sick comedy."

In late 1960, Bruce got a few classy bookings at uptown nightclubs—the Blue Angel Supper Club and Basin Street East. These were more public and controversial. "The question," *Times*'s reviewer posed "is whether the kind of derisive shock therapy [Bruce] administers and the introspective free-form patter in which he indulges are legitimate nightclub fare, as far as the typical customer is concerned." That crowd was uptight, not like the fans who attended Bruce's New York apotheosis, February 4, 1961, having arrived at Carnegie Hall mid blizzard to watch a sold-out Saturday midnight show.

Bruce's performance can be seen as an epic jazz solo. Free-associating for nearly two hours, the exultant comedian was totally in the moment. Beginning with a riff about his being booked into Carnegie Hall and an account of his travails in making the gig, he tossed off a few topical references to Cuba, waxed self-reflexively on the microphone and the nature of "toilet" jokes before settling on his favorite themes—politicians, Jews, Blacks, homosexuals, "tits and ass," and religion—lines tossed off in a staccato delivery sprinkled with movie references and casual Yiddish phrases. As the hour grew late, Bruce settled in as a raconteur who might almost be thinking out loud.[6]

6 Bruce's biographer Albert Goldman considers this performance, recorded for posterity and released as a three-LP set in 1972, six years after Bruce's death, to be the comedian's masterpiece: "Lenny worshiped the gods of Spontaneity, Candor and Free Association. His greatest fear was getting his act down pat. On this night, he rose to every chance stimulus, every interruption and noise and distraction, with a mad volley-

Following this triumph, "America's Most Controversial Comedian," as he was promoted in the *Voice*, was booked into a lengthy gig at the Village Vanguard, which four years earlier had featured Kerouac's Christmas show.

5

The coffeehouse wars came to a boil that spring with the free speech and civil rights battle tabloids dubbed the Beatnik Riot. Were unlicensed folksingers entitled to congregate on Sunday afternoons around the fountain in Washington Square Park?

Although the impromptu hootenannies had been going on since 1944, the police—acting under a directive by Mayor Wagner's new city parks commissioner Newbold Morris—began dispersing and arresting folksingers for performing without a permit. "Musicians of unsavory appearance" were panhandling in the park! In a way, the folksingers were surrogates for the Beats, the Blacks, the tourists, and the gay men who cruised the area known as the Meat Rack, along the square's western edge.

Intimations of the Hipster General Strike. On April 9 Izzy Young organized a protest, supported by Doc Humes, who a few months later would be holding forth at Les Deux Mégots: "In order to beat the System you have to understand it. The System is a collective mind and collective minds are always incompetent." Watched by a gathering estimated to be several thousand, some fifty folk bards silently marched into Washington Square; Ed Sanders recounted the moment in *Tales of Beatnik Glory*:

> An electric unification seemed to pass into the crowd when the trigger-pack, "a group of fifty, many in beatnik clothes and beards"—as *The New York Times* haughtily reported—began to march from the southwest of the park (MacDougal and West 4th) in close-order yodel formation toward the waiting-for-inspiration yodel mob, goaded all the while by trained left-leaning folklorists and known novelists.

When the demonstrators broke the silence order by singing anthems like the spiritual "We Shall Not Be Moved" and Woody Guthrie's "This

---

ing of mental images that suggested the fantastic riches of Charlie Parker's horn."

Land," the police moved in to disperse the crowd. As the poet reimagined it:

> The trigger-pack reached the fountain and began to strum, yodel, pluck, hoot, and to thicken their voices with subversive Appalachian accents. A woman auto-harpist with insolently lengthy tresses, stood then upon a hasty platform of guitar cases and began to sing "We Shall Overcome." And that was it—the police walked forward to break up the music. She was just pushing the A-Seventh bar on her harp when whonk! they shoved her and the cases went askitter.

In a show of solidarity, Joan Baez had come down from Boston, but she never made it to the square. According to the *Times*, the auto-harpist was male, and was the first person to be arrested, attempting to strum his "simple zitherlike instrument" as the police dragged him off.

Reinforcements arrived. Fights broke out. Both cops and protestors were knocked to the ground. "At the height of the battle," the *Times* reported, "hundreds of young people, many of the boys with beards or banjos and many of the girls with long hair or guitars, fought with fifty policemen in clashes across the square. Hundreds more, including some baffled tourists, watched." There were twenty serious injuries and ten arrests, among them Humes, who would be bailed out by John Mitchell. The event made front page news, occasioning an iconic headline in the tabloid *New York Mirror*: 3000 BEATNIKS RIOT IN VILLAGE.

The riot was also documented by an eighteen-year-old design student, Dan Drasin, then working as an assistant to the documentary filmmakers Ricky Leacock and D. A. Pennebaker. Drasin, who had already been recruited as the cameraman on Humes's never-completed *Adventures of Don Peyote*, was living on MacDougal Street over the Folklore Center: "I knew about the Washington Square rally as soon as Izzy posted the sign in his shop window," he recalled. "Thinking that this might be a good subject for a documentary, I borrowed some gear from Penny's place, ice-picked a bunch of long-outdated black & white raw stock from the company freezer and corralled a few friends to help out." (Among them was Frances Stillman, the gloomy suicide in Mekas's *Guns of the Trees*.)

Drasin's seventeen-minute *Sunday* begins as an urban pastoral. Children play, people enjoy ice cream, interracial couples hold hands as mounted cops look on. An NBC camera crew is briefly visible; clearly

Young and Humes have orchestrated what would later be called a media event. Presently, the folksingers parade into the square—the original guitar army—some holding homemade signs. Young, in jacket and tie, is the designated spokesman. He jaws with the seasoned cop regarding the inalienable right to sing in the square. There is some dancing around the fountain as well as sitting in. A bit later the auto-harpist is hauled away. Humes leads "The Battle Hymn of the Republic"; Young breaks into "The Star-Spangled Banner" as more police arrive. Dialogue gives way to pushing and screaming. Cops attempt to clear the square. Humes is arrested while trying to get a badge number. The movie ends as it began with the silent spectacle of cops around the fountain as kids play.

That night many prominent folkies, not all of whom had attended the riot, celebrated their victory at Gerde's—performers included Doc Watson, Gil Turner, Joan Baez, her kid sister Mimi, age sixteen, and Bobby Zimmerman, a nineteen-year-old kid recently arrived from Minnesota who called himself Bob Dylan. After hustling Joan to hear his latest composition ("Song to Woody"), Bobby went on to annoy her by hitting on Mimi. The next three Sundays saw a series of rallies, the first organized by Reverend Moody at the Judson Church, sit-ins and sing-ins. The last was to double as an "Oust Wagner" event but running for reelection as a born-again anti-DeSapio reformer, the mayor chose that moment to lift the ban. (DeSapio publicly supported singing in the square, as did the Village Young Republicans.)

The event's significance may be gauged in that two future mayors were involved. Ed Koch was a lawyer for the protestors; John Lindsay, the liberal Republican congressman, sent a telegram of support. Jonas Mekas saw a private screening of Drasin's rough cut and, several weeks after the folksingers reoccupied the square, published a brief notice in the *Voice*:

> Drasin's spontaneous camera, zooming in and out and around, caught the riot that Sunday with an authenticity and aliveness that puts it head and shoulders above most of the reporting that is going on today in film and television. The main reason for this success—I am happy to say it—is that he turned his back on all the accepted techniques of our professionals in his use of camera and of sound. He lost the slickness but he gained truth and the dynamic of life, both in sound and image.

He also integrated some of Drasin's footage into his revised version of *Guns of the Trees*. Indeed, *Sunday* had its official premiere in December 1961 at Cinema 16 on a bill with *Guns of the Trees*.

Bob Kaufman had seen *Sunday* in July at a program of "underground cinema" at the Living Theatre and gave Drasin an endorsement, handwritten in capital letters.

> THIS FILM IS THE CLEAREST CELEBRATION OF THE BASIC AMERICAN CONFLICT, THE CLASH BETWEEN BRUTAL, UNFEELING, SELF-RIGHTEOUS AUTHORITY AND THE MOST HUMAN, UNIVERSAL, AMERICAN ASPIRATION, THE ULTIMATE LIBERATION OF THE AMERICAN SOUL.
>
> THE FOLKSINGERS ARE AMERICA. THE ARTISTS ARE AMERICA. AMERICA IS PEOPLE, NOTHING MORE OR LESS. GOD BLESS THE PEOPLE SINGING, SPEAKING, WALKING, TALKING, HURTING WITHIN THIS FILM, FREE!
>
> GOD BLESS THE PEOPLE WHO MADE THIS FILM

Kaufman had some connection with the folk scene. He collaborated with Len Chandler on "Green, Green Rocky Road," based on a song he remembered from his New Orleans childhood. (It was first recorded by Dave Van Ronk on his 1963 LP *In the Tradition*.)[7]

According to Mekas, Kaufman was a regular at the Film-Makers' Cooperative. He also crashed at Ishmael Reed's apartment, hung out with Cecil Taylor (on whom he made a powerful impression), recited poetry and hustled (or harassed) tourists at Café Rienzi. New York was a bigger, meaner town than San Francisco. Touching all hipster bases and making a scene at some, Kaufman frequented Birdland, the Cedar, the Kettle of Fish (upstairs from the Gaslight), and, at the corner of MacDougal and Bleecker, the more literary San Remo.[8]

---

7 Chandler recalled that, "Kaufman was at my $34 a month New York apartment on Stanton Street for dinner. I had already put the music together. Kaufman said, 'Dooka dooka soda cracker/Does your momma chew tobacco?' and I said, 'If your momma chews tobacco/Dooka dooka soda cracker.' We were just playing."

8 A straight bar known for its openly gay habitues, San Remo boasted a list of regulars that included John Cage, Merce Cunningham, Miles Davis, and Frank O'Hara, as well as the Living Theatre crowd and the Beats. Kerouac met Alene Lee at the San Remo;

In January 1961, Kaufman dropped acid with Kerouac and the LSD-proselytizing Harvard professor Timothy Leary. In March, his wife checked herself into Bellevue and briefly split back to San Francisco with their son Parker. She would return but Kaufman was drinking heavily and often homeless. In 1963, he was arrested for walking on the grass in Washington Square Park. Incarcerated at Rikers Island, where he had landed a few years before after an incident at the Fat Black Pussycat, then shipped to Bellevue Hospital and subjected to involuntary shock treatment, Kaufman departed New York for San Francisco in October 1963.

A later poem, "Battle Report," imagines a victorious musical uprising: An unnamed city is infiltrated by a thousand saxophones, besieged by a fleet of trumpets, overwhelmed by ten waves of trombones, five hundred bass men and one hundred drummers. A secret agent flashes the signal: "Attack: The sound of jazz./The city falls." A new iteration of the Hipster General Strike: The real revolution was jazz.

6

The *Voice*'s "Gaslight Travail" issue still on newsstands, Max Roach premiered his *Freedom Now Suite*. The jazz drummer's show was late Sunday afternoon, January 15, 1961, at the Village Gate, a venue two blocks east of (and four times larger than) the MacDougal Street coffeehouse.

Art D'Lugoff's Gate was originally a showcase for folk acts and ethnic music. Over the past year, the venue had hosted several fundraising concerts for civil rights organizations and the Sunday performance of the *Freedom Now Suite*, was a benefit for CORE. The poster used a wire-service photograph from recent lunch-counter sit-ins in Greensboro, North Carolina; the same image, with one of three student demonstrators, all of whom wore jackets and ties, turning away from the counter to stare defiantly into the camera, could be found on the cover of the newly released LP *We Insist!*, produced by jazz critic Nat Hentoff for his experimental label Candid.[9]

---

it was his favorite New York bar, called the Black Mask in *The Subterraneans*.

9 Roach began working on the suite in 1959, in collaboration with the cabaret artist Oscar Brown Jr. Their intention was to present it in 1963 on the centennial of the Emancipation Proclamation. An elder statesman of thirty-seven, Roach had played with Bebop's founding fathers Dizzy Gillespie, Charlie Parker, and Thelonious Monk as well as Miles Davis and Charles Mingus; Brown, a few years younger, a multitalented

We Insist! tracked Black American history from slavery through emancipation to the current civil rights movement and, radically, put it in the context of the African anti-colonial struggle. The suite also provided a breakthrough showcase for Roach's thirty-year-old wife, the actress and singer Abbey Lincoln. The first two pieces, "Driva' Man"—Lincoln's harsh enunciation of Oscar Brown's lyrics punctuated by brusque hits on a tambourine—and the more contemplative "Freedom Day," were recorded with a piano-less sextet. (Coleman Hawkins, who played sax on the LP, would be replaced at the Gate by a fiery young Ornette Coleman sideman, Eric Dolphy.)

The last two pieces, "All Africa" and "Tears for Johannesburg" (a reference to the March 1960 Sharpeville massacre), were almost pure percussion. Already a star of world music, the Nigerian virtuoso Babatunde Michael Olatunji was joined by two Afro Cuban drummers, while Lincoln sang to the beat, most dramatically in a call-and-response with Olatunji. The centerpiece "Triptych: Prayer, Protest, Peace" was a trio of wordless duets between Lincoln's voice and Roach's drum. At the center of this primal pas de deux was an unprecedented series of screams, lasting over a minute, in which, encouraged by Roach to imagine herself suddenly coming across the corpse of a man lynched from a tree, Lincoln responded with horror and rage in what the historian Scott Saul would call "the most hair-raising ninety seconds of jazz in existence."

Roach staged the concert performance a month after the album's release. With a host of dancers, including Maya Angelou, as well as a dramatic narrator, Ruby Dee, the *Freedom Now Suite* was as much a theatrical as a musical event. "The electrifying performance brought repeated shouts of bravo from the filled house," Bob Reisner wrote in the *Voice*. "So much went on simultaneously, singing, drumming, dancing that the eye was in conflict." *New York Times* critic John S. Wilson's mixed but sympathetic review praised Roach's rhythmic compositions and Lincoln's "amazing wordless vocal calisthenics," as well as the "fierce and explosive cacophony" that concluded "Tears for Johannesburg," leaving "performers and audience limp with exhaustion."

---

crossover artist (as well as a former Communist), had not yet recorded his first LP, *Sin and Soul*. The urgency of the moment was such that, without informing Brown, the impetuous Roach recorded the material on his own.

Leading with the not-necessarily-commonplace notion that jazz had often been called "a music of protest," Wilson articulated a key idea of the 1960s, although he had employed the term "protest" only once before (as recently as July 1960) in quoting the West German jazz critic Joachim-Ernst Berendt's comment that "there is a big amount of protest in any jazz."

Protest? During the 1950s, the US government sent the Louis Armstrong, Duke Ellington, and Dizzy Gillespie bands on goodwill tours behind the Iron Curtain and to Africa. The 1960 Grove Press anthology *Jazz*, edited by Hentoff and Albert McCarthy, has nothing to say about protest except indirectly, in Paul Oliver's essay on the blues—an "often brutally realistic" mode he suggests is "unlikely to outlast the eventual complete integration of the Negro in American society" because then "the real reason for singing the blues will then have largely disappeared."[10]

Protest, however, was precisely the view that Roach and Lincoln advanced. Discussing their "protest ballet" in the hippest of the "little" literary magazines, *Kulchur*, the poet A. B. Spellman called it a "deliberate sacrifice of art for social message," adding that most people regarded Roach as a madman, particularly after he "interrupted Miles Davis's benefit for a Rockefeller-backed African research group with signs calling Governor Rockefeller down on his controlling interest in [the Congo-based, Belgian-owned mining company] Union Minière."

In early February Roach and Lincoln played a benefit for an NAACP workshop on union job bias. Along with the writers Rosa Guy and Maya Angelou, Lincoln founded the Cultural Association for Women of

10 Topical and even political blues have a long history but only a handful of jazz standards could be considered protest songs: "What Did I Do to Be So Black and Blue," "It's the Same Old South," and, most famously, "Strange Fruit" (which Billie Holliday first recorded in 1939). Dizzy Gillespie's 1947 recording of "Manteca" includes the chant, "I never go back to Georgia." Thanks to its title, Charles Mingus's "Haitian Fight Song," recorded live at Café Bohemia in 1955, can be construed as an expression of protest, as can Sonny Rollins's 1958 LP *Freedom Suite*, which featured Roach on drums. Mingus wrote the song "Fables of Faubus," mocking Arkansas's segregationist governor, Orval Faubus, in 1959 but his record company Columbia would not allow the lyrics to be recorded. The full song appeared in late 1960 on a Candid release, *Charles Mingus Presents Charles Mingus*. After *We Insist!* however, there were many, beginning with Art Blakey's remarkable seven-and-a-half-minute drum solo "The Freedom Rider," recorded in May 1961.

African Heritage and, a month after the *Freedom Now Suite* premiere, participated in what was described on the front page of the *New York Times* as "the most violent demonstration inside United Nations headquarters in the world organization's history."

As the new UN ambassador Adlai Stevenson rose to make his first formal speech, a group of some sixty veiled women and men wearing black armbands (the accessories fashioned at Lincoln's and Roach's home) interrupted the Security Council session to protest UN policies in the Congo and, revealed two days before, the murder of the nation's premier, Patrice Lumumba—"the greatest Black man to ever walk the African continent," per Malcolm X. Another 400 demonstrated outside, among them LeRoi Jones, recently returned from Cuba.

Partially performed at the Jazz Gallery that spring, *The Freedom Now Suite* received a mixed response. *Variety* noted the show's raw, "bitter mood." The critic, like Wilson, had issues with the dancing ("angry anguished writhing"), noting that "Tears for Johannesburg" concluded with the dancers gunned down to the sound of staccato drumbeats accompanied by "blinking lights"—perhaps an early use of a strobe.

Given the piece's subject matter and theatricality, it was unsurprising that Roach and Lincoln would have been involved with the first American production of Jean Genet's symbolic drama *The Blacks*, a play within a play in which a group of black actors (some in white face) reenact a trial for the murder of a white woman before the Queen and her court. The play was in rehearsal in the spring of 1961 under Gene Frankel's direction at the St. Mark's Playhouse, not two blocks from the Jazz Gallery. Roach wrote a score; Lincoln was cast as the outspoken Augusta Snow. The ensemble included Roscoe Lee Browne, Godfrey Cambridge, James Earl Jones, Lou Gossett Jr., Raymond St. Jacques, Cicely Tyson, and Maya Angelou (as the White Queen). Angelou recalled the play as "delicious to our taste":

> On that small New York stage, we reflected the real-life confrontations that were occurring daily in America's streets. Whites did live above us, hating and fearing and threatening our existence. Blacks did sneer behind their masks at the rulers they both loathed and envied. We would throw off the white yoke which dragged us down into an eternal genuflection.

A stand-in for the white audience and white authority in general, Frankel cultivated an adversarial relationship with the cast. He also encouraged Ossie Davis and James Baldwin to attend rehearsals and even hold cast meetings. The strategy had its risks. Just before opening night May 4, Lincoln quit the production and Roach withdrew his music, telling Angelou, without elaboration, that the producers reneged on an agreement.[11]

7

The struggle for Black rights was accelerating. On May 4, a bus filled with Freedom Riders was attacked in Montgomery by waiting Klansmen—the brutal assault, recorded by TV crews and press photographers, made international news.

Between the Village Gate and Jazz Gallery gigs, Lincoln recorded her own LP, *Straight Ahead*, produced by Hentoff and employing many of the musicians who had performed on *We Insist!* From the opening title song, which Lincoln co-wrote, to the final track, "Retribution," on which she also collaborated, the album was outspoken and assertive: "Just let the retribution match the contribution." Where *We Insist!* had been respectfully reviewed in *Down Beat*, *Straight Ahead* received a notoriously hostile review from the magazine's New York editor, Ira Gitler, who characterized Lincoln as "a professional Negro," writing that "pride in one's heritage is one thing, but we don't need the Elijah Muhammed [sic] type of thinking in jazz."

Controversy over Gitler's notice resulted in a two-issue *Down Beat*

11 Genet's *The Balcony* had been an off-Broadway hit, opening in March 1960; it had 672 performances, off-Broadway's longest-running dramatic play. *The Blacks*, however, was a sensation that—despite opening in the East Village at the St. Mark's Playhouse—would run for 1,408 performances. In addition to a favorable review, the *Voice* published Norman Mailer's bombastic, if confused, endorsement ("Take your family, take the kids, take the hoodlums on the corner. Take your gun . . . *The Blacks* is a Mother F. Kerr"). Lorraine Hansberry's counter-review ("a conversation between white men about *themselves*") was less a critique of Genet than Mailer, who would be defended in the *Voice* letters column by Ted Joans and Jonas Mekas. Although the audience was overwhelmingly white, *The Blacks* served as a base for its cast—actors would take roles in other plays and return. (Clebert Ford, who appeared in the play, published an appreciation in *Liberator* magazine asserting that "no play that ever had been presented on an American stage has given the Negro an opportunity to so completely express himself in both artistic and 'social' terms." *The Blacks* also established an identity for the St. Mark's Playhouse, which subsequently opened two plays by LeRoi Jones, *The Slave* and *The Toilet*, and later became the home of the Negro Ensemble Company.

symposium on racial prejudice and the magazine was obliged to deal with another controversy with the September 1961 release of Ornette Coleman's *Free Jazz*. The magazine ran two reviews—positive and negative—of an LP as radical in its way as Lincoln's gut-wrenching screams in *We Insist!* and no less insistent on liberation. Spellman concluded his *Kulchur* #5 essay with praise of the LP's existential, emancipatory quality: "*Free Jazz* beat the New Orleans method of group improvisation by starting out without head or tune, without even stating a word, thus forcing each man to use his entire store of musical materials."

Totally improvised by two combos playing simultaneously—one in each stereo channel—*Free Jazz* embodied freedom and effectively named the tendency most identified with Coleman, sometimes referred to by musicians as the "New Thing." No less than *We Insist!*, the LP cover made a statement. Not a news photo but a canvas, reproducing a section of Jackson Pollock's *White Light* (1954), one of the artist's last completed paintings—an amazingly dense web made in part by squeezing paint from the tube directly onto the canvas. (Spellman thought that if you could "freeze" the music, that's how it would look.)

Free jazz was modern art, and Coleman was understood as the supreme modernist as well as the ultimate primitive of the new era. Coleman's music was so new that the two preeminent young reedmen, John Coltrane and Sonny Rollins, were compelled to rethink their approach. In 1959, Coltrane, who, like Coleman, broke in as an R&B sideman before making his name playing with established virtuosi Thelonious Monk and Miles Davis, came frequently to hear Coleman. Rollins took a two-year hiatus and then returned for an epochal gig at the Village Gate with Don Cherry and Ed Blackwell as his sidemen.

Coleman might have been a man from Mars. (In some ways, Sun Ra—who described himself as a native of Saturn—had a similar trajectory after he arrived in New York in late 1961.) *New York Times* jazz critic John S. Wilson could not decide whether Coleman's "mixture of seemingly disjointed wails, flurried runs and peeps in a variety of tempos" was "a valid, new approach to jazz or is simply trying to raise the bizarre to the status of a style."

The same month that *Free Jazz* was released, the soon-to-fold jazz magazine *Metronome* featured an essay by LeRoi Jones that began by announcing, "There is definitely an avant-garde in jazz today." This vanguard owed nothing to European classical music, Jones emphasized. Rather, it was a modernism based on the rethinking of rhythm and melody, rooted in the blues and based on the assumption that bebop was "the most legitimately complex, emotionally rich music" to ever come out of America—and it was Black.[12]

Jones peppered his polemic with asides meant to unsettle his white colleagues: Thelonious Monk was a greater composer than Franz Liszt, the highly regarded pianist Oscar Peterson was notable for understanding that "technique *is* glibness," the popular alto saxophonist Cannonball Adderley was "*only* interesting because of bebop"—not because he plays bebop, but because "he will occasionally repeat an idea that bop once represented as profound."

Unlike Peterson or Adderley or the imitators of Billie Holiday and Charlie Parker, the avant-gardists were not classicists. Rather, they were exponents of the Now, "men for whom history exists to be utilized in their lives, their art, to make something for themselves and not as an overpowering reminder that people and their ideas did live before us." Ornette Coleman doesn't imitate Parker but uses him "only as a hypothesis." In addition to Coleman and Cecil Taylor, the musicians Jones intended to "hamper with the *nom de guerre* avant-garde" included Taylor's sidemen Don Cherry (the only "*real* innovator on his instrument"), drummers Billy Higgins, Ed Blackwell, and Charlie Haden (the only white musician whose name Jones italicized as "avant-garde"), as well as Eric Dolphy, who played on *Free Jazz*.

Jones's friend and neighbor, the saxophonist Archie Shepp

12 Underrecognized as a product of Black culture was the hip-swiveling dance called the twist. Hank Ballard's 1958 eponymous recording was inspired by the pelvic gyrations of some Tampa teenagers. Musicologists believe that the movement derives from a Congolese dance brought to America by enslaved Africans. Promoted by the Philadelphia TV show *American Bandstand*, Chubby Checker's cover of the Ballard song ignited a summer of 1960 teenage craze. In the fall of 1961, the *New York Times* reported that "the elite of the social set and celebrities of show business have discovered a sensuous dance call the Twist, performed to rock 'n' roll and are wallowing in it like converts to a new brand of voodoo." The cult's "high temple" was a mob-run sometime gay bar, the Peppermint Lounge on West Forty-Fifth Street off Seventh Avenue. By 1962, the twist was a worldwide sensation and early indicator of a revolution in cultural mores. Indeed, barely a month after the first *Times* piece, the newspaper reported a shocking outbreak of twisting at the Metropolitan Museum, during a fashion industry sponsored benefit for the museum's Costume Institute.

(unitalicized but praised for his "refusal to admit most of the time that there is a melody"), had gigged with Taylor. John Coltrane, whom Jones would soon come to regard as the greatest jazz man of his generation, was only mentioned parenthetically.

8

Before he became Amiri Baraka, Jones was a lodestar for several downtown avant-gardes. Born in 1934, he was the third youngest poet and the lone African American included in Donald M. Allen's influential Grove Press anthology *The New American Poetry 1945–1960.* He edited the little magazine *Yūgen* with his wife, then named Hettie Cohen (later Jones), while co-editing *The Floating Bear* with his lover, Diane di Prima.

A publisher as well, having established the small press Corinth-Totem with Eli Wilentz, the proprietor of the Eighth Street Bookstore, Jones befriended poets ranging from the Black Mountain eminence Charles Olson and the apostle of "personalism" Frank O'Hara to Allen Ginsberg. Jones was cosmopolitan, recounting his 1960 trip to Cuba in *Evergreen Review*, yet so closely identified with the East Village that when Dan Talbot briefly ran the Charles Theater, Jonas Mekas praised this cultural development in "the heart of Ginsberg, LeRoi Jones, and Peter Orlovsky territory."

Jones aspired to become the "Black Ezra Pound," or so his Howard University roommate A. B. Spellman told di Prima. Although friendly with Ginsberg, Jones was not close to the Black Beats (and self-identified jazz poets) Bob Kaufman and Ted Joans. Nor was he affiliated with the Umbra group, an association of young Black poets of various political persuasions who came together on the Lower East Side during the summer of 1962, read often at Les Deux Mégots and later Le Metro, and published a journal. He was, however, central to another African American vanguard that in addition to jazz musicians included Spellman and the painter Bob Thompson and had its spiritual home at the Five Spot.

In early 1962, the Jones family, expanded by two young daughters, would relocate from East Fourteenth Street to a cold-water loft on the fourth floor of an abandoned 1845 rooming house at 27 Cooper Square next door to a birdseed factory and down the block from the Five Spot (which soon after moved three blocks north to St. Mark's

Place). Rent was $100 a month. Soon the Archie Shepp family took up residence at 27 Cooper Square. Albert Ayler, Marion Brown, Ornette Coleman, Giuseppi Logan, Sonny Murray, Sonny Rollins, Sun Ra, and Cecil Taylor all lived in the neighborhood, as did Spellman and Thompson, whose Clinton Street loft was another gathering place.[13]

Born in Louisville, Kentucky, in 1937 (five years before local hero Cassius Clay) and the son of a businessman and a schoolteacher, Thompson attended but never finished college, although he did study art for several years at the University of Louisville. In 1958, he arrived in New York City by way of Provincetown. Squatting or living in a succession of cold-water Lower East Side lofts, he hung out with other young painters, most famously Red Grooms, a son of Louisville's sister city Nashville.

Impressed by the example of the figurative abstractionist Jan Müller, a German-born student of Hans Hofmann, who died at thirty-six and was something of a cult figure for young Tenth Street artists, Thompson set about fashioning a new mythology. His paintings were personal allegories often set in Edenic landscapes of rolling hills and lollipop trees, populated by nude human figures and animals, as well as an assortment of mythological creatures (harpies, angels, dragons, Biblical characters, avatars of the Egyptian dog god Anubis). More poignant than menacing, Thompson's monsters are usually black. As the other inhabitants of his cosmos were yellow, red, blue, brown, and occasionally pink, some read his work as an imagined multiracial universe—albeit charged as it is with an intermittently violent erotic pantheism.

Thompson had his first New York show in 1960 at Grooms's Delancey Street Museum and participated in several of Grooms's happenings as well as Kaprow's. While an undated Grooms sketch shows Thompson, a rangy figure hunched forward in an uncomfortably low chair utterly concentrating on a painting, Thompson portrayed himself as a musician and often painted musicians. His masterpiece, the mural-sized *Garden of Music* (1960), places

13 Forty-six years later, Hettie Jones successfully defended her right to continue living at 27 Cooper Square, compelling the builders of the Cooper Square Hotel to redesign the hotel to incorporate her building—a story that was reported in the *New York Times*.

recognizable versions of Five Spot heroes Ornette Coleman, John Coltrane, Don Cherry, Sonny Rollins, and Charlie Haden in an idyllic Thompson landscape. *Bird Party* (1961), a large, festive canvas in which pink women dance with multi-colored birds beside an alpine lake, would hang behind the bandstand in the far East Village club Slugs' Saloon, which opened in 1964, succeeding the Five Spot as the supreme jazz bar.

9

A month after "The Jazz Avant-Garde" was published, LeRoi Jones was busted. His arrest had nothing to do with the heroin he was snorting with Bob Thompson; it occurred because he was the co-editor of *The Floating Bear*.

Around 10:45 one October morning, a US marshal, an FBI agent, and a postal inspector showed up with a warrant at East Fourteenth Street (where Jones was still living). "I was awakened with these nabs standing over my head," he remembered. Jones was arrested and, along with a confiscated water pipe, taken downtown to the federal courthouse on Pearl Street. The charge—ironic in that Jones was the son of a New Jersey postal superintendent—was sending obscene material through the mail.

The Floating Bear was not sold but posted to a list of some 300 subscribers. Harold Carrington, Ray Bremser's former cellmate at the Rahway State Prison in New Jersey and one of the people on the list, was incarcerated. While reading Carrington's mail, prison authorities had been scandalized by two pieces. One, by Jones, was an account of a homosexual rape on a military base (eventually published by Grove Press in Jones's novel *The System of Dante's Hell*). The other far more scabrous piece was "Roosevelt After Inauguration," a three-page "routine" by William Burroughs, turned down even by *Kulchur* as too dangerous.

Alerted by Hettie, Diane di Prima surrendered at the courthouse where Jones was held. After arraignment, their lawyer, a prominent left-wing attorney named Stanley Faulkner, managed to get them released on their own recognizance and, rather than a trial, secured a grand jury hearing. In late April 1962, Jones spent two days on the witness stand, reading what he called "the filthy parts" from Catullus and *Ulysses*, as well as Judge Woolsey's decision on *Ulysses*, stressing Woolsey's definition of obscene literature as arousing the normal person. "I gave a John Barrymore–like speech," Jones told the *Voice*. With reference to the sadistic acts described in the accused works, he explained that he had assured the grand jury, "I'm sure none of you people were aroused." It worked. Only six of the necessary twelve voted to indict.

The First Amendment was an issue in 1961. Grove Press was preparing to publish Henry Miller's bawdy novel *Tropic of Cancer*. Indeed, *Floating Bear* #9 appeared in June, some weeks before Grove succeeded in getting the postal ban lifted on *Tropic of Cancer*. Grove publisher Barney Rosset had planned to bring out Burroughs's *Naked Lunch* once the *Tropic of Cancer* case was settled. The *Floating Bear* case stayed his hand until late 1962 even as it heightened Burroughs's notoriety.

Inevitably, Burroughs was twinned with another hipster First Amendment martyr, Lenny Bruce. Coincidentally, two days before the authorities knocked on LeRoi Jones's door, Bruce experienced his first obscenity bust, arrested between shows at the Jazz Workshop in San Francisco for, among other things, using the word "cocksucker" in his act. Jones and Burroughs employ the same epithet in their *Floating Bear* pieces. Burroughs even attributes it to Roosevelt, who he describes as "so convulsed with hate for the human species as it is, that he wished to degrade it beyond recognition. 'I'll make the cocksuckers glad to mutate,' he would say, looking off into space as if seeking new frontiers of depravity."

Often spoken of in similar terms, Burroughs and Bruce normalized profanity. They equally enjoyed spinning outlandishly desecrated pop-culture scenarios although Burroughs's performance skills would not be apparent for some decades. Both were also heroin users. Bruce was a classic hipster; Burroughs, who had the wardrobe and affect of a blasé police lieutenant, was not so obvious although a *Village Voice* review of the Olympia Press edition of *The* [sic] *Naked Lunch*, published in Paris, called the novel "by far the most successful effort to write hip; for the first time, no effort at all, just doing what comes naturally."

Jazz critics like Ralph Gleason in San Francisco and Nat Hentoff in New York were Bruce's strongest supporters; others, notably the British director Jonathan Miller, who wrote about Bruce both in the *Village Voice* and *Partisan Review*, compared his spontaneous, free-form raps to Kerouac's spontaneous prose. The two had similar deliveries: Their phrasing was jazzy, their voices were nasal and New York–inflected (although Kerouac grew up speaking Quebecois French in Lowell, Massachusetts), their raps were punctuated by hipster patois. Both dug Lord Buckley.

Of course, Bruce was also a wise guy whose anti-clericalism offended

Kerouac. Allen Ginsberg was more appreciative. As a self-aware stand-up, Bruce likely absorbed something of Ginsberg's incantatory unpatriotic rhetoric by osmosis and although he feigned annoyance that Ginsberg ("a guy with long hair, dirty sweatshirt, blue jeans, Pernod and Peter Orlovsky") was mistaken for him at a San Francisco party celebrating his first LP, *The Sick Humor of Lenny Bruce*, he may also have been pleased. Bruce was sometimes bracketed (like Burroughs) with Jean Genet and abstract expressionist painters, but, unlike Ornette Coleman, he lacked the cultural confidence to put a Jackson Pollock on an LP cover. Miller saw a similarity between Bruce's riffs and Burroughs's "jump-cut discontinuity." Burroughs was, however, more alarming. And while bisexual Bruce was upfront about balling chicks, Burroughs—who accidentally shot and killed his wife—was queer.[14]

Hentoff, who described Bruce as "so utterly free of moral euphemisms and rationalizations of all kinds that you either listen to him or leave," thought Bruce more honest than Burroughs. "Everything now is central to his basic message: 'This is an insane culture with an insane set of values.' William Burroughs agrees, but turns his revulsion into acrid, antic fleeing fantasies. Bruce lays on the line what is happening here and now." Still, as perhaps a response to the new Kennedy administration, Burroughs's "Roosevelt After Inauguration"—which imagines the appointment and subsequent abuse of the president's cabinet in hilariously scurrilous terms, while even evoking Kennedy's term "New Frontier"—might be considered as something happening here and now.

Burroughs's mildest conceits (naming "an old queen, known to the Brooklyn Police as 'Jerk Off Annie'" to be "Joint Chief of Staff," designating a female impersonator called "Eddie the Lady" to head the Atomic Energy Commission or tapping "an old-time junkie and con man on the skids" as Postmaster General) suggest Bruce at his most outrageous. The grand finale, in which Roosevelt orders his new cabinet and the Supreme Court to "submit to intercourse with a purple assed baboon" (under threat of immediate reduction to the rank of Congressional Lavatory Attendant) is well

14 Writing about *Naked Lunch* in *Partisan Review*, Lionel Abel maintained that Burroughs's novel was "rather like those pornographic films that give dispirited people pleasure. It is also like another kind of film: the documentaries shown after the war of Nazi concentration camp atrocities." In other words, his writing had its visual analogy in the collages of Boris Lurie.

beyond a Bruce routine, although, with Kennedy's inauguration fresh in his mind, Bruce did go off on a similar riff in his February 4 concert.

Positing a situation where the new president was taken ill on eve of an important announcement, Bruce imagines that his advisors scramble to find a double (whom they can always shoot afterwards). The stand-in is a stand-up "toilet comic" who, before introducing his cabinet, lapses into an impersonation of himself.

10

In the face of censorship, mimeographed magazines appeared: early 1962 brought a new one devoted to topical and protest songs, *Broadside*. The editors, sometime folk musician Sis Cunningham, fifty-three, and her husband, the journalist Gordon Friesen, fifty-two, were veteran Oklahoma leftists who relocated to New York in the late 1940s.

Living in the Frederick Douglass Houses, a city project on a super-block (100th to 104th Street) bounded by Amsterdam and Manhattan Avenues, Cunningham and Friesen published *Broadside* out of their kitchen, using a small hand-cranked mimeograph inherited from the local chapter of the defunct American Labor Party. *Broadside*'s first, February 1962 issue featured a humorous composition that, despite its studied sub-literacy, might not have seemed out of place in a more elevated zine like *The Floating Bear* or Ed Sanders's cheerfully faux loutish *Fuck You: A Magazine of the Arts*, another new mimeo inspired, according to Sanders, by Jonas Mekas's *Guns of the Trees*.

It was homespun (or rather "homespun") political satire. The writer admits "feelin' sad," as well as "blue," wondering what the world was coming to. Communists are ubiquitous, in the sky overhead as well as on the ground below and likely hiding beneath his bed. Looking for some peace of mind, he hastens to enlist in the John Birch Society, a quasi-conspiratorial patriotic group whose founder Robert Welch believed former president Dwight D. Eisenhower to have been a "dedicated, conscious agent of the communist conspiracy in the United States." Newly armed with a "secret membership card," the writer heads out on the road, giving the rebel yell and warning, "look out you Commies!"[15]

15 As the anti-white Nation of Islam rivaled the Communist Party as an internal threat, so the anti-Communist, conspiratorial John Birch Society, which supposedly had close to 100,000 members in 1961, was a vaguely comic source of menace for leftists. Alongside writing by Kerouac, Burroughs, Ginsberg, di Prima, Gary Snyder and LeRoi

The author, twenty-year-old Bob Dylan, had made his way to New York City barely a year before, having dropped out of the University of Minnesota to arrive only days ahead of the early February blizzard that buried the city under seventeen inches of snow and would elevate Lenny Bruce's midnight concert to the realm of myth. (Indeed, Dylan—no stranger to winter weather—appears to have made some money shoveling snow.)

By his own account, Dylan hitchhiked to New York, took the subway downtown and, even before finding a place to crash for the night, managed to talk his way onstage at Café Wha?, a subterranean cavern that opened at noon and closed at 4:00 a.m. Dylan had been hipped to ask for Fred Neil, a twenty-four-year-old aspiring singer-songwriter out of Cleveland with brooding good looks, a strong baritone, and a few rockabilly recordings to his credit. Neil hosted the club's daily hootenanny. After listening to Dylan noodle on harmonica, he invited him to play backup during his set. Remarkably prescient, *Village Voice* photographer Fred McDarrah documented Neil, Dylan, and the cult folksinger Karen Dalton sharing the club's tiny stage.[16]

Working his way into the heart of the scene, Dylan made repeated pilgrimages to visit his idol Woody Guthrie, hospitalized in New Jersey with incurable Huntington's Disease. Crashing on various sofas, absorbing various record collections—Harry Smith's three-disc Folkways collection *Anthology of American Folk Music* in particular—he performed at the Wha?, the Bizarre, and the Commons. Dylan was a prodigy. "A Jewish boy who changed his name!" per Izzy Young. "When he came here, he sat around the Folklore Center and lived in Bob

---

Jones, *Kulchur* #3 published the anonymous "Two John Birch Society Jokes."

16 While, as often noted, folkies and beatniks were not identical, Dalton was a hybrid and, in some ways, the anti-Dylan. Five years older, twice divorced with two kids, a few missing teeth, and a nascent drug habit, she was an "authentic" Okie of Cherokee descent. Accompanying herself on various fretted instruments, Dalton had a haunting, mournful voice and great aesthetic integrity, not to mention bad luck and negative career sense, despite promotion by handlers as powerful as Dylan's manager Albert Grossman, Café au Go Go owner Howard Solomon and Woodstock Festival organizer Michael Lang. Her lone *Voice* mention was in Annie Fisher's May 8, 1969, "Riffs" column: "She sounds like she has a terminal case of laryngitis, in advanced stages, except that it works. Earthy, sensitive, totally individual, she does eccentric justice to some fine material. Particularly tasty is Otis Redding's 'I Love You More Than Words Can Say.'"

Shelton's apartment for a month: everybody coddled him, nursed him, and encouraged him . . . I think there was more help with the beginning of Bob Dylan than anyone I ever met."

Once he befriended Dave Van Ronk, Dylan appeared at the Gaslight. A concert at the NYU folk club that spring helped him secure a gig at Gerde's Folk City. On April 11, the day after the Beatnik Riot inspired his first attempt at a protest song, "Down in Washington Square," Dylan opened for the forty-five-year-old Detroit blues singer John Lee Hooker, reinventing himself for the folk audience as an acoustic "country" bluesman. The gig, which lasted a fortnight, and for which Dylan received $90 per week, overlapped Abbey Lincoln and Max Roach's post–*We Insist!* engagement at the Jazz Gallery. (Dylan played Gerde's again in the spring on a bill with Varda Karni.)

By summer, fines were again levied against the Bizarre and the Wha? and Dylan was near ubiquitous. He opened for Van Ronk at the Gaslight, was a popular backup musician and a fixture at Folk City hootenannies, known for his hip, humorous talking blues and ragamuffin Chaplinesque persona. He was a quick study, absorbing people's record collections and bookshelves, taking in Jack Elliott's Woody Guthrie material, sponging up Dave Van Ronk's version of "House of the Rising Sun" and adopting Hugh Romney's catch phrase ("dig yourself"). Romney turned Dylan onto Lord Buckley and Dylan added a version of Buckley's recitation of the anti-lynching poem "Black Cross" to his repertoire.

In late September, Gerde's put Dylan on a bill with the Greenbriar Boys, the fast finger picking urban bluegrass ensemble founded by John Herald, red-diaper son of an Armenian American poet. Thanks to Robert Shelton's enthusiastic *New York Times* review, the booking made Dylan a MacDougal Street star, soon signed by John Hammond to Columbia Records.

In November, Dylan recorded his first album—a collection of distinctively styled blues and folk ballads—and, for $60 a month, rented a two-room fourth-floor walk-up at 161 West Fourth Street, overlooking the exhaust vent from a neighboring pizza parlor. There, living with his eighteen-year-old girlfriend, red-diaper baby and CORE activist Suze Rotolo, Dylan wrote "Talkin' John Birch Society Blues," "The Death of Emmett Till," and many lesser topical songs. "The Death of Emmett Till" was first performed at a CORE benefit (most likely at the Village Gate) scheduled for February 23, 1962, around the time that "Talkin' John Birch" was published in *Broadside.*

"Talkin' John Birch" ended with the newly minted Bircher declaring his vigilance, and looking for "them Reds" under the sink, beneath his chair, up the chimney and "deep down" his toilet bowl. The words take on additional relevance in that Rotolo and, by extension, Dylan, were under FBI surveillance.[17]

11

Protest was happening: The six-day General Strike for Peace, organized in part by Julian Beck, was prefaced on January 26, 1962, with a picket line around the *New York Times* office following the paper's refusal to publish a full-page ad announcing the worldwide general strike.

The strike continued two days later with a 1,000-strong silent demonstration outside the UN and a somewhat smaller march down Fifth Avenue from the Plaza Hotel to Washington Square. The next few days saw pickets at the downtown office of the Atomic Energy Commission and midtown Civil Defense Headquarters, and a sidewalk children's parade up Fifth Avenue to Central Park that included a Uranian Alchemy Players performance of Peter Schumann's *Totentanz.*

Save for Jonas Mekas, who documented several General Strike marches as well as leafleteers in Times Square (the marquee for *Judgement at Nuremberg* in the background), and the young painter Ben Morea, politicized by participating as an associate of the Living Theatre, the marches attracted little attention. However, a Saturday, March 3 demonstration organized by the Women's Strike for Peace protesting Kennedy's decision to resume atmospheric nuclear testing became front-page news when a man collapsed midway through a half-hour silent vigil. As the Tactical

17 *Broadside*'s editors had long been on the FBI's radar. Pete Seeger, a sometime member of the Communist Party, recalled Cunningham as a leader in the party's Greenwich Village Branch, charged with the hopeless task of getting Woody Guthrie to fulfill his party assignments. Dylan's prime press advocate Robert Shelton, a onetime member of a Communist youth group, was likely, if not rigorously, surveilled as well. So perhaps was *Broadside*, which held monthly meetings, attended by Len Chandler, Phil Ochs, Pete and Toshi Seeger (who underwrote the publication), and others, in which Dylan regularly participated into the spring of 1963. John Hammond, who signed Dylan to Columbia Records, was a non-Communist with an extensive FBI file.

Police dragged him off, a dozen marchers staged a sit-in, prompting additional police activity.

From behind the barricades Beck saw his wife Judith Malina being manhandled. He led the crowd (estimated as over a thousand and including, as described by the *New York Times*, numerous "beatniks") in screaming: "Shame! Shame! Shame!" Scores of protestors were arrested, including Malina and Beck, who suffered a punctured lung in the melee and was taken to Bellevue Hospital. The *Village Voice*, which put Beck's condition on page one, was a forum for dissident views, including that of peace activist David McReynolds, who blamed the rally's organizers for losing control, and a letter from an Upper West Side shrink who theorized that the entire event was a "psychodrama" orchestrated by "conflicting groups of lunatics."

Some, notably McReynolds, would say the same about the season's ultimate liberating expression of insane beatnik infantility: *The Flower Thief*. Ron Rice's low-budget feature arrived in New York two years after its North Beach premiere. The first New York screening was in April 1962 at Cinema 16. Taylor Mead, who was present, wrote to Rice that although about half the audience booed the film, "many more applauded + thought it was great." The Cinema 16 show was followed by screenings at the Gaslight with Mead and likely Bob Kaufman in attendance. Jonas Mekas, who'd been in touch with Rice, namechecked the film in the *Voice*.

Mekas had recently praised Jean Vigo's 1933 *Zero de Conduite*, showing at the Bleecker Street Cinema "complete and uncensored" for the first time in New York, and he considered *The Flower Thief* a kindred poem of liberation as well as social satire. "With the coming of beat and Zen, America began to regain its sense of humor," he declared in June, citing happenings, *Pull My Daisy*, and *The Flower Thief*. For what, if not reasonable behavior, patriotism, good filmmaking, adult responsibility, and authority itself, was *The Flower Thief* mocking?

12

Summer 1962: There are early intimations of the orgy to come. Students for a Democratic Society draft their Port Huron Statement. With help from the Communist Party USA (CPUSA), a group co-led by Archie Shepp and Bill Dixon brings Free Jazz to the Eighth World Festival of

Youth and Students in Helsinki.[18]

Lee Harvey Oswald returns from the Soviet Union and the Soviets prepare to send missiles to Cuba. JFK dispatches troops to Ole Miss. The French leave Algeria, Marilyn Monroe (the subject of commercial artist turned painter Andy Warhol's first one-man show) departs this earth, and *The Flower Thief* enjoys maximal visibility with a three-week run at the Charles Theater.

Encouraged by the subterranean audience, the Charles had begun monthly open screenings, or "festivals." Admission was 95 cents or the submission of one film for projection. These screenings proved popular—according to Langsford, the first had a crowd of filmmakers and friends lined up around the block.

Visiting the theater in the spring of 1962, *New York Times* reporter Howard Thompson was impressed by the intense discussion that erupted during intermissions as well as the tough audience: "The hissing auditorium sounded like a snake pit and feet pounded the floor with Rockette precision at the sight of revolving, lighted matches, a kewpie-doll's head inside a cantaloupe and an occasional stream of ball bearings"—possibly Ray Wisniewski's *Doomshow*.[19]

Six months of open screenings culminated in July 1962 with a grand, competitive Filmmaker's Festival. First prize went to Michael Putnam's *The Hard Swing*, a twenty-four-minute cinema verité portrait of a North Beach stripper. Rice, named "most promising filmmaker," was represented by two films—*The Flower Thief* and his twenty-eight-minute nonnarrative *Senseless*, the title a play on Godard's *Breathless* as well as a riff on the movie's genesis and deceptively random quality. (In lieu of a soundtrack, Rice played a Béla Bartók LP found in the Charles's projection booth.)

Brashly dedicated to Jack Kennedy (and facetiously crediting Jonas

---

18 The CPUSA also recommended the Cecil Taylor Unit, although, unhappy with his billing, Taylor decided not to attend. Funding came through the On Guard Committee for Freedom, which developed out of the protests following the death of Patrice Lumumba. Shepp and Dixon's performance was attended by Soviet poet Yevgeny Yevtushenko, who rushed on the stage at the conclusion to raise a vodka toast.

19 Among the unknown filmmakers who attended and exhibited short works at the Charles were Brian De Palma, Ken Jacobs, Paul Morrissey, and Jack Smith, who, years later, remembered the Charles screening as "wide open. People brought in their own films and saw them on the huge Charles screen—a truly surrealistic experience . . . and they looked damn good."

Mekas with the nonexistent screenplay), *Senseless* was no less Beat than *The Flower Thief*. A chunk of the movie was shot in Venice (Los Angeles), the rest mainly filmed in Mexico—where Rice had gone on a fruitless pilgrimage to the island "utopia" that Venice coffee-shop entrepreneur Eric "Big Daddy" Nord had planned and, for lack of water, abandoned—or on the road. Incidents of junkyard clowning and skid-row shenanigans, including a cameo by Taylor Mead, are juxtaposed with anti-war demonstrations and a mock wedding staged in a Mexican cemetery. Early images of social revolt give way to marijuana-infused blasphemy: like, Jesus was a Beatnik!

Along with Mead, Rice was elevated to the underground's highest echelons when the Charles gave *The Flower Thief* a theatrical run, paired with another Mead vehicle, Vernon Zimmerman's *To L.A. with Lust*. Mekas praised *The Flower Thief* as "one of the most important of modern films, a beautiful absurd poem." Unexpectedly, Rice's feature got something close to a rave review from *New York Times* critic Eugene Archer. (A mixed notice in *Newsweek* correctly characterized it as "closer to the art of assemblage and the odd theatrical Happenings of the New York painters than to anything in the tradition of film.")

The *Voice* published several hostile letters ("The Flower Thief—Invalid or Incompetent"), one written by anti-beatnik scold David McReynolds and twice as long as Mekas's review. Still fuming after the debacle of the General Strike, McReynolds had had it with the hipster politics he had called for in December 1959. Still, whatever Rice's intentions, the spectacle of a happy simpleton playing holy fool in the shadow of the H-bomb had obvious appeal for the Charles audience. Like the Bob Dylan of 1961, the openly moronic Mead was being called "Chaplinesque."[20]

20 Mead, who had a crush on Dylan, places him along among his "co-'readers'" on the coffeehouse circuit: "When Bob Dylan would come in, usually drunk or stoned, looking like a lost angel, I would stop reading and turn the podium over to him. Sometimes he was so 'out of it' he would be singing and playing the guitar to the wall, his back to the audience." Most likely, Mead was referring to the Third Side, a Bleecker Street basket house run by the Black actor Charlie Washburn, which advertised both men in a February 1962 *Village Voice* listing. Mead also claimed to have appeared with Woody Allen ("we felt he was a bit of an interloper on the scene, as his material was obviously calculated to please the audience, whereas the rest of us were more or less trying to upset and shock the general public"). A known comedy writer before he turned to stand-up,

The newspapers were filled with absurd headlines. On July 13, 1962, the *New York Times* reported a quixotic British demonstration in Red Square. Four days later, the Soviet leader boasted of a new missile accurate enough to "hit a fly" in outer space. The back-and-forth regarding the lapsed test ban treaty and need for fallout shelters culminated two weeks later in the announcement of Project Apollo, "man's race for the moon." Meanwhile, despite the Charles's lack of air-conditioning, *The Flower Thief* played to full houses for the rest of the month.

13

Broadside #3 published Dylan's anti-shelter jeremiad "I Will Not Go Down Under the Ground." Thereafter, he refocused on freedom songs. ("Blowin' in the Wind," first performed at the Gaslight by Gil Turner on April 16, 1962, appeared in *Broadside* #6 and "Ain't Gonna Grieve" in *Broadside* #11.)

Dylan's debut album had been released in March to supportive reviews and modest sales. He was already recording a second LP. *The Freewheelin' Bob Dylan* would mark the shift from white blues to protest songs. After wrapping up one recording session at Columbia's midtown studio, he appeared at a "Folk & Jazz Concert" at the nearby Palm Gardens on West Fifty-Second Street. Pete Seeger was also on the bill, as were Cecil Taylor and Archie Shepp. (This rare instance of the two downtown musical vanguards sharing a gig was most likely a benefit to fund Shepp and Bill Dixon's upcoming trip to the World Youth Festival in Helsinki.)

Broadside would publish two more freedom songs that year ("Oxford Town" and "Paths of Victory"). But in the summer of 1962, Dylan returned to nuclear angst, writing a three-page poem that would be the LP's strongest track. The crowning achievement of Dylan's first eighteen months in New York, performed by Patti Smith some fifty-four years later in Stockholm on the occasion of Dylan's Nobel Prize, "A Hard Rain's A-Gonna Fall" was an apocalyptic vision that infused the question-and-answer structure of "Lord Randall," recently recorded by Jean Ritchie in her Folkways LP *British Traditional Ballads in the Southern Mountains*, with the incantatory power of Allen Ginsberg's "Howl."

Allen played the Gaslight in December 1962, five months after Mead was there with *The Flower Thief*.

Dylan hung out that summer upstairs from the Gaslight at the Kettle of Fish or Hugh Romney's pad (a haven for pot smokers), or played cards, and, when inspiration struck, wrote. He tried out new material in Van Ronk's Tuesday hootenannies or in unadvertised late sets. Despite a common assumption that Dylan wrote "Hard Rain" at the height of the Cuban Missile Crisis, he premiered the song a month before, September 22, at Carnegie Hall, as part of the all-star "Travelin' Hootenanny" organized by Pete Seeger, and not long after he recorded a version at the Gaslight—part of an "audition" tape orchestrated by manager Grossman as a possible end run around Columbia to establish the direction of Dylan's second album.[21]

"Hard Rain" is more generally a response to the nuclear jitters of the past year. Still, the evening of October 24, when Soviet ships neared but did not attempt to cross the blockade of American ships surrounding Cuba, when Norman Mailer wondered if he was seeing Manhattan landmarks for the last time, and Sol LeWitt, then a guard at the Museum of Modern Art, observed paintings by Picasso and Matisse ("all the great masterpieces") hurriedly moved to a secret bunker, Dylan again sang the song at Town Hall. In mid-October, he had resumed recording for Columbia and would continue with sessions in November and early December.

Somewhat anticlimactic in the mass exhalation of breath that followed the Cuban Missile Crisis's resolution, a second, grimmer General Strike for Peace—again organized by Julian Beck—was held in early November. The weeklong strike began with the release of 500 white balloons at Columbus Circle followed by a chance run-in with Governor Rockefeller, campaigning for reelection in a gold-painted double-decker bus. It ended with the Uranian Alchemy Players' final performance of *Totentanz*. Scheduled for Washington Square Park, freezing weather necessitated it be moved indoors.

Voice critic Arthur Sainer was impressed by the ritual dance of death

21 Van Ronk, Chandler, and Romney were Gaslight regulars. Dylan was not. Indeed, the Gaslight's stellar attraction in 1962 and 1963 was comedian Bill Cosby, who for a time crashed upstairs in Romney's pad. Five blocks north of the Gaslight, in another universe, another twenty-year-old, self-invented musical genius and Columbia recording artist was enjoying her fourth engagement at the Bon Soir, a tiny cellar nightclub at 40 West Eighth Street. Barbra Streisand's first LP, *Live at the Bon Soir*, was recorded November 5–7, 1962, and released sixty-one years later.

and resurrection performed by children as well as adults. "To the accompaniment of a steady percussive beat, they circle about and leap until one by one they drop . . . And then, after death, they rise, to die again." However, the real resurrection belonged to the Living Theatre, saved at the last moment from a sheriff's sale when $8,300 was raised to pay down the $10,000 owed in back rent.

14

Recorded that November, *The Freewheelin' Bob Dylan* was in stores by late May 1963. "Blowin' in the Wind," "Masters of War," and "Oxford Town" were on the LP. So was "Hard Rain," which, along with "Masters of War," powerfully impressed Allen Ginsberg when he heard the record out in San Francisco. "Talkin' John Birch" was not included.

The Chad Mitchell Trio had released their satiric "John Birch Society" over a year before, yet Columbia supposedly feared offending or being sued by the Birch Society; at the label's request, the song was replaced by "Talkin' World War III Blues." For Dylan, "Talkin' John Birch Paranoid Blues," as he now called it, was a free speech issue. He insisted on performing it when booked, in a nifty bit of corporate synergy, to promote the LP, released by a CBS subsidiary, on CBS's most important variety program, *The Ed Sullivan Show*. Approved by Sullivan, the song was rehearsed three times and then censored by CBS. Dylan refused to go on. The next morning's *New York Times* ran a story headlined SATIRE ON BIRCH SOCIETY BARRED FROM ED SULLIVAN'S TV SHOW.

Dylan's brilliance as a social critic was confirmed. But, as he ascended, another self-invented musical genius was increasingly frustrated. Ornette Coleman played his last gig at the Five Spot in September 1961 exactly when, a few blocks west, Dylan was opening for the Greenbriar Boys at Gerde's. In less than two years since his sensational New York debut, Coleman had released five LPs on Atlantic—*The Shape of Jazz to Come*, *Change of the Century*, *This Is Our Music*, *Free Jazz*, and *Ornette!*

The epitome of the so-called New Thing, widely considered the single most innovative force in contemporary jazz, Coleman was a star who brought people to the Five Spot—yet his pay was insultingly low. In June 1962, his trio had a gig at the Five Spot's sister club Jazz Gallery. When Coleman learned that Dave Brubeck had been paid twice as much while drawing smaller crowds, he tripled his fee and effectively priced himself out of business.

Unable to play clubs, Coleman rented Town Hall for the night of December 21, 1962, and, in addition to his trio, brought a rhythm and blues combo and a string quartet. The concert had three components—the trio, the trio playing with the combo, and a composition written for string quartet. The event barely broke even. Coleman only made enough to pay the musicians. He would not play publicly for nearly three years.[22]

The lawyer Bernard Stollman, briefly Coleman's manager, recorded the concert. He maintains that Coleman initially licensed a portion of the Town Hall tape to him, then subsequently sold it to Blue Note records. However, in the absence of an LP, Stollman eventually issued some of the material on ESP-Disk, a label he originally founded to promote Esperanto-based music. (The remainder of the concert has never surfaced.) The LP, *Town Hall 1962*, included the string quartet but not the R&B combo. The former was deemed an interesting failure, largely because Coleman himself did not play, but A. B. Spellman, one of the few critics to write about the concert, called the R&B segment "one of the two most important works [Coleman] has ever performed" (the other being the LP *Free Jazz*).

Rising above the tight R&B beat and the polyrhythmic playing of his sidemen, drummer (and high school buddy) Charles Moffett and white bass player David Izenzon, Coleman's solo "included everything that he had learned since his early Texas days," Spellman wrote. "The piece was embarrassing in its honesty. It was as if Ornette had excavated his entire musical past to get back to the core of his work."

Why, Spellman wondered, did "other jazzmen concerned with enlarging their forms not stop and reevaluate their music?" Mutatis mutandis, the same question would be raised a bit more than two years later by Bob Dylan.

---

22 One month earlier, Town Hall had hosted another notable jazz event when Eric Dolphy's Quintet shared a bill with self-identified "metaphysical poet" Ree Dragonette, a regular as Les Deux Mégots and Café Le Metro. "Eric is working in a new field and so am I," she said before the concert. "We're breaking new ground. Here, we do it together." *Downbeat*'s reviewer wrote that the evening had "moments of true brilliance." Dragonette's friend Calvin Hernton called it "a dazzling symbiosis . . . glorious and historic."

Frame enlargement, *Flaming Creatures* (1962–63), Mario Montez at right.
Courtesy of Anthology Film Archives.

4

The Camera Shall Know No Shame, 1962–64

In which Shirley Clarke's film of *The Connection* is banned, Jack Smith's *Flaming Creatures* premieres, and Jonas Mekas declares the advent of "Baudelairean cinema." Pop Art ascends. Andy Warhol picks up a camera and establishes the Factory. Barbara Rubin shoots her shameless *Christmas on Earth*, Kenneth Anger shows *Scorpio Rising*. The Living Theatre stages *The Brig* and is evicted from their theater.

> *"Life swarms with innocent monsters." Charles Baudelaire.*
>
> —Jack Smith in *Blonde Cobra* (1962)[1]

In the beginning was the word: Shirley Clarke's adaptation of *The Connection* was banned not for what it showed but for what it said.

A former dancer and choreographer, as well as a maker of short experimental 16mm films, Clarke (born Shirley Brimberg to a wealthy New York family in 1919) purchased the rights to Jack Gelber's play in 1960; later that year, she began shooting her version of the play on a modest budget and a single soundstage that convincingly simulated a cluttered cold-water loft. Her cast was almost entirely drawn from the Living Theatre. The mellifluous Roscoe Lee Browne, soon to be cast in

1 The full quote—"What oddities one finds in big cities, when one knows how to roam and how to look! Life swarms with innocent monsters"—comes from the prose poem "Miss Bistoury," included in *Paris Spleen*.

The Blacks, was one of the few additions. Heard but not seen, his character was credited with assembling the movie from the leavings of the comically clueless director (another character within the film).

Clarke completed *The Connection* in time for the 1961 Cannes Film Festival, where it was enthusiastically received as a cinematic breakthrough as well as a fresh slice of American life. (The film was screened out of competition under the auspices of the French Syndicate of Cinema Critics; its success prompted the festival to institute a regular International Critics' Week.) Mistaking Clarke's faux cinema verité, replete with white outs, jumps cuts, and swish pans, for the real thing, *Variety* referred to the movie as a "documentary"—which, in a sense, it was. Clarke's *Connection* not only preserved the play but, largely because of her fidelity to Gelber's dialogue, managed to reproduce something of its controversial reception.

In September 1961, the Motion Picture Division of the New York State Education Department deemed the movie "obscene" and, under the state's Education Law, denied it a license. There were two objections. One was visual—a glimpse of a photographed female nude in a magazine leafed through by the pad's resident Talmudic commentator Solly (Jerome Raphel). The other was aural—the repeated use of the word "shit" (twenty-four or twenty-six times per *Variety*, ninety according to Tom Wolfe's overheated account in the *New York Herald Tribune*). The producers appealed and lost.

Thus, *The Connection* had its US theatrical premiere in Scottsdale, Arizona, January 1962, and was shown elsewhere that spring including a private screening at the White House organized by presidential advisor Arthur Schlesinger. Had the New York Film Festival been established in September 1962 rather than a year later, *The Connection* would have been a natural source of publicity. Instead, still without a license, the movie opened on October 3 at a new East Fifty-Ninth Street theater named for D. W. Griffith. The projectionist was arrested, the print impounded, and the producers went back to court.

New York Times reviewer Bosley Crowther took the bait, attacking *The Connection* as "a forthright and repulsive observation of a sleazy, snarling group of narcotic addicts." The *Village Voice* rose to the movie's defense with a Jonas Mekas jeremiad titled "Open Letter to the New York Daily Movie Critics," whom he accused of butchering what might be the year's best American film. The next week's *Voice* ran a page-one story advising readers that Reverend Howard Moody was challenging the ban with two screenings at the Judson Church. (That these occurred on October 19, three days from the height of the escalating Cuban Missile Crisis, doubtless accentuated Mekas's sense of *The Connection* as a study in nameless, existential dread.)

In the aftermath of the Crisis, the New York State Court of Appeals unanimously ruled in the film's favor and on November 9, *The Connection* reopened at the D. W. Griffith. After more than a year of legal maneuvering, the film reappeared intact and passé. Late 1962 was not mid-1959 or even September 1961; *The Connection* failed to justify the outrage or excitement it had once provoked. Clarke, meanwhile, had begun production on a more daring second feature, *The Cool World*, the story of a Harlem teenager's quest to obtain a gun and use it to wrest control of the street gang to which he belongs.[2]

While *The Cool World* would earn Clarke the best reviews of her career, the contretemps over *The Connection* was soon eclipsed by the excitement around and subsequent scandal of Jack Smith's raw, orgiastic *Flaming Creatures*, shot on the rooftop of a defunct Lower East Side movie house during that past summer and fall (and featuring several Living Theatre performers, Malina among them). *The Connection* purported to show a subculture; *Flaming Creatures* emerged from one, heralded by a manifesto in the winter 1962/63 issue of *Film Culture*, Smith's essay "The Perfect Film Appositeness of Maria Montez."

A new sensibility, dubbed Pop Art, reveled in Daniel Boorstin's despairing observation that America's "business" was the making of illusions. American artists embraced the image, and the nation celebrated itself as trademark. In the weeks following the Cuban Missile Crisis, the Sidney Janis Gallery opened an International Exhibition of the New Realists. Among the American artists were Claes Oldenburg, Jim Dine, Roy Lichtenstein, Tom Wesselmann, and Andy Warhol, who had his first New York solo show at the Stable Gallery in November.

"It's mad, mad, wonderfully mad" is how the *Times* critic Brian O'Doherty began his review of the Janis show. "It's also (at different

2 Clarke was hired by neophyte producer (and future documentarian) Frederick Wiseman to adapt a 1959 book by white writer Warren Miller. Praised by James Baldwin in the *New York Times* as "one of the finest novels about Harlem that had ever come my way," Miller's book had already been adapted with once-blacklisted Hollywood director Robert Rossen, as a poorly received Broadway play. ("*West Side Story* without frosting," as described by the *Times*.)

times) glad, bad and sad, and it may be a fad. But it's welcome." Jill Johnston published a more thoughtful and wide-ranging analysis in the *Village Voice*, identifying Happenings as "the most inclusive example of the kind of interpenetration of art and life first suggested by collage" while discussing the precedents of Marcel Duchamp and John Cage. The prescient headline writer, however, nodded to Warhol: THE ARTIST IN A COCA-COLA WORLD.

Johnston's piece was pegged to a December symposium at the Museum of Modern Art devoted to the suddenly fashionable iconography of supermarket products, comic strips, and movie stars. Even before Marilyn Monroe was found dead in Hollywood on August 5, 1962, James Rosenquist took her for a subject. The goddess had scarcely given up the ghost when Warhol was opportunistically silk-screening a promo portrait from the 1953 film *Niagara*—Marilyn's image as image.[3]

Jack Smith's take on stardom was more radical than Warhol's, as was his deployment of the kindred sensibility known as camp (popularized two years later with Susan Sontag's first contribution to *Partisan Review*, "Notes on Camp"). For Smith, the acme of cinematic expressiveness was a series of exotic, juvenile swashbucklers produced at Universal Studios during World War II as vehicles for the Dominican-born actress Maria Montez, who, by conventional standards, can barely be said to be acting at all.

For Smith, Montez's transparent role-playing, and her unconcealed delight at being the center of attention, were more authentic to him than the naturalism achieved by successfully phony actresses. "A bad actor is rich, unique, idiosyncratic, revealing of himself not of the bad script," he would write in a follow-up essay, "Belated Appreciation of VS," published in *Film Culture* #31, which defended film as a visual medium, using Josef von Sternberg's films with Marlene Dietrich as his exemplar: Sternberg's "visual projection—a brilliant transvestite in a world of delirious unreal adventures."

So it was with the Lower East Side creatures—the slum-goddess, drag-queen "superstars" of Smith's imaginary studio, Cinemaroc—whom he invited to dress up or down, to cavort and clown as he had for Ken Jacobs's

3 Warhol had dreams of stardom himself. He made his first foray into pop music in the spring of 1962 as a backup singer, along with Lucas Samaras, in a band with Walter De Maria on drums, La Monte Young on saxophone, and Larry Poons on guitar. Patty Oldenburg sang lyrics penned by Jasper Johns. The project folded after three or four rehearsals.

camera in *Star Spangled to Death.* Months before Mekas first mentioned *Flaming Creatures* in the *Voice* on April 18, 1963 (and two weeks later declared it part of "the real revolution in cinema today"), the underground was abuzz.

2

The harbinger of that revolution was *The Flower Thief.* Around the time Ron Rice's film played the Charles, Jack Smith—who, during one of the Filmmakers Festivals, had already shown *Scotch Tape*, a short film made with Ken Jacobs's camera on Jacobs's Lincoln Square "set" during the making *of Star Spangled to Death*—began populating a Lower East Side rooftop with an assortment of neighborhood poets, painters, vanguard composers, Communists, druggies, wild women, and homosexual men such as no Hollywood orgy master, neither D. W. Griffith nor Erich von Stroheim, would ever use.

Shot, like *The Flower Thief*, on outdated black-and-white film stock, *Flaming Creatures* evolved out of the photography sessions Smith staged in his roach-infested Lower East Side hovel from late 1961 through June 1962. Inspired by the Montez movies he loved as a youth, as well as *The Flower Thief*, Smith imagined a vehicle for his most important female model, Marian Zazeela, a young painter whom he met through the neighborhood savant Irving Rosenthal.

However, Zazeela's meeting and subsequent involvement with the composer La Monte Young precluded her participation in Smith's project. Thus, "La Gran Estrella Maria [sic] Zazeela," as she is known in Smith's journal, was replaced by another Lower East Side ingenue, Sheila Bick, the wife of Zazeela's high school boyfriend, Irwin Bick. Tony Conrad, a disciple of Young's who had just graduated from Harvard, was invited to stay at Zazeela's now vacated East Ninth Street studio. There, in the early summer of 1962, he discovered Smith in residence and in the process of assembling *The Beautiful Book*, which Conrad deemed "some kind of bizarre, contemptible New York art pornography."

Regarding his eccentric roommate with benign disdain, Conrad offered to help Smith transport a gigantic gray painting of a vase with flowers, identified by Smith as the backdrop for his new movie, some fifteen blocks downtown to the leaky, tar-paper roof of the Windsor Theater at 412 Grand Street. There, over the course of eight or nine weekend afternoons, *Flaming Creatures* was staged and shot. (Having established the Charles as an ongoing concern, Walter Langsford had acquired the venerable Windsor—said to be the city's oldest extant movie house—with an eye to expanding his Lower East Side exhibition empire.)

On his first visit to the Windsor roof, Conrad discovered "lots of weird substances being consumed and strange people arriving on the scene." He was "surprised when it turned out that people took three hours to put on their makeup [and] several more hours to put on their costumes" (and even more surprised when, after assigning him a dress to wear, Smith "ripped it down the back to expose my ass and turned my back to the camera.") By all accounts, Smith took great care in preparing for each shooting session. Photographer-filmmaker Richard Preston, who had produced some animated collage trailers for the Charles, took the bulkhead above the Windsor for his studio and loaned Smith his 16mm, three-lens Bolex.[4]

The shoot extended well into October. The film had to be processed and printed in Denver. Several months were required for the closely synchronized sound accompaniment that Conrad assembled on quarter-inch magnetic tape. (During this time, Conrad also cut a soundtrack for *Scotch Tape*, using Eddy Duchin's peppy "Carinhoso.") Smith showed the unfinished *Flaming Creatures* footage to friends and associates at loft screenings throughout the winter of 1963, with one publicized benefit organized by Piero Heliczer's Dead Language Press on March 9 at painter Zalman "Jerry" Jofen's cavernous West Twentieth Street loft, a dive that among other things had a reputation as a Dickensian repository for stolen pocketbooks. (In 1997, Allen Ginsberg placed it among those "little Methedrine Universities in earliest 60's, where 3 a.m. electricity

4 Preston was surprised at how "orderly" and "businesslike" the production was, although other participants remember an altogether more delirious environment. By Joan Adler's secondhand account, paraphrasing Francis Francine, the central Rape-Earthquake-Orgy sequence was shot "in broiling sunlight with the set falling all over [the performers] high as kites, Jack pouring ceiling plaster all over them (a large chunk bruised Frankie, who got mad telling about those sufferings too) and careening dangerously above on some swinging homemade contraption"—actually a ladder supported by a large, rickety stepladder and the roof of Preston's studio. While it would be an exaggeration to describe *Flaming Creatures* as having been created in a state of stoned ecstasy, the participants were well acquainted with New York's still subterranean drug culture. Marijuana, cocaine, and methamphetamine were at various times used on the set; indeed, Sheila Bick's husband (a chemist) was busted for cocaine manufacture a few months before filming commenced. Among those caught in the raid was Ornette Coleman's bassist Charlie Haden.

burned the senses recycling the ruins of Lower East Side Manhattan's demolition garbage.")

Visiting the loft with Jonas Mekas in 1963, the teenaged P. Adams Sitney experienced "the shock of another world." Some thirty-five years later, he provided a vivid memoir. One flight up from the street was "a cluttered, wildly messy series of large rooms." A long "railroad corridor led to an immense studio, heaped with monumental canvases, thick with overpainting and collage." To the right of the studio, "fronting the street, was a large room with a tall ladder in the center. It was used to hang huge sheets and skeins of plastic from the ceiling, but it also had a symbolical aura when Jofen referred to it, as if it were a distant cousin to the ladder angels traversed in Jacob's dream," suggesting that this was the source of the filmmaking equipment that Sitney was surprised to find.

Many people stayed with Jofen. Although steering clear of the loft's labyrinthian sleeping quarters, Sitney noted that it was "always filled with people, more women than men. Most of them seemed dangerous or desperate in my nineteen-year-old eyes." Sitney came to imagine the loft as a harem. The thirty-eight-year-old scion of what some thought, perhaps in exaggeration, a Hasidic dynasty—spirited out of Bialystok before the Germans arrived in 1941, arriving in the United States by way of China—Jofen was something of a cult leader. "Magnetic if you didn't find him despicable," Joan Adler recalled. "He really believed that he knew and could teach." Because many of the loft's inhabitants sat "gazing silently into the blank air for days at a time," Adler considered the place a shooting gallery. It might also have been called a crash pad or a disreputable antecedent of the Warhol Factory.

Jofen, who attended Brooklyn College in the early 1950s, was a symbolist poet turned painter and collagist, who then became interested in film—specifically the juxtaposition of unplanned superimpositions and random camera flail. Typically screened on strips of gauze, Jofen's movies were doubly ethereal. Sitney recalled that although Jofen demanded to be "taken seriously as a filmmaker," he nonetheless "made it nearly impossible to look at his work."[5]

5 According to Sitney, Jofen's films suggested subjective psychodramas:

Long stretches of over- and under-exposed, jittery sweeps of the loft; obsessive spying on the random activities visible out of its windows. Nothing was chiseled, or dramatic or even organized, it seemed. Yet after some hours of this

Rice used Jofen's loft as a location for his most ambitious work, *The Queen of Sheba Meets the Atom Man*. A sequel of sorts to *The Flower Thief*, conceived, like *Flaming Creatures*, during the summer of 1962, the movie starred Taylor Mead as a cheerfully vacant mad scientist who at one point plugs an electric cord into his nose in a discombobulated attempt to get high, opposite Winifred Bryan, an enormous, seemingly inebriated, and frequently naked Black woman, famous in the Village for taking off her clothes in public.[6]

Around the time that Smith began previewing *Flaming Creatures*, Rice showed his footage in a benefit screening at the Living Theatre. "This is a wild mad rough cut like no Hollywood director would show the public for fear of having his ideas stolen," he bragged in program notes. "We defy anyone to cop our style. This is only 70 minutes of a protracted [sic] 3-hour epic by the director of *The Flower Thief*. This is your opportunity to help challenge the Hollywood stranglehold on morals, expression, and art and what have you. Dig us." (In a handout prepared for the event, Mekas called it "the most liberating, most shocking movie since Buñuel's *L'Age d'Or*.")

Even more than in *The Flower Thief*, Mead's spontaneous shenanigans are the subject. He first appears stumbling out of bed—sock hat pulled over his ears, tongue, and fingers aflutter—making a beeline to the toilet to wash his hands with Vaseline. After completing these

---

mesmerism—this I distinctly recall—the footage became the key to a worldview, the pacing back and forth of an underground man whose observations of the random events of the street veered between paranoia and religious illumination.

Never put into distribution and largely lost, Jofen's films can hardly be titled let alone dated. A 1970 screening at the Cubilico included *Voyage*, a 1962 film featuring Ron Rice (which in its extant nine-minute form has a soundtrack by Angus MacLise) and excerpts from *Ineluctable Disaster in the Adventure of the Stairway of Infinite Wrongs Infinitely Leading Nowhere* with Taylor Mead, Jack Smith, and Joel Markman.

6 *The Queen of Sheba* was not Bryan's first movie. A onetime resident of Paris, she appeared eight years earlier in *Les héros sont fatigués*, known in English as *Heroes and Sinners*, which, set in Africa, starred Yves Montand as a former French fighter pilot turned diamond smuggler. "The French seem to be fascinated by those flea-bitten tropical ports, where the heat and humanity are oppressive and sex is rampant and raw," Bosley Crowther wrote in the *Times* when the movie opened in May 1959, calling it "a lurid demonstration of people struggling to keep from going to the dogs, while the bongo drums beat, the natives wiggle and the vermin crawl across the walls"—a description that might almost apply to *The Queen of Sheba*.

ablutions, Mead proceeds to his decrepit kitchen and attempts to cook up some "heroin" before a huge barrel of the substance falls and crowns him. Subsequent scenes show Mead strolling by the Central Park reservoir (a Chaplinesque derby balanced precariously on his head), furtively slobbering over the plastic model of a chain reaction in the "World of the Future" exhibit of Union Carbide or posing moronically in front of various modern artworks at the Guggenheim Museum.

In the film's most lyrical sequence Bryan makes a solitary trek across the city—walking through Central Park, riding alone on an elevated train, floating across the icy Hudson on an apparently empty ferry. Although she mainly serves as a good-natured foil for the regressive, manic Mead (and, later, Jack Smith), Bryan has some outrageous scenes, dallying with a young white boy whom she flings around her colossal breasts as though he were a rag doll. Still, *The Queen of Sheba* belongs to the Atom Man. When Mead clambers out of a closed trunk—festooned with confetti, wearing diving flippers, licking a football, and rubbing up, dog-like, against the air—it's to establish the outer limits of aimless, impulse behavior. An extended sequence of Mead going one-on-one with Smith in a bid for the camera's attention is a crazed burlesque of queerness that takes improvisation to the end of its tether.[7]

3

In early 1963, Mekas began a series of midnight screenings at the Bleecker Street Cinema. One of the first programs was titled "Newest Absurd and Zen Poetry," which, in addition to *Senseless*, included several movies Mekas had discovered at the Charles the previous spring and summer: Jack Smith's *Scotch Tape*, Ken Jacobs's *Little Stabs at Happiness* (still without a fixed soundtrack), Bhob Stewart's found-footage assemblage, *The Year the Universe Lost the Pennant*, and Ray Wisniewski's *Doomshow*.

There was also *Blonde Cobra*, credited solely to Bob Fleischner. As edited by Jacobs from footage shot and abandoned by Fleischner in

7 The movie would never be finished by Rice. (Taylor Mead and Rice's boyhood friend Howard Everngam each produced edited versions.) Soon after Rice's death, Alberto Moravia saw a private showing in Rome and was moved to praise the film as "a protest which is violent, childish, and sincere—a protest against an industrial world based on the cycle of production and consumption . . . Among other things, it is an excellent illustration of a certain way of life—a way of life which consists mainly in the absolute rejection of life itself."

1959, the movie is a thirty-three-minute portrait of and performance by Smith, who appears often as a demonic infant. He also riffs almost continuously on the soundtrack that, added in 1963, juxtaposes bits of dialogue from a Fred Astaire–Ginger Rogers movie, a German tango, a children's record, and taped radio news, with Smith's hysterical sing-song, free-associational confessions.

Flaming Creatures broke into print in mid-April when Mekas wrote in his column that Smith had just completed "a great movie." *Flaming Creatures* "is so beautiful that I feel ashamed even to sit through the current Hollywood and European movies. I saw it privately and there is little hope that Smith's movie will ever reach the movie theater screens." Not two weeks later and accompanied by a second version of Conrad's taped soundtrack, a further revised *Flaming Creatures* received its theatrical premiere, midnight, April 29, 1963, at the Bleecker Street Cinema on a bill with *Blonde Cobra*. (Over the next ten months, the two films would frequently be paired.)

Gregory Markopoulos described the event as earth-shattering. Viewers were "projected into a state of cosmic or filmic shock."

> Those images, scenes and sequences that they had envisioned and had wished would appear in the commercial films that they attended were unexpectedly offered before their eyes. The audience burst forth and roared while the walls of censorship began to crack.

Recalling the Bleecker screening in *Film Culture*, Ken Kelman had a somewhat different impression:

> When the first show was over, a clique, a claque of six or so, back on the west side [of the auditorium] applauded amid the numb and blind. Amid the tame, I halted, oppressed by their inertia, paused, vacillated, considered for two beats of silence or three, before I clapped solo and thus no doubt branded myself a clappy pervert, a crap happy degenerate, slobbering sadist or even, perhaps, Jack Smith.

Flaming Creatures lit up the underground with phosphorescent joy. Something new under the sun, it proposed a novel form of cine-glamour—one that owed everything and nothing to Hollywood. Smith's movie was at once primitive and sophisticated, hilarious and poignant, spontaneous and studied, frenzied and languid, crude and delicate, avant and nostalgic, gritty and fanciful, fresh and faded, innocent and jaded, high and low, raw and cooked, underground and camp, black and white and white on white, composed and decomposed, richly perverse and gloriously impoverished.

Smith's discontinuous, forty-two-minute succession of "exotic" tableaux, served with a rich stew of (mainly) dated pop music, broke the rules. Abruptly, all underground "Midnights at the Bleecker" were canceled. According to Mekas, the theater managers complained that the "low quality of the underground" was ruining the Bleecker's reputation.[8]

4

Undeterred by the loss of their showcase, inspired filmmakers pressed ahead. Weekends, there were informal screenings at Ken Jacobs's Ferry Street loft, downtown between the Fulton Fish Market and the Brooklyn Bridge. Taylor Mead showed his home movies there. So did the twenty-one-year-old twins George and Mike Kuchar. Having spent the better part of their adolescence producing 8mm travesties of Hollywood movies, largely shot on Bronx tenement rooftops and starring their neighbors, they were hailed as brilliant primitives.

Mekas's manifesto on the new "Baudelairean Cinema" appeared in the May 2 *Voice. Flaming Creatures, The Queen of Sheba Meets the Atom Man, Blonde Cobra,* and *Little Stabs at Happiness* were the four films making up "the real revolution in cinema today."

> These movies are illuminating and opening up sensibilities and experiences never before recorded in the American arts; a content which Baudelaire, the Marquis de Sade, and Rimbaud gave to world literature a century ago and which Burroughs gave to American literature three years ago. It is a world of flowers of evil, of illuminations, of torn

8 Although it is generally assumed that *Flaming Creatures* terminated "Midnights at the Bleecker," the series continued for several more weeks. Monday, May 6, there was a program of new releases from the Film-Makers' Cooperative. May 13, Stan Brakhage gave a lecture. Around this time Mekas left for the Cannes Film Festival, where his brother's feature *Hallelujah the Hills* was screening as part of the Critics Week. Thus, he was not likely to have created the ad for May 20 show conjoining Brakhage's 1956 *Flesh of Morning* with a program of Jerry Jofen's work: that the Brakhage title was given as "Flush of Morning" and further described as "a film of masturbation" was likely the final straw and consequently the last film shown—if indeed it even was.

> and tortured flesh; a poetry which is at once beautiful and terrible, good and evil, delicate and dirty.

In a subsequent column, Mekas noted that no New York City film lab would print *Flaming Creatures*, although he was soon to find one: Criterion, a midtown lab eventually busted for porn in 1977.

Using money put up by Taylor Mead, Ron Rice again screened a rough cut of *The Queen of Sheba Meets the Atom Man*, which now included Jack Smith in the cast, along with Judith Malina and Jonas Mekas. (After the screening, Rice took the money and flew to Mexico.) Jacobs started *Baud'larian Capers*, "a musical with Nazis and Jews" and his first film without Smith (the main figure was Bob Fleischner playing a gentle schlemiel). Meanwhile, as announced by Mekas in June and financed through Mekas by filmmaker-philanthropist Jerome Hill (whose grandfather founded the Great Northern Railway), Smith embarked on a color, plein air extravaganza, first called *The Great Pasty Triumph*, then (briefly) *The Pink and Green Horrors*, and finally *Normal Love*.

The season of Baudelairean cinema also brought the Living Theatre's most radical work, although the French writers that *The Brig* more readily suggested were Jean Genet and Antonin Artaud. The play arrived from left field, written by a twenty-seven-year-old, Brooklyn-born street kid, ex-Marine, and bartender: Kenneth Brown. Stationed, a decade before, at Camp Fuji, Japan, Brown was four hours late in returning from leave; he was declared AWOL and was punished with thirty days in the base's military prison. Still working out the trauma in 1960, Brown wrote a forty-page account of his incarceration, "A Concept for Theater or Film." He showed it to a friend who gave it to a friend who showed it to Al Hansen who, in early 1963, passed the manuscript on to Julian Beck.

Brown's treatment included a few scenes outside the base—cut by the Living Theatre, which ruthlessly confined the action to a single set, as well as a single day. Judith Malina staged Brown's play behind a chicken wire fence designed by Julian Beck. The cage was the proscenium. The grueling ritual of dehumanization—men with shaven heads reduced to numbers and referred to as maggots, subject to shouting abuse by capricious, godling guards—was really happening. The actors, who switched off between captors and captives, were relentlessly drilled. Malina used *The Guidebook for Marines* as a model for rehearsals.

The Brig opened with the intimidation of a new prisoner and ended with a command performance of "The Marine Hymn" during which one maggot suffers a nervous breakdown and collapses, dragged off as another new prisoner arrives. The piece was a fantastic act of aggression and reviews were generally hostile, although *New York Times* critic Howard Taubman suggested that the play warranted a Congressional investigation (into the Marines!), all but ensuring that the Living would come under additional official scrutiny. "If *The Brig* bears any resemblance to the truth, it must be hell to serve a sentence for wrongdoing in the Marine Corps," Taubman began his review, adding that sitting through Brown's play was "almost as gruesome."

As if in response, Michael Smith began his review with a bit of defensive erudition: "It is true that *The Brig* isn't a play. Neither are all the events in the Judson dance series dances . . . Nor in normal terms are John Cage's compositions always music." *The Brig* was a highly choreographed and clamorous performance in which the people on stage were defined by their activities, each of which—for the prisoners—required permission from the guards and absolute, self-effacing fidelity to regulation, and the ability to absorb enumerable gut punches. (*Baud'larian Capers* was not the only work to consider Nazis and Jews.)

Smith confessed to being blindsided. He assumed that the production's first fifteen minutes would set the scene, that characters would emerge from the ensemble and dramatic action would begin—they never do and it never does. Reducing Brown's play to an absurd, violent, abrasive routine of abuse and degradation, the Living Theatre employed the logic of a Happening. The naturalism of *The Connection* was rendered more extreme and infused with the Theater of Cruelty. Taubman may not have read Artaud but he got the idea:

> As one watches the harrowing cruelty of the guards to the prisoners and listens to the incessant roaring demanded of the condemned men, one marvels that flesh and blood can endure such bestial treatment. Then one begins to wonder how long the players can keep up the unending staccato movements and raucous bellows. And finally, as one's own ears ache and one's larynx feels sympathetic lacerations, one can became as stir crazy as the poor devils in the brig.

In rehearsal as the Becks prepared for the May 8 "Worldwide Strike for Peace," *The Brig* provided them with a master metaphor. During the summer of 1959, after they were arrested and jailed for refusing to take cover during a city-wide civil defense exercise, the couple published an essay in the *Voice* under the headline ALL THE WORLD'S A PRISON that prophesied *The Brig*.

What was the prisoner's condition?

> It is that you are robbed of your volition. It is the feeling of subjugation. It is that your body is recognized as a thing to be dealt with but that your mind is disavowed; your will is removed; and as far as functioning goes, you become an automaton to obey orders. Perhaps in this way it is not unlike the Army.

5

By mid-June, Mekas found a new venue: the Gramercy Arts was a small but legitimate theater on East Twenty-Seventh Street, only a few blocks from the offices of the Film-Makers' Cooperative. Gregory Markopoulos's hour-long, intricately structured *Twice a Man*, inspired by Euripides' *Hippolytus*, was the opening attraction. This was followed in July with a three-week run of Robert Frank's *The Sin of Jesus*, based on a story by Isaac Babel and once imagined as a companion piece to *Pull My Daisy*.

Along with the Gramercy, Mekas inherited the owner Bill Rubin's niece Barbara, just turned eighteen and newly released from the Silver Hills psychiatric hospital in Connecticut. Raised by progressive parents in Cambria Heights, a working-class neighborhood in Queens, Barbara Rubin was a high school dropout and a sometime runaway. She had been hopped up on diet pills, although it's unclear whether she was committed to Silver Hills because of a drug problem or whether the facility served to accentuate it. "Thin, frail, very young, totally scared, and totally silent" is how Mekas remembered her. "She did everything I asked her to do, but she said practically no word. Maybe she thought she was sent to some extension of the Correction House [sic]."

Mekas gave Rubin a job. Rubin, after a few weeks at the cooperative, in response to a superior remark by Mekas's assistant, Columbia student David Brooks, who, eighteen himself, regarded Rubin (per Mekas) as a "dumb suburban kid," gave them all an earful. "I don't remember what he said, but it was enough to break Barbara's silence," Mekas recalled. "She spoke up."

> No, she didn't speak up: she came out like a spitfire. Like a painful, stammering torrent of words. When she spoke, she always had these strange, painful hesitations, as if there were so many words in her mind that she didn't know which ones to choose. So she called David and everyone else "full of shit" and proceeded to inform us all on the subjects of teenagers, drugs, parents, etc, and made us all sit straight in our corners and listen to her because she knew what she was talking about, she knew it first-hand. And from there on, it was Barbara who spoke and we were silent.

Mekas discovered his most ardent disciple and one of the movement's most flamboyant personalities. Rubin found an endlessly supportive, uncritical father. In late July, Mekas reported that she was making a film: "Bursting and burning with hallucinations, shooting her first movie, with the excitement of a holy nun, feverishly engaged to rip out fragments of veiled revelations from her subconscious and the world, the sensory experiences and visions of the sad, loveless century, pouring her heart out." Hers was a fanaticism to match, and even surpass, his own.

Rubin had found an apartment on the Lower East Side and, after painting the walls white and some of her subjects black, staged marathon, drug-infused naked shooting sessions with two young friends, one of whom, Debra Feiner, was a fifteen-year-old high school dropout from the Bronx. These ecstatic gynecological explorations of female anatomy would be punctuated by close-ups of an unknown male's genitals. ("The motion picture camera has been kissed by the angel of Love. From now on, camera shall know no shame," Mekas would announce in *Film Culture*.) Rubin originally referred to her footage as *Cocks and Cunts*; later it was named *Christmas on Earth* after a line from Rimbaud's *A Season in Hell*.

Meanwhile, Jack Smith spent the summer of 1963 filming a "commercial" follow-up to *Flaming Creatures*. *Normal Love* was very much a film of its season. Except for several scenes staged once the weather turned cold around the Moon Pool, a gauzy, candle-lit, incense-shrouded mirror-strewn altar to Maria Montez that Smith had laboriously built in the middle of Joan and Robert Adler's Fourteenth Street living room, it was strictly back to nature.

Somehow, Smith filled carloads of fanciful horror movie archetypes (the Werewolf, the Yellow Hag, the Black Spider, the White Bat, the Mermaid, the Watermelon Man) driving through New Jersey and Queens, looking for locations. The Roman bath scene with comatose creatures in pink gowns lounging, as if after the ball, around the faux classical sculptures guarding an imposing swimming pool was shot in Cherry Grove, Fire Island, at John Eberhardt's extravagantly rococo Belvedere Guest House. The perfect field of goldenrod required for the Yellow Sequence turned out to be an abandoned junkyard beneath the Throgs Neck Bridge where Francis Francine mimed dying as Tiny Tim perched on the rusty roof of an abandoned car plucking his plastic ukulele.

Smith was a perfectionist; the search for the swamp where Uncle Pasty (Arnold Rockwood, the beefy, cunnilingual rapist from *Flaming Creatures*) would stalk The Girl (Diana Baccus) seemed to last for weeks. In addition to the mask worn in the earlier film, Pasty sports a set of trick-store fangs that come loose when The Girl deflects his attentions (causing him to fall out of character) with a custard pie in the kisser. A parallel scene has a handsome if slime-covered, druggy-looking Werewolf rising from the primeval muck to assault the increasingly disheveled Mermaid (Mario Montez), the equally dazed camera spinning overhead, and offer her a Coke.

On August 5, *Flaming Creatures* played the Gramercy, along with *Scotch Tape*: "At last an evening of Baudelairean Cinema," the *Voice* ad promised. The show was repeated the following weekend (and the one after that), while Smith took his *Normal Love* cast on location at the Connecticut estate of Stable gallery owner Eleanor Ward. Out in the meadow, he topped a giant pink-and-white layer cake (constructed from Claes Oldenburg's maquette) with a score of writhing, half-naked male and female chorus cuties (including Andy Warhol and a very pregnant Diane di Prima, a day from giving birth to her third child).

At the scene's climax, the Pink Faery (Francis Francine) emerges from the cake and the emerald-green Mummy (Tony Conrad, sewn into his costume) lurches out to abduct one of the cuties before being himself mowed down by the skinny, demented-looking Mongolian Child (David Sachs, a young political activist). The first *Normal Love* work print was generated in August 1963 although the shoot continued into October and, in the case of the Moon Pool sequence, through December.

Inspired by Smith and Jerry Jofen, Rice was also making a new film, shot in late summer when work on *Normal Love* had become sporadic. Rice accompanied Smith on his shoots and sometimes did his own filming; at the end of the day's work, he hosted members of the cast, filming them as, still in costume, they lazed in the Mexican hammocks he'd strung up in his Lispenard Street loft, on the top floor of a shabby building a block south of Canal.

The drug-den atmosphere (at one point Smith is shown smoking hashish or opium in a long-stemmed pipe) perhaps prompted Joan Adler's recollection of "three-day sessions," which involved "two days of waiting for Ron to start shooting." The film was essentially composed in the camera. Rice double-exposed ten rolls of color film, usually in his loft but a few times in the street outside, on one of Smith's locations, and at Coney Island.

6

Flaming Creatures was the summer's film (as *The Flower Thief* had been a year earlier). But there were signs of a brewing storm.

"When the Film-Makers' Showcase moved into the Gramercy Arts Theater, we thought now we'll be able to continue our work in peace," Mekas wrote in the *Voice*. "We were wrong."

> The censors and licensors are on our backs. They have interfered with our work. They have disregarded the fact that most of the films screened are unfinished works in progress and cannot be submitted for censorship or licensing. They are following blindly the dumb letter of bureaucracy.
>
> They say we are corrupting your morals. We would be glad if we could.

At the very end of August (while the eyes of the nation were fixed upon the March on Washington), Jonas Mekas, Ken Jacobs, Florence Karpf, Barbara Rubin, and Debra Feiner crashed the annual Flaherty Seminar in Brattleboro, Vermont. The focus was on cinema verité. "We took *Flaming Creatures* and *Blonde Cobra* to the seminar, two pieces of the impure, naughty, and 'uncinematic' cinema that is being made now in New York," Mekas told his readers. The films could only be shown at midnight. "Midnight screening in Vermont! My God, we felt underground even at Flaherty's. But a few souls saw our work and were shaken by it. Others just walked out and slept peacefully, dreaming of cinema verité."[9]

Yet it was a good season for the New American Cinema's more commercial wing. Shirley Clarke's new film *The Cool World* was shown and well received at the Venice Film Festival. Adolfas Mekas's *Hallelujah the Hills* was a surprise hit at the first New York Film Festival. In February, brother Jonas would shoot a movie of *The Brig* that would not only be featured in the 1964 New York Film Festival and named best documentary at Venice but considered a masterpiece of cinema verité.

It was also the moment for Boris Lurie and his associates, having found an uptown venue, the Gallery Gertrude Stein, located in a posh townhouse on East Eighty-First Street, off Madison Avenue. In addition to March group members Stanley Fisher and Sam Goodman, the *No Show* featured Allan Kaprow, Jean-Jacques Lebel, and, having switched from painting to sculpture, Yayoi Kusama, who exhibited her "aggregations"—furniture erupting with a profusion of white, stuffed, sewn phalluses. Richard Tyler made a rare uptown appearance as well and the show, or at least Fisher, Goodman, and Lurie, was acknowledged in the new magazine *Artforum*, established in San Francisco in 1962.

Seymour Krim characterized the work as "an appropriately brutal effort to cope with a brutish environment." In an introduction he was recruited to provide because, as he explained, he was the editor of the mass-market paperback anthology *The Beats* as well as editorial director of *Nugget* (a men's magazine modeled on *Playboy* that, for four years in the early '60s, he stocked with Beat writers), Krim extolled the show's garish "honky-tonk 'Beat Coney Island' forms and lack of shading in the materials." An ambivalent Jew, he particularly dug Lurie, Fisher, and Goodman—their art "hits you like a rock thrown through a synagogue window"—but he appreciated Kusama's "orchard of penises" as well.[10]

9 The Ninth Annual Flaherty Seminar included a half dozen distinguished documentaries and documentary hybrids including James Blue's *Olive Trees of Justice*, Robert Gardner's *Dead Birds*, Jean Rouch and Edgar Morin's *Chronicle of a Summer*, and Vittorio De Seta's *Bandits of Orgosolo* (a movie Mekas praised in the *Voice* and also programmed at the Bleecker Street Cinema).

10 Kusama emerged as the star of the show. Only weeks later she had a solo installation at Gertrude Stein, *Aggregation: One Thousand Boats Show*, in which a rowboat served as a seedbed for stuffed canvas protuberances and for which she commissioned a photographic portrait of herself naked before the camera.

On the other hand, October was a difficult month for the Living Theatre. Some $4,500 behind their rent, the group was served an eviction notice on October 16. The next day the Internal Revenue Service struck. The Becks owed the IRS over $28,000, mainly for having failed to pay withholding taxes on the actors' wages—but more likely, some thought, for having put on a play critical of the Marine Corps. IRS agents invaded the premises and tagged the theater's movable assets. Some actors refused to leave. Supporters formed a picket line formed outside, and TV crews arrived. The sit-in continued into the following day.

That night the cast reentered the building, circumventing a police barricade and making their way up fire escapes, over rooftops and through windows. "In a scene reminiscent of the Paris Commune of 1871," John Tytell writes in his history of the Living Theatre, "ladders were leaned against the building, the police pulling the ladders away while people were still climbing them."

Restoring the set that had been dismantled by the IRS, using lights from the TV crews to illuminate the stage, the actors gave a final free performance on Saturday. On Sunday, the set was carted away, the Becks and the actors were booked, charged with impeding federal officers discharging their duty. *The Brig* was no longer a "message play," Beck declared. Nor was it a play about protest—"It was a real protest," an "anarchist direct action."

7

As *The Brig* drama played out, the Gramercy Arts swung into high gear. Theater manager and projectionist Ken Jacobs may also have written the ads. When *Guns of the Trees* was revived on a bill with *Little Stabs at Happiness*, the latter's star was identified as Jack "Spiderlegs" Smith. The 149-seat theater "was always full," remembers filmmaker Stephen Dwoskin, "attracting long queues of festive people."

Films were projected from the small balcony onto what amounted to a home movie screen. Most of them had sound on tape or else records would be played since most of the filmmakers could not yet afford sound transfers. The programs included "newsreels" like Mekas's *Report from Flaherty* and *Taylor Mead Filming Jack Smith Filming Normal Love*. The Kuchar brothers had multiple shows.

Gregory Corso introduced *Happy Death*, a washed-out study in decay made in collaboration with Jay Socin, whose poem "Graffiti in a Public John" had recently been published in *Fuck You*. Dick Higgins's *Flaming*

City got a theatrical premiere—"two hours of pure nothing," per Mekas—as did Gregory Markopoulos's *Twice a Man* and the film that was to become the most widely seen of all underground movies, Kenneth Anger's *Scorpio Rising*.

A legendary figure in avant-garde film circles, Anger returned to the United States after a decade in Paris, living first in Los Angeles, then moving to New York where he stayed at the Brooklyn Heights apartment of filmmakers Marie Menken and Willard Maas. "It was like visiting a foreign country," he later recalled. "Brooklyn was as strange to me as darkest Africa." Cruising the Coney Island boardwalk during the summer of 1962, he discovered a gang of motorcyclists hanging out by a roller coaster and was inspired to make a documentary portrait. (They accepted him, he would say, as a camera nut.) Anger also discovered a twenty-nine-year-old ex-Marine biker on Forty-Second Street, Bruce Byron (born Richard MacAulay), who became his lead.

According to Byron, he and Anger went shopping at a Times Square souvenir store, purchasing motorcycle toys, T-shirts, and a button saying BORN TO RAISE HELL, snorted speed, and shot a scene in Byron's room. (Byron evidently had the James Dean pictures and Siamese cats.) For another sequence, Anger brought Byron with him to a party with the Brooklyn guys and later filmed him desecrating a church in Brooklyn Heights. Then he disappeared into the editing room. Byron was the raw material for a gaudy fugue in leather and chrome.

With its mock-heroic vision of urban youth culture, knowing homoeroticism, copious media quotations, and blasphemous juxtaposition of Hitler and Christ, *Scorpio Rising* was an instant sensation. Mekas immediately recognized it as another "poisonously sensuous" analogue to Baudelaire and, having lived under German occupation during World War II, perhaps more: "Evil attracts. Scorpios attract. The pull of fascist strength, muscle and steel and speed."

More than any other underground (or Baudelairean) movie, *Scorpio Rising* was also a lasting influence on American cinema. Smith and Jacobs had nostalgically employed dated pop music; Anger broke new ground by incorporating current Top 40 rock 'n' roll in ironic counterpoint to his visceral images.

The Baudelairean films were related to Happenings. *Scorpio Rising* was closer to Assemblage. A few weeks after its premiere, the Gramercy devoted an evening to the films of master collagist Joseph Cornell. His profile lifted by his inclusion in MoMA's 1962 *Art of Assemblage*, Cornell had made several found-footage films in the 1930s and, since the mid-'50s, some short, lyrical documentaries of various New York locations, working with Rudy Burckhardt, Larry Jordan, and Stan Brakhage. There had been occasional screenings of the latter films but the Gramercy show marked the first public screening of Cornell's *Rose Hobart* in the twenty-seven years since it was projected at the Julian Levy gallery as part of an evening of "Goofy Newsreels," in conjunction with MoMA's show *Fantastic Art, Dada, Surrealism*, and Salvador Dali accused Cornell of plagiarizing his dreams.

Taking a 16mm print of a routine Hollywood adventure film, the 1931 *East of Borneo* directed as a vehicle for the actress Rose Hobart, Cornell jettisoned the plot and condensed the movie into twenty-four enigma-charged minutes of the film's pensive star framed by jungle fauna or wandering trancelike through the palace of a graciously sinister maharaja. All chronology collapsed into elliptical mismatched reaction shots and jump-cut clusters of fade-outs. Cornell further transformed the original in the act of screening by projecting *Rose Hobart* at silent speed through a piece of blue glass while suppressing the original soundtrack in favor of selections from a 1957 schlock-bin record, Nestor Almaral's *Holiday in Brazil*.[11]

Cornell was shaken by the assassination of President Kennedy only days before his show, but Mekas assured him it was unnecessary to postpone. The underground was undeterred. Andy Warhol and his assistant Gerard Malanga spent the afternoon of November 22 silk-screening frame enlargements from Warhol's serial film *Kiss*. (A few months later Warhol would be making silk screens of Kennedy's traumatized widow.) In addition to a page-one article reporting an FBI investigation into alleged assassin Lee Harvey Oswald's supposed activities, including disrupting "pro-integration meetings in the Village during 1961 and 1962," the post-assassination *Voice* ran a Mekas column on the New York filmmakers who'd been invited

11 *Rose Hobart* had been seen by Ken Jacobs and Jack Smith in the late 1950s. Jacobs was briefly employed by Cornell as a studio assistant and Cornell had lent him the film, along with *Holiday in Brazil*, and a blue filter. "We looked at it again and again, and we were both knocked out," Jacobs would tell P. Adams Sitney. "We looked at it in every possible way: on the ceiling, in mirrors, bouncing it all over the room, in corners, in focus, out of focus [and] backwards." Inscribing a copy of *The Beautiful Book* to Marian Zazeela, Smith referred to *Rose Hobart* as "the previous greatest movie on earth."

to the upcoming Brussels Film Exposition, announced that *Film Culture*'s 1963 independent film award would go to *Flaming Creatures*, and carried an ad for the second chapter of Warhol's serial.

Kiss's first installment was premiered on the same night that *Scorpio Rising* had its 2:00 a.m. "sneak preview." Since the summer Warhol had been shooting a series of three-minute camera rolls featuring Naomi Levine (who likely gave him the idea) in the clinch with various men, notably Living Theatre member Rufus Collins, French art critic Pierre Restany (coiner of the term Nouveau Réalisme), Gerard Malanga, and Ed Sanders. (Having rented a "secret" two-room apartment in a back building on Avenue A just below Fourteenth Street and furnished it with "Jack Smith/Flaming Creatures décor"—garishly colored, flower-patterned cloth purchased on Orchard Street—Sanders was making his own film, a study of his speed-freak friends called *Amphetamine Head*.)

Kiss was a hit. (More rolls, with other participants, were shot well into 1964, eventually distributed as a forty-minute film that, along with *Scorpio Rising*, would be among the most rented items in the Film-Makers' Cooperative catalogue.) Warhol was prompted to tell Mekas about his first film, *Sleep*—also made over the summer—which consisted of half a dozen shots of his then lover, poet John Giorno, in repose, repeated in various combinations for eight (really six) hours. Mekas promised him a show. There was also, he learned, a narrative feature, not yet edited and eventually called *Tarzan and Jane Regained . . . Sort Of*, that Warhol shot on his recent trip to Los Angeles.

As much a travelogue as a riff on jungle movies, *Tarzan and Jane* was filled with LA signage and indigenous freeways. Locations included Muscle Beach in Santa Monica and Venice Beach, where Claes and Patty Oldenburg were staying, as well as the Beverley Hills Hotel, the Watts Towers, Topanga Canyon, producer John Houseman's Malibu beach house, and artist Wallace Berman's home in Beverly Glen. The stars were Taylor Mead and Naomi Levine, both half naked in the title roles, with authentic screen actor Dennis Hopper featured as an alternative Tarzan. (According to Warhol, "Taylor was supposed to climb a tree but he couldn't, so he yelled for a stunt man. Dennis appeared and climbed the tree to get a coconut for him.")

Once edited by Mead, *Tarzan and Jane* would be an underground romp in the tradition of *The Flower Thief*. *Sleep*, however, was the attention magnet—a movie that could outrage without ever being seen, a leap forward in durational works. Warhol was aware of La Monte Young's twelve-hour performances and had been present for at least part of the eighteen-hour marathon, organized by John Cage, September 9 and 10, at the Pocket Theater, on Third Avenue and Thirteenth Street.

The event made headlines. A relay team of pianists (including newly arrived Welsh musician John Cale) played 840 renditions of Erik Satie's eighty-second, 180-note "Vexations." The performance began at 6:00 p.m. on Monday, with seven people in the audience. "Note succeeded note: implacably, doggedly, swinging back and forth like the windshield wiper of an automobile," according to Harold Schonberg, the first (and last) of eight critics whom the *New York Times* dispatched to cover the event—one of whom pinch-hit for a no-show pianist early Tuesday morning.

The Pocket Theater had a capacity of 197. Attendance peaked at forty, just after midnight on Monday, following the opening of Hans Hofmann's MoMA retrospective. "The atmosphere is dreamlike and hypnotic, à la *Last Year at Marienbad*," one member of the *Times*'s relay team reported, citing the paradox of being simultaneously irritated and hypnotized by the music. By 2:00 a.m. there were half as many, "mostly male and unmistakably of the beatnik variety." The performance ended promptly at 12:40 Tuesday afternoon with one yell of "encore," possibly from Karl Schenzer, who identified himself as an actor appearing in *The Brig* and was the only member of the audience present for the entire performance.[12]

Another summer film preceded *Sleep*. Ron Rice's footage had coalesced into a twenty-six-minute film with a cimbalom score by Angus MacLise. Its title a riff on soundman Tony Conrad's pronunciation of the instrument, *Chumlum* premiered at the Gramercy in mid-December—influenced by but less ironic and, thanks to its layered color superimpositions,

12 The following week, Schenzer and Cale appeared on the popular CBS quiz show *I've Got a Secret* in which a celebrity panel vied to guess the secret whispered to the show's host. Cale's was that he had been one of the performers involved in "Vexations"; Schenzer's that he was the only audience member who stayed for the entire duration. Cale was not the first avant-garde musician to appear on the show. John Cage had been a contestant in January 1960. His first secret, "I'm going to perform one of my musical compositions," was followed by a second: "The instruments I will use are: a Water Pitcher, an Iron Pipe, a Goose Call, a Bottle of Wine, an Electric Mixer, a Whistle, a Sprinkling Can, ice cubes, 2 Cymbals, a Mechanical Fish, a Quail Call, a Rubber Duck, a Tape Recorder, a Vase of Roses, a Seltzer Siphon, 5 Radios, a Bathtub and a GRAND PIANO."

more ethereal than *Flaming Creatures*. ("A world of painful, perverse orgies and at the same time an almost spiritual vision of paradise," is how Fred Camper would describe it in *Film Culture*.) The principals include a trio of Smith creatures (Francis Francine, Joel Markman, and Mario Montez) as well as Smith himself in Arabian garb with a fake mustache. But, emerging from the gauzy webs of superimposition, wrapped in the iridescent emerald-green evening gown she wore as the Cobra Woman in *Normal Love*, Beverly Grant commands the most attention.

Chumlum was one version of *Flaming Creatures*; *Cocks and Cunts* was turning into another. As funded by Mekas, Barbara Rubin (credited but not apparent in *Chumlum*) continued filming, including, as Mekas noted in his diary, empty camera footage of Jack Smith: "She said he is like a child: as long as you film him, he is happy. So, like a good mother, she kept filming Jack. Since there was no film, she kept rewinding and shooting five times on the same roll." By the time Mekas rented the midtown Tivoli Theater—a seedy venue known for sex-exploitation films—as the venue to present Smith with *Film Culture*'s annual independent Filmmaker award, *Cocks and Cunts* was approaching feature length. Rubin had shot another extended sequence in a Ludlow Street apartment, with Arnold Rockwood, Gerard Malanga, and the dancer Barbara Gladstone, among others, engaging in naked shenanigans and some actual sex.[13]

Rubin seduced Allen Ginsberg, back from India by way of Vancouver and San Francisco, with a private screening of her rushes. Ginsberg was impressed that Rubin had "made an art object out of her vagina." He admired her spirit. "We got into a very funny rapport, we were just there alone, and we actually ended up screwing on the floor that very night. She was really young and pretty and I liked her." Rubin also persuaded Ginsberg to shave his beard. Ginsberg was discovering the youth culture; it was around this time that he met Bob Dylan, whom he shamelessly cruised at Eli Wilentz's apartment above his Eighth Street Bookstore.

December 7, moments before the ceremonial midnight screening was to begin, the Tivoli management buckled under the pressure from

13 According to Coop records and Mekas's diaries, Rubin resumed shooting in October, with the largest expenditure for film stock coming in November. A lab receipt dated December 4, 1963, indicates processing of thirty-six minutes of TriEx plus a work print.

New York City's Bureau of Licenses and canceled the show. Outraged, Mekas gave Smith his award outside, using the roofs of the cars parked along Eighth Avenue as his stage. Then a few hundred New American Cinema partisans led by Barbara Rubin occupied the Tivoli until evacuated by the police. The "slapstick disobedience" was covered by *The Sinking Bear*, a scurrilous parody of *The Floating Bear* devoted largely to gossip overheard at the San Remo. According to the anonymous informant, throughout the spectacle, "Merce Cunningham, Peter Orlovsky and ANDY WARHOL remained seated in a chauffeured limousine."[14]

8

Less than a month later, the *Flaming Creatures* crusade went international. Mekas and his two young disciples, Sitney and Rubin, arrived in Europe to promote the New American Cinema.

Mekas had been invited to judge an experimental film festival in Knokke-le-Zoute, Belgium. When *Flaming Creatures* was refused a screening, he resigned from the jury, threatened to withdraw the entries of other American filmmakers (including Kenneth Anger, Stan Brakhage, Robert Breer, and Gregory Markopoulos) and organized special showings in his hotel room. Among those present, perched on the bathtub or bed, were Jean-Luc Godard, Agnès Varda, and Roman Polanski. The word of mouth was sensational. "Two minutes after I met Federico Fellini in Rome," Stanley Kauffman reported in the *New Republic* later that winter, "he asked me whether I'd seen Jack Smith's *Flaming Creatures*."

With the irrepressible Rubin as his confederate, Mekas chose New Year's Eve to commandeer the projection booth of the festival theater. Pretending to tie up the projectionist, experimental filmmaker Jean-Marie Buchet, and screening a print of *Flaming Creatures* that had been planted between the reels of Warhol's six-hour *Sleep*, Mekas provoked a disturbance that was widely reported in Europe. A small riot broke out, and as the Belgian Minister of Justice (and honorary head of the festival)

14 Created by Søren Agenoux, with frequent assistance from Ray Johnson and Al Hansen, the first mimeographed issue appeared in late November (including an unintentionally absurd Secret Service statement in reference to the Kennedy assassination) and continued over several score smudgy issues into June 1964. One of the last issues reported that "summer is surely here. Moondog, the doorway bard on Sixth Avenue, yesterday was wearing Bermuda shorts under his army blanket robe."

arrived to quell it, Mekas projected the film on the minister's face until all power was cut off.

Ultimately, the jury awarded *Flaming Creatures* a special "damned" film prize. According to Mekas, most of the jurors thought it was a documentary. "A wild image of America we left in Knokke-le-Zout, I tell you," he noted in the *Village Voice*. "No wonder a State Department man was sitting next to our table wherever we went." Thus, *Flaming Creatures* made *Variety*'s front page—and not for the last time. But if, as the show-biz bible reported, BELGIANS BALK N.Y. 'CREATURES,' New York itself was cleaning up for the 1964 World's Fair.[15]

Although beleaguered, the Gramercy screenings continued for a few more weeks. Ken Jacobs had a benefit screening of *Star Spangled to Death* and premiered *Baud'larian Capers*. "Andy Warhol's Eight Hour Sleep Movie" screened for four consecutive evenings in mid-January as a benefit for the Film-Makers' Cooperative. Mekas reported in the *Voice* that theater manager Jacobs refused to comp a pair of journalists from *Time*; his review of *Sleep* included an account of Ron Rice's brief incarceration in Bellevue. On January 25, Rice had gone to visit Diana Baccus, a principal in *Normal Love*, committed three days before, and, having brought his camera, commenced shooting, thus resulting in his being held for observation.

By the end of January, Warhol had moved into the large East Forty-Seventh Street loft that, once the theatrical designer Billy Linich (later Billy Name) covered the walls with aluminum foil and silver aluminum paint as he had the walls and ceiling of his Lower East Side apartment, became the Factory. It was also a movie studio, the location for the three-minute portraits that would be known as "screen tests," as well as for the movie that would be a prolonged reaction shot, *Blow Job*. The act was unshown; the title alone ensured that the movie was unshowable.

15 At the Gramercy, police harassment had become a regular feature of the show. Because the films exhibited were not submitted to the New York State Board of Regents for licensing, it was deemed illegal to charge admission for their exhibition. Mekas's counter-strategy was to present the films for free and solicit contributions for the Love and Kisses to Censors Film Society. When *Flaming Creatures* was shown it was advertised merely as "a film praised by Allen Ginsberg, Andy Warhol, Jean-Luc Godard, Diane di Prima, Peter Beard, John Fles, Walter Gutman, Gregory Corso, Ron Rice, Storm De Hirsch, and everybody else."

5

New York Unfair, 1964

In which New York City cleans up. *Flaming Creatures* and Lenny Bruce are busted. The World's Fair censors Andy Warhol (who goes on to make the world's first conceptual porn film). The Living Theatre goes on trial. Harlem riots. Fluxus pickets Karlheinz Stockhausen. Bill Dixon declares the "October Revolution in Jazz." Michael Snow discovers Albert Ayler and LeRoi Jones is crowned "King of the East Village."

> *It's harassment. The mayor's all worked up about the World's Fair. He wants everything tidy. Anyway, who're the police to judge what's pornographic?*
>
> –unidentified manager of a Times Square store specializing in "girlie magazines, nudist publications, striptease films and illustrated books about perversions," CRACKDOWN HITS SMUT SPECIALISTS, *New York Times*, February 26, 1964

Monday, February 3, the Gramercy offered a "Surprise Program" of continuous showings. *Flaming Creatures* plus *Normal Love* rushes were projected every hour on the hour from 7:00 p.m. to midnight. The program was repeated on the following two Mondays, the last proving its swan song. Police shut down the Gramercy along with the Pocket Theater, which, showing avant-garde films since December, was that week offering *The Cry of Jazz*.

In late January, a federal grand jury had indicted the Becks on eleven felony counts—each carrying a maximum sentence of three years and a

$5,000 fine—alleging them to have impeded federal agents in the pursuit of their duties when the Living Theatre was closed in October. A few weeks later, the owner of the Midway Theater, where the Living had relocated, forced them to again close *The Brig*. Jonas Mekas got wind of the situation and managed to document a last performance, starting Sunday night, February 16, and extending into Monday morning.

By his own account, Mekas used three direct-sound Auricon cameras with ten-minute film magazines and, saddled with eighty pounds of equipment, shot the play in a dozen extended takes inside the Cage, weaving around the actors: "Constantly stepping in their way, disrupting their usual movements . . . I was a circus man on a tightrope high in the air." In fact, he was being steered by Judith Malina and needed to keep clear of Storm de Hirsch, who was busy filming a newsreel, *Jonas in the Brig*.[1]

On Tuesday, February 18, the Andy Warhol–Taylor Mead collaboration *Tarzan and Jane Regained . . . Sort Of* had its premiere under the auspices of Diane di Prima's Theater for Poets, now situated at the New Bowery, 4 St. Mark's Place. Mead edited the film and provided a taped soundtrack which augmented his voice-over narration with Top 40 pop and a British documentary on sexual reproduction. James Stoller, who reviewed the movie in the short-lived journal *Moviegoer*, deemed Mead a revelation, "so convincing and remarkably moving it scarcely matters that he is also mocking nearly everything he does." Two days later, Jack Smith projected *Normal Love* production slides (mostly made by Bob Adler) accompanied by a tape of Antonin Artaud's 1947 blasphemous, scatological, anti-American radio rant, "To Have Done with the Judgment of God."[2]

---

1 Mekas had two brilliant ideas. The first was applying cinema verité to a staged event. The second was having the movie cut by someone without knowledge of the play. His brother Adolfas (to whom he gave equal credit) winnowed the footage down to 65 minutes. The film, which cost about $1,200 to make, would win the Best Documentary prize at the 1964 Venice Film Festival.

2 Allen Ginsberg had been given a tape of this anguished tirade, commissioned and censored by French radio in 1947. Ginsberg shared the tape with Diane di Prima, who used it the summer of 1963 to open Michael McClure's play *Blossom, or Billy the Kid*. In her memoir, di Prima writes that her then-husband "Alan Marlowe [who played Billy] brought over two enormous speakers from his room and set them up in the front windows of the theater, so that all of Bleecker Street within a couple of blocks of Gerde's Folk City was treated to the howling of Antonin Artaud each night that *The Blossom* was running."

February 26, the same day that the *New York Times* reported a new NYPD plainclothes squad to deal exclusively with pornography, the "Infamous Surprise Program" played the New Bowery. Coincidently the *Flaming Creatures* star Francis Francine was also at the theater, appearing as Venus in Frank O'Hara's one-act play *Loves Labor*. The "Surprise Program," now augmented with Warhol's newsreel *Jack Smith Filming Normal Love*, was shown again at the New Bowery on Tuesday, March 3. There were four scheduled shows. An undercover policeman attended one; two NYPD detectives broke up the next, disrupting a near-capacity showing attended by some ninety spectators.

"It was hot enough to burn up the screen," one cop would tell the press. The police impounded both films (the Warhol never recovered) and the projector, arresting the theater manager, Ken Jacobs, and ticket-taker Florence Karpf. "The most articulate porn audience ever assembled were dressing down the cops," Jacobs recalled.

> Diane di Prima ducked out to phone Jonas. He rushed over and leaped in swinging the First Amendment. He insisted that if we were to be arrested, he be arrested as well, and forced information on them of his connection to the screening . . . At the stationhouse, Jonas was just as fiery . . . [It] was a bad scene, with movie-imitating killer cops, and I feared Jonas was going to bring it down on us. We were "fags" and "weirdos" (intellectuals) and "commies."

Mekas devoted his March 12 column to the question of obscenity: "The police, licensors, district attorney detectives, and criminal courts finally got interested in the arts." Taunting the authorities ("Mayor Wagner and Governor Rockefeller have obviously learned something from the Russians"), Mekas dared them to extend their crackdown beyond *Flaming Creatures* to other underground movies, as well as Ed Sander's poetry mimeo *Fuck You* and the revival of LeRoi Jones's verse play *The Eighth Ditch*, scheduled to open next at the New Bowery.[3]

3 *The Eighth Ditch* did in fact attract negative attention. First staged in 1961, it was published in the same issue of *The Floating Bear* that resulted in Jones's arrest. The revival, with John Vaccaro as the narrator and a set by Robert Morris, included an act of sodomy performed on stage (albeit with the lights out). "The result has been a furor over its alleged obscenity," Michael Smith reported in the *Voice*. "This is ridiculous . . . The sexual act is almost incidental to its actual content—innocence betrayed by experience."

Having issued a ringing Underground Manifesto on Censorship, Mekas next organized a *Flaming Creatures* defense benefit, screening Jean Genet's 1950 short feature *Un Chant d'Amour*—a poetic evocation of homosexual fantasy in a French prison—at the Writers Stage Theatre, 83 East Fourth Street on Saturday, March 7. Also on the bill: Stephen Dwoskin's short *Newsreel of Two Underground Film Stars Having Breakfast in Bed*, with Beverly Grant and her roommate Zelda Nelson. (It too would be confiscated.)

Mekas's strategy was to link the suppression of *Flaming Creatures* to the suppression of a film that similarly suggested graphic sexual acts and featured male nudity, by a celebrated European artist. The idea was to "push the prestigious Genet in their faces, pull in Sartre," Jacobs recalled. The plan, however, was only partially successful. The cops were unaware of *The Balcony* or *The Blacks*, approaching the third year of its run. Mekas was arrested once more but as he reported from jail: "The detectives who seized [*Un Chant d'Amour*] did not know who Genet was. When I told them that Genet was an internationally known artist, I was told it was my fantasy."

> I was [also] told that they will make a statue of me in Washington Square; that they will make 'a mashed potato' of me by the time they are through; that I was 'dirtying America'; that I was fighting windmills. One of the detectives who arrested me told me, at the theatre, that he did not know why they were taking me to the station: I should be shot right there in front of the screen.

The New Bowery, which had been screening movies free of charge, was busted yet again (a program of Japanese avant-garde films hastily substituted for *Flaming Creatures* and *Scorpio Rising*) on March 17.[4]

There were no more public showings as Mekas devoted his energies to the upcoming trial, his defense funded by Jerome Hill and abetted only by a handful of academics, an assortment of Beat poets, and the

---

4 The campaign against fags, weirdos, and commies was not restricted to New York. Saturday evening, March 7, Los Angeles police raided the Cinema Theater and confiscated the print of *Scorpio Rising*—"a purely homosexual thing," one member of the vice squad termed it. Theater manager Mike Getz was soon after arraigned, charged with "exhibiting an obscene film." Although acquitted by an all-female jury, Anger would later maintain that the American Nazi Party sued him for desecration of the swastika.

newly formed New York City League for Sexual Freedom. An article by Susan Sontag published in the April 13 issue of *The Nation* underscored "the indifference, the squeamishness, the downright hostility to the film evinced by almost everyone in the mature intellectual and artistic community." (Some twenty years later, Sontag told me that the editor who commissioned the piece was fired as a result.)

2

Flaming Creatures was not an isolated case. Three weeks after the first *Flaming Creatures* bust, *The Village Voice* ran a page-one story: CITY PUTS BOMB UNDER OFF-BEAT CULTURE SCENE. The police closed three theaters showing unlicensed movies—the Gramercy Arts, the Pocket, and the New Bowery. The Gate managed to stay open by locking out its weekly Film Club. Le Metro's poetry readings were suspended. The requisite crackdown on MacDougal Street coffeehouses now included the off-off-Broadway venue Caffe Cino on Cornelia Street.

Le Metro managed to reinstate their readings but on April 3, Howard Solomon, manager of Café Au Go Go, a new club located in the basement of 152 Bleecker Street, was busted along with his headliner Lenny Bruce—both men were charged with "indecent performance." The new NYPD Public Morals Squad had secretly recorded two of Bruce's shows and played the tapes for a quickly assembled grand jury, which determined the evidence was sufficient to prosecute. The trial was set for April 23, effectively extending Bruce's now mega-publicized engagement that resulted in a second arrest on April 7, the comic booked with Solomon's wife Ella.

The subterraneans blamed the World's Fair. Indeed, assistant district attorney Richard Kuh said as much, insisting that the question of Bruce's indecency be adjudicated before opening day. The Fair, first bruited in October 1959, would be Robert Moses's last stand. As president of the World's Fair Corporation, Moses maintained that, albeit flagrantly unofficial, the Fair would be a sure moneymaker. However dubious, Mayor Wagner and Governor Rockefeller had to take his word. The publicity juggernaut was such that, after five months in office, President Johnson elected to make his first New York public appearance delivering a keynote address at the Federal Pavilion's opening ceremonies.

The Fair enlisted the art world as well. In late 1963, the *New York Times* reported that the New York State Pavilion was to have "a decidedly avant-garde look." The pavilion's architect Philip Johnson had commissioned ten young painters and sculptors to create ten "spectacularly large works" for the exterior of the cylinder-shaped building. In addition to the relatively sanctioned painter Ellsworth Kelly and mixed-media virtuoso Robert Rauschenberg, the artists included a few outré types, notably smashed car assemblagist John Chamberlain and four proponents of Pop Art: Robert Indiana, Roy Lichtenstein, James Rosenquist and Andy Warhol, whose contribution was the simplest and the most inflammatory. Riffing on the idea of public morals, he executed a mural of cropped and enlarged mugshots presenting the NYPD's thirteen most wanted criminals. The mural was unveiled on April 14 and overpainted on April 17 (most likely at the governor's request).[5]

A celebration of New York's presumed cultural preeminence as well as space-age American enterprise, the very consumerism that Pop Art satirized, the Fair was a natural target for demonstrators seeking a wider stage. April 4, CORE's Brooklyn and Bronx chapters announced plans to protest the Fair's indifference to existing rules regarding the desegregation of the construction trades and draw attention to New York City police brutality, slum housing, and poor schools. Demonstrators would disrupt the Opening Day with a stall-in on the Long Island Expressway. CORE further intended to block Grand Central Parkway, the Brooklyn-Queens Expressway, the Belt Parkway, the Interboro Parkway, and the Van Wyck Expressway—all roads that Moses had constructed or overhauled. The Master Builder would thus be hoisted on his own petard. In response, the mayor announced that a thousand police officers in hundreds of vehicles would patrol every road leading into or out of Queens, while police helicopters—including one capable of lifting an automobile—would hover overhead.

Opening Day brought a cold rain, a third of the anticipated 250,000 attendees, and a remarkable absence of traffic on the Long Island Expressway. CORE had created a mental Happening—forcing New York's city fathers to imagine chaotic disorder. Intentional or not, the bluff worked, as did the spectacle of student demonstrators at the Federal

5 By the time the Fair opened, Pop Art had triumphed. John Canaday's mocking review of Claes Oldenburg's outsized food show at the Janis Gallery, published in the April 7 *New York Times*, was followed five days later with a more sympathetic Sunday piece that ended by comparing the artist to Walt Disney and then in late May by an article in the *New York Times Magazine* announcing that, once a "gag," Pop Art had shown surprising staying power to become "something more."

Pavilion heckling a sitting American president with taunting signs (SEE NEW YORK'S WORSE FAIR—SEGREGATED SCHOOLS FOR NEGROES, PUERTO RICANS AND RATS), something that *The Sinking Bear* was pleased to note.

Across the East River, the Committee for Freedom in the Arts—led by Julian Beck and Diane di Prima—braved the wet, chilly weather with a march from Bryant Park through Times Square and up Broadway to Lincoln Center. Jonas Mekas passed out mimeographed copies of his recent *Voice* pieces; speakers included Allen Ginsberg and Taylor Mead. Di Prima anticipated the summer's hit song when she called for "dancing in the streets."

3

A few weeks later, the Living Theatre staged what the *Voice* termed a "legal happening." Discharging their lawyer, the Becks opted to represent themselves at the IRS hearing, playing to an audience of supporters.

Dressed like Portia from *The Merchant of Venice*, Judith defended Julian, shouting "innocent!" each time the judge pronounced the world "guilty." The judge fined the Living Theatre corporation $2,500, sentenced Julian to sixty days in the workhouse and Judith to thirty days, but, not altogether unsympathetic, suspended their sentences and reduced bail to allow for a summer European tour.

The case *People of the State of New York v. Kenneth Jacobs, Florence Karpf and Jonas Mekas* was taken by the prominent civil rights lawyer Emile Zola Berman, who, according to newspaper accounts, thought he was representing the exhibitors of a film entitled "Crimson Creatures." Berman believed that *New York v. Jacobs* had the potential to go to the US Supreme Court, which it did, in a fashion, four years later. Before that, however, it went before a three-judge Criminal Court panel, which included former New York City mayor Vincent Impellitteri.

The panel refused to allow expert testimony, with the single exception of Sontag's, on the artistic merit or alleged pornography of *Flaming Creatures*. Allen Ginsberg, Shirley Clarke, and Willard Van Dyke went unheard; the prosecution case rested entirely on treating the judges to a screening, "Two of them munching cigars, watched impassively as the movie was shown in chambers," the *New York Post* reported.

On Monday, June 8, Ken Jacobs and Alan Marlowe were found guilty of "exhibiting an unlicensed film in a place of amusement for pay," a first under this New York State statute. Friday, Jacobs and Mekas were convicted of showing an obscene film. Mekas's trial for exhibiting *Un chant d'amour* was scheduled for the following week, by which time the *Flaming Creatures* case was upstaged by *People of the State of New York v. Lenny Bruce*, which ran through July in the same Criminal Courts Building.

Bruce's trial for "indecent performance" began with an agent of the New York City Department of Licenses giving a description of the comedian's act, based on notes taken on the night of March 31. But as he warmed to his role, Stephanie Harrington reported in the *Voice*, "the proceedings began to resemble the audition of a Lenny Bruce impersonator"—a bizarre version of Bruce's Carnegie Hall riff on JFK's body double. Bruce himself became ill (resulting in an adjournment). Harrington was merely aghast. The spectacle of "eight grown men spending weeks of their time and an unknown amount of taxpayer money in passionate deliberation over whether another grown man should be able to use four-letter words in public," gave her the "feeling of being present at an historical event—the birth of the courtroom of the absurd."[6]

The prosecutor Kuh employed the words for which Bruce was being prosecuted more times than did Bruce during the entirety of his abbreviated Café au Go Go engagement. Although, unlike the defense in the *Flaming Creatures* trial, Bruce's lawyers were permitted by the court to call on expert testimony, their witnesses were subject to the presiding judge's browbeating and questioning of competence.

A decision in the Bruce case was scheduled for the fall. Jacobs and Mekas received suspended sentences. Still the underground nearly went under. Although he continued to show rushes, Smith was unable to complete *Normal Love*. Having loaned his camera to a fellow underground filmmaker, Paul Morrissey, from whom it was stolen, Jacobs was working in 8mm. Ron Rice had a benefit for *The Queen of Sheba Meets*

6 Hilariously, it was during the Bruce trial that the art exhibition whose name could not be spoken—*The Shit Show*, Sam Goodman's excremental sculptures presented by Boris Lurie—opened at the Gallery Gertrude Stein. Conservative critics rose to the bait. "These aggregations of colonic calligraphy contain many formal excellences for anyone whose purist education forces him to perceive them," Brian O'Doherty wrote in the *Times* while Tom Wolfe, a reporter for the *New York Herald Tribune* popped over to the "very elegant" gallery to find "21 piles of sculpted mammal dung" lying on the floor and both artists present, seemingly annoyed that they had to explain their joke.

the Atom Man, then took off the next day for Mexico with the proceeds and possibly Jacobs's camera.

Baudelairean cinema was stalled. Under the circumstances, the major force in underground movies became the one figure who was able to subsidize his own studio: Andy Warhol.

4

Warhol and Smith collaborated throughout the summer of 1964. Their never-finished project was known variously as *A Lavender Filter Throughout*, *The Rose without Thorns*, *Silver Dracula*, and finally *Batman Dracula*.

Judging from existing camera rolls, this enterprise seems envisioned as a posher version of Smith's earlier polymorphously perverse, intermittently orgiastic dress-up fool-arounds. There was no soundtrack although it was the first Warhol production to use lights. Warhol was the producer-cameraman; Smith his star-director. Given Smith's privileged use of old movie archetypes in his previous work, *Dracula* would seem more his interest and the Pop icon *Batman* more Warhol's.

Possibly *Batman Dracula* was two movies shot concurrently. In some footage, Smith plays Dracula, dressed in black and sporting a pair of Halloween fangs. At other times, he wears a mask and cape à la Batman. One elaborate Dracula set conjures a cross between a mad scientist's lab and a discotheque crammed with Warhol enthusiasts, notably socialite Baby Jane Holzer in a tinfoil bikini. The various entanglements, scarcely more risqué than foot kissing, suggest a modified *Flaming Creatures* group grope. The scene ends as the fanged Smith twists with Beverly Grant atop a mock operating table. The wildest sequence has a bejeweled Smith first dancing and then playing footsie with a half-dressed Sally Kirkland, who, abruptly ravished by Grant, walks off abashed and puts on her skirt.

Other scenes are more sedate. Posed on the roof of Sam Green's midtown gallery, Smith twirls his cape in the company of Brown and Grant—whose picture on the cover of the summer 1964 issue of *Film Culture* is taken from this sequence. Another one, shot on a Long Island estate, has the caped Smith in long shot running across a manicured lawn toward the camera and collapsing. Holzer and Grant are also present, as is Naomi Levine, who is abducted by a naked man. (The volatile Levine herself was abducted by the police in late August, arrested for refusing a cop's order to move on when chatting with members of the newly formed League for Sexual Freedom who had set up a card table in front of the Women's House of Detention, then in the heart of the Village at 10 Greenwich Avenue, and were collecting signatures to legalize prostitution.)

Batman Dracula was never edited or even completely processed. However, *Eat*, in which the artist Robert Indiana manages to make the consumption of a single mushroom last for approximately half an hour, was shown on July 16 at Washington Square Gallery, 528 West Broadway, paired with an unannounced attraction, the wittiest of Warhol's early films, *Blow Job*. A thirty-three-minute close-up of a man's face as he is sexually serviced off-screen, it may be considered the first conceptual porn film.

Warhol was also producing the three-minute 16mm portraits referred to as "screen tests" and, in early July, the *New York Times* reported him at work on his first sound movie, *Wee Love of Life*, revealing that "several scenes, it is whispered, are played in the nude." A riff on Warhol's favorite daytime serial *Love of Life*, later called *Soap Opera*, the two-and-a-half-hour film directed by Jerry Benjamin tracked the vicissitudes of a New York couple played by Baby Jane and Sam Green in locations ranging from Madison Avenue to Avenue C, interrupted every three minutes by a TV commercial.

The same month, a less obviously epochal film was in production: Michael Snow's *New York Eye and Ear Control*. In late 1962, Snow and his wife, fellow artist Joyce Weiland, relocated from Toronto to New York, renting a loft on Greenwich Street, just below Washington Market. A jazz pianist as well as a painter, Snow offered rehearsal space for avant-garde musicians—including Cecil Taylor, Albert Ayler, Archie Shepp, Don Cherry, Milford Graves, and later the Jazz Composers Orchestra.

On one hand, the thirty-four-year-old artist was interested in making a movie that would feature his trademark icon—the Walking Woman—a stylized female profile that, for the past five years, had been the subject of his paintings, photographs, and installations. It was time for this two-dimensional creature to strut her stuff in an illusory three-dimensional world and perhaps provide Snow entrée into the underground film scene. On the other hand, he had received a juicy commission of $3,000 from a Toronto group to make a movie about the New York jazz scene. *New York Eye and Ear Control* combined the two.

Snow had already finished shooting scenes of his two-dimensional star in three-dimensional New York when his friend, the poet Paul

Haines, brought him one Sunday afternoon to the tiny Cellar Café, a basement coffeehouse on a residential block at 251 West Ninety-First Street. Composer-trumpeter Bill Dixon had organized a series of avant-garde jazz concerts, including his own combo, a Sun Ra sextet, and, newly returned from Europe, the saxophonist Albert Ayler. Soon after, Snow and Haines organized and recorded a stellar ensemble, augmenting Ayler's current sidemen—trumpeter Don Cherry, drummer Sonny Murray, and bassist Gary Peacock—with the white trombonist Roswell Rudd and the Congolese-Danish tenor sax player John Tchicai.

There was no leader. Snow's instructions proscribed previously existing tunes and all solos. The idea was that the ensemble would produce a half hour of "totally, freely improvised music."

5

The summer of 1964 became known as Freedom Summer. In the East Village, Barbara Rubin was arranging orgies for Allen Ginsberg (she also brought him to the Factory, along with Corso, Kerouac, and Orlovsky, for a *Pull My Daisy* reunion). In Mississippi, the Student Nonviolent Coordinating Committee (SNCC) was organizing voter registration.

Having missed the excitement of the *Flaming Creatures* bust, Rubin had materialized in mid-June, telling Mekas that after the Cannes Film Festival (where, according to one companion, she contracted a venereal disease) she had gone to Italy and was planning to fly to the Himalayas when the Italian authorities deported her back to the United States because she denounced a priest who attempted to abuse her in the Vatican.

Almost immediately, Rubin resumed work on *Cocks and Cunts*. (The unsqueamish midtown lab Criterion printed eighty minutes of material.) Rubin also solidified her relationship with Ginsberg, moving into his East Fifth Street apartment and escorting him to the sex commune at Kerista's Stanton Street storefront. There she met eighteen-year-old Rose "Rosebud" Feliu, a fellow speed freak and Beatles fan with whom she would hitchhike to California in late summer. ("What we experienced as two young women, not driving but at the mercy of the universe [was] far more amazing than *On the Road*," Feliu recalled thirty-five years later.)

In Washington, Lyndon Johnson signed the Civil Rights Act into law. On Second Avenue, *The Blacks* approached its 1,300th performance.

LeRoi Jones and Lorraine Hansberry were among the speakers at a contentious Town Hall symposium on "The Black Revolution and the White Backlash," prompted in part by CORE's threatened stall-in. Jack Newfield's irate *Village Voice* report, headlined MUGGING THE WHITE LIBERAL, quoted Jones's assertion that it was a waste of time "talking to these white liberals" and focused on the booing directed at *New York Post* columnist James Wechsler, who was still claiming the radical mantel he attempted to don back in 1958 at the Hunter College Beat symposium.

Uptown, community organizer Jesse Gray organized a block-wide rent strike and staged the World's Worst Fair. The banner WE DO NOT NEED A WORLD'S FAIR—WE NEED A FAIR WORLD! hung like a Pop Art caption from fire escape to fire escape across East 117th Street. More ominously, Grey had also issued a call for "one hundred skilled black revolutionaries who are ready to die." Whether or not any answered the call, Grey's pronouncement likely fed the fantasy that, as reported on the front page of the May 6, 1964, *New York Times* based on a tip from an anonymous "researcher" for the government-funded HARYOU (Harlem Youth Opportunities) organization, a shadowy Harlem group called the Blood Brothers, said to be composed of youth gang members and led by dissident Black Muslims, was engaged in killing whites.

The opposite, of course, was the case. In sweltering Mississippi, three young civil rights workers—James Chaney, Andrew Goodman, and Michael Schwerner—had gone missing. They had long since been murdered, although their bodies would not be found for several more weeks. On a hot Thursday afternoon, July 16, a fifteen-year-old Black youth, James Powell, was fatally shot by an off-duty, out-of-uniform white police officer in front of the largely white high school where the teenager was taking a remedial reading course—the incident precipitated when an irate white building superintendent turned a water hose on a group of mildly obstreperous Black students.

The temperature rose along with tempers. On Saturday, more than 200 people gathered for a CORE rally after Powell's funeral in central Harlem, then marched to the neighborhood police precinct to demand the guilty cop's arrest. By 10:00 p.m. over 500 people had assembled around Eighth Avenue and 123rd Street, a block from the Apollo Theater and Malcolm X's de facto headquarters, the Hotel Theresa. (Malcolm was then in Africa.) A police officer shouted for the crowd to "go home." "We *are* home, baby," someone answered.

Harlem was now occupied territory. Molotov cocktails were thrown, and the police fired 2,000 rounds of ammunition, not always into the air. Some shooting was point-blank. There were scores of injuries. People exiting the subway were swept into the melee. Police violence continued throughout the night and into the morning.

The uprising left some blocks ravaged and others untouched. Windows were shattered, businesses (mainly white) were demolished. Residents were wary. Dumpsters appeared everywhere. "I see Negro handymen put to work because of the riots boarding up smashed storefronts," David Henderson wrote in his seven-section-long "Keep on Pushing (Harlem Riots/Summer/1964)," named for the Impressions song that was a Freedom Summer hit.

> They use sparkling new nails
> The boards are mostly fresh-hewn pines
> and smell rank fresh.
> The pine boards are the nearest Lenox Avenue
> Will ever have to trees.

Henderson, then twenty-two, was one of the youngest Umbra poets as well as a featured reader at Le Metro. Brought up in Harlem, he relocated to the Lower East Side, writing "am I in the wrong slum?" in the poem "Downtown-Boy Uptown."[7]

A year before, New York's racial inequities—and the urban crisis in general—had been illuminated on-screen by Shirley Clarke's film version of *The Cool World.* Helped by her romantic partner Carl Lee (who plays the dealer furnishing a would-be gang leader with his gun), Clarke made the novel her own—casting young nonprofessionals and shooting interiors as well as exteriors, verité style, on location.

More underground than *The Connection*, *The Cool World* is a movie of abrupt transitions, with few establishing shots and many vignettes, its verité camerawork reinforced by a partially improvised score, composed by Mal Waldron, a member of the Max Roach Quintet, and performed by the Dizzy Gillespie Quintet. (Ed Bland, who made *The Cry of Jazz*, consulted on the

7 The poem first appeared in the July 10, 1965, issue of the *National Guardian*, the same month Henderson was published in *Fuck You: A Magazine of the Arts*, a rare poet to have graced both publications.

script.) The film's Pop Art–inspired poster identified the cast with four fat exclamation points, their red dots reading HOOKER! FUZZ! JUNK! RUMBLE!

The Cool World, opened in April 1964, two days before the Fair, at the fashionable Cinema II on Third Avenue. There were positive notices in both the *Amsterdam News* and the *New York Times*, where critic Bosley Crowther called it a film of "pounding vitality" that "gives the shattering details of an excellent newspaper exposé." Downtown at the *Voice*, Andrew Sarris was more uneasy, complaining that "by the end of *The Cool World*, the white race has been reduced to an alien presence from another planet." *The Cool World* was still playing downtown at the Art, a movie house on Eighth Street, when Harlem exploded.

Barely a week after the riot, Warhol pulled off his most outrageous stunt, planting a camera by an office window on the forty-first floor of the Time-Life Building and filming eight hours of New York's ghostly Mount Olympus, the Empire State Building. "Last Saturday I was present at a historical occasion," cameraman Mekas told his readers. "From 8:00 p.m. throughout the night and until dawn the camera was pointed at the Empire State Building, from the forty-first floor of the Time-Life Building. The camera never moved once. My guess is that *Empire* will become the *Birth of a Nation* of the New Bag Cinema."

6

Black revolution hardly topped the avant-garde agenda. Still, the issue surfaced in an unexpected fashion in a bizarre protest leveled against a bizarre Happening.

Even as the *Voice* reported a "new militancy" (members of the just-formed Coffee House Employees Guild, supported by one-time Trotskyists Dave Van Ronk and Terri Thal, were picketing two obscure basket houses), the New York Avant-Garde Festival, primarily organized by cellist and New Music devotee Charlotte Moorman, announced that its second edition at Judson Hall would feature the American premiere of *Originale* by the renowned West German composer and exponent of electronic music, Karlheinz Stockhausen. There would be pickets there too. Among the signs: FIGHT MUSICAL RACISM!

Originale's opening night, September 9, the full membership of Action Against Cultural Imperialism (AACI)—composer Henry Flynt and Fluxus impresario George Maciunas—leafleted outside the West Fifty-Seventh Street concert hall, supported by several others, including

Alan Marlowe, Flynt's friend Tony Conrad, the newly arrived Japanese artist Takaho Saito, and journalist-poet Marc Schleifer, who, increasingly radical, was now associated with the Progressive Labor Party.

The *Voice*, not unsympathetic, reported that a "stylishly designed flyer" urged "'radical intellectuals' to give up art and spend their time instead exposing and fighting the worldwide domination of 'white plutocratic' culture." The AACI targeted Stockhausen because, more than "rich US cretins Leonard Bernstein and Benny Goodman," the German was "a fountainhead of 'ideas' to shore up the doctrine of white plutocratic European Art's supremacy." Designed by Maciunas and written by Flynt, the leaflet held "art music" accountable for Europe's imperialist claim to global supremacy through the "Laws of Music," including Common-Practice Harmony, 12-Tone, and Concert Etiquette.[8]

Flynt, Maciunas, and Conrad had similarly picketed Stockhausen's April 29 appearance at Town Hall. (LeRoi Jones, invited to join them, preferred to observe from across the street.) Flynt, associated with a Trotskyist splinter group, the Workers World Party, loathed Stockhausen for his dismissal of jazz. Maciunas, as the self-chosen leader of Fluxus, claimed to oppose all art. Given the narcissism of small differences, that antipathy included not only Stockhausen but *Originale* director Allan Kaprow, who had cast several Fluxus artists in the show.

Maciunas also saw Moorman as a rival impresario, not least for her association with Norman Seaman, an experienced "niche" music promoter who—introduced by Moorman to Yoko Ono—had arranged Ono's Carnegie Recital Hall debut three years earlier. Stockhausen had stipulated that the thirty-two-year-old Korean artist Nam June Paik have a featured part in *Originale*. Still, as the newly arrived Paik had been recently written up by Jill Johnston in the context of a Maciunas event at Carnegie Recital Hall, amusingly headlined FLUXUS FUXUS, Maciunas felt that Moorman had poached him. Even more egregiously, she secured the participation of Paik's human-sized, remote controlled Robot K-456. Paik had promised Maciunas that the robot would make its American debut under the Fluxus aegis. Now, rotating its conical

8 This was not the first time Flynt protested cultural imperialism. Wearing signboards that read NO MORE ART! and DEMOLISH LINCOLN CENTER!, Flynt, Tony Conrad and Jack Smith picketed the Museum of Modern Art on February 27, 1963, only days before the *Flaming Creatures* bust.

breasts and defecating dry beans as it flailed about each night outside Judson Hall, K-456 had become the festival's unofficial mascot.

Originale (meaning "originals," a term for "real people") combined a performance of Stockhausen's hybrid live and taped *Kontatke* with appearances by a half dozen avant-garde figures, referred to as "guests," playing themselves and doing their thing. Facilitating the greatest Happening to ever confound midtown (at least since the Ringling Bros. and Barnum & Bailey Circus last played Madison Square Garden), Kaprow reconfigured the 275-seat auditorium.

Chairs were put on the stage even as rows of seats were removed or inverted and placed back-to-back. The result was a more intimate, albeit chaotic space. Scaffolds, from which Kaprow might "conduct" the action, were constructed and bedecked with aluminum foil streamers. Heightening the circus atmosphere, goldfish bowls and wicker birdcages hung suspended from the ceiling, along with an outsized alarm clock. Moreover, the theater was wired for closed-circuit TV.

No supporter of Stockhausen or the avant-garde, the *New York Times* critic Harold Schonberg had little to say about the music, preferring to focus on what seemed the piece's ridiculous pretensions. As the audience "soberly" left the hall, he reported, "there was whispered discussion as to what constituted the more sublime moments of this twentieth-century monument to drama."

> Some said that the great moment came when the guy stood on a chair, squirted himself all over with a can of shaving lather, creamed himself thoroughly, dowsed himself with rice and ducked himself in a trough of water, eagerly drinking from a shoe.

Paik began by pelting the audience with beans and wound up with a flourish, seating himself at the piano to bang the keys with his forehead—a star-making performance.[9]

"Others, more vulgar types," per Schonberg, "hailed the two girls who stripped close to the buff, trying on clothes." (The young women were

9 Although notorious in Europe for his 1960 *Etude for Pianoforte*, which had concluded with a vault into the audience to snip off John Cage's necktie and a 1962 performance of the *Moonlight Sonata* during which he stripped to his underwear, smashed a violin and pelted the audience with raw eggs, Paik was largely unknown in New York.

Olga Adorno and Letty Eisenhauer, who, in April, had participated in the "Fully Guaranteed 12 Fluxus Concerts" at Fluxhall, 359 Canal Street.) Schonberg failed to mention that percussionist Max Neuhaus also stripped while playing but did cite "the girl who played the cello sitting on the rail of the Judson Hall balcony." That thirty-one-year-old girl was Moorman, wrapped in white gauze, legs suspended over the audience.

Apples were distributed. Sound technicians dueled with radio antennae. Allen Ginsberg chanted "Hare Krishna." Jackson Mac Low, wearing a Freedom Now T-shirt, declaimed a sound poem. Music critic Don Heckman improvised on the saxophone. Barely audible above the din, someone read aloud news stories on the presidential election. Writing in *The Nation*, the linguist Faubion Bowers praised *Originale* as "so unstructured and disruptive to human reason [that] the climax comes when a chimpanzee is allowed to play percussion."

With nothing to say about the music (which could be described as stray percussive sounds and near-continuous chatter), Schonberg concluded by returning to the scene outside the Judson.

> Seven or eight pickets were demonstrating. Some said they were part of the show. Others said no, including the picketers, but nobody believed them . . . They looked like participants in "Originale," they talked like the participants in "Originale," and they were dressed like participants in "Originale."

(And, presumably, smelled like participants.)

Not only did attendees assume the picketers were participants in the performance but some participants, notably Ginsberg, attempted to join the protest. (Flynt objected but Schleifer, a friend, insisted he be allowed.) Moorman and even more dubiously Kaprow later claimed to have protested as well. Even the *Voice* critic Jill Johnston would conclude her review—a salient if personal rumination on the relationship between authorial control and Cage-ian indeterminacy—by wondering why Kaprow had not invited the picket line to take part in the production.

Two weeks later, the Bell engineer and avant-garde techie-supreme Billy Klüver (then married to Olga Adorno) wrote to the *Voice*, enumerating several acts of theft, sabotage, and harassment committed against the festival, implicitly blaming the AACI protestors, whom he called "sickening."

The following issue allowed Johnston (who had been in the cast) to offer her own impressions of the event as both participant and critic. Johnston found *Originale* derivative but intermittently affecting, noting (as Klüver did not) that the star was subject to a special attack: During the fourth and final performance, "three unexpected guests made a rush on Nam June Paik, handcuffing him to a metal bar of the scaffolding." According to Johnston, the three intruders were pushed onto the fire escape and locked out. "One of them was later found to be stuck head down in an apparatus on the roof." Whose performance was that?

Soon after, Flynt received a call from listener-sponsored radio station WBAI, offering airtime to explain the anti-Stockhausen demonstration. Unfortunately, the Workers World Party vetoed his accepting the invitation.

7

Originale was followed a month later by Bill Dixon's *October Revolution in Jazz*. History does not record the presence of Action Against Cultural Imperialism or its cohorts, although much of the *October* music was more radical than Stockhausen.

Ornette Coleman and Cecil Taylor were subterranean heroes but by and large, the inherently political jazz avant-garde was largely ignored by the generally apolitical Cage-ian avant-garde. If sometimes patronized, Free Jazz was also marginalized by the jazz establishment—even as jazz itself was challenged by the popularity of folk, the brief craze for Brazilian bossa nova, and the unstoppable force of rock 'n' roll. Yet, twenty-two months after Coleman's last public appearance in New York, it would be revitalized by Dixon.

Co-founder of the United Nations Jazz Society (a group seeking to propagate jazz around the world, particularly Africa), from which he resigned after returning from Helsinki, Dixon had been booking avant-garde jazz at the Cellar Café, a Columbia student hangout featuring folk music, films, and poetry readings, almost one hundred blocks from MacDougal Street. The following semester brought the *October Revolution*.

Admission was one dollar. Only musicians without current gigs were invited to play—twenty-three combos and soloists in all. A student reporter for the *Columbia Spectator* was thrilled. The Village scene was passé, he wrote, "musician's jazz, it seems, may be heading uptown once again." The Cellar's capacity was around ninety but, as A. B. Spellman would write in *The Nation*, "the attendance was far greater than anyone expected . . . Hundreds of people were turned away." The cream of the avant-garde—Coleman, Taylor, and Archie Shepp—were in the audience.

The sets, which began at four in the afternoon and finished at midnight, were followed by panel discussions that ran until three in the morning. Bernard Stollman, who lived two blocks away on Riverside Drive, came to all the shows. "There was no electricity," he recalled. "The only lighting was from candles on the crowded tables." True or not, the power was in the music. Stollman found Shepp outside having a smoke, and invited him to record for his new label, ESP-Disk, along with all the other artists he found.[10]

The *October Revolution* inspired Dixon to organize the Jazz Composers Guild, a collective modelled in part on the artist-run galleries that had populated Tenth Street. Members would work together in solidarity, withholding labor from low-paying gigs, collectively negotiating contracts and verifying their enforcement. Stollman attended the early meetings to provide legal advice.

That December, the Jazz Composers Guild staged a follow-up series of concerts at Judson Hall. The opening bill—the Cecil Taylor Unit and Bill Dixon Sextet—sold out the house. The remaining nights, which featured Archie Shepp, Le Sun-Ra Arkestra, and the Roswell Rudd-John Tchicai Quartet (soon to be renamed the New York Art Quartet), drew about half as many, around 150, but garnered reviews in the *New York Times.*

The Guild established headquarters in the Contemporary Space, a cramped, oddly shaped, low-ceilinged studio belonging to the dancer-choreographer Edith Stephen. Just off Sheridan Square, at 180 Seventh Avenue, it was two floors above the Village Vanguard, where, prompted

10 Bob Dylan's historic Halloween night Lincoln Center concert was staid by comparison although, as a fifteen-year-old gatecrasher, I found it fascinating. From my nosebleed seat perspective, the packed house of devotees listened with rapt attention as Dylan sang two new long, blatantly poetic songs, "Gates of Eden," which struck me as over-earnest and pretentious, and "It's Alright Ma (I'm Only Bleeding)," which, as a close reader of Donald Hall's Grove press anthology *The New American Poetry*, I thought one of the greatest poems I had ever heard.

perhaps by the *Revolution*, Ornette Coleman played his first gig since the Town Hall disappointment of December 1962. One of the Guild's last events was the New York premiere of Michael Snow's *New York Eye and Ear Control*, which, inspired by Dixon's summer series, was a cinematic analog to *The October Revolution*.

The music rarely lets up, yet, coming directly out of Snow's artistic practice, *New York Eye and Ear Control* has the insolently casual feel of *The Flower Thief*. Indeed, although more forcefully assembled, *New York Eye and Ear Control* was an even more capricious and radically desultory film. In what might easily seem a pathetic attempt at animation, a Walking Woman cutout is shown floating in the ocean before disappearing to turn up coyly positioned on some nearby rocks. Sometimes reading as positive space, other times as negative, Snow's cutout strikes a mock-heroic figure amid the buildings of Lower Manhattan. She also suffers abuse—run over by two cars, set on fire, and "undressed" to reveal an actual woman standing behind.

The compositions are informal. Exposure varies. The inscrutable visuals and blurry landscapes are another provocation. The music seems indifferent to the image and at times derisive. "I tried to do something in which the sound and image had an equal power," Snow would explain. According to him, the musicians were unaware that they were providing the soundtrack to a film although, after they finished the session, Snow filmed their "screen tests" in his loft as well as additional footage of John Tchicai in the canyons of Lower Manhattan. The final image, which might have been filmed in Snow's loft on the day the music was recorded, is a bit of underground effrontery. An interracial couple (Tchicai and his Danish wife) is shown in bed, naked and nuzzling.

That *NYE&EC* had its New York premiere in a jazz context is something Snow seemed to have forgotten. Years later, he laughingly told an interviewer that the movie's first screenings resulted in riots.

> One performance was in the New York [Film-Makers'] Cinematheque and the other was [at the Marshall McLuhan Center] in Toronto. [The movie] was partially financed by Ten Centuries Concerts, and they really hated it. They just couldn't believe how awful it was. It was shown, and there were about 300 people there, and then somebody wrote a review with a headline saying: 300 FLEE FAR OUT FILM.

The review, published on April 5, 1965, in the *Toronto Daily Star*, noted that

> of the 100 who stayed, one wonders how many hung on for the same reason as one young man who was heard to say, "Let's wait, it's bound to get dirty yet." That it did—but not before the audience had to put up with an endless stream of disconnected shots of everything from Snow's famed "walking woman" cutout to lingering, out of focus views of the ocean, woods, and New York City. All this, over the drone of a far-out jazz group. After that, even the "dirty parts" were dull.

According to Snow, the Cinematheque screening had "people throwing things at the screen . . . I showed it, and Andy Warhol showed something that he'd just finished [possibly *Poor Little Rich Girl*], and a lot of his gang were there, and they didn't like my film much—except that Andy liked it and Gerry Malanga liked it." Even without its screen tests, *NYE&EC* appeared as brash underground slapstick. What was not to like? Snow recalled Malanga "running up the aisle to the projector and saying, 'That couldn't have been made in 1964!'"

8

November 3, 1964: Lyndon Johnson was elected in a landslide. The next day Lenny Bruce was convicted, essentially for using the word "shit" in public, and sent for psychiatric evaluation.

Apart from *Originale*, the presidential election didn't garner much art-world attention. The major exception was Robert Downey's underground farce *Babo 73*, which, with its scattershot satire of Yahoos, Birchers, Southern racists, and other Goldwater types, was acutely topical. Downey posited Taylor Mead as the newly elected President of the United Status [sic], who, bamboozled by his advisors, winds up directing missiles at Albania.

Originally titled *Forget It*, the movie was inspired by the Cuban Missile Crisis and shot over a period of two years. (A scene wherein Downey managed to film Mead amid a gaggle of uniformed brass attending a military parade in Washington, DC, could not have been shot after Kennedy's assassination.) After a few private screenings at the Second City comedy club in 1963, accompanied by live music, and a single showing in Los Angeles, a month earlier, *Babo 73* opened in

October at the Nickelodeon on Bleecker Street adjacent to Bruce's scene-of-the-crime, Café au Go Go.[11]

By then, Barbara Rubin had made her way back from free-speech citadel Berkeley. On November 7 she was photographed with Bob Dylan and a still clean-shaven Allen Ginsberg backstage at the McCarter Theater in Princeton, New Jersey, before a concert at which Dylan might well have sung "The Times They Are A-Changin'" and/or "Talkin' John Birch Paranoid Blues." Rubin was likely present at Judson Memorial Church on the evening of November 16, perhaps even with Mekas, for the most outré of Happenings, an hour-plus hodgepodge of near-naked humans, dead animals, and copious body paint: Carolee Schneemann's *Meat Joy*.

The subterraneans were psyched. Premiered in Paris the previous May as part of Jean-Jacques Lebel's Festival de la Libre Expression, Schneemann's riotous exercise in "Kinetic-Eye-Body-Theater" had incurred a measure of notoriety. The police had disrupted a follow-up London presentation and, according to Schneemann, the New York audience was salted with police informants and spies from "moral decency" groups.

The Paris performance had been staged in a 400-seat theater in the American Center, sedately located in a walled garden on Boulevard Raspail in Montparnasse, and thus largely if not totally immune to French censorship. (Nude bodies were allowed only if motionless.) Schneemann, who had performed as well as directed, was ecstatic, writing to her lover, the composer James Tenney, that

> *Joy* inundated the American Center—but *totally* at the climax, crawling, slithering, twisting, in a lake of paint, battered chickens & fish, ropes, mountains of paper—drenched with buckets of red, white, & yellow, eight bodies almost naked—the men drenching us, the women struggling (joyfully) yelling, crying, howling, shouting, laughing: screaming, "Bastas, Basta, Enough."

---

11 *Babo 73* provided Mead's most substantial film role since *The Flower Thief*. It was also his first talkie, and his post-dubbed mumbling, childlike drawl was as distinctive as his slack-jawed presence. Mekas gave the movie a boost in *Voice*. *New Yorker* critic Brendan Gill called it "the funniest movie I've seen in months," memorably noting that "Taylor Mead looks like a cross between a zombie and a kewpie and speaks as if his mind and mouth were full of marshmallow."

Moreover, the locals were shocked speechless: "The impossible French audience I'd come to know & fear so well, hypnotized into a silence which no one had ever experienced before! They normally talk, yell, cheer, set up peculiar organizations of whistles, chants, cries. Instructions, jokes!" The response was mixed. The previous night Wolf Vostell stole a bit of Schneemann's thunder by incorporating raw cow lungs in his Happening. Marcel Duchamp approved *Meat Joy*; one-time Berlin Dadaist Lil Picard found the production (which featured Rita Renoir, the star *stripteaseuse* of the Crazy Horse Saloon) too close to cabaret.

Originally a painter, Schneemann had gone beyond the canvas. For *Eye Body* (1962), she objectified herself, photographed by the Icelandic Pop artist Erro as she reclined naked on a drop cloth amidst the detritus of her loft: "Covered in paint, grease, chalk, ropes, plastic, I establish my body as visual territory." Indeed, in one of the photographs, she exposed her clitoris. If not the first American body artist, Schneemann established the role. The daughter of a country doctor, she was in no way squeamish and nothing if not forthright, especially regarding sex. By her own account, Schneemann had had two abortions in her late teens and posed (and painted herself) nude while a student at Bard; looking back at her arrival in New York age twenty, she recalled thinking "men were created for my sexual pleasure."

Schneemann was a reader of Wilhelm Reich as well as Artaud. *Meat Joy* was, in every way, more excessive than the Oldenburg-Dine happenings staged at the Judson nearly four years earlier and more confrontational than *Originale*. The New York audience was primed, entering the hall to find the performers, none of whom were trained dancers, seated at a table preparing for the show even as Schneemann was heard on tape, reading performance notes mixed with a French vocabulary primer.

The show commenced with a mountain of scrunched butcher paper descending from the balcony. The first tunes, Elvis Presley's covers of "Blue Suede Shoes" and "Tutti Frutti," were total '50s but there was silence as, face-to-face, Schneemann and Tenney circled the stage in an "Undressing Walk," removing each other's clothing, one article at a time. Other actors began disrobing until everyone was down to their feathered and furred bikini underwear. Variously languid and frantic, their choreographed movements included touching, piling up and rolling around. The action was accompanied by a score that mixed recordings of Parisian street sounds with shards of current Top 40 hits.

At times *Meat Joy* seemed precisely choreographed, as when the group positioned itself in geometric formations: The women lay on their backs and bicycled their legs as the Beatles sang "From Me to You," upon which the men hoisted the women onto *their* backs. Everyone joined a circular cluster, eventually collapsing into a heap of entangled limbs. The climax came when a designated "Serving Maid" appeared bearing an outsized platter of plucked chicken carcasses, raw fish, and uncooked frankfurters. The meat was strewn over the prone performers' near-naked bodies and even stuffed into their bikinis as Jamaican singer Millie Small sang her infectious single-entendre crossover hit "My Boy Lollipop."

The cast cavorted amid the food and joyfully made a mess, writhing to the regressive words of the Supremes' #1 hit "Baby Love," still on the charts. While the men used the plastic sheeting to furnish the women with fanciful bonnets, the Serving Maid brought out pails of paint. The men employed sponges to paint the women, who responded by hurling paint on the men. It all ended with Mary Wells's "My Guy" and everyone buried beneath another mound of paper.

Infantile yet erotic, more polymorphous in its perversity than *Flaming Creatures*, *Meat Joy* similarly freed sexuality from gender—and, beginning as it did with an exclusively involved heterosexual couple to wind up in an a-orgasmic Dionysian paint-spattered orgy—not only gender. Moreover, the piece physically involved the audience. Spectators were not only engaged by what they saw but what they touched (performers occasionally brushed against them) and smelled.

Schneemann was pleased to report that one spectator vomited on opening night; perhaps less so to note that the dancer Yvonne Rainer, who appeared twenty months earlier in Schneemann's first Judson piece *Newspaper Event* and whom she greatly admired, departed mid-performance: "She hated *Meat Joy* and walked out. Messy, brainless." Rainer was not alone. Schneemann would write to the museum administrator Jan Van der Marck that after *Meat Joy* "it appeared I had lost about half my friends in the art-world-scene."

The Village Voice ran two reviews. Both dance critic Jill Johnston and theater critic Michael Smith arrived with high expectations that were not entirely fulfilled. Reporting that the spectator in front of her spent the performance tearing his program into a handful of confetti, Johnston enjoyed the return to the "muck and murk" of the early Happenings as well as "the sensual and scatological pleasures of slimy contact." The piece, however, ran out of steam. Smith thought that the basic pattern was simple—"messier and messier"—and experienced a sort of letdown. "I had expected (and wanted) it to be a violent, frightening, threatening, transgressive, possibly embarrassing experience. Instead, it was pleasant," he wrote. Moreover, Schneemann's primeval aspirations were undermined by her use of cheerful, if not brainless, pop songs.[12]

Meat Joy's reviews appeared in the *Voice* alongside a meditation on the law and Lenny Bruce. In "The Bruce Conviction: A View from the Couch," John Tarburton, a Reichian lay analyst with an interest in censorship, argued that Bruce had been "found guilty of 'crimes' that exist only in the fantasy lives of repressed people."

> Only 'when we dead awaken' will there be a true and full rebirth of erotic freedom, whereby the libido that powers and governs our bodily life will be able to express itself in open harmony with nature.
>
> Such a triumph over our 'civilized' sado-masochism cannot possibly be too soon in coming.

Schneemann would later term *Meat Joy* "an erotic rite to *enliven* my

12 As *Eye Body* was a solo performance meant to be photographed, *Meat Joy* endures thanks to its documentation. Much of its orgiastic reputation rests on Peter Moore's ring-side photographs—the minimalist painter Dorothea Rockburne, body slick, eyes closed in ecstasy as she slides into the cuddle-puddle, a raw chicken tucked under her arm, or pressed against Schneemann, both women screaming with the excited delight of kids on a rollercoaster. Schneemann had the foresight to have a performance documented at a New York TV studio by the French filmmaker Pierre Dominique Gaisseau (who had won an Oscar for his 1961 documentary of a French expedition to New Guinea, *The Sky Above, The Mud Below*). The existence of documentation permits further analysis. The art historian Elise Archias observed that, "though the performers seem to have relished the direction to handle each other's bodies without inhibition, they also seem self-conscious. The incessant smiles convey both pleasure and a sense of vulnerability or embarrassment." In any case, it seems logical that Schneemann would begin shooting her first film, *Fuses*, a densely overworked study of her lovemaking with James Tenney, soon after *Meat Joy*'s New York performances.

guilty culture." One wonders what Tarburton (or Lenny) would have made of her rampant disinhibition.[13]

The same issue included a full-page ad announcing Bruce's Thanksgiving Day Weekend resurrection. Not at the Café au Go Go but the Village Theater: SEE LENNY BRUCE SPEAK FOR PROFIT/SEE TINY TIM SING FOR LOVE. A block up Second Avenue, the St. Mark's Playhouse was rehearsing a pair of one-act plays by LeRoi Jones—*The Toilet* and *The Slave*—which, once the bill opened in mid-December, three months after *The Blacks* ended its run, would provide the neighborhood's last free speech outrage of 1964.

9

Jones had gone from verbal to staged polemics. The poet was churning out one-act plays. The new racially incendiary future sensation *Dutchman* was ready to go and soon after *The Eighth Ditch* was revived, *The Baptism* arrived at the Writers Stage on a bill with Frank O'Hara's *The General Returns from One Place to Another*.

Both *The Baptism* and *The General* featured Taylor Mead, who would receive an Obie for his portrayal of the eponymous military man, a Douglas MacArthur–type returning to scenes of his former triumphs only to discover no one cares. Both were directed by Jerry Benjamin, "a very brilliant but awry director who conceived of doing the two plays together and nearly drove us crazy," per Mead. Benjamin's previous credits included Andy Warhol's unfinished *Soap Opera* and the 1963 Judson premiere of John Wieners's *Asphodel, in Hell's Despite*, an early rock opera for which Warhol designed the sets. (As staged by Benjamin, Wieners's play ended with the principal characters dispatched to hell and the Judson audience battered with noise and light that, in retrospect, anticipated by several years the sensory aggression of *Andy Warhol Uptight* and the *Exploding Plastic Inevitable*.)[14]

---

13 According to Schneemann, *Meat Joy* resulted in an invitation to create a Happening for NBC's *Tonight Show*. Dubious regarding her proposal to incorporate the debris swept up after the previous night's broadcast, the show's producers withdrew their offer when the host Johnny Carson declined to participate in the Happening by standing on the backs of three women or, alternately, vaulting over them.

14 Benjamin subsequently founded a company called the Everyday Theatre (after Brecht) and edited a single issue of *The Everyday Theatre Bulletin*, which announced plans to stage plays by Ginsberg, Warhol, and Malanga before Benjamin left for Los Angeles and faded into a perhaps drug-induced obscurity.

Michael Smith considered *The Baptism* and *The General Returns* a "fabulous evening of theatre." *The Baptism*—a farce about homosexuality and the church—was, he thought, something new for Jones: "I cannot convey the extent of outrage it commits, the unrestrained blasphemous travesty it perpetuates on a flock of sacred subjects." (These included Jesus Christ, masturbation, and Black-white relations, which is to say, the Lenny Bruce playbook.) Arriving to be baptized, the Boy (Russell Turman, who made his stage debut at twelve in *A Raisin in the Sun*) announces his sin: "Thinking of God always gives me a hard-on."

The minister was played by another Black actor (James Spruill), while Mead portrayed the Homosexual, a devil incarnate mocking the Church and its "thin Jewish cowboy," with Beverly Grant as the outrageous Old Woman driven mad with lust by the Boy's blasphemies, pulling up her skirt to scream, "You spilled your seed in the Lord's name." That rehearsals were held at Grant's West Twenty-Sixth Street loft contributed to the "druggy atmosphere" detected by Mari-Claire Charba, one of the all-white chorus of vestal virgins who—having mistaken the Boy for the Son of God, which he in fact turns out to be—entered the theater from the street, walking through the audience holding candles and singing the Mormon children's hymn "Jesus Wants Me for a Sunbeam."

However *The Baptism* might have impressed Michael Smith, Jones was not pleased with the production. Charba remembers him being continually angry; things with Grant, who had her own history of interracial liaisons, were especially tense. Jones did not attend any of the performances and, much to Mead's frustration, refused to allow the play to move to a "real" off-Broadway theater, presumably because it might distract from *Dutchman*, which opened one day later and some blocks west at the venerable Cherry Lane (a Commerce Street venue consecrated to theater forty years before by Edna St. Vincent Millay and friends). Frustrated, Mead left for Europe.

A one-act two-hander modeled on Edward Albee's *Zoo Story*, *Dutchman* shared a triple bill with Samuel Beckett's *Play* and Arrabal's *The Two Executioners* and, as a racial allegory that, among other things, suggests that jazz and poetry are sublimated violence, got all the attention: A young Black intellectual who imagines himself the "Black Baudelaire" is hypnotized, driven mad and destroyed by a provocative white witch he encounters in an empty subway car. The play won an Obie and got a second run, billed with Albee's *American Dream*. Jones seemed poised to topple James Baldwin as New York's preeminent Black writer. Indeed, a few days before *The Slave* and *The Toilet* opened, Isabel Eberstadt crowned him "King of the East Village" in an appreciation published in the *New York Herald Tribune*'s Sunday magazine.

Eberstadt hailed Jones as a poet, critic, dramatist, and celebrity, as well as "a Flaming Seducer [and] a Rabid Racist, who Hates whites, Hates Negroes, Hates homosexuals, Hates intellectuals, Hates liberals." She made it known that she was riffing ("not all of these statements are true, obviously") but ample proof might have been found in Jones's new manifesto "The Revolutionary Theater," which demanded a theater that "must Accuse and Attack because it is a theater of Victims" (like the male protagonists of *Dutchman*, *The Toilet* and *The Slave*) and his latest poetry collection, *The Dead Lecturer*, published by Grove Press in October, which included the notorious "Black Dada Nihilismus":

Come up, black dada

nihilismus. Rape the white girls. Rape
their fathers. Cut the mothers' throats.
Black dada nihilismus, choke my friends

in their bedrooms with their drinks spilling

Jones had already recorded the poem with the New York Art Quartet for the group's first ESP-Disk release.[15]

By comparison, *The Toilet* (directed, like *The Baptism*, by Jerry Benjamin) and even *The Slave* were moderate. Set entirely in a high school boy's room, *The Toilet* centers on a Black gang who plan to stomp a white fellow student, Karolis, who had been sufficiently indiscreet to send a homosexual mash note to their leader, Foots. Violence ensues but after Karolis is beaten unconscious, Foots tearfully cradles his head. Michael Smith found *The Toilet* overwhelming but deemed *The Slave* dull. However, if Jones was talking to himself in *The Toilet*, he was screaming in *The Slave*. The play is set in the midst of an all-out race war that Blacks are apparently winning.

15 "Black Dada Nihilismus" was first published in the March–April 1963 *Evergreen Review* (cover photo by Diane Arbus).

Walker Vessels, a poet turned commander of the Black Liberation Army, crosses enemy lines to gain entry to the home of his white former wife Grace, now married to the homosexual white professor once Vessels's mentor. (Their home is a citadel of chic bourgeois culture; set designer Larry Rivers gave the white couple two large faux Franz Kline abstractions.) Vessels has come to take back his two young daughters.

In the heat of debate, Grace calls Vessels a "nigger-murderer," borne out when the men struggle and Vessels kills the professor. A bomb falls on the house, leaving Grace dead and Vessel broken.

10

The subterraneans understood Jones's plays as psychodrama. They were "personal, almost private works," Michael Smith explained, mistaken for "political statements, public pronouncements, position papers on advanced intellectual, left-wing Negro thinking."

The Toilet and *The Slave* received an enormously sympathetic *New York Times* review, forcefully, if not hysterically, rebutted in the *Voice* by Jack Newfield's page-one profile. The piece was a veritable open letter to the masochistic Eberstadts of the world: "The wilder, the more obscene, the more jugular [Jones's] thrusts become, the more [he] draws acclaim instead of blood."

A young social psychologist, Richard A. Koenigsberg, wrote in support of Newfield, excoriating the "undiscriminating" liberal tolerance for Jones's positions. The following week, a letter from Dick Higgins, identifying himself as no admirer of Jones, criticized Koenigsberg's language and ignorance of Jones's talent while making a similar point: rather than inspiring revolution, Jones's plays served only to "excite and titillate his liberal white audience." Finally, Celia Wells Willens, another young academic and Village resident, wrote in praise of Koenigsberg, declaring it was not Jones's talent but his race that accounted for the attention he received. "He is a Negro who is being shamelessly patronized." The King of the East Village had no choice but to abdicate.[16]

16 If Jones was the King of the East Village, Lorraine Hansberry, who lived on Bleecker Street, was an ambivalent observer of the West Village. Her second play, *The Sign in Sidney Brustein's Window*—a critique of Village bohemians that included characters loosely based on Art D'Lugoff, Jonas Mekas, and Edward Albee—was currently on Broadway. At one point the stand-up comedian Mort Sahl was to play the title character. The show ran 101 performances and closed the night its author died, age thirty-four.

Everyone in the neighborhood knew that Jones had a white Jewish wife, Hettie Jones, and two small daughters. (Indeed, they lived on Cooper Square, only a few blocks from the St. Mark's Playhouse.) Hettie had read *The Slave* but, home tending to her sick children, did not have a chance to see a rehearsal. "I got to the opening night unprepared for the way I'd feel. The last sounds you hear are the children screaming as the house is bombed." A few months later her husband would leave his family and relocate uptown in Harlem.

The World's Fair year ended on a dismal note. On December 21, Lenny was sentenced to four months of hard labor. Christmas Day, Ron Rice died of pneumonia in Acapulco, Mexico, where he had fled after the *Flaming Creature* bust. He was twenty-nine.

6

All Tomorrow's Parties, 1964–65

In which rock 'n' roll becomes a Thing. East Village poets form the Fugs, subterranean avant-garde musicians create the Velvet Underground, and Bob Dylan goes electric. Jonas Mekas discovers the great polymath Harry Smith, Andy Warhol discovers his most enduring superstar, Edie Sedgwick (as does Dylan), and the New Cinema Festival transforms Happenings into multimedia spectaculars.

This poem is writing itself / It learned that on the radio
—Ted Berrigan, "Fresh Windows: To John Wieners" (ca. 1963)

Fall 1964 brought Stockhausen from Germany, the October Revolution uptown, and Dylan to Philharmonic Hall. Yet, so idiotic as to be underground, the real radical movement was happening in Teenage Music.

Persuaded by a neighborhood hipster to switch its jukebox from polkas to rock 'n' roll, the Old Reliable Bar & Grill on 213 East Third Street drew a new, racially mixed crowd. Soon after, Stanley Tolkin, proprietor of Stanley's, which, together with the Charles Theater, created an Avenue B scene, persuaded Mickey Ruskin, whose previous establishments included the Tenth Street Coffeehouse and Les Deux Mégots, to absorb the overflow with a neighboring establishment, the Annex.

Off-Broadway theaters and coffeehouses had already taken root on and around the old Yiddish Rialto, Second Avenue below Fourteenth Street. BABY BEATNIKS SPUR BAR BOOM ON EAST SIDE Sally Kempton would write in a Freedom Summer, page-one *Village Voice* report: "The Lower East Side or, as some would dub it, the East Village is taking over the status of bohemia from Greenwich Village." Tolkin had just launched the Dom, a dank, dark, roomy space in the Polish National Home (Dom Polski) on St. Mark's Place. Decent whiskey was 50 cents a shot and there was a highly danceable selection on the Wurlitzer.

Barbara Rubin and her eighteen-year-old cohort Rosebud Feliu may have been there first, whether before or after they hitchhiked to Berkeley and back. Poking around the Dom Polski, the pair discovered an "incredible jukebox" and attracted immediate attention. "We weren't big old fat Polack ladies. We were girls," Feliu recalled. The "mostly older working-class men" treated them to drinks and they would dance all night with each other. One night, they went to the Metro and dragged the poets around the corner to cavort. "It became this sort of new weird place to go."

Some claimed to have spotted Jackie Kennedy's brother-in-law, the Polish aristocrat Prince Radziwiłł, at the opening. (It was, after all, the bar attached to the Polish National Home.) By November, the *New York Times* dispatched fashion reporter Charlotte Curtis down to investigate the scene: "The uptown rich, who popularized Small's Paradise in Harlem and the Peppermint Lounge in midtown, have discovered the East Village nightspots" was her unimpressed report. The Dom was "nothing more than a large room with red walls, a few subdued lights, loud music, and air that reeks of Gauloise cigarettes. The dance floor is a stage on which all variations of the twist are attempted."[1]

And so, ten months after the Beatles played *The Ed Sullivan Show* and certainly by the time LBJ trounced Barry Goldwater, rock 'n' roll was a Thing. Sally Kempton's follow-up page-one *Voice* story was pegged to the mid-September arrival of the Animals—a British blues band who had a #1 hit version of the venerable New Orleans folk lament "House of the Rising Sun," lifted from Bob Dylan, who stole his arrangement from Dave Van Ronk.

Kempton's bemused description of the Dionysian frenzy that the Animals inspired in young girls segued into a meditation on why the

1 Curtis also made a sociological observation, noting that the East Village "community is probably the most integrated one in the city, and interracial couples, some of them married, are a common sight."

Beatles had seemingly been supplanted by rock's reigning bad boys, the Rolling Stones, who, a week before Halloween, returned to the Academy of Music on East Fourteenth Street. The event provided Tom Wolfe with the lead for his profile of the first Warhol superstar, Baby Jane Holzer. "The Girl of the Year" would appear in the December 6, 1964, *New York Herald Tribune*'s Sunday magazine.

Wolfe was more excited than Kempton by the turned-on young girls—the hundreds of "flaming little buds, bobbing and screaming, rocketing around" the Academy of Music—but he was really enchanted with the near-squealing response of a mature twenty-four-year-old Park Avenue socialite.

> "Aren't they super marvelous?" says Baby Jane, and then: "Hi Isabel! Isabel! You want to sit backstage—with the Stones!"

Isabel is Isabel Eberstadt, another "beautiful" socialite a half dozen years older, who happens to be the daughter of whimsical *New Yorker* poet Ogden Nash. Isabel (whose profile of scary-fascinating LeRoi Jones will appear in the Sunday *Herald Tribune* a week after "The Girl of the Year") is also a patron the arts. Back in January she contributed $2,400 to keep Adrienne Kennedy's hallucinatory *Funnyhouse of a Negro* running at the East End Theater and was, despite the disapproval of her husband, the fashion photographer Frederick Eberstadt, particularly generous to Jack Smith, whom she had lifted from squalor to poverty. Having seen his Ludlow Street slum, she rented him a "studio" in a Grand Street loft in the still industrial neighborhood not yet named SoHo. Warhol gave Eberstadt four screen tests in 1964 and made a filmed portrait of her wrist. Wolfe suggests her polite disdain for Baby Jane's vulgar enthusiasm.

"The Girl of the Year" segues from a description of the Stones on stage to a party in their honor which somehow morphs into Baby Jane's birthday bash, an event held at fashion photographer Jerry Schatzberg's huge Madison Square loft. Entertainment is provided by Genya Ravan's band Goldie and the Gingerbreads, four girls in gold lamé tights and stiletto heels brought downtown from their regular gig in a dive on West Forty-Fifth Street a few doors from the Peppermint Lounge.[2]

2 Genya, who is the same age as Baby Jane, might be the real story. Not a transplant to but a refugee from the Lower East Side, she is a Polish-born child survivor of the

When the Stones do finally show up everyone is maniacally frugging to Goldie's version of the Supremes' huge Freedom Summer hit "Where Did Our Love Go"—the very song Jonas Mekas wanted played with his new film, *Award Ceremony for Andy Warhol*, making it the second underground movie, after *Scorpio Rising*, with an all-rock soundtrack.

2

In the art world and the underground, rock 'n' roll was *the* Thing. In late 1964, around the time Carolee Schneemann created the first pop music Happening, two Lower East Side poets-cum-mimeo-publishers, Ed Sanders and Tuli Kupferberg, were either inspired or instructed (by Rubin and Feliu) to form a rock band. First called the Yodeling Socialists, then the Freaks, the band added a drummer, Ken Weaver and, named at Kupferberg's suggestion after the euphemism coined by Norman Mailer in *The Naked and the Dead*, became the Fugs.

That fall, two stoned disciples of La Monte Young—twenty-two-year-old Welsh violinist John Cale and twenty-four-year-old Tony Conrad—got together to rehearse with a thirty-ish friend of Young's, artist Walter De Maria, who played the drums and had a big loft on Bond Street. Their mission: learn an inane would-be dance-craze catalyst called "The Ostrich." The tune was released as 45 rpm single by Pickwick International, pioneer purveyor of "sound-alike" recordings and bargain-bin LPs, and attributed to a studio band called the Primitives.

Conceived and performed by the company's resident twenty-two-year-old genius Lou Reed, "The Ostrich" was a stoned goof on the flood of post-twist dances—the Pony, the Monkey, the Fly, the Bird, the Philly Dog, the Funky Chicken et al.—as well as the ridiculous novelty songs they spawned. The 45 was pure cacophony, replete with background yelps and howls, more chanted than sung, the words were instructional ("You take it forward, put your head to your kne-e-es . . .") and exhortatory ("*now come on!!*").

Pickwick imagined they might have a hit. Consequently, a band was needed to perform "The Ostrich" at high school hops. Somehow this gig was communicated to playwright Jack Gelber's kid brother David, then living in an Old Law Tenement in the deep Lower East Side at 56 Ludlow

---

Holocaust who grew up on Rivington Street, where her parents ran a candy store. The first all-female band to sign with a major label, the Gingerbreads would eventually tour Europe with the Animals and the Stones.

Street, who, invited to an uptown party, brought a pair of musicians he knew from the building—Cale and Conrad, then sharing a $30 a month cold-water apartment. Their long hair and diffident attitude impressed Pickwick operative Terry Phillips, a Brill Building songwriter sometimes partnered with Phil Spector, who invited them to pick up a bit of cash by posing as the Primitives.

Cale and Conrad warmed to the gig even more after Reed explained that they need only tune their instruments to one note, which was basically what they had been doing with Young's Theater of Eternal Music. For several months in early 1965, Cale, Conrad, De Maria, and Reed spent their weekends playing high school dances west of Philadelphia, home of the crucial after-school TV rock variety show *American Bandstand*, which is where Pickwick vainly hoped to the break the record.

Soon after, Conrad moved out of Ludlow Street and Reed, who had been living with his parents on suburban Long Island, moved in. Before long he and Cale were doing drugs—although Cale was selling marijuana and cocaine for La Monte Young, Reed turned him on to heroin. They were also working on songs, including "I'm Waiting for the Man" and "Heroin," that Reed had written in college. Reed, Cale learned, was not just a committed rocker but during his years at Syracuse University had played Ornette Coleman on the college radio station and been mentored by the poet Delmore Schwartz. Angus MacLise, another member of Young's Theater of Eternal Music, replaced De Maria on drums and they were joined by grad student Sterling Morrison, a dorm-mate of Reed's from Syracuse whom he reencountered on the D train.

The band was first called the Falling Spikes, then the Warlocks and finally, after the title of Michael Leigh's sensational report on the sexual revolution—a paperback that Conrad found in the trash—the Velvet Underground.

3

Mid-January '65, another onetime high school rocker recorded his first (half-)electric LP: Bob Dylan cut *Bringing It All Back Home*. No less (and even more) than Ed Sanders or Lou Reed, he had poetic aspirations.

Even while Dylan was recording in Columbia's Studio A on 799 Seventh Avenue, the *Village Voice* published Jack Newfield's analysis of the *Broadside*-launched topical song movement. After his Freedom

Summer release, *Another Side of Bob Dylan*, the twenty-three-year-old "mumbling, ragamuffin genius" was understood to have outgrown topical—or as he now dismissively called them, "finger-pointing"—songs. Still, Newfield's piece was inevitably headlined after Dylan, BLOWIN' IN THE WIND: A FOLK MUSIC REVOLT.

Noting that hip supper club performers like Lena Horne and Bobby Darin were now adding topical songs to their acts, Newfield resisted the temptation to quote the title of Dylan's year-old release "The Times They Are a-Changin'." "Today every branch of culture has its own tribe of far-out revolutionaries," he wrote, citing Lenny Bruce, John Coltrane, Jack Gelber, and his colleague Jonas Mekas, along with LeRoi Jones and William Burroughs, who, a month later, on Valentine's Day, materialized on the stage of the American Theater of Poets's new venue, the 129-seat East End Theater, 85 East Fourth Street, a block once home to Yiddish cabarets, Jewish wedding halls, and Romanian wine cellars.

The Burroughs event was reported in the next day's *New York Times* (along with a page-one story that, out in Queens, Malcolm X and his family had been forced to escape their firebombed house). Burroughs, Harry Gilroy wrote, "sat at ease on the stage while he addressed what might be described as an Off-Broadway audience gathered in a little red theater."

> After some recorded music that seemed to mix a train pounding over a loose rail with North African bazaar melodies, Mr. Burroughs gave his audience a couple of clues to help their poetic impressions along.
>
> Then the author read a line here and a line there from his own works: *Junkie*, about a drug addict; *Naked Lunch*, a novel of literary bits and pieces also spliced with marijuana, and *Nova Express*, which has something to do with space. In the middle of this, he left the stage while a tape recorder provided lines read by Mr. Burroughs from the babblings of Arthur Flegenheimer, alias Dutch Schultz, on his deathbed after being shot in Newark in 1935.

Burroughs was obviously familiar with Happenings and more. The sound collage—Schultz's delirium juxtaposed with reportage on Vietnam and two air crashes—that concluded the mixed-media performance was greeted with "shock and nervous laughter."

At least one Fug was present. Ed Sanders had recently published a pamphlet edition of Burroughs's notorious "Roosevelt After Inauguration." For a few months that spring, Burroughs was New York's preeminent literary celebrity. In short order, Ginsberg brought him together with Bob Dylan at an East Village coffeehouse which, were a movie of the event ever made, would have to be Le Metro. Dylan impressed Burroughs with his self-confidence and, increasingly taken with the idea of himself as a writer, gave a late March interview name-checking Burroughs and his cut-up methodology. Indeed, something like Burroughs's experiments was evident in Dylan's just-released 45 single, a rollicking, surreal Chuck Berry riff called "Subterranean Homesick Blues." After a warning of a "must-bust in early May, orders from the D. A.," Dylan cautioned his subject that no "matter what you did," it was best to "walk on tip toes" and "watch the plainclothes."

The song would graze the Top 40, peaking at #39, but *Bringing It All Back Home*, the LP it kicked off, would reach #6 on *Billboard*'s weekly chart. A remarkable fusion of Buddy Holly and Arthur Rimbaud, *Bringing It All Back Home* not only invented what would be known as folk rock, it out-stoned the Stones, beat the Beatles to put the beat in Beat poetry and, with songs like "Maggie's Farm" and "It's Alright, Ma (I'm Only Bleeding)," took protest into the realm of pataphysics. Anticipating the Beatles' *Sgt. Pepper* by over two years, it also boasted the first LP cover that demanded to be decoded.

Daniel Kramer portrays a belligerently inscrutable Dylan at the center of a blurry vortex, hunched forward clutching his cat (said to be named Rolling Stone). The movie magazine open on his lap shows an ad for a best-selling Hollywood biography, *Jean Harlow's Life Story*. Behind him an elegantly made-up odalisque in red—Sally Grossman, the wife of Dylan's manager—lounges on a deco-striped divan flaunting a cigarette in one hand, as provocatively blank as any high fashion model.[3]

3 A high school memory: Dylan had made LP history when, back in 1962, he posed with Suze Rotolo for the cover of *The Freewheelin' Bob Dylan*. It is indicative of the "new" Dylan's enigmatic aura that the speculation about the Woman in Red did not center on her identity but the possibility that she was Dylan himself in drag. The back cover features photographs of Joan Baez, a clean-shaven Allen Ginsberg wearing an Ascot top hat (worn in another photo by impish Dylan) and, determinedly massaging Dylan's scalp, a short-haired Barbara Rubin.

The hippest couple in the universe is surrounded by assorted totems and fetish objects. These include a government Fallout Shelter sign, a copy of *Time* magazine's Man of the Year issue with President Lyndon Johnson on the cover, a harmonica, and an antique mid-nineteenth-century portrait of an unknown bearded gent. Most of the cultural markers are LPs: *The Folk Blues of Eric Von Schmidt*, *Robert Johnson: King of the Delta Blues Singers*, *Lotte Lenya Sings Berlin Theatre Songs by Kurt Weill*, the Impressions' most recent album, *Keep on Pushing*, released on the eve of the Harlem Riot. *The Best of Lord Buckley* is centrally placed on the mantle while *Another Side of Bob Dylan* looks stuck in the fireplace below.

The curation is evident as is the connoisseurship. The most significant talisman is the brand new first (and only) issue of Ira Cohen's little magazine *Gnaoua*, whose contributors included William Burroughs, Allen Ginsberg, Brian Gysin, Michael McClure, Marc Schleifer, and Irving Rosenthal (as J. Sheeper), and which included a five-photograph set titled "Superstars of Cinemaroc," by Jack Smith. All very cool although the poetic declaration on the back cover has a punchline clichéd even before Dylan dropped by Café Bizarre: "I accept chaos. I am not sure whether chaos accepts me."

4

The folkiest song on *Bringing It All Back Home* was called "Outlaw Blues." Jack Newfield's topical folkies—Buffy Sainte-Marie, Len Chandler, Tom Paxton, and, interviewed for his piece, Phil Ochs—struck him as "frontier outlaws," putting out songs that, back in the days of the House Un-American Committee and Joe McCarthy, "would have been blacklisted by every record company and radio station in the land."

On what frontier fringe would Newfield have located the Holy Modal Rounders (fiddler Peter Stampfel and guitarist Steve Weber) performing zany psychedelic revivalist folk material or the band with whom they briefly merged, the Fugs? Indeed, had Sanders and Kupferberg gone public with their invented dance song "The Gobble," the taboo-breaking teen rocker "Coca-Cola Douche," or the crazed anthem "Kill For Peace," they might have headed up Newfield's "guerilla bands of prophets and crackpots," along with Barbara Rubin, who had completed her double-screen version of *Christmas on Earth* by the time *Bringing It All Back Home* was released.

Actually, the Fugs were in the far-advanced vanguard. With the announcement that "there has never been any thing [sic] like the FUGS in the history of western civilization!!," the band made their official debut on a cold Wednesday night in February at the grand reopening of the packed Peace Eye bookstore (383 East Tenth Street) and general celebration of *Fuck You*'s third anniversary "Mad Motherfucker" issue—"Seventy pages of editorial screams, porn, poetry, and freak-vectors." The cover was a frame-enlargement from Andy Warhol's "pornographic" movie *Couch*. Having conquered the underground in late 1964, the Warhol Factory was that night a subliminal presence. Sanders had asked Warhol to help decorate the opening. Furnished with some cloth bolts from Orchard Street, the Factory silk-screened bursts of poppies on three banners to adorn the Peace Eye's walls.[4]

Sanders, one of the several men who clinched with Naomi Levine in Warhol's *Kiss* serial, originally wanted to use a Warhol Brillo box as a drum. (The poet Ted Berrigan had one lying around his East Ninth Street pad.) After the theft of Ken Weaver's buffalo-rawhide powwow tom-tom, the band made do with a Krasdale canned peaches carton.

If not Andy, at least Bill Burroughs was there. Sanders's memoir recorded Burroughs's visceral distaste for the *Time* reporter sent to cover the event but not the assassination of Malcolm X three days earlier at the Audubon Ballroom on Broadway at W. 165th Street in Washington Heights—a world-historical event that precluded the presence of *Fuck You*'s most prominent African American contributor, LeRoi Jones. "Word From the Right Wing," one of Jones's two pieces, begins "President Johnson / is a mass murder," calls his wife "weird looking, a special breed of hawkbill cracker" and ends with

Johnson's mother, walked all night holding hands
With a nigger, and that nigger's
Hard. Blew him downtown Newark 1928 . . . I got proof!

4 Not only was Warhol's studio assistant Gerard Malanga one of the three Factory stars, murky but naked, on *Fuck You*'s cover but contributions to the issue included a list of Malanga's alleged male and female paramours compiled by fellow poet and Factory scenarist "Ronnie" Tavel. The list of twenty-eight men includes distinguished poets and artists W. H. Auden, John Ashbery, Taylor Mead, Allen Ginsberg, Peter Orlovsky, Fred Herko, Rufus Collins, Willard Maas, Winn Chamberlain, Gregory Markopoulos, Alan Marlowe, Bob (Ondine) Olivo, Andy Warhol, Kenneth Koch, Tavel himself "and hundreds more which Gerard Malanga trembles in paranoia to mention." The seventeen women are more underground: Naomi Levine, Elektrah! (Lobel), Barbara Rubin, Rose (actually Kate) Heliczer and "thousands of faces and snatches in the night."

The Fugs performed on the following Saturday at Gallery 111, an English basement on St. Mark's Place, and a week or so later played the East End—four days after the Theater of Eternal Music, still featuring Conrad and Cale, appeared, one day before Allan Kaprow lectured on "The Techniques and New Goals of Happenings," and the very March 8 that saw the release of *Subterranean Homesick Blues.* (It was also the weekend of "Bloody Sunday" in Selma, Alabama.)

New neighborhood darlings, the Fugs were brought back over the next several weeks for a pair of two-day engagements. The Theater for Poets's following presentation was *The Launching of the Dream Weapon*, the mixed-media piece by Forest Hills High School buddies Angus MacLise and Piero Heliczer, twenty-six and twenty-seven, that featured the future Velvet Underground, then known variously as the Warlocks and Falling Spikes.

And later that month the Fugs found themselves uptown at the Cue Recording Studio making their first record, produced by no less an eminence than the unclassifiable Beat Generation polymath, occult animator, freelance ethnographer, collector of artifacts, and one-man counterculture, an irascible, hard-drinking, peyote-ingesting gnome—Harry Smith.

5

Smith, whom Sanders knew from Stanley's, had attended early Fugs performances. Explaining them as a jug band, he persuaded Moe Asch, the founder of Folkways records, to let them cut a disc. The recording session was lively. Smith smashed a bottle of rum (his sole payment) against the wall in praise of Kupferberg's version of the Yiddish children's song "Bulbes" (potatoes), now called "Nothing."

Smith's association with Folkways went back over a dozen years. When he first arrived in New York from the West Coast, he had drawn on his own collection of race and hillbilly 78s to orchestrate the idiosyncratic six-LP *Anthology of American Folk Music*, first issued in 1952. Not simply a compendium or even a taxonomy, the *Anthology* was an epic, intricately cross-referenced narrative played out over eighty-four songs, beginning with an Appalachian murder ballad and ending with a cheerful slide-whistle ragtime blues.

As cabalistic as it was canonical, the set had exerted a profound influence on the folk revivalists like Dave Van Ronk, the New Lost City

Ramblers, and the Jim Kweskin Jug Band. Dylan put new words to the melodies (and vice versa), as did fiddler Peter Stampfel, who with his Holy Modal Rounders partner Steve Weber adopted the high, nasal tones and hillbilly wackiness of Appalachian singers. The music was not much more than twenty-five years old when Stampfel and company discovered it, but it sounded prehistoric. It wasn't until John Cohen encountered Smith in 1962 that the folkies had any idea that "Harry Smith," imagined by some to be a pseudonymous Alan Lomax, was alive.

However ancient he might have appeared, Smith was only forty-two in 1965. A child of the Pacific Northwest, raised by Theosophist parents and afflicted with rickets, he was a genius bricoleur. Barely out of his teens and already a legendary collector of the weird 78s that would be transformed into the Folkways anthology, young Smith was also a painter in the nonobjective Kandinsky tradition, a filmmaker who did not use a camera, making abstract movies by painting/staining/scratching the emulsion, and a devotee of bebop jazz.

After relocating from Washington to Berkeley in the mid-1940s, Smith moved across the Bay in the late 1940s, taking a room upstairs from an after-hours club in the Fillmore district. He painted the club walls with abstract motifs and, to accompany the musicians, developed a mechanism that projected oils mixed on a mirror, thus inventing the light show that twenty years later would be the hallmark of Bill Graham's Fillmore. Smith came to New York around 1951. Lugging several thousand 78s, he located Asch, who was then recording Woody Guthrie and reissuing New Orleans jazz. Asch (the son of the renowned Yiddish writer Sholem Asch) had several years earlier branched out from recorded Yiddish music to folk and ethnology. He gave Smith a $200 advance against royalties, a corner in his cramped midtown office and a supply of peyote buttons to create the *Anthology*.

Surviving mainly on handouts, Smith lived in a basement in Spanish Harlem. Later he moved to a tiny upstairs apartment at 300 ½ East Seventy-Fifth Street, between Third and Lexington Avenues (around the corner from the high school that saw the shooting that sparked the 1964 Harlem uprising). There completing his first eleven films, Smith did arcane research and made impressive connections. He recorded Rabbi Naftali Zvi Margolies Abulafia at the Home of the Sages of Israel, a yeshiva on East Broadway, spent his days researching arcanities in the reading room of the New York Public Library and his nights at the midtown jazz club Birdland.

Smith met Allen Ginsberg at the Five Spot during summer 1958, when Thelonious Monk was in residence. Smith was taking notes, attempting to ascertain how often Monk played behind or ahead of the beat. Ginsberg was intrigued and the two became friendly. When he was in New York, Ginsberg enjoyed hanging out and getting high at Smith's pad and looking at Smith's movies projected on the wall, accompanied by cuts from Monk's Five Spot LP *Misterioso*. Indeed, Ginsberg had his mind blown by Smith's latest, *Film No. 12*, a fifty-minute series of animated hieroglyphics that suggest a vaudeville Jules Verne version of the *Tibetan Book of the Dead* enacted by a cast of dismembered Victorian valentines and the cutout figures of a nineteenth-century Sears, Roebuck catalog.

A masterpiece of crank art, inspired by Smith's readings in neurophysiology and the cabala, the film pushed collage animation to the outer limits of possibility. Smith's description—"consequent to the loss of a very valuable watermelon," the heroine suffers a toothache, undergoes dentistry, and ascends to heaven, returning to earth after being devoured by the philologist Max Müller on "the day Edward the Seventh dedicated the Great Sewer of London"—is not inaccurate.

Always in need of money, Smith offered to sell a reel of *No. 12* to Ginsberg for $110. In 1961, Ginsberg—then involved with Timothy Leary—organized a screening for Leary's wealthy friends to raise money for Smith's latest project, an animated version of *The Wizard of Oz*. The principal investors included supermarket heir Huntington Hartford, movie star Elizabeth Taylor, and a young millionaire, Henry Ogden Phipps, whose April 1962 suicide would effectively end the project. Discovering after a year that only twelve minutes of full color cell animation made using a multi-plane camera of Smith's design had been produced, most likely under the influence of LSD, the remaining backers withdrew. The failure of this project did not improve Smith's disposition. He began to drink heavily—but at the same time was consulted by the gallerist Richard Bellamy as to which psychedelics might best curb alcoholism.

Mekas recalled first meeting Smith at one of the Gramercy Arts' late 1963 screenings of the Warhol serial later known as *Kisses* and that, sometime after, Smith deposited his films at the Film-Makers' Cooperative. In early 1964, possibly through Leary and another crony,

Robert Frank, Smith became involved in the production of *Chappaqua*, a psychedelic vanity project directed by and starring twenty-nine-year-old cosmetics heir Conrad Rooks. That February Smith went with Rooks to Oklahoma and ran afoul of the law—held for a week in the Anadarko, Oklahoma, jail for public drunkenness and suspicion of stealing guns. While in stir he met and befriended several Kiowa who introduced him to their peyote rituals, which he taped for Moses Asch.

On returning to New York, having pawned his borrowed film equipment to purchase a train ticket, Smith found that his landlord had evicted him in absentia and had thrown his belongings—including paintings, films, books, and records—in the trash. The chronology is murky, yet it seems that, thanks to Ginsberg, *No. 12* and other film material had been entrusted to Mekas before Smith left town and, by the time he returned from Oklahoma, Mekas had had a chance to look at his films. In June 1964, Smith moved his special projector into the Coop and himself as well.

In his diary, Mekas described the "huge contraption" as "a wooden Trojan Horse with a projector, two slide machines, and various other windows and knobs and things for his square screen triple quadruple projection."

> He has been screening his fantastic cabalistic and superimposition movies and everybody is going nuts because these movies he made fifteen years ago are so fantastic.
>
> Crazy, evil, nasty, very brilliant, very learned in certain cabalistic and alchemist areas, like nobody else, and has been insulting everybody, spitting around, I don't know how I managed to make him show his films here, but he moved in and he is going to stay here with his machines and films for some time.

The first public screenings of Smith's early animations had been in October 1964 at the Washington Square Gallery, although Mekas began having private screenings of *Heaven and Earth Magic* (as he—or perhaps Ginsberg—called *No. 12*) at the Coop while planting Ken Kelman's essay in the fall 1964 *Film Culture*. But he waited until spring to announce Smith's presence on the scene.

An underground presentation at Le Metro served to whet the appetite for a member's only screening at the Film-Makers' Showcase (now at the seventy-five-seat theater, 83 East Fourth Street, next door to the East End), after which Mekas devoted most of his next *Voice* column to Smith. The lead was worthy of its subject.

> Does Harry Smith really exist? Is he a black or a white magician? Who will be the next victim of Harry Smith? What horrors is he preparing, and for whom?[5]
>
> For years, Harry Smith has been a black and ominous legend and a source of strange rumors. Some even said that he had left this planet long ago—the last alchemist of the Western world, the last magician. Then one day, last summer, a year ago, Harry Smith gave up the darkness and appeared in the open. He was still full of evil, hate, small curses, and sneers, but he came out.

Having established Smith as a match for the underground's favorite Marvel character, the Greenwich Village magus Dr. Strange, Mekas went on to describe, in ecstatic prose, Smith's films as "the most beautiful images conceivable," rewarded by the audience with "a huge ovation."

Next, Mekas scheduled *The Legendary Harry Smith* as a benefit for the filmmaker at the City Hall Cinema, a 576-seat house in the no-longer extant New York Tribune Building at 170 Nassau Street. Just down from the approach to the Brooklyn Bridge, the theater had been recommended to Mekas by Ken Jacobs. *Empire* had had its scandalous premiere there seven weeks before. Ten minutes into that projection, Mekas would report, "a crowd of thirty or forty people stormed out of the theatre into the lobby, surrounded the box office, [theater manager?] Bob Brown, and myself, and threatened to beat us up and destroy the theatre unless their money was returned. 'This is not entertainment! This movie doesn't move,' shouted the mob."[6]

---

5 Mekas may be referring to the rumor among the more supernaturally minded members of the underground that Smith had cast a fatal spell on rival sorceress Maya Deren.

6 Rudolph Siegel described a more thoughtful response in a letter published in the following week's *Voice*:

> After paying my $2 admission, I entered a comfortably appointed theatre and to the rousing notes of Beethoven's Fifth Symphony prepared myself for the upcoming presentation. About midway through the third movement the house was darkened

The crowd was incensed, as well they might be, for there were already paintings that did that very thing up at the Museum of Modern Art, where *The Responsive Eye*, a survey of perceptual abstractions curated by William Seitz, opened to much fanfare in late February.

6

By the time *Empire* premiered, *The Responsive Eye* was the most successful show in MoMA's history. Having only just grudgingly accepted Pop Art, *New York Times* critic John Canaday leapt to endorse the next big thing, inevitably dubbed Op Art.

Canaday heralded *The Responsive Eye* with a feature article in the *New York Times Magazine* that remarkably went out of its way to stress Op's affordability: "The average price of an optical painting being under $1,000, young couples are buying more optical art than any other form of abstraction." Canaday followed up with a review that began by calling the show one "worth the risk of being crushed and maimed to see, a risk that will certainly be involved." Was he speaking metaphorically? *The Responsive Eye* drew crowds as well as the animus of mandarin critics and radical artists—not least because in a third piece hailing this "brilliant show," the critic credited it with "all the theatricalism typical of avant-garde art in the past but with a most welcome difference"—craftsmanship.

Perhaps, but the precise color-based canvases of older painters Josef Albers and Ad Reinhardt, as well as the relatively subtle systematic abstractions by Frank Stella, Kenneth Noland, Ellsworth Kelly, and Larry Poons were overshadowed by the carnival midway of paintings trafficking in after-images, retinal fatigue, and optical illusions. The

---

> and a brilliant white square of light shone on the screen. It remained there, trembling slightly, for approximately 10 minutes, after which some dancing, greyish dots appeared, only to fade and be replaced by the indistinct image of a fog-shrouded Empire State Building. For the next half-hour, along with the other members of the audience, were witness [sic] to this wavering image of what the title of this presentation referred to as Empire. Upon the realization that this was going to be the whole show, I picked up my coat and left.

It is not known how many spectators stayed on or if any were present for the entire film. Certainly the filmmaker was not among them. According to Gerard Malanga, Warhol stood at the rear of the auditorium "observing the audience rather than the film": "People were walking out or booing or throwing paper cups at the screen. Andy turned to me, and in his boyish voice said, 'Gee, you think they hate it . . . you think they don't like it?'"

British painter Bridget Riley, painter of austere, overwhelming moiré patterns was the major new painter, albeit tarnished by her presence in what was perceived by some as a trendy, unserious exhibition.

As its title suggested, the show was predicated on viewer response, which might include vertigo or migraines. Some of the work was so irritating that museum guards petitioned for sunglasses. As though trying out a new dance, visitors were performing gyrations before the paintings. Critics observed them bobbing up and down, shaking their heads, even making little jumps in pursuit of ocular kicks. *The Responsive Eye* was the subject of a Mike Wallace report and a half-hour documentary by twenty-five-year-old Brian De Palma, who took particular pleasure in capturing the giddy opening-night crowd, which included women dressed in do-it-yourself op outfits.

So what if *Artforum* called the show "mindless"? (The review was written by Barbara Rose, then married to Frank Stella, doubtless embarrassed by his inclusion in the show.) Op appeared on the cover of *Vogue*. Teen magazines followed along with record covers, posters, and countless print ads. Taken as a phenomenon, the Op Art exhibit was itself a form of Pop Art. Bridget Riley took to *Art News* to complain that her work was being vulgarized in the rag trade. (The mad appropriation of Op Art designs by fashion, publishing and the media in general anticipates by some months Yves Saint Laurent's "high culture" introduction of the "Mondrian dress.")

The Responsive Eye pointed toward the psychedelic light shows and mixed-media head trips just over the horizon. Meanwhile, underground filmmakers were still pushing film toward its limits.

7

Four major underground movies and one mind-blowing masterpiece were shown that spring. These were Barbara Rubin's expanded *Christmas on Earth*, Warhol's *Empire* and *Poor Little Rich Girl*, and Michael Snow's *New York Eye and Earth Control*. The masterpiece was Harry Smith's *Heaven and Earth Magic*.[7]

7 By some accounts *Christmas on Earth* and *Heaven and Earth Magic* were screened for backers at the Coop on the same night in early March. Jealous of the attention paid Rubin, Smith hurled his projector out the Coop's fourth-story window. Yet others remember the projector being present at the City Hall screenings. In his diary, Mekas dates the projector incident some six months later and blames the fracas on Naomi Levine.

The poet Carol Bergé first saw it at Le Metro: "Smith, eyeglasses broken, irascible, nervous, says it was made from 1940–1960 roughly. He runs his own odd projector, mumbles clearly to the audience of mostly poets: 'this all takes place on the moon . . .'" If ever a movie seemed the product of an alternate universe, it was this. To call *Heaven and Earth Magic* "obsessive" scarcely does justice to the work's fantastically hermetic, labor-intensive quality and complex, paranoid underpinnings.

There is even a sort of narrative. Chasing a dog that stole her "very valuable" watermelon, the film's unnamed heroine visits a dentist, is given a powerful anesthetic, and ascends to heaven—in the dentist's chair. She subsequently toured the remarkably sinister "heavenly land," which is often located inside a giant head and is orchestrated by a dancing homunculus. Appropriate for Smith's projection apparatus, his heaven parodies Enlightenment notions of God the Clockmaker. Filled with rotating cogs and Rube Goldberg contraptions, this ethereal realm is something of a machine—although one continually on the verge of careening out of control. Despite some impressive cosmic plumbing, heaven's denizens are universally subject to violent fragmentation and dispersion.

As the heroine herself seems to lose parts of her body, the homunculus attempts a series of operations to put her back together. Nothing succeeds, however, until they are both devoured by the giant head of Max Müller, a nineteenth-century philologist and editor of *The Sacred Book of the East*. This is the climax of the heroine's trip: that the anesthetic has worn off is signaled by her dreamy descent to Earth, watermelon regained, passing through a cosmos of flying salamanders and enormous snow crystals in a roomy nineteenth-century elevator.

Bergé was knocked out: "The other viewers are mentioning Jung. I personally don't give a damn for Jung but I know art when I see it." The second screening, following a program of Smith's early animations at the City Hall Cinema on April 22, was more tumultuous. Harry, whom Bergé had befriended, was "amazed & confused by the good-sized audience." Bergé estimated the crowd at 300, although at least three-quarters walked out during the film with Smith railing at them as "fuck-ups."

Empire had provoked a riot. *Heaven and Earth Magic* caused an uproar. The City Hall screening was held the same month that Smith recorded the Fugs, and he evidently used a tape recording of the band as accompaniment for either the early abstractions or *Heaven and Earth Magic* (or both). When, according to Bergé, the City Hall projectionist put on the wrong music, Smith freaked, picking up the tape deck and hurling it from the booth into the theater. Mekas remembered the fracas a bit differently: Mid-screening "somebody said something" to Harry, who "grabbed the person, threw down the projector, and the tapes, and everything. The show stopped and he ran out and that was the end of the show. And that was also the end of the Fugs soundtrack."

In subsequent presentations, Smith accompanied his animations with the LP *Meet the Beatles*, a suggestion made by Barbara Rubin's traveling companion and Smith's youthful drinking partner and "spiritual wife," Rosebud Feliu or perhaps by Rubin herself. (It may even have been Smith's idea, as he also proposed scoring a film on Seminole craft that he shot in 1965 with the Beatles "because that's what the women hear when they're sewing.")

8

New York's reigning Beat that spring was William Burroughs. Yet Harry Smith was briefly Burroughs's equal in underground celebrity.

A photograph taken of a dinner hosted by Beat patroness Panna Grady at El Quijote, the Spanish restaurant on the ground floor of the Chelsea Hotel (where, thanks to the generosity of resident Shirley Clarke, Smith would soon be living), shows Burroughs and Smith (barely visible) as the guests of honor, seated beside Grady at the head of the table. Other illustrious diners include Warhol, Jack Smith, and Ronald Tavel.

Burroughs, however, was far more presentable. April 23, the day after Smith's raucous City Hall show, Burroughs read at a gathering in Wynn Chamberlain's Bowery loft. Invitees included Warhol, Diane Arbus, Richard Avedon, Frank O'Hara, Ted Berrigan, Larry Rivers, Barnett Newman, Jack Smith, and a reporter from the *New York Times*. Two days later Burroughs was a guest, along with Montgomery Clift, Judy Garland, and Tennessee Williams, at the "Fifty Most Beautiful People Party" that producer Lester Persky threw at the Warhol Factory. Also present was the new Girl of the Year.

More than Baby Jane, twenty-two-year-old, old-money Edith Minturn Sedgwick was zeitgeist-made material, heavy into diet pills and, like Barbara Rubin, a graduate of the Connecticut psychiatric hospital Silver Hills. Unlike the Park Avenue princess Baby Jane, Edie was emblematic of a new Upper East Side that came together in the spring of 1965 when the supremely fashionable discotheque Arthur opened on the site of the old El Morocco on East Fifty-Fourth Street and another disco, the Phone Booth appeared on East Fifty-Fifth Street, the former site of the Blue Angel supper club. Ondine, tucked up against the Fifty-Ninth Street Bridge, was one more.[8]

Having lived for several years in Cambridge while she attended Radcliffe and having come into an $80,000 trust fund, Sedgwick arrived in New York in late 1964, set up by her mother in a townhouse apartment off Madison Avenue on East Sixty-Fourth Street. Almost immediately, she introduced herself to Andy Warhol at the November 21 opening of his *Flowers* show at the Leo Castelli Gallery on Seventy-Seventh Street and encountered him more formally two months later at Persky's apartment; by March, she and her de facto manager Chuck Wein, a twenty-six-year-old friend from Cambridge, were Factory regulars.

Sedgwick first appeared in an unreleased feature called *Bitch*. On April 4, Warhol organized a shoot at the Brooklyn Heights home of the filmmakers Marie Menken and Willard Maas, hard-drinking friends of Edward Albee who were said to have inspired the battling married couple of Albee's 1962 play *Who's Afraid of Virginia Woolf?* Edie came along for the ride and was put on camera, one of four young people, including Gerard Malanga, John Hawkins, and Ronald Tavel, clustered around Menken and Maas. The couple do not seriously quarrel, and the movie is essentially a study of ensemble intoxication. Edie, whom Malanga introduces to the cast, is holding a joint as well as a glass; she becomes progressively animated and, while not upstaging Menken, establishes herself as a charismatic presence. As the movie ends, she tosses her drink in the face of an increasingly obnoxious Hawkins, prompting him to refer to her as "the daughter of a female dog," hence the title. (The movie was never released,

8 The opening of singles bars like Thank God It's Friday! and Maxwell's Plum, the arthouse preeminence of the new elegantly stripped-down Cinemas I and II on Third Avenue and East Fifty-Ninth Street, as well as the luxury department store Bloomingdale's, created a glamorous new urban arena. *Cosmopolitan* (September 1966) declared the area between East Sixty-Fifth Street and East Eighty-Sixth Street, Park Avenue, and the East River, the "Girl Ghetto": "No other parcel of Manhattan real estate is so well geared to the frantic pace of the single girl." The presumed abundance of single career women, especially stewardesses and a soupçon of call girls, as well as the well-established gay cruising area on Third Avenue in the high fifties added spice to the neighborhood.

presumably because Hawkins makes several tasteless references to Warhol's sex life.)

Impressed with Sedgwick, Warhol decided to make her the star of *Poor Little Rich Girl*, shot in mid-April in her apartment. There was no scenario: Edie was the text, both an object of study and a self-aware subject. Indeed, Warhol was so smitten with this poised ex-debutante, not only beautiful and full of grace but always "on," that he conceived the movie as the first installment of a twenty-four-hour epic that would reconstruct an entire day in the life.

Projecting a sublime indifference, the movie opens with a jerky pan and prolonged close-up of Edie's face—or to be more exact, what might be Edie's face. Her image is not only motionless but completely out of focus. Thanks to Warhol's ineptitude or a defect in the Auricon's lens, *Rich Girl* has the shallowest depth of field of any movie ever made. The image is as indistinct as a sonogram. Edie's features are veiled by the grain. This screen-filling pale oval is the pure beauty of cinema or it's nothing. ("The trouble with cinema until now was that it was always in focus," Ken Jacobs told Mekas.)

After three minutes, a male voice enunciates the title ("Poor . . . Lit-tle . . . Rich . . . Girl") and, as if on cue, Edie awakes. More erratic pans, an awkward zoom: She speaks, heard telephoning someone named "Roger." We learn that though her hair is swept up and piled in a perfect beehive she has supposedly been asleep for hours and that it is four in the afternoon. She phones a restaurant, ordering five orange juices and two coffees for delivery.

Haphazardly tracked by Warhol's camera, Edie takes off her dress and exercises, lying on her back in bed as she bicycles her legs in the air. Then, eight minutes into the movie, there is an instant of focus. Edie fidgets and ponders, sitting at the mirror amid the clutter of her toilette. She puts on a record of the Everly Brothers' greatest hits and bops a bit to the beat.

The LP plays continuously. Two cuts later "Crying in the Rain" is the heartbreaker, Edie hums and softly sings along. She is giving a performance. Intermittently, some fragment of her person (a part of her arm, the top of her head) comes briefly into focus—one such jolt is precipitated by a mere inhalation on her cigarette, the smoke from which is all but indistinguishable from her form. The first half of *Poor Little Rich Girl* is pure myopic naturalism. It is also another Warhol specialty, an exercise in frustrated voyeurism.

Upon discovering his mistake, Warhol reshot *Poor Little Rich Girl* some weeks later—this time in focus. After screening the material, he decided to combine the first reel of his first version with the second reel of the second (shot only days before the film premiered). And so, halfway through the movie, there is a shock: Form coalesces from chaos, blurry light condenses into images of fantastic richness, the Everly Brothers are supplanted, mid-song, by the Searchers singing Malvina Reynold's protest ballad "What Have They Done to the Rain." And here is Edie, still in her underwear—or rather the leopard skin brassiere and briefs she refers to in a later movie as her "special outfit." Always in character, she smokes pot from a long-stemmed Peterson pipe while carrying on a dialogue with an off-screen partner, Chuck Wein.

Edie and Chuck play at being a brittle, sophisticated couple—engaging in a form of weird domesticity after the previous night's party. It is, one gathers, late afternoon and it is all too much. While random zooms declare a democracy of interest—everything in the frame is equal—Warhol nevertheless lavishes long close-ups on Edie's wonderfully mobile, perfectly made-up face (a paint job that evidently took hours to achieve). The epitome of upper-class assurance, Edie is startled by a phone call. Off-screen, Wein adds to the confusion, blasting the Shirelles and yelling her name. Edie concentrates. Her mimed expressions as she listens and responds to the caller are a film within the film, something like a silent comic aria. Life goes on. Edie smokes more dope. The camera pans idly over her torso. Someone tosses her a dress. She disappears into the closet—emerging with a leopard skin coat over her underwear. The film begins to run out. The end credits include: "Camera by Andy."

Mekas devoted a column to it, reporting that "thirty or forty people" stayed through the movie after most of the audience, "expecting another *Empire*," walked out. Invoking the new documentaries—by the Maysles brothers, D. A. Pennebaker, Jean Rouch, and others—that had been showcased the previous summer at the Gallery of Modern Art's "Direct Cinema" series, Mekas called Warhol "the last word in the Direct Cinema."

Edie's conquest of the Factory coincided with Warhol's enhanced interest in youth culture music. He was going out to clubs. One photograph taken that spring has him posed with Malanga and Chuck Wein as a rock band at Steve Paul's West Forty-Sixth Street venue, The Scene. Another photo shows the mock Andy Warhol Fan Club that Billy Name created for a *Mademoiselle* fashion shoot.

The idea, according to Malanga, "was to equate Andy with a rock star." At the press opening of his *Flowers* paintings in Paris in May, Warhol announced that he had given up paintings and would hitherto be making only films. *Poor Little Rich Girl* had its first showing on Monday, April 26, 1965. That same evening Bob Dylan flew to London for an eleven-day British tour. Remarkably, Barbara Rubin had managed to get on the flight, handing Dylan a copy of her megalomaniacal project *Christmas on Earth Continued* to pass on to the Beatles.

That her "desired stars" included the Beatles, Dylan, and the Rolling Stones, as well as Kenneth Anger, Joan Baez, James Baldwin, Brigitte Bardot, Lenny Bruce, Marlon Brando, William Burroughs, Richard Burton, John Cale, Ray Charles, Ornette Coleman, Bette Davis, Salvador Dali, Marlene Dietrich, Diane di Prima, Walt Disney, Marianne Faithfull, Fellini, Janet Fink (later Janis Ian), Greta Garbo, Jean Genet, Allen Ginsberg, Flo and Ken Jacobs, Jasper Johns, LeRoi Jones, Sophia Loren, Norman Mailer, Groucho Marx, Marcello Mastroianni, Martha and the Vandellas, Jonas Mekas, Mario Montez, Jeanne Moreau, Picasso, Elvis Presley, Lou Reed, Soupy Sales, the Shangri-Las, Frank Sinatra, Harry Smith (who would also design the movie's "Fairy City"), Jack Smith, Ronnie Tavel, Elizabeth Taylor, Tiny Tim, Tuesday Weld, and Andy Warhol, conveys her state of mind. (In his September 1965 "Frets and Frails" column, Izzy Young reported deadpan that "it looks like Bob Dylan, the Beatles, Harry Smith, the Fugs, et al. will appear in Barbara Rubin's new movie," adding, "I'm playing Peter Pan.")

Dylan played Royal Albert Hall on May 9 and 10. Inspired by that, as well as Allen Ginsberg's presence, Rubin brought her manic organizational skills to the International Poetry Incarnation a month later at the same venue where an unexpectedly large (and mod) audience packed the hall to see Ginsberg, Lawrence Ferlinghetti, and Gregory Corso declaim with a gaggle of somewhat overawed but no less crazed British confreres.

"Rumor had it that one of the Beatles was there, hiding in a box trying desperately not to be recognized," wrote Peter Whitehead, whose *Wholly Communion*, a thirty-three-minute documentary of the event—slapdash immediacy heightened by Whitehead's improvisational technique—made the movie a planetary news bulletin. Barbara Rubin was filming as well.

9

As if in competition, Edie starred in nine Warhol films that spring. Over the next few months, four—*Kitchen*, *Beauty#2*, *Restaurant*, and *Space*—would be shown at the Film-Makers' Showcase, now located at the Astor Place Theatre on 434 Lafayette Street.

In a sense, she displaced the writer Ronald Tavel, whom Warhol had discovered in November 1964 reading from his unpublished novel at Le Metro and recruited to furnish screenplays for the Factory's new talking pictures. What the writer said was secondary. Warhol was taken with Tavel's nasal, Brooklyn-inflected drawl. The first talkie was *Harlot*, a riff on Jean Harlow with Mario Montez in the role of the platinum-haired star. The movie had its disastrous premiere in mid-January 1965 at Café au Go Go, which was then hosting regular Happenings.

Tavel's furious account was published in *Film Culture*: "A capacity crowd showed for the opening, college professors, writers, Hollywood actors, play directors, schoolteachers, artists, and reporters from a score of magazines."

> Conscienceless, the Café carted out a third-rate projector with a near-dead light bulb and focused the first reel on a tiny wrinkled bedsheet . . . And the screening was silent. The proprietor seemed impressed to learn that *Harlot* was a talkie: his machine would not carry sound. Furthermore, the screening began an hour-and-a-half late.

Still, "a good part of the audience took the fiasco good-naturedly, called it a pop happening." *Life*'s first female staff writer Shana Alexander wrote an annoyed account for the magazine, pointing out that although it was Warhol who urged her to attend the event, he himself was "too smart to waste the time." She left after watching Mario Montez salaciously devour a few bananas.

Harlot was followed by *Screen Test #1* and *Screen Test #2*, *The Life of Juanita Castro* and *Vinyl*, in which Edie had a cameo. All were written by Tavel, who appreciated Sedgwick's charisma but, despairing of her bratty unwillingness to learn lines, found it insufficient. He wrote one film for her, *Kitchen*, and another, *Shower*, which—coached by her would-be Svengali Chuck Wein to inform Warhol that she refused to be a mouthpiece for Tavel's "perversities"—Sedgwick flat out refused to make. Tavel turned it into a one-act play.

Offered first to Jerry Benjamin, *Shower* was directed by another veteran of Diane di Prima's Poet's Theater, John Vaccaro; it was paired with a staged version of Tavel's faux Cuban melodrama *The Life of Juanita Castro* (filmed and premiered in March with Marie Menken in the title role after Mario Montez declined) and, under the rubric of Theater of the Ridiculous, opened in late July at the Coda Gallery (formerly the Brata at 89 East Tenth Street). The sixty folding chairs were not sufficient. The program proved so popular that, after two weekends, the show moved to the St. Mark's Playhouse, where, along with an exhibit of "psychedelic paintings," it remained into September.

"*Shower* starts out rather promisingly," Elenore Lester wrote in the *Village Voice*. Two fully clothed actors, male (Vacarro) and female (Beverly Grant in her second off-off-Broadway dramatic role), are taking showers in adjoining stalls—"two alienated souls, encased in social trappings, separated only by a thin metal partitions."

> Soon only one shower is in use. A double striptease takes place. Sinuous Beverly Grant, Queen of the Underground Movies, stripped down to her transparent little panties and snaky black hair, pastes herself cheek to jowl against her partner and they gyrate in what may be described as a moving scene.

Acknowledging *Shower*'s appeal, Lester preferred the cross-dressed *Juanita Castro*, which she considered an excellent drag act, singling out Jeanne Phillips's Fidel Castro (in skirt and luxurious black beard), squinting defensively behind a pompously large cigar.

Clearly familiar with *Flaming Creatures*, Lester wrote that Jack Smith was a more forceful and "disturbing" proponent of the Ridiculous, whereas "the doings at the Coda are utterly comfy." More significant, she thought, was the burlesque of acting and role-playing in general, for which she credited Vaccaro who, in the spirit of Tavel's *Screen Test #1* and *Screen Test #2*, directed the actors while they were on stage.[9]

---

9 This may also be considered a Smithian strategy. Tavel was present for and may have appeared in *Flaming Creatures*; Vaccaro played the White Bat, among other roles, in *Normal Love*.

10

The summer that saw Edie's apotheosis was also the Summer of Rock. In June, the Bianchi Gallery on West Fifty-Seventh Street (infamous for having once given a show to a finger-painting chimpanzee) exhibited Bob Stanley's two-color portraits taken from action photos of the Beatles, Supremes, and Rolling Stones. None were as dynamic as Rosalyn Drexler's "Chubby Checker," exhibited the previous April, although the *Voice* dubbed Stanley "the Lautrec of the discotheque set."

The same month, the Five Spot booked a gritty white blues band, Adrian and the Hatreds, led by gravel-voiced Adrian Guillery, for a three-week gig during which, just down the block, the Fugs began a two-month midnight residency at the Bridge. Up at Columbia's Studio A, Bob Dylan—who would praise the Fugs as "very dimensional" during a rambling two-hour interview on Bob Fass's WBAI late night show *Radio Unnameable*—made twenty takes of "Like a Rolling Stone," extracted from a poem of rage written on his return from his British tour, and then recorded the rest of his first all-electric album *Highway 61 Revisited*. An unprecedented six-and-a-half minutes, "Like a Rolling Stone" was released as a single on July 20, five days before Dylan's epochal appearance at the Newport Folk Festival, backed by the Paul Butterfield Blues Band.

The Falling Spikes cut a demo that included "Heroin," "The Black Angel's Death Song" and Cale's surprisingly folkie rendition of "Venus in Furs." The band was getting gigs. April 8, the Spikes were at the East End, playing backup for *The Launching the Dreamweapon*, a mixed-media Happening coordinated by Angus MacLise and Piero Heliczer. The event included dancers, declamations, and Heliczer's new 8mm film *Dirt* projected through several veils plus a thick fog of incense. On May 28, the uncredited Spikes participated in *Rites of the Dream Weapon*, a MacLise–Frances Stillman production, advertised by flyer as an all-night "massed perfORMANCE | immense Spectacle | dark rituals of the N.Y. Underground" featuring "MUSICIANS, Dancers, STILTWALKERS | & troupe of lunar companions."

There was also short-lived stand at Café Wha? with the Warhol and future Ridiculous actress Elektrah!, who took an Indian lute called the *sarinda* as her instrument and, according to Sterling Morrison, played so strenuously her knuckles bled. And later that summer, on August 11, the Spikes were included in an abortive eight-hour spectacle held at the once grand, now moldering Broadway Central Hotel, located in the no man's land between the East and West Village. Still used for bar mitzvah celebrations, it was not yet the "Heroin Hilton" or welfare hotel it would become ("a cesspool of squalor and crime," per the *New York Times*). The Broadway Central hosted an event that Jack Smith called "Grass Busts of the Brassiere World," at which Smith would be arrested for assaulting an undercover police officer.

Dylan's "Subterranean Homesick Blues" had foretold a "must bust" in early May. One target was Allen Ginsberg, who had, along with Ed Sanders, formed an organization called LEMAR (for legalize marijuana) and thus, from a drug enforcement point of view, was Public Enemy Number 1. LEMAR held several demonstrations in early 1965 and on August 10 put out a press release revealing that days earlier four federal narcotics agents met with twenty-four-year-old musician Jack William Martin III, busted along with one Dale Wilbourne on July 29 for possession of marijuana, and offered him a lighter sentence if he helped set up Ginsberg. Refusal to cooperate, he was warned, meant his bail would be raised from $5,000 to $100,000 and he'd face additional charges. Meanwhile, Wilbourne was unable to make even $5,000.

Piero Heliczer organized a benefit, scheduled to run from 8:00 p.m. to 4:00 a.m., in the Broadway Central ballroom. According to a handbill printed for the occasion, Jack Smith would show *Normal Love* footage, Bill Vehr was bringing an early cut of his Smith homage *Brothel*, Barbara Rubin, back from London with an audiotape of the International Poetry Incarnation, would premiere a movie she shot there, *Allen for Allen*. The names Storm de Hirsch and Andy Warhol were also bruited. Heliczer, the evening's master of ceremonies, planned to read his poems. Ginsberg, Burroughs, Corso, and Gerard Malanga were promised as well. The Soviet poet Andrei Voznesensky was optimistically put on the bill along with the Fugs, the Falling Spikes, and a special performance of *Shower*. The handbill's promised "special guest appearance of 3 Federal Agents" suggested that the benefit would also be a Happening.

"It was a late summer night, narcotic night to overstimulate the Narcos and suffuse their brains with lurid imaginations," Smith wrote in an unpublished memoir. "A perfect lobster moon, full and orange, hung low in the horizon . . . The potted palms of the Broadway Central ballroom bristled and spawned strange coconuts." Jack Martin had just greeted the estimated 200 patrons when Heliczer interrupted with an announcement that gatecrashers had entered the ballroom, and that the performance would be halted until they had paid admission.[10]

Martin's observation that the narcotic agents who offered him a deal were in the room seemingly cued five men to storm the stage and grab him. "The Narco goon squad [had] altered their appearance in such a way as to appear as other than narcotics agents," Smith recalled, "But in their attempt to blend in with the beats who were actually dressed elegantly and conservatively," they appeared as outlandish caricatures, namely "moldy 1940's saloon-rioting waterfront scum of Flatulandia."

As the narcos in "pasty short sleeve Hawaiian sport shirts danced around Martin," the ballroom erupted in pandemonium. Hours later in Los Angeles, Watts would explode, triggering a weeklong uprising; at the Broadway Central, audience members demanded to see badges or a warrant. Court documents describe "a melee." The agents were "repeatedly kicked, struck and otherwise impeded" as they handcuffed Martin and dragged him up the aisle and out of the ballroom onto Mercer Street, physically confronted by the irate ticket taker Irene Nolan (featured in many of Heliczer movies) and dogged by Heliczer, who, by his own account, attempted to kick an agent, at which point he was jumped and thrown to the ground. All three were shoved into a waiting car from which they escaped but were soon recaptured.

Smith was now out on the sidewalk. Incensed to see an agent "smiling radiantly at Piero's cries of pain," he sucker-punched the narco from behind and "was instantly knocked to the sidewalk and sat upon by a gargantuan John Hall" (a reference to Maria Montez's well-built frequent leading man). Smith was arrested as well but, according to court papers, "the mob," now out on the street, "surrounded the cars so that the agents could not leave with their prisoners until they were rescued by a detail of thirty New York City policemen." The prisoners were taken to the fifth precinct in Chinatown, where, according to Heliczer, Smith was beaten by one detective; he then spent a week in the Tombs.

Ed Sanders's name had been on the LEMAR press release. In the nights that followed, his "secret" studio was twice broken into and ransacked by the narcotic agents, who, looking for drugs, instead

10 Smith remarks that the last occasion that the agents had Martin in custody they had searched him and found information regarding the upcoming benefit. Thus, their attendance was expected.

confiscated the entirety of his film footage, including two lengthy works in progress, *Amphetamine Head* and the orgiastic *Mongolian Cluster Fuck*. The following Sunday afternoon, the Village Gate hosted a follow-up benefit, "Young Beatniks Morally Opposed to Prisons."[11]

11

Three days later the Beatles played Shea Stadium. (Harry Smith and Rosebud managed to crash the gate. I did not.) Three days after that, a few miles away, Dylan appeared at the Forest Hills tennis stadium. (That very night Adrian and the Hatreds played live on Bob Fass's WBAI show *Radio Unnameable*.)

Primed by Newport, the crowd itself was electric. *Voice* reporter Jack Newfield compared the voluble struggle pitting Dylan's old and new fans to a "doctrinal fight between Social Democrats and Stalinists." The first half of the concert was acoustic. Dylan was introduced for the second half by none other than the hipster radio DJ and self-appointed Fifth Beatle, "Murray the K" Kaufman. Greeted with friendly boos, Murray told the crowd of "a new swinging mood in the country. Bobby is definitely what's happenin' baby. It's not rock, it's not folk. It's a new thing called Dylan."[12]

Soon after *Highway 61 Revisited* was released, the New Thing materialized on East Forty-Seventh Street. Gerard Malanga would call Bob Dylan's lone visit to the Warhol Factory a "non-event" but if so, it was one of the most mythologized non-events of the 1960s, not least as it has been recounted by the two men's various biographers. Self-invented geniuses with a sponge-like capacity to absorb ideas from those around them, Warhol and Dylan came from the hinterlands to conquer New York.

---

11 The case came to trial in April 1966. Martin and Heliczer were found guilty as was Smith, wearing a cast, having broken his leg in late February while in Brazil filming the Carnaval do Rio de Janeiro, a trip financed by rock 'n' roll lyricist Jerry Leiber and his wife, the actress Gaby Rodgers. The charges against Irene Nolan were dropped. The Peace Eye bookstore was busted on the night of January 1-2, 1966. Copies of *Fuck You* and *The Marijuana Newsletter* were confiscated along with Jack Smith's *Beautiful Book* and numerous manuscripts. Sanders was arrested and charged with possession of obscene literature with intention to sell—a misdemeanor that was dismissed at trial in May 1967.

12 I was there and enjoyed the tumult. Most of the kids, at least in my section, clearly supported Dylan's new material, bursting into laughter at the opening line of "Just Like Tom Thumb's Blues" (*When you're lost in the rain in Juarez and it's Easter Time to-o-o*) and singing along with "Desolation Row" and "Ballad of a Thin Man," three songs introduced that night.

Both were enigmatic personalities, prone to epigrams, fond of shades; each was the master of his scene. Best of all, their conflict—as befits two male deities—supposedly centered on a woman, Edie Sedgwick.

Looking for a genuine pop star, Warhol dreamt of shooting a movie with Edie and Bobby, while Dylan's agent, Albert Grossman, evidently had the same idea. In a sense, Dylan had already broken into movies. The verité filmmaker D. A. Pennebaker had already been commissioned by Grossman to document Dylan's British tour, resulting in the 1967 movie *Dont Look Back*.

Mid-July, Danny Fields and Donald Lyons brought the handsome singer-songwriter Eric Andersen, whom they caught at the Gaslight, to the Factory for a screen test. "Andy was excited to meet a genuine Person With A Bigtime Record Album," Fields recalled. Andersen subsequently appeared, along with Sedgwick, in *Space*. Subverted by Sedgwick and her snarky friends, Ronald Tavel's script quickly falls apart and the movie degenerates into a mock hootenanny with Andersen drafted to sing, ultimately leading the cast in a mocking version of "Puff (The Magic Dragon)."

Barbara Rubin sought to broker a more sensational alliance. Shortly before or, more likely, soon after Jean-Luc Godard's *Alphaville* opened the third New York Film Festival in early September, Rubin arranged for Dylan to sit for a screen test. Now spending most of his non-touring time at Albert Grossman's place in Woodstock, Dylan arrived in a station wagon driven by his consigliere in hipness, Bobby Neuwirth. Shepherded by Rubin, Dylan endured two uncomfortable screen tests and was also filmed with Malanga by Rubin using the 16mm Bolex that she and Malanga shared.

Dylan spoke briefly with Warhol and departed the Factory in possession of a larger-than-life silver "Double Elvis." The canvas was one of the twenty-two Warhol had silk-screened for his 1963 Ferus Gallery show in Los Angeles. The series seemed almost designed for strategic celebrity gifting and, by some accounts, Warhol had planned to present Dylan with the piece. However, according to Caffe Cino playwright Bob Heide, a witness to the transaction, Dylan simply said, "'I think I'll just take this for payment,' and walked off with an Elvis painting. Andy didn't say a word, but his face could have fallen through the floor."

Documented by Factory photographer Nat Finkelstein, the two Bobs, accompanied by Rubin, schlepped the seven by four-and-a-half feet canvas down in the freight elevator, puzzled over how to best fit it in into the station wagon, and, finally affixing it to the roof, drove back up to Woodstock. There Dylan traded the painting to his manager Grossman for a couch that, legend has it, was the very one seen on the cover of *Bringing It All Back Home*. (In 1988, Sally Grossman, still evidently in possession of that couch, sold the painting for $800,000. Now held by the Museum of Modern Art, it is valued at perhaps ten or twenty times as much.)[13]

The legend that, by way of showing his contempt for Warhol, whom he blamed for Edie Sedgwick's drug abuse, Dylan had used "Elvis" as a dartboard feeds into a narrative constructing a triangle with Edie as the tragic (or pathetic) muse for New York's two hippest artists. Each in his own way, both men were fascinated by her. Dylan may or may not have had a sexual relationship with her; Warhol was almost certainly, albeit briefly, in love.[14]

Dylan met Edie in fall 1964 through Bobby Neuwirth, who, as part of the Boston folk scene, knew her in Cambridge, and encountered Warhol soon after or perhaps before since she was photographed talking to the artist at his November 1964 Castelli show. If Warhol is to be believed, Edie eased Dylan's entry into uptown society. Warhol's memoir *POPism* mentions that in the spring of 1965, after the release of *Bringing It All Back Home*, Edie brought Dylan to a party at the gallerist Sam Green's new apartment on West Sixty-Eighth Street, where "they huddled by

13 Victor Bockris writes that it was "in Woodstock, not at the Factory that Edie got addicted to heroin" and that, as early as late summer, Warhol had decided she was impossible—"a compulsive liar and a bulimic who made herself vomit after eating [as well as] heavily dependent on amphetamine and barbiturates." (Who in the Factory wasn't a speed freak?) Jonathan Taplin, who began working for Grossman that same hectic summer, thought Sedgwick "one of the few people who could stand up against [Dylan's] weird little numbers." Grossman did seem interested in managing Sedgwick (at least according to Sedgwick), proffering recording contracts and the possibility of movies with Dylan, provided she cut her ties with Warhol.

14 Edie is widely imagined occupying a central role in Dylan's personal mythology, the supposed subject of three songs from *Blonde on Blonde* ("Just Like a Woman," "Leopard-Skin Pill-Box Hat," and "One of Us Must Know (Sooner or Later)") as well as the unreleased "She's Your Lover Now." It has also been argued that "Like a Rolling Stone" is a statement about Sedgwick and Warhol. (The 2006 movie *Factory Girl* purports to tell the story although the Dylan character is strategically renamed.) Dylan was ridiculed in several Factory productions, notably *The Bob Dylan Story*, in which a pair of groupies attack the star (played by lookalike Paul Caruso) and bind him to a motorcycle. Never released, the movie was filmed on October 6, 1966, some four months after the story of Dylan's motorcycle accident broke.

themselves over in a corner." On the other hand, Victor Bockris suggests that Edie had more Upper East entrée than Warhol, maintaining that Edie and Dylan both frequented the discotheque Arthur; he quotes one Factory source's recollection that "Andy would go there every night if they let him in. Sometimes they wouldn't let him in, but with Edie they let him in probably, and then that creep would be there."

Dylan was certainly comfortable uptown. That November, he and Brian Jones were photographed together digging the scene at the Phone Booth—there to celebrate the house band's first single, "I Ain't Gonna Eat Out My Heart Anymore," released by a New Jersey group called the Young Rascals.

12

Downtown, the Falling Spikes were performing under their new name. The band was an element in Angus MacLise's seven-part metaphysical variety show *Rites of the Dream Weapon*. The third part, "Mysteries of the Essence Chamber," promised dervish-like "random movements to the sounds of 'The Velvet Underground.'"

Rites of the Dream Weapon was but one component in the most elaborate show Jonas Mekas had yet produced. The New Cinema Festival, held at the Astor Place Playhouse for most of November, involved scores of artists, not all of them filmmakers, and some twenty presentations. Mekas hired John Brockman, a twenty-four-year-old MBA, to manage the program. Indeed, the series was originally called Festival of Expanded Cinema; Brockman changed the title in the ads. He also contributed to the event, contacting Gerd Stern and, through Stern, enlisting USCO, Jackie Cassen and Carolee Schneemann.

As all-encompassing as it was, the Festival drew from and overlapped with other presentations and was in some ways a recapitulation of work that had appeared during the past summer. MacLise and his then partner Frances Stillman had previewed *Rites* in May; Jack Smith's August benefit for his work-in-progress *Normal Love* involved musical accompaniment by MacLise and Walter De Maria; the movie itself was projected on a number of gossamer-clad dancers (Susanna De Maria, Jeanne Phillips, Mario Montez and Smith himself).

Other participants in the New Cinema Festival—notably the USCO group, sculptor turned light-artist Jackie Cassen and slide photographer Don Snyder—had been involved in *Psychedelic Explorations*, a didactic "non-verbal" evocation of "altered consciousness" staged that summer at the New Theater (formerly Arthur!) on East Fifty-Fourth Street under the direction of LSD apostle Timothy Leary. In September, Snyder subsequently showed his "light projections," accompanied by the Rebuffo Psychedelic Dancers at the Coda Gallery.[15]

In October, Nam June Paik, who had been studying video religiously for the past year, performed *Electronic Recorder* on two of the regular Monday night happenings organized by Al Hansen at Café au Go Go. The following Monday's presentation, involving composer Takehisa Kosugi, sculptor Shigeko Kubota, and cellist Charlotte Moorman, the first two associated with Fluxus, moved over to Astor Place the next evening—capping the Tuesday John V. Lindsay was elected mayor of New York. They were joined there by Paik for his *Electronic Video Projections*, an event that asked, "how to make a film without filming?" and—augmented with Stan VanDerBeek's hybrid film *Electronic Television*—proposed to convert film to live performance. VanDerBeek would have a one-man program over the Festival's final weekend while, after its premiere during the New Cinema Festival, Aldo Tambellini's *Black Zero* reopened at the Bridge on a bill with the Fugs.

Conceived as a meditation on blackness, *Black Zero* was Group Central's most ambitious work yet. Slides and films were projected on dancers, canvases, and, in some iterations, an expanding black balloon. A blinding shaft of white light was directed at the audience. Umbra poet Calvin Hernton declaimed his ferocious, Harlem riot–inspired "Jitterbugging in the Streets."

Harlem is the asphalt plantation of America
Rat-infested tenements totter like shanty houses stacked upon one
another

15 The New Cinema Festival roughly coincides with Ken Kesey's explorations in psychedelic performance. Kesey's first Acid Test was held on November 27, 1965. The next ones were staged throughout December in San Jose, Muir Beach, Palo Alto, and Portland. On January 8, 1966, there was an Acid Test at the Fillmore Auditorium in San Francisco and two weeks later, the three-day Trips Festival was staged at Longshoreman's Hall. Another parallel development was the soirees singer-songwriter commercial folkie Bobb Goldsteinn held in his duplex loft at the end of Christopher Street in late 1965. During the summer of 1966, Goldsteinn regularly staged these immersive audiovisual environments at L'Oursin, a Hamptons nightclub. According to Goldsteinn, Warhol, attended several "Lightworks" events and initially used the same term for *The Exploding Plastic Inevitable*, thus prompting Goldsteinn to send him a cease-and-desist letter.

> Circular plague of the welfare check brings vicious wine
> every semi-month, wretched babies twice a year, death
> and hopelessness every time the sun goes down

Jazz musicians Bill Dixon and Alan Silva improvised on trumpet and bass while Ben Morea's "clamorous machines" added to the cacophony one reviewer described as "a buzz saw gone berserk." *Black Zero*'s sensory overload was inspired more by the theories of Laszlo Moholy Nagy than those of Marshall McLuhan. Experiencing what he called a "theater of the senses," *Village Voice* drama critic Michael Smith was receptive yet confounded. "The eyes can't cope with the data and the sense of space goes vague; meanwhile, wild sounds have deadened the sense of time. It made me high. It also made me sleepy . . . For audiences at any future performances of *Black Zero*, I think the secret ingredient is LSD."

The New Cinema Festival brought together several tendencies. There were technology-driven productions like Paik's. VanDerBeek ("that old Barnum of cinema," per Mekas) used four movie and three slide projectors—at one point handheld and deployed in a ballet of projectionists. The climactic movie mural, created with a battery of five projectors, was greeted with prolonged applause. Snyder also employed multiple projectors in his *Epiphany of Light*. Where Mekas saw "color symphonies," Richard Kostelanetz, who published his account nearly thirty years later, less enthusiastically recalled nothing more than a boring "series of variously colored lights flashing upon a stage full of boxes, all to the accompaniment of several tapes of organized noises." Kostelanetz was similarly unimpressed by Cassen's *Polarized Light Sculptures*.

The USCO group, whose piece involved diffraction boxes, strobes, and slide projection, as well as live action, was a more rambunctious exponent of mixed media. Reporting on *Psychedelic Explorations* in the *Voice*, Mekas had deemed it something of a sales pitch. So did USCO. Bored by Leary's sanctimonious droning, they played a tape of Antonin Artaud's 1947 radio rant "To Have Done with the Judgment of God," by now an underground evergreen. "It stopped everything," recalled USCO's thirty-eight-year-old cofounder Gerd Stern, a German-Jewish refugee who had been part of the San Francisco Beat scene. "Then we stopped, and Timothy went on as if nothing had happened."

> Then about eight minutes later he was still going, and we played another little gob of Artaud screaming. Ralph Metzner [Leary's colleague] came running up to where our media control booth was and said to us, "You've broken your contract!" We just thought that was so terribly amusing.[16]

In somewhat the same spirit, Mekas claimed to be most impressed by the pre-show tuning of the projectors, slide machines, strobe lights, and oscilloscopes. He praised the more random quality of USCO's New Festival performance, *Hubbub*, which, in addition to the requisite light show, featured Carolee Schneemann and a group of dancers who, dressed as painters in white overalls that caught the images, took to the stage and began painting the screen, which would be ripped down to reveal another screen behind it.

Light shows were ubiquitous but just after 5:00 p.m. on Festival's ninth day, everything went dark. Not a blown mind but a blown fuse in an Ontario power plant killed the electricity through the Northeast. Thirty million people were suddenly without power just as the evening rush hour was underway. The Great Blackout was a cosmic component of the New Cinema Festival. Down in Philadelphia, Warhol and his entourage rushed back to New York hoping that the Blackout would still be going on. It was: "The moon was full and it was all like a big party somehow—we drove through the Village and everybody was dancing around, lighting candles," Warhol recalled. Stranded commuters were sleeping in doorways, while "cute National Guard soldiers" were helping people out of the stuck subways. "It was the biggest, most Pop happening of the sixties, really—it involved everybody." Full service in Manhattan was not restored until 3:30 a.m.

The festival within the Festival, namely *Rites of the Dream Weapon*, was a multipart exercise in low-tech music-driven total theater coordinated by MacLise, with Jerry Jofen, Jack Smith, John Vacarro, Don Snyder, and Piero Heliczer responsible for individual chapters. The pieces tended to the long and hypnotic. Their prototype was LaMonte

16 Stern remembered another disturbance caused by Harry Smith, who began screaming when he wasn't allowed in free. Leary and Metzner had a definite policy against free tickets. "Well, Harry got in free because I told Timothy that if Harry didn't get in free, there wasn't going to be a show and there'd be a riot."

Young's Theater of Eternal Music, whose events featured loud and repetitive drone music, as well as the burning of incense and the slow projection of patterns created by Marian Zazeela.

Mekas was selectively appreciative. He praised Jofen's *Rites of the Dream Weapon II: The Stagger Mass*, hailing its creator as "a master of destruction" who spiritualized reality by "dissolving time and space." Jofen's films involved multiple superimpositions that he rendered even more ethereal by projecting them on a screen of layered gauze, adding further dematerialization through the deployment of mirrors and lights. A form of glacial suspense was provided by Jack Smith, given dialogue which he pronounced so slowly that Richard Foreman recalled intervals of five, ten, and even twenty minutes between the lines (and "believe it or not: the wait was exhilarating"). Not surprisingly, Mekas reported, much of the audience walked out, thus missing what he considered "forty minutes of the most beautiful, spiritual, almost heavenly cinema experience."

According to an account in *The New Yorker*'s "Talk of the Town," MacLise's piece *Mysteries of the Essence Chamber* was set on a darkened stage resembling "the inside of a bombed-out church."

> An assemblage of objects, dimly lit by a revolving red-and-green beacon, was separated from the audience by a gauzy, see-through screen, on which two movie projectors were trained. One projector had no film in it, and the other had a short loop of film and kept repeating a few unrecognizable images [identified by another reporter as "a distorted view of a man holding his head"]. The operators of the machines occasionally held color filters in front of the lenses; sometimes they swiveled the machines around the room, so that the light from them shone briefly on the ceiling and walls.

The beam fell on members of the audience as well, the writer noted. Meanwhile, the costumed Lords of the Dream Weapon danced around the stage, intermittently accompanied by "a group of musicians known as The Velvet Underground, who specialize in 'mystical rock-'n'-roll'—a form of music that, they have explained, is attained primarily through the use of 'amplified distortion.'" *The New Yorker* found the noise level "literally deafening."

For John Gruen, who covered the event for the newly created (and short-lived) *New York World Journal Tribune*, this "confused ritual" was a two-a-half hour "endurance test" that in addition to the super-loud rock number included "endless raga scratching on stringed instruments," and a frenzied, painfully bright strobe-lit dance catharsis, capped by MacLise reading his poetry in a low monotone and near-total darkness.

Mekas faulted MacLise's two evenings for the chaotic disorganization he admired in USCO. Despite the artist's "visual mystico-ornamental flair and the beauty of texture (in image and sound)," *The Mysteries of the Essence Chamber* had "the distracting messiness of a dress rehearsal." On the other hand, Mekas praised MacLise's music for sustaining the mood of Piero Heliczer's final installment, *The Last Rites*, which he regarded as the Festival's most successful ritual. Heliczer, an Italian Jew, cast himself as a bishop: "Although he was 'acting,' there was something very real about it," Mekas felt.

Assisted by Mario Montez's Altar Boy, Heliczer blessed the projection of his 8mm film *Dirt*, a tiny flickering image cast upon a large screen flanked by six female dancers on two raised platforms. The projector itself was positioned among the musicians, who included MacLise on cimbalom, John Cale on viola, Tony Conrad on violin, and Jack Smith on tambourine. "There was something ambiguous, inexplicable in this blessing of the image," Mekas wrote. Improbably, the photographer Weegee showed up with one of his 16mm movies. "It was projected, as part of the ritual, and beautifully destroyed and incorporated into the whole by Heliczer."

Mekas also praised two theatrical rites, Smith's *Rehearsal for the Destruction of Atlantis* and Vacarro's *Rites of the Nadir*, which he associated with Artaud's Theater of Cruelty. Although the Great Blackout of November 9 would surely have impacted or greatly delayed, *Rites of the Nadir*, Mekas makes no mention of it other than to praise Vacarro as "a showman with a sense of timing and pacing." Vacarro also appeared as the Lobster in Smith's *Rehearsal*, described by Mekas as "an orgy of costumes, suppressed and open violence, and color."

Smith's piece was very much a working-through of his August 11th arrest. The script, which was later published in *Film Culture*, indicates that the show was meant to begin with the audience blindfolded and harangued by a "mad voice" asking them to imagine themselves winos, dazed and slumped on the pavement, picked up by the police, taken to a skyscraper prison and held for several days. After a diatribe on rats and narcos, the curtain rises on the twin queens of North and South Atlantis, seated together on a raised platform. Inviting the audience to remove their blindfolds, the twins begin extolling the properties of the marijuana that grows "so abundantly and legally" in Atlantis.

The two send their servant Mehboubeh for a match, over which they squabble as two narcos in rat masks and two dancers (one played by Smith) materialize on the stage. Mehboubeh reappears with a tape recorder, prompting a production number illustrating "the tawdry waste of wealthy manufacturers." The twins again quarrel over which would get the arm of an armchair that has only one arm and, as they are stuffed into a single polka-dot dress, struggle to drag it off stage. Enter the lobster with a "gigantic salad fork" and "crepe paper lettuce leaves," which he arranges around the throne platform—now an operating table—and plays the Vietnam tape.

The twins reenter carrying a pipe. They are arrested by the rat narcos and severed with a power saw as Mario Montez dances around the operating table to the music from *Swan Lake*. North Atlantis dies; South Atlantis expires in the lobster's arms. According to the script,

> The Lobster, in a daze puts lettuce leaves over the bodies & tries to cover them. The dancers, smiling like chorus girls come out one by one with the vegetables and put them on top of the littered operating table. The tape recorder and everything else in sight are placed in his arms and smoke erupts from the top of the platform as from a volcano, rises around the lobster and obscures the stage.

The play ends with the lobster screaming at the audience to replace their blindfolds and leave: "Get out I don't need you—Get out of my dressing room—*out*!!"

Rehearsal for the Destruction of Atlantis pushed the parameters of the Ridiculous into anarchic spectacle even as it elaborated on the political satire implicit in *The Life of Juanita Castro*. More significantly, *Rehearsal* was not just the only piece in the New Cinema Festival to invoke the escalating war in Vietnam—making use of a sound montage on the war supplied by Smith's activist friend David Gurin—but one of the first works of any kind to address the war.

The New Cinema Festival coincided with a season of heightened protest. On October 15, David J. Miller, a twenty-four-year-old pacifist associated with the Catholic Worker movement, was arrested after burning his draft card at a rally outside the Armed Forces Induction Center on Whitehall Street. The next day, more than ten thousand demonstrators marched down Fifth Avenue from Ninety-Fourth Street down to Sixty-Ninth Street to protest the war, heckled by an assortment of Goldwater conservatives, anti-Castro Cubans, and neo-Nazis, and later, by Conservative mayoral candidate William S. Buckley, who characterized the protestors as "mincing ranks" of epicene "young slobs." Two weeks later, Buckley was prominently featured in a pro-war march that the *New York Times* generously estimated at 25,000.[17]

The No!art group aside, protest art was rare. "End Your Silence," an open letter in opposition to the war, was published in the April 18, 1965, *New York Times* with over 500 signatories. Among the more respectable names were several prominent Beats, downtown art stars and fellow travelers: John Cage, Lawrence Ferlinghetti, Jack Gelber, Nat Hentoff, Dick Higgins, Donald Judd, Tuli Kupferberg, Jackson Mac Low, Peter Orlovsky, Carolee Schneemann. Susan Sontag, A. B. Spellman, Mark di Suvero, Stan VanDerBeek, and Israel Young.

Performed a month earlier at Carnegie Hall, Yoko Ono's *Cut Piece*—in which she sat motionless as members of the audience snipped off pieces of her clothing—has been retrospectively interpreted as a comment on American aggression in Southeast Asia. No such ambiguity exists regarding Peter Schumann's Bread and Puppet Theater. Pulling a rope affixed to a captive Jesus Christ, labelled Vietnam, their giant puppet, the snarling Uncle Fatso, was the star of the October 16 march, praised by the *Voice* as well as the old left *National Guardian*.

Soon after, Schumann began work on a Vietnam piece, *Fire*, dedicated to three Americans—Alice Herz, Norman Morrison, and Roger LaPorte—who self-immolated to protest the war. Performances began at the former Delancey Street Museum in late 1965. The piece is a series

17 I took the subway in from Queens for the October 16 march, which I joined at East Ninety-Fourth Street, and in addition to noting the friends I encountered (all, I now realize, red diaper babies) wrote in my journal that "the march was huge (more than one mile long, at least 20,000 peo.) The counterpickets were exceptional for their concentrated hatred. Signs: 'Get a Haircut,' 'May God Have Pity on Your Souls,' 'Go Back to Cuba,' 'This March is a Disgrace' etc. Plus some egg throwing and a few fights which I heard about but didn't see." The day before *Rehearsal*'s first performance, David McReynolds and four others burned their draft cards at a public rally organized by the Committee for Non-Violent Action in Union Square.

of nine tableaux in which masked players stand in for the inhabitants of a Vietnamese village. Clearly meant to represent the dead, the peasants perform routine communal actions in a ceremonial silence, ending in an atrocious cacophony as the village is bombed.

13

From *Mysteries of the Essence Chamber* to those of suburban New Jersey. One night after performing at the New Cinema Festival, the Velvet Underground was across the Hudson, at Summit High School opening for a local garage band, the Myddle Class (whose bass guitarist would later join the Fugs).

The gig was arranged by the band's manager, the New Jersey–based hipster journalist Al Aronowitz, whose three children were sometimes babysat by Barbara Rubin; Ken and Flo Jacobs came along to give their support. Still, Angus MacLise had no interest in swerving from "ritual happenings" to a high school dance (although, given his interest in rock 'n' roll performance art, Tony Conrad might have). Thus, the Velvets needed a new drummer and Sterling Morrison quickly recruited Maureen (Mo) Tucker, a high school friend's Olatunji-mad kid sister.

As recalled by Morrison, the band opened with "There She Goes Again," played "Venus in Furs" and ended with "Heroin." The set caused a stir—"the murmur of surprise that greeted our appearance as the curtain went up increased to a roar of disbelief once we started to play 'Venus' and swelled to a mighty howl of outrage and bewilderment by the end of 'Heroin.'" Half the audience left.

Back in New York, the band appeared in Piero Heliczer's latest 8mm opus *Venus in Furs* (described for a public screening at the Bridge as a movie "where a nun and a nurse go to hell for their sinful life in St. Vincent's Hospital"). It was shot in his loft at 450 Grand Street, a block east of the Winsor Theater. The shoot might be considered a Barbara Rubin production. She brought a CBS-TV news crew down to Grand Street for a story on underground movies that would be telecast on New Year's Eve. Faces painted and without shirts, Cale, Morrison, and Reed performed "Heroin," with Heliczer joining in on saxophone. Tucker, now part of the band, wore a bridal gown and a mask while a smirking Rubin (who also arranged to have photographer Adam Ritchie document the shoot) appeared as the nun.

Undeterred by the reaction at Summit High (and the fact that he thought one of the Velvets had swiped his Wollensak tape recorder), Aronowitz secured them a residency at MacDougal Street's most venerable tourist trap, the goth-themed basement cave Café Bizarre, in late December—six nights a week, continuous forty-minute sets, with twenty-minute breaks. Drums were not allowed; Mo Tucker had to make do with a tambourine. Although the band mainly played covers of Chuck Berry and Jimmy Reed, one night they performed "The Black Angel's Death Song."

According to Morrison, the owner warned them they would be fired if they ever played the song again, "so we started the next set with it" and avoided having to work New Year's Eve. It hardly mattered because, functioning as the Factory's talent scout, Barbara Rubin had been bringing her friends—including Mekas, Malanga (who was inspired to join in with his "whip dance"), Paul Morrissey (who would take credit for discovering the band), and Warhol—to hear the Velvets, and on January 3, 1966, they made their way to the Factory to jam with Warhol's new Girl of the Year, the twenty-eight-year-old German actress Christa Päffgen, recently arrived in New York. Calling herself Nico, her credentials were impeccable: in addition to modelling, she appeared in Fellini's *La Dolce Vita*, had a son by French movie star Alain Delon, hung out with the Rolling Stones and knew Bob Dylan, whom she befriended in Paris in the summer of 1964 and who gave her one of his most beautiful songs, "I'll Keep It with Mine."

Warhol brokered a melding of the Velvet Underground and Nico (for whom Reed would write two new songs, "All Tomorrow's Parties" and, supposedly inspired by Edie, "Femme Fatale"), assuming the role of manager. And so, at long last, the Factory merged with rock.

14

For Warhol, the nine-month Sedgwick era ended with a staged disaster. Warhol asked Robert Heide—whose one-act Caffe Cino production *The Bed*, among the first explicitly gay plays to be staged in New York, had been filmed in November—to write a scenario on the 1944 death of the so-called Mexican Spitfire, film star Lupe Vélez. Or rather the legend: In Kenneth Anger's tabloid version, recounted in *Hollywood Babylon*, Vélez planned an elegant suicide by Seconal but winded up drowning, face down in the toilet bowl.[18]

18 Produced in 1966, José Rodriguez-Soltero's fifty-minute feature *Lupe* featured Mario Montez as the tragic actress. A persistent mess set to a mix of schmaltzy Spanish ballads, the Rolling Stones, flamenco, and Vivaldi, it's essentially generous in providing a vehicle for Montez, the most appealing of drag queens and poignantly unconvincing, who, sinewy and big featured, carries the movie on his broad shoulders.

Lupe was shot in Panna Grady's well-appointed apartment at the Dakota on the night of December 26–27. The set was tense. According to Victor Bockris, just before shooting commenced, "Bobby Neuwirth arrived with a handful of LSD and took Edie into a side room . . . Bobby slipped Edie some acid and made a date for her to meet Dylan later that night at the Kettle of Fish." Given the lateness of the shoot, the date would have had to have happened the next night when, coincidentally or not, Warhol invited Heide for a rendezvous at the same MacDougal Street bar.

Heide arrived and was surprised to find a distraught Edie sitting alone and learn that *Lupe* had already been shot. The triangle was complete when Warhol made his entrance ("very natty in a blue suede outfit") followed by Dylan (or vice versa) who after some sullen chitchat suggested to Edie that they split, which they did, jilting Warhol—or so it would seem, as some thought they heard Edie complaining that Warhol was rejecting her. Various sources place Edie, Andy, and Bobby among the revelers at Arthur on December 28. (According to one, Dylan unceremoniously booted hopelessly uncool Phil Ochs out of an uptown-bound cab.)

Heide's dramatic account of the evening ends with him walking Warhol over to 5 Cornelia Street, the tenement from which, a year before, the dancer Freddie Herko had jumped naked out a fifth-floor window to his death. Then, according to Heide, Warhol (who had just committed Edie's faux suicide to celluloid) wondered when she would kill herself, adding that "I hope she lets us know so we can film her."

The last installment of the "Poor Little Rich Girl" saga, *Lupe* opens with Edie asleep—in focus and in color. In eight months, Sedgwick's shtick had gone stale. Face doubled in a mirror as if hyperbolizing her narcissism, she wakes, goes for a cigarette, rummages around in bed, and darts out of camera range to retrieve the telephone. Factory factotum Billy Name appears to chat as Edie fusses with her makeup. Then, as was his specialty, he gives her a haircut. Edie shrugs, flinches, responds to herself, sends him on some sort of errand, and studies her image with total absorption. The reel ends with a brief shot of her lying with her head cradled on the toilet.

The second reel has Edie dining in solitary splendor. She is trying to act or, if Bockris is to be believed, tripping on LSD. Edie nods out over her plate and then recovers with a start. As the camera engages in unmotivated tilts, she puts on the radio, toys with her food, fiddles with the table setting. She is now interesting only in so far as she is imitating "Edie Sedgwick" in an "Andy Warhol film." (A third reel featuring Jason Holliday, the subject of Shirley Clarke's 1967 *Portrait of Jason*, was unused and might be considered a footnote to Clarke's film.)

Lupe premiered in early February as a double projection, paired with *More Milk, Yvette* (based on another Hollywood scandal, with Mario Montez as Lana Turner). The bill was given a six-day run at the new Film-Makers' Cinematheque, relocated to the basement of the Wurlitzer building on West Forty-First Street. According to Bosley Crowther, who unenthusiastically previewed the event, the films were augmented by "a performance by a group of rock 'n' roll singers called the Velvet Underground. They bang away at their electronic equipment, while random movies are thrown on the screen in back of them."[19]

19 The beat went on but for Edie, the party was nearly over. She did not entirely disappear. Having initiated a month-long affair with John Cale, she did participate in the Velvet Underground's first gig at the New York Society for Clinical Psychiatry banquet. Soon after she staged her own breakdown, a public fight over money with Warhol in front of the Ginger Man bar.

7

Babushkaville Explodes, 1966–67

In which strobe lights proliferate as, conquering St. Mark's Place, Multi-Media goes Pop. Warhol and Dylan create their masterpieces. Jimi Hendrix wows MacDougal Street and Sun Ra settles in the East Village, where Timothy Leary puts on a show. The Mothers upstage the Velvets. Black Mask shuts down the Museum of Modern Art, Ridiculous Theater crosses the line, and Barbara Rubin graduates.

> *I liked the idea going from an absence or minimal sense of impression to one of a complete battering of the senses.*
>
> —Tony Conrad on *The Flicker*, *Film Culture* (Summer 1966)

Movies were no longer enough. Now there was what psychiatrists called *sensory overload*.[1]

Andy Warhol, Uptight—as Barbara Rubin named the presentation that, packaging *Lupe* and *More Milk, Yvette* with a performance by the Velvet Underground, played the 41st Street Cinematheque for a week in early February 1966—was a harbinger of what was to come, as well as the Factory's belated response to the New Cinema Festival.

1 Although traceable to the German sociologist Georg Simmel's seminal 1903 essay, "The Metropolis and Mental Life," the psychiatric term "sensory overload" (a neologism for "over-stimulation") began to turn up in scholarly journals in the early 1960s and then in the jargon of artists like Gerd Stern influenced by Marshall McLuhan and later Timothy Leary.

Having missed the boat, Warhol was playing catch up. His official contribution to the festival was, as he realized, severely anti-climactic: "Everyone is being so creative that I thought I would just show a bad movie," he explained in the *Village Voice* ad. "The camera work is so bad, the lighting is awful, the technical work is terrible—but the people are fantastic."

Shot less than a month before its November premiere, *Camp* was a disorganized impression of a TV variety show with Gerard Malanga, Tally Brown, and Jack Smith among the performers and, as a sort of joke on the Factory, jazz pianist Ramsey Lewis's hit recording of "The 'In' Crowd" intermittently heard in the background. As on a TV show, the performances were given before an unseen live audience that included the photographers Diane Arbus and Fred McDarrah. Then, Barbara Rubin led Warhol to the Velvet Underground. Mixed media followed.

The band's first appearance under Warhol's management came on the evening of January 13 at the Delmonico—the staid hotel on Park Avenue and Fifty-Ninth Street where some eighteen months before, in a historic encounter brokered by Al Aronowitz, Bob Dylan met the Beatles. The occasion chosen for the Velvet Underground premiere was the forty-third annual dinner of the New York Society for Clinical Psychiatry.

Billed as "The Chic Mystique of Andy Warhol," this wildly disruptive event was meant to acquaint the assembled doctors with the latest developments in the "creative process." It also served as a tryout for *Andy Warhol, Uptight*. Films were shown as the Velvets performed an ear-splitting set. For dessert, Rubin ran amok among the shrinks and their spouses brandishing her handheld spotlight—Mekas filming as she shouted impertinent questions regarding their sexual practices and equipment.

Headlined SHOCK TREATMENT FOR PSYCHIATRISTS, Seymour Krim's report in the *New York Herald Tribune* was truer than he knew. Lou Reed, Barbara Rubin, and Edie Sedgwick had all been institutionalized as adolescents (Reed even received shock therapy) and their performances surely had an element of payback. "I supposed you could call this gathering a spontaneous eruption of the id," one psychiatrist told *New York Times* reporter Grace Glueck while another suggested to Glueck that if she really wanted "to do something for mental health" she should "kill the story."

Two weeks later, the Velvet Underground had another uptown gig at the Phone Booth and a few days after that made a TV appearance with the Fugs. The bands had been invited to appear on David Susskind's *Open End*, a weekly discussion show telecast over WPIX. The theme was the new Bohemia. After a midtown meeting with the producers, a bus rounded up two of the Fugs and the Warhol contingent—Malanga, Rubin, Reed, Cale, and Danny Williams—along with John Wilcock of the new bi-weekly *East Village Other* (*EVO*).

Up in the studio, eighteen new bohemians formed a circle at Susskind's feet as he sat on a low stool earnestly trying to figure out where they were at. (Warhol typically positioned himself as a spectator). Hoping for ambience, the show put down a small Oriental rug and a candle planted in a wine bottle. Sanders (wearing a Fugs sweatshirt) and Kupferberg (looking near professorial in a mock turtleneck sweater and jacket) did most of the talking. The poets attempted to engage their clueless host. Reed smirked and Cale languidly ate a banana, as did Malanga, who also performed his whip dance, while camera-toting Rubin and Williams buzzed about, spooking the show's technical crew.

Joints were passed and Wilcock noted that Susskind seemed unnerved: "The roving cameramen, the disorderly group, the smell of pot, the occasional clicks, shrieks and catcalls from Barbara are apparently so much more than he expected." Discussion was cut short midway through what was intended to be a two-hour show.

2

There were other means to assault the audience. The February performances of *Andy Warhol, Uptight* had made particularly aggressive use of light. At one point, a baby spot was turned on the audience—footage taken by Williams shows the respectable looking crowd flinching and shielding their eyes. This apparently cued Rubin to rush into their midst, sun gun in hand and shouting the same questions ("Is your penis big enough?" and "Does he eat you out"?) with which she had startled the shrinks.

Williams also manned a calibrated flashing stroboscopic light, having spent nights at the Factory experimenting on himself with multiple strobes—an activity parallel to the investigation carried out over the past year by Tony Conrad. Around the time *Andy Warhol, Uptight* concluded its engagement at the Tek, as the 41st Street Cinematheque was known to habitues, Conrad screened the final version of his first film, half an hour of black and clear frames in various rapid-fire patterns that he considered the ultimate application of the strobe: *The Flicker*.

Conrad, who participated in the New Cinema Festival as a member of the Theater of Eternal Music, adapted analogous principles involving repetition and harmony to the cinematic deployment of intermittent light. Although feeling little affinity with the various light shows he did note *The Flicker*'s relationship to Op and Psychedelic art. Indeed, Conrad had been fooling around with rhythmically orchestrated light for several years. Removing the lens from a 16mm projector and running it without film, he entertained his Ludlow Street roommate Jack Smith by casting a stroboscopic beam on their next-door neighbor, *Flaming Creatures* star Mario Montez.

A tape recording of one such session dated March 5, 1963, with the label "Mario and the Flickering Jewel," preserves Smith's delighted gasps and groans in response to the effect: "Oh, Tony can you see that? Have your actual eyes, in reality, ever seen anything as exaggerated and raving as this?" Smith wondered if he might reproduce this marvelous effect in his new film although Conrad advised him it was it "technologically unfeasible." Nevertheless, Conrad's interest in the process was confirmed by the climax of a weeklong rock-and-roll extravaganza, staged at the Brooklyn Fox theater by Murray the K in May 1963, which, he would write, "built up excitement to a fantastic and nearly frenzied peak by using a strobe light."[2]

Conrad's ideas were further crystalized by William Burroughs's article "Points of Distinction Between Sedative and Consciousness-Expanding Drugs," published in the December 1964 *Evergreen Review*. "Anything that can be done chemically can be done in other ways, given sufficient knowledge of the mechanisms involved," Burroughs wrote, citing the research of the British neurophysiologist William Grey Walter, who suggested that the rapid light flashes broke down barriers to stimulate other regions of the brain, noting that this overflow ("hearing colors, seeing sounds and even odors") was characteristic of consciousness-expanding drugs. That *Fuck You*'s February 1965 "mad motherfucker issue" included doodles of a light zapping some amorphous scribbles and called itself "the magazine of the BRAIN BLOB STROBO-SUCK!" suggests additional awareness of the strobe.

2 Conrad's interest in rock-and-roll predated his brief association with the inchoate Velvet Underground. So, of course, did Warhol's. In the first chapter of *POPism*, he recalls the gallerist Ivan Karp bringing him to the New York Academy of Music for "Murray the K's Twist Party" on December 28, 1961. Murray's subterranean popularity was sufficient to rate a namecheck in *The Sinking Bear*.

By April 1965, Conrad had developed a number of strobe patterns, which he began filming that summer and spent some months editing, during which he wrote to Henry Romney (a friend of the Factory who, as an employee of the Rockefeller Foundation, was able to spirit Warhol and crew into the foundation offices on the forty-fourth floor of the Time-Life Building to film *Empire*) that his new film would be "a hallucinatory trip through unplumbed grottoes of pure sensory disruption."

Premiered at the Tek in March 1966, *The Flicker* was, per Mekas, "one of the most violently discussed movies in town." Conrad prefaced the film with a stern, somewhat snarky disclaimer—warning that the film could induce epileptic seizures in certain spectators and that audience members remained in the theater at their own risk. In a time-honored exploitation gimmick most recently employed by Willian Castle for his 1958 horror film *Macabre*, a doctor was said to be in attendance for all screenings. This was *The Responsive Eye* with a vengeance. Spectators reported headaches, eye strain, and acute nausea as well as all manner of color hallucinations.

Writing in the upstart *East Village Other*, Richard Preston noted that "by the time twenty-five minutes have passed, one's senses are completely disoriented." The screen appeared to have moved forward several yards. The theater walls of the cinema also seemed to move closer and simultaneously have a transparent quality. Much of the audience fled. "The people walking out looked rather like ghosts," Preston concluded. "They may well have been."

3

The New Cinema Festival had wound down in early December. The last presentations—notably the Theatre of Eternal Music and happenings by Claes Oldenburg, Robert Rauschenberg, and Robert Whitman—were presented at the Tek.[3]

3 *Moviehouse* was Oldenburg's last and most conceptually refined Happening—an environmental shadow play. Patrons were seated in a side section of the theater. The action was staged in the larger central section where eight performers enacted the roles of ushers and spectators. The theater was dark; the 16mm projector ran without film, producing a conical beam of white light that served to cast the performers' shadows on the screen. By way of accompaniment, an amateur pianist played the sing-song folk ditty "Oats, Peas, Beans and Barley Grow." Oldenburg did not consider the piece a success precisely because it was. Too many people attended.

USCO's *Hubbub* was revived there as well. Neither Preston nor Kostelanetz were much impressed. Bosley Crowther, who reviewed it for the *New York Times*, hated it even more than he would *Andy Warhol, Uptight*. Amid this push for visibility, John Brockman had connected with Broadway producer Michael Myerberg, who held the lease on an airplane hangar at Roosevelt Field on Long Island and—having failed to convert the hangar into a movie studio—planned to create a techno-fabulous discotheque.

Myerberg had already talked with various people—including Murray the K and, on behalf of Andy Warhol, Paul Morrissey—he hoped to enlist in his project. Kaufman's appeal for teenagers was self-evident, while Myerberg saw Warhol as a magnet whose aura and entourage could draw glamourous people from Manhattan out to Garden City. By some accounts, Warhol (who would soon take out an ad in the *Village Voice*, offering to endorse "clothing, AC-DC, cigarettes, sound equipment, ROCK N ROLL RECORDS, anything, film and film equipment, Food, Helium, Whips, MONEY!!") was tendered $40,000 to hang out. True or not, the Factory recognized an opportunity to realize a long-standing interest in the music business.

Morrissey would credit himself with the notion that the Factory should bring their own rock band to Myerberg's party. More likely, Barbara Rubin got the message and recognized an opportunity for the Velvet Underground, escorting first Malanga and then Warhol, Morrissey, and Mekas, as well as Ed Sanders, down to Café Bizarre.

Brockman chartered a bus and organized an excursion to the Myerberg's hangar, including USCO, a Factory delegation and members of Ken Dewey's Action Theater, which had also contributed to the New Cinema Festival: "We were supposed to make proposals on how to turn it into this kind of avant-garde rock music palace," Gerd Stern recalled. Likely, *Hubbub* (which had its well-publicized six-night run at the Tek in late January) and *Andy Warhol, Uptight* (which followed it two weeks later) were de facto auditions for the Myerberg club.

Warhol even imagined that the place might be called Andy Warhol's Up. Unfortunately, Myerberg was negatively impressed with *Andy Warhol, Uptight* while Murray the K, whose involvement with the project was not yet known, would later tell the *Times* that Warhol had "wanted to come in with his films, but I said, 'My God I can't have these movies of guys with whips and this whole fetish thing.' So he [Warhol] took our idea and opened his own place"—which is roughly what happened.

Morrissey and Warhol were blindsided when, two days after *Andy Warhol, Uptight* concluded its run, Myerberg announced a new "dance hall" integrating multiple-screen images with live music that would open as Murray the K's World on March 18. USCO was hired to develop the equipment. Stern remembers having thirty slide screens and an early video projector, a Swiss-made Idofor that could deliver an image twenty-five-feet across and was fed by three cameras. Feeling bad that Warhol had been passed over, Stern offered to collaborate but, "typical of Andy," Warhol had no interest. Thus, USCO supplied thousands of slides and over two hours of 16mm footage, mostly shot by their new, twenty-seven-year-old resident filmmaker Jud Yalkut.

Meanwhile, the Velvets—whom Warhol brought to the Ann Arbor Film Festival in mid-March—were still under the impression they were being considered to open the club. Back in New York, the two native Long Islanders, Reed and Morrison, visited Myerberg's disco-in-progress where they were surprised to encounter the Young Rascal's lead singer, fellow Syracuse University alum Felix Cavaliere. The Rascals' "Good Lovin'" was a #1 hit, their first LP was about to be released, and they were a popular local group. It seems overdetermined that they would open Murray the K's World, although Morrissey hints that organized crime dictated the choice.

Having promised to provide the Velvets with a venue, Morrissey scrambled to secure the Open Stage, upstairs from the Dom—a space he learned of from Jackie Cassen, who, coming off her performances as part of the New Cinema Festival, had put together a light show named *DMT* (for dimethyltryptamine, a psychedelic drug that produced brief but intense trips) that ran at the Bridge throughout March.[4]

Thus, Morrissey found his band through Barbara Rubin, his venue courtesy of Jackie Cassen, and the words "inevitable" and "erupting" from the back jacket copy of Bob Dylan's *Highway 61 Revisited*. (The word "plastic" was his own contribution.) An ad for the *Erupting Plastic Inevitable* was hastily placed in the *Village Voice*, inviting patrons to "come blow your mind." The same issue had a coincidental answer ad: "Why Bother with LSD? See the Fugs."

4 *DMT* provided the title and basis for Yalkut's three-minute flicker film. Partially scored to the Beatles' "The Word," it was constructed out of stroboscopic solo dancing, moiré patterns and Cassen's slides (clashing diagonal lines and concentric circles).

The hall "had absolutely no charm whatsoever," John Cale recalled. "You trudged upstairs to this place that smelled of urine. It was filthy and had no lights." The Factory only got access to the Open Space five hours before opening night. A hastily spray-painted banner of the sort that fluttered above MacDougal Street coffeehouses was hung from the Dom's upper windows; Gerard Malanga began whitewashing the interior walls. Warhol's crew lugged three film projectors downtown, as well as assorted lights and gels, several strobes and a Jazz Age rotating mirrored ball, found in a thrift shop, that was lying around the Factory floor.

Cassen, who received billing on the initial ads, supplied several Kodak Carousel slide projectors, as well as hand-painted slides. "They didn't have very good equipment," she recollected. "They were working on a wing and a prayer." Cassen herself was working a double shift across the street at the Bridge—in addition to *DMT* she was involved in a "Dance Light Carnival" that played for the two nights before the Warhol show opened.

The projectors were placed on the balcony; the strobes were positioned onstage. There were also moving handheld sun guns. The star effect was the mirrored ball, a triumph of strategically applied camp that soon became a disco cliché: "We revived the look," Warhol would claim in *Pop-Ism*.

4

The *Erupting* (soon "Exploding") *Plastic Inevitable* (*EPI*) had its premiere Friday, April 1. So did Murray the K's World. Indeed, such was the temper of the times that Cheetah, another techno-discotheque located on Broadway and Fifty-Third Street, was announced that day.[5]

Customers for the World were given a handbill at the door.

> Bring your shades 'cause what you're gonna see will strain your eyes! You will have a new attitude and we defy you to maintain your cool. If you're up tight. Come to where the lights change, and you'll change right in the middle the most revolutionary thing that ever happened to the world of entertainment! It's a trip!

5 In addition to "a giant dance floor and a main room seating 1,800," Vincent Canby reported in the *New York Times*, "Cheetah will have other rooms, upstairs and down, devoted to television, Scopitone, esoteric publications and movies in the Andy Warhol-Batman genre, plus a street-level boutique offering 'mod' merchandise."

It *was* a trip out to an old airplane hangar in Garden City. The *EPI* issued no disclaimer.

As observed by John Wilcock in *EVO*, "about one-third of the tables in the vast hall filled up as soon as the ticket office opened." The bar, however, did not begin serving until 10:30. Malanga was still on a stepladder painting the rear wall while the movie *Couch* was being projected on it, producing what Wilcock found "an interesting three-dimensional effect." Rock music was heard but few people got up to dance; most preferred to watch as two projectors in the balcony ran two separate movies on either side of the stage. Then the light show began: "Colored floodlights stabbed out from the corners, caressing the dancers with beams of green, orange, purple."

> At one point three loudspeakers were pouring out a cacophony of different sounds; three records playing simultaneously. Oddly, it all seemed to fit . . . [*Vinyl*] was being obscured by brightly colored slides and patterns from two slide machines operated by Jacki Casson [sic]. Slashes of red and blue, squares of black and white, rows of dancing dots covered the walls, the ceiling the dancers.

> Twice during the evening were sets by the Velvet Underground, a group whose howling, throbbing beat is amplified and extended by electronic dial-twiddling.

With a strip of strobe lights apparently positioned on the dance floor "like a demented snake who's swallowed phosphorous," the movies and the dancers seemed increasingly fragmented. Malanga, who as a Bronx teenager had been a regular on *The Big Beat* television show, New York's equivalent of *American Bandstand*, danced in front of the band while sweeping the hall with foot-long flashlights. Meanwhile, according to legend, Factory meth monsters Ondine and Brigid Berlin circulated amongst the revelers wielding syringes, freely poking pals and whomever with amphetamine.

Morrissey would maintain that 750 patrons (the legal limit) were present although Wilcock reported that only a bit more than 400 actually paid $2.50 to attend. Noting that Warhol had already been fingerprinted for a cabaret card (affixed with Morrissey's picture!), Wilcock concluded his report with the declaration that "art has come to the discotheque, and it will never be the same again." Still, the Open Stage was dark on Saturday, as Warhol attended the opening of his show "Silver Clouds" at the Leo Castelli gallery—an exhibit of inflated, hovering pillow-shaped Mylar balloons—documented in Willard Maas's four-minute film *Andy Warhol's Silver Flotations.*

"Silver Clouds" was serene and ethereal. The *Exploding Plastic Inevitable* was fantastically assaultive, sonically, visually, and mentally, a realm of ambient chaos—not all of it intentional. Mekas would later write that "Warhol has gathered toward himself the most egocentric personalities and artists."

> The auditorium, every aspect of it—singers, light throwers, strobe operators, dancers—at all times are screaming with screeching, piercing personality pain. I say pain; it could also be called desperation. In any case, it is the last stand of the ego, before it either breaks down or goes to the other side.

Protecting themselves from the lights, the Velvets wore shades and, like the new Dylan and ageing Miles Davis, sometimes turned their backs on the audience, the better to hear their band. It hardly mattered because, given the light show, the stars were the dancers and the dancers included stars: not just society swells like Cecil Beaton or Pauline de Rothschild and the daughter of Dominican dictator Rafael Trujillo, but Jackie Kennedy, CBS anchorman Walter Cronkite, Rudolf Nureyev (among other members of the New York City ballet), and Salvador Dalí, advertised as a cast member because his Factory screen test was part of the show.[6]

Warhol felt like a conquistador. "All the downtown action had always been in the West Village—the East Village was Babushkaville," he would exult. Having escaped Pittsburgh's Babushkaville, he reveled in transforming New York's, although the Dom had been a scene for eighteen months, the

6 Dalí had staged his own underwhelming happening at Lincoln Center in late February. Characterized by Grace Glueck as a "slickly packaged Bohemian cliché," the event began with a screening of the 1929 surrealist film *Un Chien Andalou*. Individual performers included an obese midget, a Parisian vedette, and the blind composer Moondog. "After slashing away with a crayon at a couple of big white cardboards, [Dali] stepped into a huge plastic bubble," Glueck wrote. "He flung pigment around its transparent walls and smeared them with a brush." As the cast frugged, the artist, who had been presented with a light-bulb vest, daubed paint on a young man's coat, then lay on the floor and contemplated his paint-smeared hands.

Five Spot at least a half dozen years, and *EVO* published its first issue in October 1965.

5

One week into the *EPI*'s run, a scandal erupted across the street. Having served a summons on the Tek for showing films of "sexual immorality, lewdness, perversion and homosexuality" (unnamed but almost certainly *Scorpio Rising* and Warhol's first attempted commercial feature and first real hit, *My Hustler*), the city license commissioner issued the Bridge with a show cause order citing the use of "obscene language" and the presence of minors in a midnight performance of Jose Rodriguez Soltero's "film-stage" piece *LBJ*.

Around 2:00 in the morning, April 9, Soltero appeared with a live chicken, strung it up by the legs from a beam over the stage, and directed the audience to evacuate from their seats into the aisle. As recounted in the *Voice* by Fred McDarrah, the house lights dimmed, a strobe was activated, and a phonograph needle dropped on the nation's #1 song, "The Ballad of the Green Beret." Carrying an American flag, Soltero and his confederates marched over the chairs to the stage. McDarrah, a former US Army paratrooper, was reminded of "a patrol of soldiers under fire on a battlefield with the mortar, machine gun tracer bullets, and screeching rockets overhead." Then the flag was ceremonially set ablaze.

"The impact on the audience was sensational," McDarrah reported.

> Although the event was clumsily performed, reaction to it was vociferous. People screamed, "Throw him out!" Others applauded wildly. Still others were dumbfounded and puzzled as to how they should react to this extraordinary anti-American theatre piece.

The Dom too received a summons that night, which seems to have been ignored. Their desecration went beyond the flag.

On the show's second weekend, which advertised a family-friendly Saturday matinee for "Teenage Tot and Tillie Dropout," the *New York Times* sent thirty-one-year-old reporter Marylin Bender to investigate Warhol's latest stunt under the rubric *food/fashion/family/furnishing*. Taking her mandate to cover the new couture, Bender wryly noted that "black tie and long chiffon or black jeans and not-recently-washed sweaters seem equally appropriate for participating in the 'total art form' that Mr. Warhol has been presenting for the last ten evenings" and briefly profiled the chanteuse. ("'Modeling is such a dull job,' Nico said, tossing her flaxen mane.")

For some, Nico's strangely accented voice and glazed affect evoked Weimar Berlin. Unimpressed, Bender found the event tacky or perhaps she pretended to.

> Guests play $2 on weekdays, $2.50 on Fridays and Saturdays for the privilege of sitting on folding chairs around tables with red checked cloths and being simultaneously bombarded by three of Mr. Warhol's underground, 16mm, unedited films, kinetic lighting and rock 'n' roll.

Still, Warhol's "temporary cinema-discotheque" had its dangerous attractions. Patrons could "grope their way to the dance floor in the blackness that is broken only by hallucinatory flashes of multicolored lights in order to wriggle, writhe and tremble to the music of the Velvet Undergrounds [sic]."

The Velvet Underground typically came on at 11:00. Coordinated if not scripted, their set was a form of aesthetic blitzkrieg. The poet John Ashbery, nearing forty and recently returned to New York after seven years in Paris, responded exactly as if someone spiked his martini with LSD: "I don't understand this at all," he is said to have cried, bursting into tears. Cale remembers that as Nico sang the ballad "I'll Be Your Mirror," the motorized mirror ball hovering over center-stage "splintered the strobe's powerful beams and sent its light skittering across the room, the band, and the screen, so that they whole mass was reduced to a throbbing entity wrapped up in color light."

The hypno-drone "Venus in Furs" triggered the fantastic new S&M dances conceived by Malanga and his new partner Mary Woronov, a twenty-two-year old Cornell art student. Malanga forewent his trademark whip and cast Woronov, even taller than Nico, as a dominatrix. Reporting for the *Columbia Daily Spectator*, two Columbia students observed a fellow in the audience clutch his tearful girlfriend, adding that the whole "*tzimmes* is really quite innocent." Malanga and Woronov also had a routine for "Heroin," which replaced the feedback frenzied "Black Angel's Death Song" as the Velvet's final number.

"They were shooting up on stage," recalled John Waters (who several months earlier had been kicked out of NYU for smoking pot). "It may not have been real, but it looked real!" In fact, Malanga used the sort of outsized bakery squeegee employed to squirt icing on cupcakes. More than anything, Waters was impressed by the attitude: "It was sort of an anti-hippie thing. And outside on St. Mark's Place was like the hippie aorta. *The Exploding Plastic Inevitable* was mocking that."

Occasionally, the *EPI* reverted to its Ludlow Street origins—when Cale was briefly indisposed, Tony Conrad's buddy, the polemicist Henry Flynt, then experimenting with avant-garde bluegrass, was brought in as substitute violinist. (Afterward Flynt formed a garage band, the Insurrections, with Walter De Maria and recorded a few demos including the sub-Fug dirge, "I Don't Wanna Go to South Vietnam.") Warhol's movies were projected on the wall, the band, and the dancers. So was *Christmas on Earth*, until Maureen Tucker objected. Indeed, mid-way through the month, Barbara Rubin contrived a moment of poet solidarity, as Allen Ginsberg joined the Velvets onstage to chant "Hare Krishna" during Malanga's whip dance.

A dedicated control freak, Morrissey feared Rubin, who was the only other filmmaker in Warhol's circle. He also loathed her as an anarchic, sexual, independent woman, not to mention a crazy, proto-hippie left-wing Jew. Ginsberg might have been the final straw. Shortly after this Morrissey successfully drove Rubin out of the club. According to Malanga, she "left the Factory one day screaming, never to return."

Soon after, Murray the K's World lost Murray. By the time Cheetah opened on May 28, the World had suffered several setbacks. Myerberg was repeatedly busted for selling alcohol to minors, and Kaufman withdrew from the project. As a *Newsday* put it: STOP THE WORLD, MURRAY THE K WANTS TO GET OFF. Nevertheless, Gerd Stern considered it a success: "It was a great scene for us because, number one, it allowed us to work with some technologies and programming that we hadn't worked with before."

But mainly, the World provided financing for USCO's upcoming show at the Riverside Museum.

6

After a month on St. Mark's Place, the Velvets toured the West Coast. LA audiences found the band too dark. Their third night at The Trip, the Sunset Strip club was shut down for disturbing the peace with a "pornographic exhibition." The San Francisco hippies hated them, and the feeling was mutual. (Malanga was arrested, supposedly for openly carrying his whip.)

St. Mark's, however, remained New York City's light show capital. Cassen began staging her own "Trips Festival." Mekas placed these presentations "somewhere between USCO and the Inevitables."

> There is the ego and a touch of perversion coming from the performers; and there is the mystical tendency on the dance floor and in the visuals—the kind of color abstraction and pattern play that by now has come to be known as psychedelic. Although much frantic movement and color and light play is going on, the show is peaceful, ornamental, and feminine, most of the time.

USCO's Steve Durkee was impressed by Cassen's use of the strobe, "hung up on wires and something that looked like shower curtains, and people would go inside and dance, under the strobes . . . I began thinking about them as showers, electrical showers."

The "Trips Festival," which variously featured the Fugs, a raga-rock band called the Seventh Sons, movies by Cassen's new partner Rudi Stern, and an assist from USCO, continued through June. Across the street at the Bridge, "Media Move," held in mid-June, included intermedia dance pieces by Judson dancers Yvonne Rainer and Liz Keen as well as Beverly Schmidt's *Moon-Dial*. Aldo and Elsa Tambellini were projecting and, as Mekas noted, performing. Turning around from Schmidt's "breathtakingly beautiful performance," he found "both Tambellinis immersed in a deep dance trance of their own, moving, with hand-held projectors and slides, shaking, and trembling, no longer conscious of themselves."

Life magazine's May 27 issue ran a cover story on the WILD NEW FLASHY BEDLAM OF THE DISCOTHEQUE. USCO's *Be-In* at the Riverside Museum (which occupied the first floor of a twenty-seven-story deco skyscraper on the corner of 103rd Street and Riverside Drive) would provide the cover image for *Life*'s September 9 story on psychedelic art. *Be-In* was less a show, like MoMA's *Responsive Eye*, than a unified environment.[7]

Arriving beneath a huge painting of a tiger marked "en/trance," visitors drifted through four rooms. One was a light garden where illuminated

---

7 USCO's use of the term predates the massive "Human Be-In" (or Gathering of the Tribes) staged in Golden Gate Park on January 14, 1967.

flowers were activated by switches built into the floor. Another contained a circular "cave" fashioned from tie-dyed cloth; inside, a similarly upholstered revolving couch allowed museumgoers to lie down and, among other things, contemplate the images of deities, demons, and mandalas silk-screened on the canopy above.

A third room juxtaposed Steve Durkee's outsized paintings of Hindu gods with images of the cosmos and Op Art patterns reinforced by pulsing ultraviolet light. Incense burned. The room seemed to revolve around a central metallic pylon. A sound mix looped the sacred syllable *Om*. The fourth room was participatory. Museum patrons could produce oscilloscopic patterns on a TV monitor or manipulate a mechanized moiré diffraction spiral. A machine assembled from old computer parts played tic-tac-toe. An outsized highway sign blinked out messages: Turn, Yield, Merge, Go.[8]

Jonas Mekas felt that he was witnessing the birth of a new religion. Grace Glueck was more skeptical. "The 'be-in' isn't easy to take," she wrote. "Its light-up paintings, frenetic machines and high decibel noises add up to a kind of programmed pandemonium that seems accurately to reflect the urban US milieu." Yet the USCO experience was far less assaultive than *The Responsive Eye*, let alone the *Exploding Plastic Inevitable.* Most surprised was the Riverside Museum's staff. While previous shows had been staid and sparsely attended, *Be-In* attracted numerous young people who took advantage the proximity of Riverside Park to toke up and groove, sometimes for hours, on the gallery.

In a way, *Be-In* was a respite. As recently as March, the *Village Voice* had run two page-one stories on MacDougal Street. Stephanie Harrington's piece depicted the scene as a Bridge and Tunnel teenage horror show centered on West Third Street around the Night Owl Café (which had incubated such popular bands as the Lovin' Spoonful and the Blues Magoos) and reported that the new Lindsay administration was considering a curfew for kids under sixteen. In fact, they briefly attempted to ban traffic from the zone. The following week, David Gurin noted that Harrington's story appeared to have inspired a TV news story

8 Jud Yalkut scored his three-minute 16-mm documentary *Down by the Riverside* to the Beatles' trippy "Tomorrow Never Knows," although if memory serves, one exited the show exalted by the strains of the Tornado's 1962 hit instrumental, the cheerfully spacey perfectly named "Telstar."

that further flooded the Village, leading to a mass demonstration against the police and a *Daily News* headline: VILLAGE HORDE FOILS CLEANUP: COPS YIELD TO 1500 BEATNIKS.[9]

Now the scene had metastasized. The June 16 *Voice* ran a piece by Harrington headlined INEVITABLE EXPLODES ON ST. MARK'S PLACE. It was finally happening, she wrote. "The Five Spot has been on St. Mark's Place for a long time."

> The boutiques and the Bridge Theatre have been there for a while, too. Café Society came, saw, conquered and left the Dom months ago. But the accumulation adds up. The bookstore, the record shop, the oriental gift shop with tiger balm and various forms of betel nuts, the antique stores, the funny buttons shop, and—most significant harbinger of all—the open front pizza stand.

In 1966 there was a mystical correlation between the cost of a slice, a subway token, and the *Village Voice* (all 15 cents). In the pizza stand, Harrington saw the future.

> The MacDougal Street vista on a weekend night is still the awe-inspiring most. Looking north from Bleecker, the street is a solid silhouette of movement. Lost legions advancing endlessly, going nowhere. Infinity described in motion. Cars streaming relentlessly southward. Mounted policemen outlined like equestrian statuary against the misty ceiling of light diffusion from electric signs and streetlamps.
> The same scene has been laid on St. Mark's Place.

Things would be crazier after the summer.

7

As the Factory prepped the *EPI*, an even wiggier avant-garde ensemble established itself. Based in the largely Puerto Rican far East Village, Sun Ra and his Arkestra had a weekly Monday night gig at Slugs', a

9 Gurin argued for decentralization. Instead of one central MacDougal Street, every neighborhood needed one. In its way Murray the K's World had been that; in another way Gurin's prescription would develop over the next decade. The 1977 movie *Saturday Night Fever* is both vision and evidence of neighborhood MacDougal Streets.

brick-walled, tunnel-like dive that was known to let musicians in for free.

Located at 242 East Third Street, between Avenues B and C, Slugs' was a former Ukrainian bar purchased in 1964 by two young devotees of the Armenian mystic George Gurdjieff and renamed for a characterization of "human beings" found in Gurdjieff's *Beelzebub's Tales to His Grandson*. Slugs' became part of the neighborhood drug scene and then, thanks to Jackie McLean, who played there without a cabaret card, the hippest jazz club in the neighborhood. Carl Lee tended bar; a Bob Thompson painting was displayed behind the tiny bandstand.

A few blocks down the street, just off Second Avenue, Sun Ra ruled a communal pad, the Sun Palace, that occupied the top two floors of a small three-story 1830s row house. The building had been the site of the Artist's Studio that, as established by the African American painter George Nelson Preston, hosted poetry readings, including the February 1959 event memorialized in Fred McDarrah's iconic photograph of Jack Kerouac, arms extended against a white curtain.

Sun Ra's Arkestra materialized in New York in late 1961, heralded by Edward O. Bland's movie *The Cry of Jazz*, which had its contentious Cinema 16 screening in February 1960. Appropriately for a band known mainly for their appearance in a movie, the Arkestra—billed as Le Sun Ra and his Cosmic Jazz Space Patrol—played their first reviewed gig at the Charles Theater on a Sunday afternoon in February 1962. Writing in the *New York Times*, John S. Wilson was unenthusiastic, devoting more attention to the band leader's philosophy, "exotically named assortment of musical weapons," and outlandish outfit (a golden headband and black- and gold-spangled cape) than to his propulsive "outer space jazz." The *Voice* dug the sounds, if not the outfits.

The Arkestra next played for the poets at Les Deux Mégots, followed by a stint at Café Bizarre where, billed as the Outer Spacemen, they were paid two dollars each a night, plus hamburgers, thus staking a claim to the weirdo realm of Tiny Tim and Moondog. The Arkestra held open rehearsals at the Sun Palace. They also made their first commercial record, *The Futuristic Sounds of Sun Ra*, for the Savoy label, supervised by Tom Wilson, who would go on to produce three early Dylan LPs and, uncredited, *The Velvet Underground and Nico*.

For a year or so the Arkestra played regularly at the Playhouse Café, located in a row house on MacDougal Street and owned by jazz pianist

Gene Harris. Ferrell Sanders, a young saxophone player up from Little Rock by way of Oakland, took a job as a waiter at the Playhouse to follow the band. (Given the new first name "Pharoah," he soon joined the ensemble.) Other gigs included a loft on Spruce Street in a deserted neighborhood near City Hall Park, the Spencer Memorial Church in Brooklyn Heights, and the Contemporary Center off Sheridan Square.

Once LeRoi Jones relocated to Harlem, the Arkestra, which partially inspired as well as participated in "The October Revolution in Jazz," joined in his Black Arts parade across 125th Street. Thereafter, according to Jones, Sun Ra was always on the scene, giving regular midweek performances that "introduced the light-show concept that white rock groups later found out about and got rich from."

Sun Ra recorded several classic LPs, *The Magic City* and *Strange Strings* on his El Saturn label during this period and, after Bernard Stollman caught the Arkestra at the "October Revolution," *The Heliocentric Worlds of Sun Ra* for ESP-Disk. The engineer Richard Alderson, famous for recording Dylan's Gaslight performances, had neither heard (nor heard of) Sun Ra before they arrived at the studio: "I was just trying to capture the force and flavor of whatever the artists were doing without editorializing . . . I mean, Sun Ra is Duke Ellington on acid."

In January 1966, ESP booked the now-vacated Astor Place Playhouse through May, providing a weekly venue for the Fugs, with performances by the label's other artists, including Albert Ayler and Sun Ra. LeRoi Jones reviewed the Arkestra in *Down Beat*, noting that the first big band of the New Black Music wants "a music full of Africa." In May, Sun Ra brought the Arkestra out to Procter's Theater in Jones's hometown of Newark, to which he had recently returned, to improvise an accompaniment to a performance of Jones's gloss on Nation of Islam mythology, *A Black Mass*.

By then, the Arkestra had established itself at Slugs'. Beneath a banner emblazoned with a white sun and inscribed "Infinity-Sun Ra," the band held forth on and spilled over Slug's tiny stage, crowded with an abundance of drums as well as musicians. Members of the Arkestra were required to play multiple instruments. Everyone joined in on percussion. Some found it difficult to distinguish between the Arkestra and the audience, which also contained many musicians. The band played from 9:00 p.m. until 4:00 a.m. without breaks. For some tunes, the lights would go out and the Arkestra played in darkness, illuminated only by the lights flashing off their leader's headband. Eventually there would be projected light shows and even dancers who held ceremonial totems that included Sun Ra's metal "sun harp."

As Slugs' performances were unique, so was the Sun Palace. Walking upstairs, one first entered a large room lit by a huge, illuminated ball suspended from the ceiling. John S. Wilson, who had developed an appreciation for Sun Ra since catching him at the Charles, visited the Sun Palace and found it a bit chaotic. The five-room floor-through was impossibly cluttered. The apartment was "piled high with a stacked, packed clutter of stringed instruments, drums, cases, phonographs, boxes, microphones, cymbals, broken umbrellas, costumes and suits in a jumble disarray."

> The walls are colored with spray paint—solid gold, silver, an orange background over which black figures have been drawn. Tacked to the back of a door are two clippings on Unidentified Flying Objects—'World's First UFO Murder' says one headline; 'Russians Concerned About UFOs" says the other.

There was also a pay phone as well as a kitchen where Sun Ra sometimes cooked for the band. House rules forbade drugs and alcohol. Nor were the musicians allowed to bring women. Another visitor, the jazz writer Val Wilmer, thought Sun Ra ran the Arkestra like an army.[10]

Sun Ra played Slugs' for a year before white critics caught on. In February 1967, Wilson reported that "a ten-piece jazz band without precedent in outlook, appearance and performance is performing Monday nights at Slugs'." Wilson recognized that Sun Ra was a precursor to the jazz avant garde who also incorporated jazz tradition. A composition "that offers twittering bird calls rubbed from a pair of single-stringed Chinese fiddles, a vast, percussive orchestral hullaballoo of grunts and squawks and a hot solo on a ram's horn will dissolve into Fletcher Henderson's arrangement of King Porter Stomp."

---

10 The Detroit jazz poet John Sinclair came to the Sun Palace in late 1966 and interviewed Sun Ra, who told him, "I'm just like a university—I've got my different courses set up—and they deal with things that are going to be beneficial to people. But it's not religious, like some people are saying—I'm not the least bit religious. I'm not interested in that. Because churches don't do anything but bring people . . . peace. What I'm talking about is *discipline*—that's what people need."

Somewhat late on the uptake, *Voice* critic Michael Zwerin wandered in with friends at 3:00 a.m. to find the place dark and near empty. "The Astro Infinity Orchestra [sic] outnumbered the audience, several of whom, including our waitress were asleep at tables."

> The orchestra was outfitted in a variety of peaked straw hats, polka dot shirts and ties, and African robes of many colors. They were surrounded by percussion instruments and an air of raunchiness . . . They stared at us without enthusiasm.

One wonders why.

A year later, the poet-critic Stefan Brecht made a study of Sun Ra's Solar Myth Science Arkestra for the *Evergreen Review*. "The audience does not really come in until midnight," he noted. The patrons were "almost entirely Negro and almost entirely male," and Slugs' itself "seems Negro-run." There was not much drinking. (Perhaps because the bar was out of beer.) "No pot or drugs as far as I could tell. The band plays *continuously*."

Identifying himself as musically untutored and untalented, Brecht did his best to describe what he heard. Sometimes, it seemed, one of the saxophones or clarinets played cool jazz, albeit "twisted and amended into ridiculous perversions of melody: squeaks, isolated in time, place relative to one another, screeches and sour slurs, hideous ectoplasmal reproductions of a composition in decomposition—awful ghosts of musical cadavers."

Compared to Sun Ra, Brecht wrote, Schoenberg was "merely an introduction, a sensitive Jewish foretaste." Schoenberg was only at Carnegie Hall once. On April 1, 1934, he joined some dozen musicians for a concert in honor of fellow émigré Albert Einstein. Sun Ra played Carnegie Hall thirty-four years later in April 1968.[11]

11 The show's printed program announces a call to adventure: "the space music of sun ra: a free form excursion into the far reaches of sound and sight—." The unlit stage was illuminated by projected slides of celestial bodies and two films: *The Magic Sun*, an abstract portrait of the Arkestra by composer Phil Niblock and Maxine Haleff 's *The Forbidden Playground* (a dance film, juxtaposing a New York playground, with documentary sequences of NASA astronauts). Dressed in colorful robes, the members of Arkestra were accompanied on stage by the Edith Stephen Dance Theater. John S. Wilson was disappointed, writing in the *New York Times* that "the Arkestra was reduced

8

The summer of 1966 was bracketed by the release of two sprawling masterpieces. New York's reigning masters of hip, the two most analyzed mid-century American artists, each produced a magnum opus. *Blonde on Blonde*, Bob Dylan's audacious double record—one of the four sides devoted to a single cut, the eleven-and-a-half-minute "Sad Eyed Lady of the Lowlands"—appeared in late June. *The Chelsea Girls*, Andy Warhol's epic three-and-a-half-hour double-screen movie, had its premiere mid-September at the Film-Makers' Cinematheque.

Album and movie both seemed fueled by the same drug (methamphetamine) and, some thought, haunted by the same lost soul (Edie Sedgwick). Both projects were voluptuously jaded, steeped in New York's New Bohemia, and had partially gestated in that Bohemia's citadel, the massive, moldering Chelsea Hotel hunkered down on West Twenty-Third Street. Warhol would never make a comparable film, nor Dylan a greater album.

Dylan wrote *Blonde on Blonde* over the tumultuous past year and had even performed acoustic versions of the album's quintessential song, eventually called "Visions of Johanna," supposedly written at the Chelsea on or about the Black-Out evening of November 9, 1965. The LP was mostly recorded in early 1966 before Dylan took off on his "electric" world tour. ABC gave him a $200,000 advance on a never-produced TV special ("The World of Bob Dylan"), but, somewhat in the spirit of a Warhol production, he was intermittently directing himself in a movie.[12]

Blonde on Blonde received few reviews outside the trade press. Yet, more than any previous Dylan album, it was understood as poetry. *Glamour*

---

to performing as a live soundtrack to a mixed-media display . . . and gave relatively little evidence of the stimulating musicianship of which it is capable." Sun Ra blamed sparce attendance on the assassination of Martin Luther King Jr. eight days before. In Fall 1968, the Arkestra left the East Village and relocated to Philadelphia.

12 On tour, Dylan tried to get D. A. Pennebaker to shoot a second film. When that failed, he decided to make a first-person film, helped by the Chicago filmmaker Howard Alk (an editor on *The Cry of Jazz*, who shot some of *Dont Look Back* and would subsequently direct *The Murder of Fred Hampton*). Bobby Neuwirth was also involved, suggesting that they pull a Barbara Rubin and begin interviewing fans. *Eat the Document* was never really released. As befits a would-be underground movie, it had its theatrical premiere at the Whitney Museum in 1972. Perversely pulverized, at once withholding and self-indulgent, it fragments brilliant onstage performances in favor of Dylan's backstage riffs with soulmate Robbie Robertson and other members of the entourage.

magazine's June 1966 issue even printed the words to "Visions of Johanna." Unlike previous LPs, there were no jeremiads. Richard Goldstein, the *Village Voice*'s new, twenty-two-year-old rock critic, was relieved that Dylan had eased up on the put-down song—"a genre he perfected in 'Like a Rolling Stone' and 'Positively Fourth Street,'" the latter of which insiders suspected to be directed at Izzy Young, who had organized Dylan's first, sparsely attended Carnegie Hall recital in November 1961.[13]

Released as 45s, the put-downs were the successors to the "finger pointing songs," as Dylan called his earlier protest material. Indeed, *Blonde on Blonde* seemed to be largely about the singer's romantic partners. Goldstein singled out "Just Like a Woman" and "Sad Eyed Lady of the Lowlands" as favorites. The former, along with the jaunty "Leopard Skin Pillbox Hat," has been identified with Edie Sedgwick while the hypnotic, droning "Sad Eyed Lady of the Lowlands" was, Dylan later maintained, written for Sara Lownds, whom he had married in a secret ceremony on November 22, 1965.

Frustrated love is certainly a theme. The anguished "One of Us Must Know (Sooner or Later)," which required twenty-four takes and provides a majestic climax to the album's first side, has the poet addressing himself as much as his lost love—or is she a one-night stand? The album suggests the outline for a novel, filled with humorous complaints "Memphis Blues Again" and "Absolutely Sweet Marie," as well as cryptic references to personalities, locations, and events.

As the British academic John Hughes—a specialist in Romantic poetry—would later write, the album is "dominated by scenarios of the self as captive, exploited, rejected, confused, betrayed, or lost," reinforced by Jerry Schatzberg's blurry cover image, upon which Dylan

---

13 Alongside a report on Ed Sanders's bust, the first issue of the *East Village Other* (October 1965) contained Young's remarkably bitter attack on the new Dylan: "He returned to the great hope of American music—Rock and Roll," Young wrote. "He electrified his guitar."

> He took the raw force of Rock and Roll. He took out the protest and vivacity and statement and hope. He added his personal bitterness and loneliness . . . He screams from the bottomless pit and it is truly heart-rending. But it is like sharing something dirty.

As it was recorded on July 29 and released on September 7, "Positively 4th Street" predates Young's screed and perhaps inspired it.

evidently insisted. An artistic triumph for the twenty-five-year-old singer, *Blonde on Blonde* opens with a drug joke—the raucous "Rainy Day Women #12 and 35"—and a sense of druggy despair.[14]

With its chortled clarion cry *Everybody must get stoned!*, "Rainy Day Women" was a song of its moment and went to #2 on the charts despite various radio bans. Drug films were ubiquitous on the underground circuit that summer. The Tek was running a "Psychedelic Film" series while the Bridge offered "Trips in Celluloid" followed by "More Trips in Celluloid." The Gate, a new venue managed by Elsa Tambellini on Second Avenue at East Tenth Street, would open in the fall with a "New Visions Festival," followed up by a program called "Psychedelia: Tune In," which, among other things, featured Richard Aldcroft's kaleidoscopic Infinity Machine projector (previously seen on St. Mark's Place and the cover of *Life*'s September 9 LSD issue).

Jackie Cassen and Rudi Stern were at Timothy Leary's Millbrook estate, ninety miles north of New York City, working out a series of psychedelic projections that Leary would stage that fall at the Village East. Even as *Blonde on Blonde* crept toward the bottom rungs of the Billboard Top 100, the Factory was busy accumulating footage, although their drug of choice was not LSD.

The summer of 1966 also brought the last great talent to pass through the West Village entertainment mill. At the suggestion of singer-songwriter Richie Havens, twenty-three-year-old James Marshall—soon to be "Jimi"—Hendrix, a veteran of the chitlin circuit and an experienced R&B session guitarist who had absorbed both Little Richard and Bob Dylan, turned up at a Café Wha? hoot and found himself fronting the house band's rhythm section—hired by owner Manny Roth to play five sets a day at six bucks a set.

Putting together an act called Jimmy James and the Blue Flames, Hendrix ruled MacDougal Street. His set might encompass soul hits ("In the Midnight Hour"), classic rock 'n' roll ("Johnny B. Goode"), and

14 Discussing "dope rock" in *The Aesthetics of Rock*, R. Meltzer calls "Rainy Day Women" "the 'How Dry I Am' of grass." The brass-band party suggests an undisciplined imitation of Sun Ra. On the other hand, the crazy free-form sound anticipates ESP-Disk's second rock band the Godz, whose first album was released in late September. Stollman commissioned a promotional film from Jud Yalkut. Set mostly in their East Village pad, the band engages in a toneless jam while watching football on TV. A party, possibly at Stollman's uptown apartment, provides the occasion for more clowning and discordant caterwauling.

Chicago blues (Howlin' Wolf's "Killing Floor"), as well as a few original songs ("The Wind Cries Mary"), a garage-band standard ("Hey Joe") reconfigured as blues, and, using a fuzz box gifted by the Fugs, the summer's #1 hit, "Wild Thing." Taking the song literally, Hendrix also amazed walk-in audiences with his loud outfits, earsplitting guitar, and a surplus of showmanship that might include playing the guitar behind his back or with his teeth.[15]

However entertaining for Village tourists, the summer was hard on American poets. Delmore Schwartz died in July. The *Voice* gave him a page-one obituary. Lou Reed, who had been mentored by Schwartz at Syracuse, furtively attended the memorial service. Eight days later, Frank O'Hara was killed in an apparent accident on Fire Island. Most famously, Lenny Bruce overdosed on morphine in early August.

Injured in a motorcycle accident on July 29, Dylan might have been among them—a near miss that, together with his disappearance from the public eye, gave *Blonde on Blonde* an additional valedictory quality.

9

If *Blonde on Blonde* was LP as novel, *The Chelsea Girls* was a movie structured like an LP. A series of discrete dramatic vignettes, Warhol's definitive film was purportedly set in various rooms of the Chelsea Hotel, with each garrulous superstar given a thirty-three-minute reel in which to perform. Twelve unedited reels were screened, originally in a random order, two reels at a time, side by side (but only one with sound).[16]

It was a three-and-a-half-hour immersion in the world of the Factory.

---

15 In early September, he had a two-week gig opening for white bluesman John Hammond Jr. at Café au Go Go and was there spotted by the Animals bassist Chas Chandler, an aspiring producer, who brought him to London.

16 The first screenings were essentially rehearsals. Two projectionists, Bob Cowan and Jerome Hiler, both filmmakers, had carte blanch, ordering the reels to suit themselves as Warhol watched. "Andy told me to play around with the image and the soundtrack as I felt like it," Hiler recalled. "You could have one soundtrack going and then change to the other soundtrack, then you might go back to the first soundtrack. Perhaps even both of them together a little bit. And then you had some gels, some cellophane, and so forth. You would hold the cellophane whenever you felt like it, over one of the projector lenses so that it all went red. And then another one went blue." Hiler remembers occasionally fluttering his fingers in front of the projection beam and once Warhol learned that it took a few minutes for the projector bulb to warm up to its proper intensity, he encouraged that effect. Hiler would "turn the bulb on when the reel started and just let it slowly come up from a throbbing purple."

Nico trimmed her bangs. The pansexual hippie Eric Emerson, an athletic dancer who made himself known to Warhol when he appeared at the *EPI*'s second weekend, dropped acid and babbled incoherently about his trip. Mario Montez serenaded a male hustler and his middle-aged john (Ed Hood) as they lolled in bed (the sequence shot at George Plimpton's townhouse) only to be driven from the set by their taunts. One of the few scripted sequences, written by Ronald Tavel, had Mary Woronov as Hanoi Hannah browbeat a room full of stupefied young fashion plates (Susan Bottomly a.k.a. International Velvet, Pepper Davis, and Ingrid Superstar). By contrast, Woronov was totally silent as Gerard Malanga's fiancée in a reel in which the couple was harangued by a seemingly drunk Marie Menken (filling in for Malanga's actual mother).

Three of the "Chelsea girls"—Brigid Berlin, Nico, and Susan Bottomly—actually lived at the hotel while El Quijote, the kitschy Spanish restaurant next door, was something of a Factory hangout. Nevertheless, half the film was shot in the Factory or borrowed apartments. *Closet*, a gloss on Sartre's *No Exit*, featuring Nico and based on an idea by Barbara Rubin, had been filmed back in February; there was also the third reel of *Afternoon*, a Sedgwick vehicle from the summer of 1965. Dropped supposedly at Sedgwick's request, it was replaced with color footage of Nico in tears, a light show that ultimately came to end the movie.

Filmed a week after the movie's mid-September premiere, one of *Chelsea Girls*'s two most memorable sequences has a jovially malignant Berlin trilling on the telephone and underscoring her pseudonym, Brigid Polk, by jabbing a speed-laden syringe into her massive, bejeaned buttock. Playing herself as a drug dealer, she made phone calls to actual clients while dumping on Ingrid Superstar—as in the "Hanoi Hannah" sequence, a convenient foil. (Legend has it that the Chelsea's switchboard operator imagined an actual drug deal was going on and called the police.)

The other sequence, shot in June, featured Ondine, the Factory's most waspish wit, shooting up and, as self-appointed pope, taking confessions from Woronov, International Velvet, Ingrid Superstar, and Pepper Davis. Ondine had developed and perfected this routine through years of hanging out at the San Remo. Although a well-established riff (frequently referenced in *The Sinking Bear*), Ondine's papal act was not universally understood. In a shocking finale that ultimately became part of *Chelsea Girls*'s last chapter, Ondine lost his cool and slapped around a young woman, Ronna Page, who snidely dared to question his authority.

A subject of a screen test, although not a Factory regular, Page was a friend of Barbara Rubin; she was then living with Jonas Mekas, who facilitated her participation in the movie. In his contempt for Page, Ondine refers to her "husband" (Mekas) as "the saint" and indeed, unperturbed by Ondine's abusive behavior, Mekas compared *The Chelsea Girls* to *The Birth of a Nation* and Victor Hugo and called Ondine's scene "probably the most dramatic religious sequence ever filmed," referring to Warhol as a "Holy Terror." (Subsequently affiliated with harmonica-player Mel Lyman's Fort Hill, Boston–based "Family," Page danced in the *EPI* when it played ICA Boston in late October.)

The Chelsea Girls had its premiere at the Film-Makers' Cinematheque on September 15. Five days into its run, the Timothy Leary show opened on Second Avenue. In a curtain-raising press conference held at the New York Advertising Club, Leary informed the world that he too had founded a new religion based on the sacramental use of LSD, peyote, and marijuana: "Like every great religion of the past, we seek to find the divinity within and to express this revelation in a life of glorification and worship of God."

Leary also noted that his League for Spiritual Discovery would be seeking tax-free status and thus "play the American social game of other religions." Ondine could scarcely have been more glib.

10

Leary's first psychedelic celebration was provocatively (or hilariously) titled *The Death of the Mind*. Opening night, the 2,000-seat Village Theatre was packed. The line outside had stretched nearly to St. Mark's Place, where the Velvet Underground was back at the Open Stage, now owned by Albert Grossman, who, supposedly at Bob Dylan's suggestion, had renamed the venue the Balloon Farm. The Velvets resented working for their bête noire and regarded *The Death of the Mind* as a pathetic rip-off. Morrissey deemed Leary a ludicrous con artist while one of Leary's associates dismissively told Richard Goldstein that the *Exploding Plastic Inevitable* was "just an amphetamine scene."

Psychedelic or otherwise, light shows continued to proliferate. The folk rock band the Byrds performed with one at the Village Gate, as did Lothar and the Hand People, a group notable for incorporating a theremin. Working the lights for both, Cassen and Stern were otherwise cashing in. The pair took out an ad in *Variety* announcing their availability for discotheques, fashion shows, commercials, and bar mitzvahs: "They can convert any room into a kaleidoscopic world of movement, light and color" or "turn a sagging club into the hottest spot in town." The USCO group were now media consultants—John Brockman brokered a meeting with the Scott Paper Company.

Brockman had been hired by Amos Vogel to work on the 1966 New York Film Festival (NYFF), which opened in mid-September, a few days before *The Chelsea Girls*. A sidebar devoted to "The Independent Cinema" included *The Flicker*, along with Victor Grauer's similarly stroboscopic *Archangel* and Peter Emmanuel Goldman's post-Cassavetes study in sexual alienation, *Echoes of Silence*, plus films by Harry Smith, Ed Emshwiller, Stan VanDerBeek, and Robert Breer. Richard Kostelanetz lectured on "The Theater of Mixed Means" and there was a panel on "Expanded Cinema," which, despite Mekas's habitual criticism of the NYFF, served as the lead article for a special issue of *Film Culture*.[17]

The underground even infiltrated the Festival proper. Jean-Luc Godard's *Pierrot le Fou* was preceded by Richard Preston's collage short *Son of Dada*; Bernardo Bertolucci's first feature, *The Grim Reaper*, by Goldman's visceral hate-Manhattan montage *Pestilent City*. Shown as a short subject with a movie by Argentine director Leopoldo Torre Nilsson, Robert Nelson's *O Dem Watermelons* served as a kind of trailer for the San Francisco Mime Troupe, who arrived in October with their satiric *Minstrel Show* (subtitled *Civil Rights in a Cracker Barrel*).

With *Death of the Mind* installed on Second Avenue and *Chelsea Girls* drawing record crowds to the Film-Makers' Cinematheque, an entity called Black Mask sent out a press release on Monday, October 10, at 12:30 p.m. The release announced that they would close the Museum of Modern Art, explaining that this action, taken while America embarked upon a "path of total destruction," signaled the opening of a new front: "WE SEEK A TOTAL REVOLUTION . . . LET THE STRUGGLE BEGIN." Obligingly the spooked museum shut itself down. Ben Morea, his Group Center cohort Ron Hahne, and the poet Dan Georgakas simply showed up and affixed a stenciled message that read MUSEUM CLOSED to MoMA's

17 A related event, conjured up by Robert Rauschenberg and Billy Klüver, "9 Evenings: Theatre and Engineering," October 13–23 at the Twenty-Fifth Street Armory, initiated the series of projects that would be known as E.A.T. or Experiments in Art and Technology; participants included John Cage, Lucinda Childs, Öyvind Fahlström, Alex Hay, Deborah Hay, Steve Paxton, Yvonne Rainer, David Tudor and Robert Whitman.

entrance and distributed a leaflet ("DESTROY THE MUSEUMS—OUR STRUGGLE CANNOT BE HUNG ON WALLS"), thus providing the first great example of Conceptual Art-cum-Political Theater in the '60s.

Morea, twenty-five, had grown up in the Amsterdam Houses, a housing project that replaced nine acres of San Juan Hill tenements. An aspiring jazz musician and a teenaged heroin addict, he benefited from art therapy and moved down to the Lower East Side in 1959 to become a painter. There he met and was deeply impressed by the Living Theatre, participating in their 1962 Peace Strike; a habitue of Tenth Street galleries, he joined Tambellini's Group Center later that year and was also part of the circle around the ecology-minded anarchist Murray Bookchin.

Claiming the mantle of Berlin Dada (whose primary spokesman Dr. Richard Huelsenbeck was alive, well, and a practicing psychoanalyst living in New York), Black Mask provided a theoretical cover for an international tendency that included the No!art group, Destruction artists, the Viennese Actionists, and the more confrontational members of Fluxus—not that they necessarily wanted it.[18]

The Black Mask position was explicit by the first issue of their self-titled periodical, sold for a nickel at an NYU symposium, "What is Art Today?" Morea's heckling ("a shattering experience for museum directors and curators," per the *East Village Other*) complemented their magazine's blunt demand for "the complete ruination of bourgeois culture." By way of example Black Mask disrupted a show devoted to the recently deceased, sometime Dada artist Jean Arp at a Fifty-Seventh Street gallery and ambushed poet Kenneth Koch with a mock assassination mid-reading at St. Mark's Church.

11

LSD was made illegal in the US on October 24. Soon after, Leary got into a dispute over money with the Village Theater ("We have been driven from the temple," he told the *Voice*) and moved the November 1 performance of *Reincarnation of Jesus Christ* to the Village Gate. Scarcely had

18 Indeed, scarcely a month before, London-based artist Gustav Metzger had organized a Destruction Art Symposium at which Yoko Ono performed *Cut Piece* and Ralph Ortiz destroyed a piano. Other participants included the Austrians Otto Mühl and Hermann Nitsch, as well as several representatives of Fluxus, Al Hansen and Wolf Vostell.

the Velvets left the Balloon Farm when the two most radical Los Angeles bands, the Doors and the Mothers (rebranded, under pressure, the Mothers of Invention), made their New York debuts.

The Doors appeared at Ondine, a posh, celebrity-friendly disco on 308 East Fifty-Ninth Street abutting the Bridge that, co-owned by Jerry Schatzberg, opened in April 1965. Seven or eight blocks up (and east) from Arthur, the joint was a Factory favorite. According to Warhol, "Edie went there all the time, throwing a lot of money around in the beginning when she still had it, picking up the check for as many as twenty people every night." Naturally, Warhol and company came to check out the Doors: "When we walked in, Gerard took one look at Jim Morrison in leather pants just like his and he flipped. 'He stole my look!' he screamed, outraged. It was true enough—Jim had, I guess, picked it up from seeing Gerard at the Trip."

The Mothers were a bitter pill. Frank Zappa's band had openly mocked the Velvets in the spring when they played together at The Trip in Los Angeles and the Fillmore in San Francisco. Moreover, although the two bands cut their debut LPs around the same time, made for Verve with same producer, Tom Wilson, the Mothers' *Freak Out!* had been in record stores for months, nearly a year before *The Velvet Underground and Nico* was released. Adding insult to injury, the Mothers' show—advertised with a handbill emblazoned with HELP LEGALIZE THERAPEUTIC ABORTION—was a critical success.[19]

19 In late October, Nico played a solo gig at The Scene. Also on the bill were Tiny Tim and Kaleidoscope, a psychedelic world-music band from California. Chris Darrow, a member, ran into Frank Zappa and the Mothers and invited them to the opening night. If Nico was typically deadpan and her material was dirge-like, Darrow recalled, "the audience was on her side, as she was in her element and the Warhol contingent was very prominent."

> In between sets, Frank Zappa got up from his seat and walked up on the stage and sat behind the keyboard of Nico's B-3 organ. He proceeded to place his hands indiscriminately on the keyboard in a total, atonal fashion and screamed at the top of his lungs, doing a caricature of Nico's set, the one he had just seen. The words to his impromptu song were the names of vegetables like broccoli, cabbage, asparagus . . . This "song" kept going for about a minute or so and then suddenly stopped. It later became 'Call Any Vegetable' off the *Absolutely Free* LP. He walked off the stage and the show moved on. It was one of the greatest pieces of rock 'n' roll theater that I have ever seen.

The B-3 was more likely a harmonium which Nico purchased that summer in California having gotten some basic instruction from Ornette Coleman. At one point, Warhol and

"The Balloon Farm became much more than a discotheque last weekend," Richard Goldstein wrote in the *Voice*. Goldstein had been unimpressed with the LP *Freak Out!*, but the Mothers in concert were something else. "They seized the stage and belted the world's first rock 'n' roll oratorio to an audience that was either too engrossed or too confused to do anything but sit and listen."

> The show was a single extended number, broken into movements by patter, and fused by repeated melody-themes. Especially notable was the use, as leitmotif, of music from *Boris Godunov*, sewn into the fabric of the song so that it became an integral part of the melody and not a sequin pasted on for class. On another evening—I have it by word-of-ear—the group lit into Stravinsky, with a rocking beat.
>
> The Mothers use the secondary technique of pop-parody with devastating effect. They goof brilliantly on the bass-falsetto hang-up of '50s teen music, and on the cocktail-clinking orchestration of the '40s. Their lyrics leave the Fugs gnawing scraps.
>
> The whole show—call it a theatre piece and tell Beck and Malina to tail it back from Europe to catch this one—is surrounded by a pulsating lightscape. Oily color globs merge and counterpoint. It all flows freely, and for once, in sync with the music.

Goldstein's panegyric was echoed by Robert Shelton three weeks later in the *New York Times*, a profile of Zappa that praised the Mothers ("the most original new group to simmer out of the steaming rock 'n' roll underground in the last hour and a half"), citing not only Stravinsky but Mozart, Holst, and Edgard Varese.

12

As the Velvets faded, *The Chelsea Girls* gained momentum. The movie returned to the Tek for a weekend and, following Jack Kroll's eye-catching write-up in *Newsweek*, played to full houses for the rest of October.

Then, heralded by Mekas's second review and a full-page ad in the *Voice*, the show moved up to Cinema Rendezvous, a posh theater on Fifty-Seventh Street a block east of Carnegie Hall. There it was reviewed

---

Morrissey wanted to package Nico, literally, by "exhibiting" her in a Plexiglass box. She refused.

by Dan Sullivan, who covered downtown theater for the *New York Times*. Characterizing the movie as "half Bosch and half Bosh," Sullivan was most impressed by Eric Emerson's soliloquy ("an authentic cry for help") and Ondine's pope: "The Roman Catholic Church has disappeared, and Greenwich Village is in its place."

Indeed. Just before Timothy Leary's farewell performance in *Illumination of the Buddha*, the Sunday *Times* published Elenore Lester's account of his "Psychedelic Celebrations." Lester provided an amused post-mortem on the "new 'turned on' Second Avenue theater scene." The barefoot, white-clad doctor's earnest hokum belied an underlying, draggy seriousness. Lester took note of the older uptown intellectual crowd, whose polite attention—"expressions faintly tinged with boredom and distaste"—reminded her of "atheists attending a religious ritual out of sociological interest."[20]

The following Sunday, the *Times* attacked another charlatan with Bosley Crowther's dyspeptic diatribe on *The Chelsea Girls*: THE UNDERGROUND OVERFLOWS. Crowther began by announcing his desire "to wag a warning finger at Andy Warhol and his underground friends and tell them, politely but firmly, that they are pushing a reckless thing too far." (And that reckless thing was . . . drugs, nudity, bad camerawork, homosexuality?)[21]

The Chelsea Girls departed the Cinema Rendezvous soon after Crowther's piece, landing at the Regency, a larger second-run movie house near Lincoln Center on Broadway and Sixty-Seventh Street. Remaining through January, the film moved crosstown to the York, a 545-seat neighborhood theater on First Avenue at Sixty-Fourth Street. Ten weeks playing the Upper East Side were followed by five weeks on

20 The audience included Columbia professor Lionel Trilling, his wife Diana (who would write a long piece about Leary for *Encounter*) and *Partisan Review* editor William Phillips, along with respectable middlebrows Marya Mannes, Leonard Bernstein, Jerome Robbins and Otto Preminger. Then very much on the scene, attending underground movies, Preminger had a professional and perhaps personal interest in LSD. His 1969 comedy *Skidoo*, arguably the strangest Hollywood film of the late '60s, has a long sequence detailing Jackie Gleason's acid trip.

21 Last February's *Andy Warhol Uptight* was bad enough, Crowther complained, but "now that their underground has surfaced on West Fifty-Seventh Street and taken over a theater with carpets . . . it is time for permissive adults to stop winking at their too-precious pranks." (Increasingly square Crowther sealed his fate, railing against movie violence and obsessing over *Bonnie and Clyde*, which he panned three times. By January 1968, the sixty-four-year-old critic had been replaced by twenty-nine-year-old novelist Renata Adler.)

the Lower East Side at the St. Mark's, a slightly larger nabe on Second Avenue, half a block from the old Dom.

From October 1966 through May 1967, when Warhol and company brought *The Chelsea Girls* to the Cannes Film Festival (where, although invited, it did not have a public screening), there was scarcely a week when their movie was not pushing its reckless thing somewhere in Manhattan. The same period brought new visibility to the thirty-year-old Brooklyn native originally commissioned to write the Factory's films, Ronald Tavel.

Back in the spring, some eight months after *Shower* and *The Life of Juanita Castro* played the East Village, John Vaccaro had directed Tavel's *Life of Lady Godiva* at a dingy makeshift storefront on West Seventeenth Street renamed the Play-House of the Ridiculous. Michael Smith called it "terrifically entertaining," a combination of *Tom Jones* and *Flaming Creatures* that managed to parody Elizabethan drama and B westerns, set in a combination brothel-nunnery.

Vaccaro played the mother superior. Mario Montez was a nun. (Jack Smith provided the costumes.) Variously brassy and demure, Dorothy Opalach appeared in the title role, originally written for Beverly Grant. Tavel recalled Opalach as "an amazing personality who was a leading soprano at the Atlanta City Opera. She was a woman in her late forties who one day decided to leave her family and her opera career and come to New York to start her life over."

That fall, toward the end of *The Chelsea Girls*'s first run at the Tek, the Play-House of the Ridiculous presented two more Tavel-Vaccaro collaborations, *Indira Gandhi's Daring Device* and *Screen Test*, a vehicle for Mario Montez. "This is more like it," Joseph LeSueur began his *Voice* review. "For months I've been wondering where the action is." LeSueur was impressed with the improvised curtain-raiser, but *Indira Gandhi* seemed the best show he had seen downtown since the early days of the Living Theatre.

The inordinate length of the opening tableaux, he thought, justified the theater's reputation as "psychedelic," just as clouds of incense authenticated the play's self-description as "smell-o-drama." Vaccaro's stunning mise-en-scène filled the stage with starving masses—most obviously a randy untouchable with a two-foot boner—writhing, rioting, and eating garbage while mimicking the positions of the Kama Sutra. "We were just shameless," Tavel recalled, although he would later blame Vaccaro for the harijan's epic erection. Subject to all manner of sexual abuse, Jeanne

Phillips, the company's only woman of color, played the title character with a bandaged nose—a reference to the Indian leader's recent injury sustained when she was hit by a thrown rock.

Tavel hoped to follow up this triumph with *Gorilla Queen*, but Vaccaro found the play too long and convoluted. Instead, the Play-House presented a one-act dramatization of the Warhol movie *Kitchen*, retitled *Kitchenette*, together with a revival of *Juanita Castro*. Fresh from *Chelsea Girls*, Mary Woronov was cast as Fidel in the latter and assumed the Edie Sedgwick part in the former. Jack Smith had a walk-on. The production was directed by Tavel's brother, Harvey, who also played the onstage directors in both.

Reviewing the Play-House for the first time, Michael Smith was caught up in the delirium: *Kitchenette* "gets wilder as it goes on, builds up a berserk hilarity and daredevil velocity, and seems in constant danger of flying apart entirely. It never quite does. Though I have no idea what holds it together, something does."

After several weeks, the Play-House added a weekend attraction: *Big Hotel*, directed by Vaccaro from a farce written by Charles Ludlam (who had emerged as the company's leading actor, cannily upstaging Mario Montez in *Screen Test*) and starring Vaccaro himself, with Mario Montez and Jack Smith featured. The play travestied early 1930s movies like *Grand Hotel* and *International House*. Panna Grady underwrote the production, which, thanks to an international incident provoked by *Indira Gandhi's Daring Device*, was shut down by the fire department.[22]

Meanwhile, *Gorilla Queen*, a pansexual extravaganza with music, was staged at the Judson Theater. Michael Smith was rapturous, calling it "an unbroken series of lewd remarks, salacious innuendos, obvious and

22 When in early 1967 *Indira Gandhi* was presented at two local colleges, Rutgers and Columbia, outraged Indian students protested with a force sufficient to trigger complaints from both the Indian Consulate General in New York, who told the *Voice* the play was "grossly obscene," and the Indian Embassy in Washington, which warned that further performances would greatly damage Indo-American relations. The affront was widely publicized in India. Tavel blamed Vaccaro, who pointed out that the play was no longer being presented. Nonetheless, the police visited the Play-House five times and issued three summonses, charging that the theater lacked a license, a certificate of occupancy, and a permit of assembly. The mailing list was confiscated, the theater shut down and its manager was hauled into court. Dotson Rader, the Columbia student who arranged for the performance (and who a year later would be a leader in the Columbia strike) lost his position as head of the student entertainment organization Humanitas.

obscure puns—beyond wit, beyond self-indulgence, beyond belief." The play drew on the jungle movies that were closest to Tavel's heart, as evinced by his first impression of a young woman, dressed to impress, whom he encountered at a "celebrity-thickened" soiree organized by Lester Persky back in early 1965.

> An arresting twenty-two-year-old blueblood sporting a brunette beehive, a leopardskin evening outfit, and a pair of the largest brown eyes I was ever to have discombobulate me. "Nyoka, the Jungle Girl!" I exclaimed. "Do you think so?" she returned smiling irresistibly.

Tavel promised to bring her to the Factory to shoot "the grainy, all-new adventures of Nyoka" and recalled that Miss Edith Minturn Sedgwick was very pleased. That was then.

13

Sedgwick disengaged from the Factory, still hoping to hitch her star to Dylan's wagon. Her fellow Silver Hill alumnus was also looking elsewhere.

Having facilitated the *Exploding Plastic Inevitable* (and subsequently been marginalized), Barbara Rubin turned her attention back to London. In early May, she convened a group of friends—Allen Ginsberg, Peter Orlovsky, Ed Sanders, Tuli Kupferberg, Jonas Mekas, *EVO* publisher Walter Bowart, and even Warhol—to create a new entity: The Creeping Kreplach Non-Profit International Cultural Foundation of Purple People Art Combine.

Named for traditional Jewish soup dumplings, the Foundation would further Rubin's mission to transform the world by connecting visionary artists and musicians in ever more spectacular mixed-media events. She imagined an International Cultural Birthday Party to be held in London's Royal Albert Hall on June 16 and 17, almost exactly a year after International Poetry Incarnation. Enlisting the aid of Bernard Stollman and ESP-Disk, Rubin planned film screenings as well as performances by the Fugs, the Velvet Underground, the Chambers Brothers, and Bo Diddley. Other popular musicians—Donovan, Paul McCartney, Eric Burdon, Cass Elliot, Marianne Faithfull—were bruited too, as was Peter Fonda and, via transatlantic telephone, Ginsberg. However, Rubin was unable to raise sufficient backing.

Frustrated by what she regarded as British provincialism (among other things she was shut out of the London Film-Makers' Cooperative that she had promoted the previous summer), Rubin's proposals were met with a general lack of interest. Letters to Mekas mention little more than a half-baked happening arranged for Italian TV and featuring Piero Heliczer, and an abortive trip to visit Fellini in Rome. In late 1966, she returned to New York and the Film-Makers' Cinematheque, where, a year after the triumph of *Andy Warhol, Uptight*, she organized an ambitious multimedia event, *Caterpillar Changes*, announced with a striking butterfly-shaped poster and a press release promising NEW YORK'S FIRST UNITED ACID-HEADSPEED RELIEF FUN BALL & GLITTER PARADE.

The program ran for two weeks, from February 18 through March 3, and involved—at least on paper—most of the filmmakers Rubin knew. There were five projectors and two jazz ensembles, the Argentine tenor saxophonist Gato Barbieri's Free Jazz quintet, soon to record with ESP-Disk, and the Free Spirits, a pioneering jazz-rock fusion band currently playing the Scene. (Rubin may not have been able to secure the Albert Hall in London but she did recruit two of the most avant new musicians in New York, Barbieri and Free Spirits guitarist Larry Coryell, both of whom would play with the Jazz Composer's Orchestra.) There was also the promise, apparently unfulfilled, that Angus MacLise would rejoin the Velvet Underground for a piece called "The Dental Destruction of the Chairs (A Mass Mental Concentration Against Furniture) by Movies Movies Movies."

Although not apparent then, *Caterpillar Changes* was Rubin's graduation. The mise-en- scène even reminded some of a high school prom. Colored streamers and blue tinsel festooned the lobby. The filmmaker Matt Hoffman, one of the few to write about the event, found the Cinematheque foyer transformed into "a new kind of space—difficult, labyrinthine, challenging, bemusing." It reminded him of a jungle or carnival. Some nights, the auditorium featured a spun fiberglass screen that curved back from the stage to form a canopy over the audience.

Hoffman attended several shows. The first, on Monday, February 20, featured Harry Smith films on all five projectors, backed by a live band. The next night was devoted to Jonas Mekas. *Guns of the Trees* was the central projection, flanked by the second reel of *The Brig* and Storm de Hirsch's *Jonas in the Brig* while, projected behind the screen and reflected in a hand-held mirror, *The Brig*'s first reel functioned as a bright, moving square.

The number of actors on the screen at any time, the constant haunting images of mass suffering; a peace demonstration from *Guns* coincided with one of the shake-ups in *The Brig* while The Mothers of Invention poured out their agonies over the sound system. A weird, fragmented, but pervasive image of multiple horror and perception flooded the auditorium. But the whole thing had evaporated in minutes, to be replaced by a ballet of loving sympathy and tenderness. The projectors were slowed down to silent speed inducing a choreographic element to *The Brig*; it became impossible to sense that shuddering horror of the suffering and instead we were presented with the beauty of all those actors working in harmony.

A jazz band on stage began to play loose and easy, feeling themselves and the situation—they could see the show from behind the screen, but the audience could not see them, except for an occasional sharp silhouette when someone would project a movie, or a slide, or a band of colored light from behind them on the screen.

The evening of Friday, February 24, was again devoted to Harry Smith but this time the show was characterized by a rigorous "cubist" symmetry. The projectors were all centered and images were doubled by mirrors. The next day's matinee featured the Free Spirits accompanying Ed Emshwiller's films. Hoffman thought that the Cinematheque had a different feel: "The material was now shredded, latticed, laced, and cobwebbed over the audience and throughout the stage. Musicians stood amid a network of spun fiberglass that most obscured them from view."

By Tuesday, most of the projectors were out of commission, leaving a "pure abstract environment." Still, the closing night was spectacular. "All the material is gone," Hoffman wrote.

> A projector hanging on the side near the stage throwing a large trapezoid on the ceiling that is a children's doodle. Rich orgiastic ballet of flesh, Barbara Rubin's *Christmas On Earth*, alternately tinted blue and pink superimposed by the incredible candy concoctions of Harry Smith's hand painted color abstractions. Tumbling, tossing—a nightmare and a fantasy. [Gato Barbieri] plays an intense atonal solo backed up by feverish drumming as images become more complex. 8mm projector backstage throws an elongated narrow band across the screen—a fluctuating zoom lens

> trained on a factory-scape. Colored balls spin about the screen. The thing becomes too fast and varied to catalogue.

Hoffman ends his account by noting that he had to rush downtown to see the Jefferson Airplane, making their second New York appearance that night at Café Au Go Go.

14

The Chelsea Girls was still playing when the Velvet Underground LP was released. Response was mixed. Admitting that the Velvets were not easy to like, that their album was derivative and often dull, ending with two cuts, "Black Angel's Death Song" and "European Son," that were "pretentious to the point of misery," Richard Goldstein appreciated Nico's "harrowing" voice and acknowledged the band's significance. "Heroin" was "seven minutes of genuine twelve-tone rock 'n' roll." By then, however, the Velvets and Nico had gone somewhat separate ways.[23]

On the first anniversary of *The Exploding Plastic Inevitable*, it was announced that the Balloon Farm would be replaced by twenty-nine-year-old, Brooklyn-born music agent Jerry Brandt's brainchild, a state-of-the-art disco light-show pleasure dome: The Electric Circus. Not only would patrons dance amid the strobes, but the place would double as a carnival midway with wandering sword-swallowers, fire-eaters, and costumed gorillas.

The gala opening, Tuesday night, June 27, 1967, was a benefit for the Children's Recreation Foundation, co-founded by Senator Robert Kennedy. Jack Newfield, who was friendly with the senator, reported on the event for the *Voice*: "The immediate reaction was that Rome must have been like this in that middle period when decline was becoming decay."

Third Avenue was clogged with rented limos. The line snaked down St. Mark's to Second Avenue. Newfield reported that some 3,000 people

23 In February and March, Warhol presented Nico at the Dom (now known as the New Mod Dom), below the Balloon Farm. Her first, unfortunate show had her singing to tapes provided by the Velvet Underground. Bill Manville, who had been covering the Village bar scene since the 1950s, made his first visit to the Dom, and upon hearing Nico sing burst out laughing. Later, she was accompanied by jazz folksinger Tim Buckley and a screening of *Hedy* (advertised as *The Most Beautiful Girl in the World* with Mario Montez). Subsequently she was accompanied by Jackson Browne and *Vinyl*. Meanwhile, Warhol presented the Velvet Underground at Sokol Hall on East Seventy-First Street, the Czech equivalent of the old Dom Polski—back to Babushkaville!

filed past the sign limiting occupancy to 740. Literati (Truman Capote, Mary McCarthy, George Plimpton) cavorted with the glitterati (Yves Saint Laurent, Gloria Vanderbilt, Diana Vreeland), stars (Bette Davis, Muhammad Ali), and rubbed up against neighborhood characters (Tuli Kupferberg, Phil Ochs), although Senator Kennedy spent the evening with a millionaire discussing his slum program for Bedford-Stuyvesant. "It looked like the cover of the next Beatles album," per Newfield, and, in the absence of air-conditioning, felt like a steam bath.

Andy Warhol was amused by the transformation from jerry-built sensory bombardment to manufactured light show, citing the evolution the small alcove off the side of the dance floor where a few funky old mattresses had been thrown for people to "lounge" and Eric Emerson to bring his conquests during the *EPI* shows: "Now, under the new Electric Circus management, [Eric's Fuck Room] was transformed into the 'Meditation Room,' with carpeted platforms and Astro-turf and a health food bar."

Jonas Mekas showed up a few days later and found the place "totally lifeless." He ran into a friend who told him, "We have to get Barbara Rubin into this show somehow, immediately, to disrupt the whole thing, make it more real." In fact, Newfield had spotted Rubin on opening night, wearing a big white button—VOZNESENSKY GLOWS IN THE DARK—celebrating a Soviet dissident poet who'd recently read at the Village Theater and aggressively interviewing the Beautiful People for a never-made movie.

II

Counterculture, 1966–71

Flo Jacobs, frame enlargement, *The Sky Socialist* (1965–66). Courtesy of Ken Jacobs.

8

Turf Wars: Destroying Lower Manhattan, Inventing SoHo, Claiming the East Village, 1965–68

In which Ken Jacobs and Danny Lyons document the destruction of Lower Manhattan. Minimalism displaces Pop, outflanking the Park Place Group. Hippies invade the East Village. Newark erupts. The Angry Arts march. John Vaccaro defeats an uprising to stage *Conquest of the Universe.* Artists find an abandoned neighborhood where Jonas Mekas inaugurates a new cinematheque with Michael Snow's *Wavelength.*

> *A great artist can make art by simply casting a glance.*
>
> —Robert Smithson, "A Sedimentation of Mind: Earth Projects," *Artforum* (September 1968)

November 1965 had been a month of utopian expectation. Not only did the Film-Makers' Showcase present the New Cinema Festival but New York elected a handsome young mayor even as the Great Blackout altered the city's consciousness.

Not since the Kennedy assassination two years before had there been a comparable universal event. Yet, "far from creating a mood of dread, the power failure created a mood of euphoria," the artist Robert Smithson would note. There was an inexplicable, "almost cosmic joy." Others living downtown recall an unexpected solidarity, a festive energy, and a collective excitement. People asked each other what was happening and what it meant. Richard Tyler materialized at Claes and Patty Oldenburgs's new Fourteenth Street loft to explain that he had caused the power failure.

The Great Blackout created jubilation in Harlem. LeRoi Jones, now living uptown, called it a "special effect."

> Suddenly, at the corner of Lenox and 125th, a group of white people were being taunted and robbed. The police swung into action—saving white people is their second most important function after their most important function, saving white people's property . . . Windows were getting smashed and commodities disappearing at an alarming rate.

That same November, the artists known as the "Park Place Group" opened a cooperative gallery on West Broadway, a block and a half north of Houston Street. The ground floor of a six-story loft building, previously the province of an electrical appliance store, it was a fantastic space. The rent for what *New York Times* reporter Grace Glueck called an "improbable" 8,000 square feet (including the basement) was, by one account, an even more improbable $100 per month.

The ten-member Park Place Group was evenly divided between sculptors and painters, although only one, Tamara Melcher, was female. Many, including Dean Fleming, Peter Forakis, Forrest Myers, Melcher, and Leo Valledor, came from the Bay Area; a number were graduates of the California School of Fine Arts. Fond of terms like *space-warp*, *optic energy*, and *four-dimensional geometry*, the transplanted Californians were relaxed regarding new technology and unafraid of *retinal kicks*.

Theirs was an inclusive counterculture. They read *Scientific American*, dug the futuristic architect Buckminster Fuller (inventor of the geodesic dome), and pondered media theorist Marshall McLuhan. Inspired by Ornette Coleman, another West Coast émigré, the artists expressed themselves through the marathon Free Jazz (or "no jazz jazz") sessions held at their original home, 79 Park Place, a five-story loft building on the eastern edge of the condemned Washington Street Market.

The building, discovered by Fleming in late 1962, was—save for the ground-floor coffee shop Walter's Cozy Corner—entirely empty. It was owned by Columbia University and slated to be razed along with the market. (Produce would henceforth enter the city via the new Hunt's Point market in the Bronx.) In the meantime, entire floors, approximately 2,500 square feet, could be rented for $35 a month. Fleming told his friends.

The Group's most prominent member was Mark di Suvero. Recovering from a spinal-cord injury suffered in a freight-elevator mishap two years before, di Suvero could no longer fashion the heroically scaled arrangements of wooden beams scavenged from wrecked buildings that made his reputation. Yet he persevered, his grit an inspiration to younger artists. Di Suvero was also a socialist. He hated Pop Art and—having severed ties with his dealer Dick Bellamy, whose uptown Green Gallery had brought James Rosenquist, Andy Warhol, and Tom Wesselmann to Fifty-Seventh Street—enthusiastically joined in a cooperative enterprise.

Spring 1963, a few weeks after Henry Flynt, Tony Conrad, and Jack Smith picketed the culture palaces, six months before the No!artists had their first uptown show, the Park Place Group turned their building's fire-damaged fifth floor into an exhibition space. Like those at the March gallery, Park Place shows were collective environments; like the No!artists, the Park Placers took an adversarial position, but with a difference. "We were having fun and not letting them be part of it," Fleming recalled. To see the show "you'd have to go up five floors in the dark with the rats jumping, shit happening [and] once in a while, we'd put up a light bulb."

Reviewing a Park Place exhibition in December 1963, the critic and sculptor Don Judd (having his first solo exhibition at Green that month), noted the Group's stated opposition to the market and dislike of Pop Art. Once, but no longer, a supporter of di Suvero's "thunderous" work, Judd professed surprise that the Park Placers were not di Suvero clones.

The group lost their lease the following spring, leaving the neighborhood as a monument to itself, an urban graveyard documented by a few stubborn artists. Danny Lyon's 1967 photograph shows 79 Park Place boarded up and standing alone, a solitary tombstone on an otherwise empty block. Lyon, a twenty-five-year-old former photographer for CORE, was a friend of di Suvero, to whom he would dedicate his book *The Destruction of Lower Manhattan.*

Lyon's pictures were relics of a lost world: "The silence left in the streets was startling," he would later write. "As one wanderer put it, everyone left one night, even the dogs and the rats."

The tectonic shift called "urban renewal" displaced artists throughout Lower Manhattan. In the late 1950s, master builder Robert Moses suggested that David Rockefeller and other financial titans develop the old city below the Brooklyn Bridge and west to the Hudson. By the time the Park Place Group got their building, the painters once clustered at Manhattan's southern tip, Coenties Slip, were largely gone.

The area around the Fulton Fish Market was also under development, although di Suvero was able to hold onto his studio. Lyon, who found a nearby place on Beekman Street, photographed di Suvero's atelier as well as an abandoned artist's loft four blocks away on Ferry Street in New York's still smelly wholesale leather district once known as the Swamp.

Also on Ferry Street, Ken Jacobs occupied a small loft—the top floor of a six-story building two blocks from the Brooklyn Bridge's Manhattan landing—which he managed to keep long enough to shoot a lyrical allegory, *The Sky Socialist*. The film was, of necessity, made on 8mm—Jacobs's 16mm camera had been stolen in 1964. After the city gave Jacobs and his wife Florence Karpf $1,600 to clear out, the couple found a loft on Chambers Street, across City Hall Park but close enough to continue filming Ferry Street and environs.[1]

Where *The Destruction of Lower Manhattan* is brusquely apocalyptic, *The Sky Socialist* is tenderly elegiac—a paean to the Brooklyn Bridge and love letter to the artist's wife. Largely confined to ancient rooftops and empty cobblestone alleys, the movie is silent and essentially gestic. The contemplation of eccentrically dressed actors hanging out amid fetishized props in a deserted urban landscape, its mise-en-scène is more understated than but not unrelated to that of Oldenburg's early Ray Gun productions or Jack Smith's orgiastic films.

The mood is shabby and bucolic. Ferry Street's weathered walls, water towers, sooty metal shutters, and ancient brick cobblestones provide an abandoned city in which Jacobs suggests more than stages a triangle involving Anne Frank (Karpf), miraculously spared, Jacobs's alter ego Isadore Lhevinne (Dave Leveson), an obscure writer whose 1931 novel of the Russian Revolution, *Napoleons All*, Jacobs discovered in a used

---

1 Danny Lyon and Ken Jacobs were not the only artists documenting the Swamp. Samuel Beckett was in town July 1964, shooting a movie with Buster Keaton under the Brooklyn Bridge, only blocks from Jacobs's Ferry Street loft. A year later, the Hollywood production *A Fine Madness* used the same location. Most uncannily, Jerry Schatzberg posed Bob Dylan near the deserted junction of Ferry and Jacob Streets for the photographs found on the sleeve of *Blonde on Blonde*, as well as that of Dylan's 45 "I Want You," and the cover of the July 30 issue of the *Saturday Evening Post* under the headline: "BOB DYLAN: REBEL KING OF ROCK 'N' ROLL."

bookstore, and Maurice, a manic sharpie in a Panama hat (filmmaker Bob Cowan). Maurice functions as a creepy reality principle, lackadaisically mocking the oblique courtship of demure Anne and wistful Isadore: He presents her with various junk treasures, she hands him a glass of clear water that acts as a lens while, plugged into a transistor radio, Maurice dances by himself.

Occasionally visited by the Muse of Cinema (Julie Motz), who ultimately supplies a happy ending, the characters bask in the sun or slip into reveries. For all the references to historical tragedy, *The Sky Socialist* is a movie about the beauty of things as they are. The artist casts a glance; the sparse narrative is put on hold so the camera can ponder the grandeur of the Bridge, the proximity of the East River, the caverns created by the arched Municipal Buildings, the top of the Tombs, the clerks spending their lunch hour on park benches. All action is digression; everything is now.

2

Jacobs spent several summers working on *The Sky Socialist*. Having first shown sequences in February 1966 at the Tek, he exhibited the film in various forms for decades before creating a digital version in 2019. This last iteration includes an addendum shot in the early fall of 1966 when the old Swamp had been gutted to create the cooperative apartment complex Southbridge Towers.

Padlocked buildings and empty storefronts give way to wrecked facades and mounds of rubble—a "half-razed ghost town" per the *New York Times* architecture critic Ada Louise Huxtable, a determined foe of heedless urban renewal whom Jacobs encountered on Ferry Street and filmed in the *Sky Socialist* addendum. Huxtable was exasperated to see the last granite lintels and columns of the pre–Civil War brick buildings "going down like tenpins on Ferry Street." The so-called Brooklyn Bridge Southwest project was, she wrote, a "total bulldozer plan" perversely realized at a time when the Lindsay administration had officially renounced the approach.

Huxtable's 1964 book *Classic New York: Georgian Gentility to Greek Elegance* hailed the superlative buildings still found along the East River south of the Brooklyn Bridge. The same was true of the nameless district just below the new Park Place Gallery. Dense with mid-nineteenth-century cast-iron structures, the blocks between Canal and Houston, from Wooster to Mercer, were the city's "richest stand of Victorian commercial architecture of the Civil War era," Huxtable wrote in a July 1966 *Times* article.

Bounded by Italian tenement neighborhoods on the east and west, the area was known as "Hell's Hundred Acres" or simply "The Valley." Once a realm of grand hotels and upscale emporia, later the hub of New York's wholesale dry-goods trade, the Valley waned and went to seed as the textile industry relocated to the South. A 1962 City Club report on "the wastelands of New York" deemed it a commercial slum, ripe for demolition. It was also something of a black hole.

In 1962, Gilbert Millstein's *New York Times Magazine* piece "Portraits of the Loft Generation" estimated that as many as 7,000 artists were holed up, working (and illegally living) in downtown lofts "scattered all over lower Broadway, the streets around Fulton and Washington Markets, Canal, Chambers, Grand and Fulton Streets, Fourth Avenue and Lafayette Street." Conspicuously absent from his Baedeker were the streets of Lower Manhattan's largest unrenewed territory—a potential Klondike for artists.

By day, huge trucks, parked on the sidewalks, clogged narrow streets left eerily desolate after dark and empty on weekends. While technically located in the South Village at 542 West Broadway, the Park Place Gallery offered a vantage point on a new frontier.[2]

3

Robert Moses thought so too. For decades, he had dreamt of spinning a steel and concrete web around the metropolitan area.

Moses envisioned Manhattan traversed by three great elevated highways. An Upper Manhattan Expressway would cross Harlem around 125th Street, linking the Triboro and George Washington Bridges. An elevated Mid-Manhattan Expressway out of *Things to Come* might snake through a thicket of skyscrapers to join the Midtown and Lincoln Tunnels. And bulldozing Broome Street through the Valley, Little Italy, and the Lower East Side, the Lower Manhattan Expressway could connect the Holland Tunnel with the Manhattan and Williamsburg Bridges. The

2 The Park Place Gallery had a precursor, the storefront Kaymar Gallery at 538 West Broadway where, in April 1964, Brian O'Doherty reviewed "the first show of the avant-garde deadpans that have been appearing in uptown galleries" (Dan Flavin, Donald Judd, Sol LeWitt and Frank Stella among them). The show turned its environs into "an original Coolsville," O'Doherty noted.

Upper and Mid-Manhattan expressways had been abandoned but, despite continuous postponements, the Lower Manhattan Expressway (LOMEX) remained live.

The Master Builder had been stymied in his attempt to "renew" Greenwich Village. Community groups prevented the extension of Fifth Avenue across Washington Square and, in 1961, blocked a Moses plan to level twenty blocks on the Village's western edge, from Hudson Street to the river. Perhaps not coincidentally that area was home to anti-redevelopment activist Jane Jacobs, who criticized Moses in her 1961 book *The Death and Life of Great American Cities*. Recruited by the newly formed Joint Committee Against the Lower Manhattan Expressway in the summer of 1962, Jacobs took up the struggle against LOMEX—a cause célèbre with its own protest song, "Listen, Robert Moses," written by Jacobs with an assist from Bob Dylan at the height of his *Broadside* phase.

After a stormy six-hour hearing in December 1962, the Board of Estimate unanimously rejected Moses's proposal. Still, the following April, he revived the plan yet again as a ten-lane elevated structure. Once more LOMEX came before the Board of Estimate, this time with Mayor Wagner's backing. A lame duck in an election year, Wagner ordered the job to commence in May 1965. Yet it did not.

As a candidate John Lindsay campaigned against LOMEX. Once elected, he thought he might slip through the plan as a trench. Thanks to community protests, the project—officially unveiled in March 1967—stalled again. Little Italy was saved. The Cast-Iron District or SoHo (the city planner acronym for South of Houston) would be preserved, if not for artists. Following the recommendations of a 1963 report that noted the area's predominantly Black and Latino workforce, the City Planning Commission sought M-I zoning laws that restricted SoHo to light industry and forbade residence. Still, as businesses continued to decamp, landlords were eager to rent lofts (or unload their buildings), prudently concealing addresses when advertising in the *Village Voice* classifieds.

Artists had found spaces on the periphery, West Broadway or Canal Street (location of the original Fluxhall), but only a hardy few colonized the interior Valley. Jack Smith occupied two top floor lofts on the corner of Grand and Greene thanks to the largesse of his patron Isabelle Eberstadt. In 1965, enterprising urban pioneer Dean Fleming moved into a loft on Broome Street, off Mercer—LOMEX ground zero—painted it white, "tapped the gas, tapped the lights, tapped the water, got everything for free." Don Judd camped out around the corner, quite possibly the only other resident in a one-block radius.[3]

Artists were careful to keep their lights dim lest they attract the unwanted attention of the fire department or building inspectors. In April 1966, a benefit "peace party" at the painters Leon Golub's and Nancy Spero's Prince Street loft was raided by several dozen police and firemen.

4

The Park Place Gallery was located on the residential side of Houston Street. Overlooking the Valley, just west of the six blocks plowed under for the construction of NYU's brutalist Silver Towers, the gallery anticipated what SoHo would become and how SoHo art would be displayed.

Recognizing a place for a large outdoor sculpture in Silver Towers, Park Place's twenty-eight-year-old director Paula Cooper suggested the project purchase a Mark di Suvero sculpture and stake a claim. She was informed that the spot was already reserved for a Picasso. Still, the Park Place Gallery of Art Research, Inc. provided the template for galleries to come. Expansive enough to encompass the Group's outsized, urban-scale sculptures, their space fostered an atmosphere and viewing protocol quite different from the uptown art scene. It was utilitarian and could be imagined as an aesthetic laboratory. "Park Place artists take the Space Age for granted and try to get it across in their work," David Bourdon wrote in a laudatory 1966 *Art News* article wittily titled "E=MC_2 à Go-Go." "The distortion of real and implied space is what gives Park Place art its 'fourth-dimensional' quality." (Emphasizing the confluence of weird angles, Peter Moore's installation photograph of the gallery's opening show suggests *The Cabinet of Dr. Caligari*.)

Park Place tempered Abstract Expressionist hubris with Pop Art fun. Fleming, considered by Bourdon to be the group's "most glamorous and doctrinaire" member, was a former hot-rodder and student of aeronautical engineering. Along with Peter Forakis and Forakis's then wife Phyllis Yampolsky, he drew avant-garde comic books; his interests

3 Dick Higgin's two-hour long feature *The Flaming City*—described as "an anti-semantic love story about a marvelous part of New York City and the people who lived there"—filmed in 1963 and largely devoted to fluxing around, has considerable footage of SoHo's cast-iron cornices, facades, and empty streets.

included Zen, Jung, the esoteric mathematician P. D. Ouspensky, and, like Myer (another teen dragster as well as a rock 'n' roll drummer), Buckminster Fuller.

Yet, by the time Grace Glueck characterized Park Place as an "off-off-Madison-Avenue outpost" for so-called minimal, pure, or systemic art, the gallery had already been preempted. "People think of our art as cool," Ed Ruda told her. "But it's really full of visual excitement and energy—the kind of thing you feel when you walk down a city street." Perhaps. But compared to rigorous minimalists like Donald Judd, Robert Morris, and Dan Flavin, as well as newer artists Carl Andre (who made art from bricks and metal plates found in the Valley) and Sol LeWitt (fabricator of modular open-cube structures and soon-to-be maker of what he called "conceptual art"), Park Place was most definitely *un*cool.

Primary Structures, the defining show of the minimal-systematic-ABC art tendency, opened to widespread excitement at the Jewish Museum in April 1966. The corrective to *The Responsive Eye*, organized by thirty-one-year-old Trinidadian curator Kynaston McShine with the assistance of twenty-nine-year-old critic Lucy Lippard, *Primary Structures* was so Now that the first *New York Times* review was provided by fashion reporter Charlotte Curtis. The exhibition was expected to be trendsetting, Curtis wrote. Sources considered it "unquestionably the zowiest (the with-it set's ultimate accolade)." The *Times*'s new art critic, thirty-eight-year-old Hilton Kramer, more soberly deemed *Primary Structures* "historic" and "the first comprehensive glimpse of a style that promises—or perhaps one should say threatens—to become our period style."[4]

Pop dispatched Abstract Expressionism and Minimalism dispensed with Pop. The easygoing Park Placers were caught in the middle. Attracted to visual sleight of hand, peripheral vision, and spatial illusions, the Group even tolerated Op Art—a despised tendency reviled by

4 Brought up on the existential *Sturm und Drang* of Abstract Expressionism and an admirer of Mark di Suvero, whom he regarded as the great new American sculptor, Kramer found *Primary Structures* a bit didactic. "I cannot recall another exhibition of contemporary art that has to the same extent, left me feeling so completely that I had not so much encountered works of art as taken a course in them." Less enthralled, Harold Rosenberg wrote in the *New Yorker* that "Minimal Art is Dada in which the art critic has got into the act." The year would bring an altogether more militant form of Dada.

formalist critics for its "trompe l'oeil tactility." Perhaps inadvertently, McShine critiqued the showmanship of Robert Grosvenor's colossal, spectacularly cantilevered, V-shaped structure by placing it in a gallery with some aggressively untitled, blandly upstaging box-like things by Judd and Morris.

The Park Placers may have been the first art world gang to frequent Mickey Ruskin's new bar Max's Kansas City—which opened a month after their gallery, not quite downtown on Park Avenue South near Seventeenth Street—but Grosvenor aside, the Group lacked presence at *Primary Structures*. Forakis was represented by a seven-foot-tall flat aluminum curlicue titled *JFK*; Myers, by an even larger aluminum bent-triangular form, and he was linked in the catalog to Buckminster Fuller. Their work seemed cute, even passé. By contrast, Flavin's piece—a sort of crossbow constructed out of four eight-foot-long deep crimson commercially produced fluorescent tubes—went straight from the Jewish Museum to Max's.[5]

In the hyper-historical New York art world of 1966, serious consideration was reserved for work manifesting the new mentalité. Thus, only months after opening their gallery—self-hyped as the home of "a *true movement* of historic importance," presenting David Bourdon–designated "young masters" Myers and Valledor—the Park Place Group teetered on the brink of irrelevance. Led by Judd, another Max's regular who in his 1965 *Arts Yearbook* manifesto "Specific Objects," declared the recognition of three dimensions as "real space" solved "the problem of illusionism and of literal space" presumably once and for all, another clique had come to the fore.

Reviewing *Primary Structures* in *Arts Magazine*, the twenty-six-year-old artist Mel Bochner recognized a new attitude that consigned the Park Place Group, among other sculptors, to a purgatory inhabited by "art-mystics," "art-existentialists," "space-arts," and retro-futurist artists merely "manipulating streamlined versions of outmoded forms." All were to be dismissed in any discussion of the New Art. Judd and the other high-minded hardcore reductivists (Andre, Flavin, LeWitt, and Morris)

5 A limited edition of three, it was titled *Corner monument 4 those who have been killed in ambush (to P.K. who reminded me about death)*. Minimalism was strictly about itself, although Flavin smuggled some political content in with a cryptic reference to a conversation regarding the Vietnam War with his friend, the artist Paul Katz.

programmatically effaced content and, as much of their work was fabricated, the hand of the artist. Despite a kindred hard-edged minimalist style, Park Place was hooked on old-fashioned expressive art.

Judd's "Specific Objects" essentially accused di Suvero of being an Abstract Expressionist–wannabe hack, using "beams as if they are brush strokes, imitating movement as [Franz] Kline did." Excluded from *Primary Structures*, di Suvero was nonetheless invited to a symposium at the Jewish Museum, presumably to strike back. He did, explaining that his "friend Don Judd can't qualify as an artist because he doesn't do the work . . . A man has to make a thing in order to be an artist."

Says who? Surely not Andy Warhol, who was closing the *EPI* just as *Primary Structures*—the zowie minimalist counterweight to his mega zowie maximalist extravaganza—was opening. Nor would Robert Smithson, who frequented Park Place and would transform the gallery by writing about it.

5

Smithson, a self-invented art-world hipster and wise-guy geek still in his twenties, was seemingly born to the scene. A native of Passaic, New Jersey, who steeped himself in science fiction and never bothered with college, Smithson moved to the lower Lower East Side, took classes at the Arts Students League, hung out at the Cedar, babysat for his neighbor gallerist Richard Bellamy, sat for Alice Neel, and began to paint gnarly looking icons spooky enough to have been planted in a field of Haitian sugarcane.

Smithson had his first solo show, *Posters from Hell*, at age twenty-one, at the midtown Artists Gallery during the *Connection* summer of 1959. The paintings are no longer extant (supposedly the show sold out), but their titles are suggestive: *Blue Dinosaur*, *Flesh Eater*, *Shark Man*, *The Spider Lady*, *Portrait of a Lunatic*, and the triptych *Walls of Dis*. Smithson even received a review from Irving Sandler in *Art News*: "These monsters, whelped by Surrealism and primitive art, are reared by frenzied Action Painting," Sandler wrote. "*Walls of Dis*, with its crude totemic creatures, would have looked well in the temple of some savage cult."

Smithson's early work flaunted a fetishized Christian religious iconography, informed by an appreciation of Byzantine art. Inspired by early Pop and *Naked Lunch*, he made sci-fi junk assemblages as well as delicately colored pencil drawings of sexually suggestive male and female nudes sometimes collaged within geometric patterns. Around 1964, Smithson abandoned figuration to become exclusively a maker of objects and soon after a writer. Brian O'Doherty included him in *Lesser Known and Unknown Painters*—an exhibition sponsored by American Express for the World's Fair's second season. His piece, titled *Quick Millions*, was neither painting nor sculpture—a geometric plexiglass construction that hung on the wall. He described it in the catalog as "emerging from a world of remote possibilities held together by incomprehensible motives."

Like the Park Placers, Smithson was taken with Buckminster Fuller. Named *Cryosphere* for the Earth's zone of solid water, his contribution to *Primary Structures* evoked the hub-connectors on a Fuller geodesic dome. But where Dean Fleming was a proto-hippie who would leave New York for Drop City, a Colorado commune notable for its geodesic domes, Smithson enjoyed holding forth and crossing swords nightly at Max's Kansas City. "Bob was a formidable debater," Mel Bochner recalled. "Wickedly, brutally, bitterly, laugh-out-loud funny."

Lost in the *Primary Structures* crowd, Smithson wrote an essay, "Entropy and the New Monuments," that, published in the June 1966 issue of *Artforum*, upended the show and put the entire tendency in a new light. "Many architectural concepts found in science-fiction have nothing to do with science or fiction, instead they suggest a new kind of monumentality which has much in common with the aims of today's artists," Smithson began, changing the frame from Fifty-Seventh Street to outer space. In addition to Judd (whose friendship he cultivated and whose pink Plexiglas box amusingly struck him as a "giant crystal from another planet"), these included LeWitt, Flavin, Morris and "certain artists in the 'Park Place Group.'"

Making a virtue of a deficit, Smithson associated their work with a cosmic listlessness, a sense of "monumental inaction," a future in which the universe itself would burn out. His favorite term was *entropy*. Grosvenor's suspended structural surfaces canceled out the notion of weight. The "brain-washed mood" of LeWitt's wooden grids and cubes pulverized the myth of progress. Time stood still in the "fossilized sexuality" of Morris's leaden brassiere and Oldenburg's "pre-historic 'ray-guns'" ("mixing the time states or ideas of *1984* with *One Million B.C.*").

Flavin was Smithson's favorite. His neon light sculptures, made from fixtures purchased on Canal Street, destroyed classical time, demolished space, and demanded a new definition of "matter." Their implicitly religious iconography might also have appealed to Smithson but as a materialist, he prized facts over values. Even while name-checking Barthes, McLuhan, Mallarmé, Borges, and Burroughs, along with various authors of science fiction, Smithson professed to compliment Judd for recognizing that printed matter was better looked at than read.

Smithson prized artificial materials (plastic, chrome, neon), writing with approval of the "alchemic fascination with inert properties" that would rather turn gold into cement than vice versa. Where the socially conscious photographer Danny Lyon was implicitly appalled by urban renewal, Smithson out-Warholed Warhol in perversely associating the new aesthetic with the proliferation of suburban shopping malls ("the lugubrious complexity of these interiors has brought to art a new consciousness of the vapid and the dull"). He appreciated the stripped-down "padded cell" look of the Cinemas I and II and the rows of boxlike glass skyscrapers along Park Avenue, singling out the Union Carbide Building with its "purposeless educational displays," an apt location for Ron Rice's *Queen of Sheba Meets the Atom Man.*

Satirical and arcane, spinning out a theory that might have conjoined Harry Smith with Hermann Hesse's *Glass Bead Game*, Smithson consigned the Park Place Group to "a space-time monastic order, where they research a cosmos modeled after Einstein [and] Fuller's 'vectoral' geometry." At a 1964 lecture Smithson is known to have attended, Fuller sarcastically noted that the experts claim that "the fourth dimension was just 'ha ha' "—meaning that it could not be modeled. Deciding to take Fuller literally, Smithson proposed relating different sorts of merriment to various shapes. "The chuckle is a triangle" and "the giggle is a hexagon" but a "guffaw is asymmetric."

Thus, he concluded, "if we apply this 'ha-ha-crystal' concept to the monumental models being produced by some of the artists in the Park Place Group, we might begin to understand the fourth-dimensional nature of their work." Their ambitions were laughable.

6

Primary Structures was still reverberating in 1967. The new *Village Voice* art critic, poet John Perreault, devoted his first column of the year to "clearing the air" regarding so-called Minimal Art: Thanks to *Primary Structures*, "we have a full-fledged 'movement' on our hands again," just born and already dying.

Minimal Art was being "strangled by the pseudo-analytical, passé Positivist, pornographically Hegelian death clasp of Greenbergian formalism," Perreault wrote with Ginsbergian panache. Still, he found it necessary to distinguish the Park Place Group from the more rigorous work produced by the Judd-Morris axis. Park Place was too easy and too . . . posh. A week later, Perreault noted that if Park Place was "almost our only downtown gallery that gets regular uptown coverings," it was perhaps

> because it is rare among downtown showplaces in its professionalism and its chic and because it has done what so few downtown galleries seem to be able to do: exhibit artists of high levels of professional workmanship, working in related areas of style. Park Place shows cool, slightly industrial, very neatly executed abstract art on the grand scale that its simple, spotless space can show to best advantage.

The group's mentor di Suvero might appreciate "professional workmanship," but the term, along with "chic," "slightly industrial," and "neatly executed," could hardly be read as praise. Nor could Perreault's sense of this downtown showplace as something like a showroom, perhaps for fancy foreign cars.[6]

Park Place sought art-world alliances, hosting organizational meetings for Experiments in Art and Technology (E.A.T.) to develop collaborations between artists and engineers, as well as music concerts by avant-garde composers like Terry Riley, Philip Glass, La Monte Young, and Steve Reich.

In April 1966, the very month of *Primary Structures* and *The Exploding Plastic Inevitable*, Fleming had recruited Reich for a benefit event at

---

6 Six months later, Perreault repeated himself, characterizing the work shown at Park Place as "chic," as well as "cool, professional, and well-designed, if somewhat derivative." Bob Neuwirth's "free-standing black door backed by a flashing light" was the standout. Perreault's judgement seems a bit unfair in that the gallery's invited artists included Morris, LeWitt, Andre, and Smithson, the minimalist painter Brice Marden, the eccentric abstractionist Eva Hesse, and future video artist Joan Jonas, as well as Bob Dylan's pal. (Briefly associated with the *E.P.I.*, Neuwirth also had a program at the Film-Makers' Cinematheque that year: His Edie Sedgwick vehicle, *A Light Look,* enjoyed a four-day run in early January. Finished film or home movie? According to the ad it "reveals the most fragile beauty of all the underground to be a real Chaplin" and cites supporting roles by Salvador Dali and Bob Dylan.

Town Hall in support of the Harlem Six—four Black youths who attempted to intervene with police in an April 1964 street altercation and were subsequently convicted of murdering the proprietor of a Harlem used clothing store.

Presented by Dick Gregory and Ossie Davis, the event also included slide projections by Gerd Stern. Reich served as sound engineer and premiered his twelve-minute phased tape-loop *Come Out*, a visceral, hypnotic, percussive piece based on countless repetitions of a phrase used by one of the Six about having to demonstrate against police brutality by making the "bruise blood come out to show them."

In May, Reich included *Come Out* at Park Place as part of a concert of "tape music." *Voice* music critic Carman Moore related Reich's "strident, reiterative work" to rock 'n' roll and mechanical fan belts. The sound loop was like a "raga exercise, distorting and distorting to incandescence." After nine months, Reich returned to the gallery to participate in Fleming's consciously consciousness-altering invitational group show, designed "to break space and change your mind."

Opening just after Barbara Rubin's *Caterpillar Changes* completed its run at the Tek, *Dean Fleming—Primal Panels/Charles Ross—Prisms & Lenses/Jerry Foyster—Mirrors/Steve Reich—Continuous Tape Music* ran throughout March 1967. Fleming's brightly colored, geometrically shaped Masonite paintings appeared to pop out of and slide back into white brick walls further warped by USCO associate Ross's liquid-filled prisms, some suspended from the ceiling, and large distortive plexiglass panels. By reflecting both, Foyster's space-expanding mirror grids further confounded the eye while Reich's contribution, *Melodica*, a hypnotic, ten-minute phased loop buzzed in people's brains. Grace Glueck praised the ingenious installation and ambient "sound effects (O.K., music)," concluding that although an "environment hardly likely to come together outside of a gallery," the show was "a stunner."

In mid-March, Reich organized an epochal concert, *Four Pianos*, as part of the exhibit. In addition to the tape pieces *Come Out* and *Melodica*, an ensemble performed three compositions, *Improvisations on a Watermelon*, *Saxophone Phase*, and *Four Pianos*. The experimental percussionist Max Neuhaus also contributed, interacting with the performance by positioning photo-sensers provided by E.A.T. on the gallery ceiling.

The *Four Pianos* performances epitomized the Park Place utopian vision—an environment conducive to shared ideas and pooled resources, a place for new technology and collaborations with nonartists. Carman Moore's laudatory review, illustrated by Fred McDarrah's photograph of the concert refracted through a bank of Ross's prisms, described "a well-attended and glittering affair" which literally blew minds: "So strong was the effect of *Four Pianos* that one of the listeners, who were all sprawled on the floor, fell into a howling kind of fit from which he emerged, shaken but otherwise (I think) undamaged."

If some assumed the seizure was drug-induced, Reich proudly credited his music.

7

Out West, the January 14, 1967, "Gathering of the Tribes" had drawn 20,000 celebrants to Golden Gate Park. This so-called Human Be-In, which brought all of the Haight-Ashbury to party in the park, was one more message from the Bay Area to New York, with Allen Ginsberg the perfect messenger.

The day before an anonymous group orchestrated a Happening in Grand Central Station, simultaneously releasing scores of balloons at the height of rush hour with the paper streamers reading NAPALM KILLS CHILDREN. In conjunction with the colorful balloons and their delicate scrolls, the protestors activated a tape recorder hidden atop an advertising display to blast a tape described by *Voice* reporter Stephanie Harrington as "the wild shrieking maddening noise of war." Harrington, who did not identify the organizers, was struck by the crowd's bemused reaction.

> There were a few remarks like "Go Back to Russia!" and "They must be some nuts." But there was relatively little hostility. There was much more curiosity and amusement and tolerance. The American public can absorb anything cheerfully—the bombings, the burnings, and even the balloons.

The Grand Central event served as promo for the "Angry Arts Week" co-sponsored by the NYU chapter of Students for a Democratic Society (SDS), the Greenwich Village Peace Center, and the anti-war Committee of the Professions. Between January 29 and February 4, hundreds of artists protested the Vietnam War with all manner of performances, concerts, readings, panel discussions, and exhibitions. Few were notable in themselves. *Voice* theater critic Arthur Sainer singled out three: Stan Brakhage's *23rd Psalm Branch* (a feature-length 8mm film that painstakingly annotated footage of Brakhage's Rocky Mountain refuge with explosive bits of battlefield imagery), Carolee Schneemann's *Snows* (a performance piece that encompassed her *Viet Flakes*, a short film composed of atrocity news photos), and an unnamed show by the Bread and Puppet Theater.

The latter began with an actual doctor's lecture on the treatment of burns, interrupted by a piercing amplified wail and the reading of a newspaper report on conditions in South Vietnamese hospitals. Meanwhile, wrapped in dirty bandages, a masked woman with outsized hands writhed in pain on the floor. As recounted in the *New Yorker*, "a long red scarf oozed from underneath her sheet, and mock bandages of shredded newspaper fluttered around her. The banshee wail of the fiddle rose like an air-raid siren and was abruptly cut off, leaving behind it a charged silence."

The least loved yet most popular work was the huge *Collage of Indignation*, for which local artists were invited to "paint, draw, or attach whatever images or objects that will express or stand for your anger against the war." Composed of twenty 10-by-6 canvas panels affixed with a clutter of paintings, statements, graffiti, and found objects, the *Collage* was displayed at NYU's Loeb Student Center, where it was visited by an estimated 10,000 people.

Critics were generally repelled. The critic Max Kozloff, one of the organizers, characterized the *Collage* as a "convocation of clichés and cretinisms." The painter Leon Golub agreed that the *Collage* was "gross, vulgar, clumsy, ugly!" not to mention bombastic, but, noting that hordes of visitors continuously packed the gallery, deemed it a success: "Largely anonymous even when huge signatures are scrawled across the canvas, [the piece was] a carrier of indignation harking back to street art, graffiti, burlesque, the carnival, the dance of death."

In short, the *Collage* existed outside aesthetics. No less than *Meat Joy* it was an unholy mess; like the Fugs it was raucously tasteless; it might almost be an instance of No!art. (Boris Lurie's name appears on the list of participants but the nature of his contribution is unknown.) Black Mask provided a painted spiral with the word REVOLUTION. Aldo Tambellini declined to join in. Instead, he postscripted Angry Arts

Week with *Black Death*, a funeral procession organized with Saul Gottlieb, that wended its way up from the East Village to arch-conservative, pro-war Cardinal Spellman's residence behind St. Patrick's Church. The action would now be in the street.

That spring, good vibes prevailed. A month or so later, Bob Fass, the host of WBAI's late night *Radio Unnameable*, called for listeners to show up Saturday midnight, February 11, at Kennedy Airport's International Arrival Building for a "Fly-In." According to *Voice* columnist Howard Smith, who covered the event, 2,000 came to hang out: "They were just there: talking love, singing, humming, sucking heart-shaped lollipops, cheering, throwing flowers on startled cops." A few weeks after the Fly-In, Smith reported on a modest Be-In that brought a crowd of 500 to Grand Central. "There were a few girls passing out flowers, an occasional waft of incense, one placard reading LOVE, and everyone was smiling. Some people joined hands and danced around in a circle sundered in thirty seconds by New York's Finest." He predicted more to come.

Indeed, publicized on a $250 budget used to print 3,000 posters and 40,000 handbills of a psychedelic-cum-yonic flower image designed by Peter Max, an Easter Sunday Be-In in Central Park made the front page of the *New York Times*: 10,000 CHANT L-O-V-E. Bernard Weinraub characterized the event as "noisy, swarming, chaotic, and utterly surrealistic." *Voice* reporter Don McNeill called it a "medieval pageant" that began at dawn when "laden with daffodils, ecstatic in vibrant costumes and painted faces, troupes of hippies gathered on a hill overlooking Central Park's Sheep Meadow." (For some time after the knoll would be known as Hippie Hill.)

Organized by anti-war activist Jim Fouratt, rock critic and *Crawdaddy!* editor Paul Williams, E.A.T. administrator Sue Hartnett, and Chilean poet-playwright Claudio Badal, a onetime associate of the Bread and Puppet Theater who managed to live rent free above a Fourteenth Street girdle shop next door to Taylor Mead, the Be-In had the tacit cooperation of the police and parks departments. McNeill, who considered the event "miraculous," noted that there was no center of activity. The field was muddy. The action was fluid as crowds surged and regrouped. It seemed open to all. In fact, the *Times* spotted the mayor's wife, Mary Lindsay, bicycling with her young son.

It was as if Dean Fleming's trippy Park Place show had spilled out of the gallery and taken root in Central Park. The Be-In was a magnet for photographers, among them Fred McDarrah, Diane Arbus, and Garry Winogrand. The latter two were featured, along with Lee Friedlander, in John Szarkowski's "*New Documents* show, which opened at MoMA in early March. So distinctive as to be given their own room, Arbus's thirty photographs were the star attraction. "Even her glamour shots look bizarre," the *Times* critic thought. Arbus's uncanny portraits of circus midgets, nudist couples, identical twins, a transvestite in curlers, and an aging burlesque queen backstage seemed to constitute a personal counterculture.

Arbus attended the show every day to eavesdrop on viewer responses and, according to her biographer, some of the most enthusiastic viewers were "East Village dropouts in beards and long hair." If she photographed such fans at the Be-In she made no prints, although she herself was photographed by Winogrand—diminutive and dressed for battle with camera and accessories draped around her neck.[7]

8

The *EPI*, *Death of the Mind*, and *Caterpillar Changes* had come and gone but their legacies continued. The Tek hosted another expanded cinema series for two weekends in June. The first was a Majik Lite show with USCO, Angus MacLise's Bardo Matrix, Charlotte Moorman, Nam June Paik, and Flux violinist Takehisa Kosugi. The other, more hippie-oriented, featured movies by Harry Smith, the Kuchar Brothers, and Paul Sharits, as well as live music and a light show provided by Group Image.

The most together of East Village "tribes," Group Image was a self-described multimedia corporation based in a loft on Second Avenue, off East Fifth Street. Group Image brought a taste of Haight Ashbury's hippie utopia, covered in *EVO* every week, to the East Village. Their band played in Tompkins Square Park and—publicly dissing the Electric Circus—on St. Mark's Place, with a regular Wednesday night gig at the Palm Gardens, where they might be joined by Village standbys like Hugh Romney and Tiny Tim.

Ultimately ephemeral, Group Image was ubiquitous throughout 1967 and into 1968. Even more so was the Electro Media Theater act that

7 The Be-In crowd was modest by San Francisco standards, but it metastasized. As organized by the Mobilization Committee to End the War in Vietnam, ten times as many rallied in the park three weeks later on April 15. Some 75 men burned their draft cards on Hippie Hill. Then, led by the Rev. Martin Luther King Jr., the crowd marched to the United Nations to protest the war in Vietnam.

premiered in mid-June at the Black Gate, a large room upstairs from the 200-seat theater. The initial *Self-Obliteration* performance was introduced with a lecture by art critic Gordon Brown, accompanied by Fluxus musician and songwriter Joe Jones, and orchestrated by the woman who would succeed Barbara Rubin as a taboo-busting downtown diva: Yayoi Kusama.

Demonstrating a genius for self-promotion, Kusama contrived to have herself appear as a Slum Goddess in *EVO*'s June 15–July 1 issue. Her press release ran beneath a half-page portrait of the artist provocatively posed lying on her stomach, naked save for her high-heel shoes, her back and posterior sprinkled with her trademark polka dots:

> The Dot Event is called Self Obliteration, an Audio Visual-Light Performance. Music for Kusama is invented by Joe Jones. He promises SOMETHING to create, endlessly—achieved by "self-playing music machines with no end and stop . . . eliminating the virtuoso . . ." A music bike will be driven around New York, to let the public know about the event; the bike will be parked in the lobby of the Black Gate. Kusama designed the bike flight suit. There will be a concert, with the sound of frogs, a frog quartet, Jones invented his own instruments, sitar-like, people can stay all night, sound will be endless, so are Kusama's dots—in blue black light. She herself is One with eternity—and promises, clad in a polka-dotted body stocking, "Extermination, Emptiness, Nothingness, Infinity, Endlessness, a trip, Self-Obliteration, Self-Destruction' and what not . . . but always it is the self and the endlessness, that concerns Kusama's obsessional mind, it's her bag . . . Patterns, Dots, Repeats—and Kusama, the center of dots on mattresses and baskets, endless/endless/endless.

The most orgiastic part of the performance was filmed by Jud Yalkut and used as the climax of his half-hour film *Kusama Self-Obliteration*, which would have its world premiere and win a prize at the Knokke-Le-Zoute Experimental Film Festival in December.

Beginning in July, Kusama staged Body Festivals in Lower Manhattan and Provincetown throughout the summer of 1967. The first was on a rainy Saturday afternoon in Tompkins Square Park. As reported by the *Sunday News*, the diminutive artist, dressed all in red (leotard, boots, cowgirl hat) and festooned with round white decals, appeared with a confederate, the Japanese painter Minol Araki, and began applying red dots to the torsos of male volunteers. Hippie onlookers joined in, while, according to Howard Smith, "Kusama, who was busy finding the reporters probably missed some of what was really happening." Smith ended his Scenes item by noting "a lady sitting on a bench, off to the side, unaware of a public celebration, gave into a private urge and removed her slacks and underpants . . . A cop stood about ten feet away, paralyzed with embarrassment."

The next day, Kusama appeared in Washington Square, painting male bodies and distributing "Love Forever" campaign pins. On July 23, Tompkins Square Park hosted a musical marijuana "smoke-in" (advertised in Spanish as well as English) while Kusama returned to Washington Square. "We have forgotten the beauty of our bodies," she told the *Sunday News*. "Why are we so ashamed and contrite? The nude body is all we own. Youth came to watch. They participated. They want love." In late August, Kusama had a weeklong engagement at the Electric Circus, staging a "Tea Dancers" happening also filmed by Yalkut.[8]

9

Kusama playtime and Hippie Hill euphoria notwithstanding, the East Village was turning dystopian. The neighborhood was roughly divided. The Puerto Ricans and Blacks who constituted some two-thirds of the population were largely concentrated in the worst slums east of Avenue B; the older white ethnics (Ukrainian, Polish, and Italian) were mostly west of Avenue A. Poets and artists were interspersed throughout. The influx of so-called hippies that began in 1966 and was estimated as high as 6,000 represented a new, potentially volatile element.

Osha Neumann, who dropped out of Yale in the mid '60s to become a painter, found a railroad flat on East Seventh Street between Avenues C and D. The streets "smelled of piss, mildew, roach powder, and rotting

8 In her autobiography, Kusama dates a "Body Paint Festival"—including nudity and flag-burning—held in front of St. Patrick's Cathedral to January 1967. This may be a fanciful description of the "Phallics Festival" of February 4, 1968, or a reference to an anti-war demonstration organized by an Angry Arts contingent that had disrupted a mass at St. Patrick's on Sunday, January 22, by unfurling posters portraying a napalm-maimed Vietnamese child. The *New York Times* reported twenty-three arrests, including Jackson Mac Low and his wife Iris, the poet Clayton Eshleman and future Motherfucker Thomas Osha Neumann. Kusama is not mentioned.

garbage." His bathtub was in the kitchen; his floor buckled with layers of cheap linoleum. Neuman's arrival coincided with that of the hippies: "Confetti blown from a party in some other part of town onto the Puerto Rican streets of the ghetto." The hippies appeared "oblivious to their neighbors. They stayed because the rents were cheap and the Lower East Side didn't seem to belong to anybody."

St. Mark's Place was theirs—the scene of a nightly Be-In. From 7:00 p.m. to midnight, the block between the Bowery and Second Avenue, home to the Electric Circus, was closed to traffic, thus creating an open-air souk-cum-acid dance party. The flashpoint was Tompkins Square Park. The neighborhood's only green space, located on the border between the Ukrainian and Puerto Rican areas, had been "a peaceful, if boring, park before the hippies came," explained Don McNeill, the young *Voice* writer who made the East Village his beat. Memorial Day 1967: The park was crowded and, as McNeill put it, the Ukrainians were sick of hippies sprawled on the grass, playing their bongos and chanting Hare Krishna. They filed a noise complaint. The police arrived—ignored and ridiculed by the hippies until they returned in force.

It was the 1961 Beatnik Riot but worse. "Sixty beatnik 'now-ists' took over a part of Tompkins Square Park on the Lower East Side on May 30 and rioted when ordered by police to quit singing, to stop making weird music, and to move on," the *Daily News* reported under the headline BAG 38 BEATNIKS IN RIOT AS THOUSANDS CHEER. More circumspect, the *New York Times* wrote that "2,000 spectators watched the brawl and many wept as the battle grew more intense." Skulls were cracked, heads were bloodied. There were nine reported injuries among hippies and police and thirty-eight arrests.

Hippies had lawyers, including Jerald Ordover, who had recently defended Charlotte Moorman when she was busted in February for playing topless at the Tek, and the local precinct was sensitive to community relations. The next day, city authorities declared the park a "troubadour area" and removed the keep-off-the-grass signs. On June 1, the police arranged for the Grateful Dead, in town for a ten-day gig at the Café au Go-Go, to bring some San Francisco good vibes with a free outdoor concert. Everything went well until, just as it ended, a group of thirty neighborhood kids began banging on garbage cans, calling for Latin music. Identified only as "anti-Hippies" in the *Times*, the group provoked a melee, pelting the hippies with debris and at one point seizing a woman and attempting to strip her.

This second riot led to another meeting with city officials and a series of more ecumenical concerts, including one by the Fugs. Tension was lowered but the bloom was off the rose. The East Village would always be contested turf. Over the course of the year, two Lower East Side experiments—the Free Store opened by a group of San Francisco Diggers on Tenth Street a block west of Tompkins Square Park and the Millennium Film Workshop, a free school-cum-equipment collective on lower Second Avenue, founded and initially directed by Ken Jacobs—would succumb to grim reality.[9]

Meanwhile, a volcano erupted across the Hudson. Boston, Tampa, Dayton, Atlanta, Buffalo, and Cincinnati all experienced racial disturbances. These were but a prologue to Newark. A Black cab driver's arrest lit the fuse. Just past midnight, July 12, a firebomb hit the police station. Looting began within the hour—"the largest demonstration of Black people ever held in Newark," according to SDS co-founder Tom Hayden, who'd spent the past four years in the city as a community organizer.

The uprising lasted five days. Hayden thought it extremely focused: "Rampaging was aimed almost exclusively at white-owned stores." This was a very particular form of Be-In. "People on the street felt free to take shelter from the police in homes of people they did not know." Touring the scene at 5:00 a.m. on July 13, New Jersey governor Richard Hughes was dismayed by the "carnival atmosphere." Then, as looting continued into the next day, Hughes called up 3,000 National Guardsmen and, assigning 500 state troopers to Newark, put the Black wards under martial law.

Poorly disciplined, panicky guardsmen ran amok, firing on Black-owned businesses and bystanders. Once the fires died down, the ongoing occupation was justified by the presence of mysterious snipers—none of whom were ever caught. At least twenty-four Black residents were killed, and many more suffered injuries. Among them was LeRoi Jones, dragged from a car, beaten by the police, and charged with

9 Funded by a federal grant funneled through the New School for Social Research and administered by the St. Mark's Church, the Millennium opened during the summer of 1966, offering open screenings at the church, as well as classes and editing facilities at the old Second Avenue courthouse. Conflict with his assistant director, the more commercially minded filmmaker Stanton Kaye, led to Jacobs's ouster after six months. The story got page-one coverage in the *Voice*. The grant was terminated. Jacobs was briefly able to keep the project afloat on his own with help from Jonas Mekas. Jacobs left and Millennium continued as a screening facility without him.

transporting two revolvers. Beside the *Voice*'s page-one story THE EXPLODED CITY: EXERCISE IN FUTILITY, the wounded poet, photographed by Fred McDarrah, glared as he was cuffed to a cop: One of Us.

Three months after Newark, as presaged by Paul Thek's sculptural self-portrait, *The Tomb*, popularly known as "Dead Hippie", the East Village bubble burst. Sunday morning, October 8, two naked white bodies—Linda Fitzpatrick, an eighteen-year-old runaway from a posh Connecticut suburb, and her boyfriend, a twenty-four-year-old drug dealer, James Hutchinson, with the street name "Groovy"—were discovered in the boiler room of an Avenue B tenement next door to the Annex and a block from Tompkins Square Park, their brains bashed in with a brick.[10]

10

Park Place closed on July 31, 1967. Grace Glueck bid farewell to "the turned-on downtown gallery." Even with wealthy angels, the cooperative had been running at a loss and the artists were at loggerheads. "Enough to say that the gallery could not hope to satisfy all of the individual inclinations," Ed Ruda recalled.

Space age to the end, the last show included a USCO dome with a black light and a strobe, which was meant to be climbed into. Nancy Graves's life-sized camels were positioned beside it. Danny Lyon's biker photographs were on the wall. "The final meeting was weird," Ruda would write. "We were all seated in the back room at Park Place enveloped by Bob Dacey's aluminum-foil environment and blinking strobe lights; the perfect science-fiction."

Still, a promised land lay just below Houston Street. Slightly more than a month after Park Place shut down, George Maciunas opened his first artists' cooperative, a new Fluxhouse in what had been a cardboard factory at 80 Wooster Street, between Spring and Broome, the very heart of future SoHo. Maciunas had his own utopian vision. Over the past year, he roamed the Valley, noting those underused buildings that could be transformed into artist cooperatives.

By November 1966, Maciunas identified ten, making down payments with funds supplied by the J. M. Kaplan Foundation. Unfortunately, Kaplan withdrew from his project to support the artist cooperative

10 Under the headline WHERE HAVE ALL THE FLOWERS GONE, the October 13, 1967, issue of *Time* magazine reported on a "Death of Hip" funeral in San Francisco.

housing developed in the old Bell Laboratories Building in the West Village neighborhood Jane Jacobs saved from demolition. Still, Maciunas soldiered on, operating a benign, if risky, pyramid scheme in which the cash advanced by prospective tenants was used to make deposits on additional buildings.

Maciunas cared little that his planned renovations (not to mention occupancies) were in violation of SoHo's nonresidential status or that making a public offering without first filing a full-disclosure prospectus with the New York State Attorney General was illegal. He put out a Fluxhouse flyer announcing the purchase of properties on Greene, Wooster, Grand, and Prince streets. Maciunas intended 16–18 Greene to be Fluxhouse I but the honor went to 80 Wooster.

Relocating his crew of "starving artists" as needed, Maciunas placed ads in the *Voice* classified section offering sizeable studio lofts for as little as $2,500 with monthly charges as low as $100, never mind that, as the *Voice* reported, federal and state agencies had tentatively agreed to pay for Lindsay's new LOMEX plan, now envisioned as part highway, part tunnel.

In September, Maciunas solicited deposits on three more buildings as Jonas Mekas—no longer using the Forty-First Street theater and now desperately fundraising for a permanent Film-Makers' Cinematheque—ran a notice in the *Voice* announcing Cinematheque I at 80 Wooster and a never-to-be opened Cinematheque II a few blocks downtown at the never-realized Fluxhouse I.

11

November brought SoHo's first official performances. The Cinematheque I was unlicensed to show movies. To book the space, Mekas hired the unproduced playwright Richard Foreman, who, despite an absence of prior construction experience, was working with Maciunas to fashion a theater on 80 Wooster's ground floor.

While the idea of having Archie Shepp play a New Year's Eve concert likely came from Shirley Clarke, whose affair with the musician was an open secret, Foreman engaged the dancer Trisha Brown (who bought the seventh floor at 80 Wooster) and Philip Glass and Steve Reich (together for the first time). Mekas booked Reich's onetime collaborators, the San Francisco Mime Troupe, then engaged in a national tour.

Friday, November 3, a few weeks before opening at the new Cinematheque, the Mime Troupe performed a comedia dell'arte agitprop *L'Amant*

Militaire at Columbia University's MacMillan Theatre, sponsored in part by the campus chapter of SDS. The play (which ended with the audience shouting, "hell no, we won't go") was "a caricature of American society from a draft-age point of view," Michael Smith wrote in the *Voice*, praising it as a challenge to other theaters to become robust and relevant.

The following Sunday, the Troupe gave a free performance of *Olive Pits*—an adaptation of a sixteenth-century Spanish farce, updated with references to Vietnam and exploited farm workers—on the Sheep Meadow in Central Park. According to the Troupe's acerbic founder-director R. G. Davis, *Olive Pits* "not only drew the hipsters but every camera freak in the underground."

> I was busy the whole performance banging into New York name photographers trying to keep them away from the front of the stage. There was one shutter-freak who paid for the right to shoot us. NBC contacted me and wanted to get shots of the troupe for publicity . . . I said we would pose—for cash. NBC paid a hundred dollars and 499 other camera flickers got it for free.

The Mime Troupe took off on a tour of New England colleges. Returning to New York in late November, Davis expected to see Fred McDarrah's photograph on the *Voice* front page. He didn't (the picture ran with Smith's review while the Troupe was in New England). Its absence may explain the downbeat interview he gave another *Voice* writer, Ross Wetzsteon. "I feel out of place in this big ugly fucking city," Davis complained. "Theatre is totally impotent here. You can't have any effect on anything."

Davis was doubtless aware of the competition. Not only was one of his idols, the Polish director Jerzy Grotowski, currently in residence at NYU but October had been a notable month for counterculture theater. On October 21 in Washington, DC, a gaggle of New Yorkers (including Norman Mailer, Allen Ginsberg, Abbie Hoffman, and the Fugs, as well as Shirley Clarke and Barbara Rubin, who were hoping to make a movie) attempted to levitate the Pentagon. As Yippies chanted, "Out demons out!" the Black Mask cohort managed to briefly breach a side entrance.

On one hand, Mailer—arrested with 600 others for transgressing a police line—spent two nights in a Virginia jail. On the other, Leroi Jones, on trial in Morristown, New Jersey, was manacled and taken from the courtroom after denouncing the white judge and an all-white panel of prospective jurors as his "oppressors."

A week after the attempted levitation, thirty-three-year-old NYU professor Richard Schechner, a producing director at the Free Southern Theatre (and another Grotowski admirer), organized an ambitious, daylong feat of guerrilla street theater involving five theatrical companies, a hundred actors, a documentary film crew, and twenty-two locations, mainly in midtown Manhattan.

The major piece, *Kill Vietcong*, published in Schechner's journal, *The Drama Review* (*TDR*), involved staging a mock patriotic rally and then recruiting a passerby who, handed a toy gun, would be directed to "execute" a designated Vietnamese guerrilla fighter. Some people thought the event was pro-war and sometimes the shooter turned the gun on the rally's speaker. (Perhaps this is what Davis meant when he suggested New York was impervious to theater.)

The meaning of Schechner's event was not apparent. At best, a *Village Voice* reporter wrote, the shenanigans produced "a sense of spontaneity which often perplexed the audience and flabbergasted the police." Schechner, however, expected more and subsequently apologized in the *Voice* for the absence of disruption. The same issue featured Michael Smith's reviews of two self-consciously with-it productions.

Imported from San Francisco by Grove Press, *The Beard*, poet Michael McClure's supposedly pornographic confrontation between Jean Harlow and Billy the Kid, a pair of archetypes in a "blue velvet" Eternity, opened at the Evergreen Theatre on East Eleventh Street. McClure's play was directed by Rip Torn and newly tricked out with a thirty-five-minute multimedia slide-movie-light-show prologue orchestrated by USCO that reminded Michael Smith of "the sleekest of discotheques."

As described by Naomi Feigelson in the short-lived magazine *Cheetah*, the audience was assaulted by "a continuous flow of images projected on the theater's cave-like walls."

> Flowers, larger than life, open and close, zooming in and out. The eyes, lips, face, and shoulder of Jean Harlow; penguins, eagles, birds of prey. A volcano erupting. On the screen up front, a lion licks her cub. Overall, this is a mixture of sound animals roaring, Eleanor Roosevelt and Lyndon Johnson, music from Bach, *Tristan*, and *Gone with the*

> *Wind*. In the semi-darkness, three musicians walk up to the stage with yahrzeit candles.

Remembering the dead, the hippie trio sang a song of "energy and love," accompanied by a sound collage that included McClure's "beast language." As the trio exited up the aisle, Billy the Kid and Jean Harlow materialized, and the play began.

The same week, several blocks farther east on Lafayette Street, Joseph Papp inaugurated his new Public Theater (the old Astor Library saved from the wrecking ball some eighteen months earlier) with the so-called "tribal rock musical" *Hair*. While he approved of *The Beard*, Smith despised *Hair*. Presenting a hippie show around the corner from St. Mark's Place seemed stupid and pointless (*EVO* agreed), although Smith decided he liked *Hair* when, now with nudity, it opened on Broadway six months later.

12

Davis could dismiss *Hair* and *The Beard* as bourgeois entertainment. He could not so easily disregard *Conquest of the Universe*.

Alert and attuned as Davis was to commedia dell'arte, the Mime Troupe's director had surely heard word of mouth regarding John Vaccaro's Play-House of the Ridiculous extravaganza, an outrageous gloss on Christopher Marlowe's *Tamburlaine* written by Charles Ludlam. The play had its premiere at the newly landmarked Bouwerie Lane Theater on Bond Street, November 21, two days before *L'amant Militaire* opened at the Cinematheque, around the time Davis first spoke with Wetzsteon.[11]

Wetzsteon's description of *L'amant Militaire* might even have described Ridiculous Theater: "The tambourines and drums, the farcical hysteria, the hilarity of content and joy of performance reach Dionysian proportions." Vaccaro's press release was so evocative that Michael Smith began his *Voice* rave with an extended quotation:

11 Davis needn't have worried about his New York reception. At the end of the 1967–68 season, the *Voice* awarded the Mime Troupe an Obie for "uniting theatre and revolution and grooving in the park." Despite an ecstatic *Voice* review, *Conquest of the Universe* was shut out.

> *Conquest of the Universe* is a paramoral study of these space-intoxicated times. Here 'camp' comes its delirious climax—Adolph [sic] Hitler's writings mingle with old movie scripts and TV ad libs in the dialogue. The dour pornography of daily Vietnam reports meets the screaming pornography of the truth.

Smith then went on the praise the production as "an explosion of talent that leaves the mind in tatters."

Having ventured downtown, the *New York Times*'s thirty-two-year-old reviewer Dan Sullivan pronounced *Conquest of the Universe* "really outré which is some trick in the unshockable 1960s." Gender was fluid if not arbitrary. A mustachioed Mary Woronov, the *Exploding Plastic Inevitable*'s resident dominatrix, played the galactic conqueror Tamburlaine, with Beverly Grant as her neglected wife, Alice.

For Stefan Brecht, *Conquest* was "a shocking display of vigorous hermaphroditic health." The embodiment of "fascism, militarism, violence and stupidity," Tamburlaine conquers successive planets unopposed. Thus, the burden of the play fell on Woronov, animated, Brecht thought, by "a frantic but steadily explosive spleen." (As in William Burroughs's scandalous "Roosevelt After Inauguration," defeated rivals submit to a ceremonial buggering.)

Conquest had a vaudevillian quality, incorporating all manner of performances. Recently returned to New York, Taylor Mead had a featured cameo as Peter Pan. Sailing into the action in Kelly green tights in the middle of the first act, he sang "I'm Flying" while perched on a drop-down swing. ("They're hiring me to wreck plays now," he told Sally Kempton in a *Voice* profile published to coincide with the play's opening.) Each night before the curtain went up, according to Warhol superstar Ultra Violet, who brought Marcel Duchamp to the November 21 performance, Ondine, King of Mars, gave himself a ceremonial speed poke in full view of the cast.

The show was quintessentially East Village, even billed as a "rock 'n' roll opera." Vaccaro fired two bands before Marsha Sam Ridge (a *Realist* staffer and member of the chorus whose previous credit was a Free University production of Factory misfit Valerie Solanas's *Up Your Ass*) recommended her boyfriend's group, the Third Eye—a local outfit that had provided loud musical accompaniment for *Trips to Wear*, the psychedelic fashion show happening that underground cartoonist-designer Trina Robbins staged in June at the Village Theater.

EVO art critic Lil Picard gave *Trips to Wear* a breathless review. "It went over fast, no pause, like a color-gale, a motor-cycle bicycle racing through the aisle right smash in the stage, unloading a girl in a short dress; it ended with a motorcycle zooming out to Second Avenue." Picard, who once ran a millinery boutique at Bloomingdale's, approvingly noted the "Freakout Frocks," singling out amid the frenzy of strobe-lit minis and mock pharaonic headdresses one performer's psycho-eyeglasses and sari ensemble.

Vaccaro commissioned Robbins, whose *EVO* comic strip *Suzie Slumgoddess* served to advertise her East Fourth Street boutique Broccoli, to provide *Conquest*'s outrageously garish costumes. "I was given a budget of about $20, but the challenge was fun," Robbins recalled, "For the chorus girls' wigs, I bought felt hat forms and sewed copper Brillo pads all over them, to look like metallic Little Orphan Annie hair. One scene called for a character to turn into a monster. I gave him huge white three-fingered gloves and mouse ears and he became a giant Mickey Mouse."[12]

Two aesthetics merged. "Was it a fashion show? It was Art," Picard wrote of *Trips to Wear*. For her, Robbins's brand of Hippie Modernism reproached the stale offerings of Tenth Street galleries. "The very young in mind and body did it, not enough people saw it, it should be repeated soon!" It was not, but, in the same issue of *EVO* that dismissed *Hair* as dramatizing the Electric Circus, Picard plugged *Conquest of the Universe* as downtown's "newest adventure."

SoHo, meanwhile, was incubating something else. In a Spring Street loft up the block and around the corner from 80 Wooster Street, Robert Wilson—a twenty-six-year-old Texan with a BFA in architecture and an interest in dance whose main credit was creating the puppets for Jean-Claude van Itallie's 1966 counterculture satire, *America Hurrah*—was putting on an enigmatic solo performance called *Baby Blood*.

The handful of spectators who attended *Baby Blood*'s five presentations found their way to a deserted neighborhood and, circumnavigating wooden debris and dismembered baby dolls, ascended the dingy staircase

12 Robbins was bemused by the cast: "Most of the actors were not very nice people—but Ondine was the worst. He was the only actor for whom I sewed an entire costume from scratch. I made him a sequined evening gown, but he was never satisfied. I had made the top in the style of Jean Harlowe gowns of the '30s, with bare arms and halter neckline, but he wanted long sleeves. 'I wanted to look like Susan Hayward, and you made me look like [ballroom dancer] Bambi Linn.'"

to Wilson's loft. A red-cowled figure collected two dollars and seated patrons. There was a wait in the darkness and then the sound of Bob Dylan's *Bringing It All Back Home*. Wilson's entry was cued by the album's second cut, the rollicking, sarcastic "Maggie's Farm."

Wearing dark glasses and a dark tank top, the artist teetered like a tightrope walker across a narrow plank. His progress was deliberate, requiring the entire duration of the song. Then a locomotive moaned and Wilson lay beneath toy train tracks, writhing like an infant in a crib. Finally, as the strident voice of a revivalist preacher was heard, Wilson draped himself with long strips of material likely found on the street and a single light illuminated a baby picture placed atop an unused piano. The piece lasted twenty minutes, ending without the sanction of applause.

Presented in the artist's (illegal) living loft, *Baby Blood* was reminiscent of Jim Dine's *Car Crash*, at once a private psychodrama—in which Wilson served as his own shaman, acting out or exorcizing a personal trauma—and a public ritual.

13

The great SoHo film had its SoHo premiere in January 1968. Michael Snow's *Wavelength* was the first movie to have a public screening at the new Cinematheque and one which Jonas Mekas, who imagined that the movie might have a commercial run, publicized with press releases and even a press screening.

A bit more than a year earlier, Michael Snow, then living on Chambers Street, walked a few blocks up to his studio, a second-floor loft on the downtown side of Canal Street adjacent to Pearl Paint, a six-story jerry-built art supply store that had been around since the Great Depression. Using a tripod, Snow planted a 16mm camera, borrowed from his neighbor Ken Jacobs, at one end of the loft; he then spent two weeks inching the zoom lens forward until it framed a photograph of the sea tacked between two of the four outsized windows framing SoHo's southern border.

Writing in *Artforum*, the painter–film critic Manny Farber, a near-neighbor living on Warren Street, would call *Wavelength* "a pure tough forty-five-minutes that may become the *Birth of a Nation* in Underground films" as well as "a straightforward document of a room in which a dozen businesses have lived and gone bankrupt." But if *Wavelength* was a straightforward document, it was also an abstract suspense narrative.

A man (the filmmaker Hollis Frampton) enters and collapses on the floor as the zoom impassively eliminates him from the frame.

The "New Art," as Mel Bocher wrote of Andre, Flavin, Judd, LeWitt, Morris, and Smithson, in his review of *Primary Structures*, "deals with the surface of matter and avoids its 'heart.'" Similarly, for Farber, "the cool kick" of *Wavelength* was "seeing so many new actors—light and space, walls, soaring windows, and an amazing number of color shadows variations that live and die in the windowpanes." Snow pleased the eye with superimpositions that functioned as material flashbacks and fed the mind with metaphor for film narrative. *Wavelength*'s final image is implicit—and even visible—in its first.

Not a minimal film but a metaphysical one: As forcefully as Warhol, Snow asserted the nature of the film object while bringing motion pictures back to ground zero. *Wavelength* was a sound object as well, with a single sinewave rising in pitch and building in intensity even as the zoom approaches its destination. Steve Reich didn't know Snow (although his studio was literally around the corner from the loft where *Wavelength* was shot) but, knocked out by the movie, he was inspired to detail his experience of the film and send it to Snow as a note.

Wavelength was in many respects a neighborhood affair. Some thirty years after Farber suggested that *Wavelength* was a document, Richard Kostelanetz would write that, by recording the wood plank floor and pressed tin ceilings of his Canal Street studio, Snow had preserved a ruin—"simply, this is how SoHo looked before artists' renovations set in."

Encouraged by Jonas Mekas, who paid for an additional print, Snow entered *Wavelength* in the Knokke-Le-Zoute festival. There, hailed as a movie that might change the course of cinema history, it won first prize. (*Self-Obliteration* won a jury prize as well. The two films, along with Storm de Hirsch's *Shaman: A Tapestry for Sorcerers*, had their New York premieres together at the Cinematheque in January 1968.)[13]

---

13 Haunted by the memory of *Flaming Creatures* and fueled by the militance of 1967, Knokke-Le-Zoute was a tumultuous festival. Jean-Jacques Lebel organized "illegal" screenings of supposedly pornographic films as well as a nude contest for Miss Experimental. Yoko Ono, on hand to screen her *Film Number Four* (a.k.a. *Bottoms*), performed *Black Bag Piece*, remaining several hours on the floor of the casino lobby concealed inside a canvas sack. In addition, a group of German students, among them Harun Farocki, disrupted the festival with demonstrations against insufficiently political avant-garde films and American imperialism.

14

Wavelength epitomized a shift among New York avant-garde filmmakers, away from the streets. Radical artists, however, were moving out of the gallery and beyond the object—to "convert [materiality] into an idea," as Sol LeWitt wrote in his manifesto "Paragraphs on Conceptual Art," published in the June 1967 issue of *Artforum*.

The same month that Snow projected his monument in time and space for a group of friends, Robert Smithson published a sequel to "Entropy and the New Monuments" that was the fruit of various expeditions the artist had made, exploring industrial landscapes of his native New Jersey (although apparently not Newark).

"A Tour of the Monuments of Passaic," Smithson's mock-pedantic riff on nineteenth-century travel writing, satirized both urban planning and the opposition to it, not to mention the new sculpture, by treating a ruined landscape as an exercise in found public art. (It also prepared the ground for Smithson's subsequent move into "land" art.) The monuments described include a wrought iron swing bridge over the Passaic River, the excavation occasioned by new highway construction (populated by machines that suggest "prehistoric creatures trapped in the mud") and a "fountain" created by the horizontal placement of six enormous pipes draining sludge into the river.

Passaic, Smithson declared, is "a self-destroying postcard world of failed immortality and oppressive grandeur." Notable for the gigantic parking lot that divides it in half, the city center "loomed like a dull adjective." The essay, which asked but never answers the question, "Has Passaic replaced Rome as the eternal city?," was accompanied by Smithson's photographs, taken with a disposable Instamatic camera and given ostentatiously neutral titles ("Monument with Pontoons: The Pumping Derrick"). Whereas a rubble-rouser like Mark di Suvero might be inspired to appropriate this material, Smithson was content to merely cite it as a Duchampian readymade.

"A Tour of the Monuments of Passaic, New Jersey" was the last feature in the December 1967 issue of *Artforum*. Having relocated from Los Angeles to New York, the journal was now positioned at the art world's cutting edge. The same issue included a Frank Stella cover story, excerpts from Dan Graham's journal, an essay by Lucas Samaras and another by Mel Bochner on the "serial attitude" that name-checked Flavin, Judd,

LeWitt, as well as Smithson (who in his essay parodied Bochner's avant la lettre by pondering a serial "set" of Passaic's used car lots).

Smithson's "Tour" began with a discussion of the reading matter brought for the bus ride, including Brian Aldiss's dystopian science-fiction novel *Earthworks* and the day's *New York Times*. (Noting the art reviews, Smithson cited the critic John Canaday's mention of Paul Thek's "Dead Hippie" although not by that name.) The essay concluded by introducing the notion of a bottomless utopia visualized as a playground sandbox that, apparently knocked together on a barren field, doubles as an "open grave."

This found *mise en abyme*—a sandbox within a "desert"—allowed Smithson to introduce the notion of cinema as "a temporary escape from physical dissolution," which might have been a way to describe Snow's ephemeral monument *Wavelength.*

15

The art world's center had shifted as well. As 1967 ended, Andy Warhol lost his lease at East Forty-Seventh Street and moved the Factory downtown to Sixteenth Street, across Union Square from its de facto commissary, Max's Kansas City. Maciunas continued to colonize SoHo.

Earlier that year, he had run two new classified ads, likely referring to buildings at 451, 465, and 469 West Broadway. Another ad listed "performing and rehearsal space" at 33 Wooster Street, a one-story garage building that, attached to the Grand Street Artist's Co-op set up and lost by Maciunas, was soon to house Richard Schechner's Performance Group and their first production, an environmental update of Euripides' *The Bacchae*: called *Dionysus in '69*.

Founded in mid-November, the Performance Group had variously found rehearsal space in the Tompkins Square Community Center on Avenue B, the Central Plaza (once the city's largest kosher catering establishment) on Second Avenue, in Robert Rauschenberg's studio at 381 Lafayette Street (a long block south of the Public Theater), in an unused part of the Electric Circus, in a community center on Avenue A, "The Real Great Society" building, and even on the rooftops of deserted, unlocked SoHo buildings.

Schechner paid $72,000 (enough to buy an entire building) for the Wooster Street garage, thus controlling the largest bloc of votes in the Co-op. His Group moved in on March 1, 1968. In addition to rehearsing

Dionysus, they used toothbrushes to scrape years of accumulated grime and grease off the floor. Meanwhile, just up the street at 80 Wooster, Richard Foreman was rehearsing *Angelface*.

The first production of Foreman's Ontological-Hysteric Theater opened for three performances in early April in what struck some participants as a work site. (Maciunas occasionally poked his head in.) *Angelface* had a script but, in the tradition of a Donald Judd box, it was as much a physical entity as a play. Radically impoverished and blatantly material, Foreman's theater privileged props over sets, activities over actions, mise-en-scène over narrative, presences over performance, and sound over dialogue. The dialogue was taped. Assured that they wouldn't have to learn any lines, Foreman's cast, basically whomever he could find, repeated snatches of dialogue when cued by the recording. No expression was necessary.

The monochromatic set included a table and chairs, a closet, a door, and a window. The sole illumination was an overhead chandelier, with another light pointed at the audience. There was no curtain, nor much of a proscenium. The play was performed on the floor. Foreman's objects were his actors and vice versa. The audience walked in to find one man sitting alone in a chair and another frozen in a doorway. After a while, they began to speak, slowly and without inflection, repeating words from the tape.

> Max: The door opens. I don't even turn my head.
> Walter: Does it turn?
> Max: What?
> Walter: Heads turn.
> Max: Heads turn. My head is a head. Therefore: My head turns. Open the door a second time.
> Walter: Why?
> Max: Find out if my head turns.
> Walter: I can't.
> Max; What?
> Walter: An opened door cannot be opened.

The lighting was such that the audience stared at the cast and the cast stared back.

Performed four times, *Angelface* ran seventy-five minutes without intermission. The sparse attendance, mainly friends of the artist or the cast, accentuated the hermetic nature of the event. The audience might find itself outnumbered by the seven-member cast—eight if one included the impassive playwright-director himself, visible at the board controlling the sound and thus cueing the action as well as the lights (operated by Michael Snow). Foreman conducted the show, which might have been taking place for his benefit alone.

Foreman's slapstick humor—exemplified by the spectacle of an angel whose wooden wings precluded his getting through a doorway—was subtle. His attenuated sense of timing was unfamiliar. As avant-garde theater, *Angelface* had competition. Foreman's closing night coincided with the first performance of Yvonne Rainer's ambitious, chastely minimal mixed-media extravaganza *The Mind Is a Muscle* at the Anderson Theater on lower Second Avenue.

"A compendium of all Rainer's formal interests" per Jill Johnston, the show incorporated several of the dancer's famous Judson pieces, ironically played off dramatic music including the Hollywood soundtracks for *Dial M for Murder* and *The Pink Panther*). There were also two short films, a juggler, and several sound interludes (the Greenbriar Boys, Frank Sinatra, a pornographic poem by John Giorno). Rainer had come around regarding rock. A salute to her hometown San Francisco, the piece ended with "She Has Funny Cars," the opening track from the Jefferson Airplane's *Surrealistic Pillow*, released some fourteen months before.

Saturday evening, on April 8, the night before *Angelface* opened—with the nation still reeling from the assassination of Martin Luther King Jr. in Memphis—another heroic performer defended her hometown. Jane Jacobs successfully deranged a hastily called hearing on LOMEX convened at Seward Park High School on the Lower East Side by the newly created New York State Department of Transportation. Ostensibly held to solicit community feedback, the meeting featured the state agency's chief engineer, John Toth, who was basically there to sell the project, which was elaborated by a glossy prospectus available at an information table.

The *Voice* account was headlined PERSECUTION OF THE CITY PERFORMED BY ITS INMATES. Jacobs noted that the microphone had been set up so that speakers would address the community rather than the officials seated on stage (who in any case refused to take questions). With the crowd chanting her name, she took the microphone, promising that "if the expressway is put through, there will be anarchy" and, as if to demonstrate, marched on stage—spontaneously joined by some fifty members of the audience—and thus delivering a message for the Department of Transportation "errand boys" to take back to Albany.

"Arrest that woman," Toth demanded as if Jacobs were Kusama. Although other insurgents took advantage of the chaos to destroy the stenotype tape of the meeting, Jacobs alone was booked and charged with disrupting a public hearing. When she showed up nine days later for her arraignment, she was informed that she now was being charged with inciting a riot and criminal mischief and enjoined from further anti-LOMEX protests. The case never went to trial, but the city took notice. In July 1969, Lindsay, who had campaign against LOMEX and then reversed his position after the election, declared LOMEX dead "for all time": it was a thought, and phrase, Robert Smithson might have savored.[14]

14 SoHo was saved. Although the city shut down the Cinematheque in August, *Dionysus in '69*, which had received an enthusiastic review from the *New York Times* in June, put SoHo on the theatrical map. Cabs were no longer afraid to go there. By then Paula Cooper opened SoHo's first gallery three flights up in a former shelving factory at 96 Prince. Cooper, who started her gallery with $1400 from the sale of a di Suvero and a $3,000 bank loan, had to renovate a space so raw "you'd get splinters if you touched the floor." Still, she had two enormous rooms of 5,000 square feet each for $300 a month. Her first show was a benefit for the Student Mobilization Committee to End the War in Vietnam. Less than two years later, Grace Glueck warned that, rather than an achieved utopia, SoHo was a "last resort" for New York arts. Two months after that the *Times* ran a story headlined COSTS FOR SOHO LOFTS ARE RISING DRASTICALLY.

NIGHT OWL

DAILY NEWS

NEW YORK'S PICTURE NEWSPAPER ®

8¢

Vol. 51, No. 52 — New York, N.Y. 10017, Monday, August 25, 1969* — WEATHER: Sunny and hot.

FEARFUL BERET BLEW LID OFF

His Role in Viet Slaying Bared

—Story on Page 2

But Is It Art? Security officer Roy Williams pleads with nude young men and women to leave Museum of Modern Art fountain, where Maillol's sculpture, Girl Washing Her Hair, reclines. Impromptu nude-in was conception of Japanese artist Yayoi Kusama (right). Crowd takes it in stride. (Some took strides to get closer). —Story on page 4

Our Noisy, Dirty, Crowded Subways—**See Page 3**

Kusama at MoMA. Front page of New York *Daily News* (8/25/1969).

9

Everything Is Now: Kusama vs. Warhol vs. the Fillmore vs. the Living Theatre and Motherfuckers, 1968–69

In which Destruction Art arrives along with *Dionysus in '69*. Political assassinations derange the national election, Valerie Solanas shoots Andy Warhol, and Kusama joins the counterculture. New York endures a garbage strike. MoMA co-opts Dada. Columbia is occupied. The Living Theatre returns from France to declare *Paradise Now* as the Motherfuckers occupy the Fillmore East and rock critics embrace Free Jazz.

> *The ultimate tactical question must be, not the seizure of power, but its dissolution!*
>
> —*Black Mask* #9 (Jan–Feb 1968)

Was ever a year more divided against itself? On one hand, the stringent Apollonian grandeur of *Wavelength*, *Angel Face*, and Donald Judd at the Whitney, not to mention *The Mind Is a Muscle* and Bob Dylan's pared down new LP, *John Wesley Harding*—self-contained, indifferent to tumult. On the other, the insanity, political and otherwise, of 1968: Johnson's abdication, the killing of Martin Luther King Jr., university turmoil at Columbia and in Paris, the second Kennedy assassination, the police riot at the Democratic National Convention in Chicago, the Tlatelolco massacre of Mexican students, and the third-party presidential candidacy of white supremacist George Wallace.

In the early afternoon of June 3, Valerie Solanas, a thirty-two-year-old playwright with a bit part in the 1967 Warhol production *I, a Man*, as well as the founder and sole member of the Society for Cutting Up Men (SCUM), took the elevator up to the new Warhol Factory on Union Square. The garrulous superstar Viva had just phoned in to tell Andy that she was right now at Mr. Kenneth's swanky Upper East Side hair salon, trying out coiffures for a small part in John Schlesinger's New York movie *Midnight Cowboy*, when she heard gunshots.

Solanas, herself one of Warhol's telephone pals, had fired three bullets at the man she called "Daddy Warhol." Two missed. The last penetrated three vital organs as well as Warhol's stomach and esophagus. Solanas also hit the art critic Mario Amaya in the hip and had her gun pointed at office manager Fred Hughes when the weapon jammed, the elevator door reopened, and Hughes persuaded the hesitant shooter to step inside. Several hours later, with Warhol's life hanging in the balance, Solanas gave herself up to a rookie cop in Times Square, saying "I shot Andy Warhol."

Thus, the social violence that characterized the spring of 1968 breached the art world. Ray Johnson saw the next morning's *Daily News* headline ACTRESS SHOOTS ANDY WARHOL, was mugged at knife point, and left New York City never to return. Solanas, too, saw the *Daily News* and fumed that she was a writer, not an actress. More to the point, she was a cultural activist and once her *SCUM Manifesto* was underlined in blood, she hardly had to wait for admirers. Even before Viva's *Midnight Cowboy* scene—a contrived loft party—was filmed, the *New York Free Press* printed excerpts of the *Manifesto*. Yippie provocateur Paul Krassner, a friend of Solanas, whom he had invited to lecture at the Free University, provided a postscript for its hastily published first edition.

Solanas was claimed by militant feminists, including Ti-Grace Atkinson and the lawyer Florynce Kennedy. She was championed by the anarchist anti-art "affinity group" Black Mask, now a self-identified gang that, further radicalized by the Newark Insurrection, had turned to political theater—or rather had instrumentalized political theater, by, among other things, staging a fake assassination of the poet Kenneth Koch. They took a new name, the Motherfuckers, initially an ironic comradely greeting, from a line in Leroi Jones's 1967 poem "Black People!": "Up Against the Wall Motherfucker."

Early spring, Motherfucker founder Ben Morea was on Eighth Street selling *Black Mask* #10 (the Berlin Dada issue) when he met Solanas. She didn't feel like paying a nickel, so Morea gave her a copy; in return she ducked into a bookstore and shoplifted a copy of her self-mimeographed

SCUM Manifesto. Morea got a deal (Solanas customarily charged women one dollar and men, two) and a highly entertaining polemic. *Black Mask* led with the cry that EVERYONE CAN BE A DADAIST! Solanas begged to differ in a most Dada-like way. Her manifesto's first sentence was a poem:

> Life in this society being, at best, an utter bore and no aspect of society being at all relevant to women, there remains to civic-minded, responsible, thrill-seeking females only to overthrow the government, eliminate the money system, institute complete automation and destroy the male sex.

Solanas was sufficiently impressed with Morea to enlist him in SCUM's male auxiliary ("we can't spare you, but we can save you for last") and took him as an advisor. A few weeks later, in the tumult of the Columbia student revolt, in which the Motherfuckers participated, Solanas made her way to the Morningside Heights campus and, seeking Morea's counsel, managed to penetrate the occupied Mathematics building. Was she perhaps thinking of the assault on Columbia professor Koch? What would happen, she asked Morea, if she shot someone. Morea recalls telling her it would depend on whom she shot and whether the attack was fatal.

Like Dada or Black Mask, SCUM was less a political organization than an art project, albeit one with a body count. Motherfucker posters parodied the long-running Famous Artists School ad in which Norman Rockwell's signature was attached to the slogan "We're Looking for People Who Like to Draw" by juxtaposing avuncular Rockwell with a holstered revolver. The Motherfuckers stashed guns but did not use them. Solanas did. Her attack on Warhol (an artist Morea loathed) was for him the ultimate Dada act. Six months after Black Mask staged a mock murder, Solanas attempted a real one.

Morea wrote a paean, PLASTIC MAN VS. THE SWEET ASSASSIN: THE CAMP MASTER SLAIN BY THE SLAVE AND AMERICA'S WHITE PLASTIC CATHEDRAL IS READY TO BURN—which he distributed outside MoMA where the show *Dada, Surrealism and Their Heritage* was enjoying its final few days.[1]

---

1 In Mary Harron's 1996 movie *I Shot Andy Warhol*, Solanas gets her gun from a character modeled on Morea—something Morea has denied, while allowing that "Valerie used to stay with me a lot."

2

The white plastic cathedral was already scorched. Three days into the new year, LeRoi Jones, who in lieu of a summation read the poem "Black People! This is Our Destiny," was sentenced to three years in prison for possession of a weapon.

North Vietnam and the Vietcong launched the Tet Offensive on the last day of January. At 3:00 a.m., nineteen VC kamikaze commandos stormed the US embassy in Saigon, killed five Americans, and held the building for six hours—long enough for TV news crews to document the action while the North Vietnamese simultaneously attacked thirty-six South Vietnamese cities.

New York's apocalypse occurred on Friday, February 2, when 10,000 sanitation workers went on strike. By Monday even the city's ritziest sections were transformed into slums. "Mounds of refuse grew higher and strong winds whirled the filth through the streets," reported the *New York Times*. In some neighborhoods, sidewalk garbage piles towered over parked cars and trash fires were becoming common.

The mayor wanted the governor to call in the National Guard. The governor refused. With 80,000 tons of putrid waste mounting ever higher, the Motherfuckers formulated an analysis ("America turns the world into garbage") and proposed an action of *cultural exchange*, transporting bags of trash from the streets of the Lower East Side up to Lincoln Center (built on the ruins of Morea's childhood community). The action, a Motherfucking first, was promoted in the *Voice* by Howard Smith's "Scenes" column and set for Monday evening, February 12. It turned out to be the day the strike was settled. Nevertheless, the show went on, documented by the recently formed Newsreel group.

Newsreel was conceived at a late December conclave of some thirty filmmakers. Jonas Mekas convened the meeting, prompted by students from the young filmmaker Allan Siegel's Free University course; having made a class project documenting the October 1967 March on the Pentagon, they were appalled by the news footage shown by network TV. Some pushed for a collective newsreel service to cover demonstrations and other "happenings" from a participant point of view. Mekas envisioned an analog to the Film-Makers' Cooperative and forestalled attempts to define a mission ("let things take their own course"). Devoting his January 25 *Voice* column to the incipient organization, he invoked the mystical world-historical coincidence that Newsreel was born on the same day that Universal News Service announced its demise.[2]

The Garbage Event was a provocatively empty gesture. The Motherfuckers' position was strategically incoherent. They identified neither with the striking sanitation workers nor with those in the community working to clean up the city, which included the more civic-minded elements of another newly hatched, LSD-fueled East Village cadre, the Yippies (for Youth International Party). Founded on the last day of 1967 when Abbie Hoffman, Jerry Rubin, and Paul Krassner dropped acid and dreamed up a plan for the summer's "revolutionary action-theater," the Yippies sought and thrived on media attention; the Motherfuckers preferred Bakunin's propaganda of the deed.

The Motherfuckers took urban detritus as their material. If anything, they identified with the garbage. Allen Siegel attended their subsequent meetings and recorded their spontaneous raps as well as a chaotic, bang-on-a-can jam session complete with a falsetto version of "God Bless America" that was worthy of ESP-Disk's fantastically haphazard, white hippie wannabe Arkestra, the Godz. Siegel and crew follow the exuberant Motherfuckers—tootling plastic flutes and shaking tambourines—on the uptown IRT to the "Lincoln Shopping Center of the Performing Arts" to rendezvous with a car crammed with bagged trash. Using a wheeled bin likely liberated from the Cooper Station post office, the Motherfuckers deliver at least some of their garbage to the entrance of the Metropolitan Opera. Spectators gawk, cops mill about, hardened New Yorkers pay no attention, although the shot of a Black janitor leaning on his broom watching a motherfucking mess being made for him to clean up provides a contradiction the Motherfuckers might not have acknowledged.[3]

---

2 Mekas saw no difference between amateur newsreels and avant-garde films; the first Newsreel productions were so casually haphazard they might have been shot by Ron Rice. The slickest aspect was the logo—a flashing graphic of *The Newsreel* set to the sounds of staccato machine gun fire. *Garbage* was Newsreel's fifth film. Siegel, whose 1967 film *The Grain* (an evocation of urban alienation in industrial Baltimore) had been screened at Millennium and praised by Ken Jacobs, was the prime mover.

3 The action in the film is post-scripted by an excited postmortem: The Motherfuckers speculate on their action's appeal for workers and their Puerto Rican neighbors. The novelist Sol Yurick took a more radical line in the new underground newspaper *Rat*, attacking the sanitation workers union for settling with the city. "Refuse! Some call it garbage but I call it I-will-not-serve," he punned. "What an opportunity we missed. The strike didn't go on long enough." As it piled up, "the Plastic Inevitable would be revealed for what it is."

Crediting six filmmakers, Newsreel's eleven-minute documentary suggests a multiplicity of views, but its perspective is largely that of the Motherfuckers. The sound is asynchronous and post-dubbed with voiceover recorded at meetings held before the action—as is made clear by a reference to the mayor's February 4 tour of Avenue C and the good-natured hippie "Sweep-In" that *Radio Unnameable* host Bob Fass organized for East Third Street on Saturday, February 10.

The *Voice* put Don McNeill's Sweep-In story on page one. Characterizing the event as "a glorious goof," McNeil compared the happening to a Central Park Be-In: "Participants passed out lunch, daffodils, incense, and chanted the glory of the now-near-sacred [supposedly psychotropic] banana. They also took pictures of each other. Every third person seemed to have a camera."

That same evening, Yayoi Kusama organized a "Body Paint Festival," which, held in a storefront on the west side of Cooper Square, also received *Voice* coverage. As described by Howard Smith, "a group of naked young men and one chubby, pantied girl, painted themselves, were painted, burned bits of flags, draped themselves in remnants of same" and, amid clouds of incense, danced to Kate Smith's "God Bless America."

3

Ever since *Self-Obliteration* premiered, Kusama had been much in evidence. Within weeks, she would be hawking 16mm prints "filmed in Wild Psychedelic SuperMod Body Color" in the pages of the *Voice*.

In late January, Kusama staged a version of *Self-Obliteration* as part of the Group Image's regular Wednesday night dance party at Palm Gardens. The movie was projected over the band, flanked by two screens showing Laurel and Hardy's 1932 World War I comedy, *Pack Up Your Troubles*. In a square black-light corral at the center of the ballroom, Kusama began painting dots on a boy's bare torso.

According to "Scenes," "several others stepped forward into the purple glow, stripping to the waist [and] began painting themselves. The crowd went on eating popcorn and apples and smiling and dancing. A few stood watching. But for the most part, it was nothing they hadn't seen before." Then, one boy "deeply moved by having his torso daubed, decided to escalate. He removed his pants."

> Amidst all that art he would have gone unnoticed had it not been for the fact that his bottom half was totally undappled. Then another paintee dropped his pants for the cause of art. Now the paint-down at the naked corral really began. Splashing paint on themselves, more and more young men stripped. Behind them, the Group Image's music built to a climax.

Flashbulbs popped as bodies melded. "The hippie crowd, although enjoying themselves, took it all for granted," Smith wrote. "They didn't realize that they had been watching an East Coast First, a totally nude body painting event in public."

Some ten days later, the show moved over to the Gymnasium, the old Czech-Slovak community center Sokol Hall on East Seventy-First Street, where in April 1967 Andy Warhol had attempted relaunch the Velvet Underground. As at Palm Gardens, the Group Image played, Laurel and Hardy were projected, and the perimeter of a boxing-ring-sized body-painting corral was established. This time *Voice* theater critic Ross Wetzsteon was there, reporting that, even as the Gymnasium manager implored Kusama's boys to put their clothes back on, "a fleshy blonde girl strode naked into the pen. [She] danced for a few minutes, then disappeared as quickly as she'd come—into clothes and into newsprint."

And that was the point. Some thirty representatives of the media waited around for another hour but . . . the fleshy blonde was it. According to Wetzsteon, *Time*'s reporter asked him ("more indignant than curious") if *this* was what's happening in New York? Wetzsteon, however, understood Kusama's gambit, anticipating her subsequent desire, expressed in a 1969 interview with a Japanese weekly, to "perform Happening exclusively for press." *Self-Obliteration* was a piece that only really existed when acknowledged by TV.

Nevertheless, the show was reprised to better effect a few weeks later as a play performed for an audience of several hundred, many of them reporters, crammed into the storefront off Cooper Square. Instead of a corral there was a stage and rather than the Group Image, a teenage band called the Dayz Beyond provided ear-splitting rock accompaniment. Kusama was painting men (and then women) clad in nothing more than American flag togas and then not even that. As the action overflowed the tiny stage, a uniformed policeman appeared.

"A negro cop starts hedging his way through the crowd," wrote *EVO*'s Allen Katzman, who covered the event for the paper he cofounded.

> A wave of expectation resounds through the audience. He yells, "You're all under arrest!" Someone screams. The band continues to play. He attacks the nude happening swinging his club like hard meat. He is grabbed, wrestled down to the ground. Hands grip his clothes pulling them from his blue and black body. He yells, "You're all under arrest!" while one of the girls pulls of his pants and shouts, "Peace Brother!" He has camouflage fatigues under his uniform. Soon he is full nude and part of the obliteration.

Not about to give away the gag, Katzman nowhere suggests that the guy was a plant.

Chaos continued with hula hoops twisted and smashed and American flags shredded into confetti. The Mona Lisa received Kusama's polka-dot treatment. *Self-Obliteration* was projected as the band pumped up the volume. Strobes flashed. The nudes returned, bearing a mock-crucified naked guy for Kusama to paint. The Dayz Beyond paused to allow Kate Smith's rendition of "God Bless America." Katzman imagined that having finished painting her Christ figure the openly genophobic Kusama lost her cool. Jumping onto the nude Jesus and kissing "her work of art," she twined herself around his body and vigorously massaged his painted stomach.

And then . . . she bowed to the audience and announced that the show was over. Katzman enjoyed himself so much he attended and reported on Kusama's May 17 "Naked Event" at the Brooklyn Bridge.

4

The night after Kusama put polka dots on Jesus, a flayed lamb was nailed to the cross on Wooster Street. Beside a *Village Voice* ad for *Self-Obliteration* (and a larger one offering the 16mm film) was a notice worthy of Hermann Hesse's *Steppenwolf.*

> introducing:
> HERMANN NITSCH
> O. M. THEATER
> orgy-mystery sense thtr.
> touch, taste, smell, hearing, seeing, believing
> ORGIASTIC TRANSCENDENCE OF SENSES
> DIRECT FROM VIENNA, MUNICH, LONDON

The venue for this sinister sounding Gesamtkunstwerk—the American debut of a twenty-nine-year-old Viennese action artist already notorious in Europe—was the Film-Makers' Cinematheque.

The Austrian filmmaker Peter Kubelka had apprised Jonas Mekas of Nitsch, a painter who graduated from *tachisme* abstraction to sacramental performances that typically involved disemboweled animal cadavers. Learning that the artist was invited to participate in the Destruction in Art Symposium that Jon Hendricks and Ralph Ortiz were organizing at Judson Church, Mekas booked him into the Cinematheque for two performances.

Nitsch, whose influences included Jung and Nietzsche, as well as Artaud, maintained that in order to confront spectators with their own existential reality, Happenings had to go deeper into "cruelty, terror, [and] ritual." His *Fifth Action*, in which performers were washed in the blood of a crucified lamb, had been the scandal of the three-day Destruction in Art Symposium held fifteen months earlier at the Africa Centre in London. Making Nitsch's name, the piece also led to the prosecution of the organizer Gustav Metzger, fined a hundred pounds for having presented an "indecent exhibition."

Mekas had no such luck, although Nitsch provided the full show. In lieu of a stage was an impromptu altar of two tables covered white butcher block paper. A lamb carcass dangled from the ceiling. Another was splayed against the wall. Brains and entrails were piled on the tables; mounds of kidneys and chunks of liver lay on the papered floor. Dressed in black save for an ostentatiously clean white shirt, Nitsch unhurriedly poured red liquid over everything, then dove into the bloody morass.

Let the cathartic sado-masochistic rumpus begin! Hendricks stuffed offal into his pants and pulled it out through his fly. A young woman in white lay on her back, staring up as bloody lamb goo dripped over her face and torso. A glistening coil of lamb intestines covered her crotch. Enforced incantatory aural domination was supplied by twenty musicians, louder than the Motherfuckers, banging on bongos, pots, pans, and washboards. Above the din the shrill whistle of the Austrian *Trillerpfeife*. There were no words, only screams. Evidently, the action went on for hours.

Lil Picard, sixty-eight-year-old doyenne of German-Jewish refugee avant-gardists, a Dada gamine in Weimar Berlin, and something of a destruction artist herself, introduced Nitsch to *EVO*'s readers. Was

America ready for him, she wondered? *Voice* reviewer Jill Johnston certainly was. "Of all the theatre of my time which I have known this is the bloodiest, the cruelest, and the best," she enthused. "Carolee's *Meat Joy* was a sweet daydream next to this nightmare of savagery." (Nothing could be further from Nitsch's Orgies Mysteries' *Sturm und Drang* than Millie Small's peppy rendition of "My Boy Lollipop.") "I am not very interested in the symbols of today, but rather the symbols of 10,000 years ago or 10,000 years hence," Nitsch told Jud Yalkut, who wrote a curtain-raiser for the *New York Free Press*, the Upper West Side weekly known fondly as the *Freep*.

Yalkut praised this breakthrough past the New York–centric avant-garde. Others, however, deemed Nitsch's Orgies Mysteries (O.M.) theater as lame as the upcoming Yip-In. "Nearly everyone around me found the piece incredibly boring," performance chronicler Richard Kostelanetz noted. The Cinematheque had become an abattoir or, as Johnston put it, "a holy mess," leaving a smelly Augean stable for house manager Richard Foreman to clean up. More taken with Nitsch's self-promotion than his stagecraft, Foreman decided to brand his new project the Ontological-Hysteric Theater.

The same weekend that Kusama performed at Cooper Square and Nitsch graced the Cinematheque, Richard Schechner took possession of the garage down the block at 33 Wooster Street. Along with his young acolytes, he undertook to scrub the oil-saturated floor, cover it with carpet remnants, whitewash the grimy cinderblock walls, and construct rude wooden platforms.

After months of exercises, some inspired by Jerzy Grotowski's theater rituals, others resembling group (or primal scream) therapy, Schechner's Performance Group had decided on a project. They would stage a radical version of *The Bacchae*, Euripides' sinister tragedy in which, proclaiming his divinity, Dionysus introduces his orgiastic rites to Thebes, and is resisted by the embodiment of the establishment, Thebes' king Pentheus, who, at the play's end, is torn apart by the god's frenzied female followers, including his mother Agave.[4]

4 Greek drama was eternally primal and newly avant-garde. Peter Brook staged an experimental version of Sophocles' *Antigone* in 1962, the same year that Grotowski began performances of his ritualistic *Acropolis* (a Stanisław Wyspiański play that drew on Greek myths). Herman Nitsch had his version of *Oedipus Rex*. Gregory Markopoulos's *Twice a Man* was inspired by Euripides' *Hippolytus*; *The Illiac Passion*, finished in 1967,

As order was dismembered in *The Bacchae*, Schechner's "environmental" staging broke numerous barriers. There were no seats. Performers and audience shared the space. Spectators perched on or lounged beneath the wooden battlements might at any moment be inveigled, even physically, by Dionysus's followers to participate in the performance. This was most dramatic during the so-called Ecstasy Dance but even more embarrassing when the god commands Pentheus to find a female sexual partner.

Before he came upon the Performing Garage, Schechner had imagined staging his version of *The Bacchae* in a place of "public assembly and direct political action" like Palm Gardens or the Electric Circus. "The event will be a dance, an ecstasy, and the audience will perform along with members of the Group," he wrote in the *Freep* in late March. The two-part article, which introduced the Performing Group to the world, was titled "The Politics of Ecstasy," a term used only weeks earlier by Ed Sanders and Abbie Hoffman in connection with the Yippies and later appropriated by Timothy Leary as the title of his book.

The Bacchae can be taken as Euripides' warning against religious (or political) fanaticism. Dramatizing the collapse of established order and the birth of a new cult, it was well suited to "1968." In his article, Schechner expressed concern that the spectacle of an unrepressed society was "perilously close to ecstatic fascism."

March 16, the same day that Nitsch's O.M. theater gave its third performance at the Cinematheque, Senator Robert F. Kennedy declared his candidacy from the Senate Caucus Room, thus joining Senator Eugene McCarthy as a challenger to the sitting president. Immediately, the Yippies, who had proposed to counter the Democratic National Convention in August with the greatest guerrilla extravaganza ever devised (a "free rock orgy" featuring the Rolling Stones, Beatles, and Bob Dylan, ending in "a huge orgasm of destruction atop giant media altar"), called a press conference at the Americana Hotel to reiterate their plan: "We will create our own reality. And we will not accept the false theater of the Death Convention."

---

draws on *Prometheus Bound* by Aeschylus. The same year, the Living Theatre was improvising on Aeschylus' *Oresteia*. After the Performance Group's *Dionysus*, Romanian émigré Andrei Serban staged *Medea* at La MaMa and Charles Ludlam parodied *The Bacchae* in *The Enchanted Pig*. In a related development, drawing on Rome rather than Greece, Federico Fellini was planning to adapt Petronius's *Satyricon*.

The Yippies had stolen the script for Barbara Rubin's grandiose *Christmas on Earth Revisited* even as Kusama, Nitsch, and Schechner pushed her confrontational happenings in a new direction.

5

The following Friday, March 22, the Destruction in Art Symposium opened at Judson. The show offered a preview of the exhibition scheduled for May at the Finch College Museum. Jon Hendricks, the young conscientious objector who had been placed at Judson and was now directing its gallery, transformed the church courtyard into an avant-garde sideshow-cum-souk. Each artist had a booth: Nitsch displayed his trademark flayed lamb, Lil Picard used a charcoal burner to create bagged feather flambés, Hendricks's sister-in-law Bici Hendricks sped up the destruction of her slow-motion melt piece by distributing ice picks, and event co-organizer Ralph Ortiz prepared to sacrifice two chickens, one white and one black.

That ritual, which Ortiz perceived as a racial allegory, was forestalled when two writers, John Wilcock and Michael Kirby, dramatically freed the doomed fowl, tossing them over the fence in the direction of the Gold Bug, a Mafia-run gay and lesbian disco in the basement of the Edgar Allan Poe house on West Third Street. Ortiz accepted this development philosophically. As reported by Grace Glueck, he and Hendricks pivoted to attack the churchyard's two trees, sawing off branches and pouring blood in the stumps. "I wasn't feeling it anymore," Ortiz told Glueck, "I'm glad the chickens were released—it was like someone making a call to the police before a murder had a chance to be committed." With that Glueck split, missing what would be the main event once the artists moved inside for the symposium.

Scheduled to perform Nam June Paik's 1962 piece *One for Violin*, Charlotte Moorman was late to arrive, thus allowing Saul Gottlieb, an associate of the Living Theatre, then planning the group's return to the United States under the auspices of his newly created Radical Theatre Repertory, to read an open letter from Jean-Jacques Lebel, published in the current issue of *EVO*. Lebel, who contributed to the London DIAS and had been invited to the New York iteration, excoriated DIAS for having allied itself to established cultural institutions like the Finch College Museum of Art, thus becoming part of the very same "power structure" that manufactured napalm. For his event, he proposed bombing Finch.

By the time Moorman arrived, taking her place behind the long table that separated the symposium participants from their audience, the crowd was restive and quarrelsome. Moorman gripped her violin by its neck, holding out the instrument waist-high and slowly raised it above her head. Even those unfamiliar with the piece understood that once she lifted the instrument to its apogee, she would smash it down on the table. A man in the back began heckling and approached Moorman. She shoved him aside. By now, Gottlieb had left his seat to join in the protest. Although taken aback by the unwarranted audience participation, Moorman resumed her performance. Gottlieb persisted, even clambering up to stage a lie-in on the table. As he twisted around to address the audience and explain his position (breaking a violin was the equivalent of murder, the instrument should be given to a needy ghetto child), Moorman completed the piece by cracking the violin on his head.

As in the Nitsch's theater, blood was spilled . . . for real. And as befits a symposium, discussion ensued. "Charlotte was contrite and ministered to [Gottlieb's] wound," Jill Johnston gallantly wrote.

> She explained the point of the piece is to show that we think nothing of killing people in Vietnam and we place a higher value on a violin. She said she didn't mean to hit him but he was in her performance space. Speaking of the therapeutic value of such actions Ortiz said Charlotte was trying to displace her hostility onto an inanimate object and Gottlieb wouldn't let her do that . . . Gottlieb said that Charlotte was unable to de-program herself.

Lil Picard published a rejoinder to Lebel in the next issue of *EVO* and provided space for other DIAS participants to say their piece regarding the Moorman-Gottlieb affair, including Ortiz, who suggested that "like a child who chases his bright colored ball into the street without looking for oncoming cars, so Gottlieb plunged into Moorman's path."

Not surprisingly, Gottlieb, given a two-page spread in the following week's *EVO*, saw it differently. Unchivalrously comparing the ample Moorman to a Mack truck while revealing that she and Picard (but not Nitsch) had accepted censorship to promote themselves on *The Alan Burke Show*—a local TV program in which the host delighted in baiting and mocking whatever publicity-seeking counterculture characters he managed to snare.[5]

"The DIAS people are two years behind the times—the time for purely *symbolic* destruction is over," Gottlieb declared. He ended by attributing the recent dynamiting of the induction center at Whitehall Street to Lebel's letter and demanding that the DIAS organizers call off the "counterrevolutionary" Finch exhibition. He threatened to stop them "*violently*" if need be and, indeed, the same evening that Moorman brained Gottlieb, the Yippies and the Motherfuckers managed to provoke a police riot in Grand Central station.

The current issues of the *Voice* and a new underground newspaper, the *Rat*, both ran stories on the Yippies when a Yip-In organized by Abbie Hoffman and Paul Krassner, largely publicized by *Radio Unnameable*, brought some 3,000 revelers, many of them suburban or outer-borough teenagers in "colorful costumes" per the *New York Times*, to celebrate the solstice in Manhattan. Sublimely irresponsible, the Yippies made no attempt to coordinate their celebration with municipal authorities. Nevertheless, police presence was considerable. When sometime after midnight several Motherfuckers climbed up on the station's central information booth and began spinning the hands of the large, four-sided clock overhead—"Time is . . . Dead!"—nightstick-wielding cops attacked.

There was no warning. Having sealed Grand Central's main exits, the police—evidently responding to a signal from the commissioner himself—forced Bob Fass's "cabal," as well as the Yippies, the Motherfuckers, and everyone else to run a gauntlet out a single set of side doors. Nor was the press spared. It was no longer the Yippies' show. "All the brass was watching," Don McNeil began his report, which reached its climax with four cops cursing the *Voice* and deliberately ramming his head into (and cracking) a closed glass door.[6]

The *Voice* would run a page-one photograph of their dazed and bloody reporter. Before that, as if anticipating a sequel, a few score Yippie sympathizers turned up on West Fifty-Third Street,

5 Previous guests included Allen Ginsberg, LeRoi Jones and Valerie Solanas, who proved so contentious that Burke threw her off the set.

6 The *Freep*'s account of the Grand Central Yip-In invoked sometime contributor Richard Schechner to describe a post police bust trek to Central Park at 3:30 a.m. for "tribal dances" and the "sharing of the weed."

Monday evening, for the Museum of Modern Art's gala preview of the exhibition *Dada, Surrealism and Their Heritage*. Their plan was to join art critic Gene Swenson's Transformation group in demonstrating ideological opposition to the show in its co-option of Dada and Surrealist politics. The cops were there too, complete with helmets, paddy wagons, and sawhorse barricades. So were the plainclothesmen.

All throughout February, Swanson had picketed MoMA from 11:00 a.m. to 1:00 p.m., carrying a large question mark as a sign, protesting his being barred from the museum (something MoMA enforced but denied) for enlivening an evening symposium on the upcoming exhibit *The Machine as Seen at the End of the Mechanical Age* with an "act of melodrama" in which, wearing a paper vest emblazoned with VIRTUE IS ITS OWN REWARD, he carried a tin cup and begged alms from museum patrons.

The thirty-odd members of the Transformation group, some wearing homemade quilts, others with faces painted, did circle dances. The dark-clad, battle-hardened longhairs—Yippies or Motherfuckers?—some complaining they'd been lured to the demonstration under false pretenses and then fingered by Swenson to the cops, took it upon themselves to point out that Dada hated museums and loudly bait the swells as "putrid bourgeois swine." (Marcel Duchamp and Salvador Dalí, guests of honor at the exhibit's celebratory dinner, would later express approval of the demonstration.)

Writing about the event several weeks later in the *Freep*, Swenson characterized it as a "massive police demonstration," suggesting that the New York art world was perched upon the "time bomb of social revolution," and subsequently published a manifesto in the *Freep* headlined WHY HAVE NONE OF MY FELLOW ARTISTS SPOKEN A WORD IN BEHALF OF THE REVOLUTION?

Surreal, if not Dada: Sunday evening, March 31, President Johnson materialized on TV to announce that he would not seek reelection.

6

The next half-week was golden. The stock market soared. The *New York Times* ran a page-one picture of Robert and Ethel Kennedy mobbed by ecstatic supporters brandishing signs that read BOBBY IS GROOVY. *Time* put Czechoslovakia's reform Communist leader Alexander Dubček on the cover. Stanley Kubrick's *2001: A Space Odyssey* opened at Loew's

Capital and the producers of *Hair* announced their move into a Broadway theater only blocks away.[7]

Four days later, April 4, Martin Luther King Jr. was shot dead by a sniper in Memphis, where he had gone in support of striking sanitation workers partially inspired by New York's February garbage strike. There were riots that night in 125 cities, Black students at Cornell held a department chairman hostage, and the Judson canceled a second DIAS (although Kusama staged *The Self-Obliteration of Bonnie and Clyde* at the 170-seat Actor's Playhouse on Seventh Avenue South). Not all destruction art was scratched. The English band the Who—led by Gustav Metzger's former Ealing Art School student Pete Townshend—did their trademark destruction thing at the Fillmore, ending their concert by trashing speakers, guitars, amps, and drums.

For security reasons, the Who played only one long set each night. Richard Kostelanetz reported that an extended improvisation of "My Generation" spiraled into a smash-up finale: "Townshend began to crash back into the speakers, which started to topple."

> He then started to bounce his guitar off the floor and various objects, losing his instrument's attachments. From time to time, he would go through the motions of playing the guitar, only to pull off a string or two, then resuming his strumming before driving the instrument down against the base of the stand-up microphone, knocking the sound out of the guitar with slaps of his hand against the amplifiers.

Townshend concluded by throwing pieces of damaged goods out into the audience.

Saul Gottlieb would have been horrified. Reviewing the Who concert in *EVO*, Jules Freemond vividly described the anxiety he felt walking east from Café au Go Go. The streets were eerily empty, populated by "some sullen looking black cats" and "a few white kids with black armbands." Nervously, Freemond and his companion jumped in a cab that brought them a half dozen blocks over to Second Avenue and the Fillmore, where they found the Who already in the midst of a long set. The sound was

7 None other than Saul Gottlieb was hired by *Hair*'s producers to generate word of mouth by salting the previews with dissident young people. I know because I was one, a classmate of his son, Steve Gottlieb, at Harpur College in Binghamton, New York.

"deafening," Freemond wrote, "If a rifle went off outside no one here would know until they read about it the next day in the papers."

Harlem had been expected to explode but Mayor Lindsay's immediate response—traveling uptown to walk the streets, at times dodging bottles, to express solidarity—had a relatively palliative effect. Some stores were ransacked or torched, but compared to other cities that brought in federal troops to restore order, incidents in Harlem and Brooklyn were minor.

New York had eluded the fate of Newark or Detroit. Still, intuiting impending breakdown, Barbara Rubin was looking to bail. Where once the love cult Kerista had epitomized the East Village, now there were the Motherfuckers. After *Caterpillar Changes*, Rubin had worked with Shirley Clarke and Ed Sanders on a fantasy film project called *The Fugs Go to Saigon*, featuring LeRoi Jones as a homosexual CIA agent, Allen Ginsberg as a reincarnation of the Heavenly Leader, and William Burroughs as prime minister.

Rubin participated in the Easter Be-In and the March on the Pentagon, but mainly she reentered Ginsberg's orbit—a letter she sent him begins with the Yiddish greeting *vos makht ihr*?—moving into his 408 East Tenth Street apartment where she took care of his partner Peter Orlovsky (hooked on meth) and Peter's catatonic brother Julius. (She also assisted Robert Frank in making a feature-length Orlovsky portrait, *Me and My Brother*.)[8]

Having once entertained thoughts of joining the Beatles or marrying Bob Dylan, Rubin now imagined she might become Ginsberg's wife or at least mother to his children. Accordingly, she set herself the task of transplanting him (and his roommates) to a healthier environment. After several months of searching, she found an old farm on ninety acres near Cherry Valley, about sixty miles west of Albany, persuading Ginsberg to purchase the place through his nonprofit organization

8 Inspired by Ginsberg's *Kaddish*, the film tracked Orlovsky's brother Julius from a mental hospital to his brother's care, and even on tour with Peter and Allen. Open Theater founder Joseph Chaikin plays Julius more precisely than Julius plays himself. Actors are identified as "Peter Orlovsky" and "Robert Frank." Amid this role-playing, catatonic Julius is a beacon of authenticity. The film ends with the startling effect of Julius breaking character to observe that "the camera seems like a reflection of disapproval or disgust or disappointment or unhelpfulness" unable "to disclose any real truth that might possibly exist."

Committee on Poetry. In mid-April—around the time the Performance Group began rehearsing *Dionysus in '69*, Rubin moved upstate to get what would be called East Hill Farm organized, along with the Orlovsky brothers and the young filmmaker Gordon Ball.

Almost in recognition of Rubin's departure, the April 14 Yip-Out was a pallid affair. Sally Kempton's page-one lede said it all: "Last year [the participants] all looked pretty and somehow authentic."

> This year, after a bad summer and a long boring winter, they appeared tired and strained. They were pale. They had flaccid shoulder muscles. Last year, at the Easter Be-In, one had noticed flower-like girls and handsome, androgynous dancing boys. This year, at the Yip-Out, one saw teenyboppers in baby doll shifts and miniskirts covering ripply thighs. One noticed boys with acne scars under their day-glo face paint.

(Like, *eeeew.*)[9]

It was the outer-borough crowd. "Nobody," Kempton thought, "seemed to be having a very good time." Still, they were well-behaved. The *New York Times* item was headlined, 10,000 CENTRAL PARK YIPPIES LEAVE NO LITTER PROBLEMS. (By comparison, the Parks Department needed three days to clean up after the 135,000 people who attended the June 1967 Barbra Streisand concert.)

Was the counterculture—newly named by California professor Theodore Roszak in a series of articles published by *The Nation*—feeling depressed? If so, things improved nine days later when militant African American students at Ginsberg's alma mater Columbia University occupied Hamilton Hall to protest the university's proposed expansion into Morningside Park. The next day, white students—led in part by the campus SDS—occupied Low Library. Soon they were joined by Tom Hayden and the Motherfuckers, who occupied the Mathematics

9 Diane Arbus, who by then was living at 120 East Tenth Street and frequenting the Dom, attended this grungier Be-In as well. Trina Robbins remembers hanging out with photographer Linda Eastman (later to marry Paul McCartney) when "this woman approaches: she's all in studded black leather, with cameras hanging on her like outsized necklaces. It's only 1968; I had never seen anyone in studded black leather. She sits down on the grass with Linda Eastman and they start discussing f-stops. It wasn't until many years later that I realized she was Diane Arbus."

Building, which, as Osha Neumann recalled, was "quickly turned into a reasonable facsimile of the Lower East Side crash pad."

April 30 at 4:00 a.m., the day after John Schlesinger began shooting *Midnight Cowboy* and the very night *Hair* invaded Broadway, New York police stormed the occupied buildings. Columbia fell, but on May 3, shortly after Ginsberg arrived at East Hill Farm, French students shut down the Sorbonne and three days later battled police in the Latin Quarter. *Life* magazine ran a picture of none other than Jean-Jacques Lebel leading a crowd of students, right fist raised, and a banner-wielding latter-day Marianne seated on his shoulders.

May 10–11 would be called the Night of the Barricades. In New York, Jimi Hendrix played his first gig at the Fillmore East on a bill with Sly and the Family Stone; out in Chicago, the Doors enflamed 15,000 fans with Jim Morrison bellowing, "We want the world, and we want it . . . Nah-ow-OW!!!" at a concert that ended with the audience twice storming the stage and twice beaten back by Chicago police. May '68! Columbia Records released a Thelonious Monk LP titled *Underground* with the jazz pianist dressed as French resistance fighter on the cover (which later won a Grammy for "album packaging").

The day after the Night of the Barricades, the Living Theatre joined students at the Sorbonne, turned them on to Artaud's "Letter to the Chancellors of Europe's Universities," soon turned into a leaflet, and later that week led the students to occupy the venerable Odéon-Théâtre de l'Europe. Factories were also occupied. The Bourse was set on fire. Street fighting spread from the Latin Quarter to Lyons.

Militant cineastes shut down the Cannes Film Festival. The same magic month, John Lennon and Yoko Ono (who, as recently as February, had herself played a gig with Ornette Coleman at London's Royal Albert Hall) spent their first night together and were thereafter inseparable. Elsewhere in the art world, the exhibit *Destruction Art: Destroy to Create* opened at the Finch College Museum of Art.

Given the worldwide tumult the Finch show seemed like the new normal. *Time* did mention an Ortiz performance that involved decapitating a live chicken but, apart from the *New York Times* critic John Canaday ("pretentious flapdoodle"), reviews were thoughtful. *Newsweek*'s critic David L. Shirley felt that "Destruction artists seem to insist that art, like life, is impermanent." Writing in *The New Leader*, James R. Mellow invoked the assassination of Martin Luther King Jr. and called the show "the simulacrum of violence." Emily Genauer, the doyenne of New York's daily art critics, wrote that—far from outrageous—the show was "rather touching and even naïve" and some of it "quite beautiful."

Up at East Hill Farm, Barbara Rubin, who had been the commune's de facto boss, gratefully gave way to Ginsberg but her fantasies were soon dispelled. Ginsberg's May 9 diary entry notes, "Barbara up here on farm in design to transform my sex marry me have infants be Jewish Cinema mother." In early June, he informed her that there could be no "loving union" between them.

At dinner that night Gordon Ball saw Rubin outside alone and weeping. Her heart was again broken by the June 5 assassination of Robert Kennedy. Rubin's dejected expression "showed a whole new bleakness on the morning of June 6," Ball recalled. "RFK's murder was apocalyptic: it spoke, loud and clear, like her relationship with Allen, of dreams unrealized."[10]

A dream realized, *Dionysus in '69* had been set to premiere on the evening of June 6. Understandably anxious, the Group met that morning, with Kennedy's body lying in state at St. Patrick's Cathedral and, after some impassioned discussion, unanimously decided that the show should go on; focusing as it did on madness, violence, and social breakdown, their radical interpretation of *The Bacchae* seemed relevant to the situation. "The misfortune that lay upon us, actors and audience alike, served to heighten the sense of shared experience," William Shepard, the play's original Pentheus, would recall.

During the sequence devoted to personal venting, cast members articulated feelings about the significance of performing in the aftermath of Kennedy's death. As observed by Stefan Brecht, *Dionysus in '69* seemed "a supplementary instrument chosen by the performers to work out their personal problems." Response to the political murder was incorporated into the play. Dionysus's climactic harangue, a mock campaign speech improvised by William Finley, delivered as he was held aloft by his followers and carried out into Wooster Street, reveled in the ecstasy of destruction.

"I am sick of reasons and laws" is how Shepard remembered Finley's

10 Ginsberg and Rubin quarreled over the summer, their disagreements displaced onto Peter Orlovsky's meth addiction. In late August, while Ginsberg was in Chicago for the Democrat's national convention, Rubin left East Hill, taking refuge in a nearby Hasidic colony.

rant. "I love the smell of riots, the orgasms of death and blood! We will tolerate no more false revolutions, no more false rituals and phony bloodbaths! We want the real thing!"

But what was that?

7

Dionysus began coming together in mid-April around the time of the Yip-Out. Parisian students were running amok when the Performance Group began holding invitational previews in mid-May. Schechner attempted to involve Richard Foreman, who declined to attend (although he was aware of the production, having allowed Schechner to use the Cinematheque for private cast meetings).

Film and theater critic Lita Eliscu accepted the invite, publishing a curtain-raiser in *EVO*'s May 31 issue. Without reviewing the piece, she detailed its modus operandi, explaining that oscillating "between themselves and character as they choose," the actors engage in a form of public introspection. While noting that this "forced self-examination" had precedents in Joseph Chaikin's Open Theater, she was impressed by the heartfelt back-and-forth—not least when members of the cast expressed panic at having just learned that only weeks after the play was scheduled to open, Schechner would be leaving for South America on a Ford Foundation grant: fear of abandonment was palpable. What, some members of the Group wondered, would become of them? Did their leader even care?

"No play I've seen before this demands participation to such a degree," Eliscu wrote although she would not reveal her own participation until after the show opened. Revisiting *Dionysus* after the previews was a letdown. The show now felt literal-minded and accusatory: "Everybody got into the act, telling the audience just where they had gone wrong. They just didn't accept Dionysus-God when he came back to spread love; they went ahead and had Newark and Watts and Detroit and Vietnam." Such finger-pointing struck her as "slightly ridiculous." In fact, she declared, "I'm not so sure I didn't see a different play in the closed rehearsal." Whether because of the Kennedy assassination or opening night jitters, *Dionysus* had changed, "much for the worse."[11]

11 Criticism of her review led Eliscu to publish a third piece, discussing her initial experience. In every performance Dionysus challenges Pentheus to find a sexual partner and as the lone invited guest, Eliscu was drafted. She felt she made the best of an awkward situation and resented being later twitted by the director: "My mood was disturbed

Voice critic Michael Smith was patronizing. Allowing that "by all means Schechner and the Performance Group should do their thing," he wrote that *Dionysus* may be "an idea of theater" but it was not his. Stefan Brecht found the play occasionally embarrassing. The cast could be childish, making up new words for nursery rhymes, chanting *Dionysus, god of joy, god of joy, god of joy. Dionysus, god of joy. Di-o-nysus!* to the tune of "London Bridge is Falling Down." He thought the actors seemed "innocent or rather naïve, somewhat awkward," as "earnest devotees of making a good effort—the opposite of Dionysiac." On the other hand, they did seem to be enjoying their riotous behavior so that, "as on hearing the party noises across the hall, we are apt to feel jealous self-pity—left out."

Nudity, profanity, and exuberant messiness weren't to every taste. *Time* (which waited a few weeks to publish its unsigned review) hated the piece—"sweaty, tangled heaps of men and women kiss and fondle each other from head to toe, all the while uttering erotic moans and groans"—kissing it off as "shamelessly alive from the waist down and shamefully dead from the neck up." But the *New York Times*'s Dan Sullivan wrote a money review, beginning with a Biblical reference, "As Jonah doubtless told the press when he emerged from the whale, it was certainly an experience."

Sullivan didn't much care for "the segment where the actors blurt out whatever has been bothering them that day—therapy for them, boring for us." But in noting the extraordinary rapport between cast and audience, he declared the piece "as faithful a production as *The Bacchae* can have received since its original performances." Not *EVO* but the *Times* outflanked the *Voice* in its appreciation of *Dionsysus* and, like Eliscu, the paper couldn't stop talking about it.

---

totally by Richard Schechner after the rehearsal telling me how uptight I was . . . [Like] they all knew—what line came next, but I didn't." William Shepard, who a decade later wrote a 500-page PhD thesis on his experience as Pentheus, recalled the incident.

> On one occasion a woman in her late twenties or early thirties seemed initially to accept my invitation. She had long, dark hair, wore some exotic perfume like patchouli, and was dressed in a colorful cotton smock of oriental or middle-eastern origin. At first she responded to my kisses and embraces. I was desperately afraid that she would be willing to go further; so I forced the issue by rather rudely attempting to caress her breasts. She pushed me away, and without looking into my eyes went back to her seat.

"A theatergoer who plays his cards right these days can have some groovy experiences with actors," Elenore Lester began a skeptical "Arts & Leisure" think piece on interactive theater, which knowledgably suggested that *Dionysus* lacked the intensity of Grotowski's work as well as the group-grope immediacy to which it aspired. A few Sundays later, the *Times*'s senior theater critic Walter Kerr weighed in to critique *Dionysus*'s critique of illusion, albeit undercutting his authority by repeatedly getting William Finley's name wrong.

The next week's Drama Mailbag featured Richard Schechner writing from Santiago, Chile, to explain that violence, not sex, was central to *The Bacchae* and, in any case, *Dionysus* was more than just "nude dancing" (a phrase neither critic used), thus defending his production's intellectual content against an implicit charge of *Hair*-y hippie-ism.

More letters followed. Inadvertently, the *Times* had raised a central question: Was *Dionysus* criticism or celebration of the counterculture? Brecht, who, unlike Eliscu, was not put off by the show's politics, summed it up: "One is tempted to call [*Dionysus*] anti-hip. However, by the form of the theatrical event, [Schechner] seems existentially committed to the hip, a hippie & engaged in converting the spectators to it." The medium was the message. The show could not but be fashionably "pro-hip."

Pro-hip with a vengeance, *Dionysus* had taken off. The cast (without their director) was giddy with newfound popularity and flush with cash. Every performance was sold out. Even with four-dollar tickets, the members of the company were taking home an astonishing $300 a week—possibly more than stars like Rip Torn and Geraldine Page, who came to the show, were getting off-Broadway. Moreover, there were fans who religiously returned week after week to get high and have sex under the towers or hope to make out with their favorite actors.

8

As the world found its way down to SoHo, Kusama took her show to the streets. There were almost as many *Anatomic Explosions* in New York that summer as *New York Times* items on *Dionysus*.[12]

12 Kusama staged a "Nude-In" at WBAI and also "Love Happenings" or orgy events at her studio, 404 Sixth Avenue, near Washington Square Park. One "Love Happening" involved only men, although female journalists were present, and was recorded by West German television. In her autobiography, Kusama describes the Kusama Sex Company, which hosted group sex parties.

Kusama staged her first naked "Press Happening" Sunday morning, July 14, outside the New York Stock Exchange. Reporting on the event, *EVO*'s star writer D. A. Latimer wrote perhaps the most appreciative, if scurrilous, interview-profile Kusama ever received. Latimer was charmed by the diminutive artist who, when questioned about her own sexual proclivities, flirtatiously told him in heavily accented English that "if you can't fuck in the streets why bother."

Kusama's press happenings were guerrilla forays. The Wall Street *Anatomic Explosion* lasted barely five minutes. With the press, a lawyer, and a lookout in attendance, the artist sprayed blue paint on her naked dancers—two men and two women. Accompanied by a bare-chested Afro Cuban conga drummer, the quartet engaged in free-form gyrations until the lookout spotted approaching police. By the time the law arrived the dancers were fully clothed but, even without an arrest, the event made front-page news as far away as Ogden, Utah.

Subsequent *Explosions* detonated on Liberty Island, in front of the First Presbyterian Church on Fifth Avenue at Twelfth Street and—dancers masked as well as nude—swarming over the Central Park statue of Alice in Wonderland. The new all-image underground publication later named *Newspaper* included a photograph of a Kusama orgy. (Diane Arbus, who had been recruited by the twenty-two-year-old publisher Steven Lawrence, had her close-up portrait of a wailing baby on the cover and two images of Bela Lugosi shot off the TV inside. By the third issue, *Newspaper* was regularly featuring work by Peter Hujar, a member of the master class taught by Arbus and Richard Avedon.)

By the end of the summer, Kusama rivaled the recuperating Warhol for notoriety. Whereas the *Voice* now regarded her with suspicion as a shameless publicity hound, the less sanctimonious *EVO* appreciated her transgressions. Cast out of the art world, she was a character in the counterculture, along with the Yippies, the Motherfuckers, and two new macho militant protagonists, Detroit's hardcore rock band, the MC5 and the left-wing superhero Trashman, the black-clad agent of the Sixth International created for the *East Village Other* by the cartoonist Manuel "Spain" Rodriguez, a twenty-eight-year-old former biker from Buffalo, New York.

A strong draughtsman with a taste for heavy lines, expressionist angles, and outré mayhem, Spain was himself something of an outlaw, having, around the time of the Garbage Strike, precipitated *EVO*'s first bust. Published in the paper's February 2 edition, the second panel of Spain's *Brink of Doom Comix* had the anti-hero on his knees before a stoical female captive, exuberantly performing cunnilingus, the act emphasized with the words *slurgh, shlosh, slurp!* Someone complained and a Brooklyn news vendor was busted for selling obscene material.[13]

Trashman made his first appearance in *EVO* in mid-June as the protagonist of *Subvert Comix*, a strip set in a rubble-strewn, fascist future Amerikkka. Some thought that the muscular black-clad agent of the Sixth International, distinguished by his dark beard and hooded eyes, was modeled on Ben Morea. An early Motherfucker poster featured a hirsute bearded figure, foot lifted to stomp, resembling Trashman as well as the iconic figure on Zig-Zag rolling paper. Thus, the Lower East Side merged with the Third World as the Motherfuckers fought turf wars with the local pigs over St. Mark's Place.

The MC5 were scarcely known outside of Michigan. Their manager, six-foot four-inch jazz poet and radical activist John Sinclair (considered Detroit's biggest beatnik), had begun using the underground press to spread the word. *EVO*'s "Kokaine Karma" column (written by Bob Rudnick and Dennis Frawley and notable for its emphasis on white rock and Free Jazz) first reported on the band, a local "legend" in early summer, citing their rock version of Pharoah Sanders's "Upper Egypt and Lower Egypt."

Installed at the bunker-like Grande Ballroom in west Detroit, the MC5 opened for and were said to have upstaged visiting bands that included Big Brother and the Holding Company, the Fugs, and Cream. Their revolutionary credentials were enhanced as the sole band to play the Yipple Festival of Life at Chicago—a performance described by Norman Mailer in his report on the convention. Without identifying the band or its vocalist Rob Tyner, albeit credibly identifying the sound with Sun Ra, Mailer extolled them in one of his book's longest sentences.

> The young white singer, his hair in one huge puff ball teased out six to nine inches from his head was taking off on a galactic flight of song,

13 *EVO* put a connect-the-dots version of the Spain drawing on their next issue's cover while Spain amended *Brink of Doom* with a four-panel recap of the last week's strip—with the naked woman slapped around and a caption: "In response to those who found last week's second panel objectionable, we submit an alternative sequence which we hope they will find more to their liking."

> halfway between the space music of Sun Ra and "The Flight of the Bumblebee," the singer's head shaking at the climb like the blur of a buzzing fly, his sound an electric caterwauling of power come out of the wall (or the line in the grass, or the wet plates in the batteries) and the singer not bending it but burning it, flashing it, whirling it down some arc of consciousness, the sound screaming up to a climax of vibrations like one rocket blasting out of itself, the force of the noise a vertigo in the cauldrons of inner space—it was the roar of the beast in all nihilism, electric bass and drum driving behind out of their own non-stop to the end of the mind.

Nothing less than "the electro-mechanical climax of the age."

9

Mailer himself was on a roll. *Armies of the Night* was published that spring to great reviews. (It would ultimately win both a Pulitzer and the National Book Award.) Not only would Mailer chronicle the "Siege of Chicago," first for *Harper's* and then in a published book, but he continued to explore a post-Warhol cinema. Mailer's first film, the improvised psychodrama *Wild 90*, had opened to overwhelmingly negative reviews in January. His second, *Beyond the Law*, would be included in the New York Film Festival, and he was now working on a third film, to be called *Maidstone*.

Warhol's cinema was in decline. Although the twenty-four-hour screening of *Four Stars* (a.k.a. ****) at the Tek in December 1967 was hardly negligible, he had not produced a major film since *The Chelsea Girls*. Nevertheless, his investigation of the medium as a means of manufacturing celebrity and stimulus to acting out was scarcely lost on other film artists. Not only Mailer but the documentary filmmaker William Greaves was that summer working on a quite different post-Warhol film.[14]

---

14 Warhol may have been a wraith, but Warholism thrived. *I, a Man*, the movie in which Valerie Solanas had a cameo, was booked into the Evergreen theater barely two weeks after the attempted assassination. *Bike Boy* opened on Bleecker Street in July at the newly renamed Andy Warhol Garrick Theatre followed by *The Loves of Ondine* in August and Paul Morrissey's *Flesh* in September. Located above Café au Go-Go, this 199-seat venue (where Sun Ra and his Arkestra had recently performed, and which Frank Zappa four-walled for the Mothers from March to September 1967) was neither owned by Warhol nor run by his associates. It struck *Voice* critic James Stoller as creepily exploitative. "They really should call it the Valerie Solanas theater,"

Reflecting his belief that American presidential candidates would now be those used to projecting their images through on-screen scenarios, Mailer cast himself as "an American Buñuel," the film director "Norman T. Kingsley." Like *Wild 90* and *Beyond the Law*, *Maidstone* had no script—it was pure existential psychodrama, shot over five days in July at several Long Island estates.

Like *Dionysus* (albeit far, far less disciplined), the movie was a game. Mailer told the cast that his character was making a film about a male brothel as well as contemplating a run for the White House and that he was being shadowed by PAXC, an acronym for the Prevention of Assassination Experimentation Control.

Cast members were divided into Kingsley supporters (known as the Cashbox) and PAXC agents while the director-star Mailer swaggered about bare-chested—having himself filmed as he chatted up a middle-aged woman wearing a McCarthy button or compared himself favorably with economist John Kenneth Galbraith, informing a bunch of black kids that he was "the best white man around." D. A. Pennebaker, who shot Mailer's two previous films, remembered a uniquely hostile environment. As the filming ended, Mailer explained that he'd been orchestrating a five-day "attack on reality."[15]

A more formally daring film, conceived by Greaves in 1967, *Symbiopsychotaxiplasm: Take One* drew on the post-Warhol sense that life itself was a "movie" and the related recognition that to record something with the camera was to necessarily alter it. No less than Warhol's films, it was based on total acceptance even as it attempted to redefine the notion of acting "naturally." (The title is Greaves's modification of a

---

he noted in a crabby review of *The Loves of Ondine*. (Stoller was annoyed that the movie, which had shown in various forms the previous winter, was billed as a world premiere, adding that "the theatre also made a claim for air-conditioning that was spectacularly unfulfilled when I was there." For her part, Lita Eliscu complained about the Garrick's broken-down projector.)

15 Having flirted with assassination, Mailer retreated into an abstruse lecture on filmmaking—until, outraged by this bad faith, the actor Rip Torn, cast as Kingsley's perhaps treacherous half-brother, refused to accept the movie's spurious ending. July 23, the morning after Mailer declared *Maidstone* over—while he was having Pennebaker take home movies of him with his wife and four children—Torn charged across the lawn and attacked Mailer with a hammer, shouting, "I must kill Kingsley." Torn pulled his blows but still drew blood. Mailer leapt upon the actor, knocked him down, and nearly chewed off his ear.

word—symbiotaxiplasm—coined by philosopher Arthur Bentley to signify the interrelationship of all creation.)[16]

As moviemaking, it is raw and profligate. The film runs out, the camera jams, mikes go dead, actors get upset, but the movie just keeps grinding on, bad sound and all. Actors work on a scene of accusation and denial, developing what appears to be a genuine mutual antipathy. The performances are self-reflexive. The male protagonist's role is all about role-playing; his female counterpart is called upon to make a scene.

Although the improvisational feel is abetted by a wildly handheld camera and an intermittent introduction of Miles Davis's "In a Silent Way," *Symbio* is highly structured, making extensive use of split-screen images to document its own making. The crew is often visible as is Greaves, explaining that he is after "a creative piece of cinematic experience." Infinitely less imposing than Mailer, Greaves supplies only the vaguest "direction" beyond invoking the Warholian or hippie credo to live in the moment and do your thing.

Maddened by endless takes of the opening scene in which a woman complaining about all the abortions she's had to get curses her husband as a "fag," the crew caucuses to vent their displeasure with Greaves: "He doesn't know how to direct. He's into blocking . . ." The debate regarding the project's "levels of reality" will be further complicated once Greaves incorporates it in the finished film.

As in *Maidstone*, there is a confrontation. One of the crew challenges Greaves, complaining that over a week has been wasted shooting this "sordid" conversation. With authority under assault, a final blast of "reality" arrives when a loquacious vagrant wanders on set to rant about the nature of sexual attraction and the rule of Nelson Rockefeller.[17]

---

16 Born in Harlem, Greaves, forty-one, began his career as an actor in "race" films after World War II. He appeared in Hollywood message movie *Lost Boundaries*, moved to Canada during the Cold War to work with the experimental animator Norman McLaren, returned to the US as an instructor in Actors' Studio, and went on to found WNET's *Black Journal*. Greaves directed documentaries and *Symbio* might be considered one.

17 Greaves tried and failed to get *Symbiopsychotaxiplasm* into the 1971 Cannes Film Festival, where it might have been shown in the context of Paul Morrissey's *Trash* and Dušan Makavejev's *WR: Mysteries of the Organism*; it was largely unseen until the Brooklyn Museum unearthed it as part of Greaves's 1991 retrospective. Having been rejected by the New York Film Festival, which included *WR*, *Maidstone* had its premiere at the Whitney Museum in September 1971.

10

The year 1968 reached its crescendo in late August. The Soviets invaded Czechoslovakia, the Rolling Stones released their 45 single "Street Fighting Man," the Beatles countered with their anti-radical single "Revolution," and all hell broke loose at the Democratic National Convention in Chicago.

Although the police riot was not televised live, guerrilla theater would never again achieve this scale. It would be described years later by Yippie organizer Jim Fouratt as a "bloodbath" staged for TV: "It was very few people and it looked like a billion people on television and it played in history as an epic moment . . . Chicago was exactly what [Abbie] always wanted it to be, a media event." A few days later, Hoffman wrote his manifesto *Revolution for the Hell of It*, which described the Festival of Life as a spectacle produced by Marshall McLuhan and directed by Mayor Daley and Antonin Artaud.

After Chicago, Kusama's *Explosions* became more political. Police presence forced the relocation of a late summer "ban-the-bomb ballet" planned for the United Nations Plaza. The following weekend, however, Kusama successfully crashed Charlotte Moorman's invitation-only Sixth Avant-Garde festival, a parade down Central Park West.

Ever resourceful, Moorman had obtained official permits, gratis TV spots, and even the co-sponsorship of New York City's electric utility Con Ed. Her own contribution was *Sky Kiss*, a piece in which she would float over the parade, playing the cello in midair as held aloft by a harness of helium balloons. Covering the event for *EVO*, D. A. Latimer kept an eye out for Kusama and found her up at Ninety-Sixth Street, where, along with her crew, she had appeared early, joining in the preparations for the parade.

Kusama solicited help from onlookers, producing "a long spread of bright red linen."

> [She] wound it around a dozen people, including a tail-end contingent of little kids. To some of these she handed flesh-colored masks of notables like Johnson and Mae West—truly hideous masks, real freakouts, people were cringing back from these little kids who looked like Lyndon Johnson, it was a good effect.

"Then she blew her scene," Latimer thought, setting fire to two flags, American and Soviet.

Latimer maintained that Kusama caused a two-hour delay, but once the parade began moving, she simply joined in. He was pleased to see this "ridiculous teeny-tiny Japanese chick strutting down the street," followed by an enormous banner reading SELF (KUSAMA) OBLITERATION. Noting that Kusama was still attached to a hammer-and-sickle flag and was, in fact, dragging it through the mud, a vigilant bystander alerted the authorities. A "racketeer type, cigar and vest and all," whom Latimer assumed came from Con Ed, threatened to cut the power on the whole parade unless the bedraggled banner vanished.

It evidently did but Kusama did not. Latimer's report ends with an outraged Moorman shrieking at the interloper to get out of her parade. Moorman had her hands full with *Sky Kiss*. "Never a minimalist," as her biographer Joan Rothfuss, noted, Moorman chose to perform in a cartoonish, somewhat Kusama-like outfit consisting of a flaming red leotard, tights, and a satin cape. "The Wonder Woman of Central Park West," as Latimer dubbed her, was betrayed by her producer (who miscalculated how much helium was needed) and an onlooker (who punctured one balloon).

By Rothfuss's account, Moorman did not so much float over the parade as bob uncertainly in its midst, often using her feet to relaunch. Defending Moorman here as she had in her version of the DIAS event, Jill Johnston wrote that the entire crowd seemed to be assisting the cellist, who once aloft blew kisses to the cheering artists below. It was "Charlotte being superbly and supremely ridiculous."

There were other startling performances that month. Following the Carnegie Hall disappointment, Sun Ra played downtown with gigs at the Garrick and the Dom, as well as Slugs', appeared uptown at the Olatunji Center of African Culture on 125th Street in Harlem, and a few weeks later made The Scene. Albert Ayler (who had been enjoying enthusiastic attention in the underground press) recorded his controversial fusion album *New Grass*. Pharoah Sanders (also highly regarded by white rock critics) was installed at Slugs'.

One Sunday afternoon, in response to the tour buses that regularly brought sightseers to the East Village, the twenty-three-year-old performance artist Joey Skaggs chartered a bus of camera-wielding hippies out to Queens, his childhood borough (and mine). Paul Krassner and the

Group Image were in tow, not to mention Kusama, who staged an *Anatomic Explosion* in front of a friendly rest stop (the Nirvana head-shop on Union Turnpike, run by a hippie couple living in a Volkswagen van parked behind the store).

Even before Chicago, Newsreel had launched an attack on the New York Film Festival as an elitist Lincoln Center production that "for all its pretentions to High Culture [served] as a cheap screening system for foreign and domestic films"—a "sop" for an alienated intellectual elite "in much the same way that anti-poverty programs pacify the disaffected poor." Published in the *Freep*, their unsigned manifesto declared an intention to "stop this Festival by any means necessary."

Coincidentally or not, the Festival (which opened in mid-September and would be the last to be directed by Amos Vogel) included a number of special programs featuring independent personal documentaries and two New Left features, *No Vietnamese Ever Called Me Nigger* (footage taken at the April 1967 End the War march punctuated by interviews with three Black veterans) and *Last Summer Won't Happen* (a downbeat East Village travelogue featuring a stoned runaway, a teenaged drug dealer, Abbie Hoffman, and Osha Neumann). Jean-Luc Godard's *Weekend* was also shown.

The event was greeted with another furious manifesto in the *Freep* headlined LINCOLN CENTER OR REVOLUTION: "Down with the Pentagon of culture."

> Perhaps it is hard to realize that we are interested in FILM in-and-of-itself, and that consequently we are not dedicated to the extension of "film culture" in-and-of-itself. Film is another tool, another weapon. It is a tool for the building of a movement for change for change . . . That struggle is, here and now, a struggle for revolutionary change in USA society.

Richard Schechner was back in New York and, after several open rehearsals, *Dionysus in '69* resumed performances on October 3. Having taken a month off (declining Saul Gottlieb's invitation to join the Yippies in Chicago), the Performance Group incorporated a few changes, rotating certain roles (mainly Dionysus) and, at the suggestion of Polish critic Jan Kott, incorporating the cleaning of stage blood off the floor into the play itself. They also experienced a greater degree of audience participation: Repeat viewers and fans began to shed their clothes and participate naked in the ecstasy dance. In response, some of the performers now stripped as well.

Actors were crazier and spectators more intimidated upstairs at Max's Kansas City, where *The Moke-Eater*, a play by Kenneth Bernard—John Vaccaro's first production since *Conquest of the Universe*—terrorized its post-midnight audience with the malicious spectacle of an obnoxious all-American gladhander trapped in a nightmare all-American town, tortured by a gibbering band of garishly made-up cannibal ghouls led by a mercurial dominatrix. "The noise level is staggering; a great deal of the violence is actual rather than represented," wrote Robert Pasolli in the *Voice*.

The Moke-Eater was topical both in its overt reference to the American scene and implicit acknowledgment of recent theater. The ritual torment began with a pledge of allegiance to the flag and a feathered Rene Ricard screeching out the national anthem. An hour or more of nonstop ranting punctuated by hyena laughter, Vaccaro's demented pageant might have been a parodic travesty of *Dionysus*, particularly as the actors were often half naked. Although the play ends with the hapless tourist being disemboweled, it seemed more about assaulting the audience.

"The imagery is perhaps the most disgusting of the season," Lita Eliscu wrote in her *EVO* review, but the main event that autumn was the return of the Living Theatre.

11

Since departing New York for London in the summer of 1964, the Living Theatre had led a nomadic existence. The troupe staged *The Brig* in East Berlin, toured West Germany, the Netherlands, Italy (where they played denizens of Sodom in John Huston's production *The Bible*), and (mainly) France. At one point they were on their own when Julian Beck and Judith Malina returned to New York during the winter of 1964–65 to serve brief sentences on charges arising from their tax evasion case.

The company's self-imposed exile ended in mid-1968. Saul Gottlieb's Radical Theatre Repertory booking agency arranged a grand tour during which Le Living, as the French called them, would premiere four new works: *Mysteries* (a series of short pieces including a dramatization of Artaud's essay "The Theater and the Plague," in which actors mimed dying in the audience), *Antigone* (adapted from Brecht's adaptation of Hölderlin's adaptation of Sophocles) *Frankenstein* (an elaborately staged, mythic presentation of the Mary Shelley novel), and the already notorious

Paradise Now, which even more than *Dionysus in '69* exuded the heady atmosphere of the French May in which Le Living itself had participated.

Paradise Now had no script. Rather, the piece was a series of "rungs" to revolution that functioned as a road map for an essentially improvised "social happening." (The audience was handed a chart specifying the revolution's stages.) During the opening Rite of Guerrilla Theater, members of the company circulated through the audience hissing or declaiming their complaints: "I cannot travel without my passport!" "I do not know how to stop wars!" "I cannot live without money!" "I am not allowed to smoke marijuana!" and, most provocatively, "I am not allowed to take off my clothes!"

These gave way to angry injunctions ("If I could drive you out of your wretched mind!") as well as various prayers, yoga exercises, a mass embrace (known as "The Rite of Universal Intercourse"), instances of possession and exorcism, an orgy of animal madness, and finally a call to leave the theater and go out into the street. The Permanent Revolution: Change! Lasting over four hours, the piece called for and depended on the audience's participation. Every performance was different. The premiere created a scandal at the Avignon Theater Festival and, after Le Living was prevented from performing it a second time, resulted in their withdrawal from the festival.

Leaving tumult in France, the Living arrived in the United States in the wake of Chicago. The thirty-four-member company (plus four apprentices and eight babies) landed on September 9. The theater had its first gig at Yale, invited by critic and dean of the drama school Robert Brustein for a three-week residency that concluded with *Paradise Now* on September 26 (four days after Joey Skaggs's magical mystery tour bus brought the East Village to Queens).

The performance ended around midnight with the exuberant cast clad in G-strings and bikinis, leading a happily chanting audience out of the Yale theater and onto the street. Half a block away five police cars were waiting. As a group of onlookers sarcastically sang "America the Beautiful," the New Haven police arrested the Becks, three members of the company, and four individuals from the audience including a Yale undergraduate and the poet Ira Cohen, who was tripping on LSD. The actors were charged with indecent exposure, the others with disturbing the peace. (The second performance sparked a near-riot after word got around and students without tickets stormed the theater. A third performance was canceled.)

On October 2, the Living Theatre arrived at the Brooklyn Academy of Music. *Frankenstein* opened with forty policemen in the theater, three squad cars parked outside, and Allen Ginsberg in the audience. (That same night in Mexico City, the police massacred an estimated 250 to 300 students protesting on the eve of the Olympic Games.) The Living's most elaborate production allegorized the creation and destruction of Mary Shelley's monster with a series of disturbing rituals and pantomimes on a huge, three-tiered set meant to suggest a cross-section of a human head. The play begins with an attempt to levitate a member of the company which, once a miracle fails to occur, turns into a mock human sacrifice. The monster is then constructed out of corpses.

Ross Wetzsteon's lengthy appreciation in the *Voice* declared that what might ordinarily be termed a performance was here a "sacrament." *Times* critic Clive Barnes was more secular and topical: *Frankenstein* is "a theater of protest, as, historically, probably most good theater is." (The next day in Washington, DC, Abbie Hoffman and Jerry Rubin made headlines with their costumed performance at the House Un-American Activities Committee. Rubin appeared as a bare-chested guerrilla fighter; Hoffman was arrested for wearing a shirt fashioned from an American flag.)

Frankenstein was performed for a week, followed by a week of alternating *Mysteries* and *Antigone*. The latter was particularly unappreciated. The play's first wordless half hour began with actors drifting on stage, shuffling about with occasional glares directed at the audience. After fifteen minutes, some of the cast dropped to their knees and began to wail. Speech was worse. Acting was never the Living Theatre's strong point, Richard Gilman thought, and the worst offenders were Malina and Beck: her Antigone was "alternately wild-eyed, coy, neurotic, and impish, a hippie heroine, while he plays a preposterous Creon, monstrous and swollen, a portrait modeled largely on Lyndon Johnson." The *Times* critic, veteran drama critic Lewis Funke, found it painfully obvious. "It is amazing how effectively they can belabor a point, a line, a scene."

Paradise Now, which had its New York premiere on October 14, was, however, beyond normal judgement. Barnes found it tediously sanctimonious, "as in church or temple," but did note that when the piece reached its climax with the chant, "I am not allowed to take my clothes off," the cast was upstaged by Richard Schechner who, sitting in the audience, stripped to his boxer shorts—"an action I had never previously observed from any of my other colleagues" per Barnes—and was rewarded with a picture in *Life* magazine's report.

Wetzsteon, a tireless defender, would write that "the difference between the Living Theatre and the Performance Group seems to be the difference between religion and therapy." *Dionysus* was "no more than superlatively imaginative theater design masquerading as the revolution," Wetzsteon thought, while *Paradise Now* was the real deal. Stefan Brecht called the Living "the civic theatre of an emergent anarchist community."

There were five more performances of *Paradise Now*. Critics came to hate it. Writing in the *Freep*, John Lahr called it "a shocking and sadly facile gesture." Yippies came to dig, although Abbie Hoffman told the *New York Times* that he didn't need to see the Becks' work to know their theater was "beautiful." The penultimate performance was transcendent. Allen Ginsberg took off all his clothes. Some people took up a collection for the actors, while others burned dollar bills. Members of the audience passed around joints and argued about the hyper-critical Eric Bentley piece ("I Reject the Living Theatre") that appeared that morning in the *Times*.

The final performance, October 21, was a nightmare. "It was a full house—full of hostility and bad humor," Susan Cakars wrote in *WIN*, the War Resisters League's quarterly journal, citing militants occupying other people's seats, while intellectuals tossed wisecracks, spitballs, and paper airplanes. There were "fraternity boys, in costumes, with paddles, drunk, rushing—it must have been a requirement to get your Greek letters to 'drop trow' at the Living Theatre freak show . . . Before the Living Theatre even whispered, 'I'm not allowed to travel without a passport,' several frat boys had stripped." During "The Rite of Universal Intercourse," Malina was surrounded, held down, and raped.[18]

12

The evening after Malina was assaulted, the Becks met the Community. The first act of *Paradise Now* was staged at the Fillmore East and for the first time, the piece was politically instrumentalized.

18 Six-and-a-half years later, Malina described the assault in the *Village Voice*. "The stage was very crowded, there was hardly any room to dance, when this group grabbed me in the middle of the crowd," she told Ross Wetzsteon. "They began to fight among each other, and in fighting to get at me they hurt me beyond my capacity to either yield or resist. Hundreds of people surround us, but the crowd is oblivious. I was no longer addressing them. They were only addressing each other, and I was their quarry."

In late winter, Bill Graham—the thirty-seven-year-old San Francisco rock impresario, a childhood Holocaust survivor who grew up in the Bronx and once managed the San Francisco Mime Troupe—bought the old Loew's Commodore, a moldering 2,700-seat movie palace on Second Avenue, then being managed as the Village Theater, and located in the same building as *EVO*'s offices.

The Fillmore East opened on March 8 with the San Francisco band Big Brother & the Holding Company topping a bill that included the former Night Owl folkie Tim Buckley and veteran blues guitarist Albert King. The main attraction was Big Brother's explosive twenty-five-year-old vocalist, Janis Joplin (her name dwarfing that of the band on Fillmore posters). Graham brought Joplin back to New York, three weeks after Big Brother played the Anderson Theater and *New York Times* critic Robert Shelton hailed her with the most ecstatic notice he had given a new performer since discovering Bob Dylan in 1962.

Without a hit record, and only recently broken through in San Francisco, Joplin was a sensation. Then, having used the Joplin juggernaut to announce the Fillmore's presence, Graham closed the theater for two weeks to complete its renovation. The official opening act was the Doors, who played the night after the Grand Central riot and, over two evenings, attracted an estimated 10,000 fans.

A *Life* photographer was on hand both to document the Fillmore's splendidly restored interior and the band's inspired performance, which was prefaced by quasi-underground promotional film *The Unknown Soldier*, in which Vietnam gets blitzed, World War II ends, and lead singer-songwriter Jim Morrison is crucified. Clad in a leather pants and an embroidered Ukrainian *vyshyvanka*, perhaps purchased around the corner from the Fillmore, Morrison was a compelling presence. Describing him, syndicated rock critic Mike Jahn invoked Nietzsche and, inevitably, Artaud.

For some the show was stupendous. "These Los Angeles boys were about to give New York the greatest rock concert they had ever," Richard Kostelanetz wrote, having experienced a show that ended at 3:45 in the morning. The Doors' extended version of "Light My Fire," a number-one hit during the previous summer's Newark riot, "made even more blatant the orgasms represented in the instrumental interludes." Moreover, Kostelanetz thought the Joshua Light Show equally spectacular. But writing in the *Voice*, James Stoller called the JLS "terrible," comparing its obtrusive vulgarity to the piano accompaniment of silent movies at the Museum of Modern Art:

> Its sloppy pulsating liquid figures apparently meant to approximate mandala explosions are ugly and tiresome. I don't know how they do any of it and I don't care. Worst of all is that it's impossible to look at the performers without seeing the light show which initiates a totalitarian atmosphere.

Stoller failed to appreciate how perfectly the Joshua Light Show matched the Fillmore aesthetic.

After the amateurish Dada demo on Fifty-Third Street, the message was clear. Who would go to Grand Central station on a weekend night when one could see rock stars in a Second Avenue movie palace accompanied by a light show spectacle beyond anything found in the Museum of Modern Art?

For a year or more the Fillmore would be the Temple of Rock; *EVO* rock critic Jules Freemond considered the Joshua Light Show itself an attraction. On the other hand, Freemond also complained that "the audience at the Fillmore is looking more and more like an upper-East-side shopping tour." The place was posh, with ushers, reserved seats, and top tickets a hefty five dollars. Smoking was forbidden, but the JLS projected stoner cartoons between the acts and the concession stand was amply supplied with tempting munchies.

All but instantly the East Village's preeminent venue, the Fillmore was the site of several notable benefits. The May 23 "Black Theater for the Black Panthers," meant to raise money for Eldridge Cleaver, featured Sly and the Family Stone, Big Brother & the Holding Company (still with Janis Joplin), and blues stars Buddy Guy and Junior Wells. Two weeks later, the Fillmore hosted a four-night benefit for the Southern Christian Leadership Conference, "A Tribute to Dr. Martin Luther King Jr." with performances by Aretha Franklin, Ray Charles, Nina Simone, Sam & Dave, and Joe Tex.

Still, while the rundown old Anderson—once a Yiddish theater—was an intrinsic part of the neighborhood and the Electric Circus had evolved organically from the Dom, the Fillmore struck some as an invasive tourist magnet. That Graham made his theater available for charitable events did not shield him from charges of exploitation—an accusation that came to a boil on the night of October 22.

The Living Theatre was one of several groups that Saul Gottlieb's Radical Theatre Repertory engaged for an evening to benefit the Columbia Legal Defense Fund. In addition to the Living and the Performance Group, the show—which at Richard Schechner's punning suggestion Gottlieb called "Up Against the Wall Theatre"—included the Open Theatre, the Pageant Players, the Sixth Street Theatre, the Bread and Puppet Theater, and a teenaged ensemble from the Soul & Latin Theater. The invited speakers, as advertised in *Rat*, were Beck, Malina, Juan Gonzalez of Columbia SDS, Ray Brown of the Columbia Afro-American Society, Bob Collier (Black Panthers), and, most ominously, Ben Morea (UAW/MF), short for "Up Against the Wall, Motherfucker".

Rat had been tremendously supportive of the Columbia strike and occupation, as had been the *Freep*. *EVO* was less interested in students and not at all friendly to the neighborhood "street gang with an analysis" which, upon learning that D. A. Latimer was planning an article on the Motherfuckers' crash pad tried unsuccessfully to commandeer the piece. *Rat*, however, was open to the Motherfuckers, literally. Before the paper went to bed, the gang would show up at *Rat*'s offices, on Second Avenue at Fourteenth Street, and lay out their analysis in a page or two of graphics. The current issue's contribution had a skeleton brandishing a banner inscribed with the exhortation "Make It Happen," and the declaration that "Your biggest enemy is your ASS . . . Support you [sic] local Revolution."

Deeper in the issue, past a piece on the Living Theatre, was *Rat* editor Jeff Shero's not entirely unsympathetic interview with the Fillmore's owner. Asked by Shero how he felt about being attacked as a rip-off artist or hippie profiteer, Graham replied that he was "up to my balls" with people criticizing him. "I say, 'come on up, let's rap, let's do it in a park, let's do it on an FM station, on an AM station, on TV, come on, stand up and explain your position. I'll explain mine.'" That would happen sooner than Graham thought.

13

"Up Against the Theatre Wall" drew an incongruously stellar crowd. As with the 1966 Leary lectures, the Upper West traipsed down to the East Village. "There were speed-freak saints doing a jig of liberation in the balcony, and West Side *liberalatti* crouched in the pews below," Richard Goldstein wrote in the *Voice*, under the headline ARTAUD ON SECOND AVENUE. "There were Black Panthers stalking Village highrisers in the aisles, their every step an indelible mince of cool. There were earth mothers with moon children in their arms." And there were a few out-and-out crazies.

Richard Schechner, who had planned a piece in which members of the Performance Group would play—as it was called—*Out in the Aisles*, had the misfortune to sit behind one such earth mother. "A few rows in front of us a heavy, muscular woman with a child wrapped tightly papoose-like kept of a stream of talking to herself. "Shit, fuck, motherfucker, bastard, prick . . .' She bounced the wrapped-up baby on her lap."

The crowd was feisty. After a lengthy anti-teacher skit broadly played by Soul & Latin's high school revolutionaries was either hooted or good-naturedly heckled off the stage, master of ceremonies Bob Fass lightened the mood and pleased the audience by bringing on "A. Yippie" (namely Abbie Hoffman).

There was an intermission and then a bit of *Paradise Now*. "You couldn't tell the dancer from the dance," Dan McCauslin reported for Liberation News Service.

> The actors lamenting, I'm not allowed to take my clothes off and I'm not allowed to smoke marijuana were undercut pretty hard by the longhair in briefs who strolled down left aisle puffing on a huge Columbian pot cigar. More clothes came off and a girl waved a pair of Levi's from the stage. The actors stripped down to jock straps and bikinis in the middle of the crowded stage and people climbed up curtains, speakers, scaffolds, and ropes.

Writing for *WIN*, Jackson Mac Low, whose history with the Living Theatre went back to the 1950s, was sanguine. "Plenty of joints were passed around," he reported. "To my surprise when the actors got to 'I'm not allowed to take my clothes off in public!' only three people really stripped, & two of them were LT actors." Not surprisingly, Goldstein saw a wilder scene: "'Oh wow,' a kid behind me said, 'Some chick back there is tripping out, screaming that she can't travel without a passport.' A tall cat with lean blond hair occupying the center aisle like an indignant stage shouting 'I don't know how to stop the war.' A lady shrank from his spittle."

> But then he was surrounded by kids who danced around him screaming, "I *do* know how to stop the war," and the litany continued for five minutes like a furious Hail Mary.

> Onstage, 100 people were dancing, chanting, or stomping away. Many who knew the scenario were stripping in anticipation. A couple started shagging stage center, surrounded by cheering admirers.

The performance ended with calls for a "free theater" and "non-violence" as the actors embraced the audience in a great, OM-chanting mass. They gathered "arms around each other rocking, humming one clear note," McCauslin wrote. And then the amplified, unmistakable nasal voice of Ben Morea filled the auditorium, announcing that "this theater is returned to the Community."

Leaflets floated through the room and were distributed outside: "The Fillmore is Open and FREE NOW. Come join the celebration Now. This leaflet printed in the Fillmore. Demand a free night." Chaos followed. Graham took the stage and, baited by the Motherfuckers to dig the liberation of his concert hall, melodramatically shouted, "If you want to take this theater by force, you'll have to kill me first." Standing serenely beside him, Julian Beck (the man who turned Morea on to anarchism) had been advised of the Motherfucker plan and told the crowd to "take" the theater with love.[19]

Order dissolved. An hour or more of confused negotiation was punctuated by further Motherfucker bulletins as well as people goofing around the stage, singing, throwing bread, and burning money. Schechner would recall being "shocked and disturbed by the take-over and the temper of the crowd." Scared, he expected a riot. As the crowd had long since occupied the stage, the Performance Group prudently voted not to play *Out in the Aisles*. *Dionysus* was a Broadway matinee by comparison.

Soothed by pacific Beck, Graham managed to clear the house with the promise of a "town meeting" to be held the following week. More tenacious than the Performance Group, the Bread and Puppet Theatre

19 Richard Schechner's account in *The Drama Review*'s "Politics" issue suggests that the Living Theatre rather than the Motherfuckers was responsible for "liberating" the Fillmore. Well before *Paradise Now* "achieved its paroxysm, people were standing on their seats, shouting at each other, deeply angered and excited—not against the Living but against the theatre itself, its ownership, the cops, the authorities—the system that repressed and harassed." Julian Beck began chanting, "FREE THE THEATRE! FREE THE THEATRE! FREE THE THEATRE! FREE THE THEATRE! FREE THE THEATRE! FREE THE THEATRE!"

hung around to perform their 1962 *King Play*, an incantatory anti-war piece in which a Great Warrior is summoned to kill a capering dragon and winds up killing everyone until he is killed by Death.

Two nights later, political theater moved uptown. Thursday, October 24, presidential candidate Alabama governor George Wallace came to Madison Square Garden. Not everyone believed the *Freep*'s anxious prediction that Wallace might carry California and win with 350 electoral votes, but "Fear," as *Voice* reporter Joe Flaherty wrote in a page-one story, "was what this evening was all about."

A ring of 300 New York policemen protected the Garden. Exceeding the Fillmore, the scene was a magnet for crazies: KKK, Minutemen, and American Nazis, not to mention gun-packing off-duty cops. Long-haired protestors—some with a sign reading WELCOME TO NEW YORK YOU RACIST BASTARD—taunted the police and attacked a Wallace bus from furthest Long Island, wresting Confederate flags from the Alabaman's partisans and setting Wallace hats aflame.

At least twenty-five kids were arrested. "From the way the believers scampered for the safety of the Garden," Flaherty thought, the crowd of protestors "must have resembled the residents of Hades." Safely inside, 17,000 Wallace supporters screamed for "White Power." Per usual, the candidate's staff proffered tickets to demonstrators thus set up as Wallace's foils. ("There would be no show without the Anarchists," Lennox Raphael observed in his *EVO* report.)

Right fist clenched, left fist jabbing, bobbing and weaving like the bantamweight fighter he'd been in his youth, Wallace delivered a flurry of punch lines: "We don't have a sick society, we have a sick Supreme Court. We ought to register Communists, not guns. We ought to turn this country over to the police for two or three years."

The crowd was ecstatic. "We don't have riots in Alabama," Wallace shouted. "They start a riot down there, first one to pick up a brick gets a bullet in the brain!" Yo! Motherfucker!

14

On the eve of the "town hall" meeting, WBAI broadcast the Motherfucker demand to "liberate" the Fillmore East for a weekly free night. The scene, as described by Dan McCauslin for the Liberation News Service, was chaotic. "A happy, hairy horde was devouring free food in the lobby and Bill Graham, frowning like a camel, squatted on the Fillmore stage next to his conception of a community meeting—six plastic chairs behind a folding table with mikes, glasses, and a pitcher of water. But $H_2 0$ was nobody's trip." Winos requested wine, bands wanted gigs, hippies who had been busted agitated for bail funds, the Community demanded space. Still, the evening ended with Graham promising that Wednesday nights would be free.

Election Day approached. Kusama staged an early morning *Anatomic Explosion* on 80 Varick Street, just below Houston. As reported by the *New York Times*, "Four long-haired young people, two of them girls, stripped off their clothes, donned masks of the presidential candidates and pranced in the nude on the rain-spattered steps of the Board of Elections in lower Manhattan." Kusama was quoted: "Let's learn the naked truth about the candidates."

Richard Nixon barely won the popular vote 43.4 percent to Vice President Hubert Humphrey's 42.7 percent. (However, if the Republican won less than a million more votes than his Democratic rival, he captured better than one hundred more electoral votes.) The following week, Kusama struck again. Once more, she made the *Times*: "Four persons stripped off their clothes on Reade Street near Lower Broadway yesterday and handed out copies of an 'open letter' to President-elect Richard M. Nixon that said that 'anatomic explosions are better than atomic explosions.'" Kusama staged one more anatomic explosion that month on the subway and included another at a gay wedding she officiated in Central Park, using the Manhattan phone book in place of a bible.

The Motherfuckers used *Rat*'s first post-election issue to announce a new "hip community" organization that subsumed UAW/MF, namely the International Werewolf Conspiracy. The first free Wednesday featured two leading uncommercial local bands, Group Image and the Fugs, as well as a brawl broken up by the police. The second free Wednesday (a night of "joyous pandemonium" per *Rat*) showcased three, more obscure, groups: the Children of God, the Purpose, and Sirocco.

The third free Wednesday was preempted by a visiting duo, the Incredible String Band, acid folk bards from Scotland. Izzy Young strolled over to the East Village to check them out and while he considered the duo to be vapidly hip as well as poor musicians, he was even more perturbed to walk out on the concert into a line of tactical police that ringed the Fillmore "not so nicely keeping out the poorer hippies that had become used to free things on Wednesday nights."

Despite or perhaps because of the election, the Motherfuckers were riding high. The November 21 *Village Voice* ran a page-one story headlined THE RADICALIZATION OF HIP that discussed not only the liberation of the Fillmore but the inexpensive coffeehouse Common Ground (a block from Tompkins Square Park), a so-called liberated space open to activists, runaways, locals, as well as street people, bums, and crazies. There was even a local defense patrol, known variously as the Anti-Pig Militia, the Lower East Side Defenders [LSD], and the Action Committee for Immediate Defense [ACID], promoted in *Rat* with a full-page illustration by Spain Rodriguez.

15

Following the fourth free Wednesday, Kusama played the Fillmore. The most notorious of performance artists was the opening act for the most political of San Francisco bands, Berkeley-based acid rockers Country Joe and the Fish.

Amended to Mike Jahn's *New York Times* review was a brief acknowledgment: "While the audience was entering the theater Friday and Saturday, nude people ran in the aisles painting polka dots on customers' faces. At one point an actor dressed as a policeman was stripped on stage." It was, Graham would concede, poor box office.

Halloween weekend, the MC5 had recorded their first LP (live at Detroit's Grande Ballroom). They also declared a new religion called Zenta. On December 5, John Sinclair announced the formation of the White Panther Party, with himself as Minister of Information, one member of the MC5 as Minister of Culture, and the other four as Ministers of War. The manifesto rhetoric was only slightly less inflammatory than that of the Motherfuckers. The White Panthers were preparing to challenge the "power structure" and, when the MC5 made their East Coast debut in mid-December, they would be "the spearhead of the attack."

Taking this literally, a contingent of Motherfuckers showed up at the Boston Tea Party where the MC5 opened for the Velvet Underground. In between the acts, the Motherfuckers commandeered the stage to demand that concerts should free. The rap ended with a cry to tear down the Tea Party, a former synagogue that had been converted into a concert hall in 1967. When the Velvet Underground (now without John Cale) came out on stage, Lou Reed declared that his band had "nothing to do" with the Motherfuckers' proposal and in fact considered it very stupid.

"This is our favorite place to play in the whole country and we would hate to see anyone even try to destroy it!"

Now blackballed from the Tea Party, the MC5 were featured on the cover of *Rolling Stone* when, along with the Group Image and the street musician David Peel, they played a Fillmore free night the following Wednesday. It was not a great scene; the band arrived late to find that members of the audience had taken over the stage. Still, they did their show and met afterward to get high and rap with the Motherfuckers. A quick trip back to Ann Arbor and then, the day after Christmas, the MC5 returned to the Fillmore.

Having rented the hall for the night, the band's new record label Elektra distributed 2,300 free tickets as part of a radio promotion—leaving less than the 500 that the Motherfuckers had demanded for the Community. These evidently sat in the theater manager's draw until at the last minute and under pressure, they were sent over to the Common Ground. The Fillmore also agreed to allow standbys fill the empty seats. Thus, scores of people were clamoring to get inside the theater when the opening act, Peel and his band the Lower East Side, began performing. Bill Graham attempted to bar the door and a kid with a bicycle chain broke his nose.

The MC5's lead singer had not mollified the crowd with a declaration that, White Panther manifesto notwithstanding, they were here to play music and not revolution. Accordingly, when the band finished their set, performed before two giant American flags, the audience stormed the stage and smashed their equipment, pelting the band with promotional 45s as they escaped into the limousine that would take them for dinner at Max's Kansas City.

Paradise lost. The debacle marked the end of free concerts (and, so far as Graham was concerned, the MC5, whom he would never again book).

Nevertheless, Sandy Pearlman, whose band the Soft White Underbelly was to share a New Year's Eve bill with the MC5 at the Broadway Central Hotel (until the fearful venue canceled the gig) gave the 5 a good review in the *Voice*—more high energy than the Doors, the Who, and Sly Stone, comparable only to Sun Ra. The following week, Richard Goldstein published a thoughtful piece on rock and the blues that, citing the lame crooning of "it's gonna be all right" on the Beatles' new single "Revolution," declared, "We much prefer the MC5, and their open hostility to all that is 'gentle' in rock." If the MC5 suffered from exaggerated expectations, their reputation was enhanced after Graham declared them personae non grata and they were dropped by Elektra.

Although hardly comparable to the Arkestra, the MC5 did share several gigs with Sun Ra. Thanks to John Sinclair's promotion, the band was associated with Free Jazz particularly in Detroit. *Voice* rock critic Robert Christgau's defense equated the MC5's relation to a respectable hippie group like Crosby, Stills & Nash with Ayler's relation to Miles Davis. "If you crave articulation and subtlety, you won't like Ayler or the 5, but if you like to listen with your body sometimes, they won't quit on you."

Christgau went on to praise Ayler's controversial new LP *New Grass*, an Impulse! release that, over a year before Miles Davis released his rock-fusion LP *Bitches Brew*, employed a soul-singing chorus and a propulsive beat, not to mention "the funky tenor breaks that filled out early R&B."

16

Progressive rock critics attempted to integrate the countercultural musical canon. *New Grass* was also praised by the *EVO* columnists who shared the byline Kokaine Karma, ranking Ayler's LP with the albums by Coltrane and Coleman. Ayler, they wrote, was a singular religious artist, having "fused spirituality, exaltation, the excitement, intensity, passion, intimacy of soul, funky jazz, gospel, rock, bebop, rhythm and blues and avant-garde sounds into a dynamic new direction for music."[20]

Kokaine Karma not only extolled Ayler but Sun Ra, Cecil Taylor, Archie Shepp, and Mike Mantler's Jazz Composer's Orchestra, demanding these artists "be played on every progressive rock FM station in the country." Intentionally or not, the *EVO* critics failed to mention Pharoah Sanders, another MC5 influence whose first two Impulse! releases, *Tauhid* and *Karma*, would be hailed as masterpieces in *The Cricket*, the jazz-oriented mimeo-zine started by LeRoi Jones, A. B. Spellman, and Larry Neal in early 1968.

The Cricket was particularly devoted to Sun Ra, an advisor to, writer for, and subject of *The Cricket*. "Under terrific opposition, I have tried to show and demonstrate my goodwill to the world," he wrote in the first

20 A prophesy was fulfilled. In the early '60s, some irate exponents of bebop and swing felt that Coltrane, Coleman, and Eric Dolphy were supported by rock-'n'-rollers drawn to a kindred sense of chaos.

issue. The journal was also loyal to Ornette Coleman, defending his cheerfully avant 1966 release *The Empty Foxhole*, controversial less for Coleman's violin than for featuring ten-year-old Denardo Coleman on drums. But in general, the publication was characterized by militant Black nationalism. The second issue included a manifesto by the poet (and Coleman devotee) James T. Stewart that began, "Our music must bring down the white empire." A significant portion of the Free Jazz audience was white.

Looking to more popular forms, *The Cricket*'s first issue had a piece praising James Brown and a half dozen Motown artists. The second issue included a eulogy for Otis Redding, teasing the idea that the Mafia crashed the singer's plane (although without mentioning the rumors that he had been marked for death because he was poised to announce his intention to become a Muslim and/or organize an independent cooperative of Black musicians). But jazz was something else. Ayler was regarded as Coltrane's heir and *The Cricket* was deeply offended by *New Grass*, which was perceived as a lame attempt to cross over or sell out.[21]

Ayler would publish a long, mystical rant in *The Cricket*'s fourth and final edition, suggestively titled "To Mr. Jones—I Had a Vision," that invoked Jesus, praised Elijah Muhammad, and foresaw a "new Earth built by God coming out of Heaven." In the same issue, Larry Neal wrote that "when most of us first heard Albert, he really blew our minds, opening us up not only new possibilities in music, but in drama and poetry as well. He was coming straight out the Church and the New Orleans funeral parades."

> But lately Albert's music seems to be motivated by forces that are not at all compatible with his genius. There is even a strong hint that the brother is being manipulated by Impulse records. Or is it merely the selfish desire for popularity in the american sense. At any rate, [*New Grass*] is a failure.

---

21 Ironically, Sun Ra—who had played Bleecker Street as well as the East Village and Harlem—did not need to sell out to sell out. In mid-April, he had been featured on the cover of *Rolling Stone*, hailed as the leader of the "fiercest, most uncompromising large American music organization in existence."

Neal deemed the rhythm, the guitar, and most of the singing to be "shitty" while the premise was worse than feeble: "Like, it's not too cool to get to the Rolling Stones or The Grateful Dead to learn things that your old man can teach you."

As if to reinforce the point, a poetic playlet called "Rockgroup," signed by LeRoi Jones as Imamu Ameer Baraka, made merciless fun of a grotesque, ultimately murderous band called the Crackers. Nevertheless, in August 1969, a year after *New Grass*, Ayler would double down with the pointedly titled *Music Is the Healing Force of the Universe*, following the earlier LP's R&B–infused path, albeit without the overdubbed "Soul Singers."

The Cricket had ceased publication by the time Miles Davis released *Bitches Brew* or played the Fillmore. In 1968, however, there was one Black musician who might have posed a political problem for nationalists: Jimi Hendrix. *The Cricket* would hardly have been impressed by the avant-garde rock critic R. Meltzer's accolade (Hendrix was either "soul's greatest master of space and time" or "space-time's greatest master of soul"), but Hendrix was an authentic Blues Person who had not only recaptured rock's citadel but was a great innovator in what Jones and Spellman argued was jazz's bedrock. In common with Trane and Ornette, Hendrix came up playing with Chitlin' Circuit R&B bands; however, once he went solo his audiences, developed in Village joints and the UK, were overwhelmingly white.

Writing in *The Cricket*'s last issue, Imamu Ameer Baraka classified Hendrix, Sly Stone, and the 5th Dimension as "integration music" sellouts, albeit acknowledging Hendrix as "an actual freak." After all, the first Hendrix LP *Are You Experienced*—an album the critic Greg Tate would decades later describe as sounding like something "an avant-garde troupe of extraterrestrial soul men left behind before heading back to Alpha Centauri"—had been available for eighteen months. Hendrix and Miles Davis were mutual admirers, although Davis evidently walked away from an LP that would feature him, Hendrix, and drummer Tony Williams.

Repeatedly approached by the Black Panthers, whom he had praised in the January 1969 issue of Capitol Records' *TeenSet* magazine, Hendrix wanted to reach Black audiences. He attended but kept a low profile at a Madison Square Garden benefit for the Martin Luther King Jr. Memorial Fund. By some accounts he was interested in playing the Apollo Theatre in Harlem (where five years before he won an amateur night contest) in support of aid to the successionist Nigerian state Biafra, but the offer was nixed by the theater owner.

Soon after, on September 5, Hendrix and pick-up group Gypsy Sun and Rainbows, who backed his epochal performance of "The Star-Spangled Banner" at Woodstock, were invited to close an outdoor festival in central Harlem to benefit the United Block Association. The gig was set up by Hendrix's friends, twins Arthur and Albert Allen a.k.a. the Ghetto Fighters. The other acts included Maxine Brown, Sam and Dave, and Big Maybelle. Too bad Hendrix didn't jam with Maybelle (name-checked in Spellman's piece on the last blues singers as authentic R&B).

The festive crowd was dancing in the street. Others were singing from their windows when hippie-clad Hendrix's racially mixed band arrived around midnight to a chorus of boos and a tossed bottle. Unplayed on New York's soul station WWRL, Hendrix was unknown in Harlem—the "true paradox of his fame" per Umbra poet David Henderson. Originally 5,000, the crowd dwindled to 500 during Hendrix's set, which opened with "Fire" and included "Voodoo Chile," which was introduced as "the Harlem national anthem." If only. Either before or after he performed, Hendrix was approached by a Black nationalist who told him, "Hey brother, you better come home."

10

No President, Scare City, 1968–69

In which Jack Smith responds to the persecution of *Flaming Creatures* and pornography seems endemic. The art world is in open rebellion. Norman Mailer runs for New York mayor. Political theater pushes its boundaries as the Crazies run amok, drag queens battle the police, and Manhattan bombings terrify the city. As the Black Panthers go on trial, the drama of the sixties reaches a climax with two astounding theater pieces by LeRoi Jones and Robert Wilson.

> *If one knew what one expected of one's president one wouldn't need a president would one?*
>
> —Jack Smith, advertising flyer (1968)

Dead of winter 1969: Jack Smith had a new film! Nearly five years since *Flaming Creatures* was busted, two years since Smith last showed rushes from his never completed *Normal Love*, two weeks after Richard Nixon's inauguration (and the Mobilization Committee to End the War's despondent "counter inaugural"), *No President* had its first public screening. Rather than midnight, it was presented at brunchtime—11:15 a.m., Sunday morning, February 2—at the Elgin, a moldering 600-seat movie house on the corner of Nineteenth Street and Eighth Avenue.[1]

1 Formerly devoted to Spanish-language films, the theater was managed by Ben Barenholtz (who ran the Village Theater before it became the Fillmore East). In some ways the Elgin resembled the old Charles.

Heading into a municipal election, New York was a mess. The past year brought soaring crime, a strike that left mountains of uncollected trash, and another strike pitting Black and Puerto Rican school boards against the heavily Jewish United Federation of Teachers. There had been the police riot at Grand Central. The student uprising at Columbia was resolved with an even more brutal crackdown. More generally, downtown theaters hosted orgies. People went naked in the streets. Acid-ripped hooligans preached disorder. The shooting of Andy Warhol was but a sideshow to the MLK and RFK assassinations, the Chicago bloodbath, and a war without end. (The week after *No President*'s premiere, a massive snowstorm would paralyze eastern Queens and jeopardize Mayor Lindsay's prospects for reelection).

How did Jack Smith process the political tumult of 1968, which, among other things, brought *Flaming Creatures* to the attention of the United States Senate? Did he? Was *No President*—a title both blunt and ambiguous, suggesting the absence or negation of the state's ultimate authority—a celebration of anarchy or a manifestation of an exhausted, even oppressive liberation?

What (if anything) prompted Smith to revisit the presidential campaign of 1940? He was eight years old when liberal businessman Wendell Willkie ran as a Republican against third-term-seeking FDR. Was Willkie a fantasy surrogate? Smith's family had recently relocated from Columbus, Ohio, to Brownsville, Texas, where his father drowned in a shrimp boat accident.

Having arranged for the *No President* screening, Jonas Mekas described it in his column as the one "truly avant-garde film" he could imagine. The artist's flyer was only a bit more forthcoming: "Wendell Wilkie [sic] . . . More Famous Than Most Presidents—He Had Farms in Indiana, Vegetative Motility, and a Willingness to be President." (By "vegetative motility" did Smith mean zombie reflexes?)

An unfixed work that, in all its iterations, was essentially performative, *No President* evolved out of Smith's November 1967 program, suggestively titled *Horror and Fantasy at Midnight*. A half dozen individual titles (*Reefers of Technicolor Island*, *Scrubwoman of Atlantis*, *Ratdroppings of Uranus*, *Marshgas of Flatulandia*, *The Flake of Soot*, and *Overstimulated*) were variously screened at the former Tek, renamed the New Cinema Playhouse (where, following its premiere at the New York Film Festival, Shirley Clarke's *Portrait of Jason* had been running for six weeks). All were silent, accompanied by a taped soundtrack by Angus MacLise's Cineola Orchestra and the Vietnam tape prepared by David Gurin two years earlier for *Rehearsal for the Destruction of Atlantis*.

Reviewing *Horror and Fantasy*, Mekas described a two-hour-plus presentation of three untitled films, each approximately forty-five minutes long: The opening piece "starred a most beautiful marijuana plant, a gorgeous blooming white queen with her crown reaching toward the sky." The second and third parts featured "Jack's creatures" in fantastic gowns and plumed hats, first in color and then faded gray and white. Another account of the program, published by the psychoanalyst Joseph Aliaga in José Rodríguez Soltero's short-lived arts journal, *Medium*, has *Reefers of Technicolor Island*, accompanied by "tooty flutes" and "the ominous tom-tom of drums," followed by images of "boys in drag."

> Seated and languidly swaying with a big fan in front of his-her face the top chief, called Lobster Man, jerks the exposed penis of a faceless naked man standing off to the side while a narrator appropriately touches, in diplomatic terms, on a corrupt official's jerking off a nation, a people, a power and it's funny.

Like Ken Jacobs's *Star Spangled to Death*, *Horror and Fantasy* mixed original material with found footage. Aliaga called the last shot, "a brilliant intuitive leap . . . a newsreel clip showing hundreds of civilians lined up on both sides of a street wildly cheering army recruits marching off into World War I." Long Live Death! James Stoller saw newsreels of the 1940 Republican Convention that nominated Willkie. Coincidentally or not, this footage appears to have been introduced around the time Senator Eugene McCarthy, an opponent of the Vietnam War, challenged the sitting president, Lyndon B. Johnson.

"I don't know what Wendell Willkie means to Jack Smith, but I was immoderately moved by this strange juxtaposition," Stoller wrote.

2

Horror and Fantasy was not the underground's only outlandish political metaphor. Tumultuous before it even opened, *Conquest of the Universe* was founded on a backstage power play. A month before the November 21 premiere at the Bouwerie Lane Theater, the autocratic director John

Vaccaro fired the egocentric playwright-actor Charles Ludlam, who took most of the actors with him, among them Smith associates Mario Montez, Bill Vehr, and Jeanne Phillips.

Hiring a lawyer to enjoin Ludlam from mounting a rival production of his own play, Vaccaro hastily recast, employing personalities associated with the Warhol factory—not only Woronov, but Ondine, Ultra Violet, Beverly Grant, Taylor Mead, Rene Ricard, and an uncredited Holly Woodlawn. According to the *Conquest* costumier Trina Robbins, Jack Smith, who had appeared in Vaccaro's previous Ludlam production *Big Hotel*, was also in the cast—at least initially, since he evidently sided with Ludlam, albeit briefly.

Ludlam would produce his own version of *Conquest* under the self-reflexive title *Queens in Collision*, but first he revived *Big Hotel*. Rehearsals took place in Mario Montez's loft in the Centre Street building also home to José Rodríguez-Soltero, then working on his political movie *Che Is Alive*. (Eventually titled *Dialogue with Che*, this crude, consciously Warholian double-screen portrait stars Venezuelan artist Rolando Peña as the revolutionary martyr responding testily to the filmmaker's off-screen direction in untranslated Spanish. In the final ten minutes, Taylor Mead, a featured performer in *Conquest of the Universe*, ambles on as a CIA agent to give a master class in pure presence.)

Smith attended *Big Hotel* rehearsals but left after several screaming arguments with Ludlam prompted by a mixture of professional and sexual jealousy. Ludlam rented Tambellini's Gate, where the current attraction, *Trips in Erotica*, included Vehr's *Brothel*, hyped by radio station WBAI as "this year's *Flaming Creatures*."[2]

Big Hotel opened three days after *Conquest of the Universe*, performed Friday and Saturday at midnight. Lacking whatever discipline Vaccaro may have brought to the play's earlier iteration, the revival was a stoned, slow-motion improvisation. Whether or not Smith was in the cast, the glacial pacing suggests his influence. One spectator remembers leaving

2 Finished in late 1965, *Brothel* was praised but never reviewed by Mekas. In addition to Smith, the cast included Mario Montez, Jeanne Phillips, Tosh Carillo, and Susanna De Maria (all of whom appear in *No President*) as well as Piero Heliczer and Francis Francine. The movie appears to have attracted police attention. The Gate's proprietor Elsa Tambellini put out a bulletin warning that "the only existing print" was in danger of being confiscated. On October 1, 1968, that print was seized by US customs officials as Vehr returned from Montreal, where he had had a show, and it has since been lost.

sometime after 1:00 a.m., going for soup at an all-night Ukrainian luncheonette, returning to the Gate an hour later to retrieve a forgotten scarf, and finding the same scene still being played.

In January 1968 (around the time *Flaming Creatures* was busted at the University of Michigan and another print was impounded by New York D. A. Robert Morgenthau), *Horror and Fantasy* moved downtown from the New Cinema, where it had been showing twice a week during the run of Warhol's twenty-four-hour ****, for a five-day run at the Gate, still presenting *Big Hotel* and now *When Queens Collide* at midnight on the weekends. Smith had been doing some new filming. The star was now his old friend Irving Rosenthal (whose novel *Sheeper* had recently been published by Grove Press, cover graced with Smith's author photo). Vaccaro has a prominent role and set of theatrical dentures.

By late March, shortly before Lyndon Johnson announced he would not seek reelection, *Horror and Fantasy* had coalesced into *Kidnapping and Auctioning of Wendell Wilkie* [sic] *by the Love Bandit*—an all black-and-white presentation starring the diminutive Rosenthal, lipstick'd and unshaven, as the infant Willkie, abducted by a mustachioed pirate (drag king Doris Desmond) and sold on the block of a slave market modeled on the one in the 1942 Maria Montez vehicle, *Arabian Nights*. Stoller again reviewed the presentation in the *Voice*, noting that it now began with the playing of a Willkie campaign speech, introduced by an announcer whose delivery was slowed down so that he sounded just like . . . Jack Smith, whose voice could be heard throughout "booming from the projection booth, complaining about one thing or another."

The same day that Stoller's column appeared, along with an ad noting the Gate's attractions as *Kidnapping and Abduction*, *When Queens Collide*, Bill Vehr's play *Whores of Babylon*—a mishmash of Old Testament and comic book sci-fi, caustically reviewed by A. D. Coleman in the *Voice* as a sub-Burroughsian cut-up—and a local band, the Seventh Sons, Martin Luther King Jr. was assassinated in Memphis.

3

The juxtaposition of Smith's Baghdad and American electoral politics proved prophetic. June 13, two days after Smith was contacted by *Playboy* magazine's editorial director, soliciting a response to the magazine's forthcoming article "The History of Sex in Cinema," lame duck president Lyndon Johnson nominated his crony Supreme Court Justice

Abe Fortas to replace retiring Chief Justice Earl Warren. (In answer to the question, Smith wrote a response on *Playboy*'s embossed note paper, "Yes, you can take your magazine & wipe your asses with it.")

In the Fortas nomination, Senate conservatives found a way to attack the liberal Warren court. Their weapon would be Fortas's rulings on pornography. A print of *Flaming Creatures* confiscated in Ann Arbor in January was flown to Washington, DC, at the behest of Senator Strom Thurmond, the ranking Republican member of the Senate Judiciary Committee.

In late July, Thurmond organized a "Fortas Film Festival," in Room 2228 of the Senate office building. A fourteen-minute filmed striptease, two other skin flicks, and *Flaming Creatures* were projected on the wood-paneled wall. Members of Congress were invited, as was the press, and Thurmond thoughtfully furnished glossy frame enlargements from the movie. The anti-Fortas forces announced plans to send prints of *Flaming Creatures* to women's groups and civic clubs in hopes of triggering further outrage. Before the Fortas nomination collapsed in September, there was talk of showing the film on the Senate floor.

Whether or not Smith was aware of these shenanigans, his summer and fall were characterized by ambitious, and likely failed, political happenings. The August 1 *Voice* ran a hand-drawn ad for a "Lobster Sunset Colored Light Spectacle," *Clamercials of Clapitalism*, presented at an East Fourth Street tenement storefront called the Breathe Gallery. Mario Montez was to appear as the Crab Ogress of Capitalism and the ad promised "Free TV from the Octopuss," while urging against buying "anything advertised on TV." (A tiny ad running the following week noted that "production problems due to Day-Glo paint not drying because of clammy weather" delayed the opening to August 9.)

Smith revived *Clamercials of Clapitalism* in late September, this time as part of a "Gala Party and Lobster Moon Pageant" at his 89 Grand Street loft, featuring the "Live Crab Ogress" as well as "music, nudity, and a slide show." On September 28, he opened Millennium's fall season with a film program called *Taboo of Farblonjet*. A few weeks later another "Lobster Moon Mixed Media Spectacle," *Wait for Me at the Bottom of the Pool*, was staged on the roof of 89 Grand Street. (To judge from Smith's notes the various *Lobster Moon* spectacles may have originated as revivals of his contribution to the 1965 New Cinema Festival, *Rehearsal for the Destruction of the Atlantis*.)

On October 12, two days before *Paradise Now* opened at the Brooklyn

Academy of Music, Smith arranged for a screening of *Kidnapping and Auctioning*, now retitled *No President*, at a West Broadway loft belonging to Japanese artist Taka Iimura. According to *EVO* cartoonist Baby Jerry, the audience was largely gone by the time Smith showed up ninety minutes late. Hanging around, he transcribed Smith's explanation:

> I really want to give this film away, if I could . . . to a big theater just for exposure, since it's a political film pertinent right *now*! And it's so confusing, chaotic . . . the rent, bill collectors, film assistants . . . you just don't know how it is just trying to bring little bits of beauty, to work.

Was Smith perturbed to see ambitious work by disciples he regarded as careerists? During this period, Ludlum revived *Big Hotel* at the Gate, alternating with *Turds in Hell*, written by Ludlam and Vehr, and featuring Jeanne Phillips and Mario Montez. More focused than *Whores of Babylon*, the play, which at one point was intended to be a black mass, began by announcing itself as a mortal sin and rambled on for four hours. Opening night was delayed by half an hour by the absence of one of the stars, either "Crazy Arthur" Kraft, a fifty-year former child vaudevillian cast as a "hunchback, pinhead, sex maniac," or Montez, who played his adopted mother Carla the Gypsy, perhaps prompting Smith to run down the aisle carrying an eighteen-year-old street kid, the future performance artist Penny Arcade, on stage for a bout of mock copulation.

Turds began around midnight and ran for hours. "I honestly thought intermission was the end of the play," Lita Eliscu wrote in *EVO*, having left at 2:45 a.m. Eliscu found *Turds* inferior to *Whores of Babylon*. *Voice* critic Martin Washburn was entranced: The loose "plot" allowed for a sinking ship to segue into an underwater ballet, a procession of flagellants and, as a set piece, "a thickly populated brothel scene (where the costuming, superb throughout, reached a crescendo). It is very ingeniously staged, with unrelated scenes—simultaneously presented, focus shifting from one to the next, somewhat in the manner of a complex baroque painting." (After the Gate raised its rates, *Turds* moved uptown to the Masque, a porno theater on West Forty-Second Street, where it ran for some months into the spring.)

Shortly after the November election, Smith was awarded a $40-per-month grant from the Friends of New Cinema. This may have encouraged him to continue work on his movie and as previewed by Mekas in the *Voice, No President*'s Elgin premiere was an Event. Andrew Sarris in the *Voice* and Lita Eliscu in *EVO* both commented on the size of the crowds. Some, it would seem, were in a daze. Mekas reported that at least one viewer thought the presentation "a remarkable first public screening of a film made fifty years ago."

No President was shown silent save for broadcaster Lowell Thomas's commentary on a Sumatra travelogue and program music Sarris identified as Tchaikovsky. The surviving version alternates scenes shot in Smith's SoHo loft with found footage—including the Thomas travelogue, a clip from a late 1940s soundie in which an unidentified couple vocalize the sentimental hit "A Sunday Kind of Love," and newsreel footage of candidate Willkie addressing the Republican convention and the Future Farmers of America.

The narrative is structured around two tableaux, similar but more confrontationally crude than those in *Flaming Creatures*. In the first, the future presidential candidate, attended by a sleeping nurse, is abducted from his crib; in the second, which features a rented fog machine and a professional belly-dancer as well as the singer Tally Brown, baby Willkie is auctioned and perhaps sacrificed. This is followed by ecstatic footage of the real Willkie accepting his party's nomination. Thus, Smith's hothouse childhood fantasies merge with entropic, harshly lit glamour scenes wherein the garishly costumed hobnob with the brazenly nude.

No President struck Lita Eliscu as calculated and joyless. That the film was almost entirely shot in the studio gives it a studied feel. (Smith may have intended some exteriors; his typically enigmatic notes suggest a plan to film Mario Montez at the April 1968 Be-In.) Sarris, aware how much Smith meant to his colleague Jonas Mekas, was measured in his dislike. "Jack Smith uses the cinema not so much to record or reveal his obsessions as to display them."

"I feel like I owe it to Smith to be shocked, and I am a little bit though not as much as I should be," Sarris wrote.

> Blame the prevailing permissiveness for the fact that fuzz didn't come down hard on the spectacle of dangling genitalia employed in semi-choreographic patterns, suggesting a collaboration between Beardsley, Busby Berkeley, and the sugar plum fairy.

Normal Love was already outmoded. Something more powerful had been unleashed.

"With the global awakening of 1968, no country or institution could defend its borders from the infiltration of the Eros Effect," historian George Katsiaficas would write in *The Global Imagination of 1968*. But the combination of love, freedom, and solidarity that Katsiaficas named also brought mass disinhibition, repressive desublimation, and naked pornography.

4

The Eros effect was ubiquitous, even reified, not least in the underground press. In late 1968, Al Goldstein launched a new pornographic tabloid, *Screw* magazine. The maiden issue's centerfold was a picture taken the previous August at Kusama's Alice in Wonderland event: the scowling artist posed with five nudes—among them, one woman wearing a Fidel Castro mask, one man with a Jackie Kennedy, another with a dangling cigarette, simply wearing a long blond wig.

On a more elevated plane, Philip Roth's *Portnoy's Complaint*, scandalous for its comic account of adolescent masturbation, was a *New York Times* bestseller. In early 1969, the Performance Group was busted for nudity at the University of Michigan. On February 7, the same day *No President* had a move-over run at Cinema 7, "a private club devoted to films for the male homosexual," a conference on censorship and pornography opened on the Notre Dame campus in South Bend, Indiana.

The student-organized event drew heavily on the New York underground. In addition to an advertised "erotic art show," the attractions included a keynote lecture by Allen Ginsberg, performances by the Fugs and the Theatre of the Ridiculous, and several film programs—one, the unannounced sneak premiere of a Warhol feature shot in early 1968 during which Viva and Louis Waldon conversed, bathed together, and, toward the movie's end, briefly engaged in coitus. The Factory called the film *Fuck*.

The Fugs dropped out. The art show was shut down before it could open. Ginsberg arrived, spoke, chanted, and split. Lita Eliscu, who flew out of LaGuardia to the wintry Midwest to cover the conference for *EVO*, reported that she spent most of three slightly abortive days in her Holiday Inn motel room watching TV with her friends. ("As a matter of routine Jack Webb fact, we were more pornographic than anything else going on.")

However, the second day's film screenings were disrupted when

Flaming Creatures, a last-minute replacement for Carolee Schneemann's *Fuses*, was yanked from the projector after two scandalizing minutes. (Smith's film was unannounced. The plan had been to ambush two representatives of Citizens for Decent Literature by showing it in a symposium on the Fortas nomination.) John Vaccaro did manage to stage *Lady Godiva* twice, but all subsequent films were canceled, and the conference blew up the following afternoon when sheriff's deputies maced students while breaking up an unauthorized screening of Andrew Noren's *Kodak Ghost Poems*.

Noren, twenty-six, had inherited Barbara Rubin's mantle as an apostle of the Eros effect. Born in Sante Fe, he grew up in California's Inland Empire and after a stint in the Army and a bit of college, moved to New York, where, working as an editor at ABC-TV, he acquired a 16-millimeter Bolex camera and began making movies. The first was a thirty-seven-minute narrative, *Change of Heart*, about an unhappy, frequently naked young couple. It was "made in 1965 when I was twenty-two, just in from the country and with a big picture of Jean-Luc Godard hanging over my bed," according to notes Noren wrote for his September 1966 screening at the Tek.

Following *Change of Heart*, Noren employed a sound-on-film Auricon to shoot several confrontational cinéma vérité interviews, each a single half-hour reel, showing these at Ken Jacobs's Millennium Film Workshop. The methodology was not unlike Warhol's first talkies. Noren's subjects included an aspiring actress, a middle-aged German co-worker who was once a member of the Nazi Party, and Harry Smith, who, according to the description Noren gave the Film-Makers' Cooperative, "refuses to be filmed, cowers inside his body, makes nasty remarks, calls me a fag, suffers temporary amnesia, long period of embarrassed silence as he tries to think of something to say. Tries to turn off the camera, etc. The NYC Culture Gestapo arrive and bust his ass for being tedious." (All of these films were subsequently destroyed by the filmmaker.)

Simultaneously, Noren embarked on a series of sketchbooks called *The New York Miseries*, short recordings of his daily life. In early 1967, a New York film lab confiscated footage Noren brought in for processing, which among other things showed the filmmaker having sex with his then girlfriend Margaret Lamarre, and turned it over to the police. (Noren won his case in court, although soon after, *Change of Heart* drew obscenity charges in California.) In August 1967, Noren screened *The Unclean*, in which, by his description, various people ("mostly women") take baths: "Everybody comes out clean & sweet. Live sound. Flesh color. Cunt-scope documentaries."

The New York Miseries became a two-hour silent work, first shown publicly in July 1968 as *Kodak Ghost Poems*. The definitive self-portrait of the male, heterosexual artist as a young boho with a movie camera, it was notable for its lush texture, lyrical idealization of life on the Lower East Side, lust for light, and graphic carnality. Without recourse to a tripod, albeit with a remarkably steady camera, Noren managed to film his lovemaking as it was happening. "Basically what I want to do is record my life," Noren told Jud Yalkut in a 1969 interview.

In any case, *Kodak Ghost Poems* (a title Noren would have to abandon in 1975 after receiving a cease-and-desist letter from Eastman Kodak) was far more celebratory than confrontational, let alone pornographic. Six weeks after the fracas at Notre Dame, an off-off-Broadway production in a Cooper Square storefront theater pushed the limits of the permissible by advertising live sex. "The effect of the sexual revolution on the arts, particularly theater, is rapidly accelerating," Howard Smith wrote in his column. "The next inevitable phase": actual sex. *Che!*, a play by the twenty-nine-year-old Trinidadian writer Lennox Raphael, an *EVO* staffer and sometime member of the Umbra group, promised to feature "real live intercourse" if only—according to director Ed Wode, whom Smith quoted and who would take credit for the play's boldness—"when the performers feel like it."

A hundred blocks uptown, Swedish director Vilgot Sjöman's *I Am Curious (Yellow)* was packing the same Cinema Rendezvous where, to the *New York Times*'s displeasure, *The Chelsea Girls* surfaced two years earlier. An instant sensation (and a triumph for Grove Press publisher and neophyte film distributor Barney Rosset), *I Am Curious (Yellow)* would be the #1 US box office attraction for the week of November 26, 1969—the first foreign-language film to top *Variety*'s weekly chart. Closer to Godardian analysis than skin-flick prurience, Sjöman's film linked his protagonist Lena's sexual curiosity to her questioning Swedish society. The most notorious scenes were comic episodes in which Lena and her boyfriend make love in public. More explicit and discomfiting was the sequence in which she is treated for the scabies with which her lover presumably infected her.

"That movie was so sick I wasn't even aroused," one senator had complained of *Flaming Creatures*. The same logic might explain the hostility directed at Sjöman's notably sober, naturalistic, politically minded, and somewhat lumbering representation of female desire. "The Trash Explosion is here, and *I Am Curious (Yellow)* is at the bottom of the garbage dump," Rex Reed wrote in a *New York Times* piece apparently designed to answer the favorable review given the movie by the newspaper's regular critic Vincent Canby. "This genuinely vile and disgusting Swedish meatball is pseudo-pornography at its ugliest and least titillating."

I Am Curious was based on a familiar trope of a young woman's erotic awakening. *Che!*, which began previews two days after *I Am Curious* opened, was a nastier manifestation of the Eros effect. The premise had a captured Che Guevara transported by a female alien intelligence agent named Mr. Mayfang to Washington, DC, to gratify the bestial desires of the president of the United States as well as a female cohort, Sister of Mercy.

The one act (which encompassed many) was confined to a single set—the Oval Office—furnished with a lumpy four-poster bed covered by an American flag. Off to the side, a silent, female "Fidel Castro" sat in a cage wearing only a cap, a gun holster, and boots. As much declaimed as enacted, *Che!* offered a lustily free-associative succession of obscene one-liners, enthusiastically delivered by a mainly naked cast while engaging in a series of essentially comic sexual entanglements.

Someone had tipped off the authorities because *Che!* was busted after its second public performance by a criminal court judge who sat through the show and, upon leaving, proclaimed it without redeeming social value—a signal for waiting police officers to arrest the cast, director, writer, and one-man crew on charges of consensual sodomy, public lewdness, obscenity, and conspiracy to commit such acts, not to mention impairing the morals of a minor (the teenaged usher). Defending their writer, the *East Village Other* posted the $5,000 bond.[3]

---

3 *Che* reopened on April 25. Lita Eliscu included a scene in the Erotic Energies Festival she organized at the Electric Circus in early May. Promising "the best in porn, avant-rock, and new jazz," Eliscu invited Sun Ra, Pharoah Sanders, and the MC5, whom she had recently interviewed for *EVO*. According to Dean Latimer who recognized activists Hugh Romney and Ben Morea in attendance, the event was shut down at 1:00 a.m. by the police, supposedly because someone had spotted somebody on the FBI Ten Wanted list. *Che* was re-busted on May 7 although it continued to play for the remainder

5

Che!, like José Rodríguez-Soltero's film, had been conceived in the aftermath of Guevara's murder. It might well have been timed to preempt or cash in on the much-hyped Twentieth Century Fox biopic that would open in late May. (In a journalistic coup, *Rat* devoted much of its May 16 issue to the movie—CHE STOLEN FROM THE GRAVE—printing a "liberated script" provided to the paper by a disgusted Twentieth Century Fox employee.)

Hollywood's *Che* was but one instance of counterculture co-option. Even before publication, James Kunen's satirical account of the Columbia uprising, *The Strawberry Statement*, had been purchased for the movies. The week after Nixon's election, Columbia-CBS Records ran a full-page spread in college and underground papers that, unconsciously high camp, posed seven dudes hanging out in a dorm room-cum-jail cell, floor littered with picket signs. One guy discreetly rolls what looks like a joint; another grooves with a stereo headset. The image is captioned BUT THE MAN CAN'T BUST OUR MUSIC. (Yet, the LPs promoted were not rock but avant-garde—Varese, Ives, Terry Riley, and Walter [later Wendy] Carlos's Moog-driven *Switched-On Bach*. Columbia-CBS, which was reprimanded by the FBI for underwriting political terrorists, had not quite figured out its audience.)

Even as the new Nixon administration cracked down on political radicals, the militant ultra-left aided the forces of repression by declaring war on the peace party. A group labeled as "crazies" by a spokesman for the umbrella organization Mobilization Against the War (or "Mobe") made its debut at the January 19 "counter inaugural" and was officially christened in *Rat*'s account of the event. Chanting obscenities while pelting the presidential motorcade with dirt clods and beer cans, the Crazies further confiscated and set fire to the small American flags distributed by the Boy Scouts.

The New York Post picked up on *Rat*'s reporting and ran a piece in late January, headlined YIPPIE IS DEAD BUT HERE COME THE CRAZIES: "They describe themselves as '200 running, screaming, hairy freaks,' call their leaders 'Groucho, Chico, Harpo and Zeppo' and emphasize ad lib revolution: 'Revolt where you live, live everywhere.'" The Mobe suspected

---

of 1969. (The iteration I saw that summer featuring a college buddy and later draft resister Phil Savath was more strenuously sweaty than salacious.) Raphael, Wode and Larry Bercowitz were found guilty of obscenity in early 1970.

provocateurs and indeed the self-appointed leader of the screaming, hairy freaks was a thirty-nine-year-old former member of the John Birch Society and current FBI informant named George Demmerle, who wore a cape over his purple, satin Cossack shirt, a Day-Glo pink helmet with two feather dusters on his head, and called himself Prince Crazy.[4]

"George was the craziest cat around," Jerry Rubin reflected. "If you wanted anything flippy done, call George. He lived on the streets and worked with the people. He never took off his Yippie button." On March 22, Demmerle was arrested along with Abbie Hoffman and forty others (including Florynce Kennedy) for "parading without a license" in a daylong commemoration of the Grand Central massacre that began at the offices of the *New York Times* off Times Square, proceeded east to a heavily fortified Grand Central, and wound up in Central Park. (The next day police raided an apartment at 333 East Fifth Street and then arrested Hoffman, who was not there, on charges of possessing guns and blackjacks.)

It seemed as though the Yippies and the Motherfuckers had merged. *Rat* bought the ruse. While scarcely mentioning George, the paper had announced that the Crazies planned to mark the first anniversary of the Grand Central police riot by disrupting liberal congressman William Fitts Ryan's annual Political Conference on World Problems and American Power at Riverside Church, and then reported on the event. The manifestation was complemented not only by *Che*'s opening night but an even more prestigious disturbance. Back from a tour, the Living Theatre fomented a modified *Paradise Now* uproar at a symposium convened to ponder the question "Theater or Therapy?"

Susan Sontag and Norman Mailer were among the 500 New York intellectuals, along with Pauline Kael, who may have brought director Arthur Penn, gathered at the Friends Meeting House on East Fifteenth Street just south of Gramercy Park to attend a $10 a head benefit for

4 According to an undated, one-page NYPD background sheet, the Crazies were composed of former members of the Coalition for an Anti-Imperialist Movement (CO-AIM), itself an offshoot of Youth Against War and Fascism, the youth organization the Workers World Party, a splinter of the Socialist Workers Party. During the 1968 presidential campaign, CO-AIM targeted "'liberal' gatherings" at which Robin Palmer and Sharon Krebs would "strip nude, carry pigs' heads, and display Vietcong flags." The Crazies were further linked to Alternate U and Florynce Kennedy's Media Workshop.

Shirley Broughton's Theatre for Ideas. A free-floating institute, Broughton's theater had over the past eighteen months staged symposia on the future of democracy, tactics of dissent, and the legitimacy of violence—all relatively civilized.

A poor sound system delayed "Theater or Therapy?" for half an hour, more time than required for the proceedings to descend into what the *New York Times* reported as "a free-for-all that sometimes verged on physical violence." The first panelist, Robert Brustein (who had brought the Living to Yale in September 1968 and soon regretted it) was subjected to a barrage of razzing that the lead heckler, Living member and former coffeehouse comedian Steven Ben Israel, called "a high seminar in brain damage repair." Doggedly concluding his remarks, Brustein was followed by Paul Goodman, a longtime Living Theatre ally, affable and clueless in his nostalgia for *The Connection* and apparent unfamiliarity with the Living's recent work. He too was mocked.

The third speaker, Judith Malina, gently chided Brustein for suggesting that she was soft on fascism. This apparently inspired Rufus Collins, another member of the company, to a frontal assault on Western culture. Collins excoriated genocide, technology, and the audience: "Fuck all liberal intellectuals and their fucking discussions." Ben Israel responded by bellowing a mantra from Artaud popularized by radical psychotherapist R. D. Laing: *If I could drive you out of your minds*. Malina seemed radiant while her husband, who at one point seized an irate woman's fur stole and tossed it on the ground, waxed prophetic. "Get used to this. It's happening all over America, in every meeting house in America. This is what is going to happen from now on."[5]

By Brustein's account, around the time that Jennie Hecht nearly broke her leg swinging down from the gallery to the stage, "other actors from the company began pounding on the railings and screaming at the top of their lungs. And now the audience began to scream back." Stella Adler cried for quiet. Richard Schechner called in vain for "five minutes of meditation to think about the beautiful thing that's happening here." Suddenly, Norman Mailer—no stranger to the Theatre of Ideas—strode to the stage.

5 Jim Morrison saw *Paradise Now* performed at UCLA on February 28. The next time the Doors played in Miami, Morrison followed the Living's lead—drunkenly taunting his audience as "a bunch of slaves" before inviting everyone up on stage.

Norman to the rescue! Striking a pugilistic pose and adopting a Southern accent, he invoked the French Revolution only to be upstaged and ultimately propositioned by the outrageously voguing Jim Tiroff, a member of the Living Theatre as well as a cigar-smoking vision in an orange velvet cape and violet plumes. Mailer retreated or rather regrouped. Ten days later he convened a meeting at his Brooklyn Heights home to discuss the possibility of a mayoralty bid.

"Theater or Therapy?" never answered its own question. Disorder reigned but then, once the uptightniks split back uptown, the event morphed into a party. Reporting for the *Voice*, Robert Pasolli wrote that "most people stayed on and on, drinking the beer and booze" that the Theatre for Ideas had provided.

> Everyone was on his feet, many on the pews in the meeting hall, talking, laughing, yelling, having a good time, really. It was impossible to know what was happening beyond a three-foot radius around one, so one stopped bothering to try. It was a nice feeling, very intimate and potentially personal.

The after-symposium lasted until 2 a.m.

Shirley Broughton wrote angry letters both to the *New York Times* ("the Becks profess a belief in anarchism but in reality they practice a new style of fascism") and more pointedly to the *Village Voice*: "One of the best weapons rightist reaction could have devised is just such directionless extremism, CREATING DIVERSIONARY CIRCUSES." So it was with the Crazies who, not twelve hours later, attacked the anti-war politicians at Riverside Church.

Their presence became known when they commandeered the church's sound system to broadcast the earsplitting, street-smart sounding, female Voice of God whose screed segued into a bit of Janis Joplin. Then, as reported by *Rat*, "from all over the room, disrupters, erupters and destroyers of many revolutionary persuasions pointed accusing fingers and hurled verbal abuse," placing a pig's head on the stage and parading Vietcong flags throughout the afternoon.

According to police files, "at the termination of the demonstration approximately twenty CRAZIES proceeded to a Peace Forum at St. Mark's in the Bouwerie Church." There, they squirted pacifist David McReynolds with a plastic water pistol and demanded that Bella Abzug, a leader of the Women's Strike for Peace, explain herself ("Where were you when I was getting my ass kicked in Chicago?"). This time the Vietcong flags were augmented by signs in support of RFK assassin Sirhan Sirhan, presumably because *Voice* reporter Pete Hamill, a friend of Kennedy and present during his assassination, had been announced as a speaker.

Meriting a page-one *Voice* story, the Peace Forum intervention would be the Crazies' last public triumph. (The following Saturday's demonstration in front of the Women's House of Detention, during which, having hoisted a Vietcong flag, they set up a mock guillotine and beheaded effigies of pig cops, LBJ and his wife Lady Bird, got only police attention.) Meanwhile, a more persistent militant group, the Art Workers' Coalition (AWC), had commenced upon a prolonged battle with the Museum of Modern Art.

6

The instigator was Panayiotis Vassilakis, a forty-three-year-old kinetic sculptor known as Takis. Three days into 1969, Takis arrived at MoMA, where a well-regarded show called *The Machine as Seen at the End of the Mechanical Age* had been up for over a month, and coolly disconnected his 1960 *Télé-Sculpture.*

A small, elegant *ballet magnetique*, in which an electromagnet mounted on a pedestal attracted a black spool-shaped form while repulsing a magnetized white cork sphere, both objects suspended by steel wires, Takis's piece was less a sculpture than a system. "You hear metal think as you watch disquieting free-floating forms move and click through invisible turnstiles," William Burroughs wrote of Takis's work, but there was nothing so modest about *The Machine as Seen at the End of the Mechanical Age.*

Two years in the planning, the show spanned four centuries, including artists from Leonardo da Vinci to La Monte Young. There were some 350 paintings, drawings, sculptures, machines, and unclassifiable objects, many of which "bleep, blare, bellow" per *Newsweek*'s David L. Shirley, who identified the show with the "new swinging museum scene" introduced by *The Responsive Eye*. MoMA, which had been given *Télé-Sculpture* some years before, stuck it into the show without securing Takis's permission.

Invited by Takis to witness his response, John Perrault reported in the *Voice* that, "in a crowded gallery, in front of stunned guards, Takis moved in on his own work, cut the wires, unplugged it," and, protected by a few well-rehearsed confederates, including the radical curator Willoughby Sharp, "gently carried the piece out to the museum garden." There, cradling his artwork against the January cold, Takis demanded a meeting with the new (and short-lived) museum director Bates Lowry, sitting in until Lowry agreed first to a conversation and then to put the piece back in storage.

A spontaneous happening at the Museum of Modern Art! Takis had distributed a handout calling his action "just the first in a series of acts against the stagnant policies of art museums" and, as Grace Glueck reported in the *Times*, "the action touched off a surprising response. Dissident attention, hitherto unfocused, zeroed in on MoMA as the Establishment beast." Taki's performance inspired the Art Workers' Coalition, whose founding members included critics Perrault and Gregory Battcock, two kinetic artists, Wen-Ying and Hans Haacke, both included in the "The Machine" show, Len Lye, represented in the show's paltry film sidebar, and light-sculptor Tom Lloyd, who did not have a piece at MoMA.

The AWC presented Lowery with a list of thirteen demands—among them a gallery for Black artists, the institution of rental fees, free admission to the museum, and an open public hearing on the question of Modern Art. Lowery stalled as the AWC raised the ante with a Sunday sit-in reported on the evening news and a mass meeting on April 10 at the School of Visual Arts. According to Glueck's account, Lloyd read "a four-page single-spaced letter to MoMA, urging more 'cultural relevance for blacks and Puerto Ricans,'" Naomi Levine denounced creeping rot in the "creative arts," the painter (and former Mambo Queen of Southern California) Anita Steckel cried, "*J'accuse*, baby!" with regard to the critics who had failed to cover her recent exhibition of sexually explicit work, and the Belgian "destruction artist" Jean Toche denounced all museums as "fascistic."

However much Glueck enjoyed reporting the AWC meeting, she made a crucial point: The changes advanced suggested a shift in the nature of art, by placing processes and ideas over objects, art would be "more concerned with effects (however ephemeral) than with collectability." (It was what was already being called Conceptual Art, theorized by Sol LeWitt and promoted by the twenty-eight-year-old Bronx-born gallery director Seth Siegelaub.) Just a few weeks later Toche subverted the second edition of *10 Downtown*, an artist-organized attempt to bypass the gallery system by inviting the public to visit their lofts and perhaps purchase their work.

Positioned at the entrance to 66 Grand Street, Toche charged gallery-goers 50 cents admission to trudge three flights to photographer Gilles Larrain's space. There they found only a white wall, blank save for a statement declaring the new "Republic of Federated Socialist States of Belgium," signed by the Government in Exile and four other groups: the Action Committee for the Liberation of Fleming and Walloon Workers, the Collective Committee for Direct Democracy, the Vigilance Committee against Centralized Authoritarian Hierarchy, and the Action Committee for Sexual Liberation Movement of May 4, 1969.

"Nobody got admitted to the studio. Nothing happened at all," Lil Picard approvingly reported in *EVO*. That was the idea. "The people went up . . . faced the wall, went down." Picard linked Toche's provocation both to "conceptual art" and a new sort of Happening: the "action-event." These included John Perrault's "Invisible Theater" and an upcoming panel discussion organized by fellow critic Jill Johnston, dedicated to the proposition that criticism was an outmoded form of communication.

7

A year after the Yippies' political theater, art-world activism was endemic. The same issue of the *Voice* that ran Joe Flaherty's account of the Crazies carried an editorial endorsement of the paper's co-founder Norman Mailer, who had announced his candidacy for mayor and was running in the June 16 primary. An elaboration on his three movies, Mailer's campaign was a performance, made by and for the media.

The candidate not only consulted a wide range of journalists, among them Robert Christgau, Richard Goldstein, Pete Hamill, Jack Newfield, Jeff Spero, Gloria Steinem, and *New Yorker* rock critic Ellen Willis, but he also engaged *Village Voice* staff writer Joe Flaherty as his campaign manager and *Daily News* columnist Jimmy Breslin as his running mate. The activists he consulted thought his act needed a wider audience. Jerry Rubin suggested that he run with a Black Panther; Florynce Kennedy thought he might put himself up as a running mate for prospective candidate Harlem congressman Adam Clayton Powell.

Twelve days after he received a page-one *Village Voice* endorsement and was heralded by another page-one *Voice* plug written by Flaherty, Mailer declared his candidacy. The field was large, and Mailer was also endorsed after a fashion in *Screw*, which, in an article on the race, imagined he might be the field's most potent lover.

Be that as it may, Mailer as a public speaker could be creative. His major idea was having New York City become a separate fifty-first state—something that had been prophetically floated in *The Bag*, Sol Yurick's newly published novel of East Village "welfare-hippieland," as one *Voice* writer put it. Mailer also favored neighborhood autonomy and, appropriating one of the most successful attractions at the New York World's Fair, proposed to encircle Manhattan with a monorail. Asked by a citizen of Queens how he would clear the snow that paralyzed the borough after winter storms, he replied, "I'd piss on it."

The *Daily News*, Breslin's own paper, published a poll of likely voters indicating that two-thirds had never heard of Norman Mailer. The campaign peaked on May 5 when it was announced that Mailer had been awarded a Pulitzer for his impressionistic first-person report on the October 1967 March on Washington, *Armies of the Night: History as Novel, Novel as History*. It sunk to its nadir two days later at an overflowing Village Gate rally.

Having been preceded by two boozy supporters (Newfield and Breslin), a similarly lubricated Mailer took to the stage at 1:00 a.m., clutching a whiskey glass and affecting his Southern sheriff's drawl, to harangue a room divided between would-be supporters and curious hecklers as "a bunch of spoiled pigs," adding insult to injury by noting that "the cops I spoke with yesterday were a more impressive group of people than you."

On the eve of the campaign's lone television debate, Mailer showed up at a public school auditorium to address the Greenwich Village Neighbors for Peace only to discover that the auditorium, packed to overflowing, had been seized by . . . the Crazies, who among other indignities displayed a portrait of their candidate for mayor, Ho Chi Minh. Joe Flaherty, author of the *Voice*'s report on the Crazies, described the evening in his memoir of the Mailer campaign.

> They mobbed the stage and stood on the seats. Volleyball was played with balloons, the participants standing in different aisles . . . Whistles blew, Vietcong flags were unfurled, paper planes flew in formation to airborne shouts of "Kill for Peace," "Bomb the Pentagon," "Free the Panthers" and "Ho, Ho, Ho Chi Minh, the NLF is gonna win."

Mailer tried to speak, according to Flaherty, but speech was impossible. "The Crazies sang, shouted, and insulted. 'Fuck you Norman,' one yelled. 'Liberals like you gave us Nixon.'" Confusing the Crazies with the Motherfuckers, Mailer set himself up for press accounts of his reckless obscenities in addressing an audience of concerned parents.

In another journalistic performance held on the evening of May 21, a week after Mailer met the Crazies, Jill Johnston organized a panel discussion at NYU's Loeb Student Center about . . . her: "The Disintegration of a Critic: An Analysis of Jill Johnston." Only Charlotte Moorman was punctual. The rest of the panel drifted on stage a half hour later in various levels of intoxication. The participants included two patrons, Walter Gutman and John de Menil, two voluble Warhol stars, Ultra Violet and Bridget Polk, plus Andy himself (who never spoke but took occasional Polaroid pictures), and two art critics, Gregory Battcock and Lil Picard. A third critic, David Bourdon, was the moderator.

The psychiatrist whom Johnston had invited never showed but Johnston did, an hour after the panel arrived. Johnston was, according to her colleague John Perrault who covered the event for the *Voice*, "smashed and all upset because her last column had been cut." Actually, Johnston had ceased to write about dance or art. ("She just writes," Perrault explained.) Printed without paragraph breaks, her columns were outrageously self-absorbed free-associational musings enlivened by art-world gossip.

Johnston read her excised column and Perrault realized that she was now an "old-fashioned poet," with a performance style akin to Dylan Thomas, Allen Ginsberg, and Edna St. Vincent Millay. Returning to print, Johnston ended her next column by referring to her event and thanking the *Voice*, which she considered an "underground paper" as long as it continued printing her.[6]

6 The *Voice*'s longstanding interest in electoral politics culminating in Mailer was not underground; the paper's commitment to memoirist criticism was. Fiercely first-person, Johnston was the most underground of *Voice* writers, closely followed by self-identified poet Jonas Mekas. Perrault, also a poet, was underground as well. The same issue in which Johnston critiqued her event had Perrault's take on a show at Paula Cooper's gallery to benefit the AWC (of which he was a founding member), a report on the latest iteration of Street Works, a series of outdoor performances to which he had contributed, and a description of his own "Invisible Theatre."

8

June 16: Mayor Lindsay lost the Republican primary to Staten Island state senator John Marchi by less than 6,500 votes. However, he held on to the Liberal line going into the November election.

In the Democratic primary, City Controller Mario Procaccino beat former mayor Robert Wagner by 30,000 votes. Norman Mailer might have made the difference; he received 41,288 votes and came in a distant fourth behind the Bronx borough president Herman Badillo. (Having also received 20,000 fewer votes than his running mate Breslin, Mailer retreated to Provincetown to write the essay on the impending Moon Shot, for which *Life* magazine was paying him a million dollars.)

Dionysus in '69 closed that month after a sensational year; the most violent of westerns, *The Wild Bunch*, opened. As usual the real excitement, though, was in the streets. Friday night, June 27, an unexpected police raid on a Mob-owned Greenwich Village gay bar met unanticipated resistance. As the raid was prompted by the Bureau of Alcohol, Tobacco, and Firearms rather than the local precinct, the management was caught unaware—even more so when the six cops who entered the Stonewall Inn began making arrests.

Once the police wagon set off for the precinct house, a taunting crowd of drag queens, cross-dressing lesbians, and teenage hustlers gathered across the street in Sheridan Square and turned aggressive. An anonymous writer for *Rat* happened to pass by the Stonewall around 1:00 a.m. and found the patrons hurling all manner of debris at the remaining cops. "The few pigs outside had to flee for their lives," he would report.

The police barricaded themselves inside the Stonewall along with *Voice* reporter Howard Smith, who had earlier come upon the scene. What the hastily summoned *New York Times* would term a "rampage," *Rat* deemed "too good to be true": "Bottles, rocks, trashcans, finally a parking meter crashed the window . . . The cops inside were scared shitless, dodging projectiles and flying glass. The orgy was taking place!" Three policemen darted outside and dragged a suspect into the bar. He turned out to be Dave Van Ronk, who, like another *Voice* writer covering the story, had wandered out of the Lion's Head, a next-door watering hole frequented by two-fisted literary types.

According to Smith, Van Ronk was beaten nearly unconscious by the besieged, panicky cops. Then, *Rat* reported, "the pigs carried futility to the extreme and turned the firehose on the mob through the door. Jeers, derision. Someone shouted to 'grab it, grab his cock.' Someone lit a trashcan stuffed with papers afire and stuffed it through the window." The cops called for reinforcements but, *Rat* exulted, by the time the "riot pigs" arrived there were 2,000 people in the street—although 400 would be more likely.

Rat saw Stonewall as more than an uprising of oppressed gay men. It was payback for Grand Central, Columbia, and Chicago. Moreover, it was leaderless. "Strangely," *Rat* noted "no one spoke to the crowd or tried to direct the insurrection." (No President!) Yippie associate Jim Fouratt saw a parallel to the Newark uprising but was frustratingly unable to persuade his Movement comrades to participate. Nevertheless, several East Village anarchists, including Ben Morea, did join a huge, largely gay Saturday night crowd, which, among other things, featured a drag-queen chorus line mocking the Tactical Police Force.

Stonewall jumpstarted a movement, inspiring first the Gay Liberation Front (which would picket the *Voice* to protest Howard Smith's article) and then the Gay Activist Alliance. *Screw*, which covered the uprising far more sympathetically than the *Voice*, soon put out a sister tabloid *Gay*, followed in short order by *EVO*'s *Gay Power*.

At the Warhol Factory, as Valerie Solanas might have predicted, female impersonators had superseded female superstars, as manifest in the unexpected commercial success of Paul Morrissey's *Flesh*, which paired hustler Joe Dallesandro with drag queens Jackie Curtis and Candy Darling. *Newspaper*'s November issue put beautiful Candy on the cover and centerfold, nude albeit—thanks to Richard Bernstein's photomontage—magically merged with another body so that her penis seemed exposed.

9

The summer was filled with portents. After many press screenings and a triumphant Cannes premiere, Peter Fonda's hippie-biker film *Easy Rider*—praised by Abbie Hoffman as "almost perfect propaganda"—arrived in mid-July. Among other things its success inspired the Factory to send up the drug culture with Morrissey's *Trash*, in which Joe Dallesandro played an impotent junkie with Holly Woodlawn as his "female" sidekick.

Days later, a manned space rocket touched down on the Moon. Ed Sanders considered it "a great gift from a slain president." Mailer, still depressed from his mayoral campaign, called the landing "the climax of the greatest week since Christ was born." Jazz poet Gil Scott-Heron was inspired to write "Whitey on the Moon," in which the miseries of slum life ("a rat done bit my sister Nell") are juxtaposed with and mock America's empty triumphalism. A week later, July 27, thirty-five-year-old red-diaper revolutionary lone wolf Sam Melville (born Samuel Grossman) bombed a United Fruit Company warehouse on a Hudson River pier at the end of West Tenth Street, initiating a seven-month-long stretch of bombings in and around New York. Four days later, *Blue Movie* (as the Factory prudently renamed *Fuck*) was busted.

August 9, twelve hours before Sharon Tate and four of her friends would be murdered in LA, the Crazies briefly occupied the Central Park bandshell, disrupting the Nagasaki Day March for Peace. In vain, Allen Ginsberg chanted a very loud Hare Krishna. But as Claudia Dreifus reported in *EVO*, "his hopeful prayers were drowned out by the choo-choo chanting of 'Ho, Ho, Ho Chi Minh, the NLF is gonna win.' "

Something similar happened in reverse a week later when half a million hippies gathered on a dairy farm in upstate New York for three days of "art and music": Pete Townshend, leader of the Who, swatted Abbie Hoffman off the stage when Hoffman popped up with a spiel for jailed John Sinclair.

Woodstock occasioned considerable analysis—politicos initially saw it as the contrivance of "rock imperialists," one more way to rip off the counterculture. The week of the festival, Jean-Jacques Lebel warned the readers of *Rat* that just as *Hair*, the Living Theatre, and *Dionysus in '69* offered "symbolic freedom, to be bought & sold, to be watched or consumed as a commodity," the so-called Peace & Music festival "plays a precise role in the anti-rebellion strategy of the Police State . . . They must sell us high-price tickets to their cultural penitentiary and ram their merchandise down our throats. They must exert physical control over us."[7]

The Motherfuckers took credit for cutting the fences at Woodstock—and, according to *Rat*, sent scouting parties to raid food caches and bring the plunder back to "liberated campsites"—but as if to prove Lebel's point,

7 Afterward, of course, Woodstock was regarded as the great event, the supreme Happening "a landmark in biologic war" per William Burroughs's enigmatic formulation and climax of the greatest week in counterculture history, not least by Abbie Hoffman, who knocked out an instant manifesto *Woodstock Nation*. It may have also inspired always competitive Kusama's most celebrated event, the *Grand Orgy to Awaken the Dead*, staged a week later in the MoMA sculpture garden.

Woodstock gave the Community a designated political area called "Movement City." It was there that neophyte bomber Sam Melville met Prince Crazy George. Melville split Woodstock, along with his old lady, twenty-two-year-old *Rat* staffer and acid-head Jane Alpert and Crazy couple Sharon Krebs and Robin Palmer. A few days after the festival ended—around 11:00 p.m., Wednesday, August 20—a powerful explosion rocked the eighth floor of the Marine Midland Bank building, a new fifty-one-story black-glass and aluminum megalith near Wall Street.

Set back from *The Cube*, Isamu Noguchi's huge red-orange rhombohedron, which featured briefly in Brian De Palma's counterculture comedy, *Greetings*, the building experienced a comparably colossal bombing: police estimated the blast as the equivalent of twenty-five sticks of dynamite. The explosion was sufficient to displace a two-ton computer, blow out windows on three sides of the building, carpet the streets with shattered glass, and leave a ten-foot crater in the concrete floor. Twenty people were injured, mainly those working one story below the blast.

Alpert was amazed if not appalled that Melville had struck out on his own but thanks to her, *Rat* received an "exclusive" communiqué on the bombing, which she wrote, typed, and slipped it under the *Rat* office door, smiling to herself as editor Jeff Shero discovered the envelope, opened it, read it, and exclaimed, "Far fucking out!" *Rat* was now the terrorist newspaper of record.

10

Until then, the two forms the underground press pioneered were comix and porn. In February 1969, with circulation figures at 65,000, *EVO* inaugurated a monthly all-comix tabloid, enigmatically named *Gothic Blimp Works*, which, marked "Adults Only," was notable for baroque violence, voluptuous naked women, and casual racial stereotypes. The first three issues featured covers and stories by the form's greatest exponent, R. Crumb. There were also multipage stories by *EVO*'s star cartoonists Spain and Kim Deitch, who then shared a sixth-floor walk-up on Eighth Street east of Avenue B, a block so menacing that after he got mugged Deitch began carrying a gun.

The pair moved to a loft above *EVO*'s new offices on Second Avenue, the same building that housed the Fillmore East; Deitch became *GBW* editor with the third issue and gave the publication artistic heft. His series *Deja Voo* was a dense, carnivalesque farrago involving time travel, doppelgangers, CIA agents, space aliens, and his character Waldo, strongly reminiscent of the 1930s animated Felix the Cat, rendered in curvilinear panels that sent the eye scattering over the page. In addition to featuring locals Bill Griffith, Trina Robbins, Spain, and Art Spiegelman, *GBW* accorded California-based S. Clay Wilson special prominence.

Wilson, largely known through Crumb's *Zap Comix*, was the most shocking of cartoonists, specializing in all-over, impacted scenes of mayhem, dismemberment, and grotesque sex acts. There was also *EVO* neophyte Joe Schenkman, a native New Yorker who worked at the Post Office and, boldly naming himself "Yossarian" after the anti-hero of *Catch-22*, produced several impossibly busy one-page urban hellscapes including a vision of deliquescing tenements that could have provided a cover image for Saul Yurick's novel *The Bag*.

During the summer, Deitch curated a weeklong show in an East Ninth Street storefront. Tripping on acid acquired by his boss as part of a business deal with Timothy Leary, he changed the exhibit daily, combining work by his underground colleagues with that of *Mad* magazine artists Wallace Wood and Jack Davis, and even Winsor McCay's *Little Nemo in Slumberland*. Deitch also dispensed free beer and copies of *Gothic Blimp Works*; the exhibition, which he considered a museum and "infinitely superior" to the one Ed Sanders had organized in November 1968 at the Peace Eye bookstore, was a farewell. Deitch quit as editor after issue #7 and moved to San Francisco with Trina Robbins. Spain followed suit. So did Bill Griffith. The final *Blimp* consisted mainly of Spain and Crumb reprints.

With no advertising and only avant-garde pornography, *Gothic Blimp Works* was a luxury *EVO* could not afford—the paper lived on sex ads and kinky personals. *Rat* was not above putting nude women on the cover to increase sales. The *New York Free Press* preferred to use a naked Kusama happening. By mid-1969, New York's underground papers were outflanked and outsold by the sex tabloids that followed Al Goldstein's *Screw*. As the *Freep* morphed into the *New York Review of Sex and Politics*, a raunchy tabloid named *Pleasure* came on the scene, courtesy of *Rat*'s business manager. "A moron can make money with a porn sheet," *EVO*'s publisher Joel Fabrikant told the *Voice*, which was interested in "the financial bonanza" of "hip pornography."

Soon *EVO* shared office space as well as contributors with *Kiss*, the most art-world of the porn-tabs which, in addition to *EVO*'s cartoonists, involved sometime contributor Al Hansen, who brought in the Factory. The July 1969 issue featured a tight close-up of male buttocks on the cover, a gossip column signed by Andy Warhol, "Beloved Ondine's Advice to the Shopworn," and promised EXCLUSIVE COVERAGE OF JACKIE CURTIS' WEDDING. ("Engaged" to Factory rascal Eric Emerson, Jackie was jilted at the altar.) Nor were Hansen's other art-world friends forgotten; Carolee Schneemann discusses her bodily performance as a form of "kinetic theatre."[8]

Writing in *EVO*, Hansen pronounced the porn papers and magazines "as culturally significant as the development of the photo cameras, the Symbolist poets, the Russian Revolution, electricity, atomic power and the Beatles." He did not mention *Newspaper*, which, although hardly pornographic, regularly ran nude portraits, male and female, and even raunchy photographs in the service of a larger artistic vision. *Kiss* lasted barely a year, by which time Warhol's Factory had its own tabloid, *Inter/View*. *Pleasure* and *Screw*, survivors of multiple busts, were each selling 100,000 copies, far more than *EVO* and *Rat* combined. Still, unlike *EVO*, *Rat* was appreciated as seriously political and refreshingly unprofessional.

In July 1969, *Voice* reporter Jack Newfield had written that out of the many new underground papers, only a handful impressed him, and *Rat* just might be "the best of the breed." Visiting the paper's cluttered two-room office across from the Academy of Music on "a seedy stretch of Fourteenth Street, one flight above a neon sign that changed PHOTOGRAPHS WHILE YOU WAIT to *HOT**RATS WHILE YOU WAIT and adjacent to a movie theater that charges $5 for a one-hour male homosexual flick," Newfield dug the youthful vibe.

At twenty-six, editor Jeff Spero was the oldest person on the *Rat* staff. Many of his colleagues were still in their teens. Some were high school dropouts. The Motherfuckers had been supplanted by radical kids. Militant politics and raw language, Newfield reported, kept *Rat* off newsstands; the

8 The porn press was steeped in the counterculture. The centerfold of *Screw*'s maiden issue was a picture taken the previous August at Kusama's Alice in Wonderland event. Steve Heller, *Screw*'s nineteen-year-old art director, having been recruited from the *Freep*, remembers Kusama's phone calls as "annoyingly routine." In heavily accented English, the artist announced that she would be arriving with new photos. "Moments later, as though she had been in a phone booth down the street, she'd arrive at the door bearing a stack of poorly printed black and white prints." Unlike most of the photos *Screw* ran, these were available free of charge. The February 7, 1969, issue of *Screw* illustrates a report on an orgy with a photograph of a naked polka-dot event taken in Kusama's studio.

rag was boycotted by affluent liberals, harassed by school principals, and, having lost some 4,000 of its 25,000 readers to the sex tabloids, broke, in debt, and harassed by creditors. "Any issue could be its last," Newfield warned. He did not mention that none of *Rat*'s writers were paid.

Even more than *EVO*, *Rat* had the doomsday vibe. A few days before Newfield's article ran, Sam Melville had held up a Bronx purveyor of dynamite and made off with four boxes. The issue of the *Voice* was still on newsstands when someone blew up a New Jersey munition plant. Attention focused on the upcoming mayor election, the *Voice* made no mention of the Marine Midland bombing but, having read the Marine Midland communique published in *Rat*, a police detective visited the paper's office in late August. There, by his own account, he encountered a "surprised" Alpert who, while admitting she received the communiqué, explained that once her piece was typed for publication, she tossed the original and the envelope in which it arrived. Like, why wouldn't she?

The detective grabbed a few recent issues on his way out, including one with a handgun on the cover. Therein he discovered a hitherto unnoticed item reporting that United Fruit bombing had been timed to celebrate "Cuban Independence Day." Who placed that tidbit? In mid-September, ten police, armed with a search warrant, paid *Rat* a visit. According to the paper's account of the raid, the "oinkers" spent two hours "turning over every loose piece of paper in the impossibly cluttered *Rat* office." Turning up Fourteenth Street, Alpert saw the squad cars and prudently kept walking.

The New York Film Festival opened that night with the bourgeoise wife-swapping comedy *Bob and Carol and Ted and Alice*. ("I must report that the audience seemed to love every minute of it," Andrew Sarris wrote.) The next day, two plainclothes cops arrested Peter Dargis, the manager of the East Side Bookstore, across from the Electric Circus on St. Mark's Place, charged with selling the fourth issue of R. Crumb's *Zap Comix* which featured the story "Joe Blow," Crumb's cheerful evocation of suburban sitcom incest.

Zap, the most artful and scurrilous of underground comic books (front and back covers marked Adults Only!) was the subject of a sting operation by the same Public Morals Squad that raided the Stonewall. On August 25 and again on September 17, an undercover policeman purchased copies at the East Side and uptown New Yorker bookstores, arresting clerks and managers upon completion of the sale.[9]

---

9 Charges were eventually dropped against the clerks but Peter Dargis and New

11

Elsewhere in the East Village, the Melville affinity group raises the ante. September 20, a few hours past midnight, a bomb made by Melville and planted by Alpert pulverizes the 40th floor of the new Federal Office Building at Foley Square. Ceilings collapse, flying chunks of concrete smash cabinets, burst pipes, and shatter windows although no one is injured. Melville splits on a mission to the Midwest, planting bombs in Milwaukee and Chicago, where the Weathermen—an SDS splinter group who took their name from a line in Dylan's "Subterranean Homesick Blues"—are planning their Days of Rage.

Up at Columbia, in the early hours of October 4, three young guys toss a Molotov cocktail into the campus ROTC office. A photo of the damage runs above the fold of the next day's *New York Times*. Call and response? Three nights later, just ahead of the Rage event, a bomb—made by Melville's associate David Hughey—blasts through the fifth floor of the Whitehall Induction Center, demolishing office partitions and blowing out forty new windows installed after dynamite damaged the building in April 1968. Melville comes back to New York to find that Hughey's bomb made the *Times*'s front page.

The Melville group is planning their most dramatic attack, scheduled to underscore the Mobe's upcoming November 15 March on Washington. Meanwhile, six explosions rock Macy's Department store over four days; the Guerilla Art Action Group (GAAG) stages its first action event at the Museum of Modern Art, replacing Malevich's *White on White* with their own manifesto (and thus, Lil Picard thought, "re-revolutionizing" the original painting); the Art Workers' Coalition organizes a Moratorium of Art to End the War in Vietnam; the perennial last-place New York Mets win the World Series; *Rat* reviews Godard's *Le Gai Savoir*; Jack Kerouac dies, age forty-seven; the *Village Voice* runs a piece on R. Crumb; Kusama licenses her name to a new sex tabloid, *Kusama's Orgy*; and *No President* opens for a midnight run at the Bleecker Street Cinema.[10]

Yorker manager Charles Kirkpatrick were convicted of promoting obscenity and fined $500 (or 90 days in jail), a ruling upheld on appeal by the New York State Court of Appeals.

10 *No President* was shown a year later, October 12, 1970, upstairs at Max's Kansas City as part of the first New York Underground Film Festival. (Somehow, I drove down from Binghamton for this sparsely attended, haphazard screening.) Alone in his praise, Jonas Mekas had already written to Smith informing him that the Selection Committee for

Crazy George returns from Chicago, where he'd been furnishing evidence for the upcoming conspiracy trial. Melville phones him with news that Something Really Big is about to happen and indeed, just after 1:00 a.m., Tuesday, November 10, the evening after GAAG issued "A Call for the Immediate Resignation of all the Rockefellers from the Board of Trustees of Museum of Modern Art," three bombs in three office skyscrapers detonate in rapid succession. The first decimates the twentieth floor of the RCA building in Rockefeller Center. The second caves nineteenth-floor walls at the new glass and marble General Motors Building on Fifth Avenue at Fifty-Ninth Street. The third, downtown, wrecks three floors of Chase Manhattan's sixty-story headquarters on Liberty Street. (A fourth bomb found at the studios of WMCA radio fails to detonate.)

New York City shakes and quakes. Wednesday morning, hundreds of bomb threats are reported, including at the UN, the Empire State Building, the Pan Am Building, the home of Hearst Publications, IBM headquarters, CBS, the General Post Office, and the Queens Public Library. That night, a Melville bomb goes off in the Criminal Court Building where the Panther trial preliminaries are to begin.

Melville enlists Demmerle to work on his next caper, and Demmerle sets him up. The two men are arrested November 11 pre-planting a bomb at the 69th Regiment Armory at Twenty-Sixth Street and Lexington Avenue. A few hours later, cops pick up Alpert and Hughey at her place, 235 East Fourth Street. "Trouble in New York is when a lovely young thing sitting under a dryer at Kenneth's thinks only thus: 'What if a bomb should explode and me sitting here in curlers,'" Sidney Zion will write in the *New York Times*. "Last week in what was rapidly becoming Scare City, no reasonable

---

the newly established Anthology Film Archives voted to include both *Flaming Creatures* and *No President* in its canon of essential cinema. Mekas stipulated the "original version" of *No President* "in the shape you projected it 15 months ago" at the Elgin. This did not happen and only one battered print was found after Smith died. Smith seldom screened *No President* after 1970. On those occasions, the footage was projected at silent speed to retard the speech and singing of the sound passages, with Smith playing records to accompany the silent footage. All screenings during Smith's lifetime presupposed his presence.

person would put the child [sic] down as paranoid." Nor would Jeff Spero.

As the bombings cost *Rat* its distributor, *EVO* made space for Spero's thoughts. Perhaps, he opines, the bomber's inspiration came from the great Northeast power blackout—it was the work of a visionary terrorist but certainly not his comrade employee Jane Alpert. "It's hard to imagine Janie working as she did at *Rat* and in women's lib and still finding time to plot bombings," Spero writes, "She seemed no more freaked out than the rest of us become living on the Lower East Side and trying to redeem a concrete jungle."[11]

The bombings cease. Janie files a story from the Women's House of Detention. GAAG takes center stage. November 14: Jean Toche enters the Whitney Museum lobby and begins dumping red pigment on the floor and Jon Hendricks douses it with soapy water. As Poppy Johnson begins mopping the foaming red mixture, Toche explains that having refused to close on Moratorium Day, the Whitney was dirty from war.

Bloodbath is a rehearsal for GAAG's November 18 performance, at the Museum of Modern Art. Hendricks, Johnson, Toche, and the feminist artist Silvianna Goldsmith enter MoMA at 3:00 p.m. and, after dropping a hundred leaflets in the lobby and explaining that the museum is funded by blood money (Rockefeller-owned Standard Oil having leased a plant for the purpose of manufacturing napalm), proceed to attack each other, rending clothes, bursting concealed bags of beef blood, screaming, writhing, and finally playing dead. It is a little *Totentanz*. All four silently rise in unison, accept applause, and split. MoMA does not press charges.

The happening would be reported in both *EVO* and *Rat*, which included a sidebar by Boris Lurie explaining that MoMA's true function is "the manipulation and promotion of market-place art . . . for the benefit of collectors-investors and dealers." A month later the *Times* will run an article headlined MUSEUMS SEEKING GUARDS TO STEM MOUNTING CRIME. A few weeks after that, twenty members of the AWC stage a

11 *Rat* not only printed Alpert in every issue but used her case to raise money. A November 21 "Benefit for *Rat* Survival and Jane Alpert's Legal Defense" was held at the Hotel Diplomat on West Forty-Third Street, off Times Square. Entertainment included a performance by Tuli Kupferberg's Revolting Theater, cartoons, and the world premiere of Newsreel's *People's Park*. The advertised speakers were Paul Krassner and Jack Newfield.

"lie-in" in front of Picasso's *Guernica* at the Museum of Modern Art, demanding a meeting with the museum's board of trustees.[12]

12

Had the sixties reached their climax? Or was it rather, as *Rat* headlined Todd Gitlin's account of the disastrous free Rolling Stones concert at the Altamont Speedway, THE END OF THE AGE OF AQUARIUS?

Elsewhere in Los Angeles, California, police arrested the alleged perpetrators of the past summer's Tate-LaBianca murders. Almost immediately, a *Life* magazine cover story introduced America to the pure personification of evil—Charles Manson, the wild-eyed, bearded ex-con LSD Svengali of a "Love and Terror" hippie cult-cum-harem that squatted in an abandoned movie ranch and, like the Motherfuckers, called itself "The Family."

Out in Chicago, where the conspiracy trial had entered its fourth month, the police raided an apartment before dawn and massacred the charismatic Black Panther leader Fred Hampton in his bed. Following their so-called Days of Rage, October 8 through 11, in Chicago, the Weathermen convened their War Council in Flint, Michigan. In New York, it was all about the impending trial of the Panther 21. Out on bail, Jane Alpert covered the story for *Rat*, which also ran an article by imprisoned Afeni Shakur, section leader of the Panther's Harlem chapter, preparing to act as her own lawyer.

On November 21, LeRoi Jones's *Slave Ship* moored at the Brooklyn Academy of Music to terrify and exalt a racially mixed audience. First performed in March 1967 at Newark's Spirit House, Jones's harrowing drama was produced by the Chelsea Theater Center at the Brooklyn Academy of Music under the direction of twenty-seven-year-old Gilbert Moses, a co-founder of the Free Southern Theater.

Moses and Richard Schechner, who had been involved with the FST, were colleagues, and Moses adapted some of Schechner's ideas

12 Back in November, the museum staff had agreed to produce a poster with the AWC that reprinted Ron Haeberle's well known photo of a corpse-lined trench in South Vietnam, asking (and answering) a TV newsman's shocked question, "And babies?" Over the staff's wishes, the plan was scotched by board president William Paley. *Newspaper* ran the poster in its January 1970 issue along with naked photos of two rock bands, the Allman Brothers and Country Joe and the Fish, that were ads placed by their record companies.

regarding environmental theater. He also brought in the Senegalese Dance Company to drill the cast and a linguist from the Olantunji Center for African Culture to teach them Yoruba. His direction of *Slave Ship* (for which he received an Obie) pushed beyond *Dionysus in '69* and stood the Artaudian theater of *Paradise Now* on its head.

A hundred minutes without intermission, beginning and often performed in darkness, the drama had three acts: captivity, enslavement, and revolt, entirely played out on the slave ship—a wooden platform split between deck and steerage, and constructed on rockers suggesting both the swell of the sea and the cosmic upheaval endured by the captives. "I had to rip up the seats, and level the floor," designer Eugene Lee explained. The audience was seated on low benches on all four sides of the ship. "They could glance upward where chained figures dragged across the upper deck."

For the first twenty minutes or more, Africans were taken one by one screaming onto the ship and forced into the hold, the horror heightened by the accompanying drums. The score by Archie Shepp drew on traditional African songs. The benches were positioned so that the lower level was barely at eye level. Not only were actors and audience impossibly close together but spectators were compelled to slouch forward to see the enslaved cargo vomiting, moaning, crying, given birth, enduring rape, and committing suicide.

Adding to the discomfort, members of the audience were directly addressed by the actors and urged to join in their cries. The pressure to participate in a theatrical situation more crazily absurd than *Dionysus in '69* invoked an appropriately terrorized sense of entrapment. *Newsweek* critic Jack Kroll reported that "on opening night screaming slaves reach out cawing for help from the *New York Times*'s Clive Barnes," while "a nausea-racked slave retched realistically" into another critic's lap. As the agitated suffering was expressed in wordless screams and bits of Yoruba, the *Times* senior critic Walter Kerr complained that he heard only two intelligible lines during the play's first half.

Whereas the opening section was accompanied by the sound of African drums, the second section—arrival in America—brought in the music of the banjo. Families were destroyed on the auction block while white audience members were invited to examine the merchandise or bid on a child. Transformed into a stylized plantation, the ship became a stage in which the slaves embodied various divisions, harangued by an invisible white voice ("I'm God. You can't kill white Jesus God. I got long blond blowhair . . . You want to look like me") supported by a collaborationist Black preacher.

Nonviolence was a nonstarter. *Slave Ship*'s third movement was a call to arms. The warrior god Ogun summoned, the plantation slaves break their chains and occupy the platform's upper deck. The audience is also liberated, able to comfortably sit up straight and follow the action at least until it spread throughout the theater. Cast members roamed free, exhorting each other "Rise, Rise, Rise, Cut these Ties, Black Man Rise" and inviting Black spectators to join in the chant. Then, after gunning down a nonviolent, integrationist preacher many took to be a stand-in for Martin Luther King Jr., the slaves tore down the cross and decapitated an Uncle Sam effigy. Abruptly the lights came on, the music turned finger-popping, and the cast started to dance. Black spectators were invited to participate in the celebration, after which performers moved through the space speaking to and shaking hands exclusively with Black members of the audience.

Thus, *Slave Ship* provided a collective catharsis—from confinement and suffering to struggle and release. Vince Aletti, who reviewed the play for *Rat*, compared it favorably with *Paradise Now* not just because of the score but for Jones's surgical precision as opposed to the Beck's "self-indulgent repetition." Whereas *Paradise Now* sought to coerce inclusion, *Slave Ship* dramatized Black separatism.

The actors had threatened a strike on opening night unless all whites were removed from the stage crew. Their demand was denied. The cast did not refuse to perform; neither did they join the opening night party. *Slave Ship* ran at BAM for over seven weeks then moved to Washington Square Methodist Church on West Fourth Street. Known as the "Peace Church," it was a large structure with a balcony that, from mid-October into late November, had hosted Jerzy Grotowski's Polish Laboratory Theater, making its New York debut.[13]

The *New York Times* called Grotowski's Laboratory Theater, subject of several lengthy *Village Voice* articles over the past year and the

13 Grotowski limited his audience, allowing only one hundred spectators for each performance of *The Constant Prince* and *Acropolis*, and only forty for *Apocalypsis cum Figuris*, thus creating an unusual degree of intimacy with the players as well as the hottest ticket in town. (Seats reportedly went for $200 on the black market.)

avant-performative event of the season, "the most overground of underground phenomena." *Slave Ship* might have been described as the most underground of overground productions. Its revival was foredoomed. The church facilities were inadequate and the cast, which had hoped to perform in Harlem, stopped the show more than once to complain that without backstage hot water and only two small dressing rooms for fourteen actors, conditions resembled those of an actual slave ship. On January 24, as noted in the *New York Times*, the play closed.

Elsewhere in the same edition, the *Times* society reporter Charlotte Curtis chewed over "the most talked-about party since Truman Capote's [1966] masked ball," a reception for the New York Panther 21 Legal Defense Fund, hosted by Mr. and Mrs. Leonard Bernstein in their thirteen-room Park Avenue penthouse; John Canaday expressed disbelief over the Jewish Museum's three-floor Dan Flavin retrospective; and it was reported that an eleven-year-old boy in East New York, Brooklyn, was arrested on a charge of selling heroin through a mail slot in the door of his home.

13

For two magical nights, *Slave Ship* shared BAM with another, quite different theatrical coup. One Thursday and the following Saturday, the large 2,100-seat theater was given over to Robert Wilson's three-hour-plus three-act "dance-theater play," *The Life and Times of Sigmund Freud*.

New York Times dance critic Don McDonagh was dispatched to Brooklyn and was properly confounded, leading with the sentence, "I thought that I had stumbled in on a stranger's group therapy session." (Because McDonagh recognized Meredith Monk's mother, the singer Audrey Marsh, in the large cast, the *Times* editors bizarrely headlined his review STORY OF DR. FREUD DEPICTED IN DANCE BY MEREDITH MONK.)

The pageant, which McDonagh described as a "Dali painting come to life," opens with sand covering the stage and a sky-blue, cloud-dappled backdrop. Was it the scene of Freud's childhood or the dawn of the world? Individuals came on stage, wandering back and forth performing simple activities. They were joined by a slow procession of outsized animals including a turtle and a walrus (Jack Smith) as well as Freud (M. Sondak, a Brooklyn jeweler, discovered by Wilson in Grand Central station) and his daughter Anna.

Suddenly, there was a moment of dervish-like sand kicking and Wilson himself appeared to restore order—in blackface drag, aproned and kerchiefed like the pancake-mix icon Aunt Jemima. He was soon joined by twenty-six similarly over-stuffed figures, waltzing to "The Blue Danube." The Black Mammy Chorus, as identified in the program, encompassed mammies in varied sizes, shapes, and genders. One can only imagine how a member of the *Slave Ship* cast coming downstairs to the main theater might have reacted, but Wilson, who grew up as a misfit in segregated Waco, Texas, was working out his past as well; the entire play was watched from the edge of the stage by a Black boy (Raymond Andrews) whom Wilson had tutored in New Jersey, as though the spectacle had been produced for him.

The sky darkened and the first act ended as a woman placed an Egyptian figure on a table. The second act, set in Freud's study, had been staged eleven months earlier at the Anderson Theatre as *The King of Spain*—a three-hour show that had no real dialogue or even a text. (Molly Haskell attended one of the two performances and gamely reviewed it in the *Voice*: "Marcel Duchamp meets Agatha Christie.") Watched by a figure seated in a large chair (the King's throne), back to the audience, the stage fills with people doing various things, including playing an inscrutable board game. The Walrus returns, as does Freud with his daughter Anna.

Although most everyone was a nonactor, the cast included several professionals: the playwright Jean-Claude van Itallie (with whom Wilson had worked), the dancer Kenneth King, and Ronnie Gilbert (one of the original members of the Weavers). Somewhat mischievously Wilson put Bob Dylan's name in the program. Even more roguishly, the act ends with a set of four twenty-foot-tall hairy legs lumbering across the stage, after which the King places a Chinese figurine on the waiting table.

The third act repeats the gradually stage-filling rhythms of the first two. Bears, tigers, and other wild animals slowly enter a cave one by one and lie down in the straw. Outside the cave young humans (including the sculptor Gordon Matta-Clark) frisk and play on the beach. At one point iron bars drop over the mouth of the cave, imprisoning the animals, who are then fed by Freud. A little boy, perhaps his grandson, cries. The play ends with Freud staring at the objects left on the table.

Allowing that "the staging had a bizarre charm," McDonogh thought that the storyline would "only be clear to an analyst." John Perreault, who briefly noted the play in the *Voice*, was well past that: *Freud* had "so little obvious meaning that it contained all meanings," he breezily opined. The production (paradoxically "static and yet full of activities") struck him as "a cross between Maeterlinck, Jarry, William Blake, and Raymond Roussel, and yet it was totally original . . . one of the strangest things I have ever seen in my life."

The same issue had a more substantial appreciation by Richard Foreman. As if channeling Jonas Mekas, who likely facilitated his review, Foreman chided *Voice* readers for resisting the need to schlep out to Brooklyn and thus deprive themselves of perhaps the major stage work of the decade. *Freud*, Foreman declared, was of a piece with those produced by advanced painters, musicians, dancers, and filmmakers whose "non-manipulative aesthetic" creates a contemplative or hypnotic "'field' situation" in which introspective spectators might find themselves.

In a sense, Foreman was providing a means to appreciate his own theater, which since *Angelface* had been further developed with his new work *Ida-Eyed*. Wilson, he maintained, was following Heidegger and Gertrude Stein in demonstrating that "profundity and holiness reenter the theatre through the proper articulation of the landscape aspect of the drama, filling the stage-space with real (i.e., impenetrable) objects and that very impenetrability is what satisfies as it produces awe and delight." *Freud* was not an object lesson but an object.

Foreman's review, which to my twenty-year-old mind made the play sound irresistible, ended by warning that *Voice* readers had "better keep their fingers crossed" that the piece would be reprised and, if so, they "better make sure they attend—because in this new Aquarian Age, or in the 1970s, or in whatever new era we're coming upon, this is the kind of the theater we need." His admonition was one more threat in a year filled with them.[14]

14 My recollection of the May 1970 revival is that the large auditorium was far less than half filled and—as spectators were free to wander throughout the theater—the piece, which began at 8:30 and ended well after midnight, was less a drama than an installation.

Page Forty-two

off off-b'way

Schedules and prices (if any) vary. So does reliability. Call the numbers below for detailed information.

Theatres

"GRAND CHICANARY," by Paul Clark, presented at 9 p.m. at the Arista Theatre, 158 West 55th Street ($2).

"THE MASQUE OF WILDE," by Joseph Addison, directed by James Murphy, presented July 13 to 17 at 8.30 p.m. and July 18 at 7 and 10 p.m. at the Cubicule, 414 West 51st Street (contribution).

"DOGS," by Serge Gorstein, directed by George Darnel, presented July 16, 17, 18, 23, 24, 25, 30, 31, and August 1 at 8.40 p.m. at the Washington Square Methodist Church, 133 West 4th Street, RY 9-3519 (contribution).

"THE MANDRAKE," by Niccolo Machiavelli, directed by Ricardo Castillo, presented by the Inner Theatre Troupe on Saturdays and Sundays at 5.30 p.m. at Carl Schurz Park, East 87th Street, near Gracie Mansion (free).

"THE TRICYCLE," by Fernando Arrabal, presented Fridays to Sundays at 9 p.m. at Cafe Deja Vu, 339 East 10th Street

Village South Theatre, 15 Vandam Street, YU 9-8639, YU 9-7736 ($3.50, $3.50).

"STREET PLAYS AND OTHER EVENTS," presented by the Pageant Players on Saturdays at 9 p.m. at 436 Broome Street (at Mercer), 4th floor (contribution).

"WITHDRAWAL FROM ORCHID LAGOON," by Jack Smith, presented by Reptilian Theatrical Company on Saturdays at midnight at Plaster Foundation, 36 Greene Street at Grand (free).

"CONRAD," by Barbara Barrett, directed by Crane Johnson, presented Fridays to Sundays at 8.40 p.m. at Royal Playhouse, 219 Second Avenue, GR 5-9647 ($2).

"BLUEBEARD," written and directed by Charles Ludlam, presented by the Ridiculous Theatrical Company on Thursdays to Sundays at 8.30 p.m. at the Performing Garage, 33 Wooster Street, WA 5-8712 ($3.50, $5.50).

"TO LANGSTON HUGHES WITH LOVE," presented Fridays and Saturdays at 8.30 p.m. Sundays at 7 p.m. at Afro-American Studio for Acting and Speech, 15

Off-off-Broadway listing, *Village Voice* (7/9/1970).

11

Withdrawal from Orchid Lagoon, 1970–71

In which death bells chime and magical thinking rules. The collective drama fissures. The underground implodes, the art world turns against itself, the counterculture seeks solace in a violent midnight fantasy. Bob Dylan returns to New York, Andy Warhol lashes out, Jackie Curtis becomes ubiquitous, Yoko Ono produces the past decade's quintessential artwork, and the author makes a modest contribution.

> IS ABBIE HOFFMAN THE WILL SHAKESPEARE OF THE 1970S?
>
> —Headline, *New York Times* (October 11, 1970)

Magical thinking or conceptual art? Wish fulfillment reigns.

On December 15, 1969, an enormous billboard went up in Times Square (and in Los Angeles, Toronto, Montreal, London, Paris, Rome, Berlin, Athens, and Amsterdam) declaring WAR IS OVER! / IF YOU WANT IT / HAPPY CHRISTMAS FROM JOHN AND YOKO.

Solidarity forever, if we want it! As the year ended, under duress (and without advertising) the jazz label Impulse! released the most idealistic of LPs. An internationalist, Big Band synthesis of Old Left and New, Free Jazz and Avant Folk, Black and White, Charlie Haden's *Liberation Music Orchestra* opened with the 1934 Hanns Eisler–Bertolt Brecht anthem "Song of the United Front." The first side continued with three Spanish Civil War *canciónes*. The second side featured Haden's "Song for Che,"

Ornette Coleman's "War Orphans," and a Dada invocation of the 1968 Chicago convention.

Haden's racially integrated thirteen-piece ensemble—including Don Cherry, Gato Barbieri, Carla Bley, Dewey Redman, Perry Robinson, Roswell Rudd, and members of the Jazz Composer's Orchestra—got great reviews in both the jazz and rock press and even *Sing Out!* It was an artistic success but a political (as well as commercial) failure: Impulse! loathed the term "liberation," and Haden's orchestra was too white to be invited to the Revolutionary Black Music Festival produced by the Black Panthers in Philadelphia, June 1970.

Perhaps Haden's concept belonged in a museum. "A museum traditionally houses and conserves objects of art but now it becomes responsible for the execution of the artist's idea," the Museum of Modern Art announced. December 30, MoMA opened an exhibition called *Spaces* in which spectators changed their shoes for paper slippers to "participate" (albeit minimally) in a series of artist-designed site-specific environments, one more pivot from the collectible art object to the art "experience"—gallery as ashram.[1]

In the realm of ideas, anything was possible. What couldn't be over if you wanted it? "I'm not a boy, not a girl, just me, Jackie," Jackie Curtis told the *New York Times,* which used the quote for a Sunday piece on John Vaccaro's production of Jackie's play *Heaven Grand in Amber Orbit*, a brothel-set, amphetamine-fueled collage of old movie lines, TV commercials, and popular songs that Vaccaro turned into a musical and in which Jackie starred until fired by Vaccaro.

Newsweek's Jack Kroll called the play, installed in the Gotham Art Theatre, west of Times Square, "the wildest and in some ways the best

1 The weary-sounding Hilton Kramer found *Spaces* worse than vapid: "On the day I visited the exhibition, most of the others in attendance were a generation or more younger than myself, and the word 'groovy' was reiterated more times than I could count." John Perreault's response was less predictable. Despite the presence of the highly regarded Michael Asher, a specialist in meditation rooms, as well as Dan Flavin and Robert Morris, New York art stars he had long championed, the *Voice* critic was annoyed: "I don't like to have to take off my boots off and shuffle around in paper slippers through an exhibition carrying them in a shopping bag." (On another front, Flavin, subject of a contemporaneous career retrospective at the Jewish Museum—compared by *Times* critic John Canaday to a cap-and-gown kindergarten graduation ceremony—was attacked by the Art Workers' Coalition for using twenty fluorescent bulbs contributed by General Electric. The company was not only a corporate war profiteer but one whose workers were on strike.)

show in New York," noting that it seemed to take the counterculture notion of freaks literally. The cast included a thalidomide baby, a set of female Siamese triplets, and the stump-armed Princess Ninga Flinga Dung (played by "authentic mad genius" Vaccaro, "as extreme a theatrician as Grotowski, as adamant in his ethos as Julian Beck"), with a carnival barker calling the shots.

Unsurprisingly *Screw* also loved *Heaven Grand* while *Times* critic Walter Kerr, who loathed it, wrote a furiously vivid description: "Girls with green faces gone spastic shake the oak leaves in their hair while revolving the red dust in their navels."

> A girl in a blue robe trimmed with ratty white fur sits on a toilet chewing at her blue-stockinged toe, abandoning the toilet only when an urgent man wishes to put his head in. A chap in bloody shorts who may or not have been castrated eventually acquires a pair of papier-mâché breasts, a fellow in a frock coat sports an enormous and apparently overused phallus, a gypsy in drag batters the heads of her/his fellow performers with a tambourine while mouths and elbows and ankles and hips twitch all about her.

Eros effect run amok, the play defied rational analysis. Kerr concluded, "When there is no evident trace of wit or talent at hand, the posture of witlessness is a life saver."

Even out of the play, perhaps especially out of the play, Jackie was a star—what the Diggers would call a "life actor." In the *Times* piece published two weeks before Kerr's tirade, freelancer Rosalyn Regelson described Jackie, twenty-one years old, five-eleven, and built like a linebacker, "grooving down St. Mark's Place in mini-skirt, ripped black tights, clunky heels, and chestnut curls," without falsies but a long Isadora scarf flying behind in the breeze.

Curtis, the grandchild of Second Avenue saloon proprietress "Slugger" Ann Uglialoro, was a one-person revolution:

> [Touring] St. Mark's Place at midnight with Jackie offers a revelation about the longhaired political activists who regard themselves as street guerrillas of the new people's revolution. They jeer at and threaten Jackie with the backlash zeal of a bunch of uptight goons.

> But Jackie sails through the machismo of the Che-Mao country unperturbed, with the confidence of one who know that she is riding the wave of the future. History is on her side.

Indeed, the January 22 *Voice* ran an ad from a St. Mark's Place boutique that captioned a willowy gender-indefinite creature with the question "Is he or isn't she?" and promised "whatever you are . . . The spiffiest He or She clothes." (The Motherfuckers were lighting out for New Mexico.)

In late November, Vivian Gornick, the *Voice*'s most prominent feminist writer, had declared in writing about the new feminism that "the next great moment in history is theirs." On January 24, *Rat*'s female staffers formed a collective and, aided by Women's International Terrorist Conspiracy from Hell [WITCH], staged a coup. As reported in the paper's February 9 issue, which also covered the opening of the Panther trial, the *Rat* office was "yielded" to them, although some of the high school boys and two male critics—Vince Aletti and Leon Gussow—hung on for a few more issues.

A manifesto published beneath a cartoon of a cute feminine rodent raising one fist and brandishing an automatic rifle in the other, saying "Up Against The Wall RAT!," ended with a utopian, anarchist assertion: "If we throw out our absurd hierarchy of Editor, Assistant Editor, etc. etc. down to the minute irrelevant divisions of labor that are dragging on both the men and the women here—we will have made a strong start in the right direction." No President! (A week later, *Rat* was busted for the S. Clay Wilson cartoon of a sliced penis that ran in the issue before the women took power.)

Where was history going? March 6, the Weathermen inadvertently blew up a Greenwich Village townhouse where they had set up a bomb factory. Drawing on one liberation to mock another, Andy Warhol that month began work on his last personal feature, eventually called *Women in Revolt*. The project, which Jackie Curtis would write (and assistant director Paul Morrissey would discourage as unduly provocative) was a wisecracking Solanas-inspired satire of the women's movement starring the Factory's three reigning drag queens: Candy Darling, Holly Woodlawn, and Curtis themself.

In April, WITCH co-founder and Grove Press editor Robin Morgan was fired for attempting to unionize editorial workers. The next day the New Left squared off against the Old when the staff of the *National*

Guardian, a paper founded in 1948 to campaign for Henry Wallace, went on strike. The day after that, Morgan's comrades staged a sit-in at Grove's offices, not only protesting boss Barney Rosset's anti-union policies but Grove's "basic theme of humiliating, degrading and dehumanizing women through sado-masochistic literature, pornographic films and oppressive and exploitative practices against its own female employees."

Naturally, as *EVO*'s report noted, the publisher of Che Guevara, Frantz Fanon, and Malcolm X had phoned the pigs: The most successful downtown action since drag queens battled police at Stonewall last June was terminated when forty cops stormed the building. Over the next weekend, members of the *Guardian* staff broke into the paper's offices and with support from *Rat*, the Gay Liberation Front, and Newsreel, created a commune that, although lasting only long enough for the landlord to call in the police, effectively split the publication in two.

2

The Sexual Revolution had turned a corner. Filmmakers and playwrights vied to dramatize the passion of Lenny Bruce. Pornography proliferated. Once a vehicle for social protest and a challenge to sexual mores, underground film passed the torch and turned in on itself. Declaring victory, Anthology Film Archives—a museum devoted to "Essential Cinema"—was set to open in the fall of 1970.

Amid the politicized counterculture, avant-garde movies engaged their materiality. The new tendency, heralded by *Wavelength*, was identified by P. Adams Sitney as "structural film." In addition to *Wavelength* and Snow's 1969 follow-up, a movie predicated on camera motion, titled by a double arrow, and referred to as "Back and Forth," the most significant example, also premiered in 1969, was Ken Jacob's *Tom, Tom the Piper's Son*. Jacobs refilmed parts of a 1905 one-reeler (directed by D. W. Griffith's cameraman Billy Bitzer), using 1905 technology to expand a few minutes of footage to a nearly two-hour exploration of motion picture possibilities.[2]

2 Other examples included Paul Sharits's flicker films, Hollis Frampton's mathematically derived conundrums and Ernie Gehr's urban studies. Even Andrew Noren had taken a formalist turn with his portrait of the ineffable, *The Wind Variations*. In addition, a score of minimalist, conceptual, and body artists turned to film: Vito Acconci, John Baldessari, Mel Bochner, Walter De Maria, Dan Graham, Les Levine, Bruce Nauman, Dennis Oppenheim, Ed Ruscha, Lucas Samaras, Richard Serra, and Robert

This introspective turn coincided with the arrival of films by European auteurs that attempted to explicate or exploit the passion of the counterculture. Early 1970 brought ostentatiously with-it movies by three European masters: Michelangelo Antonioni, Federico Fellini, and Jean-Luc Godard. The foreign invasion was presaged by Mexico-based Alejandro Jodorowsky's *Fando and Lis*, which, announced by a full-page ad in the *Village Voice*, opened at the Fifth Avenue Theatre on February 2, 1970.

Based on a 1958 play by Jodorowsky's Panic Movement colleague Fernando Arrabal, the movie premiered at the 1968 Acapulco Film Festival shortly after a Mexico City bloodbath, when the army massacred protesting students on the eve of the Olympics. Two seekers, Fando and his paralytic girlfriend Lis, travel through a wasteland to the legendary city of Tar. Jodorowsky, who directed the play in Paris, augmented Arrabal's text with sadistic, vaguely Catholic vignettes. A blind man draws blood from Lis's arm and drinks it down like wine; after she dies, mourners devour her body.

Banned in Mexico, the movie was acquired and re-edited by Cannon Productions, branching out from soft-core porn, and released in New York to mainly negative reviews. "Each new outrage invites a yawn," Roger Greenspun, newly recruited from the *Freep*, wrote in the *Times*. Opening three days later, Michelangelo Antonioni's *Zabriskie Point*, produced by MGM and titled for the lowest spot in Death Valley, was not so easily dismissed.

After two years of pre-release publicity, the film had its world premiere at a Third Avenue arthouse, the Coronet Theater. Antonioni, who hoped to open with footage of a real race riot, twice crossed the United States in late 1967 and through the summer of 1968, scouting locations and meeting counterculture celebrities. Dancer Anna Halprin's eighteen-year-old daughter Daria was cast in the lead, but production was postponed while Antonioni searched for an appropriate co-star, whom he

---

Smithson. All but Smithson would have films included in MoMA's summer *Information* show. The proliferation of video changed the media environment. On January 12, 1970, Boston station WGBH-TV broadcast Stan VanDerBeek's "Pre-Theatre-Non-Verbal-Electric-Collage" *Violence Sonata*—a mix of live action and prerecorded video played out on two channels and requiring two TV sets to watch. One channel was a montage juxtaposing space missions, riots, Martin Luther King Jr. and the Ku Klux Klan synthesized and superimposed. The other channel played the first for a live studio audience. To complete the feedback loop, home viewers were encouraged to call in their responses.

imagined as an American Che. In June, the director held an open casting call at the Electric Circus. Eventually, he chose Mark Frechette, an angry yet inexpressive young carpenter from Mel Lyman's commune in Fort Hill, Boston.

Zabriskie Point was little more than a violent anecdote opening with a conflict on the Berkeley campus and unfolding over the course of one long afternoon. Inspired by the taunts of Black Panthers (including Kathleen Cleaver), Mark steals a plane. Daria, who works for a Los Angeles real estate company in a police state skyscraper of total surveillance, is driving through Death Valley to Phoenix for a rendezvous with her boss and lover. Mark flirtatiously strafes her car, then lands so they can meet. "Conspicuously absent from the film is the 'Fuck You America' that Daria was supposed to have scrawled on the desert sands for Mark's aerial approval," Andrew Sarris noted in his *Voice* review.

Mark and Daria engage in arid repartee and then make love, occasioning a lyrical interlude in which, dramatizing the Eros effect, they are joined by a bevy of other naked young couples (members of Joseph Chaikin's Open Theater, supplemented by teenagers recruited for the "love-in" from Salt Lake City and Las Vegas.) In *Rat*'s last piece by a male writer, Leon Gussow castigated *Zabriskie Point* as irrelevant, gutless, and "so bad that even the straight newspaper and newsweekly reviewers caught most of its flaws." Antonioni insisted so doggedly that America was a horror, it was "as if he were afraid the audience might miss his point. As if he had a point."

Faring better was *Fellini Satyricon*, also the beneficiary of much prerelease publicity. "The set, it's rumored, is 'one continual orgy,'" the *Voice*'s curtain-raiser revealed. Two images from the film had already appeared in the October 1969 *Newspaper*. The cast recruited from *Hair* and various Euro hippie scenes seemed authentic. Some critics accepted Fellini's description of the movie as a "psychedelic arcane dream." Others did not. Telling tales out of school, Sarris reported that at the press review, "a covey of influential New York critics made a big show of booing and hissing." His own feeling was that the movie, which opened as a road show at the midtown Little Carnegie, was belated: "Fellini's chaste treatment of amoral antics may thereby seem too tame in the context of contemporary permissiveness."

Imagining togas as miniskirts and ancient Rome as the precursor of the Western counterculture, *Satyricon* had obvious affinities to *Dionysus in*

’69 and was admired as such. Mekas just found it depressing. *Satyricon* made him regret that Jack Smith had abandoned *Normal Love*. “It was almost painful just to think that *Satyricon* is there and *Normal Love* isn’t.”

3

Four days after *Satyricon*, Jean-Luc Godard’s *One Plus One* had its US premiere . . . at Hunter College. The movie, which featured the Rolling Stones, was already notorious. Thanks to *La Chinoise*—a sympathetic satire of French student militants—with which Godard had toured American colleges in 1968, the filmmaker enjoyed a special status.[3]

The Yugoslav filmmaker Dušan Makavejev was planning a quasi-underground documentary celebration of subterranean idol Wilhelm Reich to be shot come summer in New York’s hippie demimonde, but, unique among celebrated European directors, Godard engaged the counterculture—or seemed to. (Who remembered or paid attention to his gratuitous attack on Bob Dylan in his 1966 youth film, *Masculine/Feminine*?)

Back in the pre-Columbia spring of 1968, *La Chinoise* received mixed notices in the underground press. *Rat* published ambivalently pro and angrily con reviews. The tale of five young militants who establish their Maoist cell in a spacious Paris apartment left vacant for the summer by its bourgeois owners, then argue their way toward an act of political terror, seemed more snarky critique than model for action. But some cineastes, including D. A. Pennebaker (who undertook to distribute the movie), believed that, opening in New York at the out-of-the-way Kip’s Bay Theater on April 3, 1968, *La Chinoise* inspired the Columbia students who, three weeks later, began occupying campus buildings.[4]

Godard appeared even more prescient after May ’68 and more political as well. Unable to tempt John Lennon into playing Leon Trotsky, he

3 *One Plus One* had a notably tumultuous premiere at the 1969 London Film Festival. Bowing to commercial considerations, the producers renamed it *Sympathy for the Devil* and dubbed the song “Sympathy for the Devil” over the last sequence, at once undermining the film’s argument that Revolution is a work in progress and distracting from the majestic closing shot in which Eve Democracy (Godard’s wife Anne Wiazemsky) collapses on a camera dolly, which sweeps her up into the sky. In response, Godard assaulted producer Iain Quarrier onstage and suggested that the audience demand a refund. Right on!

4 Pennebaker documented Godard’s conversation with NYU students on April 4, 1968, the afternoon before Martin Luther King Jr. was assassinated in Memphis.

decided to secure the World's Greatest Rock Band for his first English-language film and, brushing off entreaties to participate in the Yippies' "Festival of Life" (where he might have bumped into Norman Mailer, Jean Genet, William Burroughs, and possibly Antonioni), descended on London to document the Stones' *Beggars Banquet* recording sessions, including the LP's first track, "Sympathy for the Devil."

In the fall of '68, around the time *Weekend* opened in New York to the best reviews of Godard's career, it was announced that his next film, a documentary to be made with Pennebaker for public TV, would be called *One American Movie* (later, as edited by Pennebaker, it became *One Parallel Movie* or *One P.M.*). The shoot opened in New York on the same November day that saw the Fillmore throw-down. Visiting the new economic zone that would attract Sam Melville's bombs, Godard interviewed an idealistic twenty-six-year-old corporate lawyer and future New York City council president, Carol Bellamy. Another scene had Rip Torn, costumed in a Confederate uniform, out in Brooklyn, parroting "The Wall Street Lady" for a lively class of Black public school students.

Godard also crossed the Hudson to Newark to document a free-form street jam with LeRoi Jones banging on a xylophone while chanting his poem "S.O.S": *Calling all black people, man woman child / Wherever you are, calling you, urgent, come in.* Godard crossed the country as well, flying to Oakland for interviews with Black Panther minister of information Eldridge Cleaver and SDS leader Tom Hayden. Back in New York by November 19, Godard shot his second rock band, the openly political Jefferson Airplane. Performing their chord-heavy, keening atomic-war vision "House at Pooneil Corners" on the Hotel Schuyler roof, ten stories above West Forty-Fifth Street, the Airplane rattled office windows, stopped traffic, and drew crowds as well as the police. The band ceased playing, but, wrapped only in a bed sheet, actress Paula Matter sat down at the vacated drums and as Godard hastened back to London for the scandalous *One Plus One* premiere, accompanied herself in a shrill version of the Beatles' "Hey Jude."

Leaving his footage to Pennebaker, Godard followed *One Plus One* with a second film in Britain, the strident factory "newsreel" *British Sounds*, shot in the spring of 1969, and eventually called *See You at Mao*. His next stop was Prague, where his intention to make another movie about the industrial proletariat, attacking the twin evils of Soviet revisionism and US imperialism. He was thwarted when Czech citizens refused to talk to him, and Czech authorities expelled him from the country. Nonetheless, Grove Press acquired *Pravda*, along with the British film, for American distribution.

Compared to these recondite essays, which Grove opened in New York in May 1970, *One Plus One* was relatively entertaining. As the song "Sympathy for the Devil" evolves from folkie ballad to hypnotic samba, Godard intersperses scenes in which Eve Democracy spray-paints slogans on parked cars and gives monosyllabic answers to a TV crew whose questions were drawn from a *Playboy* interview with Norman Mailer. Other sequences show Iain Quarrier declaiming passages from *Mein Kampf* and Black revolutionaries reading incendiary excerpts from Eldridge Cleaver's *Soul on Ice*. Intermittently, the soundtrack is dominated by a droll near-pornographic political thriller suggestive of William S. Burroughs that, in addition to a scurrilous episode involving the pope, includes a reference to "Uncle Mao's yellow submarine."

One Plus One received a sympathetic review from Roger Greenspun in the *Times* and a more skeptical one, calling Godard a "charlatan," from David Ehrenstein in the *Voice*. *EVO* simply ran a cartoon by Fred Mogubgub that over an abstract landscape imposed the message GODARD IS FULL OF SHIT, while *Rat* attacked the film head-on "as the cry of a straight white male who sees his whole civilization rotting," in part because of Godard's alliance with the paper's bête noire, Grove Press. Having given Godard a $25,000 advance for a never made adaptation of Marx's *Eighteenth Brumaire of Louis Bonaparte*, Grove sent the filmmaker and the other member of the Dziga Vertov Group, Jean-Pierre Gorin, out with *See You at Mao* on an American university tour.[5]

See You at Mao opened later that month at the Bleecker Street Cinema, now rented to Grove Press, along with *Pravda*. Greenspun was respectful. Sarris, who interviewed Godard at the Grove Press offices, quoted their press release in its entirety. Far more interested in the filmmaker than the film, he was nonplussed first by Godard's reference to Grove's women problems and then by the filmmaker's assertion that

5 The *Berkeley Barb* provided a lively account of Godard's packed UC Berkeley screening: "A vocal minority accused Brother Jean-Luc of being a hypocritical, male chauvinist, image-seeking, self-satisfied, arrogant poseur; a silent majority convicted him of having made a boring film."

"Czechoslovakia had been invaded by American tanks from United Artists long before the Russians came in."

On the other hand, Jonas Mekas praised *Pravda* as an abstract newsreel consumed by revolutionary nostalgia. Provocatively calling it Godard's best film to date, he welcomed him to the cause which, in addition to a new celebrity, could use an infusion of content: "With *Pravda* Godard finally abandons commercial cinema and joins the underground."

4

As underground movies lost relevance, Ridiculous Theater grew more respectable.[6] As the first anniversary of the Stonewall uprising approached, in early March *Heaven Grand in Amber Orbit* was revived downtown at Café La MaMa and received even better reviews than its first run, hailed by Dick Brukenfeld in the *Voice* as "a comic plague . . . Artaudian in effect."

In April, Charles Ludlam's *Bluebeard*, a Ridiculous gloss on the 1932 horror film *Island of Lost Souls* and at the same time a "well-made" play, previewed at La MaMa before opening to the best notices of Ludlam's career in a converted gay bar on Christopher Street. Martin Washburn gave the performance a glowing review in the *Voice*; the next issue had Richard Schechner expounding at length on its importance, explicating the plot, comparing the production to *Paradise Now* and his own *Dionysus in '69*, and paying Ludlam the ultimate compliment by bracketing him with Jerzy Grotowski (not Artaud).

A few weeks later, the *New York Times* braved Christopher Street. "A truly terrible actor like Mario Montez (as Lamia the Leopard Woman) seems exactly right and the good actors seem perfect," Mel Gussow wrote. May also brought Jackie Curtis's *Femme Fatale: The Three Faces of Gloria*. A cheerfully haphazard throwback to the anarchic Ridiculous Theater of 1968, the play featured Mary Woronov and two future downtown stars, the poet Patti Smith and performance artist Penny Arcade. Only briefly at La MaMa, *Femme Fatale* did not rate a *Voice* review,

6 The two forms were conjoined in Baltimore filmmaker John Waters's 16mm feature *Multiple Maniacs*, a gross underground farce depicting a "cavalcade of perversions" and dedicated to the Manson Family. Although the movie was plugged by Howard Smith that May in "Scenes" and played in several American cities, San Francisco most successfully, it would not be shown in New York for several years.

although the paper recognized its forebears in awarding special Obies to archenemies Vaccaro and Ludlam.

Deeper underground, Jack Smith had begun staging Saturday midnight performances (and later slide shows) at his duplex loft on the corner of Grand and Greene Streets, the Plaster Foundation of Atlantis, named for the pile of debris left on the floor after Smith knocked down half of the ceiling that separated his two floors. Evolving as it incorporated all manner of junk found on the streets of still industrial SoHo, this rubble heap surrounded a lagoon-like contraption complete with a plastic tubing waterfall the artist fashioned from an inflatable child's wading pool.[7]

Unpublicized save for a mention in the *Voice*'s off-off-Broadway listings, these pieces were organized around the lagoon, also the subject of many slides. Marie Antoinette (née Maria Antoinette Rogers), the native Apache actress married to painter Ed Ruda and currently in the revived *Heaven Grand*, was a leading performer. According to Jackie Curtis, Smith wanted him to play a "Venus figure," costumed as a woodland creature (or, to judge from the "giant wild wig of all flowers" Stefan Brecht observed at a June production of *Withdrawal from Orchid Lagoon*, simply the woodlands). "I was too tense. I didn't shut up," Curtis recalled. "Jack Smith nearly murdered me by throwing me down a flight of stairs."[8]

More overground, if equally outré, the Hollywood version of Gore Vidal's bestselling satire *Myra Breckinridge* opened at the Criterion, at

7 Richard Preston, who visited Smith's loft in late 1966, wrote a colorful description: "I wandered around his loft thru chaos, past the red velvet cushion covered with dime store jewelry, past the bust of a mannequin which looked like a bust of Caesar's whore, over a pile of grimy diaphanous costumes, around a transistor radio sputtering Spanish serenades and sat next to two elephant tusks, one artificial and one a genuine molar. Behind me were the artificial sunflowers bathing themselves in a revolting [sic] multicolored display light. To my left was a potbellied stove and a mountain of lumber. I'm not sure whether the lumber was a fuel source but I do know where it came from—the ceiling. This was conspicuous because half of it (the ceiling) wasn't there. The walls went up and up into the loft above."

8 By my own observation, Smith's performances involved listening to music, watching him make minor adjustments in the set and waiting for the unprepared actors to finish dressing. Obviously unrehearsed, they appeared confused, reading from the script whose pages were passed around the stage, while responding (or not) to Smith's direction. The action typically involved the slow burial and exhumation of artifacts from the set. *Boiled Lobster Easter Pageant* was followed by *Religious Spectacle of Atlantis*, *Fishhook of Orchid Lagoon Water Pageant* and, as summer neared, *Withdrawal from Orchid Lagoon* (a clue that the wading-pool waterfall had been dismantled).

Broadway and Forty-Fourth Street, four days short of the Stonewall's anniversary, and effectively previewed the week's Christopher Street Liberation Day March. The story of a gay film critic (played by critic Rex Reed) who undergoes a sex change (transformed into Raquel Welch) and moves to Hollywood with a plan to seize control of his uncle's acting studio and then orchestrate a realignment of the sexes reaped even more pre-release publicity than *Zabriskie Point* or *Fellini Satyricon*. Much of the press was negative; some concerned Mae West, whom the movie brought out of retirement.

West, seventy-six, graced the opening and thrilled the brazen, drag-enriched crowd outside the Criterion. *EVO* cited the "festive, often violent atmosphere" reminiscent of the Columbia building seizures—"cops, pickets, police barricades, press, television cameras, pushing, showing off, camaraderie, hurt feelings, and heroes." (The *New York Times* reported that 2,000 screaming citizens blocked Times Square and attempted to vault barriers.) Rather than a review, *Rat* simply ran a picture of Mae circa 1930, with three progressive quotes ("Communists have done a lot of good things," "A woman should be recognized for her brains," and "I resented that men could do anything they wanted"). In interviews, West expressed approval for both women's and gay liberation.

Myra nearly doubled the Criterion's previous opening day box office record, going on to garner the most hostile reviews ever accorded a Hollywood release.[9]

5

Myra Breckinridge was one slap in the face of public taste; Bob Dylan delivered another. After four years living in Woodstock, woodshedding with the Band and fending off the fans who tracked him down to his sanctuary, Dylan returned to the Village with his wife Sara and four small children, moving into a nineteenth-century townhouse at 94 MacDougal, barely a block from the Gaslight.

Could he really bring it back home, again? Four years after *Blonde on Blonde*, Dylan released a second double LP provocatively titled *Self*

9 It was not entirely unappreciated. *Andy Warhol's Inter/View* put it on the cover of its fourth issue. There is no evidence that Jack Smith saw the movie but in 1970 Ken Jacobs told me, "There's *The Birth of a Nation*, *Citizen Kane* and *Myra Breckinridge*." He may have later revised his opinion but, given its extensive interpolation of old Hollywood movies, I don't think he was kidding.

Portrait, its cover graced with a naïve expressionist likeness the artist would later claim to have painted in five minutes. What manner of icon was this? One need only compare *Self Portrait*'s insultingly grotesque cover to the complex image that graced *Bringing It All Back Home* to wonder what was left of Dylan's mind.[10]

Self Portrait appeared to flaunt its mediocrity, covering several lesser songwriters and even Elvis's crooning cover of the venerable showtune "Blue Moon." Goof or gaffe, the album was pilloried by the rock press. But in wanting to make a change, Dylan was not alone. Retreating from an early association with the Yippies, Phil Ochs, Dylan's onetime rival in *Broadside* topicality, imploded early that spring with a disastrous Carnegie Hall concert. Almost as if trying to preempt *Self Portrait*, Ochs appeared in a gold lamé suit and, in addition to performing reworked versions of his most famous songs, covered Conway Twitty, Buddy Holly, and Merle Haggard, even including Haggard's hippie-hating crossover hit "Okie from Muskogee." The crowd protested and the concert was cut short after a telephoned bomb threat.

The same season, Miles Davis coolly pulled off his own, more successful radical reinvention. As presaged by his 1969 album *In a Silent Way* and his new double LP, *Bitches Brew*, as well as successive gigs at the Fillmore East, the jazz master went electric—in a big way. Recorded at Columbia's Studio B during the Woodstock summer of 1969, *Bitches Brew* incorporated electric piano as well as electric guitar. A greatly expanded rhythm section contributed to the blues backbeat while Davis made extensive use of sound editing and studio technology.

If some recognized the influence of Jimi Hendrix and James Brown, Cecil Taylor and jazz writer Stanley Crouch, not known for their agreements, similarly labeled Davis a sellout (the LP did eventually go platinum) and LeRoi Jones dismissed Davis's audacious jazz-rock fusion as "dollar-sign music"; Jones had already rebuked Albert Ayler and even Ornette Coleman in the essay "The Fire Must Be Permitted to Burn Full Up," published in the summer-fall *Journal of Black Poetry*: Where Jr. Walker's music is "a force describing a purity. Ornette and Albert now

10 The thick brush strokes of cheerful abstraction painted by Ornette Coleman for his highly personal 1966 LP *The Empty Foxhole* seems a precedent.

describe bullshit so are bullshit." What's more, "the harmonics in James Brown's voice are more 'complicated,' if that's what you dig, than Ornette Coleman will ever be."

The laid-back jam-session quality of Coleman's SoHo LP *Friends and Neighbors: Live at Prince Street*, recorded on Valentine's Day 1970 (but not released until 1972), would have scarcely rehabilitated the artist in Jones's eyes. On the contrary. But if Ornette had gone hippie, Ayler commercial, and if even Pharaoh Sanders had been co-opted by FM radio, soul and funk would be superseded. The summer's best-selling R&B album, despite infrequent airplay, belonged to a Harlem trio that came together on what would have been Malcolm X's forty-third birthday, May 19, 1968, at a public poetry reading in Mount Morris Park. These were the Last Poets.

The men appeared that October in one of the first episodes of the public television show *Soul!* But it took eighteen months before a record was cut and the white world got the word. Robert Christgau amended his June 18 column with a report: "A few weeks ago I saw an incredible performance at the Apollo by a group comprising two shouting poets and an Afro-percussionist." The LP, he added, is "acerbic and exciting and as politically uncompromising as anything ever recorded . . . Frightening and beautiful."

Recorded for Douglas records, *The Last Poets* was released in June 1970, peaking at #3 on Billboard's R&B chart and #29 all over. The percussive chant "On the Subway" was released as a single. It would be a few years before "rap" was a familiar description for the Last Poets, but "Wake Up, Niggers," another cut from the LP, was used in the Mick Jagger vehicle *Performance* released in August 1970—Black art gospel bardic poetry, appropriated by psychedelic cinema.[11]

11 The Last Poets—originally Gylan Kain, David Nelson and Abiodun Oyewole—came together at a Harlem writers' workshop. Personnel changed, at one point, including Felipe Luciano, later active in the Young Lords (and eventually a TV newsman). In the summer of 1969, Kain, Nelson and Luciano were "busy blowing minds" (per *Jet* magazine), "blending black poetry, throbbing drums, soulful songs and hip movement" at Columbia University and the Paperback Theatre on East Second Street under the rubric Concept East Poetry. They also appeared, as the Original Last Poets in Herb Danska's documentary *Right On!*, performing their material on Lower East Side tenement rooftops. First shown at the Cannes in May 1970, the movie opened in New York in April 1971. Later that year, Kain starred as an ambivalent revolutionary assassin in Richard Wesley's *Black Terror* staged at the Public Theater.

6

Phil Ochs's failed reinvention inspired pity; *Self Portrait* was received with contempt. Understanding that the artist needed a break after the suicide note that was *Blonde on Blonde*, Dylan's fans grew to admire his sly and understated *John Wesley Harding* and tolerate, however uneasily, his prettified *Nashville Skyline*. Not so *Self Portrait*, understood to signal the artist's resignation from the Collective Drama.

"What is this shit?" Greil Marcus demanded in the first sentence of his *Rolling Stone* review. *EVO* art director Steve Heller remembers staff cartoonist Alan Shenker a.k.a. Yossarian running out to buy *Self Portrait* on its day of release, rushing back to the office, firing up a joint, and putting it on the record player. "I could hear it from my adjoining office," Heller recalled. "Sounded weird. A lot of crooning. Not the old Bob that Yossarian loved so much. Next thing I hear is CRASH, BANG, BOOM. What the hell . . .? I ran next door to find Yossarian throwing his furniture around the room."

Deriding Dylan for resuscitating the moribund music of Perry Como and the Fabulous Forties and driving a spike through the heart of rock, Yossarian used *Self Portrait* as the basis for an infuriated generational attack-cum-lament. Heller captioned an image of the cover with a dig at Dylan's most fanatical exegete: "When A. J. Weberman hears this album he'll crap in his straight jacket." A former *Rat* contributor and Yippie fellow traveler, Weberman took it upon himself to make Dylan's return to the Village a torment, in part by sifting through his garbage and reporting on his finds in *EVO* or over *Radio Unnameable*.[12]

Self Portrait was the symbol of a dispiriting summer. The counterculture had been battered by the massacres at Jackson State in Mississippi and Kent State in Ohio, followed days later by the Hardhat Riot in New York's City Hall Park—itself a foretaste of the summer's great sleeper *Joe*, in which a disgruntled worker and a deranged adman with a runaway daughter go hippie hunting. And then there was the Manson Family. Ed Sanders had gone to Los Angeles to cover the trial while, taking up most of *Rolling Stone*'s

12 Weberman's foraging, which in addition to food scraps and soiled diapers turned up a picture of Jimi Hendrix as well as letters drafted to Johnny Cash and Dylan's mother, might be considered a form of indigenous No!art. As Boris Lurie, hunkered down in a studio on the corner of East Sixth Street and Avenue B, wrote in his notebook (July 18–19, 1961): "Where does the Art of New York come from? From the garbage cans."

June 25 issue, David Dalton and David Felton's shocking in-depth report located the Family in the hippie heart of darkness, although rather than Dylan, it was the Beatles who were implicated in the cult's world view; their *White Album* was taken by Manson as sacred revelation.

Initially defending *Self Portrait* as something that the Everly Brothers or Elvis might have done, Dylan eventually characterized the LP as an act of aggression against his fans, despite its having been conceived and largely recorded before his return to New York City: "There'd be crowds outside my house," he told *Rolling Stone* some years later. "And I said, 'Well, fuck it. I wish these people would just forget about me. I wanna do something they can't possibly like.'" The double album was part of the joke—"If you're gonna put a lot of crap on it, you might as well load it up!"

Perhaps this desultory exercise in what the rock historian Peter Doggett has called "hip easy listening" was intentionally off-putting (although it quickly went gold). Perhaps the well had simply run dry. The album's most sympathetic review appeared in the *New York Times*, written by Peter Schjeldahl, himself a poet. Acknowledging the enormous pressure that Dylan was under—"every new album rocks the excitable psyche of popular culture with the force of a historical event"—Schjeldahl chose to defend *Self Portrait* as something like Dylan's version of Harry Smith's *Anthology of American Folk Music*, an almost scholarly compendium of country-western, folk, blues, bluegrass, and pop styles, "a resume of Dylan's musical tastes and whims."

But, having vouched for Dylan's mental health, Schjeldahl—enjoying a brief stint as the *Times*'s avant pop savant—would publish a piece later during the summer with a headline that asked IS THE ART WORLD HEADING FOR A NERVOUS BREAKDOWN?

7

New York's art scene per Schjeldahl was in worse shape than at any time since World War II. Schjeldahl tastefully omitted Mark Rothko's shocking suicide in February and thirty-four-year-old sculptor Eva Hesse's tragic death two months later, victim of a brain tumor perhaps exacerbated by toxic elements she used in her sculpture. ("Her death brought down the curtain on a whole period of art life in New York," Mel Bochner would say. "It closed the Sixties.")

Referring only obliquely to the events of the past May, Schjeldahl saw an unfolding catastrophe. The past 1969–70 season began "with evidence of another new, properly dumbfounding 'movement' (comprising Informal, Earth Art, Conceptual, etc)" or what, back in February, the *New York Times Magazine* declared "boulderdash." It then proceeded through a series of spectacular if premature retrospectives to end in "virulent confusion," for once, Schjeldahl thought, in accord with the national mood.

On one hand, the art market consolidated. Mid-career stars, whether Pop (Andy Warhol, Claes Oldenburg, hailed by the *New York Times* as "the Picasso of Pop," Roy Lichtenstein, one of whose canvases sold for a then record $75,000) or hardcore Minimal (Frank Stella, Don Judd, Dan Flavin), were accorded full-scale museum retrospectives. On the other, the attack on the market and all-out politicization of the art scene "visited something like terror upon dealers and curators, and heartsick or disgusted bewilderment upon apolitical artists." For the demonstrations of late 1969 had continued.

Mid-afternoon Saturday, May 2—two days before Kent State, one day after Ralph Ortiz and Tom Lloyd confronted MoMA's new director John Hightower with a demand for greater representation of Black and Puerto Rican artists—the Guerilla Art Action Group staged a supportive "art action" at the museum entrance. Jean Toche and Jon Hendricks, identified as director and trustee respectively, pulled up in a chauffeured limousine and, freeing two chickens, installed a makeshift wire barrier (enclosing selected "art works") on Fifty-Third Street. The pair used cap pistols and even a smoke bomb to defend their mock museum against a group of artists carrying placards reading "Free Museum" and "Tokenism is Dead." Three squad cars arrived only to be informed by an indulgent MoMA representative that it was just theater: "They're play acting."

Far beyond David McReynolds's dreams a decade earlier, a nationwide university strike was declared on May 5. At NYU, Richard Schechner, Joan MacIntosh, and Ralph Ortiz had already organized a guerrilla theater piece, restaging the massacre at several locations around Washington Square Park. Some students played National Guardsmen, others represented their victims (animal organs concealed beneath their clothes in anticipation of a bloody demise), harangued, brutalized, and marched around until they were executed. According to Schechner, laughing bystanders were incorporated into the piece, treated as students.

The AWC called on galleries and museums to close in solidarity. Rather than participate, MoMA announced a free day. In response the conceptual artist Les Levine printed 10,000 posters, paraphrasing John and Yoko: "MUSEUM OF MODERN ART IS OVER if you want it." Shows at the Whitney and Jewish Museum were canceled or suspended, as artists debated how best to demonstrate solidarity with striking students. A mass meeting was held at NYU's Loeb Auditorium. "They were all there," Cindy Nemser, later publisher of the *Feminist Art Journal*, began her report in the *Voice*.

> Bearded, wild-eyed, hollow-cheek artist revolutionaries; bearded, crafty-eyed, well fed pseudo artist revolutionaries; smoothly shaven, haggard eyed, slightly paunchy museum curators; meticulously kempt, sharp-eyed, nattily attired dealers; tangle-haired, glassy-eyed non-bra-wearing female artists—all the exotic individuals who make up that strange creature designated the New York art world.

The chaotic meeting was chaired by Robert Morris, who had just shut down his Whitney retrospective. ("Greater sacrifice hath no man," Nemser quipped.) Greeted with applause and a few "prophetic" boos, Morris called upon artists to do their share to undermine a corrupt system by boycotting corporate- and government-sponsored art, engaging in an optional two-week strike, calling on museums to open their lobbies for use as anti-war information centers, and tithing for peace. Meanwhile an unreconciled group located at the rear of the auditorium kept up a monotonous chant: *Art is dead!*

The art establishment had come to do the "right thing," Nemser wrote.

> They expected to applaud themselves for their liberality and leave with the good feeling of knowing that the art world had come through when the chips were down. But certain members of the radical fringe were denying them the chance to groove on their own goodness. Dealers and curators, instead of being thanked for sponsoring the one-day strike and anti-war propaganda activities, were told that they should shut their establishments for long periods of time, even for good.

Despairing of such solidarity, Nemser suggested that with regard to political activism, artists act not as artists but individuals.

Still, on the afternoon of May 9, the poet Hannah Weiner organized a protest show at Max's Kansas City. Much of the work was Body Art. Vito Acconci rubbed his arm raw to create a red blotch, the dancer Deborah Hay spent the entire hour drinking a glass of wine in super slow motion as, eyes blind-folded and ears plugged, Adrian Piper wandered around colliding with bar patrons. Other pieces addressed Max's as an environment: the painter Marjorie Strider created a faux broken window, Weiner declaimed the official instruction manual for waitresses, while John Perreault—who reported his own participation in the *Voice*—pulled the plug on Flavin's *Corner monument 4 those who have been killed in ambush (to P.K. who reminded me about death)* and taped over Warhol prints, an act that drew ridicule from Gregory Battcock in the *Voice*'s next issue.

Schjeldahl would have doubtless considered such "conceptual" shenanigans symptomatic of the logic expressed by an American officer in Vietnam that a village had been leveled to save it.

> Suddenly galleries and museums and art journals, the media, and beneficiaries of a decade of phenomenal esthetic turnover, were full of works that couldn't be removed without being destroyed, pictures of works that no longer existed or existed in remote locations, proposals for works that did not yet or never would exist—works in short that couldn't be bought. A system founded on the promotion and sale of avant-garde objects was being subverted, and by the avant-garde.

Schjeldahl had written sympathetically on the post-minimalist sculptor Bill Bollinger in an article the *Times* headlined ART: ANYTHING THE ARTIST SAYS IT IS?, but his piece focused on two shows, one of which, *Conceptual Art and Conceptual Aspects* at the New York Cultural Center, he had already attacked as hopelessly abstruse, making the sarcastic observation that increasingly "the font of genius would seem to be the cerebral cortex exclusively." By contrast, the second, at the Museum of Modern Art, had just been savaged by Hilton Kramer as "virtually mindless," echoing Barbara Rose's comment five years earlier on *The Responsive Eye*.

The show was simply called *Information* and consisted largely of photographs, documents, written instructions, and a catalogue that was intrinsic rather than supplementary. Kramer pointed out the bizarre contradiction of a major museum show devoted to attacking the very idea of museumized art. Had real Dada finally come to Fifty-Third Street? Or was it, as *Information* supporters might have added, the times were simply a-changin'? The art object had been displaced. Traditional forms were kaput.

Lil Picard saw it coming. A month before the show opened in July, she told *EVO* readers that art had entered a new phrase. The art strike had given birth to a new art form: "In the future, Art will be the political information on truth." Picard called it "Information-Art" and predicted that America, where issues of racism, repressions, sexism, and war were being fought out, would be the leading force.

MoMA curator Kynaston McShine's catalogue essay invoked Marcel Duchamp, who died in October 1968, and John Cage as well as Marshall McLuhan, the Beatles, and the *I Ching*, describing *Information* as an "international report of the activity of younger artists [in the context of] a culture that has been considerably altered by communications systems such as television and film." Artists in the Global Village were interested in ways of rapidly exchanging ideas rather than embalming the idea in an "object."

John Perreault thought *Information* as important as McShine's *Primary Structures* show, four years earlier, at the Jewish Museum. Neither video art nor light shows were included, although the Italian "Arte Povera" group did contribute a ninety-minute videotape. *Information* was heavy on Boulderdash. Some projects, like Flux artist George Brecht's proposals to exchange the Arctic ice pack with the Antarctic and to move England closer to the equator, were whimsically conceptual. Others, notably Robert Smithson's *Spiral Jetty*, were monumental.

Photography was largely used to document, as with Peter Hutchinson's photo series "Four Stages and Locations of Bread Mold," although *Newspaper* published a special issue that, more political than previous numbers, included images of the Third World, referenced Kent State, the Nixon family, and Vietnam, reprising two Diane Arbus portraits of flag-waving pro-war supporters that had run in an earlier iteration. The catalog also contained a Steven Lawrence "Environment" that, among many other found images, included stills from *Zabriskie Point, Fellini Satyricon*, and *Sympathy for the Devil*.

Inevitably, several artists riffed on the idea of a museum. Vito Acconci had his mail forwarded to MoMA. Hans Haacke was more political. His piece gave gallerygoers a proposition: "Would the fact that Governor Rockefeller has not denounced President Nixon's Indochina policy be a reason for you not to vote for him in November?" Transparent plexiglass boxes were provided for the Yes and No ballots. Hilton Kramer, who deemed the "estheticizing of political clichés" an even worse development than the politicization of art, began his review with an irritated description, noting that at the member's preview he attended, the Yes votes were slightly more numerous than the No pile. But the day Perreault attended the show, Yes votes outnumbered No ballots 5,100 to 70.

As controversial as it was, Haacke's star-making project—a de-aestheticizing of a new-minted artistic cliché—arrived and was censored some six months later. *Shapolsky et al. Manhattan Real Estate Holdings, A Real Time Social System as of May 1, 1971* was a series of 146 similarly framed photographs of Manhattan residential buildings—an exercise in serial photography differing from Ed Ruscha's gas stations or Hilla and Bernd Becher's industrial installations only in that the pictures, all tenements in Harlem or the East Village, were annotated.

Captions not only gave the location of the buildings but derived from public records, documenting their shifts in ownership structure and financial histories. All were connected to the city's ruling slumlord, the Shapolsky real estate group.[13]

8

Kramer found *Information* at once overweeningly intellectual and amusingly feeble. The abundant "junky" photographs and copious written material, not to mention John Giorno's green telephones on which one could dial-a-poem, were so much clutter: "The detritus of modern printing and electronic communications media has been transformed by an international gaggle of demi-intellectuals into a low-grade form of

13 The piece was part of Haacke's solo exhibit at the Guggenheim Museum, scheduled for April 1971. He was asked to remove it and refused, whereupon, explaining that he "had to fend off an alien substance that had entered the art museum organism," the Guggenheim's director Thomas Messer canceled the show (and also fired its thirty-six-year-old curator, art historian Edward Fry), thus inspiring the Art Workers' Coalition's last great protest. While it was assumed that museum trustees were implicated, they were not—excepting in so far as there was a class identification. In the 1982, Anita Kresofsky, who had married into the Shapolsky family, started a highly successful enterprise, originally known as the Arbitrage Gallery.

show business," Kramer wrote. "It leaves one almost nostalgic for a good old-fashioned hand-made happening."

Curiously, *Information* snubbed video. Worse, however, was the exhibition's bungled attempt to integrate cinema. Kramer was dismissive of the "visual jukebox" furnished by the Olivetti company, featuring forty films that ranged from the "merely boring to the thoroughly stupefying." In fact, this early attempt to install motion pictures in a gallery setting rendered the movies all but unwatchable.[14]

A personal note: In New York with a summer job at the Film-Makers' Cooperative, I found the show a confusing bore, albeit weirdly democratic with its basis in ideas. Interested in serial photography, I was most impressed with the Bechers' industrial images and Ed Ruscha's books. I also noted the presence of several artists, like Adrian Piper, born like me several years after World War II, and was pleased to note the inclusion of films by my teacher Ken Jacobs as well as fellow Film-Makers' Cooperative employee Ernie Gehr. (He kept the books; I inherited Andrew Noren's job as the film cleaner and shipper.) However, the art that made the greatest impression on me that summer was Jack Smith's *Withdrawal from Orchid Lagoon*.

The trek through empty SoHo, the lateness of the hour, the slowness of the action, the evocative music, the joints that might circulate through the small audience combined to create an elastic framework that seemed to successfully encompass in Smith's framework all mishaps and delays—in fact, anything that happened. Some performances had an unmistakable aura of menace, others were lighter and more relaxed, characterized by the ironic juxtaposition of music and activity and Smith's deadpan clowning.

Jonas Mekas reported on one of these in the *Voice*. Smith's loft and set struck him as the detritus of a collapsed house and the actual content of the play. Mekas noted the uncertainty as to whether there would even be a performance, followed by Smith's recruitment of actors out of the audience who were then directed on stage.

---

14 No curator was credited but the selection was comprehensive. In addition to *Wavelength*, *Sleep*, and Yoko Ono's *Bottoms* plus the numerous films by minimalists and conceptual artists, the show included work by veteran avant-garde filmmakers—among them Robert Breer, Bruce Conner, Alfred Leslie, Gregory Markopoulos, and Robert Nelson—and a score of younger structural filmmakers. In addition to Ernie Gehr, these were Morgan Fisher, Hollis Frampton, George Landow, Standish Lawder, and Paul Sharits.

The sound of the scratchy 78 recording Mekas identified as the "Dance of the Seven Veils" from Strauss's *Salome*, played at a lugubrious 33 RPM, invoked a mood: "I suddenly was very conscious that it was 2:00 a.m. in New York, and very late, and most of the city was sleeping, even on Saturday night." Smith's play struck him as "the final burial rites of the capitalist civilization."

> Only Jack Smith was still alive, a madman, the high priest of the ironical burying grounds, administering the last services here alone and by himself, because really the seven or eight people who were now his audience (the other three were on the set) were really no audience at all.

Ultimately, all the actors deserted and Mekas himself left the audience to complete the ritual.[15]

The reconstituted Performance Group was in residence at New Paltz College, not far from Woodstock, preparing a new environmental piece that would dramatize the Tate murders in the light of the *Rolling Stone* revelations and the context of American history. Writing in the *New York Times*, Richard Schechner recalled a bucolic summer:

> We ran workshops for students and faculty, rehearsed and wrote our new play, swam, sang, ate, loved, hiked, smoked, and drank with the young people there . . . Afternoons smoking and talking and swimming naked at Low Falls in the mountains were more than refreshing—they were a glimpse of Eden.

Back in New York, Yugoslav filmmaker Dušan Makavejev was making *WR: Mysteries of the Organism*, a movie about Wilhelm Reich and the Sexual Revolution. *Screw* editor Jim Buckley was interviewed. Tuli

15 I am indirectly responsible for Mekas's evocative piece. Excited to see the *Voice* listing I informed Ken Jacobs, who, although long estranged from Smith was curious enough to attend, bringing his wife Flo as well as Mekas. Ernie Gehr may have also been there. After hailing Smith as "one of the last and uncompromising great artists of our generation," Mekas concludes that "somehow there was a new hope and life in the black street again, as we walked, silently." My own recollection was as we headed up empty Greene Street, Smith turned up the volume of his record player so that one departed his realm with sounds of Les Baxter's "Quiet Village" slowly fading into the night.

Kupferberg (who in his Beat days had gone through Reichian therapy) stalked the city in combat gear: Kill for Peace. Jackie Curtis, on hiatus from *Women in Revolt*, strolled down Forty-second with Eric Emerson, slurping an ice cream cone and explaining, "I used to be a boy."

Makavejev had immersed himself in the downtown scene during his various trips to New York and had seen Curtis perform, telling an interviewer that he "was in a kind of permanent awe before Jackie, as religious people might feel in the face of Jesus."

9

Information was reinforced by the appearance of a new magazine. Employing the same slick paper-and-squarish format as *Artforum*, *Avalanche*—published by Taki's accomplice Willoughby Sharp and edited by Liza Béar—was more ostentatiously ascetic in eschewing color photography as well as more rigorous in its exclusive devotion to new, largely conceptual artists.

The enigmatic German artist Joseph Beuys, a fugitive presence in *Information*, graced the cover. Inside was Sharp's long essay on Body Art. Carl Andre and Jan Dibbets were interviewed. There was a roundtable discussion with earth artists Michael Heizer, Dennis Oppenheim, and Robert Smithson as well as a plug for Smithson's thirty-two-minute movie *Spiral Jetty*.

Avalanche scooped *Information* by including a review of twenty-seven-year-old Gordon Matta-Clark's *Museum*, solely listing its nauseating ingredients:

> Agar, water, dextrose, triptone, glycerol, sperm oil, NaCl, sugar, Pet milk, V-8, cranberry juice, corn oil, yeast, chocolate Yoo-hoo, and chicken broth; the hardware, gold leaf, local vines, galvanized pans, screw hooks, thumbtacks, and black magic plastic steel; known strains, Mucor-Racemosus, Rhizo-Apophysis, Aspergillus Niger, Penicillium Notatum, and Streptomyces Griseur.

As the concoction, exhibited at the Bykert Gallery, fermented it grew increasingly moldy and offensively aromatic. Matta-Clarke also took process art into the street. Among his earliest contributions to SoHo's most radical gallery, 112 Greene, was *Garbage Wall*, which fashioned an architectural form (and performance area) out of a mound of compressed trash.[16]

The day after Halloween, the *Times* announced an open exhibition, *The People's Flag Show*, to be held at Judson Church in mid-November. The show was organized by GAAG-sters Jean Toche and John Hendrix along with the forty-year-old painter Faith Ringgold, whose recent work included *The Flag Is Bleeding*—in which a wounded Black man, as well as two whites, male and female, are imprisoned behind its bloody stripes—and *Flag for the Moon: Die Nigger* with the words "die" and "nigger" embedded in a muted, gray-tinted American flag.[17]

Flag desecration was a political issue in New York—the Democratic candidate for attorney general expressed an opinion that flag protection laws were absurd. On the other hand, flag desecration was on the Supreme Court's docket. Held after Election Day (the Democrats retained their Senate majority and increased their grip on the House, while Nelson Rockefeller won his fourth term as New York's governor) and before the Supreme Court ruling, *The People's Flag Show* was a response to a recently adjudicated case of artistic freedom.

In late 1966, a month before Angry Arts Week, a Madison Avenue gallery exhibiting new work by Marc Morrel, a twenty-nine-year-old Black ex-marine, was busted. Morrel's work consisted largely of fabric constructions based on the American flag. Flags were wrapped around coffins and swaddled with chains. One flag formed a hangman's noose. Another was bundled in the form of an erect penis. A policeman, apparently acting on his own volition, spotted the noose in the gallery window and charged gallery owner Stephen Radich with exhibiting various flag desecrations in violation of Section 1425 of the penal law.

---

16 Matta-Clarke, who met Smithson when the artist was in residence at Cornell University and assisted on one of his projects, was perhaps Smithson's greatest disciple, having absorbed the older artist's lengthy explications of entropy. By 1972, Matta-Clarke was sculpting abandoned buildings in the South Bronx, a project that recalls Danny Lyons's photographs while urbanizing Smithson's earth works.

17 "David Rockefeller sent two people to buy a painting in 1969," Ringgold has recalled. "They came to my studio to see the American People and Black Light series. They were looking at a painting of the US flag, thinking it was like a Jasper Johns! But they ran away when they realized you can read the words 'Die Nigger' within the stars and stripes." In 2019, MoMA installed Ringgold's riotous 1967 *American People Series #20: Die* (a riff on *Guernica* complete with a bloody caricature of Andy Warhol) beside Picasso's 1907 *Les Demoiselles d'Avignon*.

Radich's case was taken up by the ACLU, working its way through the legal system until, in mid-February 1970, it wound up in the New York State Court of Appeals. Hilton Kramer, who had blown off the show with a short slam back in 1966, found himself in court years later as an expert witness who could certify Morrel's work as art: "Little did I dream that this feeble and immature attempt at creating an anti-war sculpture would ever be heard of again." Nevertheless, Radich's conviction was upheld.

Kramer would not be assigned to review the *Flag Show*, but two days before it opened, and several blocks below Judson Church, the show was upstaged by *Love America or Live*, a happening by Turkish artist Tosun Bayrak that prompted a scandalized editorial in the *Times*:

> On a recent afternoon on Prince Street, nude exhibitionists put on a nauseating performance that could only be explained as the product of demented minds. It is ludicrous to argue that this degrading spectacle represented an expression of free speech in the cause of political protest.

Nothing if not inclusive, Bayrak had invited "exhibitionists, inhibitionists, feminists, chauvinists, tourists, rapists, politicians, police, morticians, rednecks, parlour pinks, hangmen, firemen, homelessmen, pick-ups, men about town, commuters, butchers, soldiers, lechers, professors, swingers, equestriennes, pedestrians, pederasts, Bedouins, gypsies, Cypriots, and Wandering Jews" to watch or participate in his "undercover event."

Two cobblestone blocks across from Paula Cooper's gallery in the heart of SoHo were covered with butcher's paper. Over the next hour or more, naked performers emerged body part by body part from beneath the paper; animal guts were strewn; water that cascaded down from a Prince Street rooftop turned to real blood. Finally, to the horror of neighborhood onlookers, a sack of white rats was slit open. A final act of public sex was anticlimactic. Struggling not to be outdone, GAAG initiated the *Flag Show* by burning a pair of flags stitched together to create a sack stuffed with animal parts.[18]

18 It is a powerful coincidence that *Love America or Live* was staged in SoHo one day before Otto Muehl's not dissimilar but considerably stronger *Manopsychotic Ballet*—an even more repulsive countercultural attack on the art world that effectively deranged the Cologne museum's exhibition *Happenings & Fluxus*. In addition to mimicking

Containing 150 works, the show was at once single-minded and varied: The German-born sculptor Ursula Meyer baked a flag cake. The feminist critic Kate Millett draped a flag over a toilet bowl. There were flags fashioned from old soda cans and dresses of tiny, knitted flags as well as flag brassieres and bulletproof vests. There was a mirrored box of flag-draped coffins and a flag-clad crucified chicken. *EVO* writer Alex Gross created a penis-shaped beanbag. The members of Yvonne Rainer's Grand Union wrapped themselves in the flag to dance nude.

Representatives of the Black Panthers and the Gay Liberation Front spoke at the opening, as did the gallerist Stephen Radich and, wearing his notorious flag shirt, Abbie Hoffman, whom *New York Times* freelancer Elenore Lester had just hailed as the principal figure in a new "Theater of the Apocalypse," comparable to William Shakespeare in his "genius for reaching a multi-level audience."[19]

Undercover policemen were also in attendance at the Judson. Four days into the show, the church was raided. Gross's contribution was confiscated; organizers Ringgold, Toche, and Hendricks were arrested. At an emergency meeting called to discuss a legal defense strategy, Flo Kennedy informed artists they were "one of the most niggerized groups in the world." She was glad to see them "finally getting off their asses." (After factional feuding broke out, she added, "Remind me to talk about horizontal hostility as the pathology of oppressed people.")

The People's Flag Show was a scandal. Still, the great art crime of the

---

sexual intercourse, Muehl's naked performers made much of extracting and inserting various objects into available vaginas. There was also a certain amount of mutual flagellation. Two male performers urinated on one of the women and the piece reached its climax when a live chicken was ripped apart and possibly devoured. Charlotte Moorman, nude for the occasion, held a single note on her cello for twenty minutes.

19 Lester's article, published in the *Times* "Arts and Leisure" section, argued that advanced theater groups of the '60s (the Living Theatre, Performance Group, and Open Theater) had been eclipsed by the more vital and genuinely apocalyptic theater found in the streets. Hoffman had "culled the esoteric concepts formulated by Dada and Surrealist artists at the beginning of the century and worked over for years in East Village lofts and West Coast workshops and made them relevant to an audience of millions." Lester credited Hoffman with the major role in five Theater of the Apocalypse masterworks—raining money on the Stock Exchange, levitating the Pentagon, fomenting the Grand Central Station police riot, orchestrating the Yippie Festival of Life in Chicago and starring in the follow-up conspiracy trial. Hoffman, she declared, was "nothing short of what Artaud [that name again!] described as the ideal director of a brilliant nonverbal theater—'a kind of manager of magic, a master of sacred ceremonies.'"

fall season was committed by the fifty-seven-year-old painter and New York School titan Philip Guston. Opening at the posh Fifty-Seventh Street Marlborough gallery on October 17, the same day that the Beatles' *White Album* was introduced as evidence at the Manson trial, Guston's new paintings were no less shocking. Guston, a much-admired Abstract Expressionist with a reputation second only to Willem de Kooning's, had abruptly reverted to the social realism of his youth, albeit with a difference.

Painted in a style that looked back to Krazy Kat but also forward to R. Crumb, Guston's new canvases were populated by cartoony hooded figures suggestive of Ku Klux Klansmen; Hilton Kramer was disgusted. His irate review, headlined A MANDARIN PRETENDING TO BE A STUMBLEBUM, sneered that Guston, an artist who "occupied a special place in the esteem of those who found in the more painterly aspects of the New York School a satisfaction almost more religious than aesthetic," had opportunistically recast himself as an urban primitive if not "a great big lovable dope."

10

In a way, Guston's defection rhymed with Rothko's suicide. Indeed, Marlborough's next show, opening the same night the police raided the Judson, was Rothko's first posthumous exhibition.

It had been a grim year. Death bells were tolling, not just for the art world. There were now close to 50,000 American fatal casualties in Vietnam. The ongoing bombing in Laos and Cambodia had killed some hundreds of thousands of civilians. Four student protestors were shot dead at Kent State, Ohio, and another two at Jackson State, Mississippi, followed by six more fatalities during a two-day collective rebellion in Augusta, Georgia. Jimi Hendrix choked to death in late summer, Janis Joplin overdosed in early fall. (About this time, Andrew Noren was busted bringing pot into Canada and was sentenced to seven years in prison, ultimately serving a bit more than a year.)

The My Lai Massacre trial began on November 17. Around Thanksgiving, Albert Ayler's body washed up on the Brooklyn side of the East River. He was thirty-four. Unstable and depressed, Ayler blamed himself for his brother Donald's breakdown after he had dropped him as a trumpet player. Ayler almost certainly took his own life but, as with Hendrix, who was being tracked by the FBI's Cointelpro and the CIA's Operation CHAOS, and whose disgruntled manager had Mob connections, Ayler's death inspired conspiracy theories: The FBI assassinated him. Mafia hitmen threw him in the river, tied to a jukebox because he refused to make more rock 'n' roll records for Impulse! (which had canceled his contract).

The Beatles had broken up and yet the year ended with a remarkable LP to which two of them, John Lennon and Ringo Starr, contributed. *Yoko Ono/Plastic Ono Band* was released in mid-December. Howard Smith's "Scenes," which had covered John and Yoko on a regular basis for the past two-and-a-half years, tried to prepare their fans. The LP "will most likely be panned—everything she's done since she's been with John has been put down."

As expected, the LP was attacked and ridiculed. Jazz critic Don Heckman's *New York Times* appraisal of the Beatles' post-Beatles LPs, dismissed Ono's album in a one-sentence paragraph: "Yoko Ono's music consists almost entirely of wailing vocal sounds accompanied by frenzied, but essentially rather simple-minded backup rhythms. A little of it goes a long way. Too long."

Few commented on the excellence of her accompaniment—Lennon's guitar, the rhythm bass played by Klaus Voorman, a friend of the Beatles since their Hamburg days, and particularly the perfection of Ringo's rock 'n' roll beat. Lester Bangs's knowledgeable take in *Rolling Stone* was the exception. "Give it a try," he advised readers. "There's something happening here." There was: the LP represented the culmination of Ono's long and winding road from John Cage's class to Chambers Street loft concerts through Fluxus notoriety to counterculture stardom.[20]

On the other hand, *New Morning*, Bob Dylan's quickly released, optimistically titled, and mediocre follow-up to *Self Portrait*, had been gratefully received as a return to form. "You walk down Eighth Street and the face is everywhere," Lucian K. Truscott IV, who regarded *Self Portrait* as "an exquisite and unique musical statement," reported in the *Voice*. NEW DYLAN the magic-marked signs say and there he is." Dylan's expression was "squinting and wary," the LP cover as "careful and understated" as

20 Mekas, who knew Ono from her early Flux days, was pleased to promote her and Lennon as filmmakers, devoting his first column of 1971 to their recent show at the Elgin, which included two of Ono's most powerful pieces, *Fly* (45 minutes of a fly crawling over a nude female torso) and *Rape* (a feature in which a camera-crew relentlessly documented an increasingly disturbed woman): "They are neither fiction, nor documentaries, nor poems," Mekas wrote. "They are film-objects."

the music inside. *Rolling Stone* atoned for Greil Marcus's pan with Ralph Gleason's panegyric, excitedly headlined, WE'VE GOT DYLAN BACK AGAIN.

Taking *New Morning* for a sign, Gleason had a fantasy that all the cars on I-80 were tuned to the Bay Area's community rock station and "the Dylan album was blowing their minds that very minute and I looked at the drivers as they went past me and they had smiles on their faces . . . This is a hopeful album and my God how we need it." The Weather Underground picked up on the sentiment too, titling their latest communique, published in the December 17 *Rat*, "New Morning—Changing Weather."

11

The desire for a Collective Drama took other forms. Opening at the New Yorker Theater in mid-October, Robert Kramer's *Ice* dramatized a New Left fantasy of urban guerrillas in armed struggle against a near-future fascist Amerikkka. Heavy on plot but light on exposition, it was a movie of endless debates and paralyzing meetings, set on what might be a single violent night.

The unbilled amateur cast was populated largely by Kramer's friends and associates. His producers David and Barbara Stone and Dan Talbot, at whose theater the movie opened, were visible in the crowd. Pushing the movie toward psychodrama, the filmmaker gave himself a role. Familiar locations included the New Yorker Book Shop (on West Eighty-Ninth Street, around the corner from the theater), the courtyard of the massive Belnord apartments a few blocks away and, downtown, once-controversial Washington Square Village. As a New York film, *Ice*, capped the period of the underground 16mm narratives: on one hand, fueled by the passionate world-changing idealism advanced in Jonas Mekas's *Guns of the Trees*; on the other, haunted by the solitary estrangement characterizing Peter Goldman's $1,600 production *Echoes of Silence*—a film Mekas had hailed as a major debut after it screened at the Tek in February 1965.

Kramer, who was not yet thirty when *Ice* appeared at the 1970 Cannes Film Festival, grew up privileged, the son of a wealthy Park Avenue cardiologist. Educated at Swarthmore and Stanford, he joined SDS and worked with Tom Hayden as a community organizer in Newark's Black ghetto, appearing briefly in *The Troublemakers*, an hour-long documentary by Norm Fruchter and Robert Machover—before embarking in

1966 on his first feature, *In the Country*, a glacially paced consideration of an alienated, privileged white radical. Kramer's second film, *The Edge*, shot in mid-1967, elaborated on the subject: a not-so-clandestine group of armchair anarchists and anti-war activists are confounded when a member of their group announces his plan to assassinate President Johnson. The tone is both detached and paranoid, with Kramer's camera mimicking presumed police surveillance.

One of Newsreel's founding members, Kramer was further radicalized by Columbia and Chicago and became the group's most vociferous polemicist, leading a campaign against the 1968 New York Film Festival for its elitism. A 1968 manifesto (published not in the underground press but highbrow *Film Quarterly*) argued for hard propaganda: "Changing minds, altering consciousness, seems to us to come through confrontations, not out of sweet/reasonable conversations." *Ice* was already in the planning stage; Kramer began filming after the NYFF. If the movie was designed to fulfill Newsreel's revolutionary mission, it inspired no small amount of grumbling among Kramer's Newsreel colleagues once it became known that, thanks in part to a recommendation from Dan Talbot, rich kid Kramer had received a $15,000 grant from the American Film Institute.

Ice was completed in late 1969 and, unable to find a distributor, had its premiere at Cannes in May 1970. Amos Vogel, who covered the festival for the *Voice*, reported that among the several American political films shown, one of which was the Last Poets vehicle *Right On!*, *Ice* was "unquestionably" the most important: "A startling microcosm of personalities, tendencies, and hang-ups of today's New Left projected into a very possible future."

Kramer already enjoyed a French reputation. The October 1968 issue of *Cahiers du Cinema* was devoted to the new American cinema of John Cassavetes, Shirley Clarke, Andy Warhol, and Robert Kramer while, perhaps recognizing affinities to his own *Paris Belongs to Us*, Jacques Rivette declared *The Edge* his favorite film of 1968. Stuart Byron, a young, hip industry savant, noted in his *Village Voice* review of *Ice* that, if Kramer was well regarded by some American "elements," *The Edge* had established him in "nearly all elements in France (including such right-wing Hollywood loving critics as Jean Douchet) as the most important American director of narrative cinema after the Penn-Kubrick-Peckinpah generation."

Politically, *The Edge* represented an earlier stage of development than *Ice*, which, a thought experiment addressed to the Movement, made even as SDS fractured, opens with a meteorological report. ("You don't need a weatherman . . .") The movie's first half is organizational: Characters, most of whom are revolutionaries and potential fellow travelers, hold meetings (public and private), conduct interviews (formal and informal) and seek information.

A radical film is being made (in the Newsreel office). Amid the props of the Bread and Puppet Theater, radical theater is being discussed (with Saul Gottlieb). Many conversations concern a vague Spring Offensive that will coordinate various groups: the Women's, White Student, Black and Spanish-speaking Unions, the Film Division, and Deserters. (Gays are conspicuously absent.)

Characters are not easily distinguished (there are no point-of-view shots). The lighting is flat; the indifferently miked dialogue is not only oblique but hard to hear. Scenes are often a single take and Kramer characteristically joins one in media res. The focus on banal detail reminded Byron of the French "new novel" of Marguerite Duras and Alan Robbe-Grillet. As with *The Edge*, he noted, *Ice* presented "a dramatic progression within an anti-dramatic structure."

Like *The Edge*, perhaps even more, *Ice* verged on collective psychodrama. Are these angst-ridden revolutionaries role-playing? And are these amateur actors role-playing at playing a role in the moment? Beginning with a sequence in which a courier goes about her various missions in midtown Manhattan in the guise of a proper young lady, Kramer's urban guerrillas seem to have cast themselves in *The Battle of Algiers*. Her purposeful character might be planting bombs.[21]

The film's second half is devoted to the Spring Offensive. Characters continue to argue and even hector each other. Meetings become more like encounter-group sessions. As did Godard in *La Chinoise*, Kramer begins interpolating slogans: WE MUST NEGATE THE PRESENT IN ALL ITS FORMS. (This followed by some negative images.) The women's group is

21 An uncanny echo of Jane Alpert, who, on a mission to plant a bomb in the Federal Building on Foley Square, set out with fifteen sticks of dynamite in a large purse shoplifted from a midtown department store. "I boarded a bus heading downtown. I was wearing a white A-line dress, kid gloves (to avoid leaving fingerprints), and a touch of make-up. I looked as if I were going to a business lunch or matinee." Of course, Alpert was modeling herself on the female terrorists in *The Battle of Algiers*.

making bombs. A government official is assassinated. There are shootouts in Washington Square Village. Counter-revolutionary vigilantes assault and seemingly castrate a radical (played by Kramer). The revolutionaries liberate a prison and summarily shoot a designated "rat."

The guerrillas are acting in concert with the Mexican Liberation Front. Meanwhile, their group is approached by some opportunistic information specialists who want to make common cause. Kramer's despairing character starts shooting junk. Couples are too nervous to have sex. A revolutionary threatens to shoot his father for refusing to shelter a badly wounded comrade. One of the group's leaders is killed, another survives. The movie ends as self-reflexively as it began with an agitprop cartoon, presumably produced by the Newsreel group.

Dramatizing the difficulty in making a revolution, *Ice* can be understood as Kramer's missive to his comrades. By then, however, the filmmaker had moved on. Before *Ice* opened, Kramer withdrew to a commune in Vermont, announcing that he was no longer making films. The *New York Times* was respectful if unenthusiastic. Vincent Canby called *Ice* "an awfully proud and humorless film." Roger Greenspun felt the movie demonstrated that "revolution, like everything else we do, lives in our awareness as a succession of personal relationships." In a thoughtful *New York Review of Books* essay that covered all manner of counterculture productions, Elizabeth Hardwick, a writer of an age to remember the 1930s and '40s, found it interesting that *Ice* felt "old-fashioned," something that might have been produced by doctrinaire Maoists or the Progressive Labor Party and, anything but with-it, spared viewers "endless fornications and commune banalities."

On the other hand, *Ice* was excoriated by politically committed critics. Writing in *Film Quarterly*, Berkeley-based James Roy MacBean, a prominent exegete of the new Godard, called it apolitical and irrational. Essentially a paranoid thriller in the tradition of *Fantomas* and Fritz Lang's *Dr. Mabuse* (or, unmentioned, Rivette), *Ice* was "more of a science-fiction horror film than a political film" and, despite its documentary style, a personal expression of the filmmaker's "fantasies and fears about revolution."

Alienation is a given. Kramer's revolutionaries are burdened by a self-important sense of mission. Their way of life was both unattractive and elitist and, considering that the state's vastly superior power is never acknowledged, pathologically self-destructive. Joan Mellen, who reviewed

Ice at length in *Cineaste*, called it "a depressing spectacle of New Left self-indulgence," noting that "the boredom generated by this overlong film, the endless droning of ideology and rhetoric bespeak a sense of self defeat."

12

Was *Ice* masochistic wish fulfillment or a frantic attempt to ward off the inevitable? *Commune*, still in rehearsal, wanted to live as though the day were here or at least understand the impulse.

Richard Schechner drolly described his production as "several well-known scenes enacted after supper by the youth of our nation" and then, portentously speaking for a younger generation, "the play about Middle America by the children of Middle America—no copouts, no kidding."

Throughout the fall midterm election season, with students regularly attacked by Republican politicians, the play was workshopped at five New England colleges. Opening in late December, the production attracted much respectful attention. If *Dionysus in '69* had been a quintessential expression of 1968, what did *Commune* have to say about the current zeitgeist?

Incorporating bits of the Bible, *Moby Dick*, and *The Tempest*, *Commune* drew more topically on the My Lai Massacre trial of Lieutenant William Calley (which began on November 17) and most heavily on the *Rolling Stone*'s Manson Family report. *Commune* would be revised throughout its six-month run at the Performing Garage but the Tate murders were the central strand, and the play ended with the arrival of Tate's husband Roman Polanski at the murder house.

As with *Dionysus*, there was no proscenium although there was a "rolling, rippling stage—used to simulate hills, and seas, a burial ditch in Vietnam." Spectators scaled ladders to perch on narrow, multi-level wooden platforms that struck one participant as "a child's climbing gym." Even more than in *Dionysus*, the audience was encouraged—and even forced—to participate. "One is expected to leave a topcoat on the second floor, then stand in a long line on Wooster Street before being admitted to the auditorium, five at a time," wrote the critic for the soon to fold *Newark Evening News*.

Once admitted, audience members ducked beneath an American flag and then, according to Richard Gilman who wrote it up the *Drama Review*, were "*ordered*" to remove their shoes and add them to a communal pile. Walter Kerr ended his non-review by recalling that "the last thing I saw as I left was my colleague Mel Gussow, limping about the floor in search of his other shoe." (Gussow was unenthused but not hostile, praising the space more than the play.)

The event began slowly with the nine (later six) members of the company strolling about or crawling through the audience and singing the "Songs of the First Encounter," mainly "The Big Rock Candy Mountain" (a turn-of-the-twentieth-century hobo ditty that had been sanitized for Baby Boom children). The songs segued into individual reminiscences chanted by members of the group. A day at a western ranch featured a shoot-out that became a pieta.

The Manson murders surfaced for the first time, followed by a jam session featuring the late eighteenth-century hymn "Bound for the Promised Land." The Statue of Liberty (Joan MacIntosh) appeared reciting Emma Lazarus's poem in a thick Brooklyn accent and then turned into a cheerleader who inspired the rest of the cast to run a slow-motion Rat Race and frolic in a wading pool.

The aquatic orgy inevitably brought back the Manson Family and inspired the cast to deliver their individual Death Raps. A mock revival meeting again segued to the Manson Family and then into the My Lai Massacre. Some nights the audience was invited to participate, an echo of Schechner's 1967 guerrilla theater piece, and the play stopped until they agreed to become culpable. Finally, the Tate murders were recounted in gory detail to end with a Polanski surrogate being asked about the role of the artist today. Long pause followed by, "Yes, yes of course."

Uptown critics were not impressed. Rather than engage, *New York*'s John Simon turned a meaningless phrase: *Commune* had "the shape a vacuum would have if a vacuum had a shape." Writing in *Women's Wear Daily*, former *Voice* classical music critic Martin Gottfried, so taken only months before with *The Life and Times of Sigmund Freud*, found *Commune* "intellectually insipid and physically flabby"—a self-parody that swiped bits from Grotowski, the Living Theatre, the Open Theater, Daytop Village, and *Dionysus*, as well as *Rolling Stone*. But, writing for the *Voice*, Gottfried's brother-in-law John Lahr called *Commune* the Performance Group's most courageous production. "I have seen *Commune* three times, it improves with each viewing," he wrote, confessing that it was only on the third time that he willed himself to participate.

A reviewer for the *Daily Worker* appreciated the play's critical stance, albeit noting that the cast was all white. One of the few critics to address *Commune*'s dark heart, Elizabeth Hardwick found it disconcerting to find a mutant tendency like the Manson Family normalized, "caged in hymn-singing and revivalism—a quilt-and-sampler Middle America on hallucinogenic drugs." On the other hand, *EVO*'s critic P. J. O'Rourke praised *Commune* for its "non-exploitative interpretation of the Manson business." While the counterculture was still trying to wrap its collective head around the Mansons or even, in extreme cases, exonerate them, the Performance Group took the Family as a genuine American phenomenon. O'Rourke jokingly invoked W. B. Yeats: "What rough beast slouches through SoHo to perform at 8:00 p.m. Friday through Saturday?"

What indeed? *Commune*, like *Ice*, was meditating on something. Alejandro Jodorowsky's *El Topo* (The Mole), an obscure Mexican movie and a third single-noun narrative, which began showing midnights at the Elgin around the time *Commune* opened, was creating something—namely a religious ritual.

13

Jodorowsky came to New York in November with a print of his new "Zen Buddhist Western." The premiere, following a Sunday noon service at which he spoke, was at Saint Clement's Church (home of the American Place Theatre) on the western edge of West Forty-Sixth Street.

El Topo was shown twice, as was *Fando and Lis*. Not long after neophyte distributor Alan Douglas (the record producer who recorded the Last Poets, put out a posthumous Lenny Bruce LP, and put together Jimi Hendrix's live album *Band of Gypsys*) organized a private screening at the Museum of Modern Art. Elgin manager Ben Barenholtz came, saw, and booked the film.

Fortuitously, the Elgin was hosting Jonas Mekas's *7¾ New York Film Festival*, featuring new or newish films by Kenneth Anger, Stan Brakhage, and Andy Warhol, as well as Jack Smith's (formerly *No*) *Slave President*. Three of the seven programs were devoted to films by John Lennon and Yoko Ono. Barenholtz took advantage of the hippie crowds to announce an added feature. Starting December 18, *El Topo* would be playing midnights because, as put by a single ad in the *Voice*, it was "too heavy to be shown any other way."[22]

22 Midnight attractions were in vogue that month. Jerzy Grotowski was back, delivering a midnight lecture at Town Hall. That same weekend, new underground movies were having midnight screenings at a short-lived SoHo venue, the Universal Mutant Theater at 141 Prince Street. The key film was Ira Cohen's twenty-minute

Before turning to movies, Jodorowsky, forty-one, had a rich career in avant-garde theater, shuttling between Paris and Mexico City. Together with Arrabal and cartoonist Roland Topor, he formed the neo-surrealist, Artaud-influenced Panic Movement. His four-hour *Sacramental Melodrama*, staged in May 1965, was the sensation of Jean-Jacques Lebel's second *Festival of Free Expression*, a weeklong extravaganza that included readings by Ted Joans and Lawrence Ferlinghetti, as well a piece with Charlotte Moorman immersed in a barrel of water as Nam June Paik dropped his pants. Jodorowsky went a bit further. Accompanied by a six-piece rock band and a cast of bare-breasted women (each painted a different color), he cavorted atop a smashed automobile, sacrificed two geese, broke plates, then had himself stripped of his leather outfit and whipped, dancing with a honey-covered woman, two snakes taped to his chest.

Only slightly less lurid, *El Topo* was a ragtag circus sideshow, replete with dwarves and amputees, wandering through a fantasy realm part Tolkien's Middle Earth, part *Wild Bunch* bloodbath. It was also a psychodrama. Jodorowsky not only wrote, directed, and scored the picture but also played the black-clad eponymous holy killer-gunslinger saint who defeats the Four Masters of the Desert and then, betrayed by a treacherous lesbian, goes underground and shaves his head to be the clownish leader of the freaks and ultimately front their climactic revolution.

Cosmic journey, spiritual initiation, Dionysian gorefest—in short, a Trip—it was the movie version of what Elenore Lester called the Theater of the Apocalypse, addressing both the counterculture's love of the arcane and its collective paranoia. Out of the streets and into the theater! Its audience swelled by repeat viewers and a stream of converts, *El Topo* played seven shows a week starting at midnight, 1:00 a.m. Fridays and

---

Invasion of the Thunderbolt Pagoda, which, although shot in 1968, shared many of *El Topo*'s tropes, albeit in a more light-hearted manner. Basically a languidly opiated costume ball described by Cohen as "an alchemical journey born of our common consciousness," the film offers an assortment of masked and painted subterraneans, some sporting outsize elf ears, lolling about a candlelit, Mylar-lined set, blowing soap bubbles and nibbling majoun. The film is saved from preciosity by Angus MacLise's improvised pan-piping, tabla-tapping, creature-yipping score; MacLise's vaguely menacing masterpiece of Tibetan-Moroccan-Druidic trance music blossoms in conjunction with the exotic smorgasbord served at Cohen's psychedelicatessen. "No minimalism here," according to the filmmaker, "a maximalist adventure."

Saturdays, a remarkable word-of-mouth success dependent on a demographic with cheap rents and no cause to wake up early for work.

The *Village Voice* review by Glenn O'Brien, the twenty-three-year-old associate editor of Andy Warhol's *Inter/View*, captured the moment. As the credits appear on the screen, the audience settles into rapt anticipation: "They've come to see the light—and the screen before them is illuminated by an abstract landscape of desert and sky—and the ritual begins again . . . Jodorowsky is here to confess; the young audience is here for communion."

Assuming the artist, born to Russian-Jewish Communist parents in Iquique, Chile, to be Catholic, O'Brien explains that "as a good Catholic, as only a fallen-away Catholic can be, Jodorowsky makes his ritual perform the universe." Moreover, he continued, *El Topo* was a way of life—not least for its maker. "When El Topo rapes a girl, Jodorowsky really rapes her," O'Brien explained. "Jodorowsky is an actor in search of real actions who refuses to distinguish between any of the moments of himself."[23]

Not long after, Peter Schjeldahl shouldered the task of explaining *El Topo* to the readers of the *New York Times* (which had investigated but not reviewed the film). It was, he asserted, "a monumental work of filmic art," "vastly complex, genuinely profound." Jodorowsky agreed, with a caveat: "If you are great, *El Topo* is a great picture; if you are limited, *El Topo* is limited."

El Topo may have been the quintessential counterculture film, but the counterculture was not entirely behind it. "I don't know why people are going around saying *El Topo* is the greatest movie ever made," *EVO*'s new film critic "Honest" Bob Singer wondered. Singer read the film as political pandering: "When the 'Colonel' comes out of a doorway followed by a herd of swine, all the radicals snicker," he wrote, adding that "Jodorowsky's mixture of revolutionary propaganda with Christian/Zen evangelism comes down to an apocalyptic *High Noon* wherein he personally frees the people and dispatches the neocolonialist blasphemers."

23 Jodorowsky's insistence on *El Topo*'s verisimilitude came back to haunt him decades later in 2019 when his claim to have raped the actress Mara Lorenzios on camera resulted in the cancellation of a planned retrospective at El Museo del Barrio in New York. Asked for a statement, he explained that his boast was a matter of "words not facts": "Surrealist publicity in order to enter the film world from a position of obscurity."

The movie cast its spell all winter and spring. Projected seven midnights a week, the ritual coincided with a Chicago jury's convicting Dave Dellinger, Rennie Davis, Tom Hayden, Abbie Hoffman, and Jerry Rubin of crossing state lines with intent to incite a riot. It was playing when Barbara Rubin had a Hasidic wedding in Far Rockaway (guests included Allen Ginsberg and Bob Dylan), when Andy Warhol shot the last scenes of *Women in Revolt* (Jackie Curtis and Paul Morrissey nearly coming to blows on the set), when Diane Arbus's photographs were printed in *Artforum* (her famous portrait of a youth in a straw boater wearing a "Bomb Hanoi" pin on the cover), and the AWC protested the Guggenheim's censorship of Hans Haacke.

El Topo was still packing the Elgin in June when, distribution rights bought from Alan Douglas by John Lennon's manager Allen Klein, it was yanked in advance of a planned Broadway opening. (As if to mark the end of an era, a few weeks later the Fillmore East closed for good.) Materializing a year after the discovery of the Manson Family, seven months after the killings at Kent State, three months after the death of Jimi Hendrix, and two months after *Ice*, *El Topo* served as a form of collective solace. Asked if he thought viewers should be high when watching his movie, Jodorowsky replied, "Yes, yes, yes, yes. I'd demand them to be"—not perhaps what he told the Saint Clement's congregation.

14

I vastly preferred Sergio Leone's spaghetti westerns to Jodorowsky's peyote variant. Yet I sat through *El Topo* twice. Those were the days of acid fascism. Was I great or limited? Was this movie as stupefying as it seemed?

A mysterious fate brought me into contact with Jodorowsky that summer, the acme of his counterculture prestige. Somehow, he and I were both present at a living room lecture, just above the East Village, in which *EVO* cartoonist Art Spiegelman presented his analysis of "The Master Race," a 1955 comic book story by Bernard Krigstein that concerns the chance meeting of a concentration camp survivor and his onetime guard on a New York City subway. Even less likely, I stumbled upon Jodorowsky a few days later browsing the underground comics in a midtown bookstore.

Introducing myself, I volunteered the information that I would soon be going to Mexico (where I planned to stay for as long as I could make $500 last). "Incredible!" he exclaimed. "You must look me up!" When I naïvely wondered where I might find him he assured me "not to worry—everybody knows me there!" And indeed, when I asked the student residents of my Mexico City flop they were incredulous: "You know the Maestro!"

I subsequently journeyed to the depths of Chapultepec Park, where Jodorowsky was staging his psychedelic version of *Alice in Wonderland*. Maybe not so thrilled to find (hey, remember) me plus two traveling companions (oh, hello), the expansive Maestro did a good job concealing it. What, he wondered, did we want to do? Did we want to eat, to drink, to fuck? Uh, dinner sounds cool, thanks.

Jodorowsky took us out, along with his wife—who, in the hip parlance of the day, I noted was "a frizzy-haired chick, pure St. Mark's Place." Table conversation was surreal. I was reading *Impressions of Africa*. "You know Raymond Roussel?" Jodorowsky bellowed. "How do you know of him? He is fantastic! Incredible!" As if on cue, the clean-cut group of American kids at an adjacent table leaped to their feet and burst into song:

Up! Up with people!
You meet 'em wherever you go,
Up! Up with People!
They're the best kind of folks we know.

An amiable host, Jodorowsky plied us with *toritos* and showed off some Danish porn, snatching it nervously back when we began to riff on it in public. Outside, he paused to relieve himself against a parked car. "Look, he has made three streams," Mrs. J remarked proudly as we staggered toward a disco named Paz y Amor. (Not just three streams, the evening provided material for three months of stoned impersonations and the creation of a character named Josef von Chicletz: "Three streams! I . . . am . . . the Maker of the Topo!")

I was still bumming around Mexico when Diane Arbus committed suicide in her Westbeth apartment and John and Yoko took a place just around the corner on Bank Street, when the upstate Attica prison exploded (and Sam Melville was killed) and when *WR: Mysteries of the Organism* had its premiere at the New York Film Festival. I returned just after Edie Sedgwick died of a drug overdose in Los Angeles, which was just before *Women in Revolt* had its premiere in LA under the title *Andy Warhol's Women*. (Two months later it would open in New York.)

In January 1972, *Flaming Creatures* had its first public screening in New York since March 1964. Back in town, I saw it, wrote an appreciation, and, as *EVO* was on the verge of folding, sent it to the *Village Voice*. To my surprise the article ran in the February 3, 1972, issue and, although I could not imagine it then, initiated my nearly four-decade association with the *Voice*. In a sense, it planted the seed for this book, which I consider a memoir, although not mine.

Bibliography

Reportage

Sidney Bernard, *This Way to the Apocalypse* (New York: The Smith, 1969)

------------------, *Witnessing: The Seventies* (New York: Horizon Press, 1977)

Naomi Feigelson, *Hippies, Yippies, Others* (New York: Funk & Wagnalls, 1970)

Joe Flaherty, *Managing Mailer* (New York: Berkeley Medallion, 1971)

Richard Goldstein, *Reporting the Counterculture* (Boston: Unwin Hyman, 1989)

John Gruen, *The New Bohemia* (New York: Grosset & Dunlap, 1967)

Tom Hayden, *Rebellion in Newark: Official Violence and Ghetto Response* (New York: Vintage, 1967)

Jill Johnston, *Marmalade Me* (New York: Dutton, 1971)

Norman Mailer, *Miami and the Siege of Chicago* (New York: Signet, 1968)

Don McNeill, *Moving Through Here* (New York: Lancer, 1970)

Jonas Mekas, *Movie Journal: The Rise of a New American Cinema, 1959–1971* (New York: Collier Books, 1972)

Francis J. Rigney and L. Douglas Smith, *The Real Bohemia* (New York: Basic Books, 1961)

A. M. Rosenthal and Arthur Gelb, eds., *The Night the Lights Went Out* (New York: Signet, 1965)

Michael Smith, *Theatre Journal: Reviews from the* Village Voice (Silverton, OR: First Books, 2015)

Memoirs and Manifestos

Jane Alpert, *Growing Up Underground* (New York: William Morrow, 1981)

Maya Angelou, *The Collected Autobiographies* (New York: Random House, 2004)

Gordon Ball, *66 Frames* (Minneapolis, MN: Coffee House Press, 1999)

-------------, *East Hill Farm: Seasons with Allen Ginsberg* (Berkeley, CA: Counterpoint, 2011)

Amiri Baraka, *The Autobiography of LeRoi Jones* (Chicago: Lawrence Hill Books, 1997)

Carol Bergé, ed., *Light Years: An Anthology on Sociocultural Happenings (Multimedia in the East Village, 1960–1966)* (New York: Spuyten Duyvil, 2010)

John Cale and Victor Bockris, *What's Welsh for Zen: The Autobiography of John Cale* (London: Bloomsbury, 1999)

Diane di Prima, *Recollections of My Life as a Woman* (New York: Viking, 2001)

Bob Dylan, *Chronicles Volume One* (New York: Simon & Schuster, 2004)

Ross Firestone, ed., *Getting Busted: Personal Experiences of Arrest, Trial, and Prison* (New York: Douglas Books, 1970)

Richard Goldstein, *Another Little Piece of My Heart: My Life of Rock and Revolution in the '60s* (New York: Bloomsbury, 2015)

Steven Heller, *Growing Up Underground: A Memoir of Counterculture New York* (Princeton, NJ: Princeton Architectural Press, 2022)

Ken Jacobs, *I Walked into My Shortcomings: Writings, Interviews, Teaching*, ed. William Rose (London: The Visible Press, 2026)

Hettie Jones, *How I Became Hettie Jones* (New York: Grove Press, 1996)

Yayoi Kusama, *Infinity Net*, trans. Ralph McCarthy (London: Tate, 2011)

James McCourt, *Queer Street* (New York: W. W. Norton & Co., 2003)

Jonas Mekas, *I Seem to Live: The New York Diaries* v.1 (Liepzig: Spector Books, 2019)

Osha Neumann, *Up Against the Wall Motherfucker: A Memoir of the '60s with Notes for the Next Time* (New York: Seven Stories Press, 2008)

Larry Rivers, *What Did I Do? The Unauthorized Autobiography* (New York: HarperCollins, 1992)

Trina Robbins, *Last Girl Standing* (Seattle, WA: Fantagraphic Books, 2017)

Suze Rotolo, *A Freewheelin' Time: A Memoir of Greenwich Village in the Sixties* (New York: Broadway Books, 2008)

Ed Sanders, *Fug You: An Informal History of the Peace Eye Bookstore, the Fuck You Press, the Fugs, and Counterculture in the Lower East Side* (Philadelphia, PA: Da Capo, 2011)

Susan Sherman, *America's Child: A Woman's Journey Through the Radical Sixties* (Willimantic, CN: Curbstone Press, 2007)

Jack Smith, *Wait for Me at the Bottom of the Pool: The Writings of Jack Smith*, J. Hoberman and Edward Leffingwell, eds. (London: Serpent's Tail, 1997)

Kristine Stiles, ed., *Correspondence Course: An Epistolary History of Carolee Schneemann and Her Circle* (Durham, NC: Duke University Press, 2010)

Ronald Sukenick, *Down and In: Life in the Underground* (New York: Beech Tree Books, 1987)

Andy Warhol and Pat Hackett, *POPism: The Warhol '60s* (New York: Harcourt Brace Jovanovich, 1980)

Jason Weiss, *Always in Trouble: An Oral History of ESP-Disk', the Most Outrageous Record Label in America* (Middletown, CN: Wesleyan University Press, 2012)

Biographies and Monographs

Lary Bloom, *Sol LeWitt: A Life of Ideas* (Middletown, CN: Wesleyan University Press, 2019)

Patricia Bosworth, *Diane Arbus* (New York: Norton, 1984)

Mel Clay, *Jazz, Jail and God: Impressionistic Biography of Bob Kaufman* (San Francisco, CA: Androgyne Books, 1987)

Alice Echols, *Scars of Sweet Paradise: The Life and Times of Janis Joplin* (New York: Metropolitan, 1999)

Albert Goldman with Lawrence Schiller, *Ladies and Gentlemen Lenny Bruce!!* (New York: Ballantine Books, 1974)

Axel Heil, Robert Fleck and Alyce Mahon, eds., *Jean-Jacques Lebel: Barricades* (Cologne, Germany: Walther Konig, 2014)

Craig B. Highberger, *Superstar in a Housedress: The Life and Legend of Jackie Curtis* (New York: Chamberlain Bros, 2005)

Carrie Lambert-Beatty, *Being Watched: Yvonne Rainer and the 1960s* (Cambridge, MA: MIT Press, 2008)

Ed Leffingwell, ed., *Flaming Creature: Jack Smith* (New York: PS 1 Museum, 1997)

Dennis McNally, *Desolate Angel: Jack Kerouac, the Beat Generation and America* (New York: Random House, 1979)

Barry Miles, *Ginsberg: A Biography* (New York: Viking, 1989)

Alexandra Munroe and Jon Hendricks, eds., *Yes: Yoko Ono* (New York: Japan Society/Abrams, 2000)

Leslie James Pickering, *Mad Bomber Melville* (Portland, OR: Arissa Media Group, 2007)

Joan Rothfuss, *Topless Cellist: The Improbable Life of Charlotte Moorman* (Cambridge, MA: MIT Press, 2014)

Michael Schumacher, *Dharma Lion: A Biography of Allen Ginsberg* (New York: St. Martin's Press, 1992)

Judith E. Stein, *Eye of the Sixties: Richard Bellamy and the Transformation of Modern Art* (New York: FSG, 2016)

John Szwed, *Cosmic Scholar: The Life and Times of Harry Smith* (New York: FSG, 2023)

Oliver Trager, *Dig Infinity: The Life and Art of Lord Buckley* (New York: Welcome Rain, 2002)

Jon Wiener, *Come Together: John Lennon in His Time* (New York: Random House, 1984)

Emmett Williams and Ann Noël, *Mr. Fluxus: A Collective Portrait of George Maciunas 1931–1978* (London: Thames and Hudson, 1997)

New York

Ada Calhoun, *St. Marks Is Dead* (New York: Norton, 2016)

Robert A. Caro, *The Power Broker: Robert Moses and the Fall of New York* (New York: Vintage, 1975)

Anthony Flint, *Wrestling with Moses* (New York: Random House, 2011)

Joshua B. Freeman, *Working Class New York* (New York: The New Press, 2000)

Tom Goyens, ed., *Radical Gotham* (Urbana: University of Illinois Press, 2017)

Charles Kaiser, *The Gay Metropolis 1940–1996* (Boston, MA: Houghton Mifflin, 1997)

Richard Kostelanetz, *SoHo: The Rise and Fall of an Artists' Colony* (New York: Routledge, 2003)

Fred W. McDarrah, *New York Scenes* (New York: Abrams, 2018)

Kembrew McLeod, *The Downtown Pop Underground* (New York: Abrams, 2019)

Christopher Mele, *Selling the Lower East Side* (Minneapolis: University of Minnesota Press, 2000)

Clayton Patterson, *Captured: A Film/Video History of the Lower East Side* (New York: Seven Stories, 2005)

Sherill Tippins, *Inside the Dream Palace: The Life and Times of New York's Legendary Chelsea Hotel* (New York: Houghton Mifflin Harcourt, 2013)

Cultural History

Sally Banes, *Greenwich Village 1963: Avant-Garde Performance and the Effervescent Body* (Durham, NC: Duke, 1993)

Ann Charters, ed., *Beat Down to Your Soul: What Was the Beat Generation?* (New York: Penguin, 2001)

Steven Clay and Rodney Phillips, *A Secret Location on the Lower East Side* (New York: NYPL/Granary Books, 1998)

Peter Doggett, *There's a Riot Going On: Revolutionaries, Rock Stars, and the Rise and Fall of the '60s* (Edinburgh, Scotland: Canongate Press, 2007)

Stephen R. Duncan, *The Rebel Café: Sex, Race, and Politics in Cold War America's Nightclub Underground* (Baltimore, MD: Johns Hopkins University Press, 2018)

Mary Gabriel, *Ninth Street Women* (New York: Little, Brown and Company, 2018)

Jörg Heiser, *Double Lives in Art and Pop Music* (Berlin: Sternberg Press, 2019)

J. Hoberman, *The Dream Life: Movies, Media and the Mythology of the Sixties* (New York: New Press, 2003)

Branden W. Joseph, *Beyond the Dream Syndicate: Tony Conrad and the Arts after Cage* (New York: Zone Books, 2008)

Daniel Kane, *All Poets Welcome: The Lower East Side Poetry Scene in the 1960s* (Berkeley: University of California Press, 2003)

Brenda Knight, *Women of the Beat Generation: The Writers, Artists and Muses at the Heart of a Revolution* (Berkeley, CA: Conari Press, 1996)

Richard Kostelanetz, *Metamorphosis in the Arts: A Critical History of the 1960s* (Brooklyn, NY: Assembling Press, 1980)

David Lehman, *The Last Avant-Garde: The Making of the New York School of Poets* (New York: Anchor Books, 1999)

Fred W. McDarrah, *Kerouac and Friends: A Beat Generation Album* (New York: William Morrow, 1985)

James Sampson Meyer, *Minimalism: Art and Polemics in the Sixties* (New Haven, CT: Yale University Press, 2001)

Nadja Millner-Larsen, *Up Against the Real: Black Mask from Art to Action* (Chicago, IL: University of Chicago Press, 2023)

Benjamin Piekut, *Experimentalism Otherwise: The New York Avant-Garde and Its Limits* (Berkeley: University of California Press, 2011)

Melissa Rachleff, *Inventing Downtown: Artist-Run Galleries in New York City 1952–1965* (New York: Grey Art Gallery, NYU/Delmonico Books, Prestel, 2017)

Ryan H. Walsh, *Astral Weeks: A Secret History of 1968* (New York: Penguin Press, 2018)

Counterculture

David Ally, *Make Love, Not War: The Sexual Revolution, An Unfettered History* (Boston, MA: Little Brown, 2000)

Bryan Burrough, *Days of Rage: America's Radical Underground, the FBI, and the Forgotten Age of Revolutionary Violence* (New York: Penguin Press, 2015)

Martin Duberman, *Stonewall* (New York: Dutton, 1993)

Christoph Grunenberg and Jonathan Harris, eds., *Summer of Love: Psychedelic Art, Social Crisis and Counterculture in the 1960s* (Liverpool, UK: Liverpool University Press, 2005)

R. Meltzer, *The Aesthetics of Rock* (New York: Something Else Press, 1970)

Abe Peck, *Uncovering the Sixties: The Life and Times of the Underground Press* (New York: Pantheon, 1985)

Geoffrey Rips, *The Campaign Against the Underground Press* (San Francisco, CA: City Lights, 1981)

Larry Sloman, *Steal This Dream* (New York: Doubleday, 1998)

Sean Stewart, *On the Ground: An Illustrated Anecdotal History of the Sixties Underground Press in the U.S.* (Oakland, CA: PM Press, 2011)

Film

Stephen Dwoskin, *Film Is: The International Free Cinema* (Woodstock, NY: Overlook Press, 1975)

Rachel Garfield and Henry K. Miller, eds., *Dwoskino: The Gaze of Stephen Dwoskin* (London: Lux, 2022)

J. Hoberman, *On Jack Smith's Flaming Creatures* (New York: Granary/Hips Road, 2001)

J. Hoberman and Jonathan Rosenbaum, *Midnight Movies* (New York: Harper & Row, 1982)

David James, ed., *To Free the Cinema: Jonas Mekas and the New York Underground* (Princeton, NJ: Princeton University Press, 1992)

---------------, ed., *Optic Antics: The Cinema of Ken Jacobs* (New York: Oxford, 2011)

Bill Landis, *Anger: The Unauthorized Biography* (New York: HarperCollins, 1995)

Scott MacDonald and Jacqueline Najuma Stewart, eds., *William Greaves: Filmmaking as Mission* (New York: Columbia University Press, 2022)

Sheldon Renan, *An Introduction to American Underground Film* (New York: Dutton, 1967)

Jim Shedden, ed., *Presence and Absence: The Michael Snow Project* (Toronto: Art Gallery of Ontario, 1995)

P. Adams Sitney, *Visionary Film* (New York: Oxford, 1974)

Gregory Zinman, *Making Images Move: Handmade Cinema and the Other Arts* (Oakland: University of California, 2020)

Jazz

Iain Anderson, *This is Our Music: Free Jazz, the Sixties, and American Culture* (Philadelphia, PA: University of Pennsylvania Press, 2007)

Gerald Horne, *Jazz Justice* (New York: Monthly Review Press, 2019)

LeRoi Jones, *Black Music* (New York: William Morrow, 1968)

Ashley Kahn, *The House That Trane Built: The Story of Impulse Records* (New York: Norton, 2007)

David Lee, *The Battle of the Five Spot* (Toronto, ON: Mercury Press, 2006)

Ingrid Monson, *Freedom Sounds: Civil Rights Call Out to Jazz and Africa* (New York: Oxford, 2007)

Scott Saul, *Freedom Is, Freedom Ain't: Jazz and the Making of the Sixties* (Cambridge, MA: Harvard University Press, 2003)

A. B. Spellman, *Four Lives in the Bebop Business* (New York: Pantheon, 1966)

John Szwed, *Space Is the Place: The Lives and Times of Sun Ra* (Durham, NC: Duke University Press, 2020)

Val Wilmer, *Jazz People* (Indianapolis, IN: Bobbs-Merrill, 1970)

-------------, *As Serious as Your Life: Black Music and the Free Jazz Revolution 1957–1977* (London: Serpents Tail, 2018)

Theater and Performance

Pierre Biner, *The Living Theatre* (New York: Horizon Press, 1972)

Stephen J. Bottoms, *Playing Underground: A Critical History of the 1960s Off-Off Broadway Movement* (Ann Arbor, MI: University of Michigan Press, 2004)

Stefan Brecht, *Queer Theatre* (Frankfurt am Main, Germany: Suhrkamp Verlag, 1978)

----------------, *The Bread and Puppet Theatre Volume One* (New York: Routledge, 1988)

Deborah R. Geis, ed., *Beat Drama: Playwrights and Performances of the* Howl *Generation* (London: Bloomsbury, 2016)

Mildred Glimcher, *Happenings: New York, 1959–1963* (New York: Monacelli Press, 2012)

Al Hansen, *A Primer of Happenings and Time/Space Art* (New York: Something Else Press, 1965)

David Kaufman, *Ridiculous! The Theatrical Life and Times of Charles Ludlam* (New York: Applause, 2002)

Richard Kostelanetz, *The Theatre of Mixed-Means* (New York: RK Editions, 1980)

----------------------, *On Innovative Performance(s): Three Decades of Recollections on Alternative Theater* (Jefferson, NC: McFarland & Company, 1994)

Henry Lesnick, *Guerrilla Street Theater* (New York: Avon, 1973)

Judith F. Rodenbeck, *Radical Prototypes: Allan Kaprow and the Invention of Happenings* (Cambridge, MA: MIT Press, 2011)

Arthur Sainer, *The Radical Theatre Notebook* (New York: Avon, 1975)

John Tytell, *The Living Theatre: Art, Exile, and Outrage* (New York: Grove Press, 1995)

Dylan, Greenwich Village, and the Folk Revival

Agnes "Sis" Cunningham and Gordon Friesen, *Red Dust and Broadsides: A Joint Autobiography* (Amherst: University of Massachusetts Press, 1999)

Peter D. Goldsmith, *Making People's Music: Moe Asch and Folkways Records* (Washington, DC: Smithsonian Institution Press, 1998)

Clinton Heylin, *The Double Life of Bob Dylan: A Restless, Hungry Feeling* (New York: Little, Brown and Company, 2022)

John Hughes, *Invisible Now: Bob Dylan in the 1960s* (New York: Routledge, 2013)

Aaron J. Leonard, *The Folk Singers: The FBI, the Folk Artists and the Suppression of the Communist Party USA 1939–1956* (London: Repeater Books, 2020)

Dennis McNally, *On Highway 61: Music, Race, and the Evolution of Cultural Freedom* (Berkeley, CA: Counterpoint, 2014)

Robert Shelton, *No Direction Home: The Life and Music of Bob Dylan* (Milwaukee, WI: Backbeat Books, 2011)

Terri Thal, *My Greenwich Village: Dave, Bob and Me* (Carmarthen, UK: McNidder & Grace, 2023)

Dave Van Ronk with Elijah Wald, *The Mayor of MacDougal Street* (Cambridge, MA: Da Capo, 2005)

Warhol, the Factory, and the Velvet Underground

Callie Angell, *Andy Warhol Screen Tests* (New York: Abrams, 2006)

Victor Bockris, *Warhol: The Biography* (London: Frederick Muller, 1989)

----------------- and Gerard Malanga, *Up-Tight: The Velvet Underground Story* (New York: Omnibus Press, 1983)

Dominique Carré, ed., *The Velvet Underground Experience* (Los Angeles, CA: Hat & Beard Press, 2018)

David Dalton and David McCabe, *A Year in the Life of Andy Warhol* (New York: Phaidon Press, 2003)

David Dalton and Tony Scherman, *Pop: The Genius of Andy Warhol* (New York: It Books, 2010)

Deborah Davis, *The Trip: Andy Warhol's Plastic Fantastic Cross-Country Adventure* (New York: Atria, 2015)

John G. Hanhardt, *The Films of Andy Warhol 1963–65* (New Haven, CT: Yale University Press, 2021)

Larissa Harris and Media Farzin, *13 Most Wanted Men: Andy Warhol and the 1964 New York World's Fair* (Queens, NY: Queens Museum, 2014)

Johan Kugelberg, *The Velvet Underground: New York Art* (New York: Rizzoli, 2009)

Jean Stein with George Plimpton, ed., *Edie: An American Biography* (New York: Alfred A. Knopf, 1982)

Ronald Tavel, *Andy Warhol's Ridiculous Screenplays* (Silverton, OR: Fast Books, 2015)

Lynne Tillman and Stephen Shore, *The Velvet Years: Warhol's Factory, 1965–67* (New York: Pavilion Books, 1995)

Steven Watson, *Factory Made: Warhol and the Sixties* (New York: Pantheon, 2003)

Reva Wolf, *Andy Warhol, Poetry, and Gossip in the 1960s* (Chicago, IL: University of Chicago Press, 1997)

Dissertations

Sarah Elise Archias, *The Body as a Material in the Early Performance Work of Carolee Schneemann, Yvonne Rainer, and Vito Acconci* (Berkeley: University of California Press, 2008)

William Shephard, *Group Dynamics and Evolution of Creative Choice in the Performance Group's New York Production of* Dionysus in '69 (Tallahassee, FL: Florida State University, 1984)

David C. Viola Jr., *Terrorism and the Response to Terrorism in New York City During the Long Sixties* (New York: CUNY Graduate Center, 2017)

Midori Yamamura, *Yayoi Kusama: Biography and Cultural Confrontation, 1945–1969* (New York: CUNY Graduate Center, 2012)

Source Notes

Abbreviations: *EVO* [*East Village Other*]; *FC* [*Film Culture*]; *FQ* [*Film Quarterly*]; LNS [Liberation News Service]; "MJ" ["Movie Journal"]; MoMA [Museum of Modern Art]; *NYH-T* [*New York Herald-Tribune*]; *NYFP* [*New York Free Press*]; *NYM* [*New York Mirror*]; *NYP* [*New York Post*]; *NYRB* [*New York Review of Books*]; *NYT* [*New York Times*]; *NYT* A&L [*New York Times* Arts & Leisure]; *PR* [*Partisan Review*]; *RS* [*Rolling Stone*]; *TDR* [*The Drama Review*]; "TJ" ["Theatre Journal"]; *Var* [*Variety*]; *VV* [*Village Voice*]

1. The Connections

1: Dean in radio transcript: wnyc.org/story/is-there-a-beat-generation; Wechsler in Marc D. Schleifer, "Kerouac, Amis, Wechsler, Montagu: The Beat Debated—Is It or Is It Not?" *VV* (11/19/58) p1f; Charles Poore, "Books of the Times," *NYT* (10/2/58); David Dempsey, "Diary of a Bohemian," *NYT* Book Review (2/23/58); Ginsberg, "The Dharma Bums," *VV* (11/12/58); Shattuck, "The Voice and the Beat," *VV* (10/29/58). FN: A. Lee, "The Subterraneans," *VV* (2/26/58).

2: Millstein, "Books of The Times" *NYT* (9/5/57) 27; Smith, "Off the Road, Into the Vanguard and Out," *VV* (12/25/57); Wakefield, "Kerouac at the Village Vanguard," *Nation* (1/4/58).

3: Ed Sanders, *Tales of Beatnik Glory* (New York: Stonehill, 1975) 15; Young told

Wilcock, "The Boom on Bleecker," *VV* (11/26/58); "Poetry: 'Entertainment?' Police Say 'Yes'! Issue Summons," *VV* (6/3/59); "main drag" in "Changing Neighborhood," *VV* (10/7/59), 1; Louis Calta, "Theatre: World of Narcotics Addicts," *NYT* (7/16/59); Tallmer, *VV* (7/22/59); letters *VV* (8/12 & 9/2/59); Brustein, "Junk and Jazz" in *Seasons of Discontent: Dramatic Opinions 1959-1965* (New York: Simon and Schuster, 1967), 23–6; Tynan, "After Hours," *Harper's* (April 1960); Atkinson, *NYT* (2/7/60); Rivers cited in John Tytell, *The Living Theatre: Art, Exile, and Outrage* (New York: Grove Press, 1995), 157; "spectators fainted" in Pierre Biner, *The Living Theatre* (New York: Horizon Press, 1972), 48. FN: Robert Alden, "Police Pose as Beatniks in Narcotics Raid" *NYT* (11/9/59).

4: Grooms in Melissa Rachleff, *Inventing Downtown: Artist-Run Galleries in New York City 1952-1965* (New York: Grey Art Gallery, New York University/Delmonico Books, Prestel, 2017), 247–8; members of Living Theatre puzzled in Judith F. Rodenbeck, *Radical Prototypes: Allan Kaprow and the Invention of Happenings* (Cambridge MA: MIT Press, 2011), 159-60; Livingston, "Miscellany: Mr. Kaprow's 18 Happenings," *VV* (10/7/59), 11; Delany in Gavin Butt, "Happenings in History, or, the Epistemology of the Memoir," *Oxford Art Journal* v24,#2 (2001), 113–26.

5: Mekas, "MJ," *VV* (11/18/59), "MJ," *VV* (1/27/60), "November 11, 1959," *I Seem to Live: The New York Diaries* v.1 (Liepzig: Spector Books, 2019), 217; Jacobs, "New York Filmmaker (2010)" and "Star Spangled to Death (2004)," *I Walked into My Shortcomings* (London: Visible Press, forthcoming), 26, 42; Mekas, "MJ," *VV* (11/18/59); "Squaresville U.S.A. vs Beatsville," *Life* (9/21/59); "Endsville," *Time* (12/14/59), 65; Harry T. Moore, "Cool Cats Don't Dig the Squares," *NYT* Book Review (5/24/59) 1; "Rent Genuine Beatniks" [ad], *VV* (3/2/60) 6; letter, *VV* (6/8/60); "one of the foulest collections" in Ted Morgan, *Literary Outlaw: The Life and Times of William Burroughs* (New York: Avon Books, 1988), 296. FN: Letters: Amos Vogel, "Mekas Mad," *VV* (11/25/59), 4; John Cassavetes, " 'Shadows,' cont.," *VV* (12/10/59), 4f; Ben Carruthers, " 'Shadows,' cont.," *VV* (12/30/59), 4.

6: Spellman, *Four Lives in the Bebop Business* (New York: Pantheon, 1966), 79; Rivers, *What Did I Do? The Unauthorized Autobiography* (New York: Thunder's Mouth Press, 1992), 342; Wilson, " 'Village' Becomes Focal Center for Modern Jazz," *NYT* (10/27/60); Talmer, "Notebook for Night Owls," *VV* (4/13/60); Martin Williams in David Lee, *The Battle of the Five Spot: Ornette Coleman and the New York Jazz Field* (Toronto: Mercury Press, 2006), 83; Reisner, "Jazz," *VV* (11/25/60); Bley in Lee, *Battle of the Five Spot*, 58; Coleman, Eldridge, Hawkins, Garland in Nat Hentoff, *The Jazz Life* (New York: Dial Press, 1961), 228-9, 231; Davis in Joe Goldberg, *Jazz Masters of the Fifties* (New York: Macmillan, 1968), 231; Roach followed Coleman in John Litweiler, *Ornette Coleman: A Harmolodic Life* (New York: William Morrow,

1993), 83. FN: Van Ronk in *The Mayor of MacDougal Street: A Memoir* (Boston: Da Capo, 2005), 22.

7: Ellison in Tynan, "Jazz on Film: A Contrast in Black and White," *The Observer* (3/20/60); Mekas, "MJ," *VV* (3/9/60); McReynolds, "The Press of Freedom: The Hipster General Strike," *VV* (12/8/59).

2. Primitives of the New Era

1: E. B. White, *Here Is New York* (New York: Harper & Brothers, 1949), 51; Tambellini in *Inventing Downtown* op. cit., 177–8; D'Lugoff in "Outbreak of Vandalism Hits S. Village Coffee Shop Area," *VV* (9/16/59).

2: Jacobs in Lawrence Rinder, "Anywhere out of the World: The Photography of Jack Smith," *Flaming Creature: Jack Smith* (New York: PS 1 Museum, 1997), 40.

3: Uranian Alchemy Players in Stefan Brecht, *The Bread and Puppet Theatre Volume One* (New York: Routledge, 1988), 63; Oldenburg in Richard Kostelanetz, *The Theatre of Mixed-Means* (New York: RK Editions, 1980), 136–7; Hansen, *A Primer of Happenings & Time/Space Art* (New York; Something Else Press, 1965) 64; VanDerBeek in *Film-Makers' Cooperative Catalogue No.3* (New York: American Cinema Group, 1965), 62.

4: "Up-Beats," *Time* (3/14/60), 80; "Saloon Society," *VV* (6/16/60); Mekas, "MJ," *VV* (5/18/60), 11.

5: "physical disability," Air Force discharge papers (5/24/55), Ron Rice file, Film-Makers' Cooperative; "girl running nude" in Sheldon Renan, *An Introduction to American Underground Film* (New York: Dutton, 1967), 175; "more or less near-anarchy," quoted in Stephen R. Duncan, *The Rebel Café: Sex, Race, and Politics in Cold War America's Nightclub Underground* (Baltimore: Johns Hopkins University Press, 2018), 93; exposé in Francis J. Rigney and L. Douglas Smith, *The Real Bohemia* (New York: Basic Books, 1961), 158–9; Mead, "Son of Andy Warhol" (ms), 61, Reginald Gay collection, NYPL Performing Arts; Mead to Rice (6/16/60) and (6/20/60), Ron Rice file, Anthology Film Archives; Clark in "Ron Rice Biography," archive.org/web/20160303193944/http://people.wcsu.edu/mccarneyh/fva/r/RRice_bio.html; Chatterton in *Film-Makers' Cooperative Catalogue No.3*, op. cit., 20. FN: Rigney's print is held by the Pacific Film Archives, Berkeley CA.

6: Mekas, "August 11, 1960," *I Seem to Live*, op. cit., 244; *Shadows* praised, *Sunday Junction* abandoned in Mekas "New York Letter: Towards a Spontaneous Cinema," *Sight and Sound* v28 #3-4 (1959) 119; "July 14, 1960" *I Seem to Live*, op. cit., 235; "July 29, 1960," ibid., 236–7; Ken Sobol, "What Happened at Newport: Beatnik Stay

Home," *VV* (7/14/60), 7; "August 25, 1960," *I Seem to Live*, op. cit., 247; "September 11, 1960," ibid., 250; "September 25," ibid., 252; "October 7, 1960," ibid., 264. "Young cinema activity," in Mekas, "MJ" *VV* (11/17/60), 11f; Reisner, "Jazz: Lord Buckley Night," *VV* (12/8/60), 13; Mel Clay, *Jazz Jail and God: Impressionistic Biography of Bob Kaufman* (San Francisco: Androgyne Books, 1987), 20–1; Johnston, "Art: Car Crash" *VV* (11/10/60), 8; Hansen, *A Primer of Happenings & Time*, 31; Dine in Michael Kirby, *Happenings* (New York: Dutton, 1966), 184–5; Lurie in Boris Lurie, Seymour Krim, *No!art: Pin-Ups Excrement Protest Jew-Art* (Berlin: Edition Hundertmark, 1988), 58; Fisher, Vulgar Show statement in ibid., 22. FN: Malina in Oliver Trager, *Dig Infinity: The Life and Art of Lord Buckley* (New York: Welcome Rain, 2002), 211–12.

7: Johnston, "Music: LaMonte Young," *VV* (11/19/64), 14: Sherman, *America's Child: A Woman's Journey Through the Radical Sixties* (Chicago: Curbstone Books, 2007), 11–12, 15; Johnston, *VV* (11/19/64), op. cit.; Ross Parmenter, "Music: Far Out Program," *NYT* (4/4/61); Johnston, "Happenings: Ingenious Womb," *VV* (4/6/61), 13; Kroll, *Art News* (April 1961). FN: A.B. "Far-Out Music is Played at Carnegie," *NYT* (11/26/61); Johnston, "Dance," *VV* (12/7/61), 10; Johnston, *VV* (11/19/64), op. cit.

8: Markopoulos, "New American Cinema in Spoleto" (letter), *VV* (6/22/60), 4; "anguished strivings," in film-makerscoop.com/catalogue/jonas-mekas-guns-of-the-trees. FN: Jacobs in Renan, op. cit., 149f.

9: Interviews: Ken and Flo Jacobs (June 2019), Alice Meyer Wallace (Nov 2019), Richard Schechner (Oct 2019).

10: Tallmer "For Maya Deren—In the Midst of Life" *VV* (10/19/61), 11; Mekas "MJ," *VV* (10/26/61), 13; Seitz, *The Art of Assemblage* (New York: MoMA, 1961), 89; Canaday, "A Mixed-Up Show," *NYT* (10/8/61); Don Ross, "Sleeps With His Work—Fights Critics: Sculptor Hunts Junk for Fierce Forms," *NYH-T* (11/9/61); Fisher statement in *No!art*, op. cit., 40–1; Kiplinger, "Art," *VV* (1/4/62), 7; Johnston, "Doom Show," *Art News* (1/19/62), 12; O'Doherty, "Art: Three Studies in Free Association," *NYT* (1/8/62); O'Hara, *Kulchur* 5 (Spring 1962), 85; Preston, "Wide Worlds of Difference in Exhibitions," *NYT* (9/30/62).

11: Barbara Rose, *Claes Oldenburg* (New York: MoMA, 1970), 69; Johnston, "Off Off-Broadway: 'Happenings' at Ray Gun Mfg. Co.," *VV* (4/28/62), 10; Johnston, "Dance," *VV* (3/29/62), 14.

12: Smith, "Dance: Strange Excitement," *VV* (5/24/62), 7; *I Seem to Live*, op. cit., 47.

3. The Freedom Jazz

1: "Gaslight, Beatnik Spa, Extinguished Forever," *VV* (7/21/60), 1; Amiri Baraka, *The Autobiography of LeRoi Jones* (Chicago: Lawrence Hill Books, 1997), 196; "Tension Boils Up in Square But Major Riot Averted," *VV* (7/28/60), 1; Young in *Utica Daily Press*, Bedford + Bowery, bedfordandbowery.com; Polsky, "The Village Beat Scene: Summer 1960," *Dissent* (Summer 1961), 354n; J; Polsky op. cit., 342; "D'Lugoff of The Village Gate: 'Vindictive Harassment' Charged to Cabaret Police," *VV* (2/24/60), 1. FN: J.R. Goddard, "Black and Tan: Once Upon a Time Before Harlem . . .," *VV* (12/29/60), 1.

2: Young in "MacDougal St: Police Enforce Sabbath-Law," *VV* (12/2/59); *Mayor of MacDougal Street*, op. cit., 145; Goddard series, "Fruitcake Version of Inferno, Says Artist," *VV* (6/23/60), 1f, "'Run, Beatnik, Run!' To Mecca, 1960" (6/30/60), 13f, "Like, Man, Where Do We Go from Here" (7/7/60), 4f; Bonnie Bremser in *Beat Down to Your Soul: What Was the Beat Generation?*, ed. Ann Charters (Penguin: New York, 2001), 26–7; "shops selected" in Polsky, op. cit., 343; "Beatnik Café Sues in 'Hazard' Closing," *NYT* (6/25/60); Mitchell arrest in "'Village' Beatniks Heckle Firemen Closing Gaslight," *NYT* (6/11/60); "80 Beatniks Protest," *NYT* (6/13/60); Varda Karni in Goddard, "Lights Are Dimmed Along MacDougal St.," *VV* (6/16/60), 16. FN: Terri Thal interview (telephone, 12/27/2021).

3: "brutal and exhausting" in Harry Lewis, "The Circuit/New York City Poetry Public Readings: A Short History," Stephen Vincent & Ellen Zweig (eds.), *The Poetry Reading: A Contemporary Compendium on Language and Performance* (San Francisco: Momo's Press, 1981), 86; Kowitt in Carol Bergé (ed.), *Light Years* (New York: Spuyten Duyvil, 2010), 352; Atkinson, "Two One-Acters," *NYT* (6/23/60); Smith, "Café Theatre: Chance and War," *VV* (10/13/60); Hernton in *Light Years* op. cit., 292; Young, "Frets and Frails," *Sing Out!* (Apr–May 1960); Reisner, "The Press of Freedom: The Menace of Folk Music," *VV* (2/24/60), 5; Shelton, "The Press of Freedom: Listen, Mr. Reisner!," *VV* (3/2/60), 5; Goddard, "Carolyn Hester: Little Girl with The Big New Voice," *VV* (6/8/60); Goddard, "Van Ronk Fills Minetta with Passionate Wail," *VV* (8/4/60), 1; Shelton, "Folk Music Makes Mark on City's Nightlife," *NYT* (11/17/60).

4: Chandler in Nan Robertson, "Beatniks Stage a Sit-In a Café, Defying Firemen in the 'Village,'" *NYT* (1/9/61); *Mayor of MacDougal Street*, op. cit., 144; Dan List, "Gaslight Night-Of-Travail Sparked By False Alarm," *VV* (1/12/61), 1; Millstein, "Man, It's Like Satire," *NYT* Magazine (5/3/59); John P. Shanley, "TV Review: Lenny Bruce, 'Beatnik,' on 'One Night Stand,'" *NYT* (5/13/59); "The Sickniks," *Time* (7/13/59), 42; Arthur Gelb, "Comic Shocks With Moral," *NYT* (12/8/60); "Lenny Bruce at

Midnight" ad, *VV* (1/26/61), 8. FN: Goddard, "Ghouls at the Pussy Cat," *VV* (7/23/63), 1. FN: Goldman from the journalism of Lawrence Schiller, *Ladies and Gentlemen Lenny Bruce!!* (New York: Ballentine Books, 1974), 426.

5: Humes in Peter Gessner, "Espresso Underground Lays Down Party Line," *VV* (7/6/61), 3; Sanders, *Tales*, op. cit., 86; Paul Hofman, "Folk Singers Riot in Washington Sq.," *NYT* (4/10/61), 1; Drasin interview (8/13/21, email); Zimmerman hustling Joan in Clinton Heylin, *The Double Life of Bob Dylan: A Restless, Hungry Feeling* (New York: Little, Brown, 2022), 42; Mekas, "MJ" *VV* (5/25/61), 13; Kaufman endorsement in *Sunday* promotional booklet [nd] 4; "Battle Report," *Collected Poems of Bob Kaufman* (San Francisco: City Lights, 2019), 6–7. FN: Chandler in Dan Kimpel, "True Tales from the Gaslight," *Music Connection* (2/12/2014), music-connection.com.

6: Saul, *Freedom Is, Freedom Ain't: Jazz and the Making of the Sixties* (Cambridge: Harvard, 2003), 95; Reisner, "Jazz: Freedom Now," *VV* (1/19/61), 8; Wilson, "Jazz Composition of Protest Heard," *NYT* (1/16/61); Oliver, "Blues to Drive the Blues Away," in *Jazz*, eds. Nat Hentoff and Albert McCarthy (New York: Grove Press, 1959), 85–103; Spellman, "The next to the last generation of blues singers," *Kulchur* 5 (Spring 1962), 58; "Jazz Gallery, N.Y.," *Variety* (5/25/60), 66; Angelou, *The Collected Autobiographies* (New York: Random House, 2004), 790. FN: Mailer, "Theatre: The Blacks," *VV* (5/11/61), 11; "Theatre: The Blacks (cont.)," *VV* (5/18/61), 11; Hansberry, "Genet, Mailer and the New Paternalism," *VV* (6/1/61), 10; "Mailer to Hansberry," *VV* (6/8/61), 11; Joans, "Digging Mailer" (letter), *VV* (5/25), 4; Mekas, "MJ," *VV* (6/15/61), 13; Ford, "The Negro and the American Theater," *Liberator* v3 #5 (May 1963), 6–7.

7: Jones, "The Jazz Avant-Garde," *Black Music* (New York: William Morrow, 1968), 69. FN: Arthur Gelb, "Habitues of Meyer Davis Land Dance the Twist," *NYT* (10/19/61); Gay Talese, "Twist Danced at Metropolitan as Director Watches in Dismay," *NYT* (11/21/61).

8: Mekas, "MJ," *VV* (3/9/61), 11; Di Prima, *Recollections of My Life as a Woman* (New York: Penguin, 2001), 240. FN: David Kaufman, "East Village: At a Flashy New Hotel, a Pair of Eloises," *NYT* (9/26/2008).

9: Baraka, *Autobiography*, op. cit., 251; "Floating Bear Floats Free," *VV* (5/3/62), 3; Sainer, "Burroughs: Naked Lunch," *VV* (12/13/62), 17; Miller, "The Sick White Negro," *PR* (Spring 1963); Hentoff, "Second Chorus: The 'New' Lenny Bruce," *VV* (1/10/63), 25. FN: "Books: Beyond the Fringe," *PR* (Spring 1963).

10: Agnes 'Sis' Cunningham and Gordon Friesen, *Red Dust and Broadsides: A Joint Autobiography* (Amherst: University of Massachusetts, 1999), 275; Dylan, *Chronicles Volume One* (New York: Simon & Schuster, 2004), 17; Young in *Rat* (3/7/69);

Shelton, "Bob Dylan: A Distinctive Folk-Song Stylist," *NYT* (9/29/61), 31. FN: Aaron J. Leonard, *The Folk Singers: The FBI, the Folk Artists and the Suppression of the Communist Party USA 1939-1956* (London: Repeater Books, 2020), 22, 235.

11: "42 Arrested in Times Sq. In Clashes at Peace Rally," *NYT* (3/4/62), 1; Michael Smith, "The Times Square Melee: Beck's Condition Okay; McReynolds Blasts Sitters," *VV* (3/8/62), 1; Norman M. Ackerman, "Times Square cont" (letter), *VV* (4/12/62); Mead to Rice, letter (Apr 1962) Reginald Gay collection, NYPL Performing Arts; Mekas, "MJ," *VV* (3/29/62), 13; Mekas, "MJ," *VV* (6/7/62), 10.

12: Thompson, "Screen: An Experimental Program," *NYT* (6/8/62); Mekas, "MJ," *VV* (7/12/62); Archer, "Screen: 'Flower Thief,'" *NYT* (7/14/62), 11; *Newsweek* (7/30/62), 76; McReynolds, "The Flower Thief—Invalid or Incompetent," *VV* (7/26/62), 11f. FN: See *Free Jazz Communism*, eds. Sezgin Boynik and Taneli Villahuhta (Helsinki: Rab-Rab Press, 2022), *passim*. FN: Smith, "Taboo of Jingola," *VV* (12/21/72). FN: Mead, "Son of Andy Warhol," op. cit., 57; Village Bulletin Board, *VV* (2/22/62), 2.

13: Mailer, "The Big Bite," Esquire (April 1963); Lary Bloom, *Sol LeWitt: A Life of Ideas* (Middletown CN: Wesleyan University Press, 2019), 69; "Peace Strike in Quiet Start, Many Activities Planned," *VV* (11/8/62), 9; Sainer, *The Radical Theatre Notebook* (New York: Avon, 1975), 45f.

14: Val Adams, "Satire on Birch Society Barred from Ed Sullivan's TV Show," *NYT* (5/14/63); Spellman, *Four Lives*, op. cit., 135. FN: Dragonette quoted in Bill Coss, "Eric Dolphy-Ree Dragonette, Town Hall, New York City, 1963," *DownBeat*, available at hardbopjazzjournal.com.

4. The Camera Will Know No Shame

1: Dwoskin, *Film Is: The International Free Cinema* (Woodstock NY: Overlook Press, 1975), 59; "London Reacts to 'The Connection,'" *Var* (6/28/61); "Legal Brief Vs. Censoring of 'Connection' by Albany Ignoring 'That Word,'" *Var* (10/11/61); Wolfe, "Censors Ban 'The Connection,'" *NY H-T* (10/4/62); Crowther, "Screen: 'Connection' Here and Gone," *NYT* (10/4/62), 44; "Open Letter," *VV* (10/11/62), 13; "Ban By-passed: 'Connection' Film at Judson Church," *VV* (10/18/62), 1; O'Doherty, "Art: Avant-Garde Revolt," *NYT* (10/31/62), 41; Johnston, "The Artist in a Coca-Cola World," *VV* (1/31/63), 7.

2: Conrad in David Reisman, "In the Grip of the Lobster: Jack Smith Remembered," *Millennium Film Journal* 23/24 (Winter 1990–1), 63; Ginsberg quoted on flyer, Anthology Film Archives (May 1997); Sitney, "Jerry Jofen's Mystical Ladder," Anthology Film Archives calendar (May–June 1997), 6; Adler, "On Location," in

Dwoskin, *Film Is*, op. cit., 6. Sitney, "Jofen," op. cit., 6; Rice, *FC* 39 (Winter 1965), 121. FN: Preston interview (April 1996); Adler, op. cit., 12; "'Beats Panic, Toss Out Dope Kit, Bop Cop," *NYM* [undated clip], in J. Hoberman, *On Jack Smith's Flaming Creatures* (New York: Granary/Hips Road, 2001), 19. FN: Sitney, "Jofen," op. cit., FN: Moravia, "A Beat Film: Heroin for Breakfast," *L'Espresso* (2/7/65), Ron Rice file, Anthology Film Archives.

3: Mekas, "MJ," *VV* (4/18/63), 13; Markopoulos, "Innocent Revels," *FC* 33 (Summer 1964), 41; Kelman, "Smith Myth," *Film Culture* 29 (Summer 1963), 5; Mekas, "MJ," *VV* (6/13/63), 14.

4: Taubman, "Theater: Marines in Jail," *NYT* (5/16/63); Smith, "Theatre: The Brig," *VV* (5/23/63), 13; Julian Beck and Judith Malina, "The Press of Freedom: All the World's a Prison," *VV* (9/4/1957), 4.

5: Mekas, "A Preface," *FC* 80: *The Legend of Barbara Rubin* (Liepzig: Spector Books, 2018), 3; Mekas "MJ" *VV* (7/25/63); Mekas, "Some Notes on Some New Movies and Happiness," *FCe* 37 (Summer 1965), 19; Gramercy ad *VV* (8/1/63), 13; Adler, "On Location," op. cit., 13.

6: Mekas, "MJ," *VV* (8/22/63), 12; Mekas, "MJ," *VV* (9/12/63), 17; Michelle Stuart, "NO Is an Involvement," *Artforum* (Sept 1963), 36; Krim, "No! Show," *No!art*, op. cit., 24; Tytell, *The Living Theatre*, op. cit., 189; Beck in Biner, *The Living Theatre*, op. cit., 76.

7: Mekas, "MJ," *VV* (12/5); Anger in J. Hoberman, "Sympathy for the Devil," *American Film* (March 1981), 16; Byron in Bill Landis, *Anger: The unauthorized biography* (New York: HarperCollins, 1995), 103–4; Mekas, "MJ," *VV* (11/14/63); Raymond Ericson, "Music: A Long, Long, Long Night (and Day) at the Piano," *NYT* (9/11/63), 45; Camper, "Two Films by Ron Rice," *FC* 48–49 (Winter-Spring 1970), 30; "October 20, 1963," Mekas, *I Seem to Live*, op. cit., 395; Ginsberg in Barry Miles, *Ginsberg: A Biography* (New York: Viking, 1989), 334; *Sinking Bear* #3 (Dec 1963) 2. FN: Jacobs in Sitney, *Visionary Film* (New York: Oxford, 1974), 387.

8: Mekas, "MJ," *VV* (1/16/64), 13; Mekas, "MJ," *VV* (1/30/64), 17. FN: Gramercy ad, *VV* (2/6/64), 12.

5. New York Unfair

1: "Crackdown Hits Smut Specialists," *NYT* (2/26/64); Mekas, "MJ," *VV* (6/24/65); Stoller, "New American Cinema—Sort of," *Moviegoer* #2 (Summer–Autumn 1964), 67; police detective quoted in Paul Meskil, "Police Chill 'Flaming' Movie," *NYP* (3/4/64); Jacobs, unpublished letter to *Village Voice* (10/21/91), in *On Jack Smith's Flaming Creatures*, op. cit., 43; Mekas, "MJ," *VV* (3/19/64), 13. FN: Di Prima,

Recollections of My Life as a Woman: The New York Years (New York: Penguin, 2001), 382. FN: Smith, "Theatre: The Eighth Ditch," *VV* (3/19/64), 11. FN: *Scorpio Rising*, in J. Hoberman, "License for License: Underground Movies and Obscenity in the Sixties," *Banned in the U.S.A.* (Berkeley CA: Pacific Film Archives, 1993).

2: "Avant-Garde Art Going to the Fair," *NYT* (10/5/63); Homar Bigart, "Rain Soaks Crowd," *NYT* (4/23/64), 1; *The Sinking Bear* #8 (May 1964). FN: Canaday, "Art: By Claes Oldenburg" *NYT* (4/7/64), 32; Canaday, "Maybe Hopeful," *NYT* A&L (4/12/64), 19; Canaday, "Pop Art Sells On and On," *NYT* Magazine (5/31/64), 52–3.

3: Stephanie Gervis Harrington, "Becks in Legal Happening, Face Federal Court Trial" *VV* (5/7/64) 3; Paul Hoffman, "A Movie Show—in Criminal Court," *NYP* (6/3/64) 16; Harrington, "The Bruce Case: How Many 4-Letter Words Can a Prosecutor Use?" *VV* (7/16/64) 3. FN: O'Doherty, "Season's End: Groups at Castelli and Auslander—Plus a Shock at Stein's" *NYT* (5/31/64); Wolfe in *NO!Art* op. cit., 85.

4: Levine abducted in Susan Goodman, "Sex Group Demands: 'Free Them, Insure Them and Make Them Legal," *VV* (8/27/64), 1; Grace Glueck, "Art Notes: Fledgling School," *NYT* (7/5/64).

5: Sitney interview (5/5/22, telephone); Rose Feliu interview (7/15/99, courtesy Steven Watson); Newfield, "The Press of Freedom: Mugging the White Liberal," *VV* (6/25/64), 5; Mekas, "MJ," *VV* (7/30/64).

6: Thal interview, op. cit.; Ken Burrows, "The Strike Goes On: New Militancy Makes The MacDougal Scene," *VV* (8/20/64), 3; Susan Goodman, "Anti Art Picket Pick on Stockhausen," *VV* (9/10/64), 3; Benjamin Piekut, *Experimentalism Otherwise: The New York Avant-Garde and Its Limits* (Berkeley: University of California, 2011), 72; Johnston, "Dance: Fluxus Fuxus," *VV* (7/2/64), 7; Schonberg, "Stockhausen's 'Originale' Given at Judson," *NYT* (9/9/64); Bowers, "A Feast of Astonishments," *Nation* (9/28/64), 172; Klüver, "More Incidents" (letter), *VV* (9/24/64), 4; Johnston, "Dance: Inside 'Originale' " (10/1/64), 6.

7: Dan Carlinsky, "New Sounds: Jazz in a Cellar," *Columbia Spectator* (10/7/64); Spellman, "Jazz at the Judson," *Nation* (2/8/65), 149; Stillman in Jason Weiss, *Always in Trouble: An Oral History of ESP-Disk', the Most Outrageous Record Label in America* (Middletown CN: Wesleyan University Press, 2012), 22; Snow in "The Life & Times of Michael Snow," *Take One* v3 #3 (Jan–Feb 1971), 7.

8: Schneemann to Tenney (5/30/64), *Correspondence Course: An Epistolary History of Carolee Schneemann and Her Circle*, ed. Kristine Stiles (Durham NC: Duke University Press, 2010), 83; Picard in Sarah Elise Archias, "The Body as a Material in the Early Performance Work of Carolee Schneemann, Yvonne Rainer, and Vito Acconci" (PhD dissertation: UC Berkeley, 2008), 103; *Eye Body* in Schneemann, *More Than Meat Joy*, ed. Bruce McPherson (New Paltz NY: Documentext, 1979), 63;

Schneeman, *Correspondence*, op. cit., 95n; Schneemann to Jan Van der Marck (4/2/66), ibid., 106; Johnston, "Dance: Meat Joy," *VV* (11/26/64), 13; Smith, "Theatre: Meat Joy," *VV* (11/26/64), 17; Tarburton, "The Bruce Conviction: A View from the Couch," *VV* (11/26/64), 5; "erotic rite," *More Than Meat Joy*, op. cit., 56. FN: Mekas, "MJ," *VV* (10/1/64); Gill, *New Yorker* (10/17/64). FN: Archias, op. cit., 118.

9: Smith, "Theatre: Present Stages," *VV* (3/26/64), 9; Mari-Claire Charba interview (telephone, 7/11/22); Eberstadt, "King of the East Village," *NYH-T* Sunday Magazine (12/13/64), 13; Smith, "Theatre: The Slave and The Toilet," (12/31/64), 10.

10: Smith, ibid.; Newfield, "LeRoi Jones at Arms: Blues for Mr. Whitey," *VV* (12/17/64), 1; Koenigsberg, "The Jones Case" (letter), *VV* (1/7/65), 4; Higgins, "The White Problem" (letter), *VV* (1/14/65), 4; Willen "The Corrupting Dream" (letter), *VV* (1/28/65), 4; Hettie Jones, *How I Became Hettie Jones* (New York: Grove Press, 1996), 220.

6. All Tomorrow's Parties

1: Kempton, "Baby Beatniks Spur Bar Boom on East Side," *VV* (9/10/64), 1; Feliu interview, op. cit.; Curtis, "The Affluent Set Invades the East Village," *NYT* (11/29/64); Kempton, "The Animals in New York; Keep On Truckin', Mama, Truckin' My Blues Away," *VV* (9/17/64), 1; Wolf, "The Girl of the Year," *NYH-T* (12/6/64). FN: Curtis, op. cit.

2: John Cale and Victor Bockris, *What's Welsh for Zen: The Autobiography of John Cale* (London: Bloomsbury, 1999), 64–5.

3: Newfield, "Blowin' in the Wind: A Folk-Music Revolt," *VV* (1/14/65), 4; Harry Gilroy, "The Bowery: Arty and Avant-Garde," *NYT* (4/24/65); Casey Ray, *William S. Burroughs and the Cult of Rock n Roll*, available at longreads.com.

4: Ed Sanders, *Fug You: An Informal History of the Peace Eye Bookstore, the Fuck You Press, the Fugs, and Counterculture in the Lower East Side* (Philadelphia: Da Capo, 2011), 126–7.

5: Judith E. Stein, *Eye of the Sixties: Richard Bellamy and the Transformation of Modern Art* (New York: FSG 2016), 189; Mekas, "June 29, 1964," *I Seem to Live*, op. cit., 462; P. Adams Sitney interview (5/5/22), op. cit.; "Movie Journal," *VV* (3/18/65), 23; *Empire* premiere, "MJ," *VV* (3/11/65); Siegel, "Not Art" (letter), *VV* (3/18/65), 4; Malanga in Victor Bockris, *Warhol: The Biography* (New York: Da Capo, 1997), 207.

6: Canaday, "Art That Pulses, Quivers and Fascinates," *NYT* Magazine (2/21/65), 57; Canaday, "Art: Capturing the Optical Movement," *NYT* (2/25/65), 25; Canaday, "The Responsive Eye: Three Cheers and High Hopes," *NYT* A&L (2/28/65) X19.

7: Berge, "The Work of Harry Smith: Dialogue with Words," *Film Culture* 37 (Summer 1965), 2; Smith in John Szwed, *Cosmic Scholar: The Life and Times of Harry Smith* (New York: FSG, 2023), 231. FN: Richard Foreman interview (10/15/21 telephone), Sitney interview (5/5/22), op. cit., Amy Taubin interview (10/12/21 email); Mekas, "September, 1965," *I Seem to Live*, op. cit., 526.

8: Jacobs in "June 22," *I Seem to Live*, op. cit., 511; "MJ," *VV* (4/29/65), 13; Malanga in David McCabe and David Dalton, *A Year in the Life of Andy Warhol* (London: Phaidon, 2003), 137; Young, "Frets and Frails," *Sing Out* (September 1965).

9: Tavel, "The Banana Diary (Harlot)," *FC* 40 (Spring 1966), 54; Alexander, "Report from Underground" *Life* (1/28/65), 23; Lester, "Theatre: Two by Tavel," *VV* (8/5/65), 12.

10: David Bourdon, "Art: The Flip Side," *VV* (6/17/65), 11; "Bob Dylan: Every Mind Polluting Word (2nd Edition)," available at archive.org; Murray Schumach, "Broadway Central Hotel Collapses," *NYT* (8/4/73), 57; Smith, "Lobotomy in Lobsterland," *Wait for Me at the Bottom of the Pool: The Writings of Jack Smith*, eds. J. Hoberman and Edward Leffingwell (London: Serpent's Tail, 1997), 83. FN: Heliczer in *Getting Busted: Personal Experiences of Arrest, Trial and Prison*, ed. Ross Firestone (New York: Douglas Books, 1970), 24.

11: Newfield, "At Forest Hills: Mods, Rockers Fight Over New Thing Called 'Dylan,'" *VV* (9/2/65), 1; Heide in Bockris, *Warhol*, op. cit., 229; Andy Warhol and Pat Hackett, *POP-ism: The Warhol '60s* (New York: Harcourt Brace Jovanovich, 1980), 107; Bockris, *Warhol*, op. cit., 229. FN: Bockris, *Warhol*, op. cit., 230; Taplin in *The Double Life*, op. cit., 382.

12: Smith, "TJ," *VV* (12/23/65), 20; Van Der Beek in Mekas, "MJ," (11/11/65), 21; Kostelanetz, *On Innovative Performance(s): Three Decades of Recollections on Alternative Theater* (Jefferson NC: McFarland, 1994), 141; Leary in Mekas, "MJ," *VV* (7/22/65); Stern in *From Beat Scene Poet to Psychedelic Multimedia Artist in San Francisco and Beyond, 1948-1978* (interviews conducted by Victoria Morris Byerly, 1996), available at oac.cdlib.org; Mekas on USCO, "MJ," *VV* (7/22/65); Warhol in *POPism*, op. cit., 137; Jofen in "MJ," *VV* (11/11/65), 21; "Festival 1," *New Yorker* (12/4/66), 52; John Gruen, *The New Bohemia* (New York: Grosset & Dunlap, 1967), 108; Heliczer in "MJ," *VV* (11/18/65), 21; "Rehearsal for the Destruction of Atlantis," *Wait for Me*, op. cit.; Douglas Robinson, "25,000 March to Back Vietnam Policy," *NYT* (10/31/65), 1. FN: Gregory Zinman, *Making Images Move: Handmade Cinema and the Other Arts* (Oakland: University of California, 2020), 338fn100. FN: Stern in *From Beat Scene Poet*, op. cit.

13: Morrison in Victor Bockris & Gerard Malanga, *Up-Tight: The Velvet Underground*

Story (1983), 22; Morrison in Jordan Runtagh,"'The Velvet Underground and Nico': 10 Things You Didn't Know," *RS* (3/12/2017),

14: Bockris, *Warhol*, op. cit., 235; Heide in Tony Scherman and David Dalton, *Pop: The Genius of Andy Warhol* (New York: HarperCollins, 2009), 293–4; Heylin, op. cit., 382, 386; Crowther, "The Screen: Andy Warhol's 'More Milk, Yvette' Bows," *NYT* (2/9/66), 32.

7. Babushkaville Explodes

1: Warhol ad, *VV* (11/18/65), 22; Krim, "Shock Treatment for Psychiatrists," *NYH-T* (1/14/66), 27; psychiatrist in Grace Glueck, "Syndrome Pop at Delmonico's," *NYT* (1/14/66); Wilcock, "Other Scenes," *EVO* (2/15/66), 4.

2: Conrad in Toby Mussman, "An Interview with Tony Conrad," *FC* 41 (Summer 1966), 4; "Tony Conrad on 'The Flicker,'" ibid., 1; Mekas, "MJ," *VV* (3/24/66); Preston, "Voyeurama," *EVO* (4/1-15/66), 10. FN: *Sinking Bear* #5 (Jan 1964), 6. David Bourdon criticized the disc jockey Stan Z (Burns) who filled in for Murray on January 2.

3: Warhol tendered $40,000 in Bockris, *Warhol*, op. cit., 240; Stern, *From Beat Scene Poet*, op. cit.; Murray in Joan Barthel, "Youth Wants to Uh Uh Uh," *NYT* (5/15/66); Stern in *From Beat Scene Poet*, op. cit.; Cale in *What's Welsh*, op. cit., 90; Cassen in *Pop*, op. cit., 323; Warhol, *Pop-Ism*, op. cit., 156. FN: Oldenburg in Kostelanetz, *The Theatre of Mixed-Means*, op. cit., 145.

4: "Bring your shades," quoted in Mitch Susskind and Leslie Gottesman, "Keep Your Cool: An Exploding World," *Columbia Daily Spectator* (4/27/65); Wilcock, "A 'High' School of Music and Art," *EVO* (4/15-5/1/66) 3; Mekas, "MJ," *VV* (5/26/66); Warhol in *POP-ism* op. cit., 157. FN: Canby. "A New Nightclub to Have 3 Stories," *NYT* (4/1/66). FN: Glueck, "Dali Concocts a Happening—of Sorts," *NYT* (2/24/66).

5: McDarrah, "Closing Threatened: American Flag Burned in Theatre Spectacle," *VV* (4/14/66), 7; Bender, "Black Jeans to Go Dancing at the Movies: It's Inevitable," *NYT* (4/11/66); Ashbery in *Factory Made*, op. cit., 275; Cale in *What's Welsh*, op. cit., 90; Susskind and Gottesman op. cit. Not surprisingly, the *Spectator* reporters found the EPI far superior to Murray the K's World; Waters in Ada Calhoun, *St. Marks is Dead* (New York: Norton, 2016), 147. *VV* (1/22/65) reported a pot bust at NYU; Malanga in *Up-Tight*, op. cit., 37; *Newsday* (5/6/66), 2C; Stern in *From Beat Scene Poet*, op. cit.

6: Mekas, "MJ," *VV* (5/26/66); Durkee in "MJ," *VV* (6/16/66); Mekas, "MJ," *VV* (6/23/66); Mekas, "MJ," *VV* (5/26/66); Glueck, "Art Notes: A Little 'Be-In' Goes a Long Way,"

NYT (5/15/66); museum staff in Naomi Feigelson, "We Are All One," *Cheetah* 1 (May 1968); Harrington, "The Children's Hour, or Curfew on McDougal [sic] St.," *VV* (3/17/66), 1; Gurin, "MacD: A Losing Battle with a Turned-On Street," *VV* (3/24/66), 1; Harrington, "Inevitable Explodes on St. Mark's Place," *VV* (6/16/66), 1.

7: Wilson, "'Space Age Jazz' Lacks Boosters," *NYT* (2/19/62); Robert Levin, "Jazz: Space Hour," *VV* (2/22/62), 8; Baraka, *Autobiography*, op. cit., 298; Alderson in *Always in Trouble*, op. cit., 153; Jones, "Apple Cores #3," *Black Music*, op. cit., 129; Wilson "Sun Ra: I'm Talking About Cosmic Things,'" *NYT* (4/7/68), 17–18; Wilmer, *Mama Said There'd Be Days Like This: My Life in the Jazz World*, (London: The Women's Press, 1989), 98; Wilson, "Sun Ra, Jazz Avant Savant, Digs Into Infinity," *NYT* (2/11/67); Zwerin, "Jazz Journal: One for Two," *VV* (5/25/67), 17; Brecht, "Sun Ra," *Evergreen Review* (May 1968), 88f. FN: Sinclair, "Sun Ra and Interview: Collision of the Suns," *Warren-Forest Sun* (4/1/67). FN: Wilson, "Sun Ra and His Space Arkestra Give a Show With Mixed Media," *NYT* (4/13/68).

8: Goldstein, "The Pop-Bag: Blonde on Blonde," *VV* (6/30/66); Hughes, *Invisible Now: Bob Dylan in the 1960s* (New York: Routledge, 2013), 133. FN: Meltzer, *The Aesthetics of Rock* (New York: Something Else Press, 1970), 280.

9: Mekas, "MJ," *VV* (9/29/66), 27; Robert E. Dallos, "Dr. Leary Starts New 'Religion' With 'Sacramental' Use of LSD," *NYT* (9/20/66), 33. FN: "The Chelsea Girls: An interview with Jerome Hiler," vimeo.com/108790392.

10: Leary's associates in Goldstein, "Pop Eye," *VV* (10/20/66), 13; *Variety* ad cited in Richard Goldstein, *Reporting the Counterculture* (Boston: Unwin Hyman, 1989), 84; Morea interview (10/3/23); Lil Picard, "Voyeurama," *EVO* (11/15/66), 12.

11: Leary in Howard Smith, "Scenes," *VV* (11/3/66), 13; Warhol in *POP-ism*, op. cit., 99, 189; Goldstein, "Pop Eye," *VV* (12/1/66); Shelton, "Son of Suzy Creamcheese," *NYT* (12/25/66), 11. FN: Darrow in *Music Connection*, musicconnection.com/chris-darrow-an-appreciation.

12: Sullivan, "Andy Warhol's 'Chelsea Girls' at the Cinema Rendezvous," *NYT* (12/2/66); Lester, "Taking a Trip with Leary," *NYT* (12/4/68); LaSueur, "Two Plays by Ronald Tavel," *VV* (10/13/66), 25; Tavel interview, *Criticism* (Spring 2014), 329f; Smith, "TJ," *VV* (1/12/67), 24; Smith "TJ" *VV* (3/16/67) 21; Tavel, *Andy Warhol's Ridiculous Screenplays* (Silverton OR: Fast Books, 2015), 39. FN: Crowther, "The Underground Overflows," *NYT* (12/11/66). FN: Don McNeil, "Appeal to Washington: Theatre of the Ridiculous Isn't Funny to Indians," *VV* (3/9/67), 3f.

13: Hoffman, "Caterpillar Changes," *Film Culture* 44 (Spring 1967), 76.

14: Goldstein, "Pop Eye: Albumin," *VV* (4/13/67), 19; Newfield, "Electric Circus Opens: Hippies & New Frontier on Desolation Row," *VV* (7/6/67), 1; Mekas, "MJ," *VV* (7/20/67), 20. FN: Manville, "Later . . . : A Night at the Dom," *VV* (3/16/67), 15.

8. Turf Wars

1: "Entropy and the New Monuments," *Artforum* (June 1966); Baraka, *Autobiography*, op. cit., 323; Glueck, "Turning Them On Downtown," *NYT* (12/5/65) X23; "Oral history interview with Dean Fleming, 2013 August 6 and 7," Smithsonian Archives of American Art; Judd on Park Place, "In the Galleries," *Arts Magazine* (Feb 1964), on Di Suvero, "In the Galleries," *Arts Magazine* (Oct 1960); Lyon, *The Destruction of Lower Manhattan* (Toronto: Macmillan, 1969), 12.

2: Huxtable, "Project, Planned 10 Years, Has Been Called Unsound," *NYT* (10/21/66), 43; Huxtable, "Noted Buildings in Path of Road," *NYT* (7/22/65), 33; Millstein, "Portraits of the Loft Generation," *NYT* Magazine (1/7/62), 207f. FN: O'Doherty, "Avant-Garde Deadpans on Move," *NYT* (4/11/64).

3: "Listen, Robert Moses," thebobdylanproject.com; Fleming "Oral history interview," op. cit.; "City's Might Knocks Out Artist's Peace Party," *VV* (4/14/66), 1.

4: Bourdon, "Park Place: New Ideas," *VV* (11/25/65), 11; Bourdon, "Art: Parallelogram Backflip," *VV* (12/23/65), 13; Glueck, "Turning Them On," op. cit.; Ruda in ibid.; Curtis, "Gallery Hoppers Extend East Side Rush Hour Into the Night," *NYT* (4/27/66); Kramer, "Art: Reshaping the Outermost Limits," *NYT* (4/28/66); Bourdon (12/23/65) op. cit.; Judd, "Specific Objects," *Arts Yearbook* 8 (1965); Bochner, "Primary Structures," *Arts Magazine* (June 1966); di Suvero in James Sampson Meyer, *Minimalism: Art and Polemics in the Sixties* (New Haven: Yale University Press, 2001), 83. FN: Rosenberg, "Defining Art," *New Yorker* (2/25/67).

5: Sandler, "New Names This Month," *Art News* (October 1959), 18; Bochner, "Secret of the Domes," *Artforum* (Sept 2006).

6: Perrault, "Art: Minimal Art, Clearing the Air," *VV* (1/12/67), 11; Perrault, "Art," *VV* (1/19/67), 11; Moore, "Music: Park Place Electronics," *VV* (6/9/66), 17; Glueck, "The Park Place Puts On a Stunner," *NYT* (3/11/67); Moore, "Music: Park Place Pianos," *VV* (3/23/67). FN: Perrault, "Art," *VV* (3/23/67); Cinematheque ad, *VV* (1/5/67), 22.

7: Harrington, "A Happening: Ballooning at Grand Central Station," *VV* (1/19/67), 3; Sainer, "Speak Out on the Arts: If War Is Still With Us, So Are the New Works," *VV* (2/16/67), 19; "Talk of the Town," *New Yorker* (2/11/67), 30–1; Kozloff, "A Collage of Indignation . . ." *Nation* (2/20/67), 248; Golub, "The Artist as an Angry Artist," *Arts Magazine* (April 1967); Smith, "Scenes," *VV* (2/16/67), 28; Bernard Weinraub, "10,000 Chant 'L-O-V-E,'" *NYT* (3/27/67), 1; McNeill, "Be-In, Be-In, Being: Central Park Rite Is Medieval Pageant," (3/30/67), 1; Jacob Deschin, "Photography: People Seen As Curiosity," *NYT* (3/5/67); "East Village dropouts," in Patricia Bosworth, *Diane Arbus* (New York: Norton, 1984), 247.

8: "Youth: The Hippies," *Time* (7/7/67), 22; Smith, "Scenes," *VV* (7/20/67), 16; Alfred Carl, "Call Her Dotty," *Sunday News* (8/13/67), 10. FN: Will Lissner, "23 War Protesters Arrested in St. Patrick's After Disrupting a Mass," *NYT* (1/23/67), 1.

9: Neuman, *Up Against the Wall Motherf**er: A Memoir of the '60s, with Notes for Next Time* (New York: Seven Stories Press, 2008), 35; McNeill, "Tompkins Square: The Youthquake and the Shook Up Park," *VV* (6/8/67), 1; Sylvan Fox, "9 Hurt, 38 Arrested as Hippies Clash With Police," *NYT* (5/31/67), 1; "Anti-Hippies Disrupt Concert in Tompkins Sq. Park," *NYT* (6/2/67); Hayden, *Rebellion in Newark* (New York: Vintage, 1967), 29; Marlene Nadle, "The Exploded City: Exercise In Futility," *VV* (7/20/67), 1. FN: Leticia Kent, "East Side Project: Film Head Fired: 'Alienated' Revolt," *VV* (3/9/67), 1; "Hippies: Where Have All the Flowers Gone?," *Time* (10/13/67).

10: Glueck, "Art News: Switching It Off Downtown," *NYT* (7/23/67); Edwin Ruda "Park Place 1963 1967: Some Informal Notes in Retrospect," *Arts Magazine* (Nov 1967); Maciunas ad, Studios & Lofts, *VV* (11/9/67), 43, *VV* (11/23/67), 42, *VV* (11/30/67), 44; Cinematheque notice, *VV* (12/14/67) 48.

11: Smith, "TJ," *VV* (11/9/67), 27; Davis in Wetzsteon, "S.F. Mime Troupe: Theater of Revolution: Protest or Celebration," VV (11/30/67), 32f; Carter Braxton Horsley, "Guerrilla Theater I: Killing the Cong in New York Street," *VV* (11/2/67), 18; Schechner, "New Road to Peace" (letter) *VV* (11/9/67), 4; Feigelson, "We Are All One. Who R U?," *Cheetah* (May 1968), 30.

12: Wetzsteon, "S.F. Mime Troupe," op. cit.; Smith, "TJ," *VV* (11/30/67), 33; Sullivan, "'Supreme Comedy of the End' Opens," *NYT* (11/27/67), 76; Stefan Brecht, *Queer Theatre* (Frankfurt am Main: Suhrkamp Verlag, 1978), 56; Mead in Kempton, "Taylor Mead: The Homosexual Clown as Underground Stars," *VV* (11/30/67), 19; Picard, "Trips to Wear," *EVO* (6/15–7/1/67), 6; Robbins, *Last Girl Standing* (Seattle: Fantagraphic Books, 2017), 92. FN: Robbins, op. cit., 93.

13: Farber, "Canadian Underground," *Artforum* (Jan 1969); Bochner, "Primary Structures," op. cit.; Reich, "Wavelength by Michael Snow," *Presence and Absence: The Michael Snow Project*, ed. Jim Shedden (Toronto: Art Gallery of Ontario, 1995), 91–3; Kostelanetz, *SoHo: The Rise and Fall of an Artists' Colony* (New York: Routledge, 2003), 189.

14: Smithson, "The Monuments of Passaic," *Artforum* (Dec 1967).

15: Foreman interview, op. cit.; Richard Schechner interview (6/15/22); Joan MacIntosh interviews (1/8/22, telephone), (1/24/22 email); Johnston, "Dance Journal: Rainer's Muscle," *VV* (4/18/68), 29; Leticia Kent, "Expressway Hearing: Persecution of the City Performed by its Inmates," *VV* (4/18/68), 3. FN: Paula Cooper interview (1/15/22, Skype); Glueck, "Neighborhoods: SoHo Is Artists' Last Resort," *NYT* (5/11/70), 37; Leslie Gourse, "Costs for 'SoHo' Lofts Are Rising Drastically," *NYT* (7/26/70), 200.

9. Everything Is Now

1: Ben Morea interview op. cit., FN: ibid.

2: Emanuel Perlmutter, "Shots Are Fired in Refuse Strike; Filth Litters City," *NYT* (2/8/68), 1; analysis in Smith, "Scenes," *VV* (2/1/68); Smith, "Scenes," *VV* (2/8/68), 13; Mekas, "MJ," *VV* (1/25/68); McNeill, "Sweep Out on 3rd Street," *VV* (2/15/68), 1; Smith, "Scenes," *VV* (2/15/68), 26. FN: Yurick, "Garbage," *Rat* (3/4/68), 16–17.

3: Smith, "Scenes," *VV* (1/25/68), 16; Wetzsteon, "The Way of All Flesh: Stripping for Inaction," *VV* (2/1/68); Katzman, "Watching Girl," *EVO* (3/8/68), 6f; Katzman, *EVO* (5/24/68).

4: O.M. Theater ad, *VV* (2/29/68); Nitsch in Mekas, "MJ," *VV* (3/28/68); Picard, "Art: Crucifyin' and Chicken Pluckin'," *EVO* (3/1/68), 14; Yalkut, "Napalm Art 2: Dead Bees, Wine, Luke-Warm Water & Urine," *NYFP* (3/7/68); Kostelanetz, *Innovative*, op. cit., 111; Schechner, "Critique: The Politics of Ecstasy," *NYFP* (3/28/68), 10; Jerry Rubin, *Do It! Scenarios of the Revolution* (New York: Simon & Schuster, 1970), 161–2.

5: Ortiz in Glueck, "Art Notes: You Can Almost See Bedouins," *NYT* (3/31/68); Lebel, "An Artist with Balls is Worth Two in the Gallery," *EVO* (3/22/68); Johnston, "Dance Journal: The Holy Hurricane," *VV* (3/28/68); Ortiz in Picard, "An Artist with Balls is Worth Two in the Gallery/Round 2" *EVO* (3/29/68) 20; Gottlieb. "Yesterday Whitehall, Tomorrow the Finch Museum," *EVO* (4/5/68), 12–13; "3,000 Hippies Sing and Hurl Objects In Grand Central," *NYT* (3/22/68); McNeil, "Yip-in at Grand Central," *VV* (3/28/68), 1; Swanson in Gregory Battcock, "Art: Museum of Modern Art Hires Guards to Keep Swenson Out," *NYFP* (2/29/68), 6; Duchamp and Dalí in Grace Glueck, "Hippies Protest at Dada Preview," *NYT* (3/26/68); Swenson, "Art: The Corporate Structure of the American Art World," *NYFP* (4/25/68); FN: J. B., "Yip-In Stops Trains at Grand Central," *NYFP* (3/28/68).

6: Kostelanetz, *Fillmore East: Recollections of Rock Theater* (New York: Schirmer Books, 1995); Freemond, "Pop, Rock & Jelly," *EVO* (4/12/68), 12; "Fugs Go to Saigon," in Sanders, *Fug You*, op. cit., 275–7; Kempton, "Sunday in the Park: Yip-Out or Has-Been?," *VV* (4/18/68), 1; "10,000 Central Park Yippies Leave No Litter Problems," *NYT* (4/16/68); Roszak, "The Counter Culture Part I: Youth and the Great Refusal," *Nation* (3/25/68), 400f; Neumann, op. cit., 82; photo "Caroline de Bendern on the shoulders of Jean-Jacques Lebel," Jean-Pierre Rey/Gamma; "Exhibitions: Destruction Can Be Beautiful or Can It?," *Time* (5/24/68); Shirley, "The Destroyers," *Newsweek* (5/27/68), 93; Mellow, "On Art: The Limits of Destruction," *The New Leader* (6/3/68), 32; Genauer, "Sublimation of Violence," *Newsday* (5/14/68); Ginsberg diary entry, *The Fall of America: Journals, 1965-1971*, ed. Michael Schumacher (Minneapolis: U of Minnesota Press, 2020), 362; Gordon Ball interview (12/16/22, telephone); Ball, *East Hill Farm: Seasons with Allen Ginsberg* (Berkeley: Counterpoint, 2011), 48; William Shepard, *Group Dynamics and Evolution of Creative Choice in the Performance Group's New York Production of "Dionysus in 69"* (PhD dissertation: Florida State University, 1984), 321; Brecht, "Theatre Reviews: Dionysus in 69, from Euripides' The Bacchae, The Performance Group," *TDR* (Spring 1968), 156. FN: Bosworth, op. cit., 253; Robbins, *Last Girl*, op. cit., 98.

7: Joan MacIntosh interview (3/21/23, email); Eliscu, "Theatre? Dionysus in 69," *EVO* (5/31/68); Eliscu, "Theatra?," *EVO* (6/14/68); Smith, "Theatre Journal," *VV* (6/13/68), 41; "New Plays: Dionysus in '69," *Time* (6/28/68); Sullivan, "Theater: 'Bacchae' Updated in Garage," *NYT* (6/7/68); Lester, ". . . Or the Wave of the Future?," *NYT* A&L (6/30/68), 1; Kerr, "The Delusion About Illusion," *NYT* A&L (7/21/68), 1; Schechner, "Drama Mailbag: Beyond Nude Dancing," *NYT* A&L (7/28/68), 3; Brecht, "Dionysus," op. cit., 159. FN: Eliscu, "Theatre?," *EVO* (6/28/68), 5; Shepard, *Group Dynamics*, op. cit., 279–80. MacIntosh interview op. cit.

8: Latimer, "Polymorphous Polkadot," *EVO* (7/19/68), 11f; Don McLeese, *Kick Out the Jams* (London: Bloomsbury 2005), 68; Mailer, *Miami and the Siege of Chicago* (New York: Signet, 1968), 142. FN: Alexandra Munroe, "Obsession, Fantasy, and Outrage," in *Yayoi Kusama: A Retrospective*, ed. Bhupendra Karia (New York: Center for International Contemporary Arts, 1989), 29; Midori Yamamura, *Yayoi Kusama: Biography and Cultural Confrontation, 1945–1969* (PhD dissertation: CUNY Graduate Center, 2012), 325f; Kusama, *Infinity Net* trans. Ralph McCarthy (London: Tate, 2011), 106.

9: FN: Stoller, "16mm" *VV* (8/12/68), 32.

10: Fouratt in Larry Sloman, *Steal This Dream* (New York: Doubleday, 1998), 156; Latimer *EVO* (9/20/68); Rothfuss, *Topless Cellist: The Improbable Life of Charlotte Moorman* (Cambridge MA: MIT Press, 2014), 229; "60 Hippies in a Bus See the Sights of Quaint Queens," *NYT* (9/23/68); Paul Spike, "The Hippies Tour Queens: The Freak Circuit Goes Home Again," *VV* (9/26/68), 59; Newsreel's attack on NYFF in *NYFP* (8/15/68) and *NYFP* (9/19/68). Robert Pasolli, "Theatre: The Moke Eater," *VV* (9/26/68), 45; Eliscu, "Thilm," *EVO* (10/4/68).

11: William Borders, "Indecent Exposure Charged to Becks," *NYT* (9/28/68); Robert Pasolli, "Becks in New Haven: Collisions in Paradise: Love-Zap or Provocation?," *VV* (9/26/68), 1f; Eliscu, "Thilm," *EVO* (10/4/68) Wetzsteon, "TJ," *VV* (10/3/68), 34f; Gilman, "The Theater of Ignorance," *Atlantic* (July 1969), 38; Funke, "Stage: Brecht 'Antigone,'" *NYT* (10/11/68); Barnes, "Stage: Living Theater's 'Paradise Now,' A Collective Creation," *NYT* (10/15/68); Westzeon, "TJ," *VV* (10/17/68), 45; Brecht,

"Revolution at the Brooklyn Academy of Music," *TDR* (Spring 1969), 48; Lahr, "Theater: Trouble in Paradise," *NYFP* (10/31/68), 7; Hoffman in Elenore Lester, "The Living Theater presents: Revolution! Joy! Protest! Shock! Etc,!," *NYT* Magazine (10/13/68), 53; Cakars, "A Bad Night," *WIN* (11/15/68), 12. FN: Ross Wetzsteon, "The Living Theatre at the Pittsburgh Station," *VV* (4/21/75).

12: Jahn, "Jim Morrison Is a Sex Symbol," *Pop Scene Service* (4/6/68); Kostelanetz, *Fillmore* op. cit.; Stoller, "16mm," *VV* (3/28/68), 49; Freemond, "Pop, Rock & Jelly," *EVO* (4/26/68); Latimer "Decomp," *EVO* (1/10/69), 5; Shero, "Bill Graham Part I," *Rat* (10/18-31).

13: Goldstein, "Theater of Cruelty Comes to 2nd Avenue," *VV* (10/31/68), 45; Schechner, "Radicalism, Sexuality, & Performance," *TDR* (Summer 1969), 92; McGauslin, "Graham the Cracker or Paradise Next Wednesday or Motherfucking Works," LNS #113 (10/23/68), 15; Mac Low, "Up Against the Wall Theatre, or Where Have All the Flowers Gone, Motherfucker?," *WIN* (11/15/68), 13; Flaherty, "Wallace Rally: The Legions of Fear Huddle Against the Night," *VV* (10/31/68), 1f; Raphael, "Georgie Buoy at the Garden," *EVO* (11/8/68), 5. FN: Schechner, "Radicalism" op. cit., 93.

14: McCauslin, "Fillmore East Round II," *Rat* (11/1-14); "'Bare Facts' Presented in a Political Protest," *NYT* (11/4/68); "4 In Nude Protest the War in Vietnam," *NYT* (11/12/68); *Rat* (11/15/68), 13; "Space Energy Revolution," *Rat* (11/29/68), 3; Young, "Folklore Center-Fretted Instrument Newsletter," (12/5/68).

15: Jahn, "Country Joe's Fish Make Heads Swim To Electric Sounds," *NYT* (12/9/68); Reed in Ryan H. Walsh, *Astral Weeks: A Secret History of 1968* (New York: Penguin, 2018), 106; Pearlman, "Riffs: Revolutionary Moments," *VV* (1/2/69), 17f; Goldstein, "Pop Eye: Why the Blues," *VV* (1/16/69), 27; Christgau, "The Continuing Saga of the MC-5," *VV* (6/5/69), 32.

16: Bob Rudick and Dennis Frawley, "Kokaine Karma," *EVO* (3/19/69), 12; Stewart, "The New Black Music," in *The Cricket: Black Music in Evolution 1968-69* (Brooklyn: Blank Forms Editions, 2022), 67; Ayler, ibid., 143–6; Neal, "New Grass/Albert Ayler," ibid., 153; Baraka, ibid., 157f; Meltzer, *Aesthetics*, op. cit., 222; "Integration Music," *The Cricket*, op. cit., 121; "Jimi Hendrix," *Flyboy 2: The Greg Tate Reader* (Durham NC: Duke University Press 2016; "Hey brother" in Frank Owen and Simon Reynolds, "Why Hendrix Still Matters" *Spin* (Apr 1991), 32. FN: John Burks, "Sun Ra," *RS* (4/19/69).

10. No President/Scare City

1: Mekas, "MJ," *VV* (1/30/69), 49; Mekas, "MJ," *VV* (11/16/67); Stoller, "16mm," *VV* (12/7/69), 37.

2: Smith and *Big Hotel* in David Kaufman, *Ridiculous! The Theatrical Life and Times of Charles Ludlam* (New York: Applause, 2002), 77; Stoller, "16mm," *VV* (4/4/68), 49. FN: Mekas, "MJ," *VV* (2/17/66).

3: "Yes, you can take your magazine," in Ed Leffingwell, "Jack Smith: A Working Chronology" (9/5/96), 67; Baby Jerry, "Sprockets," *EVO* (10/25/68), 8; Penny Arcade interview (6/8/2023); Eliscu, "Thilm," *EVO* (11/15/68), 14; Washburn, "Theatre: Turds in Hell," *VV* (12/5/68), 47; Sarris, "Films in Focus," *VV* (2/6/69), 55; Eliscu, *EVO* (2/7/69); Mekas, "MJ," *VV* (1/30/69), 49; Katsiaficas, *The Global Imagination of 1968: Revolution and Counterrevolution* (Oakland: PM Press, 2018), 134.

4: Eliscu, "Video," *EVO* (2/14/69), 16f; Stoller, "16mm," *VV* (8/17/67), 23; Yalkut, "Film," *NYFP* (7/23/69), 10; Smith, "Scenes," *VV* (3/13/69); "I wasn't even aroused," in Samuel Shaffer, *On and Off the Floor: Thirty Years as a Correspondent on Capitol Hill* (New York: Newsweek Books, 1980), 92; Reed, "I Am Curious (No)," *NYT* A&L (3/23/69), 1D. FN: Latimer, "Decomposition," *EVO* (5/7/69), 5.

5: "Yippie Is Dead But Here Come The Crazies," *NY Post* (1/29/69); Rubin in "Remembering George Demmerle: Portrait of a Police Informer," *CounterPunch* (10/1/2008), 6; NYPD Bureau of Special Services report, "Demonstration by 'Crazies' at N.Y. Times, Grand Central, Central Park, and Midtown Manhattan" (3/23/69), NYPD Intelligence Records, Municipal Archives; "Yippie Leader Held in Raid on Lower East Side," *NYT* (3/24/69); "Crazies Go to Church (and take their friends)," *Rat* (3/29/69); Frank Moses, "Freedom? Boredom? Fascism?," *NYT* A&L (3/30/69), 1; "Fuck all liberal intellectuals" in Brustein, "Monkey Business," *NYRB* (4/24/69); Pasolli, "Fracturing a Forum: Beck Cast Zaps the Elite: 'It's Coming Attractions," *VV* (3/27/69), 14f; Broughton, "Drama Mailbag: Did the Living Theater Do All the Disrupting," *NYT* A&L (4/6/69) and "The Beck's Circus" (letter), *VV* (4/10/69), 4; "Crazies Go to Church" op. cit., NYPD B.S.S. No. 313, "Demonstration by Crazies at Riverside Church, Clairmont Ave" (3/29/69), NYPD Intelligence, op. cit.; Flaherty, "Crazies at Peace Forum: The New Purists: Water Gun Wrath," *VV* (4/3/69). FN: "Crazies" undated fact sheet, NYPD Intelligence op. cit.

6: Burroughs in Wayne Andersen, *Takis: Evidence of the Unseen* (Cambridge, MA: MIT Press, 1968), 30; Perrault, "Art: Whose Art?," *VV* (1/9/69), 16–17; Glueck, "Art Notes: 'J'accuse, Baby!' She Cried," *NYT* A&L (4/20/69); Picard, "You can't win 'em all: Non-Art-Event," *EVO* (5/14/69), 11f.

7: *Screw*'s endorsement in Joe Flaherty, *Managing Mailer* (New York: Berkeley Medallion, 1971), 48; *Daily News* poll, ibid., 112; "spoiled pigs," ibid., 99; meeting the Crazies, ibid., 120–2; Perrault, "Art," *VV* (5/29/69), 14.

8: "Queen Power: Fags Against Pigs," *Rat* (7/9/69); Fouratt in Martin Duberman, *Stonewall* (New York: Dutton, 1993), 198; Arcade interview op. cit.

9: Dreifus, "Up Against the Wall, Crazies!," *EVO* (8/13/69), 16; Lebel, "Containing Hip," *Rat* (8/12/69), 26; Morea interview, op. cit.; "liberated campsites," in *Rat* (8/27/69), 15; Jane Alpert, *Growing Up Underground* (New York: William Morrow, 1981), 27. FN: Burroughs, "Woodstock," *Rat* (10/29/69).

10: Fabrikant in Steven Lerner, "Press of Pornography: Bonanza or Best," *VV* (5/28/69), 18; Hansen, "Index Card for a Decade," *EVO* (2/11/70), 9; Newfield, "The Durable Rodent of the Underground," *VV* (7/10/69), 17f; David C. Viola Jr., *Terrorism and the Response to Terrorism in New York City During the Long Sixties* (PhD thesis: CUNY Graduate Center, 2017), 181–3; The Black Rat, "Rat Raided," *Rat* (10/8/69), 4. FN: Steve Heller, *Growing Up Underground: A Memoir of Counterculture New York* (Princeton NJ: Princeton Architectural Press, 2022), 116f.

11: "Arson Incident at Columbia," *NYT* (10/5/69), 1; Picard, "On Art," *EVO* (11/15/69); Zion, "Bombs: To Topple 'Establishment,'" *NYT* (11/16/69); Spero, "Reports on Bomb Plot," *EVO* (11/29/69); Alex Gross, "Blood Donors Rescue Museum," *EVO* (12/10/69), 4; Lurie, "More Mind Control: MOMA As Manipulator," *Rat* (12/25/69); Edward C. Burks, "Museums Seeking Guards To Stem Mounting Crime," *NYT* (12/12/69), 57.

12: Lee, "Slave Ship: Notes and Design," *Yale/Theatre* (Fall 1970), 32; Kroll, "Dark Voyage," *Newsweek* (12/1/69); Kerr, "Slave Ship," *NYT* A&L (11/23/69), D3; Aletti, "LeRoi Jones' Slave Ship," *Rat* (1/26/70), 26; "Cast of 'Slave Ship' Quits Stage After Protest About Conditions," *NYT* (1/24/70).

13: McDonagh, "Story of Dr. Freud Depicted in Dance by Meredith Monk," *NYT* (12/20/69); Haskell, "Theatre: The King of Spain," *VV* (2/6/69), 42; Perreault, "Art," *VV* (1/1/70), 16; Foreman, "Speak Out the Arts: 'The Life and Times of Sigmund Freud,'" ibid., 41.

11. Withdrawal from Orchid Lagoon

1: Kramer, "Participatory Esthetics," *NYT* A&L (1/11/70); Rosalyn Regelson, "Not a Boy, not a Girl, Just Me," *NYT* A&L (11/2/69), 1; Kroll, "Ridiculous!," *Newsweek* (11/3/69), 94; Jim Buckley, "Dirty Diversions," *Screw* (11/3/69); Kerr, "Mindlessness Is the Essence," *NYT* A&L (11/16/69), D7; Regelson, op. cit., 1; Gornick, "Women's

Liberation: The Next Great Moment in History is Theirs," *VV* (11/27/69), 11; Grove's "basic theme" in Irvina Shusnik, "The Grove Press Nine," *EVO* (4/21/70). FN: Perreault, "Art," *VV* (1/15/70). FN: Canaday, "Art: Jewish Museum Retrospective for Artist of 36," *NYT* (1/24/70); Flavin attacked by AWC in Grace Glueck, "Museum Beckoning Space Explorers," *NYT* (1/2/70).

2: Sitney, "Structural Film," *FC* 47 (Summer 1969), 1f; Greenspun, "'Fando and Lis' a Film Calculated to Shock," *NYT* (2/3/70); Sarris, "Films in Focus," *VV* (2/12/70); Gussow, "Zabriskie Point," *Rat* (2/24/70); Angelo Quattrocchi and Jill Neville, "Fellini 'Satyricon': A Pagan Dolce Vita: 'Faces Are My Words,'" *VV* (1/22/70), 55f; Sarris, "Films in Focus," *VV* (3/19/70); Mekas, "MJ," *VV* (5/14/70).

3: Majorie Heins and Leon Gussow, "La Chinoise (2 Views) or: Who the hell does Godard think he is & What does he think he's doing?," *Rat* (4/19/69), 17–18; Greenspun, "Screen: 'Sympathy for the Devil' ('1+1')," *NYT* (4/27/70), 42; Ehrenstein, "Film: Sympathy for the Devil (One Plus One)," *VV* (4/9/70); Mogubgub, *EVO* (5/19/70), 15; "More Sympathy for the Devil," *Rat* (6/5/70), 20; Sarris, "Films and Focus: Godard and the Revolution," *VV* (4/30/70), 53; Greenspun, "Godard's 'Mao' and 'Pravda' Begin Run," *NYT* (5/22/70); Mekas, "MJ," *VV* (6/4/70). FN: Lemmy Caution, "Godard in Berkeley," *Berkeley Barb* (5/1/70), 9.

4: Brukenfeld, "Off-Off," *VV* (3/12/70), 51; Washburn, "Theatre: Bluebeard," *VV* (4/16/70), 44; Schechner, "'Bluebeard' & 'Stomp': Two Exemplary productions," *VV* (4/23/70), 44; Mel Gussow, "Laughs Pepper Ghoulish 'Bluebeard,'" *NYT* (5/5/70); Curtis in Gaby Rogers, "Jackie Curtis and John Vaccaro Together Again," *Soho Weekly News* (9/23/76); Brecht, *Queer Theatre*, op. cit., 12; Arthur Irving, "Mae West at the Myra Premiere," *EVO* (6/23/70); "Misses West and Welch Mobbed at Film Debut," *NYT* (6/24/70), 43; *Rat* (7/15/70).

5: Taylor, Crouch, and Jones in Adam Shatz, "The Sorcerer of Jazz," *NYRB* (9/26/2016); anthologized in Imamu Amiri Baraka, *Raise, Race, Rays: Essays since 1965* (New York: Random House, 1972); Christgau, "Rock & Roll," *VV* (6/18/70), 34.

6: Marcus, "Self-Portrait," *RS* (6/8/70); Heller in Lynda Crawford, "Remembering Yossarian, 'Original Hipster and Legendary Cartoonist,'" available at localeastvillage.com; Alan Shenker, "It Ain't My Cup of Meat," *EVO* (6/23/70), 16–17; Dylan interview with Kurt Loder, *RS* (6/21/84); Doggett, *There's a Riot Going On* (New York: Cannongate 2007), 345; Schjeldahl, "Pop: Dylan, No Longer Tormented," *NYT* A&L (6/21/70); Schjeldahl, "Is The Art World Heading For A Nervous Breakdown?," *NYT* A&L (8/23/70).

7: Bochner, "About Eva Hesse: An interview with Joan Simon," *Solar System & Rest Rooms* (Cambridge MA: MIT Press, 2008), 154; Roy Bongartz, "It's Called Earth Art—And Boulderdash," *NYT* Magazine (2/1/70); John Canaday, "Art: Oldenburg as The Picasso of Pop," *NYT* A&L (7/28/69); Glueck, "Art Notes: Yanking the Rug From Under," *NYT* A&L (1/25/70), D25; "They're play acting," in "Museum Here Gets A First-Hand View of 'Art' of Protest," *NYT* (5/3/70); Nemser, "The Press of Freedom: Artists & the System: Far From Cambodia," *VV* (5/28/70), 20f; Battcock letter, "Turned Off," *VV* (5/21/70), 50. Schjeldahl, "Art: Anything The Artist Says It Is?," *NYT* A&L (5/17/70); Schjeldahl, "Don't Just Stand There—Read!," *NYT* (8/9/70); Kramer, "Show at the Modern Raises Questions," *NYT* (7/2/70); Picard, "Teach Art—ACTION," *EVO* (6/2/70); McShine, "Essay," *Information* (New York: MoMA, 1970), 138–41; Perreault, "Art," *VV* (7/16/70). FN: Gary Carrion-Murayari and Massimiliano Gioni, eds., *Hans Haacke: All Connected* (New York: Phaidon Press/New Museum, 2019), 289–90.

8: Mekas, "Jack Smith or the End of Civilization," "MJ," *VV* (7/23/70); Schechner, "After the Blow-Up in the Garage," *NYT* A&L (12/13/70), 3f; Makavejev interview with Edgardo Cozarinsky and Carlos Clarens, *Film Comment* (May–June 1975).

9: "Rumbles," *Avalanche* (Fall 1970), 4; Kramer, "A Case of Artistic Freedom," *NYT* (3/1/70); "Episode on Prince Street," *NYT* (11/16/70); Perrault, "Art," *VV* (11/19/70), 22; Lester, "Is Abbie Hoffman the Will Shakespeare of the 1970's?," *NYT* A&L (10/11/70), 3f; Kennedy in "Flag bust unites artist," *VV* (11/19/70), 30; Kramer, "A Mandarin Pretending to Be A Stumblebum," *NYT* (10/25/70); Perreault, "Art," *VV* (11/5/70). FN: Faith Ringgold, *Black Light Series #10: Flag For the Moon: Die Nigger, 1967*, available at faithringgold.com.

10: Andrew Noren file, Film-Maker's Cooperative; Ayler blamed himself, Val Wilmer *As Serious as Your Life: Black Music and the Free Jazz Revolution 1957-1977* (London: Serpents Tail, 2018), 145–6; "Scenes," *VV* (2/19/70), 16; Heckman, "Pop: Two and A Half Beatles On Their Own," *NYT* A&L (12/20/70); Bangs, "Plastic Ono Band," *RS* (3/4/71), 49f; Truscott, "Riffs: New Dylan?," *VV* (11/5/70), 39; Gleason, "Perspectives: We've Got Dylan Back Again!," *RS* (11/26/70).

11: Kramer, "Newsreel," *FQ* (Winter 1968–69); Vogel, "Moviegoing at Cannes: One Festival Plus One," *VV* (7/9/70), 51; Rivette in J.D. Copp "My Gleanings: Jacques Rivette – 10 best films – Cahiers 1954-1966," available at jdcopp.blogspot.com; Byron, "Film: Ice," *VV* (10/22/70), 63; Canby, "'Ice': Finally Getting the Revolution Straight," *NYT* A&L (10/25/70), 1f; Greenspun, "Film: Insight Into World Revolution," *NYT* (10/16/70; Hardwick, "Militant Nudes" *NYRB* (1/7/71); McBean, "The 'Ice'-Man Cometh No More (He Gave His Balls to the Revolution," *FQ* Summer 1971), 26f; Mellen, "Ice," *Cineaste* v4 #2 (1971), 30. FN: Alpert, *Growing*, op. cit., 112.

12: Schechner, "After the Blow-Up," op. cit.; Joan MacIntosh interview (2/23/23, telephone); "Child's climbing gym," in Mary Cambell, "Theater," Associated Press (12/20/70); "One is expected," in Edward Sothern Hipp, "Theater Based on

Discomfort," *Newark Sunday News* (1/3/71), E3; Gilman, "Theatre Reviews: Commune," *TDR* (Spring 1971), 126; Gussow, "Schechner's Performance Group in 'Commune,'" *NYT* (12/21/70), 50; Kerr, "Two That Try to Break the Rules—and Fail," *NYT* A&L (12/27/70,) 1f; Simon, *New York* (1/11/71); Martin Gottfried, *Women's Wear Daily* (12/21/70); Lahr, "On-Stage," *VV* (12/31/70); Paul Cassidy, "Snatches of American history," *Daily Worker* clipping [nd] *Commune* file, NYPL Performing Arts; Hartwick, "Commune: Together Is Not Enough," *Vogue* (Feb 1971); O'Rourke, *EVO* clipping [nd] *Commune* file, op. cit.

13: *El Topo* ad, *VV* (12/17/70), 73; O'Brien, "Film: Midnight mass at the Elgin," *VV* (3/25/71), 61; Schjeldahl, "Should 'El Topo' Be Elevated To 'El Tops'?," *NYT* A&L (6/6/71), D11; Singer, *EVO* (2/14/71). FN: News Desk, "Alejandro Jodorowsky Speaks Out After El Museo Del Barrio Calls Off Retrospective," *Artforum* (01/31/2019).

Index